ANGELS of MERCY

FAR WEST & FAR EAST

LYNETTE RAMSAY SILVER

DEDICATION

For Aunty Bid and the people of the Far West,
and for the Sisters of the Australian Army Nursing Service

SALLY MILNER
PUBLISHING

First published in 2019 by
Sally Milner Publishing Pty Ltd
734 Woodville Rd
Binda NSW 2583 AUSTRALIA

Design: Natalie Bowra
Editing: Kathryn Lamberton, Bridging the Gap
Printed in China

A catalogue record for this book is available from the National Library of Australia

10 9 8 7 6 5 4 3 2 1

Contents

Author's note

This book tells the story of two very different nursing sisters, who overcame two very different challenges. In the 1930s Marjorie Silver, the outback's flying sister, fought almost single-handedly against the isolation, poverty, heat and dust of the far west of New South Wales to bring vital medical assistance to her far-flung patients. Sister Pat Gunther, who served in the Far East on the battlefields of Malaya and Singapore, then fought a desperate battle for survival in the prison camps of Sumatra.

Angels of Mercy has been compiled from their edited memoirs, supplemented by various conversations and interviews. Interspersed throughout their first-hand accounts is a 'second voice', which I am privileged to supply as the historical narrator. These sections, easily identifiable as they are in italics, contain information that falls outside the knowledge or experience of the two nursing sisters. The historical narrative is secondary but, when read in tandem with the autobiographical strands, it expands each story in a way that would not otherwise be possible.

These two remarkable, highly resilient women may not be remembered as great Australians, but they will be remembered for making Australia great.

Lynette Ramsay Silver
April 2019

Note: Place names are spelled as they appear on wartime maps and documents. If there is a modern-day equivalent, it has been added in brackets. Distances are given in both empirical and metric measurements.

Acknowledgements

The author gratefully acknowledges all those who so willingly provided assistance, information, memorabilia and photographs, especially Judy Balcombe, Craig Berelle, Colleen Chidson, the late Eddina Churcher, Derek Emerson-Elliott, Di and Paul Elliott, Jonathan Moffatt, the late James MacKay and the MacKay Family, Barbara Orchard, Eunice Ramsay, Alyce Simmonds of The Royal Hospital for Women Foundation, Royal Far West Children's Health Scheme, the late Mary Turner, Sue Williams and the Setchell Family, and the late Arthur Weston.

The author particularly recognises the outstanding contribution to this book and to the nation's military history by Di and Paul Elliott, who spent many weeks researching and compiling the Nurses' Nominal Roll; the support and encouragement of Libby Renney and Ian Webster at Sally Milner Publishing; and the unstinting financial and moral support of her husband, Neil Silver.

ANGEL OF MERCY

FAR WEST

PROLOGUE

The phone shrilled demandingly one hot morning in late 1986. I answered it and an immediately identifiable voice said, 'Is that you, darling? I'm Bored with a capital B.'

It was my husband's aunt. Baptised Marjorie Dobson Silver, she was known to the family as Aunty Bid and to the rest of the world as Margot Weiss. No one can quite remember how Marjorie morphed into Bid, but the transition some time after her marriage from Marjorie or Marj, which she loathed, to the more sophisticated sounding and upmarket Margot was entirely her own doing.

Now aged 76, she was laid up at home with a broken leg. It was from a fall, sustained after eating too much bran. Her sister, Jean, who was really into health food and expounded its virtues at every opportunity, had told Bid that a good dessertspoonful of raw bran on her cereal each day would do her digestive system a power of good. At their age they needed the additional roughage, Jean had said. On the basis that, if one spoonful was beneficial, then three or four would be even better, Bid upped the dose.

Within a day or two she was in agony. The bran had impacted, necessitating a trip to hospital to unblock the blockage. The procedure went without a hitch but, still disoriented and groggy after the anaesthetic, Aunty Bid fell out of bed, hit the floor with a thud, and broke the top off her femur.

Never a good patient at the best of times, and now encased in plaster for at least six weeks, she was fretful, bored witless and in need of diversion.

'I'll come over for morning tea,' I soothed.

She perked up considerably at this and gave orders to her husband Charles to rustle up some ham sandwiches.

By the time I arrived, the bone china teacups were set out, along with delicious cake from a local luxury-style bakery and the ham sandwiches. The packaged biscuits that I had bought at the supermarket as my offering were totally superfluous. If Aunty Bid did eat shop-bought biscuits, she preferred those that came from David Jones – the large and prestigious department store in Sydney that had a mouth-watering food hall.

The conversation turned to the recent publication of a book I had written. It had been featured on ABC TV News nationally and I had been interviewed on several high-rating radio and television programs, something that had greatly impressed Aunty Bid – a niece (albeit by marriage) who had made the news, and nationally, just as she had done herself on quite a few occasions.

'Darling, what is your next book going to be about?' she asked. Not intending to do anything much in the foreseeable future, I laughingly replied, 'Well, Aunty Bid, I could write down your story. You've led a pretty interesting life.'

It was a throwaway line said in complete and utter jest, but Aunty Bid caught it and ran with it like an international Rugby winger towards the try line. As far as she was concerned, the problem of her boredom was solved.

And so it was. Over the next six weeks, accompanied by countless pots of tea, always served in fine bone china cups, and delectable eats provided by the ever-helpful Charles, she told me her story.

CHAPTER 1

Basic Training

I'd always wanted to become a doctor. It was a dream I had nurtured for as long as I could remember. My imagination had been fired when I was a small girl, by family legend, that I, along with my father's side of the family, was related to Sir William Harvey, a famous 16th century surgeon who had unlocked the mystery of blood circulation. Of course, I had never been shown any documented proof of this relationship and had never thought to question it, believing implicitly that it existed. So, apparently, did everyone else in the family, so much so that no one had ever bothered to undertake the necessary genealogical research to compile a family tree to prove the connection. In any case, tracing long dead relatives in faraway England was extremely difficult, not to say horrendously expensive.

Many very ordinary families at that time harboured similar, often fanciful, notions. Everyone knew someone who had an unclaimed inheritance held in Chancery in London, which should rightly have passed to relatives who had emigrated to Australia. Others boasted of a tortuous, but unfortunately incomplete, genealogical line, linking the bastard side of a family to those born on the right side of some Royal blanket, or claimed a relationship based on an unusual surname they shared with some famous or notable member of British or European society.

In Marjorie's case, the kinship to the eminent doctor was said to be via her grandmother, Emma Harvey, who had emigrated with her family to Australia in 1854 at the age of 16. A most independent young woman, not unlike Marjorie in her youth, Emma was educated, but her father George was an agricultural labourer and could neither read nor write. Any bloodline linking Sir William to Emma's grandchildren had never been investigated beyond the three Australian generations, but this did not stop Marjorie, along with her sister Jean, and brothers Aubrey and John, claiming him.

Australia at that time had been settled for less than 150 years, largely by felons transported from Mother England: a period far too short to encourage genealogical digging lest a most 'unsuitable' ancestor emerge, even among those considered to be aristocracy. Had the Silvers been able to chart even a rudimentary family tree, they would have soon realised that any relationship with William Harvey, if it existed, was extremely distant. The relationship had never been challenged by anyone inside the family and, with no outsider pressing for details or demanding to see the necessary evidence, the story persisted.

Despite my supposedly illustrious relative and my personal aspirations, to become a doctor was a dream destined to remain unfulfilled. For a start, in those days it was generally considered that higher education was wasted on girls who, on marriage, were forced by convention and social pressure to give up work – assuming, of course, that they joined the workforce at all. It was a matter of pride for the males in the family to provide for the women. Many girls, who at that time left school at the age of 14 or so, stayed at home, learning housekeeping and homemaking skills from their mothers until they were old enough to be married. Even if they had aspirations, and were game enough to say so, further education, especially medical school, required a great deal of money – money that was far better spent educating the boys, the potential breadwinners of the family.

I was born on 16 June 1910 at Wickham, in the steel city of Newcastle, and was third in the Silver household's pecking order, after my two brothers, Aubrey and John. While I realised that neither might ever wish to go to university, I knew that, being boys, they were entitled to the best education the family could afford which, in this case, meant private secondary schooling in Sydney, at the very least. As a mere female, there was no hope of my entering university, so I kept my dream to myself.

When I was still a toddler, my father, Richard Lancaster Silver (who was always known as Lang), decided to move to Scone in the Upper Hunter Valley. Set amidst lush green countryside, and backed by misty blue hills, Scone was a far cry from the then grimy, pollution-laden Newcastle, where the tall smoke stacks at the BHP steelworks belched forth smoke and gases twenty-four hours a day.

Renowned for its thoroughbred horses and solid, middle-class values, Scone was a prosperous country town with a wide main street lined with numerous shops and emporiums. It boasted a substantial railway station, a public school, a police station, a small hospital, and also had several fine churches. The Roman Catholics, who got in first, had bagged prime position on the high side of the town, where they built a large and impressive stone church. Known as the Blessed Virgin Mary Queen of Peace, or St Mary's for short, it eclipsed, architecturally, the less flamboyant but nevertheless substantial St Luke's Church of England, which nestled, English-style, in a grassy field surrounded by ageing tombstones on the other side of the railway line. Being C of E, this is where I attended church and Sunday School.

Although the family was C of E through and through, the name sounded Jewish and on occasion people assumed it was, as Silver was a common Anglicisation of names like Silberman and Silverstein. However, our family came from Thame, a small English town on the Thames River in Oxfordshire, where the name Silver is very localised. There are still Silver relatives living there.

Scone Post Office, 1931

Like all country towns, the community in Scone was tight-knit and everyone pretty much knew everyone else. We lived in town, where I experienced a carefree and pleasantly predictable childhood until January 1916 when, at the age of five and a half, I started school.

Although the family on both sides were from England and were staunchly C of E, my mother Maud, for reasons that I never quite fathomed, enrolled me at St Mary's Convent School, rather than at the state-run school. However, my early childhood education, under the guidance of the ironically named Sisters of Mercy, was destined to be of short duration. Although I was not a particularly naughty child, I was considered to be bright, and was naturally high-spirited and independently minded, even at that young age. This combination was bound to land me in trouble sooner or later and, sure enough, I managed to commit a misdemeanour. What it was, I can't recall. I am sure it was only minor, but whatever it was it certainly riled the nuns.

My punishment was incarceration in a cell-like cupboard, into which not a single ray of light penetrated. The period of detention could have been for no more than 10 minutes or so, but to a child of six years, as I then was, it seemed an eternity. When I arrived home and reported that the nuns had locked me in a dark cupboard for hours and hours, my mother, who was quite a formidable lady, sallied forth like a battleship at full speed and withdrew me from the control of the papists. Deciding that I might fare better in more neutrally religious surroundings, she enrolled me the very next day at the local infants' school.

I soon settled into the rhythm of things, enjoying the company of the other children. I did quite well and at the end of Grade 2 was one of four pupils to receive a merit certificate. So did my sister Jean, who was one year behind me. These accomplishments were evidently deemed to be newsworthy, because they were reported in the *Scone Advocate*. I enjoyed the formal lessons and, being quite outgoing and with a good singing voice, also had no problem performing in public at school concerts. Jean was also musical and we often teamed up to do a double act.

With the memory of the dark cupboard a reminder of what might happen if I misbehaved at school, I tried to stay out of strife in case punishment by the state proved to be worse than that of the church. However, despite my best efforts, towards the end of 4th grade I came unstuck.

After a frustrating day, on which several pupils had been particularly trying, our teacher, a normally mild-mannered and gentle woman, uncharacteristically let forth a stream of invective on the impropriety of our behaviour. Finishing her tirade with the comment that she was at a loss to know why the culprits set out to deliberately disrupt the class, she asked if someone could enlighten her as to why the troublemakers persisted in playing up. I was only 10 years old but, as I generally had an opinion on most things and was not the slightest bit reticent in voicing them, I blurted out, 'The trouble is, Miss, we all think you're a bit soft.'

That did it! Believing that I had inferred she was soft in the head, the teacher scolded me severely for being so cheeky, silencing all attempts to explain the misunderstanding with a wagging finger and a look that would have withered the toughest mortal, let alone a 10-year-old. As additional punishment I was detained, sitting at my desk in resentful silence until 5 pm, two hours after the normal going home time. It was summer and there was plenty of daylight left, but my mother was not pleased. Furious that I had been kept in for so long and, on the basis that a grave and unforgivable miscarriage of justice had occurred, she decided to remove me from the control of the public school system.

As the educational philosophy of neither church nor state were to Mother's liking, after the summer school holidays I was enrolled as a day girl in yet another school – Narwonah, a Private School for Girls or, as the principal, Miss Bode, liked to say, a Private School for Young Ladies. In actual fact, the school wasn't exclusively for girls. The practical Miss Bode also accepted boys in the junior school – but only if they were under the age of 10.

The school, reminiscent of a large comfortable home, was constructed of mellow brick. Deeply shaded on all sides by invitingly cool verandahs, it was set in the centre of a very large garden, filled with flowering trees and shrubs, and with plenty of room to play. The curriculum offered by Miss Bode, the owner as well as the principal, was specifically designed to cater for the academic and social needs of the young ladies who daily entered its genteel walls.

Miss Bode was a very C of E lady born at the height of Queen Victoria's reign. She was always referred to as Miss Bode. No one had any idea of her Christian name, and would not have dared to use it, even if they did. Like most young people, I had difficulty in imagining she was ever a child. Being C of E, she had strong affiliations with St Luke's. It was a fairly 'high Anglican' church and Helen Cadell, the Canon's daughter, was in my class.

Several other women assisted Miss Bode in looking after our day-to-day education and welfare. Two whom I remember particularly were total opposites: Miss Kent, who was said to be entirely without any sense of humour whatever, and the far more loveable Miss Mabel Corbett, the Matron, who was adored by everyone, day girls and boarders alike. Lurking mysteriously in the shadows was a Miss Gertie, whose last name I can't recall and whose precise role in life I never actually determined. Rumour had it, however, that her sole function, at the direction of Miss Bode, was to spend her day earnestly in prayer, her petitions evidently directed at our wellbeing and spiritual protection.

Miss Amy Maria Jane Bode, born in 1874, was 44 years old when she opened her school, situated on the corner of Liverpool and Waverley Streets, Scone. Advertisements in The

> Scone Advocate *from 1920 onwards, promoting the school and its virtues, revealed that prior to this she had taught at Astroea College, a Private Girls' School (sold to the Church of England in 1919) in the Sydney suburb of Chatswood and at a Church of England Girls' School in Goulburn, a prosperous sheep town south-west of Sydney.*
>
> *Besides the 3Rs, the subjects offered at Narwonah ranged from French, English and Australian history to geography, mapping, drawing, and painting and music. Elocution and dancing classes were also available as extracurricular activities. Miss Bode stressed that 'backward and delicate children' would receive 'every care and attention'.*
>
> *The school functioned continuously from 1920 until 1952, when it became a pre-school, under the auspices of St Luke's. The redoubtable Miss Bode died eight years later at the age of 86.*

My mother had also decided to remove Jean from the state school and enrol her at Miss Bode's. Close in age, we were just one grade apart. We got on quite well together and, with potentially bothersome older brothers safely installed in boarding school in Sydney, life was a most pleasant mixture of lessons, horses and friends, although not necessarily in that order.

Although still outspoken and referred to as 'outgoing', I performed well enough on the academic front. However, I could act the fool when the mood took me, and was prone to indulge in practical jokes when things became boring. The most memorable prank occurred one hot and somnolent summer afternoon when, during a particularly tedious English grammar lesson, I accepted a dare designed to put Miss Kent's famous lack of humour to the test. The instigator was Helen Cadell, the Canon's daughter and, to make sure I wouldn't back out, she told the entire grade about it. Fully aware of what was about to unfold, my classmates waited in delicious anticipation as I framed my question.

'Excuse me Miss, but I am having a bit of bother with my grammar,' I said. 'I am wondering which is more correct: the yolk of an egg is white, or the yolk of an egg are white.' Miss Kent, busily marking books while we worked on the exercise she had set, took the bait. With a look of utter contempt, she spat 'IS white, IS white, you stupid girl'. Feigning a look of total innocence, I replied in as meek a voice as I could manage, 'Excuse me, Miss Kent, but I believe the yolk of an egg is yellow.'

Miss Kent's normally pale complexion rapidly turned a remarkable shade of puce. Clutching the collar of her high-necked gown, she dropped her red marking pencil and looked as if she might have a stroke, while the rest of the girls stuffed handkerchiefs in their mouths in an attempt to smother guffaws that might have otherwise summoned Miss Bode to investigate the cause of the disturbance. Meanwhile, I stared at an invisible spot, just above the blackboard, fearful that I too might explode into uncontrollable giggles.

There was no escaping punishment: 400 lines, to be completed after school that day. Four hundred lines, written in my best copperplate handwriting and in pen and ink, took some time, so long that my unexpected lateness almost prompted my mother to call the police to investigate my whereabouts. Fortunately, although it was almost dark when I arrived home, Mother had more important matters on her mind that day and did not press me for details. The whole school knew I was in trouble, but Jean, being a loyal sister, did not dob. When the girls congregated on the verandah before classes the next morning, the opinion was unanimous. I had very definitely proved a point: Miss Kent had absolutely no sense of humour.

Apart from a proper grounding in basic education, Miss Bode expected her girls to be well versed in the arts, particularly music. She was an accomplished pianist and, in this post World War I period when entertainment was mostly of the self-made variety, she believed that to be musically proficient was an essential requirement for any young woman whose parents could afford a piano and tuition. For the majority of my friends, music lessons were a painful ordeal to be endured, with reluctant fingers stumbling woodenly over difficult pieces and mindlessly thumping out monotonous scales and hated arpeggios.

However, I had the good fortune to be born into a family of considerable musical ability. My mother was particularly talented and could play anything, from improvised, often racy music to accompany the silent films screened at Uncle Aubrey Dobson's Olympia Picture Theatre, to the work of great composers. I had inherited her love of music and, for me, playing the piano was as natural as breathing. As soon as my feet could reach the pedals, I had begun formal lessons. Unlike most of my classmates, who gave up once an acceptable level of competency had been achieved, music tuition continued throughout my teenage years.

Playing the piano was pure joy, so much so that I abandoned my secret dream for one that I believed was attainable – if I couldn't be a doctor, I would become a concert pianist. Miss Bode, realising my talent in this field, encouraged me to perform in benefit concerts held at the school or in town on a regular basis. Although these events were attended by uncritical townspeople and biased family members, it didn't take much imagination for me to see myself on the world stage, with adoring fans giving me a standing ovation and calling 'encore' as they showered me with roses.

Highly motivated by these images, I had no problem finding time for the mandatory four hours' practice each day required to reach a level of expertise to sit for the Licentiate of the Royal Academy of Music. Without this qualification, known as the LRAM, along with an equally important recommendation from the examiner, aspiring musicians had no hope of securing a place at the prestigious New South Wales Conservatorium of Music, a crenellated, castle-like colonial structure overlooking Sydney Harbour.

On the appointed day, the all-powerful examiner steamed into town on the morning train. Aware that my future depended on how well I performed, I had tried to leave nothing to chance. My theory was well rehearsed, my technique as perfect as I could make it and the works to be examined practised with unrelenting determination. As none of the three candidates presenting for the examination was keen to go first, we drew lots to determine the order of appearance. I drew the short straw.

I played competently enough, but the enormity of the situation was too much. Although I had performed at quite a few concerts in town, I was overcome with stage fright and my nerves disintegrated. The kind but realistic examiner let me down gently. Diplomatically praising my theoretical ability and near perfect technique, he nevertheless made it absolutely and abundantly clear that, although very talented, my temperament was not suited to the pressures of the highly competitive and sometimes cut-throat world of the concert pianist. I received the much coveted LRAM, but there would be no recommendation to attend the Conservatorium of Music to further my career.

Although bitterly disappointed, I tried not to show it and reassessed my options. What was this product of Miss Bode's School for Young Ladies going to do now? Career opportunities for young women, in fact women at all, were very limited. Most educated girls of my age and background who didn't remain at home opted for secretarial work or teaching, where they marked time until they snared a suitable husband. I had no desire to do either. The world was a far too interesting place to spend my time drumming the 3Rs into unwilling pupils, or tapping out reams of letters for unappreciative bosses from nine until five, five days a week. It was all so frustrating. A musical career as a concert pianist would not only have opened up new horizons, it would have been the perfect way to avoid that other career option: tedious domesticity, centred on husband, child-rearing and endless afternoon tea parties, at which guests were expected to indulge in polite conversation while sampling thinly sliced cucumber sandwiches and Victoria sponge cake.

Although I had reluctantly put aside my secret dream, and had failed in the concert pianist stakes, I suddenly realised that the medical world was not closed to me entirely. Nursing was a viable and socially acceptable alternative. Furthermore, I would not be depleting the family finances because nurses were actually paid while they trained. It was not a fortune by any means, but full board and lodging, free training and an allowance of 10 shillings a week – the going rate at the time – were not to be sneezed at.

As the minimum age to begin nursing training was 18, I filled in the next 18 months by opening my own music school. My exposure at Miss Bode's concerts now stood me in good stead and, as my mother was a well-known pianist, I soon had enough pupils to keep me going. In early 1928, after informing my surprised but supportive family of my rather unexpected career change, I applied to the Maitland Base Hospital for an interview with Matron Stacey. This time my nerves did not let me down, despite the machine-gun rapidity with which Matron, who was all starch and crackle, fired off the questions. Finally, after a grilling worthy of the secret police, I was ordered to present myself for duty on 16 June 1928, my 18th birthday.

With the admonitions of my mother that I must try and save something from my measly pay packet ringing in my ears, buckets of tears freely flowing and 5 shillings, all my worldly wealth, jingling in my pockets, I boarded the train for the great unknown with high hopes and great expectations. For a relatively naive country girl, who considered an excursion to a neighbouring town a noteworthy event, this translocation to Maitland, fully 40 miles (60 kilometres) away, was on par with emigration to a foreign country.

The base hospital was an imposing, three-storeyed brick building, housing surgical and medical wards and surrounded by large, open-sided verandahs providing plenty of fresh air for the 'chest' patients. About one hundred yards away was an infectious diseases ward for the specialised nursing of patients suffering from scarlet fever, diphtheria or measles. The nearby Nurses' Home, which was to be my accommodation for the next four years, had a large number

Maitland Hospital

of single rooms. We six 'commencers', however, were housed for the probationary period in the one dormitory. To my delight, I spied a piano in the sitting room and looked forward to some lively jam sessions when off duty.

After unpacking my few belongings, I proudly presented myself on my first day of duty, dressed in a crisp uniform consisting of a traditional blue-striped dress, starched collar and cuffs, sensible black lace-up shoes with low heels, black lisle stockings and a stiffly starched white apron cinched with a wide belt. Covering my hair, tortuously scraped clear of my face and neck in the approved regulation manner, was a rather jaunty white cap. The uniform was the same for all trainee nurses except for the difference in the number of small blue bars embroidered on the front of the cap, one for each year of seniority.

First-year trainees, being the lowest in the hospital pecking order, began at the bottom and worked their way up. I was rostered to the Men's Surgical Ward where, on arrival, I was greeted with wide smiles from the patients and a bottle of metal polish and rags by Sister Mendham, who pointed me in the direction of the nearest plumbing fixtures. Feeling somewhat deflated, I was busily shining taps in the sluice room when I heard the magical call of 'Nurse!' It was a patient, and he wanted attention. A second call galvanised me to action. The moment had come to be a ministering angel.

The patient who had called out was a grumpy individual, who ordered me to bring a 'bottle', and be quick about it. Hurrying to the anteroom, I looked around. I had not the slightest idea what kind of a bottle was required so I selected two from a crate awaiting collection, one soda and one lemonade. The patient was not impressed. 'What do you think I am, Nurse, a bloody horse?' His voice was loud and by this time he had the full attention of every patient in the entire ward. On being told exactly to what use the bottle was to be put, and where to find it, I told him that, as he was allowed out of bed, he could use the bathroom. Gathering what dignity I had left, I retreated to the safety of the sluice room where I resumed my tap polishing, red faced with embarrassment and confusion.

However, despite my rather bad start, and the good deal of ribbing that followed, I soon came to enjoy working in the men's ward. In actual fact, I looked forward to being rostered there, as it was the one place in the hospital sure to revive flagging spirits.

I'd only been at Maitland for about six weeks when I was bitten on my lower leg by a red-backed spider. If this sounds dramatic, it was. The pain was excruciating, and while I was assured that, as I had just been bitten once, I had not received sufficient toxin to kill me, it was a most unpleasant experience. There was no antidote in those days, so treatment consisted of cutting across the bite mark with a scalpel and rubbing in a solution of Condy's crystals. As the doctor had predicted, I didn't die, but my leg swelled alarmingly and I had a few weeks off work.

One afternoon after my return, the patients were all quietly reading when someone gave a whistle. To a man, they slid under the bedclothes feigning deep sleep, books abandoned where they fell and conversations cut off in mid-sentence. The reason for this odd behaviour was evidently a female visitor, who entered the ward loaded with sweets, cigarettes and books, but, in spite of her swag of goodies, no one stirred. I watched, fascinated. After surveying the two rows of seemingly comatose forms, the bewildered woman retreated. With her departure, the ward was restored to noisy normality. She seemed harmless enough to me, but apparently none of the patients could stand her, so much so that they preferred to forgo the goodies than put up with her company.

Like all rookie students, I spent an inordinate amount of time in the 'pan room', mastering the art of emptying and washing a seemingly endless supply of bedpans. Weeks of pan detail were followed by lessons in bed making, an exacting science peculiar to hospitals – not unlike precision engineering, but studied only by trainee nurses. The corners of a hospital bed had to be absolutely exact, mitred to a precise angle of 45 degrees before being tucked under the mattress, with sheets and blankets stretched as tight as a drum, so tight that I wondered how patients managed to breathe. After beds had been made to a standard to satisfy Matron, woe betide any patients who rumpled the sheets before she arrived on her rounds, or allowed visitors to sit on the bed. It was only after I graduated from bed making that I was actually allowed to be let loose on patients. Even then, my tasks for some time did not extend beyond the taking and recording of temperatures, under the watchful and very strict eye of a senior sister.

Once I managed to master the basics and ceased to be a probationer, a distinction that gave me a room of my own, I was given more responsibility and was rostered on the night shift. I was working in the men's ward one evening, when a practically naked psychiatric patient, who had been secured to the bed to limit his movement, somehow freed himself from his bonds and made a beeline for the front door. Raising the alarm, I chased after him, but he was up and away, putting on a great burst of speed as he passed beneath the Maitland bridge. By the time the police took over the chase and cornered the fugitive, he had reached the main street, where his dignity was partially restored with a strategically placed sugar bag. He then passed what was left of the night in the cells, which were deemed far more secure than the hospital.

If security was lax at the hospital, it was non-existent at the Nurses' Home, which was totally open, front and back, day and night. With such free and easy access, we were honour-bound to check in after an evening out and the night sister would also do the rounds to see that all was well. This arrangement worked admirably, but did not take into consideration unauthorised entry by members of the public.

One night, after an extremely busy day in theatre, I flopped into bed, exhausted. I fell instantly into a deep sleep, only to be awakened in the early hours of the morning by someone, or something, trying to push me off the bed. The light from the shaded lamp at the end of the hall was far too dim to allow me to see properly, so I staggered to the light switch, bleary eyed and not a little apprehensive. Light flooded the room to reveal a strange man, fully clothed, trying to huddle under the bedclothes. It was obvious, from the stale, beery odour emanating from every pore in his body, that he was in a state of gross inebriation.

Ripping the covers from the bed, I dragged him onto the floor. In response to my demand that he tell me what he wanted, and how he had gained entry, he mumbled, 'I wanted a bloody bed for the night, and as the front door was open I bloody well came in, and now I'm here, I'm bloody well going to stay.'

With a great deal more serenity than I felt, I said in what I hoped was my sweetest, most cajoling voice, 'If you come with me, I'll find you a bed for the night, and arrange for breakfast in bed in the morning.'

The ploy worked. He padded obediently down the hall and followed me into the empty night sister's office where I invited him to wait, saying that I would find the night sister and arrange for someone to show him his room. He received both the promised bed and breakfast: in response to the night sister's urgent call for help, two burly police officers arrived and escorted him to the local lock-up. The following morning when I awoke, rather later than usual, I found that word had circulated about my adventure and I was now considered to be a heroine.

The euphoria did not last long. In fact, it ceased the very next day when I received A Summons From Matron. This was not a good thing. A Summons almost always meant that a breach of discipline had been detected and, for the guilty party, this meant trouble with a very large capital T. Furthermore, any judgement handed down was absolute. There was no hope of any appeal to a higher court, because Matron was at the very top of the hospital pecking order.

Scurrying along the highly polished floors as fast as my leather-soled shoes would allow, I racked my brains to figure out what I could possibly have done to attract the unwelcome attention of Matron, especially after my well-publicised heroics of the previous day. Never one to indulge in preliminaries when dealing with trainees, Matron came straight to the point.

'How many cigarettes a day do you smoke, Nurse?' she barked.

I immediately realised that this was no idle question as a forerunner to a lecture on healthy living. It was a loaded question, a question that, if answered in the affirmative, would lead to instant dismissal. Smoking by nursing staff in the hospital precincts or, heaven forbid, anywhere at all in public was a Cardinal Sin.

Taking a deep breath, I looked her straight in the eye and replied, 'I have never smoked in my life.'

Compressing her lips into an even thinner line, Matron fixed me with a glacial stare before continuing in a voice heavily laced with sarcasm.

'How then, Nurse, do you account for the fact that every morning, when the cleaning staff arrive, your room smells strongly of cigarette smoke.'

Well I couldn't, so I didn't. I had no defence, save the truth, and so I used it. Making a supreme effort to overcome the feeling of doom that threatened to engulf me, I squared my shoulders, returned her gaze and replied in as firm a voice as I could manage, 'Matron, I do not smoke.'

There was no question of Matron allowing me to be placed on remand, much less acquitted. The sole judge at this trial had already made up her mind before one word of a plea had been entered by the accused. The verdict? 'Do not report for duty until the matter is investigated.' In other words, I was suspended.

However, all was not lost. One of the senior sisters, on hearing that I had been carpeted, embarked upon some extracurricular detective work. The following day she told me to follow my usual breakfast routine but not to return to my room.

While I twiddled my thumbs in the sitting room waiting for the time to pass, Sister and Matron made their way to my bedroom. Bursting in, for there was no other word for it, they caught three trainees puffing away. As the sole judge and jury, Matron convened an on-the-spot hearing and handed down the mandatory sentence. By morning tea time the culprits were on their way, and our six trainees had been reduced to three. From then on, I always made sure that the door to my room was locked – I'd had quite enough of unauthorised entries in the past two days.

As nursing was very much 'on the job training', lectures and study had to be fitted into an already heavy workload. However, despite broken shifts, lack of sleep, the constant physical and mental demands, and Matron's ingrained habit of publicly humiliating any trainee who failed to meet her exacting standards, I loved every minute. It seemed no time at all before I had a full set of blue bars on my cap, signalling to everyone that my training period was almost over.

With final examinations looming in May, I grabbed what spare time I could to furiously study. I had to do it on my own, as by this time my remaining companions had fallen by the wayside and I was the only trainee from my group left. Matron Stacey was also no longer at Maitland. She had departed, during my third year of training, to greener pastures at a newly opened Masonic Hospital in Sydney. I don't know if I was sorry to see her go or not. Although she was tough on junior staff, we were assured that she had a softer side, which she displayed to others, but we only heard about. Her replacement was Sister Mendham who, on elevation to Matron, proved to be just as steely as her predecessor.

As I was due for a day off, I decided to combine some study with a day at the beach in Newcastle. Surrounded by lecture notes and various books on anatomy, I started out with good intentions but, seduced by the warmth of the sun and the rhythmic sound of the surf, I fell asleep.

The following morning was sheer agony. Unable to report sick without revealing how badly sunburnt I was, I arrived for duty at the isolation ward pinned into a theatre gown, all that I could bear to wear. My valiant attempts to disguise the severity of my condition came unstuck, however, when Matron Mendham and the doctor arrived on their daily rounds. The loose theatre gown, often worn when attending to isolation patients, attracted no comment, but the odd way in which Nurse Silver was moving about most certainly did. What a battering my ears took as I was escorted to the Nurses' Home where, every day for the next four weeks, my blistered back was subjected to Matron's cure for sunburn: a thorough swabbing with methylated spirits, followed by immersion in a hot bath.

Fortunately, my back healed in time for the final oral and written examinations, held at Newcastle Base Hospital. As Matron was less than confident in my ability to uphold the honour of the hospital and pass the finals, I was not exactly overcome with confidence myself, particularly as she had remarked that it would be a miracle if I struggled through the exams. To add extra sting, she also observed that it would have been far better if my brain had been given to someone who may have made better use of it. Looking back, perhaps it was a ploy for me to work hard enough to prove her wrong.

Nevertheless, she had undermined my confidence. Worried that she might be right, I made my way to Newcastle with a feeling of dread and foreboding. The first part of the oral section, conducted by two doctors, involved the identification of various surgical and dental instruments. As Maitland had a dental ward, with a set of tools identical to those on display, I had no trouble at all in passing this test with flying colours.

The second stage of the oral was conducted by the hospital's Matron Hall, a woman said to be even more intimidating than her counterpart at Maitland, and whose reputation for posing tough questions was legendary. What questions, I wondered, would this coldly efficient arm of the nursing service spring upon a hapless final-year trainee? Would it be a full dissertation on blood circulation, or perhaps a complete rundown on some tropical disease encountered nowhere outside the remote jungles of the Belgian Congo? Would she expect detailed knowledge, in precise medical terminology, of the most obscure parts of the body or, worse, throw in a question based on an area of study that the tutor sisters had somehow failed to cover?

I sat nervously while Matron framed the two questions that, in her opinion, would confirm beyond all doubt my degree of nursing ability, thereby allowing me to sit for the written exams and, provided I passed, to become a registered nursing sister. At last, after a theatrical pause that I felt sure was simply a ruse to create a deliberate state of tension, my inquisitor was ready.

'What is a leech and what is its use, medically speaking?' Matron asked.

I was sure that it must be a trick question but, as I knew of only one kind of leech, I identified the blood-sucking creature and described the medical uses to which it could be put, all to Matron's obvious satisfaction. I then waited in silence, unable to gauge from her deadpan expression what the next question might be. It was even more amazing than the first.

'Tell me Nurse, how does one make a bed in the correct hospital fashion?'

This was best answered by practical demonstration, rather than a verbal account, so under the steely gaze of the highest authority possible in terms of bed making, I set to the task with an energy that would have astounded many, lest Matron change her mind and substitute another question. How many perfectly made beds had rolled off my personal production line so far, I wondered, as I smoothed into place a bed entirely free of wrinkles and with corners that would have satisfied even Pythagoras. Matron Hall was evidently impressed by the depth of my medical knowledge and my level of bed-making expertise after years of intensive training, for I was soon on my way for the last and final test – the written examination at a Newcastle college of education.

Aided by a moderate amount of study and a fairly retentive memory, I found that the questions were well within my capabilities. Despite Matron Mendham's poor opinion of my intellectual capacity, I left the exam room far more buoyantly than I had entered, satisfied with my attempt and confident that I stood a good chance of passing. All I could do now was to return to Maitland and await the results.

Finally, the long-awaited summons from Matron arrived. After dashing into a bathroom to check that nothing was amiss with my appearance, and that no stray hairs were peeking out from beneath my cap, I hurried to the administration block where, after a short but nail-biting wait, I was ushered into Matron's immaculately tidy office.

As usual, there were no preliminaries or any social chitchat. Neither was I invited to sit. In a style reminiscent of a Supreme Court Judge handing down a most unexpected verdict, Matron, without the vestige of a smile, simply intoned, 'I congratulate you, Sister. You passed your examinations well.'

This news was delivered in such a bland style that it took me a second or two to absorb the implication of her words. I'd passed! And passed well! The one and only candidate from Maitland Hospital that year had actually passed her final exams!

Presuming the audience was at an end, I thanked Matron and turned to leave. I had almost made it safely through the door when her voice stopped me mid-stride. Although the hospital's newest nursing graduate had just enjoyed a fleeting moment on centre stage, there was no way Matron was going to allow me to have the last word. Predictably, she added the sting that I knew she could not resist. 'I thought, Nurse Silver, that YOU would be here forever.'

CHAPTER 2

Triple Certificates

1932–1934

Glorying in the title of Sister Silver, and with the results of my examination success printed in the *Sydney Morning Herald* and the local paper for all the world to see, I was preparing to return home to Scone to bask in the warm glow of admiration from family and friends, when I found myself in hospital. Not as a nurse but as a patient, to have my appendix removed.

As this was a most unexpected development, it was reported in the *Scone Advocate*, along with details of my examination success, ensuring that, after I was discharged from hospital and allowed to return home, I had a stream of visitors and well-wishers for the week or so that I was in town.

With my convalescence complete, and now a Registered Nurse, I took the train to Sydney and the prestigious Royal Hospital for Women in Paddington, where I had been accepted to study midwifery, an essential additional qualification in those days when many births took place at home.

The Royal Hospital for Women in Paddington began life in 1820, during the governorship of Lachlan Macquarie, whose wife, Elizabeth, chaired a committee of the Benevolent Society to establish an 'asylum for the poor, blind, aged and infirm'. The building, erected near Turnpike House, in what were then the outskirts of Sydney, also provided care 'for the poor married women during their confinement ... so that the deserving and virtuous poor, in that hour of trial may experience all the sympathy and relief which female tenderness and commiseration can administer'.

The first delivery took place in October 1820 and by June the following year six women had been confined. In 1866, 129 mothers were accommodated in a newly completed northern wing, the Lying-in Hospital of New South Wales. A nurse 'sent by Miss Nightingale from England' was appointed Matron in 1870 and seven years later the hospital embarked upon a formal, organised training program for midwives and nurses. In 1888, it became a training hospital for Sydney University's School of Medicine.

In 1901, the historic buildings that formed the Benevolent Asylum and the Lying-in Hospital were resumed. Part of Central Railway Station now occupies the old site. A seven-acre property on the hills of Paddington was acquired and the large residence on it became the Hospital for Women, Paddington, until a new building was opened in 1905 on Glenmore Road. That same year, the hospital assumed the title of 'Royal' under the patronage of King Edward VII and Queen Alexandra.

Twelve months later, a department was created for the welfare of infants – the first baby health clinic in Australia – to which mothers could bring their babies for consultation and advice. The clinic boasts the longest continuous period of service of an antenatal clinic in the British Commonwealth. The Hospital continued to occupy the Glenmore Road site until 1997, when it moved to nearby Randwick.

The hospital was dubbed 'The Royal', but I discovered that the suburb in which it was located was anything but.

Royal Hospital for Women, Paddington

As I alighted from the tram in busy Oxford Street and made my way along the narrow streets and lanes towards the hospital, exploring my new environment, I wondered why, with so much space available, the early inhabitants had not given themselves a bit more room. The houses here were just as crowded as those in many English industrial cities. The streets were, for the most part, fairly steep and twisting, and lined with row upon row of terrace houses, some small, some quite large, the pattern broken only by the inevitable corner shop. Here and there, an old detached single dwelling, constructed from faded cedar planking or beautiful hand-hewn sandstone, relieved the monotony of the smug facades of the more ornate Victorian edifices.

Occasionally, I spotted a solitary grand mansion, a relic of colonial days when gentlemen of substantial means built country estates in an area that was, at that time, far removed from the squalor of a Sydney struggling for identity. However, by 1930, Sydney, like most of Australia, was in the grip of the Great Depression and, with so many out of work, parts of Paddington were looking decidedly down-at-heel.

After Maitland, which was a reasonably large hospital, I found The Royal rather daunting, with hundreds of beds accommodating women suffering from a huge variety of gynaecological and obstetrical disorders. However, it was definitely the place to gain experience and I couldn't complain about the pay – there wasn't any – just a small weekly allowance. Worse, on enrolment, all graduate sisters were demoted to the rank of plain nurse, with conditions of 'employment' to suit.

Midwifery was about confinement of the mother and the safe delivery of a healthy baby. It followed that the more babies a nurse could deliver, the more proficient she could become. Aware that most babies seemed to arrive in the wee small hours of the morning, I volunteered for the night shift. I had no trouble securing all the hours I wanted, as my fellow nurses were far more interested in spending the night curled up in a warm bed than hanging about a draughty delivery room, especially in winter. My strategy worked and I was amply rewarded. While I was at The Royal, I notched up 103 deliveries, 32 of them solo.

But it was the antenatal room that really tested my level of expertise. With no ultrasound, and X-rays only used as a last resort, trying to determine the position of the unborn child by feel alone could be tricky. Was this its bottom or its head, or heaven forbid, could there be more than one foetus? It was important to know this in advance because, unless the patient was a first-time mother, or there was some complication, we midwives, not doctors, were responsible for all deliveries.

If a medical emergency occurred and a Caesarean section or some other surgical intervention was warranted, we were often called to assist the surgeon. One evening, after a particularly hectic few days and feeling unusually tired, I was on duty when a call went out for my urgent assistance in the theatre. Bruce Williams, a most eminent obstetrician and the hospital's medical superintendent, was about to undertake a rare emergency procedure, one usually confined to textbooks. All other available staff members were urged to report to the observation gallery to witness the decapitation and surgical removal of the body of a baby who had died before being fully delivered. It sounded very gruesome and I was not at all keen to assist, but I scrubbed up as requested and was managing quite well when, about half-way through the operation, Dr Williams stopped and said in a very loud voice, 'Nurse, what on earth's the matter with your leg?'

Nonplussed, I replied, 'Why, nothing, Sir.'

'Nothing!' he roared. 'Have you noticed the size of it?'

His voice boomed around the small confines of the theatre, and beyond it. From behind the glass of the observation gallery, the eyes of 200 interns and nurses swivelled from the anaesthetised patient, lying draped upon the table, to my swollen left leg. Feeling an explanation was in order, I shrugged my shoulders and, with my voice a little muffled by the surgical mask, said, 'Well, Sir, I WAS bitten by a red-backed spider', only to be cut off mid-sentence.

The surgeon, his patient forgotten for the time being, drowned out the remainder of my words, bellowing that I must report to the registrar at once and stay in bed until the swelling had subsided. I turned and fled, not to the registrar, but to my room. I stayed there, in bed, in luxuriously wicked bliss, blessing the spider that had given me this most unexpected rest, five years after I was bitten. The only long-lasting effect had been to my lymph glands, which were blocked and tended to cause my leg to swell, especially if I spent many hours on my feet, thereby earning me a few wonderful hours of illicit respite.

Despite the 12-hour duty rosters and periods of intensive study, nurses sometimes managed to have some free time. No one was over-endowed with cash, but there were always plenty of books to read, or tennis to play or, if relatives or friends had been generous, perhaps a trip to the pictures. One evening, being unusually flush with funds sent by Mother for Christmas, I splashed out on tickets to a live show for myself and a fellow nurse.

It was an evening performance. We arrived back at the respectable hour of 11 or so to discover that, in accordance with hospital regulations, all entrances to the Nurses' Home had been securely locked at 10 pm and that no one had remembered to unofficially leave a side door open for us. There was no other way in. This was no Maitland Base Hospital with its wander in, wander out attitude. This was The Royal.

After circling the building several times, we had all but given up any thought of gaining entry before dawn when I spied a small window ajar in one of the first-floor bathrooms. I was the taller by far so, clambering onto my friend's shoulders, I managed to push up the sash and haul myself onto the narrow sill. Balancing precariously, I swung my legs around and dropped through the opening, landing squarely in the open toilet bowl. With one foot, clad in one of my best leather shoes, wedged in the S-bend and the other in the bowl, I was wondering how to extricate myself when the night sister arrived to investigate the commotion. To my relief, she burst into laughter and effected a rescue, along with the admonition not to make so much noise next time.

The night sister did not strike me as a 'dobber', but I was re-evaluating my assessment the next morning when told to report to the Sister-in-Charge – a most powerful and intimidating woman. Known to junior staff as 'The Flying Squad', she habitually patrolled the corridors on the lookout for real or imagined transgressions. Fortunately, she was endowed with such ample proportions that, with veil starched to board-like stiffness billowing out behind her like a spinnaker in a stiff breeze, we usually managed to see her before she saw us.

Despite my assumptions, my summons to report to the Flying Squad did not, as I so guiltily had imagined, herald a reprimand for my unconventional nocturnal ablutions. As I now had acquired the necessary level of obstetrical skill, I was being assigned to undertake 'district nursing' – a service that required medical staff to be on call 24 hours a day, to undertake home visits to the impoverished, the frail and the house-bound. I was to be in charge of a squad, consisting of a raw, rather nervous male intern and a junior nurse. The appointment was effective immediately.

The first shift passed quite without incident until about 5 pm, when we were called urgently for a confinement in The Rocks – a very sleazy part of the city on the western side of Circular Quay and the haunt of cut-throats, petty criminals and just the plain poor for generations. The roads were badly paved, the rat-infested alleys poorly lit and many of the houses were merely shacks. Carrying our obstetrical gear, we picked our way across the overflowing drains and narrow, refuse-strewn streets to a dilapidated shanty. Above, and completely dwarfing the pitiful hovels huddling beneath, were the towering granite pylons of the recently completed Sydney Harbour Bridge. Viewing the decaying wood of the lopsided, filth-encrusted front door with some distaste, I delegated the job of knocking on it to the intern, who gave a substantial rap. The sound echoed hollowly, but brought no response.

'Give it another jolly good bang,' I whispered, 'and belt it a bit harder if you can.'

The intern rapped again, more loudly. This time a gruff male voice roared from the dim interior, 'Get to 'ell out of 'ere!' Quite unperturbed, we stood our ground and knocked yet again. This time, we were rewarded with a faint and gentle, 'Come in.'

We three entered a scene of the most abject poverty. The shanty, for it hardly qualified as a house, consisted of just one room with a lean-to kitchen and lavatory. Lying on the floor of the kitchen area was the man, a boarder, who had responded so belligerently to our knock, and who now bluntly told us in words of one syllable to shove off. He was on the floor because the one and only bed was occupied – four children, a man inebriated to the point of unconsciousness who was evidently their father, and a woman, well into labour with offspring number five.

With a great deal of pushing, pulling and dragging, we managed to evict the comatose father from the communal bed and onto the floor, where he slumbered on, completely oblivious to what was happening. The four wide-eyed children were bedded down on the floor with two mouldy-looking pillows and two tatty pieces of clothing, which barely covered their thin little bodies. With great trepidation, in these less than ideal conditions, I turned my attention to the patient, who soon delivered a remarkably healthy-looking baby. After swaddling the child in worn but clean baby clothes that the mother had ready, I tucked them both into bed.

It was with a feeling of great relief that we picked our way past the father, still out to it, and the hostile boarder, still scowling at us from the floor, to the front door, still standing open on its sagging hinges. But our relief was short lived. Emerging into the gloom of the poorly lit street, we were greeted by a barrage of stones and abuse, hurled by local residents whose sole aim was to chase from their patch, and as quickly as possible, anyone who smacked remotely of authority. Stopping only to sling a few rocks back at our tormentors, we took to our heels to the relative safety of Lower George Street.

The joy I had felt at the safe delivery of the baby was now completely overshadowed – not

Typical slum housing

by the hostile rock-throwing reception committee but by an overwhelming sense of pity for the woman and her family, condemned to a life of misery that I realised was pretty much without hope and from which the chance of escape was slim. It was the first time I had ever come face to face with such misery. My comfortable, you could say sheltered, life in Scone and the clean and efficient hospitals I had worked in had not prepared me in any way for the shock of District Nursing. It was sobering to see at first hand the dreadful conditions in which many people lived, and even more sobering to realise that there was not a single thing I could do to improve the lot in life of the tiny helpless baby I had just helped bring into the world.

Fortunately, District Visiting was not usually so traumatic. Irrespective of the mother's social standing, I found the safe delivery of a healthy, bawling infant an immensely satisfying experience. Each new arrival was as precious and special as the last, and even after so many deliveries I still marvelled at the wonder of it all.

I gained my Midwifery Certificate, but had I known what was in store when these tiny scraps of humanity grew into less than docile children, I may have been content to call a halt to any further study. However, with two certificates now to my name, the third, for Tresillian training, called enticingly. Once again, I was relegated to the status of trainee, but although it was 'on the job' training, unlike midwifery, there was no allowance.

The Tresillian Welfare Home for Mothers and Babies in the lower North Shore suburb of Willoughby was, from the outside, serene and quite beautiful, so much so that many passers-by assumed it was a large private residence. However, those who ventured inside soon discovered that serenity stopped at the front door. Apart from providing specialised care for mothers and babies, this particular institution was also the domain of babies and small children with feeding problems, and the Tresillian-trained nurses whose task it was to teach them to eat normally.

Upstairs, beyond the sweep of the handsomely balustraded staircase, it was peaceful enough, for here the mothers with very small babies rested in private, well-appointed wards. Downstairs

Tresillian Home, Willoughby

was where all the action took place. Downstairs was where recalcitrant children, who made meal times a nightmare by throwing their food about and refusing to eat, were 'educated'.

Basically, the strategy was one of smiling non-aggression by the nursing staff, who calmly cleaned up the mess and offered another plate of food until their charges realised the futility of the game and mended their ways. It could take days. Spoonfuls of oatmeal, sometimes entire plates, were upended and splattered about. Not even that old Australian standby, buttered bread and Vegemite, did the trick. The baby brigade outwitted the adults at every turn and day after day the pantomime continued, until some of the little darlings caved in under the relentless pressure. Deemed to be 'cured', they would be packed off home, only to be replaced by another lot of equally delinquent toddlers. If nothing else, this part of my training, which lasted three very long months, taught me the art of infinite patience and never to underestimate the cunning of small children.

Fortunately, my stint at the food education centre was followed by a far more enjoyable period at the Baby Clinic, offering advice to first-time mothers. I must have done something right, because I was presented with my third and very precious certificate. The news did not escape the attention of the local press, which later broadcast the fact that I was one of the youngest nursing sisters in the state to possess all three certificates.

Now a fully qualified, triple-certificated sister, my next and very pressing step was to find paid employment. As my bank balance after more than a year without pay amounted to precisely £4, I immediately registered for work at the Manly Nurses' Club, which also offered accommodation. After paying for the room, I then rather recklessly boarded a ferry to the city, where I blew almost every remaining penny on a slap-up meal.

On my return, and now virtually impoverished, I learned that in my absence I had been offered a job as night nurse for the next three months in the general hospital at Kurri Kurri, a coal-mining town north-west of Newcastle. I was elated. I could replenish my bank account and Kurri Kurri, being so close to Maitland, would provide me with a ready-made and agreeable social life. There was only one catch – having spent all my spare cash on that gastronomic feast I didn't have enough for the train fare. Fortunately, Jean, who was now living at nearby Dee Why, came to the rescue.

Kurri Kurri Hospital was quite large but, for some obscure reason, was situated in an area surrounded by quarries, deep cliffs and water-filled gullies. After a quick inspection to gain my bearings, I began tackling the important task of re-establishing my social network. A few quick calls to Maitland, only a few miles away, were all that was required to ensure invitations to the picnic races, race ball, and any other important event scheduled for the coming weeks.

Night duty was most pleasant, except for one thing. As there was no kitchen in the isolation ward, for 30 minutes each evening I was required to swap places with the sister there, so that she could have her evening meal. Built between two cliffs and surrounded by towering rocks and shadow-filled quarries, the isolation ward was indeed isolated, and a most eerie place. It was also deathly quiet, so much so that when a door banged I nearly jumped out of my skin. I spent the entire time there nervously counting off each minute, until the isolation sister reappeared, allowing me to escape to the cosily familiar surroundings of the main hospital.

It was routine procedure, when I came on duty each evening, to review any new admissions scheduled for surgery the following day. One night towards the end of my employment period, and just before I left for the half-hour stint in the isolation ward, I made sure that two recently admitted women patients were sedated and sleeping peacefully. I was therefore somewhat surprised, on returning from isolation, to find one of the newcomers' beds empty. The junior nurse, who had not seen any patients at all roaming about, let alone one in a state of drug-induced semi-consciousness, could offer no clues to her whereabouts. After a thorough search of all the bathrooms and every conceivable hiding place, I came to the appalling conclusion that I had 'lost' one of my patients.

I informed Matron, who ordered me to contact the police as a search party must be organised without delay. While the local constabulary and their civilian helpers combed the area by the light of hurricane lamps, I telephoned the patient's husband in the hope that she may have returned home. She hadn't, and the hospital now had to cope with a frantic husband, who immediately joined in the search, spurred on, doubtless, by the same mental image that was torturing me – a nightdress-clad body lying at the bottom of a cliff or floating in a water-filled gully.

The search continued throughout the night and it was nearly dawn when one of the junior nurses, who had admitted the two women, suggested that maybe we were looking for the wrong person. She suspected that the 'missing' patient might be the one still in bed, sound asleep, and that it was her companion who had wandered off. With the husband still out searching, and therefore unable to provide positive identification of the sedated woman, I telephoned the other household. The nurse was right. The missing patient, who had turned up at her house at about midnight in a dazed condition, was in her own bed, fast asleep.

If the hours of darkness brought occasional dramas, so too did the days, although not in the medical sense. One of the nurses, who came from the country town of Dungog, had brought her horse with her, which she kept in the hospital paddock. In conversation one day, she asked if I liked riding. Never keen to admit a lack of experience in anything, especially to my contemporaries, I conveniently forgot that it was simply years since I had been on the back of a horse and somehow managed to convey the impression that I was an accomplished horsewoman.

'Good,' she said. 'He's been eating his head off for days and could do with a long, hard gallop. I can't do it because I'm on duty, but he's all yours.'

Ensnared in the web of deceit I had so foolishly spun, I was now stuck with the consequences. As there was no way I could wriggle out of equine exercise duty, I said I'd take him for a gallop early the next morning, while it was still cool. It was my day off and my plan was to ride the 18 miles (29 kilometres) into Maitland very sedately, at about walking pace. Even I, with my limited riding experience, could surely manage that.

When I arrived at the paddock the following morning, I coaxed the horse into his bit and bridle, gently placed the saddle on his back and gingerly mounted for my leisurely trip into town. The horse, however, had other ideas. As soon as we hit the open road, he picked up speed and, with head down and tail up, took off. I clung on for dear life, shouting for someone to help, but there was not a soul to be seen. By some miracle, I stayed upright and was still in the saddle when we finally reached Maitland, having covered the 18 miles (29 kilometres) in what must have been record time. Somewhere en route I lost my hat and a shoe, along with my pride and any vestige of confidence I had left.

Pulling with all my might, I slowed the beast to a trot, just in time to see a group of friends gathered on the lawn in front of their house. Greetings were cheerily exchanged, but I declined the offer of a cup of tea: not because I didn't want one, but because I dared not, and could not, get off the horse. In any case, the decision was taken out of my hands. As I loosened my grip on the reins to wave goodbye, he took off again, and it was with great difficulty that I clattered to a noisy stop at the home of a friend and her husband, with whom I had arranged to stay the night.

My host put out his hand to help me down, but I couldn't move. My legs were stiff as posts and my backside was in an indescribable condition. With two helpers holding the horse's headgear, and another firmly grasping the saddle, I made my first voluntary movement since leaving Kurri Kurri. Sensing the weight shift, the horse braced his legs, arched his back and unceremoniously dumped me onto the ground. I lay there, not moving an inch, for the simple reason that I couldn't. After ascertaining that I was still alive, the two helpers carried me indoors, away from the stares of interested passers-by, while a third tied the horse to the fence.

As nothing would ever induce me to go near the brute again, I sent him back to his owner in the back of a truck, along with a message that I had been unexpectedly taken ill. After spending two days recovering in bed at the home of my friends, I returned to work, where the Dungog nurse expressed concern for my welfare and her disappointment that I had been laid low and couldn't ride him back. However, as the trip to Maitland had done him wonders, she extended an invitation for me to take him for a gallop at any time I liked.

Fortunately, I didn't have to invent an excuse to decline the offer as I was due to depart the next day. My three-month contract at Kurri Kurri was up.

Kurri Kurri Hospital

I headed home for a break. It was wonderful to spend time with family and friends, catching up on gossip and revisiting old haunts, but after a while I was vexed by the inactivity.

In the New Year I treated myself to a holiday of a voyage to Lord Howe Island, a magical tropical volcanic remnant in the South Pacific Ocean, about 370 miles (595 kilometres) east of Port Macquarie. It was the first time I had been any distance from home and it certainly whetted my appetite to broaden my horizons.

After that, my return to Scone was a bit flat. I realised that I was simply not cut out for life in a small, conservative country town. What had been comfortably predictable was now mind-numbingly boring, and the local social scene claustrophobic.

The wide open spaces were calling and, almost without realising it, I came to the conclusion that I really needed to get away, to go bush, not to the relatively civilised bush of the Hunter Valley, but to the real bush, the bush so loved by poet Dorothea Mackellar – the vast, limitless plains of the outback.

CHAPTER 3

The Far West Children's Health Scheme

1935

Even today the words 'going bush' conjure up images of wide, open spaces, of red dust, brilliant blue skies and over-bright colours. In the mid-1930s, going bush often meant intense isolation, with tracks rather than roads linking towns, some not much more than outposts of the nation. For someone anxious to escape from the cloying, repressive atmosphere of a country town that was not quite bush and not quite city, this vastness was its very attraction.

All I needed was to find a job, preferably way out west. There were plenty of nursing positions available, but most were for general nursing posts in the city or in large country centres. I was beginning to resign myself to the fact that finances might force me to go down this path when, in mid-March, I spotted a small notice in the classified section of Saturday's *Sydney Morning Herald.*

POSITIONS VACANT

Nurse, trebly trained, required for country position.
Applicants to state age, qualifications, when available, and forward copies of testimonials and personal references to:
General Secretary, Far West Children's Health Scheme, Box 3277PP GPO Sydney.

The Far West! That definitely sounded like the bush. And as three certificates were mandatory,

Stanley Drummond

the actual job should be interesting. Hoping that my three months at Kurri Kurri would be of sufficient duration to qualify as 'experience', I posted off my application and was granted an interview with a man named Stanley Drummond. Within days I was on my way to the beachfront at Manly on the northern side of Sydney Harbour where, rather incongruously, the Far West Children's Health Scheme was based.

The Far West Children's Health Scheme was the brainchild of Stanley Gillick Drummond, son of James Drummond, a saddler born in the Victorian town of Beechworth in 1852. In his twenties, following the death of his first wife, Elizabeth, and their baby son, James decided to become a schoolteacher, a profession he rated very highly – second only to that of the clergy, and superior to medicine. Joining the New South Wales Department of Public Instruction, James Drummond taught in Sydney and in various country towns, including Albury, Wagga Wagga, Tamworth, Appin, Laguna, Barrington and Lostock, on the Paterson River.

During the 21-year period from 1879 to 1900, his second wife, Mary Jane (known as Polly), nine years his junior, whom he married at Albury in 1879, bore him a total of eight girls and three boys, of whom three died in infancy. In 1903, while posted to Nimmitabel on the Monaro, ill-health forced James to return to his former trade, which he was able to combine with teaching at a subsidised school at Springfield, a property on which he worked.

Stanley, his second eldest son and fourth child, was born on 22 May 1884 at Attunga, a small town about 500 kilometres north-west of Sydney, between Tamworth and Manilla.

Unlike his younger brother, Norman, Stanley showed no inclination to follow in his father's footsteps, much preferring to be outdoors playing cricket rather than sitting inside with his nose in a book.

James Drummond was undoubtedly most disappointed when Stanley left school to become a junior clerk in the Queanbeyan office of the New South Wales Department of Lands and even more disappointed when, following a severe bout of pneumonia, he resigned from his office job in favour of outdoor manual employment. Stanley, who was good with his hands, returned to Nimmitabel and soon found employment as a carpenter's mate, working mainly on the construction of timber buildings. With his health fully restored, he was visiting a family who lived in Colombo (now Bemboka, on the Nimmitabel–Bega road) when he felt 'called' to the ministry. The decision to give up carpentry and become a clergyman met with his father's complete approval.

In 1905, at the age of 21, Stanley entered the Evangelical Training School run by the Central Methodist Mission in Sydney, where he displayed a hitherto hidden talent for study, topping the final examinations at the end of the three-year training period. His first posting, in 1909, was as a probationary minister based at Bulahdelah, a timber town on the New South Wales mid-north coast. However, Stanley had not completed his first 12 months 'on the circuit' when he was thrown from his sulky, landing with great force against a tree-stump and injuring his hip so severely that he was fitted with an iron splint extending from ankle to armpit. Forced to give up his ministry, he moved to Bowral in the New South Wales Southern Highlands, where he passed the time studying art and painting. In 1911, he married Lucy Doust, a qualified deaconess, whom he had met while studying for the ministry.

For the first two years of his enforced retirement, Stanley moved about with the aid of crutches. He could stand and lie down but, as the splint was not jointed, sitting was impossible. In the hope of restoring some mobility to his injured muscles, he embarked upon an intensive physiotherapy program. After several months, he was able to walk without the aid of either splint or crutches.

With his mobility restored, Stanley Drummond returned to the ministry in 1914. His first appointment was as probationary pastor at Rylstone, on the fertile western slopes of the Blue Mountains, where he and Lucy somehow managed to survive the next four years on a single man's salary. From Rylstone they moved to Canowindra, where Stanley and a local parish priest, Father Donovan, joined forces to help establish a hospital, dedicated to the memory of those who had lost their lives in the Great War. In 1924, after a 12-month posting at Yass, Stanley accepted the position of Superintendent of the Far West Mission, based in the mining town of Cobar. The area he was to administer covered 233,000 square kilometres.

On Good Friday 1924, he and Lucy left Sydney by train for Cobar – a town of just 1,250 souls, but once a thriving metropolis of 10,000 people, 2,000 of whom were employed by the Great Cobar Copper Mine. This massive enterprise, with its 14 smelters and 64 metre high smoke stack, had closed down in 1919, following a drop in the demand for copper after the Great War.

The closure of the mine, and others, had dealt the community an almost fatal blow. Where previously there had been a prosperous town with well-stocked department stores, late Saturday night shopping, live theatre, horse racing (the most notable turf fixture being the famed Longworth Cup), four brass bands and a cordial factory, now there were abandoned houses and boarded up shops. The exodus from Cobar itself was so great that empty timber houses were dismantled and transported to Sydney, notably the suburb of Bankstown.

Within a month of their arrival, Stanley and Lucy set off to visit as many homes as possible, scattered widely across their vast domain. The train line went no further west than Cobar, so travel was in a large, canvas-roofed Vauxhall car belonging to Tommy Clapperton, the local hire-car proprietor. Perched alongside the spare tyres, spare parts and other paraphernalia strapped to the vehicle's wide running boards was Vaux, the Drummonds' recently acquired cocker spaniel.

Even in ideal conditions, it took the best part of two days to cover the 260 kilometres of sandy track linking Cobar to Wilcannia on the Darling River. Fortunately, the weather remained fine, allowing the Drummonds to reach Allendy Station the first night. The following morning, as Stanley reversed the car from its parking space beneath the high-set verandah, a key on the pinion's differential sheared off. Their host, Mr Hudson, was able to fix it, but their arrival at Wilcannia was delayed by 24 hours. A rather impatient and impetuous man, Stanley chafed at the delay. He had yet to learn that, to people who lived this far west, time was of little consequence.

In earlier times, the Murray–Darling river system was a vital communication link between Victoria and South Australia and the interior of New South Wales, and Wilcannia, on the east–west overland track, an important inland port. Although the 'Queen City of the West' no longer handled anything like the number of river craft as in days gone by, steamers still plied for trade between Adelaide, Echuca, Goolwa, Wentworth and Bourke, provided the Darling had sufficient flow. Wilcannia, an important mail centre, had excellent facilities, including a police station, court house, school and hospital, but with many of its citizens lured further west by the rich silver, lead and zinc deposits at Broken Hill, the town's population now stood at around a thousand.

Their host during their stay was a fellow clergyman, George White, who had volunteered to assist with services and pastoral visits on the trip. Before they set off, Stanley spent some time poring over maps and, more especially, water charts showing the position of artesian bores and tanks, all drawn up by George's predecessor, Reverend Keeling. Much of their journey, as they progressed further into the interior, would be cross country, so Stanley studied this material with more than passing interest. Despite its obvious importance, it was not until they were well on the track to the opal-mining town of White Cliffs that they realised that the maps and water charts had somehow been left behind. Unaware of just how desolate the region beyond White Cliffs would be, they decided to push on.

The next day, after taking careful note of directions supplied by the locals at White Cliffs, they headed north-west, hoping to intercept the road linking Broken Hill to Tibooburra. The trio carried some water and had taken the precaution of having the car overhauled at White Cliffs but, as the country became increasingly barren, Drummond and White grew uneasy. As far as the eye could see, treeless plains stretched in all directions, the grey–green saltbush broken only by vast clay pans, their salt-encrusted surfaces dazzlingly white in the brilliant sunlight. If the Vauxhall broke down, or was delayed in any way, water would be a problem. Creeks were few and far between, and those they crossed were bone dry.

Fortunately, there were no breakdowns and it was with a feeling of relief that, at about 3.30 pm, they reached Yancannia Homestead, situated just south of the rather grandly named Yancannia Range, an area of high ground in the otherwise flat and featureless landscape. After a refreshing cup of tea with the station owner, they set off again. They hoped to make Morden Station by nightfall but had only travelled about 25 kilometres when the differential broke again, forcing them to spend the night in the open. Lucy, being the only female, bedded down in the comparative luxury of the car. The men draped themselves across two partially inflated inner tubes, twisted to form a figure eight, and slept behind the only stretcher, turned on its side to form a windbreak,

With the sunrise came the reality that they were stranded at the edge of Sturt's Stony Desert, with few tools, limited water supplies and only a very small amount of food. Breakfast for each consisted of half a wholemeal biscuit and half a pannikin of water mixed with condensed milk. After spending the entire day under a blazingly hot sun, the men succeeded in putting a new key in the pinion and the following morning, after another frugal meal, they set off, with no idea of where, or if, they would find water. Fortunately, about 6 kilometres further on, they spotted a slight rise, which on closer inspection proved to be the earthen wall of a government tank.

With their water supplies replenished, they continued along the track, the surface of which was extremely rough. Twelve months before, following heavy rain, a camel train had passed over it, churning the mud into thousands of peaks and troughs, which had then baked rock hard in the sun. The Vauxhall negotiated this bone-jarring section successfully, only to become bogged in the dry sand at the Palgamurie Creek crossing. Fortunately, the travellers had been following a lorry, whose driver stopped and pulled them free, before pointing them in the direction of the Broken Hill–Tibooburra road.

Towards sundown, they reached an impassable sandhill. After scouting around, they found traces of a 'road', evidently the Broken Hill–Tibooburra track, which led to a low point in the hills. Gunning the engine, Stanley took a run at the dune only to stop dead, well short of the crest. Undeterred, he rolled the car back and tried again, with Lucy and George adding their combined strength to push it just that little bit further. This process was repeated, making a little more progress each time until, finally, the vehicle broached the top of the rise and slithered down the other side.

It was dark by the time they reached the shores of Cobham Lake. To their dismay, they discovered that, while they had water in abundance, they had no means of making a fire – there was not a stick or a tree to be seen. With the aid of the headlamps, the two men began to scour the area, eventually locating the tip of a small tree stump buried in the sand.

The next morning, they discovered that the sandhill they had crossed the previous evening was the first of many, extending for another 12 kilometres. By employing the same technique as previously, they managed to get through, despite a heavy landing on the far side of one dune when the car became airborne, crashing to earth with a terrific thud, which snapped the wing of the hood frame and scattered luggage and gear in all directions.

To their relief, this 'terrible experience' in the dunes came to an end when they located the track again, leading to Coally Homestead. After recovering from the surprise of seeing a Vauxhall car emerge from the wilderness with three passengers, one of whom was a woman, the station owner and his wife immediately extended their hospitality. Refreshed, the intrepid travellers headed north to Milparinka.

Surrounded by stony plains, this once thriving township, situated near the Grey Range about 270 kilometres north-west of Wilcannia, had once served the Mt Browne goldfield and appeared at first sight to be deserted. The abandoned roofless houses, stripped of their corrugated iron when the gold ran out, coupled with crumbling ruins of cement and brick buildings, were, Drummond recorded, 'So dreary and desolate that it brought the words "Sodom and Gomorrah" into one's mind'.

Adding to this air of desolation was an almost complete lack of vegetation for, apart from the gums lining the nearby Milparinka Creek and Waterhole, there was not a tree to be seen. There were not many people either, for the town's entire population stood at less than 20, with two families, the Bonnetts and the Bakers, running the post office, general store, garage and hotel. The travellers received a warm welcome from Mrs Bonnett, the licensee of the one and only hotel, the postmistress Mrs Baker and the district's sole policeman, Constable Hughes.

For the next 40 kilometres, they passed through a very lonely stretch of countryside until, in the distance, jagged granite rocks loomed from the monotonously level horizon. Within their rim lay Tibooburra, another former gold town of about 300 people, and a vital centre for the surrounding sheep properties. Far more prosperous looking than Milparinka, Tibooburra boasted amenities that included several stores, a bank, post office, police station, undertaker and a hospital. The sandy main street was bordered with houses built entirely of corrugated iron, with a more substantial cement building here and there. The one constant and notable architectural feature of each dwelling, irrespective of the method of construction, was an extended roofline, which sloped steeply towards the ground to reduce the glare. Looking forward to a good soak in a hot bath, the travellers checked into the Hotel Central Australia, only to have the licensee, Mrs Best, present them with a dipper. It held their daily water ration, to be shared among all three.

They were now in an extremely remote area of the state. After organising the repair of a spare axle, they pushed on to Yalpunga, which consisted of a post office cum general store, a blacksmith's forge and one other house. As they drove up, Drummond ran over what he thought was a sandy hump, only to discover, when the front tyre burst, that it was a heap of half-buried beer bottles.

With the tyre changed, and with the population of Yalpunga, one woman and two men, treating them with indifference, they set off for The Corner, where the state boundaries of New South Wales, Queensland and South Australia met, the limit of their journey. Basing themselves at Onepah Station, just inside the New South Wales–Queensland border, they

The Overland trip

made numerous trips in various directions, determined to visit as many people as possible, irrespective of their religious beliefs. State lines meant nothing to Drummond, as he criss-crossed the entire area, calling on station owners, doggers, boundary riders, stock inspectors and workers at lonely out-stations, especially those who had children.

After a stopover at Olive Downs, where they learned that the wool clip was taken by camel train to the nearest railheads at Bourke and Broken Hill, they visited Mt Wood Station and then Mt Stuart. During their stay at the latter, their hostess Mrs Agnes Poole, now a grey-haired woman of about 60 years, revealed that she had come as a bride to Mt Stuart in 1884. Leaving a comfortable lifestyle in Melbourne, she had travelled by train to Hay, and then by Cobb & Co coach to Wilcannia, where she transferred to a horse and buggy for the rest of the gruelling journey. Besides battling 28 severe droughts and helping her husband on the property, she also managed to raise eight children and care for the station hands and Aborigines camped along the creek.

After retracing their steps to Onepah Station, the expedition returned to Milparinka, no longer a semi-ghost town. Word had spread to the 300 or so people who lived in the surrounding area that the preachers were coming back to conduct a service. Leaving George behind to do the honours, the Drummonds struck off cross-country towards the south-west and the South Australian border, hoping to reach Yandama Station, the most remote of the many outposts on their visiting list. First stop was Mt Sturt Station, named for the explorer Captain Charles Sturt, best remembered for his futile search to find an inland sea. The comfortable homestead, with its dark green trees surrounding the home paddock, was a welcome change from the otherwise dun-coloured landscape.

The next afternoon the Drummonds were on their way to nearby Mt Poole when the car broke down in a dry creek crossing. With little likelihood of anyone passing by on such an isolated track, they were forced to undertake an arduous trek through heavy sand and then across rough stony ground to the homestead, which they reached shortly before 9 o'clock that night. A tow was arranged, and by midnight Stanley had the car ready for the following day's journey.

Morning revealed a scene of great beauty. In place of the featureless desert, which had been so much in evidence for most of their journey, were the cliffs of Mt Poole, at the foot of which wound a beautiful, water-filled creek. A short distance from the homestead, nestling against one of the cliffs, was an outcrop of castle-like rocks, parts of which resembled the pipes of a giant organ.

It was here, in 1844, that Charles Sturt and his companions – the first Europeans to penetrate the region – had created 'Depot Glen', camping beside the life-sustaining water until the weather moderated sufficiently to allow them to return to civilisation. While they waited, James Poole, the expedition's second-in-command, had died. After visiting his grave, and against their better judgement, given the condition of the road and the previous problems with the differential, the Drummonds headed for Yandama, about 80 kilometres away.

Their goal successfully achieved, they collected George from Milparinka before heading to Morden Station, which the broken differential had forced them to bypass on the inward journey. At Morden they picked up a couple of passengers: a postal inspector and his friend who needed a lift to White Cliffs. From there, it was a relatively quick trip to Wilcannia.

The trip had been far more arduous and nerve-wracking than Stanley admitted in his diary. He failed to mention many of the breakdowns and flat tyres, and that the vehicle had sustained more damage than a broken roof strut. No one was more pleased to see the lights of the Darling River township than George White, who had not previously travelled beyond White Cliffs. As he began to recognise familiar landmarks, George whistled and sang, improvising words of thanksgiving to well-known hymn tunes. He was certainly overjoyed to be back, but it would be 10 days before the Drummonds could go home. Stanley's hip injury had flared up, provoking an enforced rest with a local family, before embarking upon the final leg to Cobar. The pair had scarcely unpacked their belongings and resumed normal life before they were on their way to Sydney, and hospital, on the orders of Dr Holland. Stanley had been diagnosed with gallstones.

A master of understatement, Drummond later described their epic journey across scarcely made roads into some of the remotest areas in Australia as 'educational'. However, the impact was far greater than that. Although struck by the extreme isolation of many of the families they had visited and appalled by the hand-to-mouth existence of so many of them, he and Lucy were greatly affected by the plight of the children, many of whom were fatherless as a result of the dreadful loss of life sustained during the Great War.

Others, whose fathers had survived the bloodbaths of Gallipoli and the Western Front, lived on soldier settlement blocks: Crown land granted by a grateful government to its wartime heroes; land which, the returned soldiers discovered, was generally situated in areas of extremely marginal rainfall and far too small to sustain viable farming of any kind. With timber scarce, and bricks far too costly, the roughly built cottages of so many struggling settlers and government bore keepers were constructed entirely of corrugated iron. Although tough and resilient, it absorbed and retained heat to such a degree that, during the hottest months, the occupants were forced to live in rough bough shelters on the shaded side. In winter, when the temperatures dropped to below freezing at night, the iron huts were colder than an icebox.

Cut off from outside contact, and often poorly nourished and in ill health, many of the children who lived on the remote out-stations that the Drummonds visited were the hidden victims of outback isolation. A large number suffered from disfiguring bone malformations, trachoma (a blinding condition caused by sandy grit lodging under the eyelids and commonly known as 'sandy blight') and congenital disabilities which, while not life-threatening, were serious enough to warrant specialised medical treatment. Socially they were misfits, excluded by sheer distance from contact with other children or, for that matter, anyone outside their immediate family. Their parents, struggling to eke out an existence among the dust, flies and searing heat of the long summers, were powerless to improve the situation. Stanley decided he must do something.

Inspiration came on 6 December 1924 while he was convalescing at Manly beach, following the removal of his gallbladder at Royal Prince Alfred Hospital. Surrounded by a sparkling blue ocean, towering Norfolk Island pines, refreshing breezes and a carefree holiday atmosphere, he was struck by the tremendous difference between the children laughing and playing on the beach and those who lived in the dry west of the state. He must bring the outback children to the seaside! For those who had seen nothing but dust and flies, brown earth, stunted semi-arid scrub land, half-dried water holes and the pathetic muddy trickles that passed for rivers, a holiday at the beach would be akin to a trip to paradise.

Lucy agreed. The idea was barely conceived before she and her irrepressible husband, now recovered from his surgery, headed west once more. Leaving others to organise mundane but necessary details, such as accommodation and food, they drove to Cobar in grand style, in a chauffeur-driven, brand-new Vauxhall car, provided for their exclusive use by a wealthy supporter, Mr William Arnott, the well-known biscuit manufacturer.

Leaving Lucy and the Vauxhall in Cobar, Stanley and the chauffeur set off along a rudimentary track in a Willys-Overland car for Bourke where Stanley, as head of the Methodist Far West Mission, was to attend an annual committee meeting. After being forced to detour cross country, owing to an unexpectedly heavy downpour, and losing their way, they had decided to camp out until, eaten alive by voracious mosquitoes, they had pushed on, only to become hopelessly bogged. They missed the meeting, but it was not a wasted trip. Before he returned to Cobar, Stanley had the enthusiastic support of Bourke's Town Clerk and leading businessmen to help him find 20 local children who would benefit from a seaside holiday.

One of those who pledged his assistance was the Mayor, Sid Coleman. Born in Central Queensland on 1 March 1899, Sid was a true child of the outback. At the age of 12 years, with virtually no education other than that offered by an itinerant schoolteacher, who covered the back blocks of Queensland in a horse and buggy, Sid began working for Cobb & Co. His job was grooming horses, for which he was paid £2 15s a fortnight, but he had to find his own board and lodging – in this case a tent. After six months of solitary existence under canvas, he quit his job and took up droving. Four years later, having narrowly missed death when hostile Aborigines attacked his camp one night, he re-joined his former employer. Working as a coach driver, he enjoyed a spell of notoriety when, after waiting a week for the ferry to put in an appearance, he swam the flooded Diamantina River, which was almost 5 kilometres wide.

In 1924 Sid, now married, moved to Bourke, where he opened a hire-car service and garage. He was a popular figure and there was much consternation when, during a typhoid epidemic in 1926, a rumour ran around town that Sid, proprietor of the town's only taxi service, had died. However, the story was soon scotched by a local identity who put paid to any further argument by declaring, 'That can't be right. Coleman promised to take us to Barringun for football in April and he's never gone back on his word yet.'

True to form, Sid Coleman kept his promise to help Drummond in his quest. As news spread, Stanley was inundated with applications from all over outback New South Wales. In February 1925, 58 boys and girls, accompanied by six mothers whose children were very young, were on their way by train to a holiday camp by the beach. Some, who came from very poor families, were dressed in clothes made from hessian sugar bags. However, volunteers soon rallied round, providing adequate clothing and any other necessities required. By the time these campers returned home a fortnight later, Drummond had rounded up another 128 children.

The first camp at Cronulla, and the second, at Collaroy, were almost entirely under canvas. The concept was fine while the weather held out, but the inadequacies of the system were soon revealed when a disastrous soaking during a torrential rainstorm at Collaroy resulted in Stanley contracting an ear infection, leaving his hearing permanently damaged. In any case, the tents were only a stopgap arrangement.

Drummond was grateful for the generosity of the Salvation Army and the Church of England, which had made their properties available and provided food for the campers, but he wanted to establish something more permanent. More importantly, he wanted to shift the focus from recreation to one of health, by providing the outback children with much needed medical treatment. To date, potential candidates had been excluded from the camps by illness or disability. From now on, they would be selected on the basis of physical need. And so, the Far West Children's Health Scheme was born.

When Drummond suggested to Gordon Wynn, head of the well-known Sydney department store and already a generous benefactor, that he should experience outback conditions first hand, he took up the challenge. Wynn, his wife and his assistant, Oscar Robson, a returned World War I soldier, drove to Cobar in May 1925 to join Stanley on his next trip, visiting the Darling River towns of Bourke, Louth, Tilpa and Wilcannia, before moving further west to Menindee and Broken Hill.

The journey was nowhere as gruelling or as desolate as the expedition to the north-west corner of the state, but the sight of soldier settlers living in dirt-floored shacks, with rough

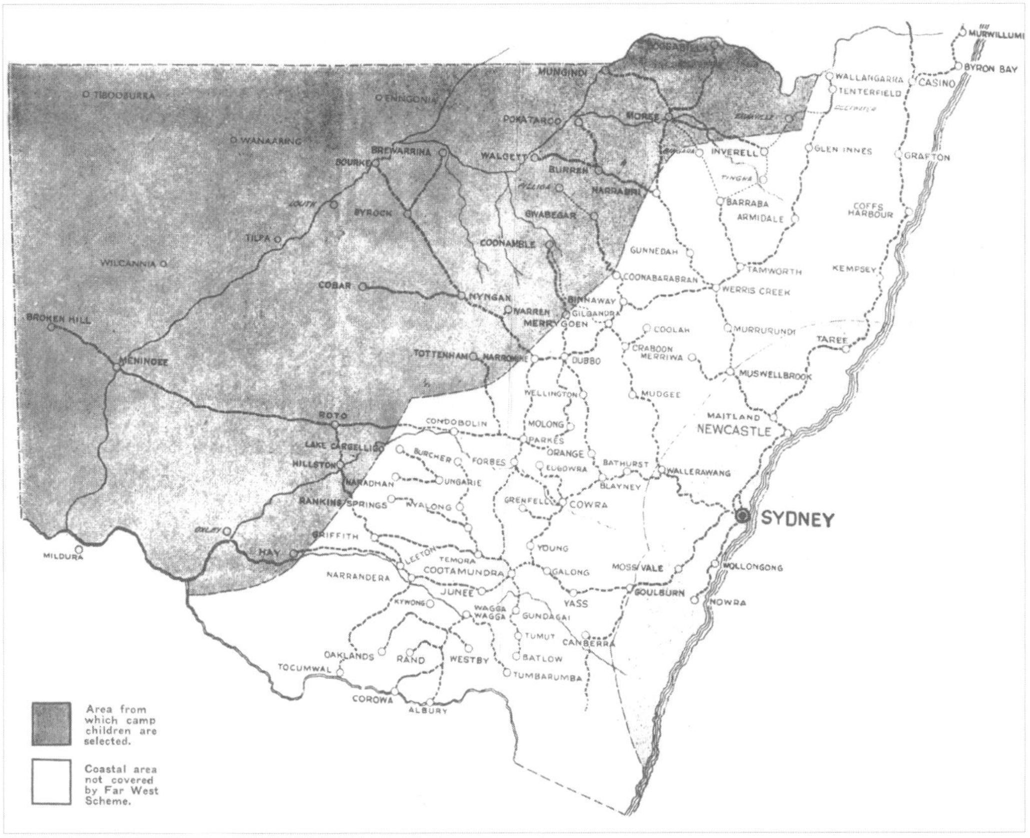

Map of NSW. The shaded section shows the area from which the children were selected for a trip to Manly

wooden boxes their only furniture and their ragged children suffering disabilities which could be cured so easily, were more than enough to shock the city visitors from their complacency. When they returned to Cobar, Gordon Wynn and Oscar Robson pledged their unqualified support.

Accepting the role of the Scheme's honorary treasurers, they scoured Sydney's beachside suburbs in search of a suitable property in which to house the children. Just in time for the first camp of 1926, they located a house at Fairlight, near the Manly ferry terminal. The house was old and dilapidated, but its owner, Mr Cross, had no objections to it being used as a holiday camp, provided George Moncreiff Barron, the doctor in charge of the cottage hospital next door, agreed. He did more than agree. Greeting Drummond at the ferry terminal, he offered to call on the children each day and organise whatever medical treatment was needed, free of charge.

One of those who benefited from Dr Barron's contacts with the Sydney medical fraternity was an 11-year-old girl. She came from the far north-west corner of the state and was so crippled she could not walk. Even so, it had taken hours of argument by Drummond and Coleman to persuade the mother to allow her to come to Sydney. The first physically handicapped child to be treated under the Scheme, she received expert specialist attention from Barron's colleagues, enabling her to return home with only a slight limp.

In order to accommodate as many able-bodied children as possible, a large tent was erected in the backyard of Mr Cross's house to serve as a dining room. Mrs Thomas, a local woman, organised the general housekeeping and distribution of the meals, which were prepared by Monty, a rugged ex-shearer's cook recruited by Mr Cross. Although the pair worked tirelessly, they could not hope to cope with the huge load. The labour shortage was relieved when Mrs Elsie Hill, who had met the Drummonds when they had stayed at her guesthouse in Sydney Road during Stanley's convalescence in 1924, arrived with a small band of helpers. Elsie, a countrywoman whose small son had died from want of on-the-spot medical treatment, knew better than most of the value of Drummond's work.

Elsie volunteered to accommodate the post-operative patients, while another supporter, Mrs Cluett, offered her home at Balmoral Beach for the medical cases. Three of the latter, suffering from trachoma, were treated at the Sydney Eye Hospital at Drummond's expense.

The New South Wales Education Department now began to take an interest, following a suggestion by Dr Bruce, of the School Medical Service, that his routine medical reports be used to form a basis for the selection of children for the next camp. The Headmaster of Cobar Public School also suggested that the 1927 camp should be held during the January school holidays. Although the teacher's prime motivation was to try and ensure that the already disadvantaged children did not miss lessons, it set Drummond thinking.

By this time, Mr Cross's house had been demolished and, despite a concerted effort, they had not found alternative accommodation for the next camp. Manly, a popular holiday destination at almost any time, was packed in the summer months. However, throughout the six-week school vacation the local public school stood empty. Drummond paid a visit to the headmaster, Mr Brown, and had no trouble securing his cooperation. Brown's son, a medical practitioner, had died at Bourke from pneumonia.

With the wholehearted backing of the Minister for Education, Mr Brown agreed to make the school available for the entire holiday period, as well as part of the Manly Literary Institute, which was being used by the Department for home science classes. Essential furniture, along with crockery and cutlery, was scrounged from various sources. The problem of providing sufficient bedding was solved when Drummond hired a sailor to make mattresses, by sewing three chaff bags together and stuffing them with straw. For the sake of propriety, the girls slept upstairs and the boys, down. However, any potential problems with the coeducational nature of the camp were lessened by the decision to lower the maximum age for those attending from 18 years to 14. That year it was also decided that the needs of mentally handicapped children could be better met if they attended a specially organised camp.

By this time, screening had become more rigid. An infuriated Drummond had discovered that some applicants were not the children of 'battlers', but offspring of well-to-do and unscrupulous people seeking a free beachside holiday. Others whose names had been submitted were discovered to be strapping, healthy youngsters, teachers' pets, or proteges of clergymen favouring those of their own faith.

Drummond immediately put paid to this deception by asking Sid Coleman at Bourke and the Shire Councils of Wilcannia and Brewarrina to isolate the deserving cases. Those who passed muster were taken to the home of Tommy Clapperton and his wife at Cobar, where they were bathed and fed before boarding the train to Sydney. On one occasion, with fares to find for four children, Drummond discovered he had 10s 3d, and Clapperton 5 shillings. However, the piggy bank was swelled to bursting point the next day when Clapperton's car was hired for a trip to Bourke, resulting in a massive fare of £10, half of which was given to the Scheme.

Although Drummond received donations from supporters, it was often a hand-to-mouth existence. Fortunately, small gifts of cash and petrol kept them, and the car, going. They never returned alone. On one trip, Tommy and Stanley collected eight children – two with poliomyelitis and six with trachoma so severe that it was necessary to cover kerosene lamps with brown paper to reduce the glare. When they reached Wilcannia, Clapperton sent a telegram to his wife: 'Bringing eight home. All crook. Tom.'

In January 1927, with hordes of children running around the normally deserted Manly Primary School buildings and a huge dining-room tent erected in the playground, the locals and holidaymakers began to take notice. Not all of the attention was welcome, for there were some who feared that such obviously underprivileged children might introduce and spread disease. Once these irrational concerns were allayed, all kinds of people willingly offered their time, services and goods. Discovering that the number of children requiring urgent dental treatment could not be accommodated during normal working hours, Mr Bolton, the school dentist, gave up his New Year holiday, extracting 154 teeth from 62 mouths in a mere space of five hours. Sheer fatigue and a severely cramped forearm prevented him undertaking any more surgery that day, although two more children were anxiously waiting to be relieved of their painfully decayed teeth.

As it was obvious that the annual camps, which depended on the Drummonds being granted leave, were insufficient to cope with the demand for medical treatment, it was decided to operate the Scheme throughout the year. With school buildings unavailable during term time, the sympathetic Elsie Hill offered the use of her guesthouse. Among her first guests were seven-year-old Jimmy and his sister, Mary, aged five, from Tibooburra. Both were suffering from trachoma so severe that when Drummond found them they were sitting in a darkened room with their eyes bandaged. After spending 18 months in the Eye Hospital, they were transferred to the care of Mrs Hill, who looked after them for almost six years, by which time their sight had been restored.

In early 1928, the Scheme faced a problem. Stanley Drummond was due to be moved to a new parish, in all likelihood far away not only from Cobar but also from the children who so desperately needed his help. As he could not possibly organise the holiday camps and look for other children requiring medical treatment in his spare time, he sought official help from the Methodist Conference in Sydney, hoping that the church would agree to take over the maintenance and administration of the Scheme. Reverend Raywood, a senior member of the conference, recorded that there was 'a long and sympathetic debate'. But it was not sympathetic enough. The proposal was denied.

Shattered, Stanley was now forced to make a choice between his professional ministry and Far West work. Should he, at the age of 44, resign his post, forsaking his only source of income, in order to devote his energy to the Far West children, or should he remain with the church until retirement and see his hard work go for nought? The Drummonds took the plunge. Stanley submitted his resignation. On 31 March, they left their little wooden parsonage at Cobar and took the train to Sydney.

They arrived back in Manly without a home, car, private income or, indeed, any guaranteed source of financial assistance. Their accommodation was provided in the short term by Elsie Hill, who made room for them in her house although she had a fair number of convalescent children still in residence. The following day Gordon Wynn and his father solved their immediate financial problems with a cheque for £75 to cover immediate living expenses.

Shortly afterwards, Drummond was run over by a car at Circular Quay. Far from being a disaster, the accident, described by the injured victim as 'fortunate', saved him from insolvency by providing £265 in insurance and compensation. Although laid up for four months with a broken foot, Stanley used the time profitably in compiling the Far West's first brochure. In it he penned several heart-wrenching stories – of children blinded by trachoma; of women, their husbands away working, dying alone in childbirth, and their tiny babies with them; of mothers carrying desperately ill children in their arms along dusty tracks in a vain attempt to find help; of a treatable illness taking the life of a father, leaving his motherless children orphaned. Drummond's impassioned and blatantly sentimental pleas for help did not go unheeded. When the brochure, with its logo featuring Sturt's Desert Pea, was posted out to people likely to be interested, it raised over £600, allowing him to resume his work.

Discovering that Stanley was unable to travel out west to locate children in need as there were insufficient funds to purchase a car, the Wynn family came to the rescue with a good low-mileage second-hand Vauxhall. There was no trouble finding suitable candidates for the month-long summer camp held at Manly School in January 1928, which was attended by 118 children, 30 of whom required specialist eye treatment. Another 32 underwent surgery. Demand for dental services was so great that school dentist set up a clinic. At the end of January, it was found that 31 campers would have to remain behind for pressing or on-going medical treatment. As the school buildings were not available in term time, Mrs Hill offered her home to accommodate these children, as well as others arriving throughout the year. As this situation could not continue indefinitely, funds would have to be raised to secure a permanent building, for the exclusive use of the outback children.

Freed from his obligations to the church, Stanley was now devoting his entire energy to the Scheme. Nothing stopped him, not even the heart attack he suffered while covering the area north-east of Cobar. The trip of 800 kilometres in just three days had been too much. Leaving Clapperton to continue to Brewarrina, where five children were waiting to be picked up, he had a short rest in Bourke at the Post Office Hotel, as the guest of Mrs Fitzgerald, before resuming his work, his energy and enthusiasm undiminished.

When not touring the outback in the faithful Vauxhall in search of needy children, Drummond was busy soliciting help, by whatever means he could devise. Assistance was

Off to the Far West camp, with sugar-bag luggage

sought from every strata of society – government officials, doctors, professional businessmen, local tradespeople, outback folk, charitable agencies and service organisations, as well as ordinary citizens. His pleading and coaxing, wheedling and begging paid dividends. The State Governor agreed to be patron, which in turn encouraged conservative members of the establishment as well as the socially ambitious to take an interest. Wealthy medical specialists donated their services and Joe the Barber cut everyone's hair free of charge. The Sparklers, a concert party composed of Australia's leading entertainers – organiser Rus Garling, Maggie Foster, Reg Harrison, Peggy Dunbar, Lurline Hammond and Herbert Crellin – toured the western towns in their leisure time, raising £350 in five nights, and £600 by the end of the year.

By January 1929, there were enough funds in hand to put down the necessary 10 per cent deposit to purchase a substantial brick house with nine rooms. Costing over £2,000, and dubbed 'the depot', it was at 25 Wentworth Street, not far from the surfing beach. It was large enough to accommodate children requiring medical treatment, as well as the Drummonds, who took up residence in a small glassed-in verandah. Although she had no formal training, the much loved Elsie Hill was unanimously appointed as Matron.

As news of the Scheme's work spread, aid poured in. The Country Women's Association (CWA) pledged its support, Far West Committees were established in both urban and rural areas, the Education Department supplied a full-time hospital teacher and individuals from all over the state offered money and assistance.

Quite suddenly, Stanley Drummond's modest little plan blossomed into a fully-fledged operation. By 1931, seven years after the first children had arrived for a holiday at the beach, the Far West Children's Health Scheme was sufficiently well established to run the holiday camps, supply accommodation and board for all those requiring medical treatment throughout the year, and staff out-station clinics in remote areas.

It was to this man of vision that I now presented myself.

I knew virtually nothing about how the Scheme functioned or who did what, apart from Mr Drummond himself, who was the Superintendent. However, during my Tresillian training I had heard about the Scheme's mobile baby clinics. They operated from three railway carriages, which travelled the western lines to such far-flung places as Cobar, Bourke, Mungindi and Walgett. The rolling stock and the steam locomotives required to haul them from one town to the next were a gift of the New South Wales Railways. Stripped of unwanted or unsuitable fittings, the former railcars were well appointed and surprisingly comfortable, with a fully equipped clinic, waiting room and self-contained living quarters for the sisters.

The railcars, as they were known, visited a number of places on various lines every six weeks. The dates were advertised in the local press, and the clinic remained in town for as long as was needed. When it was time to move on, the railcar was hitched to the back of the next train that came along and hauled to the next town on the list.

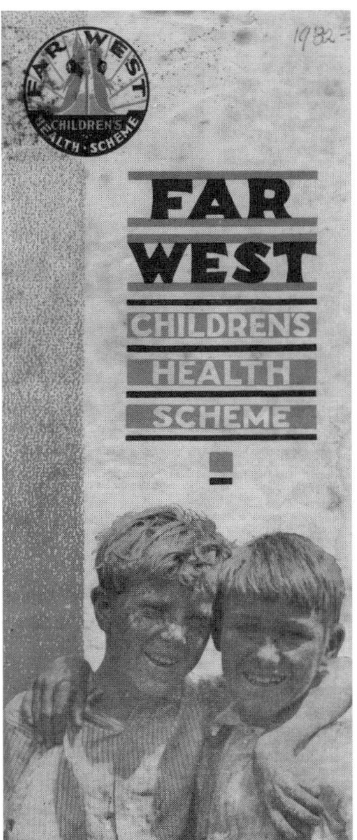

Cover of the 1932 publicity brochure, written by Drummond to raise funds

Mr Drummond must have been satisfied with my credentials and experience as he offered me a job at the Far West Clinic at Pallamallawa. He explained that he had established a clinic there after the incidence of diphtheria and trachoma reached alarming proportions. I didn't know a great deal about trachoma and had certainly never heard of Pallamallawa but, as Mr Drummond assured me, it was definitely in the bush and that I would be the sole sister in charge, I accepted his offer on the spot.

Trachoma has been around for centuries and is mentioned in ancient Egyptian and Chinese records. It reached Europe during the Napoleonic wars, when tens of thousands of British and French troops suffering from trachoma returned home from fighting in Egypt. The infection spread quickly through European armies, where soldiers lived in crowded and unsanitary barracks. It then infected the general population, as people abandoned a rural lifestyle to live in overcrowded slums during the industrial revolution.

Rampant in Europe and North America during the 19th century, trachoma was brought by early settlers to Australia where it rapidly spread due to poor living conditions, as well as flies, dust and heat.

Baby Health rail car

With improved housing, separate beds, clean water, and adequate sewerage and rubbish removal, trachoma was virtually eliminated from white Australia by the end of the 1930s. By the year 2001 it had been eradicated from all developed countries except *Australia, where in 2016 it remains a common cause of blindness in remote Aboriginal communities.*

From 1976 to 1978, Trachoma Program Teams visited every Indigenous community in Australia, examining more than 60,000 people and treating more than 40,000. At the end of the program, guidelines and recommendations for the eradication of trachoma were established.

During the next 20 years, although progress was made in larger towns and cities, the trachoma rate among children in some outback areas, where housing and sanitation was poor, changed not one iota. In 2001, a study of Aboriginals living in areas with severe trachoma revealed that one in five of the older people had ingrowing lashes, and about half of these were either blind or would eventually go blind. It was estimated that it could take 100 years before trachoma was completely eliminated, unless the living conditions of Indigenous people improved to a level enjoyed by other Australians. A further study in 2013 revealed that, while some progress had been made in the past 12 years, the speed was 'glacial' compared to changes being made in undeveloped parts of the world.

All but two of the 27 children at Pallamallawa diagnosed with trachoma came from very poor families, unable to afford any medical treatment or to improve their living conditions. The other two were the children of the secretary of the local Country Women's Association. The CWA ladies were so alarmed by the prospect of 25 of the town's children going blind that they contacted Drummond and struck a deal. The CWA would provide a clinic building and accommodation; the Far West Scheme, a nursing sister.

After consulting a gazetteer that listed and described all towns in New South Wales, I discovered that Pallamallawa was situated on the Gwydir River between Moree and Warialda. It was very definitely in the bush: it was off the rail line and the closest town of any size was Moree, almost 400 miles (650 kilometres) from Sydney. My area of responsibility also included the towns of Gravesend, Biniguy and Warialda.

I set off for Moree by train a few days later, and then took a service car to Pallamallawa, 24 miles (38 kilometres) away – 16 of them along a very rutted dirt road. Just as I suspected, it was pretty much a one-horse town. The dusty main street was fringed with an odd assortment of wide-verandahed buildings, but not much else, not even a general store. About 50 houses, occupied by local farm workers, straggled untidily on either side of the single road leading into, and out of, town. On the outskirts, between the cricket pitch and the road, was my new home – a small, nondescript weatherboard house, loaned to the CWA branch for use as a clinic. Square in shape, it had open verandahs on all four sides and a corrugated-iron roof. Parked alongside was the clinic car, around which cavorted about 90 goats.

The soon to be departing Sister Pender met me at the door, along with her large and ferocious looking guard dog, which was baring all its teeth in a most menacing way. Keeping a wary eye on it, I sidled into the cottage at the invitation of my colleague, who took me on a guided tour. There was a kitchen with a fuel stove, a fair-sized living area, a bathroom and two bedrooms. At the rear was the laundry, equipped with a wood-fired copper, a tub and a mangle. A narrow path linked the house to the pit toilet or dunny, which sat in solitary splendour in the backyard.

One bedroom was for me. The other had been converted to a clinic, and the only bed was occupied. A glance revealed that the recumbent form was female, and that she had been badly burned. Wondering why she was in the clinic, and not in hospital, I asked if her condition had been reported to the doctor at Moree. My colleague, who was a Far West transport sister temporarily manning the Pallamallawa clinic, did not seem overly concerned by the woman's condition and shrugged off my enquiry with a 'she'll be all right'.

She didn't look all right to me, at all. So, fully aware that I was about to create a ruction by stomping into territory that was not yet mine, I took a sterile sheet, wrapped her gently in it and placed her on the back seat of the car.

My actions were not appreciated. Sister Pender, who obviously saw me as a brash young interloper, refused to concede that hospitalisation was necessary. However, as the patient was about to be mine and, as I would be responsible if she died, I ignored her protestations. Sister refused to come along, so I slipped behind the wheel, started the motor and headed towards Moree. Worried about crunching the gears, I stayed in first all the way. In any case, the road condition was so bad that I doubt I could have built up enough speed to change gear, even if I had wanted to.

The necessarily slow journey along 16 miles (26 kilometres) of rough road with a very ill patient on the back seat was nerve-wracking enough, but I was also very anxious as I knew I was breaking the law: I didn't have a driving licence. Had never had one. I knew more or less how to drive, thanks to the efforts of my brother John, a motor mechanic, but I had never owned a car and had never sat for a test.

Fortunately, I didn't encounter a single vehicle along the way and managed to negotiate the ruts without mishap and reach Moree in one piece. Greatly relieved, I handed over my patient to the doctor on duty, who scolded me and demanded to know why he had not been summoned hours earlier. I told him, and he replied that he was duty bound to make a report to Mr Drummond. I don't know if he did or not but, by the time I arrived back at Pallamallawa, a journey that took twice as long as it should because I drove all the way with the handbrake on, the sister and her dog had vanished.

Unexpectedly alone, I took time to look around my new domain. I was surprised to find that such a small clinic was equipped to cover any kind of accident or condition, from snake bite to eye infections, lacerations, abscesses, burns, food poisoning, confinements and concussion. In short, just about anything that did not require the attention of a doctor.

After unpacking my belongings, I gave the house a good clean, lit the bathroom chip heater and had a relaxing soak in the tub. I had settled into bed for a welcome night's sleep and was in that state of dreamy semi-consciousness when I was suddenly wide awake. It sounded as if an entire army in hob-nailed boots had invaded the verandah. I looked out the window and saw that I had indeed been invaded – by the goats. With the guard dog gone, they had taken up residence. I shooed them away, but it was a losing battle.

The goats finally gave up their cavorting around dawn, only to be replaced at about 8 am by about 40 kids – of the human variety. Some had come to have their eyes treated, but most had come to take a look at the new Sister. With their eyes attended to and their curiosity evidently satisfied, they scampered off to school to excitedly deliver their 'news' which, in turn, generated a new influx of children as soon as the afternoon bell went.

The very next day there was a cricket match. Seeing it as a good opportunity to meet some of the locals and, with nothing else to do, I wandered down to the oval, which was practically next door. With introductions over, I took a seat on a bench in the shade of a tree, beside the rickety shelter that passed as a pavilion. Ranged around the field, the other spectators were watching, drinking or dozing as the game proceeded, at a pace that is best described as leisurely, even for cricket. The drowsy peace of the afternoon, punctuated by the occasional shout of 'good shot' or 'howzat', was suddenly shattered by a frenzied shout from the clinic as a figure ran helter-skelter towards the oval.

'Snake bite! Snake bite!

Rocketing to my feet, I took off for the clinic where I found a man lying on the verandah, almost comatose, after being bitten by one of the hundreds of death adders that infested the area. As his companion watched anxiously, I placed a tourniquet around his thigh and gave him a shot of antivenene.

This dramatic medical emergency, my first, and the highlight of my day, caused hardly a ripple at the cricket match. Although the spectators, who were easily distracted by the slow progress of the game, wandered over to see if the victim was dead or alive, the players, after a brief glance in my direction, decided that the matter was well under control and continued with their game in the time-honoured tradition. The sound of the willow bat on ball soon recalled the remaining spectators, leaving me suddenly alone to scribble a quick note to the doctor, before sending the patient on his way to Moree Hospital in his friend's car, thereby saving me from breaking the law for the second time in 24 hours.

The following week I set about organising and supervising the installation of a goat-proof and child-proof verandah. After a blessedly peaceful goat-free night, I woke the following morning to find that, although the railings and gate had put an end to the goats' nocturnal visits, they had turned their attention elsewhere – to the washing on the clothes line. My white uniforms and veils, along with the sheets and towels from the clinic, all laboriously boiled in the wood copper, were hanging forlornly in shreds. I was furious. Not only had the goats divested me of my clothing, they had also stripped my pay packet, as all my uniforms would need to be replaced. As I cursed them under my breath, I added goats to my list of unloved creatures, along with horses and large dogs.

However, the goats, if nothing else, provided a distraction in my increasingly tedious existence. The townsfolk were friendly but, from a medical point of view, Pallamallawa was a real backwater. I was so bored: the locals were rarely ill, the trachoma treatment was well in hand and everyone in town had been immunised against diphtheria. I did have a slight diversion when I offered to extend the program to children at the quaintly named Terry-Hei-Hei, about 30 miles (48 kilometres) to the south-west of Moree, and the distinctly feminine sounding Gurley, a whistle stop on the north-western rail line.

While trachoma cases required constant monitoring and treatment, sometimes for months, or even years, I found that, apart from attending to the odd crack on the skull from a misplaced cricket ball or treating an occasional snakebite, there was little demand for my services.

One very disappointing thing about my posting to Pallamallawa was that, although I had plenty of spare time, I did not have the authority to treat the local Aborigines who lived in various camps scattered around Moree. I was very interested in their welfare, but it was made clear to me that this was the sole prerogative of the overworked doctors. Nevertheless, I was fortunate enough to meet the Queen of the tribe, who would come out of her hut to greet me with a royal wave every time I went past. This stately and dignified lady was albino, a great rarity among Aboriginal people, and her pale features added to her regal air one of mystery and awe. I often wondered if the three doctors who were her official health custodians ever realised what a unique and rare privilege they had been given to be in regular contact with these proud and gentle people.

With so little to do, I was beginning to doubt the wisdom of accepting the post so readily, and regretted that I had not found out a little more about the position before agreeing to come. However, with the goats making me virtually bankrupt, I couldn't resign without another job lined up. In any case, apart from the lack of ready cash, there was also my obligation to Mr Drummond. I had decided I would stick it out for another month before deciding what to do when the phone rang.

Stanley Drummond's warm voice filled the line. It took me a few moments to realise that he was offering me another job. It was way out west, in the outback. Not only that, he wanted me to take to the air and become the Far West's first permanent flying sister. This was a startling enough announcement, but there was more to come. The pilot he had hired was a woman – aptly named Nancy Bird.

CHAPTER 4

The Far West's Aerial Service

1935–1936

After I recovered from my surprise, Mr Drummond explained that for some time he had been toying with the idea of putting on a permanent footing an intermittent, rather ad hoc aerial medical service, established three years before. An aerial medical service? This was news to me!

Drummond's ambition to create an aerial service was fired in May 1924, when he and his wife visited a soldier settler in a remote part of the state. On meeting his host's two young daughters, Drummond asked if there were any boys in the family. He was appalled to learn that there were two sons, but both were dead. One, aged 18 years and the other 17, had died within a year of each other – the first from a ruptured appendix and his brother from a severe and sudden illness. Although in both cases medical help had been on its way, it had arrived too late.

Drummond, fuming at such a tragic loss of life, resolved to do something about it. He was not alone. That same year, his counterpart in the Presbyterian Church, Reverend John Flynn, had also begun thinking along similar lines. Twelve years earlier, Flynn, then aged 31, had been appointed Superintendent of the Australian Inland Mission, which built a number of out-station clinics in remote regions of Australia.

The first, in Oodnadatta, South Australia, and the next, in West Australia's Port Hedland, were staffed by trained nurses and were dedicated to 'suffering humanity without preference for nationality or creed'. However, establishing and staffing clinics was not enough. Flynn, like Drummond, knew that the best medical care in the world was of no use to outback people without an effective transportation and communication system.

As far back as 1917, Lieutenant J Clifford Peel, a 23-year-old pilot from Inverleigh, Victoria, who had put his medical studies on hold to enlist in the Australian Flying Corps, had come up with the idea of an aerial ambulance. However, the aviation industry was still in its infancy, with flimsy open-cockpit planes and, with the Great War still on, a shortage of qualified pilots. The first flight to demonstrate the practicability of such a service was made by Dr George Simpson on 2 August 1927, when he flew from Cloncurry, in Central Queensland, to pick up a miner with a broken pelvis at Mt Isa, about 100 kilometres to the west. The plane, a De Havilland DH 50A, hired from the fledgling Queensland and Northern Territory Aerial Service (QANTAS), was piloted by Norman Evans. Unfortunately, Clifford Peel did not survive to see his dream of an aerial ambulance fulfilled. He was killed in action in France in September 1918.

However, while great strides were being made in aircraft design and construction, and many former Flying Corps pilots were looking for work, the problem of providing efficient and easily accessible communication, on which an ambulance service depended, remained unresolved. An experimental wireless transmission, using cumbersome equipment, had been made in South Australia in 1926 by George Towns to confirm the feasibility of long-distance wireless communication, but it would be another two years before an Adelaide electrical engineer named Alfred Traeger perfected a pedal-powered wireless from an idea conceived by Flynn. Capable of receiving and transmitting messages, the wireless had a range of about 480 kilometres. No technical knowledge or skill was required to operate it.

By May 1928, the Australian Inland Mission had established a base at Cloncurry for the 'Australian Aerial Medical Service', the name by which The Royal Flying Doctor Service was known until 1941. It operated from the vestry of a church, where a transmitter had been installed. Also stationed in the town was the service's first full-time doctor, K Vincent Welch, the QANTAS De Havilland plane and pilot Arthur Affleck. In the first year, the doctor flew 32,000 kilometres and treated 250 patients. In 1931, another doctor, Allan Vickers, flew 2,092 kilometres from Normanton, on the Gulf of Carpentaria, to Brisbane in a vain attempt to save the life of a hotel licensee, critically injured when a kerosene refrigerator exploded.

Although in 1929 the 'flying padre', Reverend L Daniels, a Church of England clergyman based at Broken Hill, made his aircraft available to fly urgent medical cases to hospital, it was not until four years after the Queensland service became operational that Drummond's dream of establishing a similar service in New South Wales had the chance to become a reality.

In 1932, Hilda Brooks, the Far West's first rail clinic sister, began travelling the line to Bourke every two months, extending her territory whenever possible by car from the railhead. By hitching a ride with a local Presbyterian clergyman, Reverend S A Faulkiner (known to all as 'the padre') whenever he made his parochial rounds, she had managed to make spasmodic but very welcome visits to outlying areas. One grateful mother was Mrs Swift Treweeke, who lived at Waverley Downs station and completed a round trip of more than 160 kilometres by car to the clinic, held in the one-room, one-teacher school at Wanaaring, in order to receive professional advice on how to care for her baby.

Aware of the vast area Sister Brooks had to cover, often in temperatures exceeding 40 degrees Celsius, Sid Coleman, who was still Mayor of Bourke and one of the Scheme's most hard-working supporters, suggested the possibility of using an aeroplane to cut down travelling time. Coleman, who had his pilot's licence, had been running an aerial taxi service since early 1931.

His first plane, a De Havilland Gypsy Moth, delivered at the end of 1930, was available for joy rides at a cost of 5 shillings for two passengers, or for charter at one shilling a mile. Sid ran his business from a tin shed sited alongside a newly constructed strip behind Bourke Railway Station. Although the surface was as yet unsealed, the strip was a vast improvement on the old landing ground – the old racecourse at North Bourke, 5 kilometres from town on the other side of the river.

The aerial taxi business got off to a rather shaky start when Sid crashed the plane into a roller during landing but, by the end of 1931, things were looking up. In November, Sid replaced the Gypsy with a three-seater Glenairco and hired Mr 'Robbie' Robinson as his chief pilot and engineer. Although Sid's plane was used occasionally to fly doctors to remote locations, it was not until July 1932 that Drummond's proposal to hire a plane was agreed to by the Far West Council.

A much publicised mercy dash by a Bourke doctor to Tibooburra, in the far north-western corner of the state, was all Drummond needed to put his plan into action. He approached Coleman, who offered the use of the plane, and Robbie, free of charge.

On 5 October 1932, Sister Brooks, suitably clad in goggles, leather coat and flying helmet, and with Robbie at the controls, took off on her first tour. Packed into the cockpit were a set of baby scales, bottles of a tonic referred to as 'emulsion' and cod liver oil. They were farewelled by Sid, the Drummonds, Reverend Faulkiner and members of the Bourke Far West Committee, all of whom had turned out in force for this special occasion dressed in their finest. As the plane gained altitude, Sister Brooks acknowledged the importance of her mission by dropping a note: 'A message from the air. My wish to visit outback mothers and babies has at last come true. Good luck to you all below.'

The first stop was at Louth, a small hamlet on the Darling River downstream from Bourke. The plane was met by a crowd of excited well-wishers, including the entire school population, which had been given a half-day holiday in honour of the occasion.

Sister Brookes and Sid Coleman with the the Bouke Far West Committee, before her inaugural flight

When the fuss died down, the local policeman drove the visitors to the town's only hotel, where the licensee had made a room available for use as a baby clinic. After seeing seven babies and their mothers, some of whom had travelled up to 130 kilometres, Sister Brooks left for Wanaaring on the Paroo River, where the entire population of 30 was waiting by the airstrip. As no plane had landed at Wanaaring for three years, the enthusiastic teacher took the opportunity to give a lesson to his class on the wonders of air travel.

While at Wanaaring, Sister Brooks learned that three of the expected patients would not make it in time as their car had broken down. One of those stranded was Mrs Treweeke of Waverley Downs and, by the time the car was fixed, the clinic would be well and truly over. However, Robbie saved the day by agreeing to fly the plane to them, and fortunately managed to find a suitable place to land.

After spending the night at Wanaaring, Sister flew to Yantabulla, where the King of the local tribe, King Billy, proudly wearing a crescent-shaped brass necklace bearing his title, wanted to take possession of the plane. However, he changed his mind when Robbie offered him a ride, promptly scaling a nearby tree. After visiting Ford's Bridge on the Warrego River, the aircraft returned to Bourke late in the afternoon. Sister Brooks reported that in the two-day aerial tour she had visited 30 children.

As Drummond enthusiastically reported to his Committee, flying was far superior to driving. The five to six day journey was now reduced to two, the distance of 880 kilometres had been cut back to 530 kilometres, and the cost was £12 instead of £25 – a big financial consideration. The flight was so successful that Sister agreed that, in addition to her railcar work, which reached 400 children, she would conduct baby clinics at Louth, Wanaaring, Yantabulla and Ford's Bridge every two months or so, weather and landing grounds permitting.

More often than not, they weren't. The area was frequently plagued with dust storms or inundated with floodwaters, and the landing grounds were, at best, improvised. Sid's notoriously poor eyesight had resulted in several mishaps, without Sister Brooks aboard, which required lengthy and expensive repairs to the aircraft, and a near-miss when she was, which put an immediate stop to the flights in mid-1933. However, the entrepreneurial Drummond, who had no wish to jeopardise the safety of his staff, capitalised on the incident to lobby the government for £3,000 to establish or upgrade a total of 25 airstrips, under the Unemployment Relief Programme. At the same time, he announced his intention to set up a full aerial medical service, based at Bourke.

With airstrip construction underway and a public appeal launched in July to raise the £1,675 needed for the Far West to purchase a cabin plane large enough to carry a nursing sister and a patient, Drummond hoped that Sister Brooks would soon be flying again. However, her announcement in February 1934 that she must return home to her native England the following month threw a spanner in the works. Early that same year, due to his wife's ill health, Robbie had left Bourke and moved to Western Australia. His departure was a great loss. Not only was he an excellent pilot, he was the only aircraft engineer between Bourke and Charleville, in Central Queensland.

In March, Sister Irene Webb, a railcar sister who replaced Sister Brooks, took to the air. The first attempt was thwarted by a dust storm, but a few days later she tried again. The route had been expanded to include Urisino Station, where she stayed the night, allowing her to travel 215 kilometres by car to visit a number of isolated out-stations. The following morning, she flew to another new destination – Hungerford on the Queensland border – before moving on to Ford's Bridge.

Although in April Drummond was granted an annual Defence Department subsidy of £150 to assist with landing grounds, bad weather was a constant worry. Rounds were completed in May and June, but in October floodwaters led to the cancellation of clinics at all destinations, except for Louth.

Flights continued on and off until mid-1935, encouraging Drummond to proceed with a plan to transfer Sister Webb from the railcars and open a permanent baby clinic in Bourke, in anticipation of the aerial service. However, as Sid was no longer able to afford the upkeep and repairs to his plane, he sold it – a move that left Sister Webb without air transport. This setback, as well as the unpredictable weather, led to the cancellation of the August flights. Although more than 40 children as well as adults received treatment during the June rounds, it seemed as if the various problems would put an end to the aerial service. Drummond, however, had other ideas.

Due to Drummond's lobbying, the recently upgraded Bourke airfield now had two narrow all-weather landing strips so, in October 1935, he decided to try again, this time on a more permanent, better organised basis. He hired a couple of rooms at the old court house to serve as a clinic and, with Sid's plane no longer available, secured the services of pilot Nancy Bird and her open-cockpit Gypsy Moth.

Twenty-year-old Nancy de Los Bird was born in 1915 at Kew, on the mid-north coast of New South Wales. When she was about five years old, the family moved to the Sydney seaside suburb of Collaroy.

She had been fascinated by aircraft and flying since she was a small girl, jumping off fences pretending to be an 'eppy plane', and gazing entranced at the sight of skywriters. The first aircraft she saw, up close, was at the age of eight when a plane made an emergency landing on Dee Why Beach, not far from her Collaroy home.

Her interest was further increased by a photograph, hanging on the wall of the lounge room, commemorating the 1928 flight across the Pacific by aviator Charles Kingsford-Smith. Kingsford-Smith, or 'Smithy' to his adoring public, was a much admired and charismatic figure who had performed many great feats in aviation. He had risen to international prominence when he and co-pilot Charles Ulm flew from Los Angeles to Brisbane, a distance of 12,000 kilometres. Nancy was further inspired by the pioneering aviation exploits of Australia's Bert Hinkler, who had made the first non-stop solo flight from England to Australia that same year, as well as America's Amy Johnston and Charles Lindbergh.

Nancy disliked school. As soon as she could, she persuaded her father, who had left the family in Sydney to work in the country during the Depression, to allow her to leave. He agreed, on the condition that she undertake a business course. She quit school and moved to Mt George, in the rich dairy country along the Manning River, west of Wingham, where her father ran a small general store and 'cream concession' with his brother. Nancy, not quite 14 years old, helped in the shop and did the housekeeping and bookkeeping.

Nancy was still 'aeroplane mad'. A joy ride in a Gypsy Moth in September 1930, during an air pageant held at the nearby Wingham racecourse, clinched it. She was now determined to learn to fly and began saving every spare penny.

Three years later, in June 1933, she met the legendary Smithy when his colleague Mr O B 'Pat' Hall took her for a joy-ride during a barnstorming tour at Wingham – an unforgettable experience that had cost her the equivalent of a week's pay. After taking an instructional flight with a Captain Leggatt in Sydney, she was hooked, but had to wait until she was 17 to begin proper training. In the meantime, as proof of her determination, she ordered a leather flying helmet from Miss Martin's shop in the Strand Arcade, Sydney.

By August that year, Nancy had saved up £200 from her job, supplemented by an insurance policy that matured when she was 16. Over the protests of her father, who declared he would disown her, and her mother, who would much rather she indulge in more feminine pursuits, she left Wingham to learn to fly.

Although Smithy had expressed a widely held view that aviation was not a suitable career for a woman, he agreed to accept Nancy as a pupil in his flying school, Kingsford-Smith Air Service, at Mascot in Sydney. Before he left for England and an attempt to break the England–Australia solo flying record, which he did, Nancy had a few lessons from the famous airman. She was then handed over to chief instructor Pat Hall, who had taken her on the joy-ride at Wingham and would now prepare her for her first solo flight.

Nancy learned quickly and, six weeks later, had her private licence. However, it would be another 18 months before she could qualify for a commercial licence. As Smithy did not have a 'hood' to screen the Gypsy Moth for blind-flying instrument exercises, she transferred to the tuition of George Littlejohn at the Aero Club. Since she did not have the necessary cash, navigation lessons were supplied to her free of charge by Patrick G Taylor, who had filled the role of co-pilot and navigator to both Smithy and Ulm – with Smithy to New Zealand and back in 1933, and in 1934 with Ulm to England and back, and with Smithy on a flight to the USA.

Taylor was an excellent teacher and, with a 30-minute solo flight at night over Sydney completed, in April 1935, aged just 19, Nancy became the youngest woman in the British Empire to hold a commercial licence.

Using a £200 legacy from her great-aunt, Annie Thomas, and another £200 borrowed from her father, whose attitude had mellowed considerably, she purchased her first plane at a bargain-basement price. It was actually a wreck, a De Havilland two-seater Gypsy Moth, co-owned by experienced English pilot Mr R T Richards and fashion expert Lady Chaytor.

Lady Chaytor, who had been taking flying lessons, had made a well-publicised flight from England to Australia in 1932 to deliver talks on women's fashion in the hope of raising funds to maintain her family seat, Witton Castle. The 30-bedroom crenellated ancestral pile, complete with dungeons, a moat and drawbridge, had started out life as a manor house in 1410. It had been in Lady Chaytor's family for 200 years, and she wanted to keep it that way.

Smashing a bottle of champagne over the propeller, Nancy's great-aunt and benefactor christened the plane, which had taken six weeks to rebuild, 'Vincere' – a Latin word meaning 'to conquer'. It was a distinct improvement on 'Beefix', the name selected by the previous owner. In 'Vincere', Nancy and her friend and co-pilot Peggy McKillop, the only other woman in New South Wales to hold a commercial licence, decided to embark on a barnstorming tour at country shows in north-western New South Wales.

To supplement her income, Nancy had struck a sponsorship deal with Eric Baume, editor of Sydney's Sun *newspaper, who paid her the massive sum of £10 a week for the privilege of having the name of the newly launched magazine,* Woman, *painted in large letters on the underside of the plane's wings. Many years later, Eric, a crusty columnist and commentator renowned for his conservative and right-wing views, ironically hosted a television program entitled* Beauty and the Beast, *designed to put female panellists in their place.*

The first stop on their tour was Tamworth, where they sold joy-rides for 10 shillings a time to anyone game enough to try. After spending three weeks in the area, they flew further south for a further three weeks. The venture proved to be highly successful, with 101 joy-riders in two days at one location.

Nancy was barnstorming in Dubbo, where Tom Perry, a well-known grazier and member of the nearby Narromine Aero Club, was trying to drum up interest to establish a local airline. He organised a combined air pageant at Dubbo and then Narromine, which both Stanley Drummond and Nancy attended. By sheer luck, the pair met up in Bell's Hotel, Dubbo.

Providing joy-rides to the public, even at 10 shillings a time, was a precarious way to earn a living and Drummond seized the initiative. As Nancy was in need of a proper job, and he was in need of a plane and pilot, he offered her one. Provided all went well on a trial run, he was willing to pay her a retainer of £100, plus an additional one shilling a mile for Far West flights, with £100 guaranteed over six months – the length of the initial contract – by which time the Far West hoped to have its own aircraft. As part of the deal, Nancy would be permitted to engage in other charter work to supplement her income, provided the Far West clinic had first call on the use of her services. She told Drummond that, if he wanted a trial run, she could combine it with a barnstorming tour to Bourke.

For the next part of the air pageant, which included an air derby, Nancy and Peggy flew to Narromine, where Nancy received a call from Drummond, asking if she could carry out the trial run from Bourke in a fortnight or so. In anticipation of a steady income, the manager of the Bank of Australasia in Narromine agreed to grant her a loan, with Tom Perry as her guarantor, allowing her to place an order for a DH 85 De Havilland Leopard Moth. It had an enclosed cabin and was large enough to carry two passengers in comfort. With the finance arranged, Nancy and Peggy flew to Bourke, arriving on Saturday, 12 October, four days before Nancy's 20th birthday. If everything went to plan, the baby clinic contract was hers.

The following Monday morning, the Gypsy Moth took off for Louth, Urisino, Hungerford, Yantabulla and Ford's Bridge. As the cockpit was at the rear, Sister Webb, decked out in mandatory goggles and helmet, was in the front seat, baby scales at her feet and clinic equipment stacked around her. To be on the safe side, water and emergency rations were stowed in the tail locker.

The trip could hardly be described as uneventful. They followed the Darling River downstream from Bourke to Louth, where the airstrip, reported to be 'good', turned out to be nothing more than a small paddock, its surface dotted with paddy melons and perforated by numerous rabbit holes. The first attempt to land was aborted when a willy-willy blew up from nowhere. However, on the second try they landed without incident, which was just as well as the entire school, given another half-day holiday by the teacher, had turned out for the event. From Louth they flew to Urisino Station, landing on a rather rough paddock after a 70-minute flight that saw the aircraft constantly tossed and buffeted by rising thermals. The next day Sister Webb visited outlying posts by car before continuing on her way by air the following day.

The landing ground at Yantabulla was one of the worst in the far west. Built in thick scrub, it had been created by flattening out numerous rabbit warrens. However, as it was rarely used, the rabbits had returned and drifting sand had piled up against tufts of grass, creating numerous bumps. There was a more suitable site closer to town but, rather than re-route the telegraph line, the powers that be had settled on the warren-riddled site.

The policeman's wife gave them a restorative cup of tea, despite the searing heat. In return. they gave her fresh fruit and vegetables from Urisino, along with an ice-cold drink of water from a thermos flask. With no electricity at Yantabulla, this was quite a treat for her children.

An excellent airstrip at Ford's Bridge had been constructed recently at a cost of between £400 and £500 but, as was the case with Yantabulla, it too was sited in thick scrub. As the Gypsy was only a small aircraft, Nancy landed without too much bother, but made a mental note to look for an alternate landing ground, if and when she returned.

The most hair-raising event of the trip occurred at Hungerford when Nancy, with the engine's throttle wide open, swung onto the propeller. The engine fired and the unchocked plane moved off, with Nancy, who miraculously escaped decapitation by the spinning blades, in hot pursuit. Fortunately, she reached the cockpit and the controls in time to prevent the aircraft crashing into trees at the end of the strip.

None of this was reported in the press. Nancy, however, capitalised on the flight to promote her own interests. Describing her as Sydney's 'youngest commercial airwoman' and the owner and operator of two aeroplanes (a claim that was incorrect as the Leopard had not yet arrived), several large newspapers reported that Miss Bird had recently concluded an aerial clinic tour of the outback 'accompanied' by Sister Webb and had visited 'several hundred children'. Keeping the focus firmly on herself, Nancy had told the press that 'we' had found that the children's eyes were affected by sandstorms and flies, something with which Sister Webb, who had spent years on the railcars travelling the outback, was very well acquainted. The report also included the rather amazing but unchallenged claim that, while visiting these hundreds of children, Nancy had flown a massive 11,000 miles (17,700 kilometres) – the distance she had flown on her barnstorming tour.

The account in the local Bourke paper was far more low-key. Under the headline, 'Louth News. Visit of Clinic Sister', the journalist reported: 'Sister C I Webb, of the Far West Children's Health Scheme, came here by plane on Monday. She was piloted by Miss Nancy Bird. After a short stay Sister Webb and Miss Bird flew to Urisino.'

Although the trial run, from a medical point of view, was successful, there was one drawback. Sister Webb, a former Australian Army nurse whose pluck and bravery had sustained her through the horrors of the Great War, confessed that she was terrified every minute she was in the air. The thought of being based there permanently and repeating the ordeal on a regular basis, as well as ferrying ill patients to hospital, was not to be endured.

Her decision to remain with the baby clinic railcars was regarded as only a minor setback by Drummond, who was upgrading, not abandoning, his plan. Inspired by Sid Coleman and the Queensland service, whose planes had been used to transport the doctor to the patient, Stanley Drummond wanted to bring the patient to the doctor. For this, he would need a plane capable of carrying a nursing sister and a patient. He was in luck. Nancy, who had returned to Sydney after the trial flight, was unemployed and keen to log more experience and air time. Furthermore, her new plane was already on its way from England by sea, which was fortunate because the engine of the Gypsy Moth had packed up. It was later purchased by the South Australian Aero Club.

The new aircraft had cost a massive £1,700. Because of Nancy's age and inexperience, the plane was uninsurable, so Tom, her guarantor, had taken out an insurance policy on her life instead. It was a two-edged sword – if she crashed, she had to die before he got his money.

Nancy Bird takes delivery of her Leopard Moth (Geoff Goodall)

Nancy Bird with the Leopard Moth and her old Gypsy Moth

The Leopard Moth had a cruising speed of 200 kilometres an hour – far superior to the Gypsy, which battled to maintain 130 kilometres per hour. It was due for delivery in November, so Drummond decided to go ahead with his plan to expand the Aerial Baby Clinic into an Aerial Medical Service.

After taking delivery of her new plane, which she christened 'Spots', as in leopard, Nancy completed a few circuits at Mascot to the satisfaction of De Havilland's Major Murray-Jones to gain the necessary endorsement. On 23 November, with only two hours' solo experience, she then took off for Narromine, where she spent the night before continuing to Bourke, arriving in good time to begin the clinic round the following day.

Sister Webb, despite her fervent wish to be assigned only to the railcars, had been persuaded against her better judgement to do one more aerial tour.

This time she visited 42 patients and 22 children. Everyone who had heard about Nancy's new plane turned out to inspect it, including the entire population of Louth. Fortunately, the anxiety of landing at Yantabulla on its rabbit-warren airstrip was avoided by a message that the entire population had gone to Ford's Bridge to either watch or play in a cricket match. They were able to skip Yantabulla but, as Nancy was not keen on using the scrub-ringed landing ground at Ford's Bridge, she put the Leopard down on a rock-hard clay pan.

It was just as well, as part of the official airstrip was being used for the cricket match. Sister Webb had chosen a good day to arrive – the ground as well as the cricket ball was hard and injuries came thick and fast: a whack in the eye with a ball, another on a leg and a damaged hand for one of the fieldsman, along with other sundry smaller injuries. Despite the very high temperature, there was no suggestion that the game be curtailed and, surprisingly, no one was treated for heat exhaustion, although all players made a beeline for the water bottles at every opportunity.

The fact that she was in such obvious demand, and her transportation was in a much larger and far more comfortable plane, did not change Sister Webb's mind about flying one iota. If anything, the trip strengthened her resolve never to fly again. Flies were in plague proportions, the weather was so hot and the going so rough that, when finally released from her ordeal, she declared, 'If I ever go to England, I'll go by ship.'

Irene Webb may have been very unenthusiastic, but Nancy was not. Again demonstrating great flair in the PR department, she had issued a press statement to the newspapers to further promote her own interests, a move that would create ongoing friction between her and Drummond.

On 15 November, the Western Herald *reported:*

> Aerial Transport in the West
>
> MISS BIRD MAKING BOURKE HER HEADQUARTERS
>
> Miss Nancy Bird, one of Australia's clever lady flyers, has taken delivery of her new Leopard Moth, which she imported from England. It is Miss Bird's intention to station the 'plane at Bourke, with the object of servicing the west with aerial transport and all types of charter and taxi work. Her first trip with the new 'plane will be on November 25, when she will take Sister Webb of the Far West Health Scheme, on her tour of inspection to Louth, Tilpa, and other outback centres. This machine is designed to give the pilot and passenger every possible comfort when travelling, and is a three-seater cabin model. The passengers are provided with deep-cushioned seats, with adjustable head-rests and arm supports, soft carpeted floors, and a clear view all round. It is also provided for cold weather or flying at high altitudes. Noise has been reduced by the long, low, exhaust pipe and by insulated walls, so that conversation is as easy as in a closed car. Miss Bird hopes to encourage the people to fly for both business and pleasure, and in case of sickness she can offer them speed, safety and comfort.

CHAPTER 5

Back of Bourke

1935–1936

After giving me a very brief outline of his plans to date, Mr Drummond explained that, as Sister Webb had returned to the railcars, he needed a nursing sister to replace her. However, the new appointee would not only attend to mothers and babies in town, she would also fly to remote areas to conduct baby clinics, carry out emergency treatment and transport hospital cases or patients requiring specialist services. He had a permanent clinic organised and a plane and pilot hired for the next six months. All he needed was a sister with triple certificates who didn't mind flying and would agree to be permanently based in Bourke.

He hoped that his phone call to Pallamallawa would find her.

'What do you think of the idea?' he asked.

What indeed? The job sounded right up my alley but, never having been in a plane, let alone with a woman pilot, I was very undecided. On the one hand, ministering to families and especially children in remote outback areas interested me immensely. The downside was that, in order to do it, I had to flit about the desert in a tiny plane, piloted by a woman. This, and my impulsive move to Pallamallawa, uncharacteristically put the brakes on any on-the-spot decision.

'I'll think about it,' I told Mr Drummond, 'and give you my answer tomorrow'.

Things always have a habit of looking better after a good night's sleep. By morning, the plane of my imagination did not seem quite as fragile, nor so likely to fall out of the sky, and the woman pilot not so female and, therefore, by the standard of the day, so potentially incompetent.

I figured that Nancy Bird must be able to fly or Mr Drummond would not have hired her. And he must be confident that the plane would stay up in the air when it was supposed to, or he would not put his precious cargo, the outback children, into it.

As his offer seemed a good deal better than uniform-eating goats, occasional cricket injuries and gossipy picnics, I booked a long-distance call to Mr Drummond in Sydney the next morning.

'I'm going to Broken Hill,' I announced.

'What are you going to do up there?' he asked.

Reminding him that it was he who had called me to offer me a job there, I was very surprised when he informed me it was Bourke, not Broken Hill, that needed a flying sister.

Well, geography had never been my strong point. Broken Hill, Bourke, Brewarrina, Boggabri – they all started with a B and were all out in the bush, miles from anywhere. So I said that Bourke was just fine with me.

After making sure that I was happy to give it a go, even though I had never flown before, Mr Drummond got down to tintacks. Nancy was to live in town at Fitzgerald's Post Office Hotel, so that she could maintain close contact with me. I was to board nearby with a middle-aged couple – Bill Glover and his wife Henrietta – members of the Bourke Branch of the Far West Scheme and local pillars of society. I was expected to divide my time between the Bourke Baby Clinic, the aerial baby clinic and the general community, which to my joy included the Aborigines at various camps around Bourke as well as those on the aerial run. Places close to Bourke would be visited every three weeks. Those further away, every six. Nancy was contracted to the Far West Scheme, so I had first call on the aircraft, but she could take on private work provided Mr Drummond and I were informed in advance. My wages were £2 a week, with an additional 10 shillings per week 'danger money'. All out-of-pocket expenses were to be paid by the Far West Scheme.

By the time Mr Drummond explained all this, the long-distance call became very protracted. I lost count of the number of times the operator asked if we were extending, and I'm sure she was listening in, because everyone in Pallamallawa seemed to know I was leaving, almost before I did. In those days, there were no automatic telephone exchanges in the bush, where telephones were something of a rarity, so it was very tempting for the local operator to 'monitor' a call.

Satisfied with the arrangements, and more than happy to swap Pallamallawa for something a little more challenging, I packed my bags, returned to Scone briefly to see the family, reported to Mr Drummond at Manly and bought a one-way train ticket to Bourke – 500 miles away.

Five hundred miles by rail. Five hundred miles by rail. Say it fast enough and it doesn't sound all that long or all that far. However, in 1935, 500 miles (800 kilometres) on the New South Wales Government Railways was hardly a leisurely journey. When we think nostalgically of steam trains today, we conjure up romantic images of hugely powerful locomotives gobbling up miles of track as they speed towards their destinations. Decades on, we forget about the soot, the lack of air-conditioning in the summer, the freezing cold carriages in winter and the hard, upright bench-type leather seats that did not recline.

At that time, an extensive rail network of main and branch lines, now sadly long gone, operated throughout country New South Wales, providing a lifeline in areas where roads were poorly made or non-existent. Trains usually ran to timetable, but could not be relied upon to reach a specified destination at a specified time, unless it happened to be on one of the important, well-patronised intercity routes. Bourke, being in a remote area of the state, did not have top priority for either special timetable considerations or the latest rolling stock. Some carriages were the corridor type, with compartments off to one side or, worse, the old-fashioned non-corridor, 'dog-box' variety, in which passengers were confined, eight at a time, in compartments from which there was no escape until the train stopped.

The toughened leather seats, with their ramrod straight backs, may have been conducive to good posture, but were both uncomfortable and hard. There was no buffet car or any sleeping berths, forcing intending passengers to come prepared with their own rations as well as blankets and cushions. On an overnight journey, particularly in winter, blankets were a necessary supplement to the Government Railway heating system – a type of flattened metal cylinder filled with a heat-absorbing substance. Shortly before the train departed, the station attendant placed a cylinder, preheated to a very high temperature, on the floor of each compartment where, with any luck, it radiated warmth until morning.

I left Sydney's Central Station on Friday, 6 December on the 8 pm train for Bourke. It was the express service, not the much slower mail train, but from similar experience with country rail travel I knew that it would be a long night. Despite inane chatter from a fellow passenger, who thought it his duty to keep up a one-sided, non-stop running commentary about anything and everything, I managed to doze off once or twice, only to be rudely awakened by blasts from the train's whistle, which sounded from time to time and for no obviously apparent reason. As it was night, the further west we travelled, the cooler it became. By the time the train had crossed the Blue Mountains and reached Orange, on the central western tablelands, the temperature had dropped considerably.

It was with some relief that I heard the conductor bellow down the corridor that the next stop was Dubbo. Dubbo meant Railway Refreshment Rooms and Railway Refreshment Rooms meant a hot and reviving cup of tea. But tea, alas, was only for those blessed with extreme fleetness of foot.

As there was no way known that the Railway Refreshment Room could possibly serve every passenger who alighted from the train, it was very much a case of first in, best dressed. My long legs and my seat near the door of the compartment in the middle of the train gave me a head start, helping me secure a place at the top of the refreshment room queue, but others were not as lucky. With the steaming beverage almost within reach, their hopes were dashed by the blast of the whistle, accompanied by the ringing of an equally loud brass bell and a roar from the conductor to reboard the train. Gulping the last of my tea, I joined the lemming-like exodus to the carriages, having no desire to find myself stranded on Dubbo station until the next train arrived.

The trip seemed endless as the train made its painful progress across the western plains. The scenery had long ceased to hold my interest, and I was feeling hungry and tired when, just before 4 pm, a very long and tedious 20 hours after leaving Central Station, the conductor announced that we were about to arrive in Bourke. Thankful that I was not on the mail train, which took 23 hours to cover the same distance, I had just enough time to brush the soot from my hair and clothing and repair my ravaged make-up before we arrived at the station, bang on time.

Emerging from the stuffy confines of the compartment into the still, warm and sultry air of the late afternoon, my nostrils were assailed by a powerful and nauseating odour, bad enough to make my stomach flip. I modified my breathing and was trying to figure what it could possibly be when a welcoming committee of enthusiastic Far West people, dressed in their Sunday best and sporting wide, friendly smiles, introduced themselves.

There was no way I could have slipped into town unnoticed. As *The Sydney Morning Herald* had interviewed me in Sydney at Mr Drummond's insistence, my appointment had been well publicised. Not that I really minded. It had taken a lot of effort to launch the new aerial medical service, as well as establish a permanent clinic in Bourke (the only one west of Sydney), and he was determined to get as much publicity as possible for his cause.

Consequently, not only the welcoming committee but the entire town knew pretty much everything there was to know about me, apart from my birth date, before I put one foot on Bourke's soil. The *Herald* had not only broadcast the time of my arrival in that day's edition, but had included details of my previous experience, my triple certificate qualifications, the undeniable fact that I was 'very young', my home town, the names of my parents and that I was 'thrilled at the prospect of visiting cases by plane' as I had never been in the air before. The reporter also disclosed that I had brought my tennis racquets, golf clubs and plenty of books. The story was taken up by other newspapers, ensuring widespread publicity for the Far West and its 'flying sister', before the week was out.

Trying to ignore the pong, I returned the greetings of the welcome committee members, hoping that we could soon get away from the stench, which they didn't seem to notice or, if they did, were masterfully ignoring.

After exchanging pleasantries, at the same time trying to shut my nostrils down, I tentatively asked if there was a problem with the town's sewerage or gas system. They looked blank for a few seconds before breaking into peals of laughter.

'It's the Gidgees,', they explained. 'When it's going to rain the gidgee trees give off that smell.' That figured, as the weather forecast in the area was for storms. While I appreciated that for people who daily scanned the skies for promising rain clouds welcomed such a sign, the stink of the gidgee tree was something I could have done without.

The gidgee (Acacia cambagei), also known as 'stinking gidgee' and 'stinking wattle' is endemic to Australia. A slow-growing tree that reaches about 10 metres in height, it is resistant to termites, is extremely hard and tough, makes excellent firewood and is often used for fencing. While it is no good for stockfeed, it has colourful roots that can be turned on a lathe and polished. Found mainly in arid and semi-arid regions of Queensland, the gidgee also extends into the dry areas of Northern Territory, South Australia and New South Wales. When the atmosphere is humid, the bitter tasting grey-green leaves gives off a strong odour that carries on the wind for miles, giving notice that rain is on the way.

A short drive in the car of the committee's president took me to my hosts, the Glovers, who lived in a very attractive and roomy white timber house close to the aerodrome. They had a long association with the Far West Scheme and were active in town affairs. Bill, the local Ford agent, was a Director on the hospital board, while Henrietta, a former nurse who had worked at Bourke Hospital from 1911 to 1914, was a member of the CWA and P&C Associations.

I woke the next morning bright and early and decided to take a look around the town before it became too hot. After studying Henrietta Glover's mud map, scratched in the dirt with a stick, I set off along the main street.

Bourke Court House

Oxley Street, Bourke

Bourke, in 1935, was a thriving community. There was a European population of just under 2,000 which, as far as I could see, appeared to enjoy a wide variety of amenities and services. There was a sizeable park, showing signs of distress from the drought, and a modern tennis club, complete with courts floodlit for night games.

It was Sunday morning so all the businesses and shops, apart from the milk bar, were shut. However, I could see that deep in the shade of wide verandahs, which extended the full width of the footpath, were a pharmacy, three butchers, two bakers, Rodda's department store, the large Hales and Company's store, and various other shops selling general goods, hardware, fruit, vegetables and groceries. There were also no fewer than four ladies' hairdressers, two tailors, a saddler, a welding works, ice works, three motor garages, one of which belonged to Sid Coleman and another to Bill Glover, the Palais Royale picture theatre, Fitzgerald's entertainment hall, *The Western Herald* office and seven pubs, including the one where Nancy boarded.

For those who preferred non-alcoholic beverages, Miss Menis's Refreshment Rooms offered locally produced cordials and carbonated drinks, tea and milkshakes. There were also two solidly built private banks (a magnificent two-storey, multi-arched edifice owned by the Commercial Banking Company of Sydney and a less impressive, but nevertheless not insubstantial, building housing the English, Scottish and Australian Bank), two agencies of the Commonwealth Bank, one of which was located in a large two-storey post office with a colonial lace verandah, a Pastures Protection Board, Stock Inspector's Office, Mechanics' Institute, Literary Institute, CWA Rooms, the Diggers' Club, the volunteer Fire Brigade and a Court House.

Side streets revealed a motley collection of houses, which ranged from substantial residences to corrugated iron shacks, but most had gardens in which late blooming roses were almost at an end. There were any number of sporting clubs, a C of E and Catholic Church, a convent school run by the Sisters of Mercy, and the state-run Bourke Superior Public School for pupils aged between 5 and 14 years, who were kept in line by the headmaster, Mr Murray, and six teachers. The majority of pupils were white, as schooling for Aboriginal children was not compulsory. Aborigines technically did not exist. Their numbers could only be estimated, as they were not included in the government census and were ineligible to vote in elections.

Bourke's population in 2018 still stands at around 2,000, about one-third of whom are indigenous. The first white people to enter the area were explorer Charles Sturt and his party, who discovered the Darling River in February 1829 while searching for an inland sea. The town's actual roots go back to 1835, when colonial surveyor and explorer Sir Thomas Mitchell made camp on the western bank of the Darling, the course of which he was surveying, near its junction with the Bogan River. Fearful of attack from hostile Aboriginal tribesmen, he and his party constructed a small stockade, which Mitchell named Fort Bourke after the then Governor, Richard Bourke.

In the 1850s settlers began arriving to take up land, and in 1859 Captain W R Randall sailed his twin-hulled, single paddlewheel boat Gemini *from South Australia up the Darling as far as Brewarrina, east of Bourke. With the Darling providing a navigable link to the Murray River and the states of Victoria and South Australia, the area began to flourish.*

The town of Bourke, named after Mitchell's stockade, was soon established as a hub of trade and a transport centre for the whole of south-west Queensland and western New South Wales. Small towns like Barringun, on the New South Wales–Queensland border, became conduits for the wool trade from western Queensland, with bullock teams and camel trains transporting bales to the Bourke Port, where Cobb & Co coaches and several paddle steamer companies set up business.

Up until 1885, when a rail line was completed, linking Bourke to Sydney, paddle steamers carried the wool clip downstream to the Murray. Although the steamers continued to bring in bales to the Bourke railhead and provided vital transportation to and from many places along the Darling, an ever expanding road and rail network reduced the number of steamers until, by the 1960s, there were none.

My attention was diverted from the plight of the hapless Aboriginal community by the sight of a polished brass plate. It belonged to one of the town's two doctors and I was pleased to note that there were also two dentists and a hospital, which I could not actually see but whose existence was confirmed by a signpost pointing in the direction of the Brewarrina road.

The polished plate, with its smeary brick surround caused by an over-zealous application of Brasso, reminded me that it had been my intention to find the clinic, and that I had been distracted by the sightseeing. Leaving the exploration of the town until another time, I took my bearings and quickly relocated Fitzgerald's Hotel. Mrs Glover's map had indicated that the clinic was close by, in the old superseded courthouse.

Sure enough, there it was – a substantial two-storey brick building dating back to 1876, shaded by peppercorn trees and right alongside the new courthouse. Following Mr Drummond's decision to establish a permanent clinic, part of the old courthouse had been rented to him for the grand sum of one shilling per annum. A family with two small children occupied the remainder of the building.

Local mythology claimed that the new court house, a handsome colonnaded building in Oxley Street topped by a resplendent square tower, was built by mistake in the 1890s because a government clerk had entered the wrong name on the Public Works authorisation papers. As a result, it was widely believed that Bourke now boasted a splendid hall of justice intended for Wagga Wagga, far away in the southern part of the state. The circuit magistrate held regular sittings at the court, but actual law enforcement was in the hands of Sergeant McClintock and three constables, two of whom were mounted policemen.

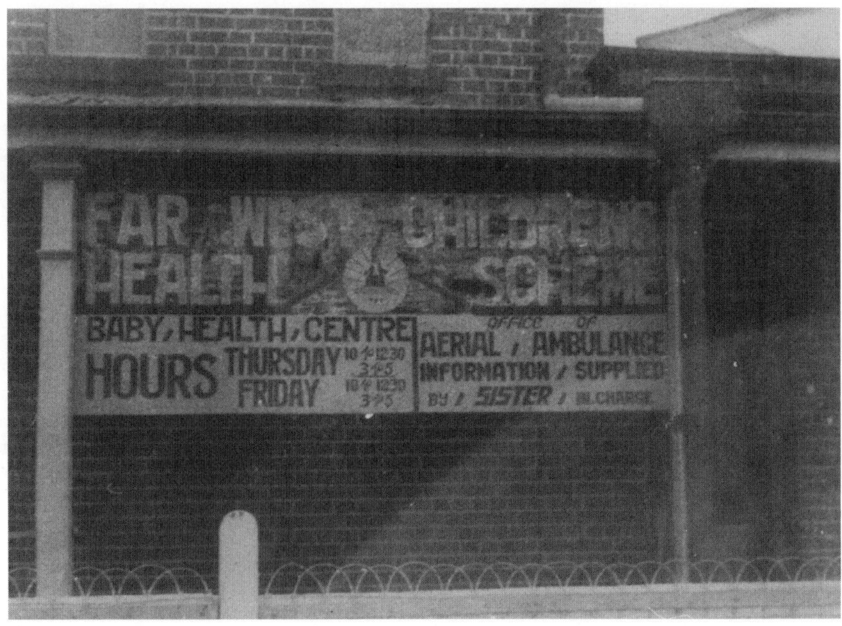

The Far West Clinic in the Old Courthouse

I let myself in and headed straight for the medical cupboard, which proved to be quite well stocked, apart from one or two items that would be needed. Continuing with my inventory, I was on my hands and knees, poking about in the cupboards, when Nancy Bird wandered in or, more correctly, bounced in. Small of stature at not much more than 5 feet (152 cm) in height, she was rather unconventionally attired in mid-calf culottes and bush shirt. Covering a mop of unruly ginger curls was a pith helmet, of the type usually worn on an African safari, shading a cheerful face already freckled by the outback sun. I later discovered that the locals did not quite know what to make of Nancy – no other female in Bourke wore culottes or short shorts, or painted her fingernails black to match a dress.

Nancy, who had only just discovered that I was replacing Sister Webb, was keen to show off her new plane and offered to take me for a spin. Right there and then. As I was dying to give it a go, I gave the inventory the flick for the time being and followed her out the door.

It was only a short walk as the aerodrome was practically in town and separated from it only by the railway line and station. Recently upgraded, it consisted of two blue-metal, all-weather intersecting runways, both about 600 yards (550 metres) in length and with a turntable at each end.

At the side of the strip was an old camel watering trough and a recently completed hangar, about the size of a domestic garage. It had been especially built, as the Leopard Moth was 2 feet (60 centimetres) too long for the existing hangar – a corrugated iron affair belonging to Sid Coleman, in which Nancy had garaged the Gypsy Moth. The new hangar had cost her £70 and took four days to construct. I couldn't work out how a plane could fit into a space just large enough for a car until I realised that the wings folded back against the fuselage for storage.

It was only a basic shelter, but was an absolute necessity as the temperatures of mid-summer made the aircraft too hot to touch, and were sufficiently high to shrink the canvas cover from the wooden framework. Of equal concern was the wind, as a good gust could make the plane turn

The hangar at Bourke airstrip, situated just behind the Far West clinic. The railway station is in the background.

The cockpit of a Leopard Moth (Ross Stenhouse)

turtle, even if tethered. Nancy had been worried sick until the work, delayed for several days by rain, was completed. She had secured it to the ground with ropes and tent pegs but, when she learned that a windstorm was on its way, was so anxious that it might tip over, or blow away, that she had climbed into the cockpit to add extra ballast. I doubt if the bare 100 pounds (45 kilograms) she weighed made the slightest bit of difference, but at least it made her feel better.

Nancy carefully pushed the plane, which only just fitted through the hangar doors, into the open. She could manage to manoeuvre it out by herself (only just), but needed assistance to get it back in. However, as planes were still a great novelty, if she were on her own she would buzz the town, a signal that she was back and an open invitation for anyone who wanted to come and help.

Unfolding the wings, which reminded me of a brolga preparing itself for flight, we stood back to admire the new plane in the late afternoon light. While Nancy proudly recited the aircraft's vital statistics – *length, 24 feet 6 inches; height, 8 feet 9 inches; wingspan, 37 feet 6 inches; a Gypsy Major engine, fuelled by two 17.5 gallon tanks, with a cruising speed of 120 miles per hour* – I cast an interested eye over its more aesthetic qualities. This was no flimsy-looking, open-cockpit, two-seater Tiger Moth, of the type I had seen at country air shows. There was no doubt about it. Nancy's new Leopard Moth was beautiful.

The plywood fuselage was French grey with a jaunty red stripe and registration VH UUG painted in huge letters along the side. On the tail rudder was an advertisement for a sheep lick – a large merino ram with the words 'VITA-LICK grows more wool'. The fee Nancy received from the company helped pay for the plane's petrol. The wings were high set and the cabin was fully enclosed, making unflattering flying goggles and hideously unglamorous leather helmets a thing of the past. The windows were large and the door handles were of shiny chrome. The interior trimming and the upholstery of the pilot's bucket-type seat, centred in front of the wood-panelled controls, along with the two passenger seats set side by side in the rear, gave off a luxurious 'new leather' smell. They were all grey in colour and toned beautifully with the light charcoal carpet. There was no room for a stretcher, but a patient could be transported in relative comfort by reclining the passenger seat. There was also a generously sized luggage locker in the rear, as well as a heating system and air-chutes for ventilation.

As my landlady had wasted no time filling me in on the terrifying experience with the runaway Gypsy Moth at Hungerford, I waited until Nancy had swung on the twin-bladed propeller and taken her seat before I clambered aboard. As the pilot opened the throttle, the engine hummed reassuringly and then, with what seemed incredible speed, the plane gathered momentum, bouncing along on its three small wheels until, quite suddenly, we were airborne.

I was hooked. Flying was sensational. Moreover, the view was breathtaking.

The trees were vast grey oceans, swirling in broad patterns across the black-soil plains. The Darling River, its twisting course clearly identifiable by coolabah trees and towering red river gums, was instantly recognisable, as were the huge levee banks, built after the disastrous floods of 1890. Also easily recognisable was the tabletop, Mt Oxley, to the east of the town and the Gundabooka Range to the south.

As we swept in a graceful arc over the town's neat collection of iron roofs, reflecting the brilliant rays of the late afternoon sun, I spotted a golf course, tennis courts and a handsome iron bridge spanning the river. There was also an old landing strip to the north, a straight railway track fading into the distance towards Nyngan, and a network of roads and telegraph lines radiating out towards Cobar, Louth and the far-off Queensland border.

Now, immediately below, was a Chinese market garden, with its regimented rows of vegetables and a gardener busily at work, judging by what appeared to be a coolie-type hat. Further out was a grove of dark-green, glossy leaved orange trees, growing in the irrigated fertile soil of the internationally renowned Pera Bore Orchard. Formerly a government experimental farm, the orchard now belonged to a pastoral company and was famous for its Washington Navels, which were in such demand that the fruit rarely reached the open market. The few for sale in Bourke were extremely expensive.

Pera Bore had started out as a government experimental farm in 1895, about 20 kilometres from Bourke. Twenty 20-acre blocks, covered in gidgee scrub, were offered to settlers to test the viability of irrigating small agricultural holdings using artesian water. Nineteen blocks were taken up and, although the settlers were beset by crippling drought and flooding rains, by 1912 the place was flourishing, with a school, post office and even its own cricket team. Visitors, after toiling from Bourke through heat and dust across barren saltbush plains, were confronted with a wondrous sight of fields of millet and maize, groves of olives, almonds, grapes, nectarines, peaches and plums, plus a huge variety of vegetables and heavily laden date palms and orange trees.

Less than 10 years later, this oasis in the desert was abandoned. Drought, flood and increasingly corrosive artesian water, with a flow reduced from 2.3 million litres a day to a mere 230,000 litres, had taken their toll. The government closed the farm, removed all improvements, and the settlers left.

By 1920 the government had leased Pera Bore, including the navel orange orchard established during the Great War by a German settler, to the Fort Bourke Pastoral Company. The orchard not only survived but prospered, producing some of the finest Washington Navel oranges in the world. The fruit's reputation was such that King George V ordered that four cases be dispatched annually to the Royal Household.

In 1938, navels from Pera Bore, described as 'the best on earth', were selling in Sydney for 14 to 17 shillings a bushel, compared to other navels that sold for between 2s 6d to 6 shillings.

However, success was short lived. By the mid-1940s the Pera Bore Orchard had vanished, killed by rising salt contaminating the water table because of incorrect irrigation practices. Similar salt overload also killed thousands of citrus in the Murrumbidgee Irrigation Area before the authorities realised where the trouble lay and how to avoid it. Citrus experts in the late 1940s agreed that 'Pera Bore oranges had never been equalled, let alone excelled'.

Today, all trace of the Pera Bore orchard is gone. All that is left is the actual bore, designated as a public watering place, and controlled by the Bourke Pasture Protection Board.

As the fruit trees slid from view, they were replaced by clumps of native vegetation, from which dusty-fleeced sheep appeared and reappeared. Square blots that I knew must be cars spat out twin tunnels of dust, marking the erratic potholed paths of the unsealed tracks.

The interior of the cabin, which was insulated, was amazingly quiet, but I was not interested in conversation. Instead, I sat with my face glued to the window, fascinated. And in no time at all, it seemed, Nancy was banking the plane and I was on the ground again to find, disappointingly, that the scenery had reverted to its normal perspective.

I could hardly wait to take off again, but I had other important things to do first, such as holding an informal gathering of mothers and babies on Monday morning, just two days after my arrival. I discovered that the local grapevine must have been working overtime because, within minutes of opening up, the waiting room was overflowing with mothers eager to view the new Sister, and to introduce themselves and their babies. Large woven-cane prams, roomy enough to hold six infants, were parked in every possible corner, while the mothers perched on wooden chairs, chatting.

The babies, gurgling happily in their prams, looked well and contented, so I picked up one chubby-faced specimen. His mother was obviously delighted that her pride and joy had been singled out for attention and stood beaming graciously at the other mothers, who were not being similarly honoured by having their babies 'officially' cuddled.

She may not have smiled so broadly had she known what I was going to do next. Holding junior firmly with one arm, I used my free hand to turn over his pillow. Sure enough, just as I

Pera Bore

suspected, was the baby's dietary supplement – jelly beans and a well-known brand of arrowroot biscuits manufactured, ironically, by one of the Far West's greatest supporters, Mr William Arnott, who had successfully marketed his arrowroot biscuits for decades with the slogan 'happy babies are Arnott's biscuit babies'.

Handing over the baby to his mother, I ushered her into the clinic room where I gently but firmly advised her on the type of food baby should be eating – milk, baby cereal, mashed vegetables, a little egg, fruit – but definitely not biscuits and definitely not jelly beans. Tucking the baby into his pram, I assured her that I would work out a proper diet for her by Thursday, the regular clinic day. I then returned to the waiting room to give the other women the same advice, only to discover that almost all of them had left, doubtless to dispose of their hoards of sweets and biscuits before Sister found them.

With regular baby clinics scheduled all day for Thursday and Friday of each week I spent the next couple of days meeting local medical staff, completing the inventory of equipment and supplies, and scrounging reading material to distribute to isolated women. With the new schedule calling for regular visits by plane to outlying areas every six weeks, the next round was not actually due until the New Year. However, I decided to bring it forward so that I could become acquainted with my patients well before Christmas.

I needed three days to cover the area. Mr Drummond was due in town on the 17th to attend a meeting of the local Far West Committee and, as I had to be back in time to give him a rundown, I put Nancy on notice to fly out early Saturday morning.

Because the people living in the remotest areas were my priority, I decided to fly direct to Urisino Station, a vast sheep property about 160 miles (260 kilometres) to the west of Bourke. After I had seen everyone on the overland route, we would stay the night before proceeding to Hungerford and Barringun, on the New South Wales border, then Engonnia, Yantabulla, Ford's Bridge and home. On the third day we would visit Louth and Wanaaring. If anything grounded the plane that day, I would still be able to reach Bourke in time for the Far West meeting.

After briefing Nancy, I posted a notice on the clinic door advising I would be out of town from Saturday morning until late Monday, and telephoned George Henderson at Urisino to let him know our estimated time of arrival and to check on the barometric reading. The news that crackled through the receiver was not encouraging. The barometer was falling, indicating that we might encounter some rough weather. However, Nancy was not particularly concerned about the forecast. Reasoning that she could always land on the road and sit out a storm or return to Bourke if the turbulence became too great, we decided to give it a try. Having agreed to go ahead with the flight, I was a little apprehensive when Nancy, somewhat as an afterthought, volunteered that the strip at Urisino was a bit on the short side, with a heavy growth of trees at one end.

We followed the Bourke–Wanaaring road before turning west for Urisino, another 25 miles (40 kilometres) to the west along the Tibooburra road, at that time a barely discernible track. On the way the weather deteriorated and the going become rough as we neared our destination. When I finally saw the airstrip, which looked about half as long as I had expected, I began to have second thoughts. My fears, however, proved groundless, for Nancy put us down with practised ease. Despite the turbulence, there was only a slight bounce as the wheels hit the strip, which had been constructed by dragging three iron cartwheel rims, attached to a truck, across the paddock in order to smooth out the worst of the bumps.

Although I had no preconceived ideas on what to expect, after flying across miles of arid desert Urisino came as a surprise. With the help of a jackeroo who had come out to meet us, we tied the plane down before plodding along a bare sandy track leading to the homestead, obscured from our sight behind a hefty 9 foot (3 metre) and very ugly corrugated iron fence. As we passed through an equally hefty gate, we entered a veritable Garden of Eden. On one side of the barricade was a no-man's land of drifting, shifting sand. On the other were velvety green lawns of the most startling green, disciplined hedges, brilliantly coloured flowers, and a range of succulent fruit and vegetables of a variety and excellence not generally seen outside displays at major agricultural shows.

The zinnias, geraniums and other heat-tolerant plants were a blaze of colour, but the roses, even the late-blooming variety, were just about finished. However, the trees in the orchard area were dripping with luscious peaches, grapes, figs and oranges. Apparently, in the winter, the variety of flowers was greater, as the days were warm and the garden was protected from frosts on the nights when the temperature plummeted.

The jackeroo told me that, although the nearest stream was 25 miles (40 kilometres) away, the secret of Urisino's wonderful garden was an unlimited supply of water, tapped from the Great Artesian Basin by bores sunk deep into the sand. A total of 25,000 gallons (113,000 litres) was used each day to supply the sprinklers watering the groves of grapes, figs, oranges and peaches, as well as the huge kitchen garden.

The station itself covered 1.25 million acres (505,900 hectares). The homestead complex was like a mini-town complete with an historic rambling homestead, a beautiful creeper-covered store and a post office – all with iron roofs and pisé walls. Being composed from the very earth on which they stood, the man-made structures were at one with nature. I could scarcely credit that 50 years before, when Urisino was settled, the finely proportioned homestead and magnificent gardens did not exist.

An unlimited supply of water, tapped from the Great Artesian Basin by bores sunk deep into the sand

The house had all mod cons, including electric lights and a large refrigerator, and was fully screened against pesky flies and other insects. The interior was beautiful, elegantly furnished and a perfect backdrop for the formal dinners hosted by owner George Henderson, who believed that standards should be maintained even (and possibly especially) in the bush. In the evening his guests, who dared not wear anything other than formal clothing, dined on exquisite food, served by a white-jacketed butler, while a chamber orchestra, brought up from Sydney, played quietly in the background. It was as if we had stepped into another world.

Urisino was founded in 1885 by an Irish immigrant, Samuel Wilson, who started out his life in Australia working on the Victorian goldfields in the 1850s, before buying up pastoral land for improvement. Within 20 years he had made a considerable fortune and owned vast properties in Victoria, New South Wales and Queensland. At one time he was credited with owning more sheep than any other person. In 1874, he endowed Melbourne University with £30,000, a gift that saw his name immortalised in Wilson Hall. He was knighted in 1875 and dabbled in state politics in Victoria, but in the early 1880s went to England where he became a conservative politician.

Sir Sidney Kidman, 'The Cattle King', who owned or controlled 68 stations covering up to 107,000 square miles (280,000 square kilometres) and was said to own more land than anyone else on earth, had used Urisino as a watering hole for his stock.

In 1924 Urisino, along with Elsinora, Thurloo Downs and Wanaaring stations, was sold to the Killen brothers, who had formed the Elsinora Pastoral Company with the intention of converting the properties from free-ranging cattle to sheep. In 1927 George Henderson, who was related to the Killens by marriage, bought into the company and became general manager. He lived at Urisino, which he turned into the oasis and social centre of the outback that Sister Silver was fortunate to experience.

In 1941, at the age of 43, he married Margaret Doyle, the first female announcer on

the ABC and a woman who loved music as much as he. However, when World War 2 depleted Urisino of much of its workforce, the glamorous pre-war social life ceased and the Hendersons spent their time tending to the most vital needs of the livestock. George, who became one of Australia's richest men, died in 1991 at the age of 93. Following the death of his widow in 2002, the residue of his estate, amounting to $16 million, was given to the Conservatorium of Music in Sydney to foster young musicians.

In 1963, Urisino was sold to the stock and station agents, Dalgety's, but in 1975 it was sold again. The new owners abandoned it shortly afterwards as the property had become unproductive due to overgrazing by cattle and prolonged drought. In 1992, Andrea Rudd and Paul Hansen, who were passing through the area on camels, came across the once beautiful homestead in a state of great disrepair. With the help of the Australian government's New Enterprise and Incentive Scheme, and with the co-operation of Urisino's absentee owners, they restored the historic homestead for paying guests. They now own the property and have embarked upon a regeneration project, relocating the feral goats and horses that overran the place and undertaking substantial reafforestation. The aim is to bring Urisino back to its former glory, and to host fabulous dinner parties, just as George Henderson did.

Because of the huge labour force, the men's quarters, which were more like army barracks, were almost as big as the homestead. Dominating the entire place was a huge wireless aerial, made from an iron pipe that must have been 100 feet (35 metres) in height, with stay wires radiating from it like a gigantic spider web. Hundreds of galahs, the cheeky grey and pink clowns of the parrot family, perched upon the wires and seemed to regard the aerial as their personal funfair as they flitted back and forth, dive bombing and chattering to each other.

After a quick cup of tea, it was time for me to look the part by changing into my white uniform and shoes, before setting off on a 200 mile (320 kilometre) overland journey to visit the outlying homesteads. I was surprised, given the terrain I had to cover, that the vehicle placed at my disposal was not the utilitarian Overlander I had envisioned but a very snappy 1928 green Chevrolet roadster, drawn up in the shade of an overhead trellis. The car had two comfortable seats, with plenty of leg room for my medical bag, personal gear, refreshments and small treats for the mothers and children, as well as a packed picnic lunch, a good supply of water and other odds and ends. In the rear was a dickie seat, below which perched the spare wheel. Under the long bonnet purred a powerful six-cylinder engine, which could have sped along at a very fast rate had the roads been in a fit state. The car was a convertible, but it was far too hot and dusty to drive in an outback summer with the roof down.

The roadster also came with a chauffeur – the jackeroo – who seemed to know everyone on my visiting list. Somewhat to my embarrassment, I discovered that my driver was not a jackeroo at all, but Charles Weiss, owner of the car and manager of Thurloo Downs, a sheep station 40 miles (65 kilometres) to the north-west of Urisino, way up in the red soil country. Having spent the previous six years as overseer and head stockman at Urisino, he had been recruited by George as my personal driver because of his bush skills and his knowledge of local conditions,

1928 Chevrolet Roadster

both of which were essential to navigate the bewildering maze of unsignposted tracks. Leaving Nancy behind to relax and enjoy Urisino's hospitality, we set off to follow a route that looped in a wide circle south from Urisino almost to White Cliffs, the opal mining settlement.

Once outside the home paddocks, we followed a winding track through fairly scrubby country for some miles. Apart from a few sheep and cattle clustered around an occasional earthen dam, we saw not a living thing. We bypassed our first port of call, a small adobe homestead, whitewashed to a dazzling intensity. Charles explained that the family who lived there – husband, wife and seven children – had left shortly after Sister Webb's visit to holiday in Broken Hill. I was surprised by the destination because Broken Hill in summer was just as hot and sandy and dusty as where they lived. However, at least they were having a holiday, and had a car to take them there and back.

Our itinerary took in a number of soldier-settlement blocks or 'selections', scattered at random across flat mulga country. On paper, these properties of 70,000–80,000 acres (28,000–32,000 hectares) appeared most impressive. The reality, however, that a 'land fit for heroes', as the government put it, was composed of very poor country, capable of carrying only one sheep to every 12 acres (5 hectares). Add to this a scant and erratic water supply, and the result was heartbreak country. Charles warned me that the current depression, which had reduced wool prices to almost nothing, on top of poor grazing country, unreliable rainfall and no capital for improvements, did not make for affluent living and that the home of the next family on the list, about 15 miles (24 kilometres) further on, was in complete contrast to the tidy whitewashed cottage.

Despite this, it did not really prepare me for the grinding poverty, the like of which I had not seen since my midwifery days in the slums of Sydney. The little house, typical of many that I visited, was made entirely from flattened kerosene tins and corrugated iron, lined with brittle sheets of newspaper, their moisture sucked dry by the unrelenting heat. Life was tough in the depressed areas of Sydney, but it was much tougher for the outback people struggling to keep body and soul together in conditions that could only be described as extremely primitive.

The next home was set in stony country, with not a blade of grass to be seen, although the owners had attempted to make a small garden inside a fenced-in area, where several large

Corrugated iron hut

sunflowers were coming into maturity. The outside was humble, as was the interior, which, despite its lack of proper furnishing, was kept spotlessly clean. A family of nine, with seven children ranging in age from a toddler to a 16-year-old, lived in the house and managed to eke out a living from the sheep that they ran in this really poor country. They had just finished shearing; the so-called shearing shed was as basic as the house – just a few posts with a dilapidated iron roof, in which one sheep at a time was shorn with hand shears.

One member of the family, a small girl named Elsie, aged about nine or so, had been selected for a holiday at the seaside home at Manly. Her excitement knew no bounds when I told her that I knew Manly and Mr and Mrs Drummond well, and would be going there myself after Christmas to help out at the Home and also with the holidaymakers.

As we drove on, Charles warned me that we would soon be visiting six children left motherless after a medical emergency that did not have a happy ending. In fact, it was the recent death of the mother that had spurred Mr Drummond to establish the aerial service. Charles knew her, of course. I forget her name after all these years, but she had become very ill with pneumonia. Her husband tried to get help, but she died on the way. Had an aircraft been available, the journey to hospital would have taken just over an hour. The children were now in the care of a young woman, aged about 21, who had a baby of her own, bringing the number of patients at this particular stop to eight.

The woman whose death so touched Stanley Drummond was Elsie Jackson, who lived with her husband Ernest on a sheep station, Colane. In February 1935, 32-year-old Elsie, mother of seven children aged between 15 years and 7 months, had been laid low with a cold which, after four days, developed into a severe chest infection. Placing her on a mattress in the back of a truck, Ernie set out to seek medical treatment. The nearest town with a bush nurse was Wanaaring, 50 miles (80 kilometres) away over an appalling rough road. The closest hospital was at Bourke, a further 140 miles (225 kilometres) distant. Ernie had not even reached Wanaaring when Elsie's condition deteriorated rapidly, and she died.

At each stop we made, at the sound of the car's engine, lonely mothers and painfully shy children, some dressed in clothing made from adult hand-me-downs and calico flourbags, emerged from hessian, corrugated iron and rough slab timber shacks to welcome us. From the reception I received, it was obvious that their need for contact with the outside world was just as great as their need for medical assistance.

Bore keeper's hut

Boundary rider's hessian home

The situation was the same with the families of boundary riders and the government bore keepers. However, while many of the keepers' huts were as pitiful as those of the soldier settlers, a steady water supply made their immediate surroundings a great deal more pleasant. The bores attracted a variety of animal life, birds in particular. Galahs congregated at the tanks in their thousands, rising as one at the approach of the car to fill the sky with raucous cries and feathery wings.

As I continued on my overland trip, I was gratified to discover that, although most people were extremely poor materially, their health was comparatively good, apart from the usual eye complaints and a nasty ear infection or two. However, as the day progressed I became increasingly aware that for them to know that help was now at hand was just as important as any drug or medical advice I might be able to dispense.

Not that such medical treatment was always welcome. We called at one home where there were five children. One, a girl, had eye trouble that was proving a bit of a challenge. Mr Drummond had arranged for her to travel to Sydney for treatment. However, she was not used to people outside her family and was as wild as a feral kitten. As she wouldn't let anyone touch her, she had been sent back home, untreated. With a bit of patience, some sweets and the cajoling of her mother, she eventually submitted, allowing me to do what I could.

As the day progressed, I was pleased that I had a driver who was quite good looking as well as good company. Apart from knowing where we were going, Charles kept up an interesting running commentary and, as I had now seen for myself how difficult life was for these outback people, he went on to impress upon me how tough some of them could be.

Just a short time previously, he and the station hands at Thurloo Downs had been mustering cattle in very isolated country about 90 miles (150 kilometres) from the homestead. The muster was proceeding quite normally until late one afternoon a ringer (a stockman circling the herd on horseback) somehow managed to impale himself on the end of a gnarled and twisted branch of a mulga tree. The branch had entered his abdomen, skewering him through the soft flesh of his belly and out his back before snapping off, complete with auxiliary twigs and clusters of leaves.

It was obvious that the branch would have to be removed, but how? They were a couple of hundred miles by road from the nearest hospital and many hours away on horseback from the homestead. There was only one option available to save his life. Someone must somehow pull the branch out.

Charles, commonly known as the 'horse doctor' because of his skill in castrating horses, was the only person capable of attempting it. Fortunately, he had with him his castrating knife, wrapped in a kerosene-soaked rag. By carefully cutting away the foliage, bark and knobbly bits until only clean ends remained, he was able to withdraw the branch backwards through the abdominal wall.

The wood came out, followed by glistening coils of slippery intestines which, despite the best efforts of the horse doctor to push them back in, refused to stay put.

He solved the problem by pushing the innards firmly back into the wound with one hand and then quickly binding the patient's middle with strips of kerosene-soaked mosquito netting with the other. The elasticity of the netting did the trick and a few deft turns of baling wire held it all in place.

The ringer was then carried to the cook's wagonette, a converted ex-Cobb & Co coach, minus its original cabin. Pulled by four strong horses, the wagonette normally carried the rations and cooking gear from one mustering camp to another. Leaving the wagonette to follow an established track, Charles headed cross-country to the homestead, figuring that with a 30 mile (50 kilometre) short cut and a reliable, sure-footed horse, he could dispatch a vehicle to meet the patient.

Keeping the evening star on his back, he headed due east, his ability to find his way in the dark rewarded by the early rescue of the ringer, who was then transported immediately by road to Bourke hospital, a journey that took more than 24 hours.

Although, amazingly, the branch had not perforated the intestines or caused any internal damage, the doctors were very worried that infection might set in. It didn't. Against all the odds, the patient not only survived but turned up chirpily for work four weeks later, his own cast-iron constitution and a combination of the disinfecting kerosene (which worked just fine on horses) and the unconventional mosquito net bandaging doing the trick. Listening to this incredible, but true tale, I nevertheless observed that Mr Drummond's aerial service had not arrived before time.

Using kerosene as a disinfectant or antiseptic was not confined to outback Australia, where it was applied to any cut or abrasion. In America it was also often mixed with sugar as a salve on wounds and as a poultice for puncture wounds, including snakebite.

With the maze of tracks and sidetracks criss-crossing our route, I marvelled that not once did we get lost, especially when we had to deviate around a boggy area that had been churned during the wet season, but was now a mass of dried-out hollows and ridges, all as hard as concrete. Several cars, which were old and impossible to move from the bog, had been stripped of everything remotely useful and now sat like skeletons, as they waited for time and the elements to render them into some kind of weird desert sculpture.

I was not particularly worried about breaking down as we carried vital spare parts, including a set of springs strapped to the bumper bar. And even if we suffered a major breakdown, I was not concerned about being stuck in the middle of nowhere. Apart from being an experienced bushman and knowing the area like the back of his hand, I had discovered that Charles was also an accomplished tracker.

We had stopped for our picnic lunch and, while waiting for the billy to boil, he told me that he had acquired this skill by necessity, as he wanted to find out what his Aboriginal station hands were doing each day. Suspicious of the number of 'missing' horses that reportedly needed to be rounded up, thereby excusing the workers from other chores, he had decided to track them to see what they were up to. Following their footprints to a shady tree, where he found them having a peaceful siesta, he realised how handy it was to be able to track, and from then on practised at every opportunity, until he was more adept than some of his experienced Indigenous trackers.

His skill proved to be life saving when, while riding along a boundary fence, he noticed an erratically swerving set of prints. Backtracking, he found a completely disoriented and hopelessly lost swagman, minus his swag and supplies, beneath one of the few trees in the area. In an effort to conserve precious bodily fluids, the swagman had plugged his mouth and covered his body with leaves to slow down the rate of evaporation. The zigzagging marks in the red soil, left by his boots as he dragged his weakening body towards the shade of the tree, showed that he was nearly on the point of death when Charles found him. But for the swaggie's own survival skills and the skill of his tracker, the unforgiving desert and the merciless sun would have claimed yet another victim.

I was so fascinated by my driver's commentary that I hardly noticed the dusty miles slip by. By the time we arrived back at Urisino in the early evening, my knowledge of the outback in general, and of bores, dingo trapping and sheep in particular, had improved out of sight.

That night we dined out in legendary style with George Henderson, a most congenial host. The following morning dawned relatively clear, enabling us to fly as planned to Hungerford, a whistle-stop town on the New South Wales–Queensland border. Before we left, Nancy topped up the fuel, using a funnel to transfer petrol from a can into the wing tanks.

Urisino had regular deliveries of 600 gallons (2,700 litres) of petrol, plus a good amount of oil and kerosene which, along with other supplies, was brought on a robust Thorneycroft truck and trailer. With the refuelling complete, we set off, taking with us a supply of fresh fruit and veggies to distribute, all picked from the station garden and orchards. Again, there was no danger of getting lost. All Nancy had to do was to fly due east along the road to Wanaaring, and then follow the Paroo River to the border. This was easily identified by the wire-mesh dog fence, built to keep dingos out of New South Wales and South Australia and running in a straight line west to east. It had been cleared for some distance either side to make sure trees did not fall on it, and had doggers' huts spaced along it at 25 mile (40 kilometre) intervals.

Known officially as the Wild Dog Barrier, the Dog or Dingo Fence was built in the 1880s to keep dingos out of the sheep-grazing lands of south-eastern Australia and South Australia. It is one of the longest structures in the world, stretching 5,614 kilometres from Jimbour on Queensland's Darling Downs to the towering cliffs of the Eyre Peninsula in South Australia, on the Great Australian Bight.

Straddling the border was Hungerford which, apart from the post office, was on the Queensland side of the border. It wasn't much of a town – just a police station, a hotel, a general store and a house. The clinic was held in the post office, which meant that many of the patients had to cross the border, which was simply a matter of opening a gate. Before we left, I wandered into Queensland. It looked exactly the same as New South Wales.

Queensland border gate at Hungerford

Situated on the Paroo River upstream from Wanaaring, Hungerford started out in the 1860s as a drovers' camp. In 2006, the population stood at 59, but back in 1900 it was a much larger centre, with a police station, court house, post and telegraph office, four churches, a school, three hotels and several stores. Today there is just one pub, The Royal Mail.

The town was immortalised by Australian author and bush poet Henry Lawson who, in the searing heat of summer in 1893 walked the 215 kilometres from Bourke to Hungerford. Lawson reported that the town on the New South Wales side consisted of two houses, a humpy and a post office, and five houses, two pubs and police barracks in Queensland.

Since each state in Australia at that time was autonomous, there was also a Customs House hard against each side of the fence. According to Lawson, who wrote a humorous short story entitled Hungerford, most altercations broke out on the Queensland side of the fence, where the pubs were. If a row started in New South Wales territory, he claimed that the only option for the police, being in Queensland, was to contact Brisbane and apply for an extradition warrant. If the fight was on the Queensland side, they generally didn't bother to do anything at all.

Lawson didn't think much of Hungerford, which he said was named because of the hunger experienced there by early explorers and the ford across the (usually dry) Paroo. 'I believe Burke and Wills found Hungerford,' he wrote, 'and it's a pity they did.'

After Hungerford came Barringun. Although there was no road directly linking the two, all Nancy had to do was follow the dog fence for another 80 or so miles (130 kilometres).

Barringun developed as a border crossing at about the same time as Bourke. By 1878 it had a hotel, The Tattersalls, where bush poet Harry 'Breaker' Morant later drank, and within five years was sufficiently large and lawless to warrant a Court of Petty Sessions. In 1894, there were two hotels and a Customs House on the Queensland side of the border. On the New South Wales side were several houses, a bonded warehouse, post and telegraph offices, two hotels, the Commercial Bank, a brewery, two butcher shops, the Court House, a gaol and a public school. All this for a population of 180, including 30 school-age children.

By the time Sister Silver began her clinic in early 1936, the court house had been closed for two years and the customs houses were long redundant, following the federation of the states in 1901. The town was also minus one of its pubs, The Royal Mail, which burnt down in 1895. Today, the population of Barringun is less than 10, and the only pub left is The Tattersalls.

With the closest dairy hundreds of miles away, fresh cow's milk was unprocurable in the outback. There were, however, plenty of goats in and around Hungerford and Barringun. I conducted special workshops at both to show mothers how to convert fresh goat's milk to a suitable infant formula. From Barringun we flew south, to Enngonia. As had been the case with the two border towns, there were no major complaints at Enngonia that required ongoing attention.

Enngonia is on the Mitchell Highway, about 100 kilometres from Bourke and 40 kilometres south of the Queensland border. Settlement was slower than in some of the surrounding towns, but by the late 1800s large properties were employing a substantial amount of labour and the town became an important stopping point for travellers and bullock teams between the border and Bourke.

The origin of the name is said to be a corruption of Erin's Gunyah – a simple shelter erected by one of the first settlers – into Eringynyah, which was also spelled as Eringunla and Eringonia, before becoming Enngonia.

If anyone has ever heard of Enngonia, it will most likely be in relation to its colourful bushranging history and the two incidents that took place in 1868. At that time, according to the local squatters, the area was infested by 'lazy, idle, loafing scoundrels', whose sole aim in life was to live without working.

The first incident occurred when the ironically named horse thief and bushranger, Thomas Law (known to police as George Gibson and Henry Wilson and to the public as Midnight), was shot and killed by police to the west of the town. He was on the run after a shoot-out with police at Dubbo, in which Sergeant Wallings was killed.

The second involved the murder of Constable John McCabe, who was shot by bushranger Frank Pearson, known as Captain Starlight. Constables McCabe and McManus were searching for Starlight and his companion, Charles Rutherford, when they stopped at the Shearers' Inn at Enngonia for supplies. While they were there, the two bushrangers arrived and attempted to bail up the publican and patrons. In an exchange of fire between the police and the outlaws, McCabe was hit in the chest. Infection set in, and he died a month later.

Today, Enngonia is a small service centre for surrounding properties. The post office, built in 1898, burnt down in 1941. The settlement now consists of a police station, school, a hotel and several houses.

Assuring my patients that I would return in about three weeks, we headed cross-country for Yantabulla, which required concentration on Nancy's part. So did the landing, as the airstrip had been created, amid a thicket of scrub, on old rabbit warrens that had supposedly been flattened. However, as the strip was seldom used, the rabbits had returned and had begun to make new homes for themselves. As the plane rolled to a bumpy stop, squashing paddy melons in its wake, almost the entire population of the village swarmed out to greet us, keen to put the new sister under the microscope. I looked at them, and they looked at me, and when the looking was over we all chattered away nineteen to the dozen while the children amused themselves inspecting the aircraft. The women, who had dressed in their best clothes and scrubbed their children until they glowed, confided that they were greatly relieved to have regular clinic visits at last.

The name Yantabulla, which is Aboriginal, meaning stones around a spring, and also plenty to eat, was derived from a station originally known as Yantabulla-bulla and owned by Vincent Dowling, whose homestead stood on the Bourke Road. The town was once a camel camp, where the teamsters rested for the night and watered their animals. This small but thriving community in the 1930s was, by 2008, home to just 17 people.

In the reception committee were 17 school-age children. Four were 'white' and the remainder were Aboriginal or part-Aboriginal. It was Sunday, and also school holidays, but normally they all attended school in an old converted shop, shaded at the front by a rusty corrugated-iron verandah. In summer, school hours were from 7 am to 12.30 pm to avoid the hottest part of the day.

I held the clinic in the local pub, the Yantabulla Hotel, a low timber building with a narrow, shaded verandah running along the front. The publican had brightened up the interior with vases and urns filled with artificial ferns of a startling shade of brilliant emerald green and impossibly exotic flowers. For some reason, diners were instructed by prominently displayed signs to 'pay the waitress'. I never did find out if this was to remind them to pay, or some kind of internal accounting system.

Apart from checking that their vaccinations were up to date, and spending some time making friends with the publican's two small daughters, who were as alike as two peas in a pod, I left Yantabulla feeling faintly superfluous. Apart from one or two people who were suffering from colds, everyone else was disgustingly healthy.

So far, I had not done much except distribute advice, reassurance, magazines and the odd aspirin or two. It was not until we reached Ford's Bridge, about 50 miles (80 kilometres) away along the main road to Bourke, and were almost home that I had a chance to demonstrate my

Children line up for medical inspection outside Yantabulla school house

medical skill. Waiting for me at the clay-pan strip was a farm worker with an iron spike firmly embedded in the calf muscle of his leg. As the tissue damage was extensive and very inflamed, I urged him to come with me in the plane to Bourke, as he required immediate hospital treatment. However, he had no intention of becoming the Aerial Medical Service's first airborne patient. With a look approaching sheer terror, he backed off, spike and all, and declared that, although 35 miles (55 kilometres) of dusty, bumpy kilometres lay between him and the hospital, he would much prefer to make the journey by car. Before he escaped from my clutches completely, I managed to give him a tetanus shot, much to his chagrin and the amusement of the onlookers, still clustered around the clay pan.

In 2006 the population of Ford's Bridge was 31, with males outnumbering females by more than three to one.

Next morning, day three of the rounds, we flew to Louth and Wanaaring, which we had bypassed on the way to Urisino. Some dust was encountered en route to Louth, a tiny community about 60 miles (100 kilometres) south-west of Bourke. However, we could hardly get lost as it was on the Darling, which we just had to follow. The so-called landing strip was nothing more than a rough paddock strewn with paddy melons that popped under the wheels.

The town of Louth was established in 1859, following the advent of paddle steamers along the Darling. The first building to be constructed was the Daniel O'Connor Hotel, built to cater for passing river trade by Irishman Thomas Mathews who named the settlement after his home county in Ireland. A post office was opened 10 years later and by the 1890s the town included a school and a police station. The expansion was due largely to the transportation of wool upstream to Bourke, and copper ingots from the Cobar mine shipped downstream by steamer

High level bridge at Louth

and barge to Morgan in South Australia. Before a high-level bridge was constructed above the flood line, a ferry carried sheep, pedestrians and Cobb & Co coaches from one side of the Darling to the other. In times of flood today, the town's population relocates to the sturdily constructed iron bridge, camping out until the water subsides.

With a present-day population hovering around 100, Louth's main claim to fame is its annual race meeting, held early each August and attended by more than 5,000 people.

I met the locals in the sitting room of The Royal Hotel, a low-set timber building, barely clear of the earth and with a few ferns (real ones this time) planted outside that somehow managed to stay alive in spite of the heat and dust. As it was clinic day, the publican, Mrs Emma Okely, had put aside the pub's sitting room, whose walls were adorned with a rather bizarre mixture of pictures of flamingos and shaggy Scottish cattle and portraits of various ancestors.

Mrs Okely, aged in her sixties, had bought the pub with her first husband, Harry Gillette, using part of her £6,750 windfall from a winning ticket in a Tattersall's sweep in the 1900 Melbourne Cup. Fred, her second husband, whom she married in 1911, died in 1917, and she had run the pub on her own ever since.

She was most welcoming and offered me a glass of water, kept in a canvas waterbottle behind a bar, whose offerings in the way of alcoholic, or indeed any other kind of beverage apart from beer, appeared to be very scant. We were not in town for long. The population of Louth was small so, as soon as I had met the handful of mothers who turned up, we headed for Wanaaring. It was about 85 miles (135 kilometres) or so away – but not as the crow flies.

Following a north-westerly compass heading, and with a road map balanced on her knees, Nancy headed out across some very desolate desert – flat, red-soil plains as far as the eye could see, broken by bits of scattered scrub and shimmering clay pans. Occasional wedge-tailed eagles soared on the rising thermals, which Nancy kept well clear of, as the birds were large and she didn't relish the thought of colliding with one. With such featureless country below, she didn't need to encourage me to keep a sharp lookout for the Bourke–Wanaaring Road, roughly 40 miles (65 kilometres) distant. It was nothing more than a bush track, but when we spotted it she altered course to the west and followed it into town. I say town, but the commercial business district consisted of one hotel, a general store, post office and a one-man police station.

Although the town was situated on the Paroo, there were no gardens to speak of, apart from a few flowers and some surprisingly healthy citrus trees, planted in the grounds of the police station. I soon discovered why the locals were not into gardening. The Paroo is an apology for a river, and usually nothing more than a string of muddy waterholes – except in times of flood, when I was assured it became a raging torrent. Looking at it shrivelling before my eyes under a scorching December sun, I could hardly credit that this could be the case.

Arriving back in town, I headed for the Glovers' house for a quick cuppa before checking on the situation at the clinic. I was scarcely inside the front door when I heard a voice call urgently from the hallway, 'Sister! Sister! Phone!'

'Typical,' I thought. 'Hardly home and someone wants me already.'

I trudged up the hallway only to find that when I lifted the receiver, there was no one there. Returning to the lounge, I kicked off my shoes only to be summoned again by an insistent 'Sister! Sister! Phone!'

Repeating the pantomime, and finding no one on the end of the line, I went into the kitchen to tell Henrietta that I had answered the call, but that something was wrong with the phone.

Scarcely able to contain her mirth, she beckoned me to follow her onto the front verandah. There in a cage sat the biggest, fattest, most magnificently plumed white sulphur-crested cockatoo that I had seen for some time. He put his head on one side and fixed me with a beady stare. He then scratched himself and nonchalantly preened his snowy feathers before strutting up and down like a prima donna on the stage of Albert Hall. Certain he had my undivided attention, he looked at me patronisingly, raised his yellow crest, opened his beak and called 'Sister! Sister! Phone!' He then cast another penetrating look my way before turning his attention to the contents of his seed tray.

As Henrietta explained that this was his latest party trick, I wondered what he would look like minus his feathers. However, as he had fooled me, I figured he would also fool the neighbours, which would do wonders for my image if everyone within earshot thought that I was in such demand.

Before heading off to the clinic, I took out my road map to show Henrietta where I had been. We added up the mileage and could scarcely believe the distance I had covered in the past three days. Although I was feeling a bit weary, and looking a little on the dusty side, I realised that this was nothing compared to the fatigue and dust encountered by the sisters who had attempted to cover much the same route by car. Small wonder that the clinic rounds had been few and far between.

As I pushed open the clinic door, my spirits plummeted. Red dust was everywhere. It coated the tables, the sink and the cupboards, and clung, defying gravity, to all vertical surfaces, including the recently cleaned windows. It sat in neat rows along the skirting boards and picture rails and clouded the cushions and upholstered seats. The baby scales wore a delicate tracery of apricot, the dust outlining every intricate swirl of the neatly woven cane. The floor was also thickly coated, apart from the broken line made by my footprints, which revealed traces of the brown linoleum beneath. As no one was there to hear, I let a swearword slip. And little wonder. This was more than the usual accumulation of dust, the bane of all outback housewives, which seeped on a daily basis under closed doors and around the window sashes. While I was away, Bourke had been hit by a dust storm. I should have realised this was a possibility, because we had encountered dust as we neared Louth.

This storm, although it had made a mess, had obviously been quite mild, for relatively little sand had been driven in under the door, even though I was not on hand to take the usual precautions. Mr Drummond who, early in his Superintendency, had experienced a storm so severe that trees had been uprooted and the sand sucked from beneath his car, made sure that his outback sisters knew the warning signs and acted accordingly.

The first indication, which always sent me scurrying to close all windows and pack rags in the gaps under the doors, was an unnatural decrease in the intensity of the sunlight and a

A camel train brings the wool clip to Bourke

blurring of normally sharp shadows upon the ground. As the dust cloud closed in, diffusing the rays of the sun and turning the light to a sepia brown, the birds ceased their chirruping and the air became unnaturally still. But not for long. With a frightening, roaring intensity, the storm would erupt, turning day into night, driving dust and grit into every nook and cranny.

Those indoors were safe enough, but the stockmen at Urisino told me that, if caught in the open, I must take whatever cover was available and stay put until the storm had passed. The stockmen had assured me that the only living creature able to remain in the open without any ill effects were the camels.

> *Descended from animals imported by Afghan traders in the 1800s to transport goods and material for the construction of the Overland Telegraph Line, camels were still used to transport the wool bales to the railhead at Bourke, sometimes from as far away as Wanaaring. Perfectly adapted to the conditions by their evolution in the sandy wastes of the Middle East, they simply closed off their nostrils, shut their eyes and settled down to wait, seemingly indifferent to either wind or dust, while man cursed the storm with all the vehemence he could muster.*

I cleaned up the mess in time for an inspection by Mr Drummond, who arrived the next day, as expected, for the committee meeting of the Far West's Bourke branch, held in Fitzgerald's Lounge. As 170 children were about to leave numerous outback towns for the annual seaside camp at Manly, the departure of the Bourke contingent by train for Sydney on 20 December was high on the agenda. This was to be the first camp actually held at Christmas.

As was always the case, the problem of finances loomed large, but my suggestion that we hold a monster raffle, at the outrageous price of £1 per ticket, was adopted. Although it was a very substantial amount of cash, the people of Bourke responded magnificently, aware that the Far West Scheme was a lifeline to the people of the outback.

Christmas was now only a few days away. The Committee had asked me on my arrival in town if I would consider undertaking a special trip to Urisino to distribute treats and toys to the children, dressed as Santa Claus who, in those days, was generally referred to as Father Christmas. Nancy had volunteered to provide the transport in a private capacity as her contribution so, although by mid-afternoon the mercury would be nudging around the century mark on the old Fahrenheit scale, I readily agreed.

As Santa could not arrive without a bulging sack, the local Far West Committee, the CWA ladies, Nancy and I had been soliciting firms and individuals for the past fortnight for donations of cash and goods. George Henderson, along with the staff and station hands at Urisino, chipped in, as well as the drinkers in the town's pubs, the mothers at the clinic and the wider community. People were so generous that, well before our 23 December departure, we had sufficient funds to buy enough presents at Mr Rodda's shop and at Hales and Company's department store to ensure that no one would be left out. A list of names had been prepared, along with age and sex, so we had some idea of what to buy. The gifts included an assortment of dolls, a small cane doll's pram, books, games, tea-sets, cricket bats and balls, toy animals, rattles, a wooden horse, tops, skipping ropes, marbles, and balloons and party squeakers. Nancy had also persuaded Nestle's management to donate 40 red cardboard stockings, filled with small cheap items and other little treats.

On the day of our departure, the sun rose with its usual brilliant intensity. In spite of the early hour, I was already sweating as I donned a white coverall, all I could bear to wear under the Santa suit. Borrowed from Rodda's store, which always had a Santa as part of its Christmas promotion, my traditional 'Father Christmas' outfit consisted of a red hat, a long, flowing cloak and shoulder cape edged with cottonwool fur, and an enormously thick and enormously hot cottonwool beard. The cloak, designed for a man, was a bit big around the middle but, since I am fairly tall, the length did not need adjusting.

The Drummonds and a party of well-wishers came to see us off. Posing for the mandatory group photograph beneath the plane's wing, we made a diverse group: Nancy, in her bush rig and sandals, leaning nonchalantly on the frame of the open hatch; Ellis Oates, a local man, equally at ease against the wing strut, attired in a short-sleeved undervest and braces; and a beaming Lucy Drummond dressed in what appeared to be her Sunday best, complete with hat and handbag. I stood next to Lucy. I just fitted. Being much taller than the others, my head only just cleared the underside of the upswept wing. Mr Drummond also took a photo of me dressed in the Santa suit, which he intended to use for publicity purposes. It was so hot that I wondered how I would ever manage the overland trip from Urisino the next day.

Jammed into the back seat of the Leopard Moth, with piles of donated toys, stockings and treats on my lap and taking up all the available space on the spare seat and floor, I then set off to become not only the first Santa, but the first Flying Santa, the outback children had ever seen.

We stayed at Urisino for the night. The next day was Christmas Eve. It was much hotter than I predicted, about 115 degrees Fahrenheit, which is how we measured temperatures in those

Top: Sister Silver waits to board the plane for her Christmas flight, watched by (l to r) Nancy Bird, Thomas Ellis Oates and Mrs Drummond.

Above: Sister Silver with Nancy Bird at Bourke airstrip, prior to take off.

Left: Father Christmas and Nancy Bird.

days. It always seems to sound much hotter than 46 degrees Celsius. We loaded the car and set off early to beat some of the heat. It was far too hot to drive all the way in my Santa suit, so I put it on just before reaching each stop. It was just as well. We had three punctures, the first one only about 7 miles (11 kilometres) from Urisino, which involved a complete unpacking of the car in order to reach the jack. To make matters worse, we drove through a dust storm practically the whole way and the windows had to be wound up tightly to keep the sand and dust out.

What a sensation we created! For children who had never before laid eyes on a toy, let alone a crimson-robed Santa, it was a wondrous moment when, in place of the Far West Sister, out of the

Two children visited by Father Christmas. Note the hessian bag dress on the younger girl.

car stepped a real, live Santa Claus. The looks of undisguised joy on the children's faces and the tear-filled eyes of their mothers wiped out any discomfort I felt inside the sweltering, sauna-like suit. The little ones were so excited that no one noticed that Santa's rather unorthodox footwear was a pair of white leather lace-up shoes with a fringed tongue, remarkably like those that Sister Silver had worn on her visit a few days earlier.

The reactions of the children varied from shy acceptance to whoops of delight, as they frenziedly ripped the wrapping paper from the gifts. The noise was deafening as they ran around, scattering the contents of the stockings on the floor, in their excitement to show other members of the family what Santa had brought.

One home we visited was deserted – much to my disappointment. However, in the bush no one ever locks a door, and we were able to leave the presents on the kitchen table as a surprise for when they returned.

Drummond, who was keen to promote the work of the Scheme, distributed details of the proposed trip to the press, along with the photo of Sister Silver, dressed in her Santa costume, beside the plane at Bourke. However, other coverage of the event, evidently based on material supplied by Nancy, was less than accurate, according to one report, which cast Nancy in the starring role. Under the headline, 'A New Role for Girl Flier', 'a clinic sister' had accompanied Nancy who, 'acted as father Christmas to hundreds of little children' and, despite the heat, 'wore the conventional robes of Santa Claus' as she distributed the gifts. In yet another report, Nancy and the unnamed Sister were 'Father Christmases to scores of little Westerners this festive season. Starting early from Bourke, this gallant girl flew on Christmas Day to Urisino Station, distant 125 miles, and then round the settlements.'

The report continued: 'A Sydney firm supplied the aviatrix with toys and presents for the round trip and Miss Bird safely negotiated it. Though the temperature was well over 100, Miss Bird wore the conventional robes of Santa Claus . . . She gave real joy to scores of kiddies who never before had known the real pleasure of Christmas.'

The claim that Nancy had dressed up as Santa Claus was so entrenched that, in 1938, the famous airman P G Taylor, as a foreword to a series of articles by Nancy, wrote:

'At Christmas she thought of the children in those places, organised a toy supply, loaded her Leopard with teddy bears, dolls, toy trains, Christmas stockings and the small things beloved of children, and, landing at each place dressed in conventional costume, played Father Christmas to them all.'

The next day, with George Henderson, Charles Weiss and the eight or so remaining staff, I tucked into my first outback Christmas dinner. As George was the host, it was a most traditional affair, in spite of the heat. The huge dining room table was draped in a snow-white damask cloth, on top of which was placed Urisino's finest china and heirloom silver, polished to perfection for the sumptuous feast that had been prepared. The table groaned under the weight of succulently baked turkeys and chickens, surrounded by bowls of fresh vegetables, picked that morning from the station's own garden. The steaming plum puddings, cooked several weeks before and hung to cure in the pantry, were smothered in a mouth-wateringly rich brandy sauce. For those who could manage it, there were slabs of Christmas cake, nuts and fresh fruit.

Urisino Station December 1935 (l to r) Charles Weiss, Sister Silver, George Henderson, Nancy Bird

We also spent Boxing Day at Urisino, flying back on the 27th. It was then off to Sydney for me as I had volunteered to spend my 'holiday' with the outback children at the brand-new Drummond Far West Home at Manly. I arrived far too late, of course, to join in the Christmas festivities, which included a 4 am visit on Christmas Day from Santa. The Far West Auxiliary had also erected a huge Christmas tree filled with gifts and organised a Punch and Judy Show – always a great favourite.

Nancy remained in Bourke, hoping to pick up some charter work. She certainly did. The drought broke shortly after I left and the heavens opened up, making roads impassable. Bourke had 5 inches (125 millimetres) of rain in 24 hours, cutting all roads in and out. Dry creeks and rivers ran a banker and then overflowed – the road to Barringun was under a record depth of 4 feet (120 centimetres) of water. People with urgent appointments, or trains to catch, and who had the means to pay, suddenly realised how handy a plane could be when hemmed in by floods. Nancy also made several runs carrying mail and food to cut-off areas.

Sydney had more rain than usual that January, but the storms brought relief after the hot, sultry days. Of course, nothing dampened the spirits of the children, even if it rained, as the Drummond Home was virtually on the beach and was far grander than 'the depot', now used as an overflow for the new building. The local school housed the campers, a concession granted by no lesser person than the Minister for Education.

By 1932, it had become obvious that the Far West house at 25 Wentworth Street, which was bursting at the seams, was no longer adequate. On 4 December that year, Drummond had convened a meeting at Government House and launched a special building appeal. The New South Wales Government set the ball rolling with a donation of £3,000. Other donations quickly followed, including a cheque for almost £1,200 from Charles Kingsford-Smith, who had met Drummond during one of his country air shows.

Learning that the Scheme was trying to raise sufficient cash to build a new Home, Smithy had suggested they hold a 'Kingsford-Smith Testimonial Fund', launched by Drummond on 6 May 1933. In only one week the aviator had raised enough money from a barnstorming tour to build an entire accommodation wing, which was named after him. He arrived at the depot to present the cheque in person, much to the joy of the small patients, especially one handicapped boy, who was taken for a ride to the mid-west in Smithy's plane.

Generous patronage from such a high-profile public figure generated a great deal of publicity. New branches and auxiliaries were formed and Eric Baume launched a special appeal in the Sun *newspaper. In December 1934 the foundation stone was laid by the State Premier and, five months later, The Drummond Far West Home, a name insisted upon by the members of the building committee, was officially opened by the Governor General of Australia, Lord Gowrie, at a ceremony attended by 5,000 people.*

The huge Georgian-style building was a palace compared to the old depot. A wide front door, flanked by substantial columns and a wide, open-sided verandah, led to a broad central corridor,

Drummond Far West Home at Manly

flanked by four children's wards, a schoolroom, dining room, main kitchen, reception room and other ground-floor facilities. The babies' suite, comprising nursery, bathroom, feeding room, small kitchenette and dining area, was upstairs, along with a sunroom for the use of all patients. The mattresses in all wards were covered with bedspreads, onto which the Far West badge had been embroidered. Characteristically, the Drummonds did not make the move to the palatial building that now bore their name. They remained at the depot where, no longer confined to their tiny glassed-in verandah, they now had the 'luxury' of two rooms.

I knew a few of the patients as one of my tasks at Pallamallawa had been to assess those needing treatment. Apart from Elsie Martin, my young friend from Urisino, most of the 180 holidaymakers were strangers to me. Elsie, who had a fine singing voice, was very excited when she was invited to perform a solo item on Radio 2GB and equally excited when the New South Wales Premier asked for a command performance when he came to visit.

The campers, as they were still called, even though they were no longer holidaying in tents, certainly needed a break from the outback. Twenty-five children had problems with their eyesight and 20 were tested and had glasses prescribed. Fourteen had their adenoids and tonsils out, while four others needed surgical attention. More than half, ninety 90 in fact, needed dental treatment, a task carried out by Mr Hyder of the Education Department and Mr Perdriau, who voluntarily gave his services, along with Dr Wearn who assisted in more difficult procedures.

Many, suffering from malnutrition, were given Parrish Food and Malt, as well as plenty of milk, meat, fruit and vegetables. In the three weeks that the camp lasted, the children ate their way through 610 loaves of bread, 625 kilograms of meat, 120 kilograms of fish, 2,100 litres of milk, 360 dozen eggs, 1,450 kilograms of peas and beans, 35 cases of tomatoes, 110 cases of fruit, 760 kilograms of potatoes and 150 dozen lettuces. The average weight gain per child was more than 2 kilograms.

The selection criteria for campers was fairly straightforward: any child whose economic circumstances warranted it could be selected for a holiday as long as they had never seen the sea. Some children had not only never seen the sea, they had never laid eyes on a train, a bus, boats, trams, a lift or an escalator, or eaten ice-cream.

However, some newcomers who had been in contact with former Far West campers had definite ideas on what the sea would be like. One small boy, on arriving at Central Station after his long train journey, had been asked by one of the sisters if he had any idea what to expect. Speaking with the confidence of one who is in possession of prior knowledge, he replied that 'the sea is like a big dam without banks, where the water knocks you over and makes you sick if you swallow it'. Although amused by the response, I really could not imagine what it must be like to see the vast Pacific Ocean for the first time. The look of rapture that lit up the children's faces was a clue, but I felt that, for those accustomed to an unremitting vista of featureless dirt, dust and flies, the sight must have been almost beyond belief.

Another child, on seeing jellyfish for the first time, became concerned that they might puncture the hull of the ferry, or even make it capsize. Yet another wanted to know 'How did a bloke hop over the harbour before you got the bridge?'

Although most patients at the Home had come to receive specialised medical treatment, a few had come to gain relief from 'tropical pallor', a condition caused by intolerance to severe heat. Some children, who failed to thrive in extremely hot climates, developed diarrhoea, feverishness, listlessness and a peculiar jaundice of the skin, hence the name. The malnourished, in particular, benefited from the plentiful and vastly improved diet. After a few weeks of fresh, wholesome food, legs that had once resembled matchsticks became strong and sturdy, with tanned muscles in place of bony protuberances.

Children with medical problems arrived in a steady stream throughout the year, so the convalescent wards were always full, even at Christmas. As soon as they had been released from hospital, where they had received expert attention from compassionate specialists, they returned to Manly, where the fresh air and sunshine soon restored their health and vitality.

It was not merely good food, the beach and medical treatment that raised their spirits. There

Far West children at Manly, 1934

were no flour-sack dresses, ragged blouses, holey shirts or baggy, hand-me-down shorts here or at the holiday camp. On arrival, each child was provided with new clothing, either donated by the public or sewn especially for them by a small team of volunteers. The Far West Home was a place where, through the tireless efforts of Stanley Drummond and his staff, miracles happened every day.

Although it was a rather topsy-turvy existence, I volunteered for the less popular nightshift at the Home. The daytime shift, which the other sisters preferred, tended to border on the chaotic, with three meals plus morning and afternoon tea to serve and clear away, dressings to change, medicine to dispense, and doctors and specialists to escort around the wards. As there was a standing invitation issued by Drummond for any member of the public to visit the Home between 2.30 pm and 4 pm, there was always a sizeable group of sightseers as well.

The nights were far more peaceful, apart from the whimpering of an occasional homesick child, who could always be cured by a cuddle and a story, whispered secretly in the dark. After breakfast and a refreshing sleep, I spent the afternoons with the campers – playing on the beach or down at the park, or going on picnics and sightseeing excursions. Fabulous treats were organised – trips to the Zoo, the Harbour Bridge, the circus, pantomimes and the ever popular picture shows. The ladies from the Mosman Branch of the Country Women's Association hosted morning teas and lunches at the Zoo.

The days passed quickly and in no time the fortnight was up and it was time for me to go home – but not by train. This time I was flying in a Butler's Airways plane.

I turned up at Butler's city depot in plenty of time, as failure to make the flight could mean a delay of two or three days. Arriving at Mascot in the company bus, passengers were driven

Mr Drummond and the Far West children on an outing to Taronga Zoo

directly to the hangar, where tickets were issued. Commercial flights were still a novelty, with few regulations and even fewer passenger comforts. The airport, itself, was little more than an untidy collection of tin sheds scattered along an airstrip surrounded by grassy paddocks, tidal swamps and market gardens. There were no ground facilities, other than a few hard-backed chairs and out-of-date newspapers discarded by previous travellers. The passengers, irrespective of their social standing, had to wait in these spartan surroundings until the pilot came to collect them.

The plane on which I was returning to Bourke was a single-engine Avro. When ordered to board, the eight or nine passengers, lugging their baggage as well as provisions for the trip, straggled across the grassy verge to where the plane was waiting. Entering by the rear door, we manoeuvred ourselves and our parcels up the sloping floor to our seats, arranged in two single rows either side of a narrow central aisle. With everyone safely settled, the pilot slammed the rear hatch and clambered on board himself. For the next five or six hours we were at the mercy of the pilot, a bloke with a perverse sense of humour, who called himself 'Chief Makem Sick'.

For those not up to the rigours of air travel, a paper bag was provided, the contents of which, in the absence of any flight attendant, had to be disposed of by any passenger unfortunate enough to use it. There were no other concessions. The flight ticket did not include refreshments of any kind and visits to the lavatory had to wait until the plane landed at one of the many stops en route. It was not without some sense of relief that I disembarked from the aircraft, six hours after leaving Sydney.

With the holiday over, I tackled my work with renewed vigour. My first task was to organise the first of my three-weekly visits to Byrock and Brewarrina. I was especially anxious to visit Brewarrina, or Bre, as the locals called it, because part of my job was to keep an eye on the health of babies and children in the local Aboriginal Camps there and in Bourke.

A few days later, with my medical bag restocked and a load of fresh fruit and vegetables on board, I left for Brewarrina, stopping first at the small settlement of Byrock. Of all the places I visited, Byrock was the only one where we did not have to walk or find transportation into town. After landing, we simply taxied down the road to the Police Station, where the clinic was held.

Quite a large crowd, also dressed in their best clothes, had gathered at the strip. Some had come purely to rubber-neck, but a good proportion had come seeking medical advice. This stemmed not from confidence in my medical ability, but was motivated by pure economics. Bourke, with its superior medical facilities and qualified doctors, was only a relatively short drive away, but my services, unlike those of the town doctors, were free. Because of the unexpected crowd that packed into the Police Station, it took several hours to complete all the consultations. A rather stern lecture pointing out the folly of boycotting the local medicos made not one scrap of difference. At every visit, the people of Byrock continued to turn up in force, thereby sidestepping the need to part with any cash.

In 2006, Byrock's population stood at 90. This little town is named after a rock hole, called Bai by the local Nyammba tribe, which in time evolved into Bye Rockhole, then Bye Rock before becoming Byrock.

Patients greet the plane at Byrock

In comparison with the tiny communities I had called on to date, Brewarrina, my last stop, was a thriving metropolis. It was the only town on my circuit besides Bourke to have a proper clinic building and a proper airfield.

My plan was to leave Nancy at nearby Quantambone Station, where she could relax while I completed a hefty workload. However, this plan was ditched when Nancy received an urgent telephone message shortly before we left Bourke. A man living on a station about 130 miles (210 kilometres) away wanted to charter a flight to Dubbo, so that he could catch up with the night train and reach Sydney in time for his father's funeral. He had no hope of joining the train at Bourke, as it left at 9.30 am on its 23-hour journey to Sydney.

Nancy calculated that, after dropping me at Brewarrina, she could fly back to Bourke, pick up her passenger and then fly to Dubbo in time to meet the train. As I would be fully occupied at the clinic and Aboriginal Camp all day, I couldn't see any reason why she should not accept the charter. With this settled, I headed for the clinic, filled to overflowing with mothers and babies. Picking out a likely suspect, I repeated the old pillow trick, and was not at all surprised that sweets and biscuits were just as popular in Bre as they had been in Bourke. This time, the mothers did not retreat, but listened attentively as I outlined the diet I wanted them to follow. It was not until some hours later that I was free to visit the Aboriginal Camp, about 4 miles (6 kilometres) out of town.

The government-funded camp consisted of a number of basic iron-roofed timber houses and a school, staffed by a schoolmaster and his wife, who lived in the adjoining residence. The welcome was genuinely warm and everyone was keen to meet the new Far West sister, especially when she handed out sweets to the children and fresh fruit and vegetables to the schoolmaster's wife.

In most one-teacher schools in the state, the wife usually taught sewing and basic cooking. Here, however, she cooked the meals for the entire camp, assisted by the older tribal women, who were willing and able kitchen hands, and a very supportive branch of the local Country Women's Association, which ensured that supplies of fresh food were delivered regularly.

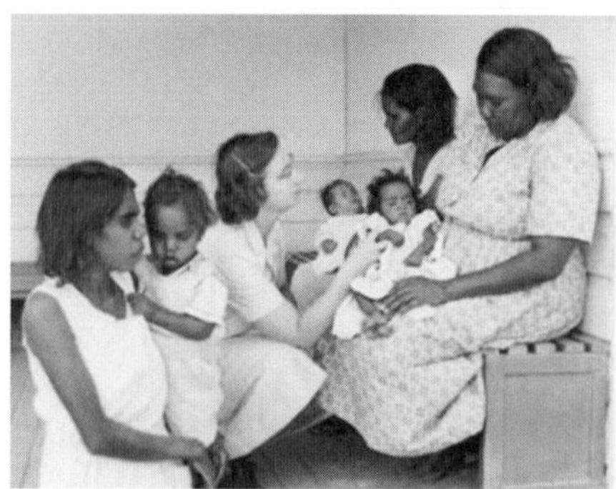

The work begun in 1936 by Sister Silver at the Aboriginal Camp at Brewarrina

Although I monitored the general health of the camp's population, my most important task was to conduct regular leprosy inspections. Aware that this disfiguring and potentially fatal disease could be easily cured if caught in the early stages, I was always on the lookout for the first sign of infection – a small black ring. If any patients managed to slip through the screening net and advance to the next stage, they were doomed, even though treatment was available. Advanced leprosy meant a one-way ticket to the leprosarium at Darwin – a fate that the Aboriginal people avoided at all costs, as they were terrified at the thought of dying away from their people and the home of their tribal spirits.

Nancy arrived back in town early the following morning, after successfully chasing the train and spending the night at Narromine. She had been lucky enough to find a man wanting to fly from Brewarrina to Bourke so, after dropping him off, she headed north-west to pick up her charter passenger. Refuelling at Bourke, she then began the chase to catch up and overtake the train, which had a six-hour start. The distance to Dubbo was 230 miles (360 kilometres), and as the Leopard Moth had a cruising speed of 120 miles per hour, she made it just in time for her passenger to board at 5.30 pm.

About three weeks later, the story appeared in the press. It came hot on the heels of newspaper reports on Nancy's flood flights but, once again, there was no mention of the Far West, or of Nancy being released from duty to allow her to take the charter. As the details published in the press could only have come from Nancy, Mr Drummond was most annoyed.

Nancy admitted many years later that Drummond was 'displeased', particularly by the articles about her flights during the floods, reprimanding her over her failure to help promote the Far West Scheme. She claimed ignorance, stating that it had 'never entered my head that it was news or that I should report it even to the Far West Children's Health Scheme'. However, a check of newspaper files from 1933 onwards reveals that Nancy certainly knew the value of the media, supplying details of her life and flying to the press, agreeing to frequent interviews and engaging in well-publicised public speaking engagements.

The first mention of Nancy's successful effort to overtake the train was on 11 February when the Dungog Chronicle *reported:*

> Miss Nancy Bird one day last week gave an exhibition of what is saved by planes. She left Bourke 10 minutes after the train for Sydney, flew to Byrock, then to Brewarrina, back to Bourke, up to the Queensland border, picked up an urgent passenger, back to Bourke to re-fuel, and then to Dubbo, and beat the train by 15 minutes. She covered 450 miles [725 kilometres], with many stops. She returned to Narromine for the night and left again the next morning for Brewarrina.

We flew back to Bourke in good time for me to visit the Ngjamba people at the Aboriginal Camp, downstream from the town. I decided to walk, as it was not all that far, and on the way called in to check on the C of E's Bush Brother. Brother Jeff, as he was known, was one of a hardy band of Bush Brothers who worked throughout outback Australia.

Brother Jeff belonged to an order known as the Brotherhood of the Good Shepherd, founded in 1903 in Dubbo, New South Wales. The energetic and dedicated young priests who undertook to administer to folk in remote rural areas were at that time mainly from England. As they were required to take vows of temporary poverty, chastity and obedience while they fulfilled their missionary work, they were either single or had left their wives behind. Their parishes extended over vast areas which, in the early days, they covered on horseback.

Brother Jeff had arrived in Bourke not long after me. His predecessor, Brother Fred, had been farewelled on 23 December, at a night-time garden party, held at Dr Horsely's house. Just about everyone in town had attended, including the Drummonds, but Nancy and I had missed out as we had flown off to Urisino that very morning. Not that it mattered. We were newcomers, so we barely knew Brother Fred, but that didn't stop the locals from telling us what a great party we had missed. From all accounts, it had been a great social event, with the garden festooned with fairy lights.

Surviving on a paltry 5 shillings a week, which equated to half of what I received as my danger money, Brother Jeff worked with great energy to bring practical and pastoral help to his far-flung parishioners. As I left a bag of chokos, purloined from the vine that covered the Glovers' outdoor dunny, on his verandah, I reflected that Brother Jeff and I were a kind of team – he looked after his people's souls, while I looked after their bodies.

My ultimate destination was situated on the banks of the Darling, regarded as Utopia in the parched west where rivers of any kind, let alone those that had water in them, were few and far between. To city people, the Darling was just a river, and a fairly uninspiring one at that, with its high banks and often sluggish flow. To the locals it was everything. Apart from the life-giving water, it had other advantages that I came to appreciate.

A hot, dusty walk was rewarded by a pleasant interlude, feet dabbling in the water while I and local children fished for a juicy cod or a fat yellow belly, deemed to be just right for dinner. Later, I would experience the river's other, not so pleasurable, side. It looks peaceful enough as it wends its way across the black soil plains, but it is a deceptive and changeable waterway. At times, it is nothing but a miserable string of stagnant waterholes. At others, without warning, it is a

Paddle steamer towing a barge loaded with wool bales on the Darling River

raging torrent of muddy water that can rise overnight to inundate the surrounding countryside for miles in every direction. The floods from the temperamental but life-giving Darling are as unpredictable as the rain that causes them, but once the water has receded and the country has dried out, it is difficult to imagine that a flood ever occurred.

The Aboriginal Camp was a complete contrast to the well-run one at Brewarrina. It was obvious from the amount of rubbish and heaps of old junk lying about that the camp had not been inspected by anyone in authority for some time. The conditions, also compared to Brewarrina, were deplorable. Collaring a couple of young men, I introduced myself and told them I would return in three days to carry out a major inspection, by which time I expected the camp to be clean and tidy.

I then made my way to a huddle of lean-to gunyahs where I found five men and women lying listlessly inside, severely undernourished and very ill with bronchitis and pneumonia. It was little wonder they were sick. Living in the same flimsy, open-ended shelters summer and winter, most did not have the resistance to ward off infection. The children were not much better off, suffering from malnutrition, colds, ear infections, contagious skin complaints and suppurating sores. Although the entire camp was poorly nourished, the condition of the children was exacerbated by the behaviour of the adults, who took the lion's share of the communal food, leaving very little for the youngsters. By the time I finished my assessment, it was late afternoon, allowing me time only to arrange for the seriously ill to be admitted to hospital and to try to organise a more equitable distribution of rations.

Doing a quick circuit of the camp to locate the two young men to whom I had spoken on my arrival, I was gratified to find that the clean-up was well underway. As the workers were obviously keen to improve their situation, I came back the next day, and the next, to offer support and encouragement. When I returned on the third day, with a doctor in tow, the camp passed inspection.

The doctor was answerable to the Public Health Department. Now that I had intervened, he had no alternative but to visit the camp on a regular basis and provide the medical treatment that had been so sorely missing. After the initial clean-up, I called once a week to conduct the baby clinic and to give everyone else the once over. I enjoyed my visits greatly and, before long, I thought of the people there as my extended family, finding that any effort or kindness on my part was repaid threefold in affection and loyalty.

Before my six-weekly clinic round, which now included Byrock and Brewarrina, I spent a few days stockpiling food for the camp and children in outlying areas. The inadequate diet of the latter, who seldom saw fresh fruit and vegetables, and fresh milk not at all, was of major concern. Supplies of fresh meat were also a problem, and not only for those living out of town. The nation was still weathering the effects of a severe depression and, for all but the well-heeled, fresh meat was a rare, barely affordable luxury. Consequently, the staple diet for many families was damper, black tea and salt meat. Although an adult could survive on these very basic rations, it was definitely not a proper diet for a growing child.

The flights to Louth and Wanaaring passed without incident, and the clinics were well attended. The Urisino round included all the outposts I had visited on the Santa Claus trail, and the 40 or so children on my list were still bubbling about the special Christmas visit. 'What a pity you couldn't have been here to see him, Sister', said the mothers, a comment wholeheartedly and naively endorsed by the little ones.

Despite the isolation, many of the women required nothing more than reassurance that their pregnancies were progressing normally or that their children's rates of growth and development were fine. For others, my visits provided a unique social opportunity to down tools, make a cup of tea and catch up eagerly on the news.

CHAPTER 6

Doing the rounds

1936

Now the settling-in period was over, the remainder of 1936 was one of consolidation and growth. The baby clinics were going from strength to strength and, with mothers aware of the need to provide balanced meals, the health of their infants improved dramatically. Eager to do the best for their children, they religiously followed a proper feeding program and reported regularly to the town clinic. Gone were the days of jellybeans and biscuits. The babies were now into pureed spinach and pumpkin, fresh fruit and rusks. The effect of the new diet was very apparent in the improved general health of the infants and in the relaxed faces of the mothers, confident that they were doing everything possible to help their little ones.

The aerial clinics, once an oddity, were now an integral part of outback life, with patients congregating at the airstrip, or some central place in town, to receive attention, along with the latest news.

It had not taken long for Sister Silver to become a household name in and around Bourke. As the sole health-care worker over such a vast area, her patients, as well as the press, called her the 'Angel of Mercy', a variation on 'Angels of the Outback', a term often used when referring to bush nurses.

The success of the 'clay-pan consultations' was soon evident in the 'tone' of the children. The experience I had gained during the messy three months of Tresillian training allowed me, at a glance, to assess a child's general health by the look of its skin, eyes and muscle condition – otherwise known as 'tone'. As I had also learned to gauge an infant's weight by simply picking it up, I was thankful it was not necessary to take the cumbersome woven wickerwork basket, scales and weights, every time I ventured from the Bourke clinic. All I carried was my medical bag containing blood-pressure instruments, pain-killers, snake and spider bite antivenenes, syringes, vaccines, suture materials, a comprehensive first aid kit, bandages, lotions and, last but by no means least – a supply of wool and knitting needles.

These had become an essential part of my equipment when the novelty of flying had begun to wear off. Settled in my comfortable leather seat, I found great satisfaction in mid-air knitting, and was amazed to find how many booties, socks and jumpers I managed to complete as I notched up the miles. It was also a most rewarding hobby for my patients, who were delighted to receive an unexpected present when Sister arrived on her regular visit.

I had my wool and needles with me, as usual, on a routine visit to Urisino, when we were forced to land at Louth because of the extreme heat. It was a searing hot day, so hot that the air seemed ready to explode. Feeling rather peckish, despite the temperature, I enquired what was on the menu at the one and only café. The barman leaned across the counter and drawled, 'Goat 'n galah. The goat is finished and the galah is a bit orf, but not too bad if yer really hungry.'

I gave both a miss and, since coffee was also 'orf' the menu, we were offered a glass of water, which Nancy and I accepted gratefully. It was lukewarm, but at least at Louth it was free, unlike Wanaaring where water was a shilling a glass – the same price as a glass of beer! Our thirst slaked, we retreated to the shade of the verandah to wait until the temperature dropped sufficiently to allow us to take off for Urisino.

Petrol vaporisation was a real problem in extremely hot weather and neither Nancy nor I fancied a forced landing in conditions of the type we were now experiencing. Even if we ran into trouble and made a successful emergency landing, we were only too aware that, despite the mandatory water flask we carried, we would die of dehydration before anyone realised we were missing.

By four o'clock we calculated it was safe enough to leave. If we waited any longer, it might be dark before we reached our destination, which was even more risky than flying in the heat. The plane took off without any trouble but, as expected, the superheated air rose from the sunbaked plains below, giving the plane a severe buffeting.

Unfazed by the rough ride, I settled back in my seat, took out my needles and cast on stitches for a baby's bootie. I was not at all alarmed by the erratic updraughts, or by the weird sinking feeling as my stomach was left behind in the downdraughts. Unlike Sister Webb, I had never experienced the slightest sensation of anxiety or worry, a serene state that Nancy, who had a rather offbeat sense of humour, often tried to upset. Taking full advantage of the adverse conditions, she picked a particularly bumpy sector before shouting over her shoulder.

'Are you knitting, Silver?'

'Yes,' I replied, wondering what was coming next.

'Well put your needles away. I think we have broken a strut.'

I was used to Nancy's attempts to disturb my equanimity, and was not about to fall for this latest trick. Still calmly knitting, I replied, 'Well Nancy, that will be just too bad, for if you really have broken a strut, then your struts will be broken, my struts will be broken and my putting aside my knitting will not make the slightest bit of difference to the outcome.'

There was silence from the cockpit. The knitting continued unabated and uninterrupted. By the time we landed at Urisino, the bootie was almost finished.

With the thousands of air miles that I was logging, flying had become as routine as catching a tram in Sydney and the red sands and drab olive vegetation as familiar as the shops in the city streets. I had discovered that, by keeping one eye on the knitting and the other on the passing scenery, I would not miss anything interesting happening below.

Occasionally, disturbed by the unfamiliar sound of the plane's engine, large mobs of kangaroos would stir themselves from the lethargy of a daytime siesta, emerging onto the open plain to move as one, as their huge, rhythmic bounds covered the ground with graceful ease. Monotonous as the scenery sometimes became, I never failed to be moved by the sight of these beautiful creatures or wonder at their magnificence.

The flight paths we took on the six-week and the three-week rounds were not always the same, and not always on the same weekdays. Sometimes we reversed the order of the visits, cut out one of the stops if we were not needed, or detoured to see a patient who required special attention. Sometimes, if the weather was too poor, we had to return to base, and wait until things improved. So much depended on prevailing weather conditions. With no radio to make navigational contact, or keep up to date with weather reports, the best route to take was often a calculated guess. My navigational skills became better as I learned to recognise landmarks in what appeared at first to be a featureless landscape – the particular shape of a patch of vegetation, the way a track deviated around a watercourse, the patterns made by the clay pans or the ripples of sand in a dry river bed.

Sometimes, it was a case of dead reckoning, in which case Nancy was forced to use a compass and keep an eye on the time in order to navigate from one place to the next. The roads, railway tracks, telegraph lines and the dog fence were a great help. By flying a couple of hundred metres above them, Nancy could navigate to faraway destinations such as Cunnamulla, on the far side of the New South Wales–Queensland border. She often joked that the land was so flat there was no danger of crashing into a mountain – the only danger was running into another plane, following the road or telegraph line from the opposite direction!

Cunnamulla, about 70 miles (110 kilometres) across the border from Barringun, was in Queensland and wasn't on my regular schedule, but we had occasion to make the trip there to attend a dinner dance to farewell a nurse at the local hospital. As Nancy had also been invited, she was happy to leave Bourke after the baby clinic finished at 4 pm and return the following day at first light, so that I could go too.

I remember the date, because it was the only Black Friday that year – Friday, 13 March. By pure coincidence, we both wore green, a colour that suited us both, especially Nancy with her red hair, but also a colour considered by those who are superstitious to be very unlucky.

There were no landmarks to guide us after leaving Bourke but, since all we had to do was to follow the main road, navigation was not a problem. It was also fairly good weather. We were making quite good time so, when Nancy spotted a huge flock of emus, she decided to break the monotony of the flight by flying low over their heads. At the noise of the plane's engine, they scattered, their huge and powerful legs covering the ground in enormous and surprisingly graceful strides. Although I couldn't see her face, I could tell by her whoops of glee that Nancy was having the time of her life. As the emus wheeled, so did she.

However, the high jinks ceased abruptly when she glanced down and realised that the road was no longer in sight. To make matters worse, grey clouds had suddenly rolled in and rain had begun to fall, making the already fading autumn light much dimmer. Nancy confessed with some alarm that she had no idea where she was. I didn't either, but hazarded a guess that by this time we might be somewhere in central Queensland. This sarcastically unhelpful remark did not go down well with Nancy, as the sun had dropped below the horizon and the sky was becoming blacker by the minute.

Suddenly, just as I was thinking that we might be lost in the sandy wastes forever, some lights appeared. Assuming they were the lights of a small town, Nancy turned the plane in their direction only to find, on closer inspection, that they were the headlamps of cars, moving along the road. Alarmed that the plane was overdue, the people of Cunnamulla had come to look for us. By flying so low that the wheels barely cleared the vegetation, Nancy was able to make out the glow of the headlamps well enough to be guided to the airstrip, which was immediately behind the dinner venue at Davis's Hotel.

As every actor knows, there is nothing quite like making a spectacular entrance. After the procession of cars lighting the way to the landing strip, there was the excitement of the actual landing, made possible only by the headlamps turned to illuminate the field.

Not surprisingly, there was not a soul within cooee of the hotel who didn't know about our narrow escape. However, our very unorthodox arrival, with the added novelty that we were from out of town, ensured that we both had a wonderful evening, surrounded by partygoers avid for a first-hand account of the drama.

One of those who introduced himself to me was a businessman from Bourke who was desperate to return home as quickly as possible and asked if he might fly back with us. The trip to Cunnamulla was a private arrangement, and therefore not under my control, so I referred him to Nancy, who negotiated a suitable charter fee. The deal having been struck, the prospective passenger was instructed to be at the strip at daybreak.

When he arrived at the plane the next morning, it was obvious that he had developed cold feet. What had been a good idea last night with a few drinks under his belt was a terrifying proposition in the cold, sober hard light of day. To add to his anxiety, it was raining, with no sign of an immediate let-up. As the rain was insufficiently heavy to cancel the flight, there was no question of staying an extra day. Besides, an epidemic of trachoma had broken out among many of the children in Bourke and I had issued instructions that, as soon as they heard the plane arrive, they were to report to the clinic for treatment.

It was still raining as we took off and the road was flooded, but by keeping beneath the low cloud bank, Nancy could see the telegraph line well enough not to lose sight of it. While I was quite enjoying the early morning ride, the same could not be said for our passenger, who was pale with fright and shaking uncontrollably. He turned to me and spluttered, 'I c-c-can't bloody well s-s-stand it much longer.'

It was now my turn to feel anxious. The last thing we needed was a passenger so overcome by terror that he might do almost anything to get out of the plane. Using the calm, soothing tone I generally reserved for highly traumatised accident victims, I took his hand and said, 'Now really, there is nothing to be worried about. We have a very experienced pilot, and if you look out the window you can see the road heading towards home. Saint Christopher is also keeping watch from the instrument panel and I have a back-up, if we need it – and I'm sure we won't – with the rosary beads an old Irish nun gave me. With all these things going for us, there is no possible reason for you to imagine that we will not land safely back in Bourke.'

He remained unconvinced. Not even the sight of Saint Christopher smiling from the instrument panel or my Irish rosary, pressed into his hand, allayed his fear.

I understood how he felt. On a recent flight from Quantambone Station, surrounded by the full fury of a storm, complete with pelting rain, deafening thunder and brilliant lightning flashes, I had begun to think that perhaps God and Saint Christopher were not on my side this time and that, Irish rosary beads or not, we might not make the airstrip safely.

The current weather conditions were benign compared with the Quantambone tempest, but no amount of persuasive talk could reassure the passenger. The last 20 minutes of the flight, when visibility improved enough to spot the landmark hill rising out of the flat plain near Bourke, were a time of agony for him and apprehension for me – I dared not take my eyes away from him, lest he decide to make a mid-air exit. Fortunately, he managed to keep his terror in check long enough for Nancy to put the aircraft down safely. As the plane rolled to a gentle stop, he leapt from his seat and headed for the nearest hotel to steady himself with a much needed, and very stiff, drink.

The unexpected charter was a help to Nancy financially, but a chronic shortage of money was always of huge concern to Mr Drummond, for without a decent cash flow the aerial clinic could not possibly continue. The stress of trying to juggle finances was wearing him out so, in an attempt to drum up contributions from the locals, he went to the press.

Far West Children's Health Scheme

AERIAL AMBULANCE. APPEAL FOR SUBSCRIBERS.

The Far West Childrens' Health Scheme earnestly request the cooperation of the people of Bourke and districts in establishing a permanent Aerial Service at Bourke, for the purpose of Ambulance work and the convenience of the public.

The following circular has been widely distributed, and those interested are invited to interview Sister Silver at the Far West Children's Health Scheme Baby Clinic, Oxley Street, Bourke, for further details or communicate with Mr D F Martin, the Hon Secretary, at the E S and A Bank, Bourke:

Dear Sir/Madam.

A serious attempt is being made by the Far West Scheme to make provision for the transport of Doctors or patients by air in cases of emergency, and to facilitate matters your co-operation is earnestly desired. While it is recognised that transport by car is sufficient in most instances, and patients have but little difficulty in making the necessary arrangements, there are times when roads are impassable, or when the nature of the case requires haste. This need can be met by an Aerial Ambulance Service, which, it is our desire to establish permanently.

To meet the expense of the retaining fee, the Bourke Branch decided that an effort be

> *made to secure annual subscribers at £1/1/0, such subscriber to receive the benefit of a reduced rate of hire of the plane in cases of sickness. The usual charges are 1/- per mile, but subscribers will only be charged 9d per mile, when the plane is required by them, or their dependants, for transport in cases of sickness. It must be distinctly understood that no guarantee can be given that the plane will be available after the termination of the arrangements with Miss Nancy Bird. However, if experience both as to work and support justifies a continuation of the aerial transport service, a serious effort will be made to purchase an Ambulance Aeroplane, or to secure in some way a continuation of an Aerial Ambulance Service. Will you become an annual subscriber, or assist in any way? Please reply by return if practicable.*

By this time, the value of the aerial clinics had become very apparent, something that Mr Drummond wished to convey to a wider audience at the upcoming April conference, held in Sydney, and which I attended. I was able to report that I had notched up more than 3,000 miles (4,830 kilometres) in the air, and another 1,400 on the ground, attending to 41 adults and almost 300 babies. In addition, 225 patients had attended the clinic in town, while the treatments for trachoma during the recent epidemic, 70 children twice a day, reached a staggering 1,730.

Drummond used this report to raise the awareness of the public through the media. Rather than make a direct appeal for help, the Sydney Morning Herald *took a different approach, under the eye-catching heading 'Things that matter – and don't'.*

> It will be a thousand pities if sufficient support is not forthcoming to keep the Far West plane going. This is the plane which Miss Nancy Bird pilots, and which takes Sister Marjorie Silver on her rounds every six weeks. Out in the distant country west of Bourke the settlers and their wives and children have found this service of inestimable value. Doctors are far away, but the Conqueror, as the plane is called, overcomes the difficulties and brings them aid in case of sickness.
>
> Sister Silver is a sort of 'flying doctor' herself; and in addition to carrying medicines and rendering nursing assistance when it is required, she distributes books and magazines among the outback folk.
>
> The plane is fitted up as an ambulance, and if occasion calls for it a patient can be transported to a doctor. But funds are needed, and without them the work cannot be carried on.

Fund raising button 1935

We certainly needed to keep the aerial clinic going. In the past few months, because of the regular check-ups, there had also been a marked increase in the number of children I was referring to Sydney for specialised treatment. Once they had been assessed, and the referral approved, I would bring them into Bourke on one of the routine flights, and then see them off on a Butler Airways flight accompanied by a transport sister. If I had a meeting or conference to attend in Sydney, I often took the children myself.

I was away on one such visit when John Kingsford-Smith, a friend of Nancy and cousin of Charles Kingsford-Smith, arrived in Bourke.

Now in his mid-twenties, John had begun flying at the age of 18 and had flown as a co-pilot for the next two years with Australian National Airways, an airline founded by Smithy and Charles Ulm. However, John's commercial flying career had come to an abrupt end in 1931 when the fledgling airline was forced into voluntary liquidation, following the crash of the plane Southern Cloud *in the Snowy Mountains of New South Wales, killing the crew and the eight passengers on board.*

As no other commercial airline existed, John accepted a job as a Laboratory Assistant at Cinesound Productions, a company known throughout Australia for its documentaries and newsreels, which were shown in every cinema.

His love of flying and his skill with the camera brought him to the attention of the public when, in May 1935, Smithy and Taylor made an inaugural airmail flight between Australia and New Zealand. Their plane, Southern Cross, *a tri-engined Fokker piloted by Smithy, was out over the Tasman Sea, returning from New Zealand, when one engine lost a propeller and one of the two remaining engines ran short of oil. As Smithy fought to keep the wheels out of the water, Taylor saved them from certain death by climbing out onto the wing six times and transferring oil, drop by drop, into a thermos flask, from the propeller-less engine, while tethered to the fuselage by a rope. The graphic running commentary by the plane's radio operator was broadcast to thousands of anxious listeners tuned into their crackling receivers.*

John flew out in a Gypsy Moth to meet the plane. The dramatic film footage he captured for Cinesound News of the stricken plane limping back to port was seen by hundreds of thousands of cinemagoers around the nation.

John had told Nancy, but not me or Mr Drummond, that he wanted to make a newsreel for Cinesound on the work of the Far West Scheme, to be entitled 'Angel of Mercy', the name that had been coined for me by the locals. Nancy had also not said a word to either of us about John's plans. Oblivious to the fact that a film was to be made about our work, Mr Drummond had arranged for me to fly to Sydney for a meeting.

Nancy did not tell John Kingsford-Smith that I would be out of town. She had, however, gone to the trouble of checking with me that on the appointed date I was going to be in Sydney, as planned. I thought it a bit odd that she had checked, but figured that there must have been a charter she wanted to do, if I didn't need her.

Unaware that I was unavailable, John Kingsford-Smith arrived with all his paraphernalia to discover that the 'angel' was missing. However, to a filmmaker who was well known for his inventive skill in design, production and special effects, the loss of the central figure was of no great consequence. Nancy's friend, Nancy Skinner, daughter of the town's electrician, was recruited as a substitute. Dressed for the benefit of the cameras in a white uniform and veil, which I never wore while flying, the stand-in 'flying sister' acted out her assigned role, allowing Kingsford-Smith to shoot the necessary footage.

At a Women's Conference on Child Welfare, held in Sydney in September 1936, it was decided that Australia's contribution to a film festival in Paris would be a film 'showing the work of Miss Nancy Bird who pilots a plane used by the sister of the Far West Children's Health Scheme to the outback districts of New South Wales'.

On my return from Sydney, the locals wasted no time in describing the antics that had taken place in my absence. When I finally went to the local cinema to view the end product, I discovered that it had been renamed 'Flying Angel of the Outback', and that the main focus was on Nancy. John's inventiveness, in my 'unfortunate' absence, was not confined to the stand-in nursing sister, dressed in white. Although the Leopard Moth seemed to take off and then dash dramatically across the parched country, with Nancy piloting 'Sister Silver' on her mission of mercy, the entire sequence was filmed at Bourke airstrip. The subterfuge gave the townspeople something to talk about, but by the time the newsreel reached Bourke, I was occupied with other, far more important matters.

There was no nursing service available in Bourke, other than that provided by the local hospital. Concerned by a pressing need for specialised nursing of patients whose condition was so poor that a round-the-clock vigil had to be maintained, the doctors asked me to lend a hand. Although 'specialling' at either the hospital or the patient's home meant I was on-call 18 hours a day, 7 days a week, I agreed to assist whenever possible.

Some of these cases, such as that of a young woman thrown from her horse, resulting in severe lacerations and concussion, ended happily. Others did not. One of the hardest cases I was asked to 'special' was that of a very good friend, Anne Sheaffe, wife of the Department of Lands surveyor and a Deputy Commissioner. Anne, who was a keen tennis player and worked tirelessly to help returned servicemen, had been ill for some time and had to undergo a major operation.

The doctors anticipated that she would need a minimum of 12 hours' intensive nursing care after the surgery, which would be completed by 6 pm. I would take over until 6 am, grab three hours' sleep and then conduct the normal clinic in town before doing my usual check on the Aboriginal Camp.

Unfortunately, Anne's post-operative condition was critical. Despite my efforts and that of her doctor, her blood pressure fell to such a level that I was unable to get a reading. There was nothing that I could do at all to save her and she faded away just before dawn. All I could do was shed bitter tears, snatch a couple of hours' sleep and then get on with the job of caring for the living.

Fortunately, the amount of time I needed to spend with the Aborigines at the Bourke Camp had eased considerably. Once the rubbish and junk had been cleared away, the tribal elders had taken responsibility for seeing that the grounds were maintained and the food distributed equitably. As conditions improved there, so did the general level of health, which in turn lessened the number of serious cases of bronchitis and pneumonia. However, chest complaints were still of great concern, with nine out of ten children suffering.

I was also called on a regular basis to extract pebbles from the ears and noses of the youngsters who, like children all over the world, had a great propensity for poking foreign objects into the most inconvenient places. Usually, the pebbles were removed without any drama, but if a number were actually swallowed, the minor inconvenience escalated to a medical emergency. The trauma caused by the subsequent emergency operation did little to discourage the practice, so that admittance to Bourke hospital for rock removal was not as rare as people might imagine.

There is only one medical emergency that I can recall during Nancy's contract that necessitated my using the plane as an ambulance. Jim Russell, a grazier, lived at Dunoak Station, 18 miles (30 kilometres) south of Tilpa on the eastern side of the Darling River between Louth and Wilcannia. Born at Wanaaring, Jim had served in World War 1 and on his return to civilian life had taken up Dunoak as a soldier settlement block. Now aged in his 30s, he had become very ill with pneumonia. His wife could not drive, and their children were too young to ride for help, so it was fortunate that a boundary rider who happened along realised the seriousness of the situation and raised the alarm.

It wasn't far to go and, provided there was a suitable area to land, the evacuation would be straightforward. Nancy's plane was fairly robust and she always called ahead to check on the situation. As long as the worst of the bumps were flattened, and any tree stumps or serious obstacles flagged, she generally had no trouble.

In the absence of a nearby road, or clay pan, the station owners were instructed to do a test run with a car to flatten the area, and to use a bed sheet to mark out the best landing spot. To indicate wind velocity and direction, smoky fires were lit alongside the proposed trip. Fortunately, Mr Russell was evacuated without any undue drama to Wilcannia, the nearest hospital, where he recovered well.

With my increased workload, I sometimes did not lay eyes on Nancy for days at a time. Apart from emergencies, the clinic tours were regularly spaced, enabling her to engage in charter work, which she was free to do under the terms of her contract, provided she informed me of her movements. As Mr Drummond had been unable to raise the funds necessary to purchase a plane, Nancy's employment period had been extended, but only for another six months. At the end of that period another woman pilot, May Bradford, had been contracted to take over. Nancy's contract had another few months to run when I received a phone call from Mr Drummond, asking if I knew where she was.

'Down at Fitzgerald's I expect,' I replied.

In a tone of extreme annoyance, he replied that she wasn't – she was in Adelaide, something that came as a huge surprise to me as we were due to fly to Urisino the next day. I had no idea that she had left town, let alone travelled as far as Adelaide. He told me that, when she turned up, I was to 'ground her'.

'Ground her!' I exclaimed. 'She is in Adelaide and I am up here, so how on earth can I ground her? I really think you should deal with this.'

Nancy's contract, which had just been extended for a further six months in May 1936, was terminated by Mr Drummond when he discovered that she had flown to Adelaide without permission to make enquiries about the Brisbane–Adelaide Centenary Air Race, to be held in December. I later discovered that he had given her three months' notice, effective in August.

When Nancy returned a few days later, we set off belatedly for Louth and Urisino, where we stayed overnight as usual. The weather in the outback can be very cold in winter, and the next morning when I awoke it was to discover that there had been a heavy frost overnight and the homestead lawns and roof were coated with a good layer of ice. As, too, was Nancy's plane, so it was fortunate we were not flying off that day.

As usual, I left on my car rounds as soon as it was daylight, but this tour was in stark contrast to the summertime trips. There had not been any substantial rain for a while but, because of the much lower winter temperatures, the ground had not dried out, especially in areas we knew were prone to be boggy. The surface could look all right, but it was an illusion. Aware of this, I was forced to curtail my route, and expected to be back earlier than normal.

We weren't. Deceived by what appeared to be solid ground, we drove into an unexpected bog, which saw me and the driver labouring for some hours, digging channels in the mud for the wheels and then lining them with cut branches to provide enough traction. It was hard and exhausting work before we were finally free of the morass. Covered in mud, bone weary and looking very dishevelled, we finally arrived back at Urisino just in time to stop a search party going out to look for us.

Nancy had spent the day tinkering with the plane's engine, which had been running a little rough, but we had no trouble with it and the flight to Hungerford went smoothly. However, I had calls to make at Yantabulla, which meant landing on the sub-standard strip, which was in a worse state than usual. It was covered in ripe paddy melons, which popped and squashed disconcertingly under the wheels as we landed. No damage was done but, as there were so many vines and melons, Nancy cleared a path for take-off while I held the clinic.

In mid-August Nancy flew me to Urisino for what was to be the last time. A few days after completing the usual rounds, she packed up her things and was gone. She didn't say goodbye. And there was no farewell from the townspeople or the patients as, like me, they had no idea she was leaving. I was standing in the main street chatting with a couple of friends when we heard the sound of a plane's engine. We looked up just in time to see the Leopard Moth pass overhead and then disappear towards the east. It was many years before I saw her again.

However, Nancy was not out of the public eye for long. In December that year she participated in the air race that had cost her her job. She was a keen competitor in air pageants and in

January 1936, while Sister Silver was in Sydney, Nancy entered the Leopard Moth in an air derby at Narromine and, later that month, flew in the Mudgee Aerial Derby – a circuit race that was part of the program for the Diggers' Air Pageant.

One of the first pilots to enter her name for the Centenary Air Race, Nancy had flown to Adelaide on a much publicised flight at the end of May, before flying to Brisbane to trace the route of the race. After taking what Drummond regarded as unauthorised leave for a week, she returned to Bourke. Nancy left Bourke for the last time on 24 August, when she flew as far as Narromine. The engine log was then ruled off until 20 November, when the engine was overhauled in Sydney, prior to flying to Melbourne via Cootamundra. Nancy flew in the Centenary Air Race as planned, and won the Women's Handicap Section.

Although the press reported in early September that Nancy's contract with the Far West Scheme had 'ended', in later years Nancy was often evasive about just how long she was flying for the Far West Scheme, giving rise to a belief that she flew for the entire three years that the aerial clinic was in existence. Her claim that she had lost her job as the Scheme could not afford to pay her was untrue. Apart from the fact that the Scheme received a subsidy from the Commonwealth Government, the cost of doing the rounds by car far exceeded the cost of covering the same distance by air. Furthermore, money, although always tight, was not an issue. Pilot May Bradford had already been engaged by the Far West to take over from Nancy on the expected expiration of her contract in November.

The sudden departure of Nancy and her Leopard Moth was a great blow. In the nine months that the updated aerial service had been operating, I had flown 5,130 miles (8,250 kilometres) and covered another 4,210 (6,770 kilometres) by car, visiting 344 homes and seeing a total of 696 babies. As I was now pilot-less, the aerial clinic rounds would have to wait. I did not know what had taken place between Mr Drummond and Nancy, but she had really blotted her copybook this time and evidently there was no going back. I considered her an able enough pilot – if a little unthinking on occasion and prone to seek publicity for herself – but I put that down to her lack of maturity, as she was only 20 years old.

Although I was in desperate need of a plane and pilot, and Nancy was now out of work, Mr Drummond made no move to rehire her. She later said that she wished she had confided in him more, but I think the real problem was that Mr Drummond believed that she put her own self-interest before that of the Far West Scheme. The chances of finding another pilot were slim, but Mr Drummond hoped that May Bradford would be able to rearrange her plans and fill the position immediately.

Unfortunately, May was not free to start until the agreed date in the New Year, after the annual camp at Manly. As this was five months away, we were forced to abandon any idea of continuing with the aerial clinic for the time being. Taking advantage of the unexpected and unwelcome disruption, I exchanged places for the next month with the Sydney-based Sister Leach, who also held triple-certificates and was more than pleased to hold the fort at the town clinic while I spent some time with the children at the Far West Home.

While I was there, I and another sister, whose job entailed a lot of train travel, were interviewed by a Sydney paper. Mr Drummond, always with an eye to free publicity, decided to highlight the problem caused by Nancy's departure to raise public awareness of the Scheme.

Thursday 3 September 1936

SISTER M SILVER SEES ANOTHER PART OF THE WORK OF THE FAR WEST SCHEME.

She has just returned from nine months at the clinic at Bourke. She will spend the next few weeks at the home at Manly, looking after the babies, and will then return to Bourke. She travelled 4,000 miles [6,440 kilometres] by aeroplane visiting sick people and looking out for sick children to be recommended for treatment at the home. In Bourke her work is mostly with babies, and, as well as tending the sick, she gives advice to mothers upon their treatment. As well, she keeps in touch with the children in her vast district who have been in the home, and sees that they are not allowed to slip back in health.

"I am hoping that there will be an aeroplane to travel in when I go back," she said. "Miss Nancy Bird, who was under contract with us, took me on all my trips by air, but her contract has expired, and at the moment there is no plane for that part of my work.

After rains in Bourke, the roads are impassable, and a plane is the only possible way of getting to the isolated cases. It is not so much the poverty as the utter isolation of the settlers in the outer areas that is so sad. Mothers with sick children have no hope of help when the roads are bad, unless we can reach them by plane."

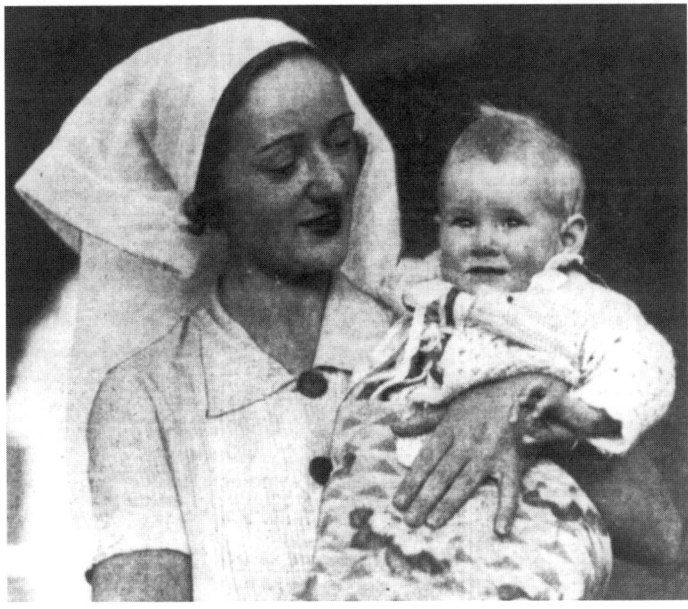

Sister Silver with Nellie, at the Far West Home at Manly

Visiting the Home at Manly was good for the soul, as I never ceased to be amazed on witnessing the results of the work of Mr Drummond and his hard-working team. The disabled children who came in twisted and bent, almost blind, their bodies ravaged by scurvy, polio or tuberculosis, went out weeks, months or in some cases years later, with limbs straight and whole and with eyes that could see. As the number of children receiving treatment each day now averaged 132, fundraising was of prime importance to Mr Drummond.

The man never seemed to sleep. When not at Manly, he was out on the campaign trail, encouraging groups of already committed CWA and Far West Committees and organising the formation of new ones.

Media coverage, when the children arrived for their holidays, was a great help to his publicity campaign. Since the very first camp, when the children had run in terror at the sight of the breaking surf and a huge python at Taronga Park Zoo, the newspapers had never tired of reporting the reactions of the 'far westers' to the city, the harbour, the bridge and, most especially, the ocean. Many children had also never before seen rain, drunk milk, had a ride on a merry-go-round or eaten ice-cream.

Their obvious delight in experiencing these pleasures, taken for granted by their city cousins, plucked at the heartstrings of many people. Well-heeled society matrons opened their beautiful homes and magnificent gardens to host lavish parties, while department stores, such as Grace Brothers, conducted basement-to-rooftop tours, with unlimited rides on escalators and lifts. Not to be outdone by a rival retailer, Mr Wynn and his assistants arranged a party each year for all children whose birthdays fell during holiday time. The centrepieces of the gargantuan feasts were two huge cakes – one in blue for the boys and the other pink for the girls – with the name of each child emblazoned in thick icing on the top.

Unwilling to allow commercial enterprise to steal the show, the Lord Mayor of Sydney, Alderman Stokes, opened the Town Hall for inspection, providing refreshments for all after conducting a personally escorted tour of his grand domain. After much gaping, first at the resplendently attired Mayor in his fur-trimmed robes and golden chain-of-office, and then at the wonderfully ornate, almost wedding-cake-like exterior of the building, the children had climbed onto the balcony to view the busy streetscape provided by the intersections of George, Park, Druitt and York Streets. Exposed to the public gaze, they waved excitedly to the crowds below, which delighted in the spontaneity of the young visitors.

The visit to the Town Hall was eclipsed only by an invitation to attend a special reception at Government House, hosted by the Governor himself. If the rare privilege of this vice-regal occasion was lost on some of the children, the groaning tables of ice-cream and ginger beer, thoughtfully provided by the governor's staff, were not. The ice-cream, a great favourite with the small guests, was consumed with gusto on the manicured lawns of the gardens, while wide eyes took in the fairy-tale magnificence of the crenellated sandstone towers of the residence.

There were also visits to Parliament House, fun parks, pantomimes and concerts, and free rides on harbour ferries operated by The Manly and Port Jackson Steamship Company. The resulting press, newsreel and radio coverage was an immensely powerful tool in Drummond's search for funds. Contributions from a fascinated public, backed up by year-round donations from the Far West and CWA Committees, ensured that the Scheme was able to keep up its vital work at a time when the economy was generally in a depressed state.

Being term time, the campers were not yet in residence, but I had plenty to occupy my time with the patients. However, after about six weeks, homesickness set in. Although Mr Drummond had not found a temporary pilot or aircraft, and Sister Leach was coping well at Bourke, I was anxious to resume the clinic tours, even if it meant travelling by car until May Bradford arrived.

When I returned home in mid-October, I moved from the Glovers' house and into a good-sized room at the Post Office Hotel. Mrs Fitzgerald insisted that I pay no board – my room and meals were all free, as this was to be her donation to the Far West Scheme. The room, painted a pale shade of green, was adequately, if indifferently, furnished and faced east, which meant that there was no glaring afternoon sun. Being in the centre of town, there was no view, other than the rear of the nearby general store and sundry iron roofs.

I was back in the swing of things at once as, in my absence, Mr Drummond had managed to secure the services of Mr Sullivan, a local pilot, who agreed to take me on the much postponed clinic tour. Unfortunately, as he was not available for any further trips, Santa was grounded for Christmas 1936, being stranded in Bourke without a sleigh.

CHAPTER 7

Just part of the service

1937–1938

Routine, a much hated word, had been drummed into my head every single day during my basic nursing and Tresillian training. I loathed unnecessary regimentation and, although I had to be organised in my work, I was not a naturally methodical person. However, my duties were now so diverse and my patients so widely scattered that, unless I stuck to some kind of routine, it was difficult to fit everything into an already overextended working week. No plane meant, at best, a tedious six-day car trip just to do the Urisino round, jolting over rough tracks, and surrounded by never-ending clouds of dust as the temperatures soared above the 40 degree mark and stayed there. The towns closer to Bourke were visited whenever I could fit them in.

Although I knew more or less how to drive and had driven (albeit in first gear) from Pallamallawa to Moree and back, I had never managed to find the time to sit for the test. How I wished that I had made a greater effort. While I could flaunt regulations when the mood took me, I was not game enough to undertake a round trip of 600 miles (1,000 kilometres) to Urisino and back without a licence.

Pallamallawa to Moree was one thing; Bourke to the Never-Never quite another. In any case, there were more serious aspects to consider. To travel alone across vast tracts of land, in conditions where dying of thirst was a very real possibility, or where sudden monsoonal downpours could cause flash floods, was foolhardy in the extreme – particularly as I couldn't even change a flat tyre, let alone fathom the mysteries of the internal combustion engine. So, when a local man offered himself and his comfortably solid sedan for hire, Mr Drummond accepted, before he could change his mind.

The journey was sheer torture. Road conditions were atrocious, with deep bone-jarring ruts and rough, dried-out creek crossings that sorely tested the constitution of both driver and passenger, and the car's durability. If it rained, the trip was postponed until the glutinous soil had dried out, by which time the gouged-out tracks made by bogged vehicles had set into concrete-hard, teeth-rattling obstacles. If it didn't rain, there was still the problem of the extremely arid terrain.

Midway between Bourke and Wanaaring was an escarpment. From the Bourke side, the access was a steep slope, rising out of an otherwise flat plain, and known, for some obscure reason, as the Gin Bottle. The mound was a formidable obstacle to most vehicles at the best of times but more so when the wind deposited a layer of soft, shifting sand over the generally relatively stable surface. If the driver could not take a sufficiently long run or build up enough speed, the car's wheels spun madly and the engine faltered. After a few aborted attempts, the driver had no option but to detour, backtracking for two or three miles, eyes peeled for tyre tracks disappearing into the scrub – a sign that another motorist had found a more navigable route, either up or around the obstacle. The return trip was not a problem. Vehicles, after pausing momentarily on the edge of the escarpment, simply plunged headlong down the slope in a wild confusion of sand and dust to land, quite miraculously, I always thought, right side up at the bottom of the hill, none the worse for the unorthodox tobogganing.

The entire excursion was not only rough, hot and dirty, it was also very slow and exceedingly tedious. Trips that had taken two hours by plane now took two days by car, leaving little time for anything other than the basic essentials. A lingering chat over a mug of hot tea was a now a thing of the past, as was time off to play with the babies and small children, activities that I missed very much. It was only the knowledge that May Bradford and her 'Golden Eagle' would arrive in mid-February that kept me going, as I bounced over the interminable corrugations, each one seemingly deeper and rougher than the last.

My hopes of returning to the air were shattered in the last week of January, when I received news of the sudden and tragic death of May Bradford. I stood stunned, my knuckles turning white as I clutched the black bakelite telephone receiver, listening in disbelief to Stanley Drummond relate the details. The day before, May, the only woman pilot in Australia with a commercial licence and an A and B Class engineer's certificate, was taking off on a joy flight at Mascot when her plane slewed out of control and hit a stationary aircraft. May's Klemm-Eagle monoplane, having gained a height of less than 10 feet (3 metres), ripped apart its undercarriage as it tore the wing from the other aircraft. The Golden Eagle, full of volatile fuel, pitched forward and nosedived into the ground, erupting into a huge inferno. May and her two passengers died

May Bradford

instantly. The news was a devastating blow. Not only had the nation lost its finest and most accomplished aviatrix, but I had lost my urgently needed pilot.

With no aircraft available in the foreseeable future, a few days after May's death I set off by car to collect six-year-old Eileen from a soldier settlement block beyond Urisino. Since the age of two, she had been suffering from a severely turned eye, which obscured her vision and contorted her face. On the way back, I also collected Enid, aged 7, who was suffering from a similar complaint. Once back in Bourke, we boarded the train for the 500 mile (800 kilometre) journey to Sydney. Mr Drummond publicised the story, in the hope of raising public awareness and more funds. In the meantime, he agreed that the overland clinic trips would continue and, should a real emergency arise, a plane would be sent from Sydney.

After delivering my two small charges to the care of the specialists, I returned home with the intention of organising the next overland tour. However, the plan was temporarily shelved when the matron at Bourke Hospital suddenly fell ill, leaving five wards, including the isolation wing, staffed by only two nurses and a sister. A frantic call for my urgent assistance was sanctioned by Mr Drummond – he was not only aware of the need to pool all available resources, but he also realised that this was a chance to promote the work of the Scheme while providing a vital community service.

For the next month, by juggling the baby clinic and leaving a succession of notes pinned to the door giving details of my whereabouts, I was able to spend three days a week at the hospital, three on my usual work and, provided all went well, one day off. It was a hectic existence but, in spite of the long hours, I enjoyed the return to hospital life – so much so that, once the crisis was over, I accepted an invitation to help on a regular basis.

Situated about two miles (3 kilometres) out of town on a dusty patch of ground, the Bourke Hospital was a rambling, old-fashioned, single-storey brick building, whose iron-clad roof heated the interior to a blistering level in summer. As the town was only just making the transition from kerosene-generated power to electricity, electric fans, which were standard equipment in city hospitals, were unheard of. There were no washing machines or electric coppers, so the hospital laundry was boiled in a huge wood-burning copper. Set low on a side verandah, the copper was in constant use and required the services of a full-time attendant to keep it on the boil.

One day, when coming off duty, I rounded the corner of the verandah just as the laundress's small son, about four years old, fell head-first into the boiling cauldron. I pulled him out immediately, but the burns to his tiny body were horrific. Aware that a charter plane, due to return to Sydney the next day, was unexpectedly available, I offered to transport him to the city for specialist attention, only to be brushed aside by a doctor, who considered I was overreacting.

As a mere nursing sister and part-time hospital employee, I was in no position to argue and, in any case, I was forced by hospital regulations to accede to his instructions. It was of no comfort that my medical superior assumed full responsibility. The boy died during the night, while the plane that might have saved him stood uselessly on the runway.

My next critical case also involved a small boy. One morning, the clinic routine was interrupted by a call to drive immediately to Narromine, about 150 miles (250 kilometres) away, and then fly to Broken Hill to pick up a desperately ill patient in a charter aircraft, currently en route from Sydney. Medical bag in one hand and a small valise containing a change of clothing in the other, I was out the door and ready to leave by the time a hire-car and driver arrived to collect me.

Aware of the urgency, he hit the road at high speed, dust and dirt spewing from the rear wheels and shock absorbers strained to breaking point as the vehicle bottomed every pothole. The bone-jarring dash was not in vain for we screeched to a halt at Narromine to find the charter flight had just landed. It took off immediately for Broken Hill where a local doctor, waiting with the distraught mother, handed over the patient – a five-year-old boy suffering from a fractured skull, lacerations and severe shock.

The doctor had done everything possible with the facilities available. It was now up to me to deliver the lad to the brain surgeon, on stand-by in Sydney. Never had a plane trip seemed so long. Keeping vigil over the pathetically small shape strapped to the stretcher beside me, I could do no more than monitor his condition and pray that we would arrive in time. We did, and he recovered fully, once again vindicating Drummond's faith in the value of his aerial medical service.

I caught the next flight back to Bourke and had barely resumed work at the clinic when I was ordered to return to Sydney on the next available Butler's flight. This time, I was to escort home a local woman who had been released from hospital after sustaining shocking injuries in an accident. Although it was a scheduled commercial flight, the pilot made a most unscheduled diversion to Tooraweenah, on the western side of the Warrumbungle Mountains, to pick up a nurse and her patient, an ex-soldier suffering from shell shock, who required psychiatric treatment in Sydney. As this was a period of extreme flexibility in aviation and as there were two empty seats in the otherwise full plane, the unplanned detour was by no means unusual and of no consequence to anyone, least of all the paying passengers.

I was seated in the rear seat. About 30 minutes out of Tooraweenah, I heard a loud noise coming from the port side. Detecting a difference in the engine pitch, which sounded as if it were losing power, I took a look out the window. The propeller, whose blades were normally an indistinguishable blur, was definitely slowing down. I shifted my gaze to the ground, which looked very much like the countryside around the Hunter Valley – rolling hills, great stands of very substantial looking trees and lots of sheep. As we were too far north for the Hunter, I reckoned we were somewhere near Dunedoo, to the north of Mudgee. I also thought that, wherever it was, we were going to have to land.

As if on cue, the pilot stuck his head out the cockpit door and shouted for the passengers to move to the rear and strap themselves in, three to a seat. It was an emergency landing, but we must not panic. As there was nothing else I could do, I took another look out the window.

The trees lining the paddocks now seemed very close, very thick and very numerous, while the sheep seemed to have trebled in size and number. A few seconds later, a fence slid past. The sheep scattered, clearly terrified, as the pilot dodged trees with the same nonchalance as if he were steering a routine obstacle course. I held my breath as another fence slid by. There was a sudden bump and the wheels touched down – not on the treetops, or the sheep, or the scattered murderous stumps, but on soft, dry grass. As the aircraft rolled gently to a stop, the passengers swarmed from the plane, congratulating the pilot and one another on their narrow escape. By the time I emerged from the rearmost seat and joined the chattering throng, the pilot had his head in the engine and the fault diagnosed: 'Magneto has gone. Bloody thing.'

He fetched his toolbox to take care of the repairs, only to discover that the box was locked and the keys were hundreds of miles away in Charleville, where he had left them. Not to worry. A few good belts on the lid with a hefty branch and the lock gave way. With the box opened, the rest was easy – old magneto out, new magneto in.

At the pilot's 'Righto. Get in again', all the passengers reboarded, bar two. With her feet planted firmly on the ground and her patient held firmly by the elbow, the nurse from Tooraweenah was insisting on a trial run to make sure the plane could take off. With everyone else on board and the light rapidly fading, the pilot was in no mood to tolerate any dissent or enter into any debate. He issued the ultimatum to 'Get in now, or bloody well stay here on your own'.

The nurse, her patient in tow, abandoned any further thought of protest and scrambled aboard. The door slammed shut, the engine roared to maximum revolutions and we were off, bumping over the grass as the sheep scattered. One or two trees came horribly close, but then, suddenly, we were airborne, sailing over the fence like a carefree bird. The passengers slumped back into their seats, exhausted and limp as rag dolls for the rest of the flight, which was mercifully uneventful.

My next trip was far less harrowing. It involved a transfer to the Royal Alexandra Hospital for Children in Sydney's Camperdown. My patient was an eight-year-old boy, 'Smiler' Bill Elletson, who had been in hospital for the past six months. He had been down at the local cricket oval, playing about as young boys do, when he fell off the back of a wagon, injuring his spine and losing the use of both his legs. His father was temporarily out of work, so the locals had set up a fund to help pay for Bill's medical expenses. When the Far West stepped in to help, I flew to Broken Hill, where Bill was transferred to the regular Inter City Airways flight, two seats having been removed from the cabin to make room for his stretcher. His plight and his cheery disposition, despite his terrible injury, had touched the hearts of the townspeople, who turned out in substantial numbers to wave us off.

A few months later Mr Drummond gave me some excellent news. Bill's father had won a substantial prize in the lottery that had paid for the best surgeon available, and Bill would walk again.

Meanwhile, Mr Drummond's search for a permanent pilot and plane continued. Although there had been an announcement the previous November that the Queensland-based Australian Aerial Medical Service intended to set up a base in New South Wales, there was no sign of anything eventuating in that department. Consequently, while I resigned myself to the necessity of yet another overland tour, Mr Drummond continued with the tedious job of combing the country for a pilot prepared to work for him on a regular, but not full-time, basis.

Although the press publicised the difficulties being encountered since Nancy's sudden departure, there was no response to Mr Drummond's pleas for assistance. The situation was inadvertently resolved, however, on my very next overland trip.

The car was negotiating a fairly remote section of the route when the driver pulled off the track and detoured into the scrub. Switching off the engine, he leaned across the front seat, leaving me in no doubt that he had things other than driving on his mind. A few well-chosen words soon cooled his ardour and, realising that any idea of a dalliance among the dunes had not the slightest chance of success, he restarted the engine. Having received an earful, he did not attempt to rekindle negotiations, the decidedly frosty atmosphere leaving him in no doubt that he must seek gratification elsewhere. Once safely back in Bourke, I phoned Stanley Drummond to tell him that any further overland excursions were 'not on' and that unless something was done I would resign.

I was now both driver-less and pilot-less but, when word got out that I was contemplating leaving, several male pilots offered to come to Bourke. They did not want a retaining fee, and were prepared to exist on commercial work as long as they had the guarantee of the Far West flights, and the use of a hangar. This enabled Mr Drummond to come up with an acceptable compromise by the end of May.

He would hire a local plane for the routine clinic visits, which would resume without delay. For emergency and special flights to the city, I would continue to use a charter aircraft sent from Sydney, which would meet me at the closest landing strip. For any other non-urgent cases to Sydney I was to take a scheduled Butler's flight. The cost would be high but manageable, and less than overland trips.

In August, Mr Drummond's money worries ceased when an anonymous benefactor gave the Scheme £16,000. This very generous donation was sufficient to pay off the £12,000 still owing on the Drummond Home, buy up adjoining property, on which nurses' quarters were to be constructed, and pay for the new aerial clinic arrangements.

An urgent summons shortly after Mr Drummond implemented the new system saw me once again pinning a notice to the door to inform my long-suffering mothers that the town clinic was postponed, as I had been called to a homestead just out of town.

The attending doctor, who was waiting for me outside the house, informed me that the patient was an acute alcoholic. After his latest drinking bout, he had been admitted to The Old Durham, Bourke's private hospital, only to be discharged into the care of his wife when the overtaxed staff could cope with him no longer.

She had managed admirably until her husband had taken exception to a program being broadcast on the radio. Not content to merely turn the knob to switch it off or change to another station, he had silenced the radio by taking a shotgun from beneath the mattress and blasting it to bits. His terrified wife, who had taken cover without delay, sought assistance from the doctor, who advised immediate transfer of the patient to a psychiatric hospital in Sydney.

As there was no question of transporting him on a scheduled Butler's flight, his family had arranged for a private charter. The plane that was arriving from Sydney late that afternoon was *Southern Cross*, the plane made famous by Charles Kingsford-Smith.

> *After landing at Mascot airstrip in Sydney after the fateful cross-Tasman attempt, with Taylor, seaweed festooning the wheel struts and salt spray coating the plane's undercarriage, Smithy had announced that* Southern Cross, *his 'old bus', had earned its retirement. It was sold to the Australian government for £3,000.*

Smithy, however, was not quite ready to call it a day. Shortly afterwards, he announced that he and co-pilot Tommy Pethyridge would make an attempt to break the existing England–Australia record in a new aircraft, now known as Lady Southern Cross. *The original name,* ANZAC, *had been withdrawn on the orders of the Australian government, which did not allow the name to be used commercially.*

The plane had reached India and was en route to Singapore when it disappeared on 9 November 1935 when over the Andaman Sea. In mid-1936 a wheel strut and wheel were found by fishermen on Aye Island, off the south-east coast of Burma (now Myanmar). This section of the undercarriage, all that has been recovered to date, is on display in Sydney's Powerhouse Museum.

While an adoring public mourned the loss of one of its most famous and talented sons, various plans were formulated to preserve 'the old bus' as a memorial. Although it was announced after Smith's death that Southern Cross, *stored at Richmond aerodrome, would be placed in a museum at Mascot, a purchase transaction was not actually finalised for some time, leaving the plane in limbo. In June 1937, the press reported that it had been reconditioned in preparation for removal to Canberra in the expectation that it would be put on display at the Australian War Memorial. Despite much media hype about a 'last flight' to Canberra, nothing eventuated. In the meantime, the old bus made the unscheduled trip to Bourke.*

Although *Southern Cross* was an historic aeroplane, it was still airworthy, and at that time was available to anyone who had sufficient funds to charter it. As my patient was a man of considerable means, his family was well able to afford it, and me. The deal having been struck, I agreed to accompany him to Sydney provided that the gun was surrendered to the police, that a thorough search was conducted for firearms in case he had any more hidden away (which he did, under the bed), and that once on the plane he must be securely restrained and kept heavily sedated.

I also demanded extra supplies of sedatives in case the flight was delayed by bad weather or mechanical trouble, both of which, in my experience, were regular occurrences. With the conditions met, and the necessary arrangements completed for his reception in Sydney, I loaded my soundly sleeping patient into the aircraft. The Fokker, painted a dull grey-brown, was quite roomy inside and a good deal larger than Nancy's Leopard Moth.

The cockpit accommodated the pilot, co-pilot and radio engineer. In the rear were two bunks on either side of the fuselage – one for the patient and the other, converted to a seat for this trip, for the flight engineer. I sat in a regular seat between them. As a huge dust storm was looming on the horizon to the west, the pilot was anxious to be well clear of the town before it hit.

The flight was jinxed from the start. While taxiing for take-off, one of the propellers fell off and cartwheeled across the strip. Fortunately, it had not suffered any damage. Keeping an eye on the rapidly approaching storm, the crew replaced it in record time, enabling them to lift off before the first dust started to swirl.

Southern Cross

Once we were in the air, I noticed that the flight engineer could not take his eyes off the patient, viewing him with the same apprehension a trapped rabbit regards a carpet snake. The slightest movement from the patient, who was so well trussed he could not possibly free himself, elicited an urgent request to 'give him another shot'.

In spite of the engineer's anxiety, the flight passed without incident until we were 90 minutes out of Nyngan. Almost simultaneously, the condition of both weather and patient began to deteriorate. Despite the drugs, he began thrashing about and pulling agitatedly at his restraints so that I was compelled, much to the engineer's relief, to administer a further dose of sedative.

By this time, the rain, which had progressed from drizzle to downpour, was pelting against the windows, reducing visibility to almost zero. Unable to leave my seat because of the turbulence and unable to be heard above the roar of the engines, I scribbled a note to the pilot, requesting an estimated time of arrival in Sydney, as I was becoming very concerned that I might not be able to keep the patient under control for much longer. The answer, passed backwards from the cockpit, was telegram-like in its simplicity.

> Unable to cross Blue Mountains.
>
> Heavy icing on wings.
>
> Land Narromine 10 minutes.

Narromine! We were almost back to where we had started. Still, Narromine offered firm ground and medical assistance, which I figured was a good deal better than I had at present. I pulled the curtain back and took a hurried look out of the window. Pilot Jack Larkin, who happened to be my cousin, was not exaggerating about the ice. The grey-brown paint on the wings was coated in a sheet of crystalline white, which looked dangerously thick. Jack was the New South Wales Aero Club Champion Pilot, so I had faith in his flying ability, but I knew that unless we landed soon, there was a very real danger of the plane falling to earth like a gigantic hailstone. It was useless to attempt to fly higher in an effort to clear the bad weather, for an increase in altitude only increased the risk of further icing.

On landing at Narromine, I sprinted to a public phone and asked to be connected to the doctor on duty at the local hospital. This local keeper of the public health took a decidedly parochial view of my plight. He denied me access to the local hospital on the basis that he was not prepared to risk disturbing his mothers and babies by what was, in his opinion, a raving lunatic. Eager to be rid of us, he instructed an ambulance to transport me and my patient to Dubbo Base Hospital where, I assumed, patients were less likely to be fazed by erratic or irregular behaviour.

Topping up my unfortunate charge with more sedative, I remained awake at his bedside all night, in case his condition should suddenly deteriorate. The crew, fortunately, enjoyed a good night's sleep in the comfort of the plane, in order to be ready to leave at first light. The day dawned bright and clear, enabling them to collect me from Dubbo and complete the journey without further drama. Once we landed in Sydney, the still sedated patient was handed over to trained psychiatric staff. Jack later told me that the flight had been the last 'passenger' flight undertaken by the 'old bus'.

Evidently, after the actual 'last flight' to Bourke and then to Sydney to carry out the mercy mission, the plane remained at Mascot, where it slowly deteriorated. By 1940, the press announced that Southern Cross *was falling to pieces. The next year, following the War Memorial's rejection of the plane for its collection as it was not a war relic, the aircraft was transported on the instructions of the Department of the Interior to Canberra, where it was stored in a civil aviation hangar. A proposal to place it in Sydney's Technological Museum came to nothing when it was revealed that the plane was too large to be displayed inside the building.*

In 1945, Southern Cross *was made airworthy for a feature film, but by 1949 was once again in a poor state. It had been left standing abandoned behind a hangar at Mascot, where vandals had scratched their names on the fuselage and removed items as souvenirs.*

It was not until August 1958 that the historic relic of Australia's pioneering aviation days was finally restored to its former glory and found the home it deserved – a purpose-built glass and aluminium display hangar at Eagle Farm Airport in Brisbane, constructed at a cost of £31,000. Southern Cross *now rests only metres from the spot where Smithy, Ulm and their American crewmen, Harry Lyon and James Warner, touched down after making the first air crossing of the Pacific from California in 1928.*

At the hospital I bumped into an old friend who, on learning that I was stationed at Bourke and was about to return, gave me a pitying look and remarked, 'But my dear, how ghastly for you. Fancy being stuck out there, in the back-of-beyond. You must be bored witless.'

Bored? Apart from having no time to be bored, my range of duties was now so great that no two days were ever the same.

While gala social events were not common, the Annual Bourke Picnic Race Meeting and associated events in May had lasted an entire week and swelled the town's population to at least double its normal size. Attracted by the race balls, one of which was always fancy dress, and the numerous pre-race and post-race parties, as well as the actual races, punters came from near and far to join in the festivities. Anyone who could possibly find transport turned up. Arriving on horseback, by train, in cars and trucks, on bicycles and on foot, they made a colourful crowd, cheering on their favourites as the horses thundered past on the dirt track. I always enjoyed race week and found that, with regular invitations to see a film at the town cinema, dances, concerts and private parties, my social life was more than adequate.

Four months later, Bourke experienced the excitement and glamour of a vice-regal visit. The recently appointed Governor of New South Wales and his wife, Lord and Lady Wakehurst, along with their entire entourage, embarked upon a grand tour of the outback.

Staying at various outback grazing properties, the King's representative was anxious to gain first-hand knowledge of how His Majesty's far-flung subjects were faring. The honoured visitors finally made their way to Bourke, arriving in great style on board a special train. The townsfolk, aware that this was the closest thing to a royal visit that Bourke was likely to experience in their lifetime, rose to the occasion, organising functions and sightseeing tours to amuse the guests.

I was invited to every event but, because of my workload, had to decline some invitations, even though I risked offending those hosting the entertainments. I made sure I was at the Far West Committee's dinner, but was unable to manage the public reception at the Bourke Town Hall. My friends, however, gave me a full and detailed account of the event the following morning, just to make sure I knew what I had missed. Although the visit was hailed an outstanding success, in my opinion it could not compare with the Picnic Races, undoubtedly the social event of the year.

My professional life also kept me on my toes. Even the basic work, revolving around the Bourke clinic, the aerial service and the Aboriginal Camp, provided endless variety. Many of the ailments, unfortunately, were as familiar as ever, although the incidence of trachoma and malnutrition had decreased dramatically. Each time the hot weather returned, sunstroke took its toll, particularly among the children, who were prone to run alarmingly high temperatures. A simple but effective home remedy was to place the child on the floor with wet towels or ice packs (a rarely seen commodity) around the neck.

Anxious to restore the patient's depleted body salts, I made a game of it, encouraging the child to suck on fingers that had been dipped into jars of Vegemite, which is rich in salt and a favourite with most children. The incidence of tropical pallor – that debilitating condition which plagued almost every child to the west and north of Bourke – also increased as the mercury rose. Sometimes the symptoms – diarrhoea, vomiting and jaundice – were so severe that frightened mothers phoned or telegraphed me to transport the children to town and then down to Manly for treatment. With the illness caused by a combination of extreme heat and often unavoidable malnutrition, a move to the coast was often the only recourse available. Emergencies were always the wild card, so I kept a well-stocked Gladstone bag by the door, ready to move at a moment's notice.

Horses accounted for a fair proportion of the injuries. A few deft sutures and a tetanus shot were often all that were required, but fractures were far more difficult. After immobilising the broken limb with anything to hand – fence palings, strong sticks, ripped-up floorboards – I flew the victim to Bourke where simple fractures could be set, or sent them by charter flight to Sydney if the break required specialised orthopaedic treatment.

However, by far the most common injury was the accidental slicing of various body parts by the indiscriminate wielding of axes, knives, saws and machetes. The attitude of many farm workers to these potentially dangerous implements was very casual, resulting in severed fingers and toes and badly lacerated limbs. The less serious cases I treated on the spot, demonstrating sewing skills that would have greatly surprised Miss Bode.

Of all the emergency calls, the one I most dreaded was childbirth. No matter how skilled the midwife, even one who had notched up 103 births during training and a good number since, a difficult confinement in an isolated area could easily result in the death of both mother and child. Aware that Bourke Cemetery had more than its fair share of stillborn babies and mothers who had died giving birth, I kept a careful watch on my pregnant patients, making sure they were safely installed in Bourke, close to proper medical facilities, well before term.

While main centres had a telephone, communication between patient and nurse was often via telegraph. As soon as a message arrived, I was on my way, hopefully in time to render assistance. Time was always against me in cases of dire emergency, but with the plane I was far better off than my predecessors, who often arrived in time to see the patient buried. Communication was still, however, the weak link.

I was only too aware that a speedy response to a call for help was the difference between life and death. The wife of a small landowner, living between Bourke and Wanaaring, had become suddenly very ill. Although a telephone line actually ran through the property, they were not connected to it as no additional subscribers could be accommodated. The distraught husband, unable to send word to Bourke, had taken the only course possible. Laying his desperately ill spouse on the back seat of the car, he had attempted to make the long overland journey to Bourke, the vehicle's speed reduced to a walking pace by the ruts and sandy drifts that passed as the Bourke–Wanaaring road. He lost the race. His wife died on the track, frustratingly out of reach of the aircraft that could have saved her. An appalled Stanley Drummond, shocked by yet another needless death, used this unhappy incident to pressure the government into upgrading the telephone system, so that such a tragedy need never again occur.

Since its inception, the Scheme had the capacity to attract publicity but, in spite of this, funding was still sometimes a problem. The cost of running and maintaining the railcars, the clinics, the plane, the Aboriginal Camps, the seaside holidays and the Drummond Home at Manly was horrendous. By establishing more and more support groups willing to raise money and appealing to the medical profession to continue to act in an honorary capacity, Mr Drummond somehow or other managed to keep the bank account in the black. Aware that there was nothing to compare with a first-hand account of life at 'the front line' to prick the social conscience of those at the rear, he asked me to speak at fundraising rallies two or three times a year.

The aid we received was not always purely monetary. Fares on private and government transport for Far West children were reduced or waived, clothing was made, jumpers and layettes knitted, food donated, and time, talents and resources freely given by all members of the community. For years, the townsfolk of Leeton, situated in a rich, fertile fruit-growing district, sent cases of oranges to remote areas of the state, where such produce was seldom seen. Yet, in spite of this overwhelming generosity, there were children who were occasionally denied help –

not by bureaucratic red tape or unwillingness to accommodate a special need, but by their very own parents.

Not infrequently, I encountered a reluctance by some parents to allow their children to receive medical treatment in the city. Often it stemmed from a natural hesitancy at the thought of being parted from the child, the idea of travelling so far away, or from apprehension about the operation. Sometimes, however, the motive for withholding permission to allow the child to be treated was entirely mercenary.

Having an ill or handicapped child entitled the family to a special government allowance. Consequently, a couple of children with congenital hip deformities, turned feet or trachoma ensured that the family income was quite well supplemented by a steady stream of funds from the government coffers. When I realised that some children were being deliberately denied help by their parents, I decided to take direct and immediate action. Aided by tip-offs from concerned members of the public, I began calling unannounced at houses in which ill or handicapped children were being hidden.

Sometimes what I found defied belief – malnourished, partially or totally blind children, uneducated and confined to a hot corrugated iron hut, day in, day out. Their eyes were so unaccustomed to the light that when they emerged outdoors the strong sunlight made them wince with pain. When confronted, some parents would only allow their children to obtain treatment if the precious government cheque remained in their control.

The dedication of the Angel of Mercy to the children in her care did not pass unnoticed. At the annual general meeting of the Bourke Branch of the Scheme, the president publicly paid tribute to Sister Silver in his opening address:

> During the year the work of the Clinic had been carried on in an efficient manner. The people of Bourke cannot be too thankful for the presence of Sister Silver who has maintained her attention to the children to the utmost of her capacity.
>
> Bourke should be ever grateful to the Scheme for sending such a capable and energetic worker.
>
> This was the biggest meeting he had ever seen, the President continued, and he believed the credit for it was due to Sister Silver and the work of the Secretary. The fact that the branch had a credit balance at all was due to the generosity of Mrs Fitzgerald who has supplied Sister Silver with meals free of charge.
>
> The installation of a plane at Bourke was still in the balance. A permanent 'plane' would be an asset not only to the Scheme but to every citizen.

Although the Far West relied to some extent on its own funds to subsidise the cost of a child's treatment, which sometimes took years, Mr Drummond refused to entertain any thought of mere money coming between his far-westers and proper care. If parents were intractable, we bowed to their demands and paid for the treatment out of Far West funds. The cases of hidden children decreased dramatically when the public, on learning of the work being done and of the opportunities being offered, overcame their reluctance to 'dob' on a neighbour or acquaintance.

Not all my successes were medically related. In October of 1937, with Spring well and truly in the air, I witnessed the satisfactory conclusion of an affair of the heart, in which I had been involved for two years.

When I first arrived in Bourke, I had met, on the overland section of the Urisino route, a charming young widow who suffered greatly from the loneliness of her isolated location. Further along the track was an unattached and reasonably well-off grazier, his eligibility made even more attractive as he owned a car. Discovering that he craved the company of someone with whom he could share his life, I mentioned that I had just visited a woman in much the same situation who, having no car, felt very isolated and might enjoy a social visit.

On a subsequent trip, I was delighted and immensely satisfied to discover that the grazier was no longer living alone. However, two years later, by which time two children had been born to the happy pair, my sense of propriety told me that perhaps it was time the liaison that I had so blatantly engineered was formalised.

The following month, I arrived at Urisino with Bourke's Presbyterian Minister in tow – the knowledge that he might be able to perform a marriage and two baptisms, as well as enjoy a free plane ride, proving an irresistible temptation. I let him off at the homestead while I continued with my rounds, returning later to learn that everything had been concluded most satisfactorily and that a bride, bridegroom and two bonny children had been added to his flock.

With Christmas looming fast, I arranged to borrow the Santa suit again. As expected, the townsfolk rallied to the cause, providing presents and treats galore, while the pilot, delighted to be part of such a joyous occasion, gave his services free of charge. The year ended on a high note – for the children, parents and Santa, as well as the driver of the sleigh, who enjoyed the Christmas flight as much as anyone.

My feeling of elation and happiness was heightened by a special Christmas/farewell dinner held at Urisino. In July, while on my rounds, I had received and accepted a proposal of marriage from Charles Weiss, the 'jackeroo' who had escorted me on my first round in his snazzy green Chevrolet roadster. We had met many times since.

The groom-to-be, born in 1907, was the eldest son of Charles Weiss, a farmer of German descent who owned a small sheep property with a post-office concession at Swan Dale, near Glen Innes. After falling ill with influenza in 1913, he contracted pneumonia, which took his life at the age of 52. His Irish-born wife, Theresa, 13 years his junior, was left to raise the three children still at home – a daughter, Nan, aged 17, Charles aged 6, and an infant son, Lewis.

Charles attended Swan Dale Public School, but with the outbreak of the Great War anti-German sentiment became rife. When the harassment at school became too great, his mother enrolled him at De La Salle College in Armidale. He had completed his primary education and was about to begin his second year of high school when he left to help his mother run the farm.

Diagnosed with breast cancer, she was forced to move into Glen Innes, where she was cared for by her eldest daughter, Kate. With Theresa unable to return to the land, Charles remained on the property, supplementing his income with casual work at the local stockyards. He also trained as a wool classer, becoming fully qualified at the age of 19. However, he was unable to find a job owing to his extreme youth.

After the death of his mother in 1926, the property was sold. Charles left Glen Innes and headed west to Borambil, a large holding near Condobolin, to work as a jackeroo/bookkeeper for nine months. From there he went to Murrawombie Station at Nyngan, where he sustained a serious injury when a horse reared and fell on his leg, dislocating his knee and tearing the cartilage. Unable to ride or walk unaided, he spent the next 18 months employed as the station's bookkeeper and storekeeper. He then went to Mundiwa Station, Brewarrina, before finally ending up as head stockman at Urisino, and then station manager at Thurloo Downs.

As our friends at Urisino toasted our health, I reflected that it was indeed fortunate that two people who so loved the outback were to marry. My new home, as wife of the station manager, would be at Thurloo Downs. So, although I knew I must leave the Far West Scheme which, in keeping with the social mores of the day, did not employ married women, I was not leaving the far west.

With my wedding date set for April, and my sister Jean's wedding to take place less than three weeks before, I submitted my resignation on New Year's Eve, effective in mid-February. With so much clinic work to be completed in a scant six weeks, I cancelled my usual trip to Manly for the

Sister Silver and some of her outback friends, dressed in their Sunday best, at Hungerford

summer holidays. The time passed in a blur, with visits to the Aboriginal Camp at Bourke, clinic sessions in town, sessions at the local hospital and, finally, my very last aerial medical tour. It was with a heavy heart and more than a feeling of regret that I boarded the plane for that final flight.

The route was much longer than usual as I insisted on saying goodbye to everyone and visiting every out-station. Louth, Wanaaring, Urisino, Hungerford, Ford's Bridge, Yantabulla, Byrock, Brewarrina and Enngonia – I stopped at each of them as well as every hut and homestead on the car route from Urisino.

Saying goodbye to my friends at the Aboriginal Camps at Bourke and Brewarrina was very difficult. It had been a privilege to know them. Their knowledge of the bush was remarkable, and they taught me many things about their way of life that I would otherwise never have known. Looking back across so many years, I have a tremendous sadness when I realise that, in many places in Australia, hardly a thing has altered for these warm and gentle people, despite great strides made by the white community. Their main problems are still the same – poverty, poor health and lack of proper housing.

All too soon, the farewell tour was complete and I was back in town. After making sure that all was in order, I handed responsibility for my far-flung patients to Sister Leach. As no replacement had been found to take over my duties, she had been transferred to Bourke from the Far West Home at Manly as a temporary measure.

And then it really was time to go. With hugs and waves, accompanied by tearful promises from dozens of well-wishers that if ever they happened to be near Thurloo Downs they would pay me a visit, I took my leave from my outback family.

Finding a suitably qualified sister to take over the aerial service was unsuccessful and, to make matters worse, Mr Drummond became very ill. With no resident nursing sister in town, the mothers and babies were now reliant on the reintroduction of the railcar and Sister Webb, who arrived once a month to open up the town clinic, where she remained on duty for a week.

However, while Sister Silver's resignation put paid to the end of the Far West's Aerial Clinic, it was not the end of aerial medical services in the far west. Indeed, it was an entirely new beginning. The void created by her departure was filled, partially at least, by another agency that also had long recognised the need for an efficient aerial medical service in outback New South Wales. Established at Broken Hill in 1937, it now serviced an area covering 400,000 square miles (1 million square kilometres). Before long, the welcome drum of aircraft engines, bringing medical assistance to those in need, was once more heard above the lonely rooftops of the homesteads and out-stations around Bourke.

At long last, the Flying Doctor had come to town.

CHAPTER 8

A new beginning

As Jean and I were being married less than three weeks apart, the next two months were filled with more than the usual amount of pre-wedding activity. Although my parents thought that, at the age of almost 28, it was high time I married, and were very pleased that I was at last taking the plunge, they were not exactly enthusiastic that I was relocating to an even more remote corner of the state.

At the end of March, I was chief bridesmaid to Jean who, like me, had become engaged to a practising Roman Catholic. Charles's Irish mother was Catholic and his father, who remained C of E, had agreed to have the children raised in that faith. In what was a first for the hitherto very C of E Silver family, Jean was married at a Catholic Mass, conducted in St Mary's Cathedral in Sydney. As neither of us was superstitious, my bridesmaid's dress was green chiffon. On 19 April, at 7 pm, it was my turn to be the bride, at the very same Cathedral.

The ceremony was followed by a reception at Schofield House, Point Piper. The magnificent old mansion, set amid velvet lawns and beautiful gardens on the shores of Sydney Harbour, was an idyllic setting. At night, the grounds were transformed into a virtual fairyland, with tiny festooned lights reflected a thousand times over on the rippling harbour waters.

As I cast my eyes over the fashionably dressed ladies, the elegantly attired men, the masses of fragrant floral arrangements, the sparkling cutlery and glittering glassware, the culinary delights gracing exquisitely decorated tables and the string orchestra playing softly in the background, I was acutely aware that the scene unfolding before me was a far cry from the outback. The scene of opulence and extravagance took on an air of unreality as I recalled the raw, earthy simplicity of my outback life. How the eyes of my far western friends would bulge if they could see the brand-new Mrs Charles Weiss dressed in a filmy bridal gown that was far removed from the often dusty garb of Sister Silver.

The press covered both weddings. Jean's attracted attention, not simply because 'The Flying Sister' was her bridesmaid but, because one of the groomsmen was Jack Fingleton, a well-known test cricketer and friend of the cricket-playing bridegroom, H J 'Tom' Byrnes.

Two other well-known cricketers, Stan McCabe and W J 'Bill' O'Reilley, school friends of the groom, were also among the guests.

The marriage of the well-known and much loved Flying Sister was also reported in detail by several newspapers.

> Sister M D Silver, who was the first trained nurse in Australia to travel by 'plane in the course of her duties outback, was married at St Mary's Cathedral, Sydney, on 19th April, to Mr Charles Weiss. The bride is the elder daughter of Mr and Mrs L Silver, of 'Dee Why,' Scone, and the bridegroom is the eldest son of the late Mr and Mrs C L Weiss, of 'Swan Vale,' Glen Innes.
>
> A gown of parchment angel skin cut with an overshadowed pattern of maple leaf with a tudor cap were worn by the bride, who carried an ivory prayer book with a trail of lily of the valley. Mrs Tom Byrnes, sister of the bride, was matron of honour and wore a gown of lavender blue chiffon, with a Juliet cap of real lavender, matching her old world posy also of lavender. Mr Lou Weiss was best man.
>
> The reception was held at 'Schofield House,' Point Piper. The vestibule, ballroom and reception rooms were a mass of glorious blooms. The bride's mother received the guests, wearing a black sheer frock heavily embossed with steel beads and wore a coronet of silver lame and a shoulder spray of mauve orchids.
>
> The bride added a beautiful fur coat, the gift of the bridegroom, to her wedding gown as she left the reception for her honeymoon, which will be spent touring Melbourne and Adelaide, from where Mr and Mrs Weiss will proceed to 'Thurlow Downs,' Bourke, where they will make their future home.

As we drove away from the reception, I could hardly credit that the entire day had gone without a hitch. However, I had not reckoned with the honeymoon, which was an unmitigated disaster.

On paper it all looked perfectly straightforward – a motoring holiday to Adelaide and Melbourne, via Cobar and Broken Hill, to be taken at a leisurely pace to combine the scenery of the outback we loved with the delights of stately cities and the lush green of Victoria's coastal districts.

We were at Orange, a mere 160 miles (260 kilometres) from Sydney, where we were to spend the second night of our honeymoon, when trouble struck. Orange is not, as its name suggests, a warm and temperate place set amid orange groves. Orange can be very chilly, even in April, and the temperatures can suddenly plummet. The two thin and skimpy blankets supplied by the hotel management were woefully inadequate but, by the time we realised this, it was far too late to ask for supplementary bedding. My beautiful fur coat was no match for the bone-chilling air so, with sleep impossible, we huddled together until dawn, talking.

As soon as dawn broke, more asleep than awake, we continued on to Cobar and fell thankfully onto the bed, only to discover that the hotel had been selected as the venue for a rip-roaring wild-west party. The racket continued unabated until dawn, when the last of the revellers collapsed into alcoholic unconsciousness. While the partygoers slumbered on, we dragged ourselves to the car at first light for the next leg of the journey across the red plains to Broken Hill.

The sight of the familiar grey-green scrub and gently rolling dunes beneath a sky of brilliant blue restored our spirits. The autumn air was crystal clear, and the sleeplessness of the past two nights was soon replaced by a feeling of optimism and wellbeing. Reaching Wilcannia, I settled back as the car negotiated the long, straight stretches leading to Broken Hill.

We had only a few miles to go when I realised that my throat felt a little sore. By nightfall it was so painful that I barely slept, and by morning was unendurable. A doctor summoned by Charles took one look, diagnosed diphtheria and put me in hospital, where I was placed in total isolation. As the nurses erected a screen round my bed, I overheard a patient say, 'Don't make too much noise. They are putting a screen round her, so she must be dying.'

The mass of injections pumped into me day and night kept me alive, but the screen remained. After a couple of days, when I realised that the head of my bed was directly beneath a window, Charles and his friends made use of the privacy it gave to bypass the isolation rule and hand over all kinds of goodies, which lifted my spirits enormously.

After a week, I was pronounced 'diphtheria free' and allowed to continue on our honeymoon. We didn't get far before I began to itch. The drugs had created a severe allergic reaction, which saw my entire body covered in a hideous and intensely itchy rash. Adelaide, the city of churches, remained unseen, as from the confines of my bed I heard, rather than viewed, the church bells chiming the hour and quarter-hour round the clock for a whole week.

With the rash and the itching having finally settled down, we headed for Geelong, driving along the picturesque coastal route. At long last we began to relax, admiring the scenic drive through pretty timbered country, now lush and incredibly green from recent rainfall.

While negotiating a steep incline on a twisting section of the road, the king pin – a mysterious mechanical gadget that held the steering together – snapped. In an instant we were hurtling down the slope, with the car completely out of control, and with large and very deep rainwater culverts on either side of the roadway. Just as it looked as if we were destined to meet a sticky end in the abyss-like ditch on the next bend, the brakes finally grabbed. The car swerved to the left, became airborne and neatly cleared the ditch to smash into a fence, landing nose down on a patch of grass. By some miracle, it appeared neither of us was hurt. As the steam rose from the fractured radiator, a farmer driving a pick-up truck arrived. Taking in the scene, he laconically enquired, 'Have an accident?'

Seeing the funny side of this remark, I replied, 'No thanks. We've just had one.'

My flippancy was lost on the farmer, who gave me a vague look before bundling us, and our luggage, into his truck. He drove us to Geelong, where Charles arranged for the car to be collected and repaired. The only upside was, because of the luggage and the distance to be travelled, we had opted for a more spacious and more robust Ford sedan, instead of the glamorous green Chevy roadster.

We continued by train to Melbourne, eager to revel in the luxury and peace and quiet of a suite at the Menzies Hotel. It was certainly peaceful. The abrupt stop to our mid-air flight over the ditch had rearranged the bones in Charles's back. It was now his turn to be confined to bed, unable to move until the pain subsided. It took five days – long enough for the car to also be repaired. I added Melbourne to my list of places unseen, although the interior of the hotel became very familiar.

We decided to drive to Sydney, and then on to Scone to visit my family before turning at last to the west. The mechanics and body builders at the Ford Motor Works had done an amazing job, and the car was as good as new. We motored without mishap through the pretty rural countryside and historic towns of Victoria and New South Wales, and then to Sydney. The city was at its seasonal best, with deciduous trees in full, glorious autumnal colours and the waters of the harbour a dazzling blue.

As we continued on towards the Hunter Valley, we revelled in the fine weather and relaxed holiday atmosphere, but fate had not quite finished with us. As we rounded a bend, stretched out across the road was a large feral pig intent on suicide. I shut my eyes. Charles sounded the horn and stamped the brake pedal to the floor. The pig did nothing at all and we hit it with some force.

Miraculously, the car and the pig were undamaged, but Charles's back was not. The impact had locked up his spine, and he was in agony. He spent the remainder of our honeymoon in bed, at the home of his in-laws, until he regained sufficient mobility to drive again.

Fortunately, the last leg of our incident-packed journey passed without any further drama and, as we neared Thurloo Downs, I scanned the horizon for the first sight of my new home. It was with a sense of deliverance that I spotted the roof of the homestead, glinting a welcome in the late afternoon light. Although our honeymoon had not been what I had expected, I took great delight whenever anyone asked where we had spent our honeymoon in replying, quite truthfully, 'in bed'.

Thurloo Downs, a sprawling pisé homestead, was set on the banks of Thurloo Creek. The wide verandahs and open breezeway combined with the thick mud-brick walls to create a cool haven on all but the hottest days. Encircling the house was an earthen levee bank about three feet (a metre) high, designed to keep back floodwaters. Looking at the khaki-coloured puddles

Marjorie Weiss c1938

The huge shearing shed at Thurloo Downs built in 1928

that constituted the creek, I wondered how a flood could ever threaten the solid old homestead, perched so far above the present water level, especially when bores had to be sunk to keep the 750,000 acre (300,000 hectare) property watered.

Nearby was a vast 32-stand shearing shed, only half of which was ever used by the teams that took five weeks to shear the thousands of sheep. As wool prices were at an all-time low because of the effects of the Depression, the unused portion of the shed was stacked with hundreds of bales of low-grade wool that could not be sold until the market improved.

When summer arrived, I discovered that the temperatures at Thurloo Downs far exceeded those at Bourke. During one particularly hot spell, the temperature did not fall below 100 degrees Fahrenheit (38 degrees Celsius) for 38 consecutive nights. When the mercury soared to these extremes, not even the thick pisé walls of the house could cope, and everyone moved out of doors at night, sleeping on stretchers on the lawn. With the temperature so high, work schedules were rearranged to begin at 3 am and end at 9 am.

Dust storms were horrendous, with the dust so thick that midday became midnight and stayed that way for two or three days at a stretch. Tons of sand were deposited, choking the bore drains, burying the fences and filling the roof space of the homestead. The minute normal breathing became possible, I would send an army of jackeroos up into the ceiling space to sweep it clean, before the whole lot came tumbling down. Charles even found a use for the station camels, usually considered to be a real pest, by harnessing them to a V-shaped, plough-like delver, which they dragged along to unblock the sand-choked bore drains.

With my resignation from the Far West Scheme, I had naturally assumed that my nursing days were over. However, while the Flying Doctor catered for medical emergencies, people living far away from a hospital or a bush nurse were still very much on their own. As Thurloo fitted into this category, one of my first tasks was to unpack the contents of my Gladstone bag and convert one of the spare rooms into a two-bed clinic. The property supported a considerable labour force, so one or both beds were usually occupied by ill or injured station hands. It felt just like old times as I lanced and sutured, injected and bandaged, bathed and dressed – and generally kept an eye on everyone's health.

Although normal to me, having medical attention was quite a novelty to the station hands, who often had trouble reconciling my dual roles as 'Mistress of the Station' with 'Sister-in-charge of the Clinic'. Sometimes I was 'missus', the wife of the boss and a lady of refined sensibilities; at others, I was the chief medical officer who could hear and handle almost anything.

One day, when wearing my missus hat, a station hand named Alec came galloping up to the station in a state of extreme agitation, calling for the boss who, as it happened, was absent. Hearing the kerfuffle, I went out onto the verandah to investigate and, realising that something was obviously the matter, asked if I could help. Alec scuffed his boots in the dust, fidgeted with his hat and looked around in confusion.

'Come on, Alec. Out with it. I'm quite sure that if anything is wrong I can deal with it.'

Alec stared at me in incredulous disbelief. Tell me? The missus, a lady, a mere fragile female? Obviously thunderstruck at such an idea, he blurted out, 'Gawd no, missus, YOU can't come! He looks DEAD.'

Telling him that I'd seen more dead bodies than he'd had breakfasts, I ordered him to lead the way. With the 'Chief Medical Officer and Sister-in-charge of the Clinic' now in control, he did so.

I could see that the body of Jimmie, one of the hands, was indeed very dead. He had suffered a broken neck after falling from his saddle, which had not been tightened properly. There was nothing that I could do for him, as death had been instantaneous.

With such high temperatures, the only course of action after alerting the police was to knock up a coffin on the spot and transfer the body back to the homestead for a speedy burial.

Charles arrived in time to take charge of the joinery work and the men rallied round with planks of timber, nails and hammers. When the coffin was almost finished, Charles asked one of the workers, a fellow named Jim, to try it for size.

'Me?' squawked a horrified Jim.

'Yes. You. You're about the same size as Jimmie. We need to make the lid, so hop in for a second to see if it is big enough before we go any further.'

That was enough for Jim, who backed off with a 'No bloody fear. I won't get into THAT thing. I'm orf. Where's me horse?'

And he was, in a cloud of dust and with the speed of a desert willy-willy.

Jimmie's mates who, up until now had been shocked by the sudden finality of his death and had been uncertain of just how to act, dissolved into helpless laughter, storing up the vision of the terrified Jim for the next camp-fire yarn, when the story would become part of the rich outback folklore.

About 250 miles (400 kilometres) away to the north, across the Queensland border, lay Mt Margaret Station, which the Peel River Pastoral Company had recently sold to the Elsinora Pastoral Company for £50,000. The Killens and George Henderson were sheep men, so Charles had been instructed to purchase and hold 25,000 sheep at Thurloo for transfer to Mt Margaret, formerly a cattle station.

There is an old saying – new home, new baby. Well, in my case, it came true, and in July 1939 I gave birth to a son, Tony, who demanded my attention, as all small babies do. I made the best of it while I could. One of the drawbacks of living in the outback is that, if children are to be educated as soon as they are of school age, they must leave home and go to boarding school. The year 1939 also brought the Second World War in September and a transfer for both Charles and the sheep to Mt Margaret in December. The station, our home for the next 18 years, was

Mt Margaret homestead

huge and would become the largest sheep property in Australia, running 70,000 sheep and 6,000 cattle, and with 40 workers on the payroll by the time we left.

The property fronted the Wilson River for 50 miles (80 kilometres) and was well watered by way of numerous bores, dams, wells, tanks and natural watercourses. It covered a diversity of land types, ranging from Mitchell grass floodplains to undulating country covered in mulga and gidgee trees, providing a range of vegetation to feed stock in the dry season. The closest settlement was Eromanga, 20 miles (36 kilometres) away.

Although Mt Margaret was a sheep station, the cattle herd was developed from a poll Shorthorn stud that Charles began in 1942, with champion Antrim bulls bought from Edward Killen's stud in New South Wales and Kaluga and Nalpa cows. The venture was successful as well as profitable.

At the time of our transfer, Mt Margaret was rather rundown, unfenced in places on the outer boundary and infested with dingos. The homestead was not in very good condition and there was no garden to speak of, but Charles was confident that this would soon be put to rights. Some internal fencing had been started, but the advent of the war made labour and materials hard to get. As there were no fenced paddocks for the 25,000 sheep to be sent from Thurloo Downs, arrangements were made to put them on agistment at neighbouring stations.

While improvements were being made to the homestead, I went home to Scone with the baby. Charles, who had to supervise the movement of stock, camped out in the house until our belongings arrived.

The sheep were moved in flocks of 5,000 along the stock routes, by five drovers from Thurloo Downs, the exact track taken dictated by the availability of water. The route to Mt Margaret crossed the Bulloo River, a fan-like mesh of intricate, and usually dry, waterways connected to higher ground. However, in this land of violent contrasts, the creeks, which spread in vast webs from New South Wales to Queensland, could fill with very little warning, trapping man and beast alike.

One mob of sheep became completely isolated when a midnight thunderstorm, followed by heavy rain upstream, created a huge surge of water that poured without warning down the almost dry riverbeds. Marooned by the floodwaters and without any fodder of any kind, the mob stood forlornly and soggily on the small island created by the newly rejuvenated river.

An attempt to swim the frightened sheep across the torrent was a complete failure and resulted in 300 drowned corpses. With the anticipated loss of the rest from slow starvation, the outcome seemed inevitable.

However, help was at hand in the form of Captain Moody, a well-known pilot.

'Skipper' or Captain P H Moody, aviator and adventurer, had flown in the 1936 Brisbane–Adelaide Air Race and had served as a fighter pilot with the Royal Flying Corps in World War 1, before becoming a test pilot with the Royal Air Force. Post-war he held the post of chief mail pilot with QANTAS and also flew in New Guinea. Besides running his own charter service, he was a pilot with New England Airways, which operated along the Queensland coast to Sydney, and he later flew an air ambulance. An interest in pastoral pursuits had led him to purchase a sheep property on the Warrego River, a tributary that joined the Darling just to the north of Louth.

Stationing his small plane at Thargomindah, he flew south over the stranded mob time and again, while a young lad, with great delight, dropped bags of corn from the open cockpit, two or three times a day for the next six weeks, until the floodwaters receded. With the river reduced to a safe level, the mob continued its walk to Mt Margaret, where it was shorn of fleece worth £2,000 – the exact cost of six weeks of fodder and plane hire. The drovers, who had successfully herded the mob to safety, were as pleased as punch to learn that their sheep had the distinction of being the first to receive fodder by air.

While I was occupied with our infant son, Charles was kept busy overseeing improvements to the property and the homestead. Dingo netting along boundary fences and some paddocks were completed, and lawns and gardens were coming along nicely around the homestead, which was now painted white. However, it was not for some months that sufficient material and labour were obtained to build a shearing shed and accommodation for the shearers, enabling the remainder of the sheep on agistment to be shorn. More sheep were brought up from Thurloo, with another 5,000 from Landsdowne Station near Charleville. By 1944, Mt Margaret was running 62,000 sheep.

However, the shed was not big enough, and with no prospect of building a new shed until the war was over, the only way to cope was to employ two teams of shearers, a couple of months apart. After the shearing, 32,000 sheep were sold – 8,000 young ewes sent to Urisino and Thurloo Downs, 8,000 sold for meat and 16,000 sent to a station at Winton, leaving us with a more manageable 30,000.

We also ran 12,000 head of mixed cattle. My expertise lay in nursing people, not animals, but I put my knowledge to good use following a difficult birth, when a calf became stuck during delivery and died. The body had to be dismembered to save the mother, who became very ill with an infection. Charles was about to shoot her, when I decided to intervene. As there was nothing to be lost, I dosed her with sulphur drugs – the standard treatment before penicillin became available. My patient recovered and went on to produce many fine calves.

As the station spread across 1,800 square miles (1.2 million acres or 500,000 hectares) and was 86 miles (145 kilometres) from Quilpie and the nearest hospital, the isolation and the war ensured that my nursing skills were in demand. Again, I set up a two-bed clinic, which was always occupied, as there were even more station hands at Mt Margaret than at Thurloo.

Charles volunteered for military service, but was rejected on the grounds that his contribution to the war lay in keeping the country supplied with food. Many nursing sisters who had trained at the same time as me enlisted and, had I still been single, I would have been off to the recruiting office like a shot. However, when I discovered that recruitment of medical staff to the war effort had created a crisis at Quilpie Hospital, I volunteered my services, allowing the matron, who had been working for months without any time off, a period of well-earned relief. By this time, my mother had come to stay with us, bringing Jean's small son with her – a perfect playmate for Tony. When not needed at Mt Margaret, this meant that I could travel into town and stay for a few days, before heading back home.

In late 1943, the Aerial Medical Service, now known officially as the Flying Doctor Service, established a new base at Charleville, about 250 miles (400 kilometres) east of Mt Margaret, greatly relieving the pressure on the Cloncurry base. Dr Allan Vickers, who had returned to the service after a stint in the army, was placed in charge of an area that extended from the northern extremity of the Broken Hill base to the southern edge of Cloncurry's redefined territory, taking in the towns of Quilpie, Birdsville, Thargomindah, Eromanga and Windorah. The plane and pilot were supplied by QANTAS.

Each station in the Charleville area was provided with a medical kit, packed with carefully numbered drugs and measuring spoons, and a 'body chart'. With the aid of the chart, patients requiring assistance described their symptoms via pedal wireless or telephone to the doctor, who issued instructions on which medicine to take and in what amount. This innovative system often relieved the need for further consultation.

Dr D Allan Vickers beside one of the Flying Doctor aircraft, 1935 (Geoff Goodall)

Ironically, the arrival of the Flying Doctor enabled me to extend my services. With diagnosis confirmed and treatment sanctioned by the doctor, I was now able to undertake minor surgery, for which a general anaesthetic was not required. To take the edge off the pain, I knocked out the patient with a good swig or rum or whisky, allowing me to extract an abscessed tooth or clean and sterilise a deep tissue wound, while the victim lay oblivious in a happy alcoholic haze.

Unfortunately, long-distance diagnosis was not infallible, and became complicated if Dr Vickers, who was in verbal communication with his far-flung patients, was absent for some reason or another. This was tragically demonstrated one day when one of the drovers, Bob Cain, aged in his fifties, fell into a fire in a state of stupefaction. He was quite badly burned, and the men, who had no first-hand information of the incident, assumed that he had been drinking. So did Dr Vickers' locum.

I wasn't at all convinced – Bob didn't smell of liquor. Rather, I believed he was suffering from meningitis, which was a far greater threat to his life than the burns he had suffered. However, my plea for the plane to come immediately fell on deaf ears, leaving me to cope as best I could. I rotated two volunteer jackeroos, suitably masked to protect them from infection, at Bob's bedside in 12-hour shifts as he needed to be watched around the clock.

The patient's condition deteriorated and, by morning, he was clearly critically ill. A frantic call to the doctor finally convinced him that I was not some hysterical, overreacting female, but by the time he got his act together, it was far too late. The patient, officially diagnosed by hospital staff as a confirmed meningitis case, did not recover.

This was fortunately an isolated case and the Flying Doctor saved many a life in circumstances that would otherwise have resulted in death. Sometimes, in dire emergencies, operations would be carried out on the kitchen table, with the patient usually none the worse for the experience.

One emergency I was not involved with, as we were away at the time, occurred when two of the station hands became involved in a fight at the shearing shed, 8 miles (13 kilometres) from the homestead. One of those involved had pulled a knife, slashing his opponent across the abdomen. The cut was deep and had penetrated his stomach wall.

The victim was Norman Francis Timms, aged 34, a station hand, who had become involved in a fight with Samuel Duggan, aged 30, on 22 May 1949. When questioned by police, Duggan stated that he had taken a knife with him when Timms challenged him to a fight after an altercation over alcohol. Duggan said that, as the two men closed, he 'slashed everywhere with the knife. He punched me several times and I kept slashing at his body … I didn't care whether I killed him or not. I just slashed his guts as hard as I could.' Duggan appeared in court on a charge of attempted murder. He pleaded guilty to grievous bodily harm and was sentenced to 18 months gaol with hard labour.

The fight had taken place at around 9 pm. By the time the alarm was raised and an ambulance dispatched from Quilpie, the victim had been six hours without any medical assistance. Using an acetylene lamp, the doctor carried out an emergency operation to save the life of the patient.

Shortly before this incident, the station overseer became seriously ill with pneumonia. We had been cut off by monsoonal floodwaters, so the station hands built an emergency strip on a ridge so that Dr Vickers could fly in and attend to his patient. However, although he landed safely, he was grounded by poor weather conditions and had to wait 24 hours to evacuate the overseer, before flying off again to attend to his next patient, in what amounted to a 400 mile (250 kilometre) round trip.

Recognising the great work being done by the airborne doctors, the local community was always willing to join in the vital fundraising efforts needed to keep the service going. One of the highlights of the yearly calendar was the Eromanga Flying Doctor Races, when people came from near and far to join in this anything-but-ordinary race meeting.

Local property owners supplied the 'racehorses' by donating the use of their animals for the day. An auction was held for 'ownership' of the participating horses, which were passed temporarily to the highest bidder. Bidding was brisk as people eagerly sought the opportunity of being a racehorse owner and a potential winner, if only for a few short hours.

Jockeys were chosen from a huge pool of willing jackeroos, who were given added status by dressing in brilliantly hued silk shirts, although the elastic-sided boots and well-worn moleskins betrayed more humble origins. Bookmakers set up their stalls, the punters poured in and the fun began.

For first-time racegoers there was no mistaking the venue. A huge red plume of dust, not unlike that of an atomic cloud, billowed into an otherwise clear sky as the movement of horses round the track and the coming and going of motor vehicles stirred up the fine, talcum-like soil. At the completion of the eight or nine card events, a dance swung into action to the sound of a visiting band.

For those who survived the revelry of the night there was a rodeo the following day, in which anyone in a fit state could participate or watch from the sidelines. The evening brought socialising of a different kind – a cosy, subdued get-together, where folk cemented old friendships and made new ones.

Reminiscing about the old days in the bush and recounting of yarns was well underway one race evening when I noticed that it was raining – and had apparently been doing so for quite some time. No one else seemed to notice, as the sound of the rain drumming on a nearby iron roof and slapping against the sides of the marquees was drowned out by the hum of conversation and good cheer.

Towards midnight, mindful that we had a few creeks to cross on the way home, I decided to broach the subject of the downpour with Charles and his Mt Margaret cronies, who were busily engrossed in the serious and singularly masculine art of 'mateship'. My interruption was not welcome, and I was told it was only a shower. After some persuasion, I managed to convince them to take a look outside. One look and they abandoned their drinks. With any thought of further socialising forgotten, they jumped into their vehicles, followed by a convoy of cars filled with 20 overnight guests.

We led the contingent across red-soil plains that were now a sea of boggy mud. The creeks were running a banker but, in spite of my fear that we would all be washed away and drown, we negotiated the first two crossings without mishap. The third, however, stopped us dead. The creek, surging in a knee-high torrent across the plain, snuffed out the engine.

Realising that we were marooned, Charles set out to wade the short distance to the homestead, while I sat in the vehicle with a jackeroo, praying that the water would rise no further. Stretched out in a dog-legged line behind us were the cars of our house guests, the lights from the rapidly dimming headlights casting eerie patterns across the water.

Charles seemed to have been gone for hours, and I was dying of thirst as well as shivering with cold. It was at this point that I really learned that jackeroos were, if nothing, resourceful. Digging into his kitbag, he produced two tin mugs and a small flask of overproof rum, which he watered down by opening the car door a notch, admitting a small amount of creek water. The toddy soon had my spirits revived, my circulation restored and my thirst quenched. We had just finished our nightcap when the headlights of the large station lorry cut through the driving rain, announcing that help was at hand.

With the vehicles winched from the floodwaters, we returned to the warmth and safety of the station. The general consensus was that, although the races had been a little soggy, it had all been enormous fun and without a doubt everyone would be back next year. Such was the camaraderie of the bush; it took an event of great magnitude to upset this equilibrium.

The shearers' strike of 1956 was one such event.

Shearers are vital to the wool industry, for without the annual clip there is no income. Mt Margaret was a large wool producer, once more running 64,000 sheep, which yielded a clip of well over 100 bales, weighing in at around 12 tons. This particular shearers' strike occurred when some of the union leaders decided that the best way to contest an Arbitration Commission decision, regarding rates of pay, lay in direct action rather than renewed court proceedings.

The strike was announced, the shearers downed tools and the shearing sheds stood idle and empty. With hundreds of thousands of sheep on its various properties in need of shearing, and quite a few shearers who wanted to carry on as usual, the Elsinora Pastoral Company decided to break the strike by flying in the necessary labour. With the arrival of the first of 33 strike-breaking shearers and their offsiders, the action started. Striking shearers declared Mt Margaret 'black' and provided a noisy picket line, which issued plenty of colourfully phrased and bad-tempered threats, but was kept in check by the presence of the local constabulary.

Invasion of the property was repelled by securely locked gates and by armed boundary riders protecting the fence lines. During the three months it took to shear the sheep, the strike-breakers were kept virtual prisoner on Mt Margaret and I was run off my feet attending to their medical needs.

The hospital was enlarged, overflowing into the main bedroom. Charles's pyjamas were commandeered as I admitted patients with burns, cuts, lacerations, abrasions, torn muscles, fractured wrists, sore backs, severed fingers and concussion. On top of this, there were the usual stomach bugs, coughs and colds. At one stage it looked as if war had broken out and the homestead had become a casualty clearing station.

The medical emergencies that stretched me and my limited resources to the limit were not, as might be expected, the result of punch-ups between the opposing forces, or by violent infighting from cooped-up shearers. The cause was simply inexperience. With the top shearing teams on strike, their replacements were a less-than-competent and rather motley crew, with ages ranging from 15 to 60 or more years. Inexperience, coupled with fast-moving machinery, heavy sheep and sharp equipment, spelt trouble. In the 12 weeks that the shearers were in enforced residence, the sheep were eventually shorn, in a manner of speaking, and I gained enough experience to qualify for a special gilt-edged accident and emergency certificate.

Not long after the strike had been resolved and after 18 years as general manager, Charles decided he needed to move on from Mt Margaret. He was by this time pastoral supervisor for all of Elsinora's Queensland holdings, and did not agree with a company decision to shear the sheep at the height of summer. Rather than go against his principles, he refused to stay at Mt Margaret. However, he did not leave the employ of Elsinora and accepted a transfer to New South Wales to manage Gundaline, a merino stud property near Carrathool on the Murrumbidgee River. We then took long service leave for a year, visiting sheep and cattle holdings all over the world, before returning to the outback and the company's Welltown Station, 40 miles (65 kilometres) to the west of Goondiwindi, between the Macintyre and Weir Rivers. This stud property was one of the oldest and most prestigious in Queensland. For the next two years Charles's time was divided between visiting sheep and cattle studs overseas and completely restructuring the property's management, before we finally severed our ties with the outback and Elsinora.

Foolishly believing that a complete change of direction was in order, in late 1960 we headed for the green pastures of the New England district of New South Wales. We had convinced ourselves that on our own property, surrounded by lush paddocks, fat lambs and permanently running streams, we would become immersed in a new life and forget the vastness of the unique land on which we were reluctantly turning our backs.

CHAPTER 9

Back to the wide brown land

It was useless, of course, just as, deep down, we always knew it would be. Nocoleche, situated on the McDonald River, near Woolbrook, with its pretty verdant surroundings, reminded me of an insipid watercolour, reminiscent of the gentle English countryside. Enveloped in subtle, muted tones, the soft tranquillity only served to underline the dramatic and stark nature of the lusty oil-painting country we had left. The very name of our new property was enough to transport me to another Nocoleche – a large sheep station out on the Paroo, just south of Wanaaring. We had plenty of sheep at our new home – Border Leicesters – but how I missed the depth of colour and the three-dimensional effect of the interior, which looked so empty but was so deceptively alive.

With good medical facilities within reach at Tamworth to the south and Walcha to the north, I had resigned myself to the fact that my nursing days were over. However, I had not counted on the harsh New England winters, which resulted in intensive care nursing of two sick lambs, rescued at the height of a snowstorm. One, which I immediately dubbed 'Lambie', was huddled beside his dead mother. The other, 'Oscar', was just one week old. He was suffering from white muscle disease and had lost the use of his legs.

White muscle disease is caused in winter–spring lambs by a deficiency of selenium, an essential trace element, in the pasture. The situation is aggravated if the ewe is already selenium deficient. Lambs are generally affected from one month of age and the disease results in muscle damage, usually the most active muscles (thigh muscles), which become pale, giving rise to the name.

We put a strong wooden box under some low pine trees near the house, where Lambie was kept warm with bedding and bottles of milk that I delivered at regular intervals. He learned to answer to his name and, when he was strong enough, came running to the kitchen door for his milk as soon as he heard my call. People say that sheep are dumb but, months later, long after he had joined the other sheep in the pasture, all Charles had to do was call and Lambie would bound out of the flock.

Lambie was just an orphan in need of a surrogate mother. Oscar took much more of my time. He was too weak to stay outdoors, even in a warm shelter, so I put him in the laundry where I could keep a close watch on him. For the next three months he was hand fed and given numerous injections in search of a cure, on the advice of the Tamworth vet. I had almost given up hope of his making a recovery when the vet suggested something new. The result was miraculous. Oscar got to his feet and stayed there. However, it was some time before he could lie down and get up again without assistance.

The very fact that I could devote so much of my time to looking after two lambs is a fair indication that Woolbrook was not the most exciting place in the world. It was pleasant enough, but Charles was becoming increasingly restless, with not enough work to keep him occupied physically and not enough challenges to make life interesting. After enduring almost four years of pastoral purgatory, we were at a stud cattle sale at Gunnedah where, by sheer chance, Charles ran into Geoffrey Killen, his former employer and a director of Elsinora Pastoral Company. On learning that we were both missing outback life, he told us to expect a telephone call from his son, Bryce.

That phone call was our salvation. The King Ranch Pastoral Company, a subsidiary of the King Ranch Corporation of America, wanted Charles to manage its latest acquisition – the three million acre (1.2 million hectare) Brunette Downs cattle station on the Northern Territory's Barclay Tableland, a vast savannah grassland between Mt Isa and Darwin.

King Ranch had purchased Brunette in 1958, at the height of a crippling drought. By 1964 the property needed overhauling and the company had advertised widely in an effort to find a competent general manager. Almost 400 applicants had been interviewed and rejected before Charles received his phone call.

Brunette ran Shorthorns and a few Santa Gertrudis cattle, but King Ranch wanted to convert entirely to Santa Gertrudis. Although, being a Shorthorn man, Charles did not have a particularly high opinion of the Santas, he didn't need to be asked twice. Appreciating Brunette's potential and welcoming the challenge, he agreed to meet the managing director and accepted the position on the spot. All I could do was shake my head in wonderment and start packing.

Peter Baillieu, the managing director, set a two-year time limit for Charles to prove his worth. Local cattlemen, however, were not impressed by the appointment. As word circulated that a 'cow cockie' from 'down south', who had spent more time with sheep than cattle, had been given the job of running Brunette Downs, the general consensus was that the newcomer wouldn't last a week.

Leaving Nocoleche in charge of our newly married son and his wife, we headed for Brunette by air. I couldn't wait to return to the outback and it was wonderful to see the look on Charles' face as each mile took us closer to 'home'. As the plane lost altitude and circled the station, I pressed my nose to the window, anxious for the first sight of the enormous holding, which covered 4,500 square miles (7,250 square kilometres).

A prolonged drought had been relieved by welcome rain in January, just three months before our arrival, so there was quite good grass cover. Trees, mainly beefwood, were scattered here and there, along with thousands of termite mounds, many of them well in excess of 6 feet (2 metres) tall. I could also see a few of the 3,000 miles (almost 5,000 kilometres) of graded tracks that criss-crossed the open plains, a racecourse alongside some large stockyards, and a number of the famed turkey's nest dams – an insurance against drought, minimising the distance that cattle had to walk to find water.

However, it was not until we were on the ground that I was able to appreciate the complexity of Brunette, which was more like a small country town than an isolated cattle station. As I walked from the airstrip and across the road to the homestead compound, dark heads popped shyly around the corners and little black faces, topped by unruly black curls, peered from the verandahs and odd recesses of the buildings, only to vanish when I glanced in their direction.

Apart from the spacious homestead, there were quarters for the station hands, the bookkeeper, the schoolteacher, the storekeeper, the veterinarian, the house staff, the pilot, the mechanics, the saddlers and the gardeners. Various other buildings housed the school, sundry storerooms, garages, stables, a general store and large workroom, where a full-time saddler was kept busy making saddles, reins, bridles and every kind of tack imaginable for the station's 1,400 workhorses.

But it was the small hospital that, not surprisingly, caught my attention as this was the first station I had known of to be equipped with medical facilities. It was quite well set up and was staffed – at least in theory – by a general certificated nursing sister. In practice, medical staff didn't stay long and there were often very long periods when no nurse was in attendance.

Brunette Downs homestead

With a fully equipped hospital, hundreds of potential patients and a frequent lack of nursing staff, I realised that there was a very distinct possibility that I would be able to turn my hand to my old job, and looked forward to the prospect with growing enthusiasm.

Fortunately, I did not have to deal with the burden of any household chores, including cooking, although I did like to cook and was said to be quite a good chef. To take care of the routine domestic arrangements was a small army of delightful Aboriginal house girls. They met me for the first time wearing broad smiles and hideously striped uniforms and caps, reminiscent of the days of slavery in the Deep South, a legacy of the previous manager.

The striped dresses and everything they represented were too much for me. A few weeks later, with giggling girls in tow, we made a visit to the station store where the old trappings were abandoned in favour of brightly coloured floral dresses, purchased by the hundred at my request when Charles visited Sydney. A brilliantly hued hibiscus, placed jauntily behind one ear, made the transformation complete. The hated striped numbers were passed on to less fashion conscious family members at the tribal camp.

Brunette Downs was Australia's third largest cattle station, after Alexandria Downs and Wave Hill. When Charles took over at Brunette, it had a population of more than 200, of whom 130 were Indigenous; a quarter horse stud; and 46,102 head of cattle, of which a mere 102 were pure-bred Santa Gertrudis – 100 cows and two bulls. Improvements had been made since its purchase six years before, but the property was still underdeveloped and had yet to reach its potential. With Charles' management expertise and a massive injection of capital, Brunette became the envy of cattlemen the world over.

Additional bores were sunk and the network of innovative turkey's nest raised circular dams extended, so that no beast was more than a day's walk from water. With extensive improvement to facilities, the establishment of a TB/brucellosis testing laboratory, and careful breeding programs that greatly increased the quarter horse stud to 200, the Santa Gertrudis herd from 102 to 4,000 and the commercial herd to 54,000, Brunette Downs became an international showplace.

Shortly after our arrival, Charles revised his poor opinion of Santa Gertrudis cattle, when he realised, first hand, their amazing capacity to withstand the searing heat of the Northern Territory. He was particularly impressed by the way in which the cows protected their newly born offspring. A shorthorn calf unable to get to its feet would literally bake to death on the ground, watched by an indifferent mother; the Santa Gertrudis calf was up within minutes of birth, its survival almost certainly guaranteed by its mother, who used her body to shield her newborn from the sun by creating life-saving shade.

Because of the lack of proper facilities, progress in building the Santa Gertrudis herd was slow at first. The homestead paddocks and yards were the only ones fenced and, as the station hands were required to draft and load cattle for shipment, the breeding program was put on hold until proper facilities had been constructed – a project that took about two years to complete. Once the breeding program got underway, the results were very impressive. Calf brandings shot up from 11,500 to 17,000, eventually averaging out at about 14,000 head a year. Five years later, when the commercial herd numbered more than 50,000 head, there was not one Shorthorn to be found.

While improved stud facilities were important to the property's continuing viability, they paled into insignificance against two other changes Charles introduced. Both were innovative and were to revolutionise the cattle industry in northern Australia.

Prior to his arrival, cattle destined for market in New South Wales and Queensland were walked either all or part of the way from Brunette to their destination. In 1965, realising that these long overland journeys had a detrimental effect on the condition of the cattle, Charles introduced road-train transport. The trial run was so successful that, before long, the station's road trains were transporting cattle to Darwin, Katherine, Wyndham, Alice Springs and the McArthur River. By the end of the 1960s, road trains were the norm, rather than the exception, throughout northern Australia.

Equally important to the development of the beef cattle industry was the establishment of the fully equipped TB/brucellosis laboratory. In 1972, when the cost of testing got out of hand, Charles, who was now the General Manager of all King Ranch holdings in the Northern Territory, came to the conclusion that the time had come to build a fully equipped laboratory and employ a full-time technician.

It was a most prudent move. Prior to the construction of the laboratory, completed in April 1973, cattle had to be yarded, tested and then held in mobs of 1,500–2,000 while blood samples were flown in the company's plane to Alice Springs for analysis – a process that took more than a week. Under the new system, laboratory technician Frank Shiel and his assistant were able to have the results reading within 24 hours. Within four years, the incidence of brucellosis and TB in the commercial cattle herd was down to .05 of one per cent, while the Number 1 stud herd, permanently contained within a 400 square mile (1,000 square kilometre) double-fenced area, was recognised officially as being free of both diseases.

The laboratory and its on-tap technicians were a great boon to me, as Frank was also adept in analysing human blood. He was able to diagnose illnesses on the spot, instead of my waiting many days, enabling me to get on with relevant treatment immediately. This was especially useful as we had a big Aboriginal population, for whom I took responsibility, health-wise.

The camp, about a mile from the homestead on the banks of Brunette Creek, was well run, with individual housing for each family, as well as a communal dining room. All meals were cooked at the homestead's main kitchen and were taken down to the camp at mealtimes. The station's nurse made sure that the children ate first and received adequate helpings. As I had discovered at the Bourke camp, the adults loved their children, but they also loved their tucker, and would wolf down the children's share unless supervised.

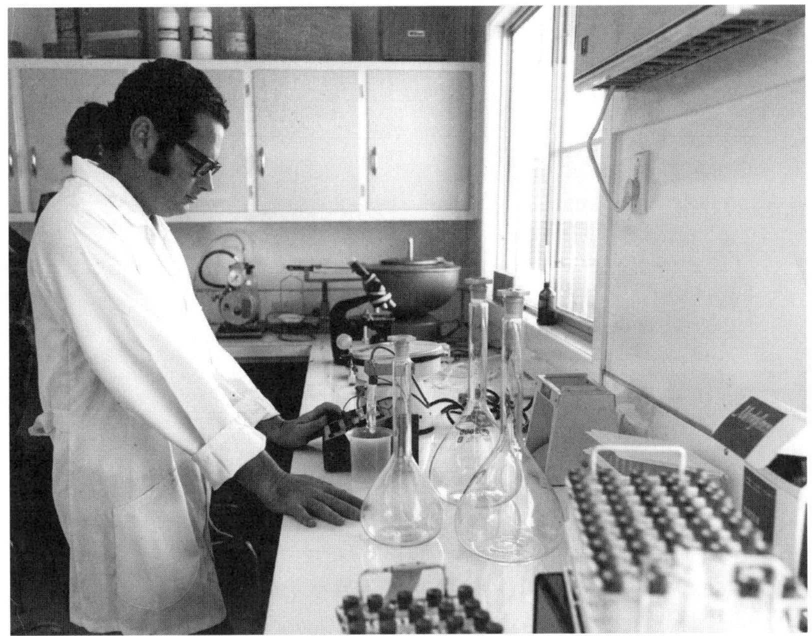

Technician Frank Shiel carrying out tests for brucellosis in the laboratory at Brunette Downs

Apart from the control over food, there was no interference in Aboriginal affairs by the station management. A few of the men worked as stockmen and quite a few women helped in the house, but there was no pressure for them to conform to a European way of life. The tribe was left to pursue and preserve its age-old customs, undisturbed for the most part by outside civilisation. This live-and-let-live approach worked exceptionally well, and it was only rarely that I had to become involve in Aboriginal matters.

One day, the wife of one of the white station workers came to the homestead to ask me to take a look at her small son, Bobby, aged about eight years. He had been playing quite happily with his three Aboriginal friends after school when he suddenly became very sleepy. The station nurse, who had already been consulted, thought that he was simply tired and told the mother not to worry. But being a mother, she continued to worry and came to me for a second opinion.

Taking the station jeep, I made straight for the tribal camp and rounded up Bobby's playmates, two of whom were skylarking in the creek while the other was satisfying his hunger in the dining room. I asked them if they would like to have a ride in the jeep, as I was going back to the house.

'Too right, missus,' they chorused, and scrambled aboard.

Once back at the homestead, I lined them up and said, 'Righto. Which one of you sent Bobby to sleep this afternoon?'

Although my question met with much foot shuffling, no one offered any information. I took a new tack.

'Look at your poor friend Bobby. He's been lying there asleep for two hours while you have been having a lovely time in the creek. Aren't you sad that he's missing out on all the fun? If I could get him to wake up soon, there would be a holiday tomorrow for everyone.'

The prospect of allowing a holiday to slip from their grasp struck the right chord and, after a great deal more foot shuffling, the smallest, shyest boy stepped forward.

'Did you put Bobby to sleep?' I asked. 'How did you do it?'

'It was easy missus. I just made a circle with my finger on his forehead and he went to sleep.'

'Good! Now can you show me how easy it is to wake him up again?'

Without another word, the boy sidled up to the sleeping Bobby and traced a cross on his forehead, muttering a couple of tribal words as he did so. Bobby opened his eyes, stretched and said, 'By jingo. That's the best sleep I've ever had in my life.'

I had no doubt that this was true, because hypnosis has a revitalising but relaxing effect. Fortunately, having been found out, the young hypnotist did not attempt the same trick ever again, although there was plenty of opportunity with all the children mixing freely and happily, day in, day out.

The Aboriginal and European children were taught together in the same little schoolhouse. While at school, the Aboriginal children literally shed their tribal way of life and temporarily entered the world of the white man. Each morning they happily lined up at the bathrooms provided by King Ranch to shower and dress in going-to-school clothes. At the end of the day, with the trials of book learning over, they shucked off their clothes, which were whisked away for washing and ironing, and with yells of delight ran to the creek to once again become children of the bush.

Sometimes, as they made the transition between the two cultures, the children had trouble fathoming the baffling concepts of the white man, especially in the area of religion. One teacher, keen to impress upon her pupils the significance of Christ's crucifixion, had gone to great lengths to reinforce the story, especially the role played by Pontius Pilate.

Convinced that the dramatic events of Easter week must have sunk in, she quizzed the class the following week by asking if anyone could tell her about Pontius Pilate. Attracted by the reward of a half-day holiday for the correct answer, one little girl was emboldened to deliver it, only to be shouted down by a fellow pupil who declared, 'That's not right miss! Pontius Pilate drowned hisself in the Brunette Creek, not long ago!'

There was no disputing this, so the teacher invoked the wisdom of Solomon and gave both children the afternoon off.

On the whole, the Aborigines were quite comfortable with the broad concepts of Western religion, since they themselves believed in an omnipresent being who had watched over them since the Dreamtime – a time so long ago in Aboriginal mythology that it cannot be calculated. One of the most wonderful aspects of my time at Brunette was the tribe's acceptance of me, even to the extent of inviting me to share its rich cultural heritage and hear the Dreamtime stories.

They also showed me their secret tribal places, and explained the special significance of the paintings on the rock walls of the faraway Kimberley region, as well as the sacred and spiritual significance of Uluru – the tourist destination known to Europeans as Ayers Rock. Absorbing this precious knowledge as a sponge absorbs water, I began to understand the gentle tribal folk in a way I had never thought possible. As I trusted them, they learned to trust both me and Charles. Their respect for Charles became so great that, on the death of their tribal elder, King 'Jacky', they took the

King Jacky's gorget

unprecedented step of handing over the title of 'kingship' of the McArthur River tribe to Charles. As a symbol of this high office, they presented him with a brass crescent-shaped breastplate, on which his title had been inscribed as 'King Jacky, of MacArthur River Station'

Also known as king plates, or Aboriginal gorgets, these breastplates were a type of regalia, handed out by the various colonial state governments to recognise those perceived to be leaders. This was an alien concept to Aboriginal people who did not have kings or chiefs, but lived in small groups, led by tribal elders who consulted and made decisions for the group. The McArthur River tribe had decided it was time to put an end to the practice and gave the gorget to Charles. He was greatly humbled by the gesture, and appreciated what the giving and accepting of the breastplate represented. Today, the gorgets are rare collectors' items.

The mutual acceptance we all enjoyed was a rare thing – we were invited to attend special corroborees. They were a major event and it took an entire day for the male members of the tribe to decorate their bodies in the ritualistic and traditional way. Step one was to puncture the skin with a multitude of tiny dots, using a sharp needle or flint. The blood that oozed out was then used as glue to secure a mosaic of small pieces of cotton wool or downy feathers in place. The remaining bare skin, including the face, was filled in with intricate red and yellow ochre patterns, and the whole wonderful 'costume' topped off by the addition of elaborately woven fowl and turkey feathers to create a headdress, bracelets and anklets.

Carrying a fighting stick and a didgeridoo, the magnificently attired warriors made their way to the centre of a large circle, formed by the women who sat cross-legged, clapping their hands and banging their wooden rhythm sticks. For the next hour no one spoke as the men performed ancient tribal dances to the accompaniment of hypnotic chanting which, had I not made myself resist, would have drawn me unprotestingly into the ring by its sheer magnetism.

This close and constant contact gave me a unique opportunity to observe my dark-skinned friends in their day-to-day activities. Corroborees were only a part of tribal life, and there was many a fun-filled goanna hunt, which provided a bit of sport as well as a chance to supplement the white man's tucker.

Men and boys would swarm across the sandy soil following the tell-tale signs of the goanna's tracks, as easily as I would follow a bitumen road. Caught by the tail, the goanna would be stunned by a hefty crack on the head with a nulla-nulla and its fore and rear claws hooked together before being thrown onto the fire. The cooking process didn't take long as the meat was consumed while it was still half raw. They didn't bother to cook the fat, protein-filled witchetty grubs, which were eaten raw, on the spot.

Each year, the Aboriginal station employees were granted leave to go walkabout with the rest of their 'mob'. A walkabout is a spiritual 'time out', providing the opportunity for the tribe to reconnect with nature, rediscover 'country' and perform age-old traditions and rites.

Every year, after Christmas, all members of the tribe disappeared into the bush to a walkabout camp. The elders always selected a site that was near a waterhole, as the walkabout could last two months or more. With most of the station's white staff on annual leave, I was supposed to drive out to the camp site occasionally to check on everyone's health, especially that of the small children, who suffered most from being placed on a sudden and inadequate bush-tucker diet. However, unless there was an extreme emergency, in which case someone would send for me, I left them undisturbed and waited until the tribe returned, usually in dribs and drabs over a few weeks.

I was always overwhelmed by the subsequent need for medical attention, which ranged from burns and scratches to bronchitis and life-threatening illnesses such as severe gastroenteritis. Malnutrition was the most common complaint and the easiest to deal with, unless severe, requiring nothing more than a return to normal rations. Other ailments were trickier, and the widespread habit of pebble poking always ensured that at least one or two children were admitted to hospital for the removal of pebbles that had been stuck in nostrils and ear canals, sometimes for weeks. However, even relatively simple treatments were beyond my capabilities if complicated by input from the medicine man.

One day, a baby with a badly burned foot was brought to the hospital for treatment. After removing the burned skin and carefully cleansing the wound, I applied antiseptic cream and a sterile bandage, instructing the mother to keep the bandage clean and dry and to return the next day to have the dressing renewed. The following morning she arrived bright and early at the clinic door. She had brought the baby with her, but in place of the bandage was a layer of ashes that the witch doctor had applied. The baby was in some distress from the burn, which was red and tender.

I cleaned and dressed the injury a second time, and warned the mother to keep away from the witch doctor. She didn't take a scrap of notice – the witch doctor's magic was greater than mine. I eventually won the battle by sending the child to hospital at Tennant Creek, 250 miles (400 kilometres) away and far from the witch doctor's reach. We flew in the station's Cessna, which was always available if the Flying Doctor was busy or likely to be delayed.

Because of Brunette's isolation and the sheer enormity of the holding, the all-weather landing strip was in constant use. Apart from medical cases, normal transportation requirements for staff, daily aircraft movements of stock, well and fence inspections, and weekly mail and passenger services, there were constant plane arrivals and departures from all over the world, carrying both invited and uninvited guests. Brunette's size, its modern management techniques and its truly 'outback' way of life attracted a steady stream of visitors, many of whom arrived unexpectedly and unannounced. They ranged from cattlemen and government officials, to ambassadors, tourists and royalty. Irrespective of their social status, all were welcomed and accommodated in the guesthouse for the duration of their stay.

Brunette's visitors included the Queen's cousins, Prince William of Gloucester (who came incognito) and the Duke and Duchess of Kent (who didn't), Governors General Lord Casey and Sir John Kerr and their wives, the colourful United States Ambassador Ed Clark, the Netherlands Ambassador, the Administrator of the Northern Territory, senators, state premiers, government ministers and sundry politicians, along with cattlemen from all over the world, including King Ranch Chief, Robert Kleberg, who arrived with an enormous entourage. Guests always wrote to thank me or, if they were quite important people, their secretaries did. One notable exception was Prince William, who penned his letter himself.

At Mt Margaret I had entertained VIP guests, including the Queensland Governor, Sir John Laverack, and his wife so, with the invaluable assistance of the station cook, Bob Foulston, a colourful identity who answered to the name of Pommie Bob, I took these visits to Brunette in my stride. Unexpected visitors, no matter how high up the social pecking order, fazed Pommie Bob not a skerrick. An excellent chef, he was capable of putting on a sumptuous barbecue for 60 at a moment's notice – a talent that was put to good use during Race Week at Brunette, when hundreds of people came in by road and air to join in the festivities that always accompanied the running of the Brunette Cup.

Before we arrived at Brunette, a small plane piloted by a young American adventurer and his friend arrived without warning. The aircraft, a top-of-the range and very expensive Beechcraft Queen Air, was filled with fuel drums, as the plane had flown almost non-stop from the United States. The intrepid travellers were ready to drop with fatigue and slept for two whole days. When they were ready to move on, one of them signed the visitors' book. Name: Rockefeller. Address: New York. Shortly afterwards, the guest, and heir to the Rockefeller billions, disappeared in the jungles of New Guinea.

Michael Rockefeller

The visitors who flew into Brunette in 1961 were Dutch anthropologist René Wessing and his friend, 23-year-old Michael Clark Rockefeller, son of the immensely wealthy Nelson Rockefeller, Governor of New York and later Vice-President of the United States. Both were bound for Dutch New Guinea where they wanted to record the culture and collect the art of the Asmat tribe in a remote area of Dutch New Guinea, now Irian Jaya. On 17 November 1961, the pair was in a 12-metre twin-hulled dugout canoe about 5 kilometres from shore when their boat was swamped and overturned. Two local guides swam for help, which was slow in arriving, leaving the other two clinging to the hull. After drifting for some time – they were about 20 kilometres from land on 19 November – Rockefeller told his companion 'I think I can make it'. He swam towards the shore but was never seen again. Despite a huge search, his body was not found and his fate remains unresolved. Whether he was taken by a shark or crocodile, drowned, or was killed and possibly eaten by hostile tribesmen has never been established. Wessing was rescued the next day. Rockefeller was declared legally dead in 1964.

Another visitor to Brunette while we were there was Elly Beinhorn. It was a return visit for the pioneer German aviatrix, who had landed at Brunette on her flight to Australia in 1932, 35 years previously. She was a friend of Nancy Bird, who had also called in briefly while co-piloting a plane around northern Australia for the Netherlands Ambassador in 1966. I had not seen Nancy, who was now married, since she parted company with Far West.

After losing her job with the Far West in August 1936, Nancy relocated to Cunnamulla in October before taking part in the Brisbane–Adelaide Air Race two months later. In need of an income, the following year she tried to interest the Queensland government in starting up an aerial ambulance, without success. As was the case with New South Wales and the Far West Scheme, the extended Flying Doctor network had made an aerial ambulance service redundant.

Nancy did some charter work out of Cunnamulla, but decided to call it quits in early March 1938 during a flight from Sydney to Goodooga in Queensland. Encountering bad weather over the Blue Mountains, she lost her nerve and had to turn back to Mascot. As she later revealed, 'I never wanted to fly again – not even in a Link trainer, which never leaves the ground.' However, she told the public that she was giving up flying as 'there is no future in the air for women pilots'. Instead she would 'concentrate on commercial ground organisation'. Twenty years later she changed her mind, took flying lessons and renewed her licence to co-pilot a plane in the 1958 air race for women, held in the USA and known as the 'Powder Puff Derby'.

Nancy had close ties with Dutch airline KLM and the Dutch. In late 1938, after she gave up flying, KLM's subsidiary in the Dutch East Indies offered her promotional work and a free flight to Europe. While there, she visited a number of countries before returning to Australia by sea, via America, in July 1939, shortly before the outbreak of war. On board ship she

The crashed Leopard Moth (Geoff Goodall)

met John Walton, known as Charles, a wealthy businessman who worked in his father's importing company. After a whirlwind romance, the pair became engaged in November and married four weeks later. The officiating clergy, in what was a very private ceremony held in Scots Presbyterian Church, Sydney, was the Reverend John Flynn, who had started the Flying Doctor Service.

Before departing overseas on her promotional work, Nancy had sold the Leopard Moth and the hangar at Cunnamulla to local grazier Gordon Young, of Overshot Station, a transaction that left her with a £400 surplus – the exact amount she had saved to buy the Gypsy Moth.

In February 1940, the Leopard's new owner, who had just returned from a flying school in Sydney, was taking his cousin on a late afternoon joy-flight over Cunnamulla when he was forced to make an emergency landing in a paddock near the hospital. The plane's wing hit the ground and the aircraft crashed nose first, killing the pilot and critically injuring his passenger, who was thrown clear on impact. The aircraft was a write-off, but the engine and airframe were later salvaged and sold.

Taking a leaf from George Henderson's book, I had decided that just because we were slap-bang in the middle of the Northern Territory, we didn't have to forgo the niceties of social life. The large, comfortable homestead was beautifully furnished with antique-style furniture so, when we had visitors, everyone dressed for dinner. Nancy must have forgotten that at Urisino this had been normal practice, or had assumed that Brunette Downs was far too far from anywhere civilised to bother, not even in the presence of an Ambassador. Years later, when commenting on her visit, she remarked that tiaras would not have been out of place. I took it as a compliment.

Not all the visitors came for pleasure or to discuss business matters with Charles. In late 1965, a full bench of the Arbitration Commission, whose judgement was to have a great impact on our Aboriginal community, arrived. President Sir Richard Kirby and Mr Justice John Moore, along with senior Commonwealth Conciliation Commissioner James Taylor, had been appointed by the Arbitration Commission to decide if Aboriginal and white stockmen should receive the same rate of pay. As part of that enquiry, Sir Richard adjourned the next stage of the hearing to Brunette.

At the time, a top Aboriginal stockman was paid £12 a week, plus keep. His white equivalent earned £18. However, at Brunette any Aboriginal stockman whose work reached the required standard was paid what he was worth. We had on our books 130 adult Aborigines, of whom only 40 could be described as full-time workers. The rest simply did odd jobs if, and when, they felt like it. The arrangement suited everyone.

I don't know what Sir Richard expected, but he was not too impressed with the type of clothing some of the stockmen wore while at work, and was horrified that, when they went walkabout, they reverted to a simple loin cloth. In defence of the Indigenous workforce, Mr Kerr, QC, stated that Aboriginal stockmen were suitably dressed and generally took great pride in their appearance.

It was not until March the following year that the Arbitration Commission handed down its decision that all employees were to receive minimum award wages. Although this was not to be implemented until the end of 1968, it effectively put an end to the odd-job brigade – a decision that pleased no one, apart from the Commission. Whereas previously any Aborigine who wanted to earn a bit of spare cash could do so on an hour-to-hour basis in return for an agreed sum, the workforce was now restricted to full-time employment at a minimum award wage. The result of the ruling was that, for every Aboriginal 'employee' on Brunette's books, three others would be out of work. Part of Charles' brief was to find a way around the problem of the reduced workforce.

Peter Baillieu had given Charles two years to prove himself, and he did. In his second financial year at Brunette, the station returned a profit of $275,000. In 1968, he was promoted to General Manager of the company, which resulted in his being in Brisbane for a great deal of the time. During this period, we also travelled to Texas to visit the King Ranch headquarters, but in 1972, following problems at Brunette, we were back there permanently. The way we flitted from here to there by jet aircraft with comparative ease made me realise just how far aviation had come since I had taken my first flight with Nancy at Bourke, 30 years before.

Brunette, of course, had its own plane and it was in constant use. Apart from domestic work and ferrying the rich, the important, the famous or the just plain adventurous for jaunts around the station, the aircraft really came into its own at Brunette during the floods of 1973–74.

Situted in an area where summer rainfall was fairly predictable, the property was kept reasonably well watered with an annual rainfall of 16 inches (40 centimetres). However, in the 14 months between January 1972 and March 1974, a total of 63 inches (160 centimetres) of rain fell on the tableland, inundating the flat grasslands. It was later dubbed 'The Big Wet' – and it was.

Normally, when we had heavy rain at Brunette, the outer fringes of the lakes flooded, soaking into the black soil and creating very boggy conditions. Cattle stranded on higher ground had to

The Big Wet, Brunette Downs

stay put until the water evaporated along the roads and ridges, providing a safe path for them to walk to safety.

This time we faced a flood, the likes of which could not be remembered. Fifteen inches (38 centimetres) of continuous rain fell in January 1974, on top of the massive 38 inches (96 centimetres) received the previous year. The outer fringes of the lakes did not dry out and, as the rain continued, water spilled rapidly across the land. The level crept up steadily as the deluge continued until the depth rose to 20 feet (6 metres) above any previously recorded level. In February, the rain-swollen Anthony Lagoon on an adjoining property overflowed into the Brunette Lakes (Sylvester, Corella and De Burgh) to form one vast inland sea of 1,400 square miles (almost a million acres), or almost one-third of the holding. The homestead and most of the station buildings remained out of reach of the floodwaters, along with the nearby airstrip, but only just. Stuck on various patches of high ground in the middle of the lake were 8,000 head of valuable cattle.

Marooned like Robinson Crusoe, they faced certain and slow death from starvation. Normally, they could be walked to safety, and could also be coaxed to swim short distances across deeper water, but it was impossible for stockmen to reach them.

Faced with the loss of thousands of head of valuable stock, Charles decided to use the Cessna to encourage them to move. The first attempt was only partially successful, owing to the difficulty of getting the cattle to budge, let alone make progress. On more than one occasion a mob was coaxed off its island, only to return when the Cessna flew off to refuel.

A new strategy, using the Cessna in tandem with a helicopter, was devised. Since almost every available chopper was on stand-by for emergency rescue work in flood-affected Queensland, one was only obtained with a great deal of difficulty. While the helicopter encouraged small mobs of cattle to move from higher ground into the water, the Cessna coordinated a path by radioing advice about obstacles and very boggy fringe areas. This approach, although slow, was successful, resulting in 5,000 head reaching safety.

A further 3,000, which could not be transferred to dry land without a very long swim, were moved in small batches to three large islands within the lake. Losses during these exercises, which took about four hours to complete, were practically nil. Although the young calves had to swim most of the time, they were able to take a rest by leaning on the sides of older cattle. We also managed to get hold of a couple of aluminium dinghies fitted with outboard motors, which helped considerably.

However, in February, rising water levels diminished the size of the island refuges alarmingly. Unless 900 cows and calves now on the island closest to the shore were moved, all would starve. An attempt to wade out 100 head across 4 miles (6 kilometres) of shallower water was a dismal failure. The ground beneath the floodwaters was so boggy that, after 400 yards (365 metres), the leaders turned and the mob was left to flounder its own way back to firm ground.

A further attempt to move a herd from the other end of the island across a three-mile stretch of water appeared at first to also be doomed to failure. Although the cattle started out well enough, the helicopter was not able to push the tail-enders along fast enough, or to keep the leaders from drifting in the wrong direction.

However, while the helicopter was refuelling, the mob split into two sections, and on its return the rescue team was astounded to discover that, far from being exhausted, about half the cattle were swimming strongly in the direction of dry land, while the remainder were floating on their sides or making their way back to the island. Sixty eventually reached the shore unassisted, after swimming about four miles (6 kilometres) – a distance previously thought to be impossible.

By throwing their heads back along their flanks, the cattle had floated like enormous balloons, their air-filled stomachs providing the necessary buoyancy. The realisation that they could float for days at a time, and also swim long distances, meant that the rest of the stranded herds could be saved, provided they could be shepherded in the right direction. Employing two helicopters and the outboard dinghies to round the stock up, and the Cessna to supervise, the team was able to encourage the beasts to move in groups of about 250 from one island to the next by using a combination of swimming, floating and drifting to cover the distance. The 50 head that were too timid to enter the water were kept alive by fodder drops.

This innovative move did not go unnoticed, and media attention was substantial, especially when journalists sent back footage and photographs showing the rescue teams at work and a homestead surrounded by floodwater as far as the eye could see. Charles, dubbed 'The General' by the press, had reason to be satisfied. For an outlay of $33,000, all but 50 of the 8,000 cattle marooned by the Great Flood had survived.

By the time Charles retired in 1976, he had become one of Australia's most respected cattlemen. Accolades poured in, as government officials, agricultural experts and cattlemen worldwide paid tribute to the enormous services he had made to the cattle industry. Recognised as an expert in the control and eradication of TB and brucellosis, he had also become renowned for his excellent and progressive management techniques, which resulted in Brunette owning one of the nation's largest and finest Santa Gertrudis herds.

In 12 short years, the cow cocky from down south, who wouldn't last a week, had made Brunette Downs the jewel in the crown.

The floodwaters dropped, but did not disappear for many months, creating a massive wildlife refuge. Land that had once been semi-desert, supporting kangaroos, emus, rabbits and the like, had miraculously turned into wetlands, filled with freshwater prawns and fish that attracted a vast number and variety of birds, including tens of thousands of pelicans.

Some of the station hands built boats and spent long hours fishing in waters up to 25 feet (8 metres) deep. Others, who were keen ornithologists, kept a record of the birds they saw, with one stockman reporting 175 different species.

As life gradually returned to normal, and the days once more merged into weeks, and the weeks into months, I suddenly realised that time was running out and we were staring retirement in the face. As the inevitable countdown began, I tried to impress upon my memory the incredible beauty of a land that would soon be lost to us.

On the morning of what would be our last day, 31 October 1976, I decided that keeping busy was the only way to cope. To take my mind off it, I had intended to keep myself occupied with packing up various goods and chattels, but all that went by the board when a medical emergency arose.

It was shaping up to be a scorcher of a day. As I sauntered from the shade of the verandah and onto the lawn, I could see that a recently engaged gardener from down south was looking decidedly unwell. Aware that he might not yet be acclimatised to the hot daytime temperatures of the Territory, I suggested that he take it easy for a while. Stalwart that he was, he insisted he would be fine and after a few minutes' rest returned to his work.

Shortly afterwards, the station nurse came running in to commandeer the Cessna for an emergency evacuation. The new gardener, she said, had suffered a heart attack. I examined him but, as I couldn't detect any symptoms to support her diagnosis, suggested that heatstroke might be the problem. She insisted it wasn't and, as she was technically in control, she had the last word. Bundling the gardener into the plane, she left me to get on with my packing.

The aircraft had barely taken off when I heard the most enormous commotion outside, along with a most insistent hammering on the front door and cries of 'Missus! Missus! Can you hear? Come quick. Someone burnt bad.' As I streaked across the lawn to the clinic, it seemed that half the station's population was crowded inside the building, while the remainder were squeezed onto the verandah.

I soon saw why. One of the stockmen had been enveloped in fire while filling a gas container. Although still conscious, he was dreadfully burnt. Clearing the sightseers, I cut away his charred clothing while Helen, my unflappable personal assistant, soaked sheets in cold water and supervised the brewing of pints of sweet, weak tea. I managed to coax him to drink a fair amount of it before giving him a shot of pethidine to sedate him and ease his excruciating pain.

It was obvious that he would not survive unless I could get him to hospital for specialist treatment, but the Cessna, now on its way to Tennant Creek with the alleged heart attack victim, was now out of radio range. The closest Flying Doctor was at Alice Springs. For the 90 minutes that it took the plane to arrive, I could do no more than continue with the cold water and pethidine treatment and pray that it would not be too late. Fortunately, it wasn't, but the burns were so severe that the stockman spent the next eight weeks in hospital.

By the time I cleaned up the clinic, the station aircraft had returned from Tennant Creek, along with an astonishingly healthy gardener, who had not suffered a heart attack but had succumbed to the tropical heat. For once in my life I bit my tongue, deciding that on this occasion silence was golden.

If nothing else, the day's dramas had taken my mind off the emotion-filled hours that were to come, as I toured the homestead and the station buildings to make my farewells. The most poignant goodbye was saved until last when, as darkness fell like a velvet cloak, we made our way to the tribal camp to sit with our adopted family for the last time. Drawn into the centre of a large ring, formed by 150 Aboriginal friends, I spent the next hour seated on a large rock while our hosts talked of the Dreamtime, of their beliefs older than time itself, of the ancient tribal ways now lost forever and of their hopes for the future. As I sat, surrounded by people whose culture predated all other civilisations, I knew that, no matter how far I might be physically removed from the land and its people, my heart would belong in the outback.

As the plane circled the station early the following morning, I could see them all, tears rolling down dusky upturned faces as their voices called in a continuous unbroken rhythm, like an ancient and ritualistic lament, 'Ba de bah – come back soon'. With my own tears spilling unchecked down my cheeks, memories of a varied and most wonderful life came flooding back – the pesky goats at Pallamallawa, the 'Flying Santa' Christmases, the outback medical tours, the frisky driver, the hair-raising flights with difficult patients, the happy days at Manly with the Far West children, the clumsy learner shearers at Mt Margaret, the wonderful years at Brunette and, finally, the indomitable spirit of the outback people, which had enveloped and sustained me from the first day I set foot on the dusty streets of Bourke.

I knew that I had been blessed with a richness of life and had experienced a sense of fulfilment known to only a few, ever since that day so long ago when, in fear and trepidation, it had fallen my lot to be the first to play the piano for the music examiner. The failure to keep my nerves in check had been the turning point in my life. As the plane dipped its wings in final salute and I brushed away the tears to catch a final glimpse of all those whom I had grown to love, I had the most intriguing thought.

What would have happened if I hadn't drawn the short straw?

EPILOGUE

Aftermath

After leaving Brunette Downs, Aunty Bid moved to Brisbane, but in the early 1980s relocated to the Sydney beachside suburb of Mona Vale. It was here that she decided to take sister Jean's advice and supplement her diet with bran, which led inadvertently to the writing of this book.

Sister Silver and babies celebrate the 75th Anniversary of the establishment of Baby Health Centres

It was not until 1988, the bicentenary of white settlement in Australia, that she received any public acknowledgement for a lifetime spent serving the people of the outback. Using some of the information she had given to me, supplemented by other research, I nominated her in response to a nationwide quest to find 200 unsung heroes and heroines, sponsored by the Bicentennial Authority and the National Library of Australia.

Sister Silver's story was one of those chosen from many thousands of entries. An account of her work with the Far West was included in 200 Unsung Heroes and Heroines of Australia, *an official bicentennial publication. For some years afterwards, a copy of this inspiring book was presented to all those being honoured with special bravery awards.*

Her story was also featured nationally in the Australian Women's Weekly, *as well as in the press. To commemorate the 75th anniversary of the establishment of Baby Health Clinics, she was photographed in one of her beautiful hand-knitted creations, cuddling two babies on her lap. When questioned by the reporter about the difficulties she had faced at Bourke, she replied, 'It was no picnic, but I couldn't get there fast enough.'*

A reception was held at Government House, Sydney, to launch the book and to present special medals to those whose stories were featured. Aunty Bid was not well at the time, so I accepted the award on her behalf from Governor Sir James Rowland. It was the first time that she had ever received any recognition.

I also nominated her in another special Bicentennial project, 'Women 88', aimed at identifying outstanding Australian women who had made a significant contribution to the nation. Unlike other awards, this one was designed to salute women whose achievements were significant, but relatively unknown; whose contributions were unrecognised outside their own communities or circle of friends.

It was tailor-made for Aunty Bid. Never one to seek the limelight or blow her own trumpet, this quiet achiever had simply got on with the job, when the job needed doing. Although it had been reward enough for her to know that she had made a real difference to the lives of so many outback people, I knew that she found Nancy's take on events annoying at times. Rising above it, she had maintained a dignified silence over the years, never publicly attempting to correct misconceptions that had arisen and, thanks to the internet, persist to this very day.

From more than 1200 entries to 'Women 88', Sister Silver was one of 10 to receive a major award. Her fellow recipients at a glittering presentation dinner in Melbourne in December that year included nuclear activist Helen Caldicott, solo round-the-world sailor Kay Cottee, legal activist Jocelyn Scutt, environmentalist Christine Milne, Aboriginal activist Betty Colbung, advocate for the ordination of women Patricia Brennan and humanitarian Helen Moyes. Special commendations went to 10 others, which included the well-known Olympic sprinter, Marjorie Jackson.

Women 88 finalists. Sister Silver is on the far right, front row. The author is in the back row, 2nd from the right.

The 20 prize-winners were all presented with a stunning ebony and gold-leaf commemorative brooch, designed by artist Diane Appleby. Each major award winner was also invited to commission a valuable artwork from leading Australian artisans. To make it a little easier, various examples were on display. Given that Aunty Bid was a most accomplished knitter, a skill she claimed was honed by many long hours spent in the air, and also her love of fashion, I was not surprised by her choice: it was wearable art – a simple, long-line but very elegant dress, hand woven from fine Merino wool in a design and colours inspired by the outback she loved so much.

Aged 78, Aunty Bid was by far the oldest of the group. Still tall and slender, she was dressed for the gala black-tie occasion in a long gold-coloured gown. When her name was called and her lifetime of service read to the audience, she moved regally to the stage, using an ebony cane topped with a gold knob to steady her. As she mounted the podium to accept her award, the last and most prestigious to be presented, the huge crowd rose to its feet to give her a tremendous standing ovation. It was her first and last public appearance. Plagued by continuing ill health, she died in June 1991, shortly after her 81st birthday.

Charles, her devoted husband of 53 years, died two years later, at the age of 86. They were survived by their son, Tony, and two grandchildren.

While Sister Silver was fighting a battle against the harsh elements and isolation of the Far West, another dedicated woman of about the same age had graduated as a nursing sister, with a view to longed-for overseas travel. Little did she know that she would shortly embark upon a sea voyage to the exotic Far East, where she would engage in a battle for survival as an unwilling guest of the Emperor of Japan.

ANGEL OF MERCY

FAR EAST

PROLOGUE

I first met Pat Gunther on Anzac Parade in Canberra in February 1997. As honorary historian to the 8th Australian Division Association, I was representing the members at a ceremony to dedicate a site for the construction of a memorial to honour all Australian nurses who had served in war. Pat, who had enlisted in 8 Division in WW2, was one of them. On 2 October 1999, many months later, we both returned for the dedication of the completed memorial, built at a cost of more than $2 million. The nurses had been waiting a long time – since September 1945, when the idea of a national memorial was first floated.

Following the ceremony, a number of the surviving nursing sisters from 8 Division attended a reception. After serving in Malaya and Singapore, many had become prisoners of the Japanese, including the well-known Vivian Bullwinkel, sole survivor of a massacre, and Lorna Whyte, the last nurse still alive of a group of six, who had served in Rabaul, on the island of New Britain, before being captured.

The 8 Division nurses sat in a group, and I was invited to join them. I had met one of their colleagues many years before and the nurses, aware that I knew a great deal about the war in the Far East, especially prisoners of war, spoke very freely about their experiences – or at least one of them, Lorna, did. I had the distinct impression that those who had spent their captivity on the Indonesian island of Sumatra were holding something back. In fact, they said as much, with Pat and her friend, Wilma Oram, candidly admitting that there were some incidents that they had agreed never to talk about. Knowing that there was a conspiracy of silence was intriguing, but it would be some years before enough pieces of the jigsaw fell into place for me to work out what their secret might be.

Since 1997, I had met Pat at various prisoner of war (POW) functions, but I did not learn of her story in detail until early 2000, when she invited me to her retirement apartment in Mosman, a northern harbourside suburb of Sydney. She handed me an account of her experiences and asked me to appraise it for her, saying that life in a POW camp was very tedious and that the story might be too boring to be of interest.

The story was far from boring, and deserved to be told, but it was not substantial or detailed enough to make it commercially viable. However, with additional material elicited from our further conversations, and with my input as a third-person narrator, I realised it would be an interesting companion piece to the story of Sister Silver – the outback's first permanent flying sister, who fought a battle of a different kind against isolation and harsh conditions in the remote north-western regions of New South Wales. Pat agreed. She provided further details to expand her story, and gave me free rein to edit her original narrative.

However, the project did not reach fruition for another 20 years. Pat's original memoir, supplemented with details that came to light during our conversations and other in-depth interviews, now forms the basis of the story of Sister Gunther, an army nurse who went to war.

CHAPTER 1

To Malaya

It was 1937. I was 23 years old and had just gained my general nursing certificate at Sydney's Royal Prince Alfred Hospital, generally known as RPA. I don't quite know why I decided to be a nurse. I had a variety of interests and my mother always wanted me to write. That's all she ever said to me, 'Write child, write.' I told her that I didn't have the educational background, but she insisted that I could write very well, and that it was what I should do. As a teenager, I had sent contributions to the *Bulletin* magazine, which had a couple of pages devoted to local events or issues, described by the editor as 'Aboriginalities'. I also sent items to *The Sydney Mail* to earn a bit of pocket money, but I can't remember much about it now.

In 1924, a few days after Pat's 11th birthday, she had the following item published in the children's section of the Sydney Mail.

> I have always liked the frilled lizard, and was very proud of myself years ago when I first learned his name — chlamydosaurus. A reason why I was inclined to make a pet of him, too, was because his tail was not so liable to come off if touched. 'Chlamy's' tail is quite firmly fastened on; but don't pull it; it makes him feel fearfully vexed. I know he eats hairy caterpillars, and is a good, harmless fellow, though he does pull faces. There is no name for little lizards unless we invent one; they are neither chickens, cubs, kittens, nor tadpoles. Next time I find a little one I think I'll call it a 'Lizette.'

By the age of 14, Pat had progressed to inventing puzzles for the newspaper, described as 'clever', and children under the age of 17 were invited to solve them. A certificate was awarded to the girl or boy with the neatest and best entry.

Writing was something that my mother should have done because she really could write quite well. Dad had been a journalist at one stage in his life and, if they'd left me alone, I might have become a writer. However, writing is a precarious way to make a living and I felt that training for some kind of a profession was important. There were not a lot of openings for a country girl who had left school at the end of primary, so I decided to follow in the footsteps of my sister, who was training to be a nurse at Sydney Hospital.

However, when I announced at the age of about 16 or 17 that I also wanted to be a nurse, one of my aunts, who had studied medicine and had been a resident doctor at RPA, said 'Well there's only one hospital for you to go to, and that's the Prince Alfred.' A great admirer of the Royal Family and a proud member of the Empire, as were we all, she told me that the hospital had been named in honour of one of Queen Victoria's sons, Alfred, Duke of Edinburgh, who was shot while on a royal tour.

During the royal visit of 1868, Prince Alfred, the second son of Queen Victoria, was attacked at a picnic at Clontarf beach, on Sydney's Middle Harbour. The would-be assassin was Irish-Australian Henry James O'Farrell, who professed to be Fenian. Before he was overpowered, a determined O'Farrell fired a second shot into the foot of an unfortunate onlooker. However, all attention was on the Prince, who was evacuated on HMS Morpeth *to Government House. Two days later the bullet was extracted by a ship's surgeon, using a gold probe.*

Mortified by the attack on their royal visitor, the citizens of Sydney attended public meetings, where it was resolved to construct a hospital as a thanksgiving for the recovery of the Prince. The University of Sydney Senate granted a parcel of land from the Grose Farm estate and, in September 1882, Royal Prince Alfred Hospital opened with 146 beds.

The hospital, which became the teaching hospital for Sydney University, quickly expanded in physical size and status. The course offered to trainee nurses in the 1930s was a four-year general training syllabus, similar to that provided by most other hospitals at the time. Pat was one of 27 from RPA to pass her final exams for a general nursing certificate in November 1936.

I had left school at the age of 13 to help out at home. Although I didn't have my Intermediate Certificate or indeed any secondary school education, it was possible in those days to take up nursing by sitting for a nurses' entrance exam. I didn't find it at all difficult and in 1933 I began my training when I turned 19.

The day was broken into shifts, ranging from four to eight hours, with time off in between, or a straight stretch of 12 hours. Probationers had one and a half days off a week but had to attend lectures in off-duty time. We were rotated between wards about every three months, and I started off in the children's ward. One of my first tasks was to give a bedpan to a little girl, a cheeky little red-headed thing aged about 9 or 10. She was suffering from a terminal lung abscess and was terribly spoilt. I had never been in hospital myself, so had never seen a bedpan before and gave it to her the wrong way round. She looked at the bedpan, turned it around and said, 'This is the way you do it, nurse.' After a couple of weeks, I had a good relationship with her, but shall never forget the humiliation of that first introduction.

As a junior probationer, I was allowed to do only the simplest things for the first 12 months – taking temperatures; delivering, collecting and washing out bedpans; cleaning out bedside lockers; making beds with hospital corners; giving sponge baths and learning how to make patients comfortable. Humdrum stuff. Probationers rarely did so much as a dressing until their second year.

As the Depression neared its end, wards that had been closed due to lack of funding were reopened and trainee nurses whose competence was considered to be above average were pushed ahead. I was in this group and, consequently, half-way through third year, I was doing fourth year work. I worked as a head nurse for two terms in third year and four terms in my final year, which included night duty.

Matron and the deputy matron visited each ward each day. They expected a high level of nursing care, with beds and patients immaculate. We also had to be on our toes, ready to answer questions about the treatment of patients in our care.

Although RPA was a large city hospital, I was not a city girl by any means and it took a bit of adjustment living with a lot of people in the Nurses' Home. I was raised on a farm and my entire childhood was spent in the bush, riding horses, playing tennis and enjoying a simple life. When I left school, I helped my mother at home. I did very little around the actual farm – occasionally a little bit of milking or something like that.

My mother's roots were Scottish, but my great-grandfather on my paternal side was of German descent – with a name like Gunther he could hardly be anything else. He was actually Lutheran, but was ordained as a priest in the Church of England and eventually became an archdeacon. His son, my grandfather, who also entered the C of E priesthood, went to England, where he studied at Oxford. After completing his MA and Doctor of Divinity, he came home and married an English woman. He served for many years as rector of St John's Parramatta, and was also an archdeacon. Evidently two archdeacons in the family were enough, for my father did not follow in their footsteps. Instead he took up farming, and not very successfully.

Janet Patteson Gunther, known as Pat, was born on the family dairy farm in the Hogarth Ranges near Piora, 14 kilometres to the west of Casino, on 31 August 1913. She was named for her aunt and her father, Arthur Patteson Theo Gunther. Pat was one of eight children, four boys and four girls (William, Thomas, Philip, Kenneth, Meg, Pamela, Sybil and Pat), born to Arthur and his wife Jane. Pat attended local primary schools at Mongogarie and Deep Creek.

Despite being a German Lutheran, Pat's great-grandfather James, who had a strong vocation for missionary work, joined the Church of England. After training at the C of E's Missionary Society College in London, he was ordained in 1836 and came to Australia, where he worked at an Aboriginal mission near Wellington before taking up the post of Rector at Mudgee, where he remained until his death in 1879, by which time he was an archdeacon.

His son (Pat's grandfather), William James Gunther, was born on the mission station in 1839. A Broughton Scholarship from the Anglican Church enabled him to study Classics and Divinity at Oxford. He was ordained in England, but returned to Australia in 1866 to take up the post of Curate at Sydney's historic St Philip's Church, Church Hill, before becoming priest at the equally historic St John's Parramatta. He remained there for 42 years and was closely associated with The King's School, an exclusive Anglican boys' college noted for its military-style uniform. William declined several senior posts, including two bishoprics, but was appointed Archdeacon and Vicar General of Sydney Diocese.

My mother had plenty of wealthy relatives, but my father was hopeless with money and it was an embarrassment. We led a simple life, but certainly not one where there was very much money. I had a difficult time as a child because it wasn't the sort of situation into which you could invite friends.

Mum considered being well bred more important than anything else in life. Nothing compared. Her father, a member of the squattocracy and a magistrate, was James Thomson, who lived at Burrier House on a family property on the upper reaches of the Shoalhaven River on the New South Wales south coast. He was the first parliamentary representative of the St Vincent electorate, but served only one term as he found the travelling from Burrier to Sydney too difficult. My mother, Jane, was directly descended from Mary Reibey, an emancipated convict, who received the land at Burrier as a grant from the Crown.

Many Australians whose forebears had arrived in the early days of the colony had a convict ancestor – a fact that families often tried to keep secret. However, my mother and I were proud of our connection to Mary Reibey, one of the few convicts who became famous – famous enough to be featured on the Australian $20 banknote.

Mary was born Molly Haydock, in the town of Bury, Lancashire, in 1777. Raised by her grandmother after the death of both parents, she went into service as a housemaid. However, at the age of 13, she ran away. Masquerading as a boy by the name of James Burrow, she was found guilty of horse stealing and transported to New South Wales for seven years. On arrival in Sydney in 1792, Molly was assigned as a nursemaid to Major Grose, of the New South Wales Corps, on whose land, 90 years later, RPA Hospital would be built.

Two years after her arrival, at the age of 17, Molly (now Mary) married a junior officer with the East India Company, Irishman Thomas Reibey, whom she had met on the transport ship. Thomas, a successful businessman, also owned numerous farms. He died in 1811, leaving Mary to raise their seven children.

She proved to be a canny businesswoman, opening a new warehouse the following year and then extending her trading fleet with the purchase of two more ships. By 1816, her business concerns were valued at £20,000, or almost $700,000 in today's money. A founding member of the Bank of New South Wales, she was welcomed into the Governor's social circle and was highly respected, despite her humble origins. Using her status and influence, she tackled education and social issues, and was appointed as governor of the Free Grammar School in 1825.

She died in Newtown, Sydney, in 1855, shortly after her 78th birthday. One of her daughters,

Eliza, married Thomas Thomson. Their grand-daughter, Jane Eileen Thomson, was Pat's mother. This relationship allowed Pat to proudly claim the feisty Mary Reibey as her great-great grandmother.

We were fairly poor but at least, being on a farm, we had plenty to eat. During the Depression, men would drop in to see if they could have a bed and a meal for the night. Attached to the barn was a room with an iron-framed bed and also a small shower room, normally used by farm workers. We couldn't afford to have paid labour during the Depression, but when these sad men shuffled in, they were always given a meal and a bed. Next day, after breakfast, they would pay for their board by chopping a pile of wood.

I was the fourth child in the family. I was only about five months into my nursing training when my mother died at the age of 53. Fortunately, I was able to continue with my studies as my elder sister, who had her nursing certificate, went home to look after the house and Dad and the boys. The two little girls went off to boarding school in Sydney. By the time I finished training, my elder sister had married and had a household of her own, but Pam, my younger sister, who had left school, was quite happy to stay home, allowing me to continue with my nursing.

After passing my final exams, I joined the Nurses' Club – an organisation that helped registered nurses find suitable positions in the private nursing sector. Private nursing would be a useful string to add to my bow, I thought, and one that would help me obtain employment if I worked overseas. I had always harboured thoughts of travelling to England one day, and figured that the extra experience would be a definite plus.

The Nurses' Club was in Sydney's Potts Point, one of the most vibrant parts of the city. Although much of it, as Kings Cross, would become Sydney's most notorious red-light district and home to numerous underworld figures, in the thirties it was the city's most cosmopolitan suburb. Situated on the southern shores of the harbour, a stone's throw from Woolloomooloo and the nearby Garden Island Naval Base, it was an eclectic mix of grand homes, naval establishments, stylish apartments, Victorian terraces and down-at-heel tenements. Macleay Street, the main thoroughfare, was a pleasant tree-lined boulevard leading down to the harbour foreshore, while nearby Darlinghurst Road was dotted with numerous flower shops, small boutiques and cafés. There was also a charming interior design studio, run by Margaret Jay, who looked like a piece of Dresden china.

In September 1939, I was only into my second year of self-employment when war broke out in Europe. I was nursing a doctor's wife at Dover Heights in Sydney's eastern suburbs at the time. Because of the Nazi purges, at the end of the 1930s quite a number of refugees, particularly Jewish, started to arrive in Sydney. Most settled in the eastern suburbs, in Rose Bay and Bellevue Hill, so much so that to racist (and very politically incorrect) Sydneysiders, Rose Bay became Nose Bay and Bellevue Hill, Belljew Hill.

I had a reasonable grasp of the political situation in Europe as I had read two very insightful books on the subject. One was by John Gunther, an American and no relation, who wrote *Inside Europe*. The other was Douglas Reed's *Insanity Fair*.

So, with Europe on a war footing, any thought of travelling to England was clearly impossible, but the upside was that there was plenty of work about. Besides taking on private patients, I worked at nearby Gemma Private Hospital and in a private wing of St Vincent's Hospital known as Gloucester House, as well as doing 'special' nursing at St Luke's.

Christmas of 1939 came and went. When the war was not over by then, as so many had confidently predicted, and with the army actively recruiting nurses, I decided to put my name down for enlistment. I qualified age wise, as the minimum age was 25, and had the necessary experience, which was also mandatory. At that time, the Australian Army Nursing Service (AANS), formed when the Great War broke out, was the only women's military nursing service.

> *The Royal Australian Air Force didn't establish its nursing arm (RAAFNS) until 1940, and the Royal Australian Navy (RANNS), not until 1942. Some 4,000 nurses served in World War 2. However, the AANS was by far the largest and made up the bulk of those who went overseas.*

At the urging of a friend, the first person I had met when I enrolled at RPA, I put my name down at the nearest recruiting office, which was at the colonial sandstone army base on Oxford Street, Paddington (known as Victoria Barracks). I don't quite know why we did it – we just thought it was the correct thing to do. I then left for a new assignment in the country.

I was still out of town when the phone call came to tell me to report for duty, so I missed my first call-up. My friend was already in the army when I returned and encouraged me to contact the recruiting depot and find out if we could be together, but I am a bit superstitious and thought it might be tempting fate. So I let it ride, and on 27 November 1940 I finally received my second call. After a satisfactory interview with Matron, I was given a week or so to get my equipment and uniforms together, before leaving Sydney on 7 December.

Pat Gunther in uniform

I had been posted to a base-camp hospital at Tamworth, a rich farming area on the Liverpool Plains of New South Wales. The work wasn't hard because seriously ill patients went to Tamworth Hospital. As the soldiers were physically fit, most of my patients were suffering from a reaction to smallpox vaccinations and typhoid and tetanus injections. While a few had a very bad reaction to the smallpox vaccine, resulting in a high fever, most of them were not really sick. Of course, the nursing sisters also had bad reactions, but they stayed on duty!

Experience had shown that, when a line of soldiers was waiting for an injection, there was a tendency for one to faint, which could start a chain reaction. So the usual practice was to vaccinate the nurses first. When we came out rubbing our arms, the men would say to each other, 'There you are, you see. She didn't faint so you're not allowed to.'

Although most other nursing duties were confined to relatively minor injuries and illnesses, such as ingrown toenails caused by long route marches, working at the base camp was a good introduction to army life. I volunteered to stay on duty over Christmas, and so had 14 days' leave in the New Year.

On my return to Tamworth, I was rostered on night duty and was only about two hours into my shift when, at around 10 pm, I was told I had been recalled to Sydney and was to catch the midnight train. I managed to report as ordered and learned that I had been posted to 2/10 Australian General Hospital, generally known as 2/10 AGH, which was going overseas.

When the 2nd AIF was formed, it was decided to recycle the numbers assigned to WW1 units, preceded by the numeral 2, instead of following on chronologically for WW2. Consequently, 10 AGH from WW1 became 2/10 AGH. However, if the WW2 units surpassed the WW1 numbers, the 2 was dropped. As there was no 113 AGH in WW1, the WW2 unit was simply 113 AGH. The same rule applied to a unit that had no forerunner, such as an anti-tank regiment, there being no anti-tank units in WW1.

As I had already had my injections, I only needed a chest X-ray before being given pre-embarkation leave. Where I was going the army didn't say, but my expectation and hope was that it would be to North Africa, where my brother was serving at Tobruk. At that stage, there was no clue whatsoever that our destination would be Singapore.

Up until 1941, all focus had been on the war in Europe and the Middle East, where Australians had taken up the fight with British forces against the Germans and Italians. However, when the Japanese, the third partner in the Axis tripartite pact, occupied French Indo-China on 22 September 1940, attention was diverted much closer to home – to the Far East.

Britain's defence of this region was centred on Singapore Island and the 'Singapore strategy' – the heavily defended naval base, from which warships would be dispatched should there be any threat to British interests in the area – Malaya, British Borneo, Australia and New Zealand.

Twenty-seven strategically placed guns, ranging from 15 to 37 centimetres in calibre, protected the approaches to the naval base from the sea, making a seaborne assault impossible. There were also four airfields – two near the naval base, one at Tengah in the north-west and the other just to the east of the city at Kalang.

According to one enthusiastic journalist, reporting for the Sydney Morning Herald, *there were 'more guns on Singapore Island than plums in a Christmas pudding'. Hailed as 'the Gibraltar of the East', this 'bastion of British might' was considered to be impregnable, with its giant guns and air power repelling any attempt at invasion from the sea, while any assault from the land was regarded as impossible. Protecting Singapore's back door was Malaya – steamy, inhospitable, mountainous, jungle-covered, impenetrable Malaya.*

Although concerns were raised about Singapore's security, Britain's Prime Minister Winston Churchill shouted down the 'alarmists'. Time and again he expounded his belief that the island was impregnable, safe through the awesome firepower of its guns and further defended by the 'splendid broad moat' that surrounded it.

Australia and New Zealand were not nearly as complacent. Under the 'Singapore Strategy', they had agreed to assist Britain in time of war by sending troops to Europe in return for the promised naval protection. With almost all their trained troops earmarked for service in Europe and the Middle East, the two countries believed they were now vulnerable to attack. However, Churchill constantly reassured them that war with the Japanese was virtually beyond the realms of possibility.

In December 1939, he had declared that 'Singapore is a fortress armed with five fifteen-inch guns and garrisoned by almost 20,000 men. It could only be taken after a siege by an enemy of at least 50,000 men . . . such a siege would be liable to be interrupted if at any time Britain chose to send a superior fleet to the scene . . . It is not considered that the Japanese would embark on such a mad enterprise.'

However, by June 1940, the goalposts had shifted. The war in Europe was not going well. France fell, Italy entered the fray and the British Expeditionary Force was evacuated from Dunkirk. With the collapse of France, it was now highly unlikely that any naval force could be sent to Singapore.

When Churchill, in Britain's bleakest hour, declared, 'We shall not flag or fail. We shall fight on the beaches. We shall fight on the landing grounds. We shall fight in the fields and in the streets. We shall fight in the hills. We shall never surrender', the British defence chiefs faced up to the fact that Britain was now fighting for survival. Dispatching a fleet to defend the Far East was a pipe dream. If it came to all-out war, the whole of Malaya would have to be held by air and ground forces. To do this, many more troops and planes would be needed. But who would supply them?

Australia had already committed No. 1 Squadron RAAF and its 12 Hudson bombers. In response to a further plea, Australian Prime Minister Robert Menzies announced that another two squadrons would be provided – 12 Hudsons from No 8 (General Reconnaissance) Squadron and No 21 Squadron's single-engine, Australian-made Wirraways, used mainly for training.

But it was still not enough. Another 336 aircraft, at least, were needed. Two additional infantry divisions were also required, along with a third until the Air Force reached its required strength.

Pressure was put on Australia. After much deliberation, the government offered to dispatch to Malaya one brigade (three battalions) of the still-forming 8 Division on the proviso that, as soon as more Indian troops were recruited, the Australians would join their countrymen fighting in the Middle East. At the beginning of December 1940, Churchill accepted the offer.

Eager to lessen Australian anxieties, he also declared that the situation in the Far East had now eased and that the danger of Japan going to war against the Empire was far less than previously, following the fall of France. In any case, even if Japan did enter the war, he was 'persuaded' that the United States would 'come in on our side, which would put the naval boot very much on the other leg, and be a deliverance from many perils'.

He also contended that the Allies' successes in Europe would not be lost on Japan – a convenient argument, given that he knew it would be impossible for the British fleet to leave the Mediterranean. Despite this, he told the Australian government he was hopeful of knocking out the Italian Navy, which would allow him to send strong naval forces to Singapore 'without suffering any serious disadvantage'. However, until this result could be achieved, the Empire's 'Eastern anxieties' would have to be borne 'patiently and doggedly'.

Of course, aircraft were a bit of a problem – the changing situation made it 'difficult to commit ourselves to the precise number of aircraft which we can make available for Singapore', and flying boats could not be spared to 'lie about idle there on the remote chance of a Japanese attack' when they could be put to far better use elsewhere. However, 'if Australia were seriously threatened by invasion, we would not hesitate to compromise or sacrifice the Mediterranean position for the sake of our kith and kin'.

With Churchill accepting Australia's offer of troops for the Far East, arrangements were made for 8 Division's 22 Infantry Brigade and attached troops – 5,850 all told – to prepare for embarkation. Final leave was taken and tropical kit issued, a sure sign to the recipients that they were headed for somewhere hot. On 1 February 1941, the troops converged on Sydney and began boarding the 81,000 ton Cunard liner Queen Mary.

The great passenger ship had arrived in Australia earlier that year for refitting as a troopship. With Cunard Line's distinctive livery obliterated by a coat of camouflaging grey

Queen Mary in Sydney Harbour

paint, 'HTQX', as the ship was now known, was moored at Athol Bight in Sydney Harbour, near Taronga Zoo. At Darling Harbour, the troops, who had travelled by rail, transferred to a fleet of passenger ferries that ran a continuous shore-to-ship shuttle. Consequently, the embarkation, far from being a low-key affair, became a great and festive public occasion.

As the 45,000 ton Aquitania, *which had also served as a troop transport in World War 1, and the slightly smaller Dutch Liner* Nieuw Amsterdam *– both bound for the Middle East – were also included in the convoy, word quickly circulated that the departure of the vessels, escorted by the Royal Australian Naval cruiser HMAS* Hobart, *was an event not to be missed.*

The ultimate destination of 22 Brigade, code-named Elbow Force, was supposed to be a secret, but the security precautions were a waste of time. Stacked along the wharves, in full view of the passing parade, were crates of supplies clearly marked 'Elbow Force, Singapore'.

I spent 10 days of my pre-embarkation leave back home before returning to the Nurses' Club to await orders to move out. In early February I, along with nurses from all over the state, congregated on the docks, where we boarded smaller boats for the transfer to *Queen Mary*.

Once on board, we met our Queensland counterparts. They had received a visit the previous day from Lady Gowrie, wife of the Governor-General, and were still in a state of feverish excitement. The Queenslanders reported that, although her ladyship was not able to give any hint as to our destination, she had added to the already high state of speculation by remarking that we were the luckiest nurses to leave Australia. Why, she didn't say, but it sounded very good and very exciting. We speculated on where we were going. I always said Trincomalee – for no other reasons than it is a pretty word and Ceylon, as it was known then, is a pretty island.

The ship was beautiful, if very crowded, but we nurses were assigned some very nice cabins. *Queen Mary* was at that time Britain's largest ocean liner and, although converted for use as a troopship, much of the opulent interior, synonymous with the luxury and privilege of the British upper classes, remained intact. After stowing our gear, we made our way to the crowd lining the rails to join in the farewell celebrations. *Aquitania*, a graceful four-funnelled ship, led us out the harbour entrance.

The departure date was 4 February, and it was certainly a gala, but chaotic, affair. Relatives, friends and sightseers were crowded into dinghies, rowing boats, yachts, ferries and launches, or were massed on headlands and other vantage points. Those lucky enough to manoeuvre their small craft close to the ships 'coo-eed' to attract attention and held placards aloft in an effort to deliver one last cheerio. However, attempts by well-wishers to intercept bottles tossed overboard containing last-minute messages were invariably thwarted by patrol boats that circled endlessly, and usually got there first.

After Lord Gowrie had delivered his farewell speech, the bands played 'Auld Lang Syne', followed by 'The Maori Farewell'. Slipping their moorings, the ships steamed down the harbour, the cheers of the 12,000 troops all but drowned out by the shouts and cries of the spectators. With final cheeky toots from the tugboats, sirens and hoots from the rest of the spectator fleet and a blast from Queen Mary's *huge bass-note foghorn, the convoy passed through the Heads and into the open sea.*

As all on board were convinced they were bound for a warm climate, they were surprised when, instead of heading north beyond the Heads, the ships turned south. It was a good tactic. A scant 20 hours later, the radio operator picked up a message that an enemy raider had been within 63 kilometres of the convoy, evidently in anticipation that the fleet would track to the north.

When we arrived in Melbourne, more medical personnel came on board. These included our commanding officer Colonel Glyn White; our Matron, Dorothy Paschke, who was slender, in her 30s and dubbed 'Dashing Dot' due to her refreshing personality, enthusiasm and leadership qualities; and her second-in-command (2 IC) Sister James. There was also a gynaecologist and obstetrician whom, we assumed, had been sent for his gynaecological, rather than obstetrical,

Matron Paschke

expertise since we were all single and going off to war.

Apart from seasickness caused by the swell off the Tasmanian coast, the passage across the Southern Ocean was uneventful. Lectures, physical fitness exercises and bayonet training helped the troops wile away the daylight hours, with concerts, band recitals and cinema screenings filling the evenings. The only excitement occurred on 8 February, two days out from Fremantle, when a ship painted in the same camouflage grey joined the convoy. It was Mauritania, *another Cunard liner converted for use as a troopship and now carrying reinforcements for the Middle East, who had embarked in Melbourne.*

The number of 22 Brigade personnel on Queen Mary *numbered about 5,750. Besides Brigade Headquarters, there were three infantry battalions – 2/18, 2/19 and 2/20 – all raised in New South Wales; 2/10 Field Regiment from Queensland; a battery from 4 Anti-tank Regiment; 2/10 Field Company; 8 Division Signals; Pat's unit, 2/10 AGH; 2/4 Casualty Clearing Station; 2/9 Field Ambulance from Victoria; 2/2 Motor Ambulance Convoy; 2/5 Food Hygiene Section; 2 Mobile Bacteriological Laboratory; 17 Dental Unit; 4 Supply Personnel Section; a Reserve Motor Transport Company; a field bakery; 2/4 Field Workshop; 2/2 Ordinance Store; 8 Division Cash Office; 8 Division Provost Company; and other headquarters' details.*

Also on board was a small kangaroo, Joey, the mascot of 2/19 Battalion, smuggled aboard from the training camp at Bathurst, with the help of men from the Pioneer Platoon, who made a special wooden crate, and with the connivance of the battalion's Regimental Medical Officer (RMO), Captain Richard Lloyd Cahill, on whose suggestion it was painted white with huge red crosses on the sides and labels identifying the contents as 'medical supplies'.

However, once on the train, the crate had been separated from the troops. There was no sign of Joey or the box on the battalion's arrival in Sydney, but any concern that Joey might not make it on board were dispelled when a Shell Oil Company lighter with the box as

Joey, the 2/19 Battalion mascot

cargo came alongside Queen Mary. *In a few minutes the crate, with Joey safely inside, was hoisted aboard.*

All medical staff had been on duty from the moment we stepped on board. With such a large number of troops, some were bound to be ill with some complaint or another, which included an outbreak of mumps and occasional appendicitis. All were admitted to various wards in what were the vessel's previously fashionable tearooms. At Fremantle we took on more troops and medical staff and transferred ill patients to a hospital ashore.

Aquitania *and* Queen Mary *anchored offshore as the harbour at Fremantle was too shallow to accommodate such large vessels. The troops on the smaller ships were allowed ashore, but the others had to make do with sending a brief telegram to their families. Oblivious to, or possibly wilfully ignoring, the security restrictions that were in force, small boats circled the moored vessels to collect 600 parcels and letters, but all were intercepted and confiscated However, instead of burning the offending items, when* Queen Mary *was 36 hours from Singapore, the ship's security officers soaked them in water and dropped them over the side. Some floated ashore, where they were retrieved by civic-minded individuals in Dutch Indonesia and forwarded to Singapore for further delivery.*

On 13 February, the day after the convoy left Fremantle, Major Whitfield addressed the troops. He now confirmed what everyone who had seen the booklets entitled 'Tactical Notes on Malaya', liberated from an Elbow Force crate, or deduced from the daily lectures on malaria and tropical hygiene, had already guessed – but hoped was not true. Their destination was Singapore.

All who still clung to the possibility of seeing action in the Middle East were bitterly disappointed. They had volunteered to fight, not sit out the war twiddling their thumbs in the backblocks of the Far East. Now that their destination was no longer a secret, the lectures stepped up. Topics covered included flora and fauna, with an emphasis on tigers, poisonous snakes, scorpions, killer wasps and mosquitoes, of which there were many – including those which spread malaria and dengue fever.

Other nasty complaints that troops might encounter were enteritis, yellow fever, cholera, dysentery, sandfly fever and hookworms. Fungal infections included ringworm, tinea, Singapore ear and dhobi's itch – a nasty complaint that affected the scrotal sac and took its name from the dhobi (laundry) boys, who were thought to be responsible because they had not rinsed the clothes properly. There were many other skin irritations, either too numerous to mention or about which very little was known. However, as the most common and most debilitating illnesses were venereal disease and malaria, troops were instructed at all times to 'beware of women and mosquitoes'.

For the rank and file, the voyage was a unique, if overcrowded and uncomfortable, experience.

The accommodation for the nursing sisters, officers and senior non-commissioned officers (NCOs) was in keeping with their rank, but the few troops lucky enough to secure berths on one of the upper decks found that eight hammocks occupied a space usually reserved for two. Nevertheless, this was a good deal better than sleeping on mattresses, placed on the floor 30 centimetres apart, or in tiered bunks set up in an empty indoor swimming pool.

On 16 February, as the convoy neared the Cocos (Keeling) Islands, five nerve-shattering blasts from the ship's siren signalled that the time had come for parting of the ways. As those on deck jostled for a better view, the British naval cruiser HMS Durban *appeared from over the horizon and took up its station alongside HMAS* Canberra, *which had replaced HMAS* Perth *at Fremantle. As if on cue, 'Mary' gave a single blast on the foghorn before swinging to port and circling behind the other ships, which formed a line.*

Each ship had a band, fore and aft, which now struck up 'The Maori Farewell' – that beautiful, haunting song, sung whenever Australian troops left for overseas. We waved goodbye as *Queen Mary* steamed slowly and majestically past her honour guard but, on reaching the end of the line, the huge vessel suddenly changed course to starboard and put on a tremendous burst of speed. As *Canberra* shepherded the depleted convoy west into the setting sun, *Durban* and *Queen Mary* headed north, for Singapore.

It was a slightly eerie feeling being on our own, but we were assured that *Mary* was so fast nothing could catch her. As I didn't want to know the answer, I didn't ask what would happen if we ran headlong into the enemy.

As we moved further north, conditions on board became very uncomfortable. The ship had been built for the cold North Atlantic run, not the tropics and, to make matters worse, most of the air-conditioning had been disconnected to make more power for the engines, if needed. The only air-conditioned room on the ship was a comfortable lounge room. It was for officers only, but we had our meals there as well. I shared a double cabin with Kath Neuss, who was a bit junior to me, but had trained at RPA. The cabin wasn't air-conditioned but we did have a porthole.

It became very hot in the wards, so all medical staff on night duty were ordered up on deck into the fresh air for 10 minutes in every two hours. Our patients, who suffered dreadfully from the hot, humid and stuffy conditions, had no such relief. They begged us to take them with us. If only we could.

As the ship moved even further north, the situation became almost unbearable. At night, in an effort to escape the heat and get some sleep, many of the able-bodied left their berths and moved topside into the fresh air – a sizeable number venturing onto the 'officers only' decks where they resisted all attempts by the duty officer to evict them. However, sleeping under the stars came to an abrupt end when someone, in defiance of the blackout, was caught smoking on deck.

Nursing sisters on *Queen Mary* waiting to disembark in Singapore

One of the sisters was afraid of the dark. Either forgetting or oblivious that blackout restrictions were in force, she took her torch with her to light her way along the deck. The sentry's angry shout when he spotted her gave her such a fright that, if it had been possible to fall overboard, she would surely have ended in the sea.

Two days after leaving the main convoy, those gathered along the railings on the port side had their first glimpse of Singapore Island. Unable to dock at Keppel Harbour because of her size, Mary *kept heading east, towards the Straits of Johore (Johor) leading to the great naval base. Near the eastern entrance of the strait, guarded by batteries of guns, the white barracks buildings, solid and squat, and the distinctive black-and-white officers' bungalows at Changi Camp were clearly visible against the lush green of the foliage. As the ship moved slowly up the narrow waterway, those on the starboard side could almost touch the palm-thatched huts of fishing villages, jutting out on stilts from the Malayan shoreline.*

As they edged closer towards the naval base, a smart cream-coloured launch with blue trim, manned by Malay Police dressed in spotless white uniforms, came out to meet the vessel. A Jacob's ladder was lowered and, to the sound of much cheering from the troops, up scrambled 8 Division's Commanding Officer, Major General Gordon Bennett, accompanied by 22 Brigade's Brigadier Taylor.

There were more uniforms at the dock, where a large contingent of British military personnel, including some very senior officers, was waiting to greet the newcomers.

The high-spirited Australians, described as 'tall, lean and tan', certainly made an impression on the welcoming committee. The Straits Times *reported it was rather like a carnival, with soldiers hanging over railings and sitting in portholes, waving and shouting to all and sundry, playing two-up in the corner of the deck and drowning out the sound of the welcoming bands with their strange songs, to which the 'choir's' conductor kept time with a shirt on the end of a stick. Some yelled questions about the price of local beer and whisky, while others tossed pennies among the crowd and the top brass. Unaware that some of the copper coins had been heated to a high temperature with cigarette lighters, people who picked them up dropped them even faster.*

When Governor Sir Shenton Thomas arrived with his wife they too were showered with coins. As the journalists remarked, the Australians were 'full of practical jokes'. One soldier, spotting a general in the entourage, demonstrated that anti-authoritarianism, so prevalent in the Great War, was still alive and well by bellowing 'this is going to mean a lot of extra work for you, brass hat!'

Four months later, the local radio compared the 'unorthodox antics' of the exuberant colonials with the behaviour of recently arrived British troops. Unlike the Australians, they had come quietly. 'And when the bands played, they listened, and clapped in appreciation at the end.'

It was noted, however, that the AIF did manage to disembark in an orderly fashion. After the Governor had delivered a speech of welcome and taken his leave, along with his entourage, the 'bronzed carefree orang putih [white men] who sang such weird songs', left the ship without hurry or bustle – admirable discipline in this 'democratic army' where, as the Malaya Tribune *and even more class-conscious* Straits Times *pointed out, 'you find a solicitor as a private in a company commanded by one of his clerks'.*

Having disembarked from the ship to the overwhelming satisfaction of the press, Pat Gunther and the rest of 22 Brigade had no time for sightseeing. The anticipation of a day or so in Singapore, with its strange and wonderful sights, and even stranger aromas, had been quashed by the announcement that all personnel would be sent immediately to their bases in Malaya.

By 4 o'clock that afternoon the transfer was well underway. A march of about 400 metres took the rank and file, sweating profusely in the sauna-like heat, to a railway siding and a waiting train, and they were off.

The three infantry battalions were based at Port Dickson and Seremban, about 300 kilometres from Singapore on Malaya's west coast, along with the field ambulance and hygiene units. Roughly 70 kilometres to the north-west of Seremban was Kuala Lumpur where, on 20 February, General Bennett established his divisional headquarters. The signallers were nearby, the 2/4 Casualty Clearing Station was at Port Dickson, while the artillery, engineers, supply units and Pat's 2/10 AGH were at Malacca, an old pirate haunt south of Port Dickson. The Motor Ambulance Convoy was stationed at Kajang, between Seremban and Kuala Lumpur.

The 2/10 hospital staff – 43 nurses, three physiotherapists and Matron Paschke – were posted to Malacca, about 150 miles (240 kilometres) away from Singapore on the west coast of Malaya. After being handed two thick sandwiches and an apple to sustain us on the journey, we disembarked at 7.15 pm and boarded a comfortable sleeper train for Tampin, where we transferred next morning to ambulances for the final part of the journey.

At 3.30 am we arrived at Malacca where we were allocated quarters in the Colonial Service Hospital. I was on the top floor of the maternity wing where some of the sisters had a room to themselves. Others shared, either two or four to a room. However, every room was light and airy with good but basic facilities, and we had a small army of amahs (maids) to look after our every wish and need.

Opened in 1934, and with full medical and surgical facilities, the hospital itself was a large modern five-storey building set in almost 20 acres (8 hectares) of grounds and on a hill to catch the breeze. The patients were accommodated in spacious airy wards with verandahs on all sides.

Now renamed the Malacca General Hospital, the building was dubbed 'The White Elephant' by the locals, due to its size, colour and lack of patients. Although it had been constructed as a purpose-built hospital, the standard was much lower than in its Australian counterparts, with primitive facilities and scant offerings in the way of equipment.

The nurses had to improvise, making do with what was at hand, but were severely handicapped when dealing with the local community, whose culture was alien and whose languages they did not speak.

There was plenty of work. With medical officers removing tonsils and circumcising any soldier who was not, in order to forestall potential problems later, there were hundreds of operations, resulting in hundreds of patients.

The hospital was originally equipped for 400 beds but this was increased soon after our arrival to 600.

2/10 AGH, Malacca

Lieutenant-Colonel Albert Coates, a most brilliant man who was later knighted, was the senior surgeon. Major Maynard was in charge of pathology, while Major Burnside was responsible for diagnostic routines, such as testing for malaria and dysentery. Although we were on the seaboard, the port and approaches were too shallow for ships large enough to transport patients to dock. However, this was not a problem as the road system was good.

Members of the male medical staff were assigned to small houses in the grounds and the auxiliary staff to tents. Close by the hospital was a large atap (palm-thatch) building that served as a mess for the nurses. The botanic-like gardens were filled with bougainvillea, frangipani, hibiscus and other exotic shrubs and, to my further delight, there were also two tennis courts.

We had plenty of time for socialising and often received invitations to attend battalion dinners and dances. However, we were only allowed to associate privately with officers. If someone had a friend who was not an officer, she could go out with him, provided another officer tagged along. Anyone who decided to break this rule to go it alone was liable to be confined to barracks for a fortnight.

Physiotherapist Edith 'Bonny' Howgate wrote candidly in her diary about swimming and tennis parties, picnics, dancing and dining, and her romantic liaisons, including a 'daring' association with a married man – tall, dashing Captain Charles Cousens, of 2/19 Battalion, whom she met in Singapore while on leave. A popular announcer on radio 2GB in Sydney, Cousens was a ladies' man whose wife Dorothy had divorced him when he fell in love with Mrs Winifred (Grace) James. He married her in 1938. In an interesting twist, Dorothy then married Grace's former husband Otto.

The work was straightforward at first but increased in variety as patients with injuries, sustained either during army exercises or sporting activities, as well as those suffering from a variety of illnesses and tropical complaints, were admitted. Dhobi's itch was particularly troublesome, so troublesome that some patients had to be sent home to the more temperate climate of Australia. 'Singapore ear', a fungal infection, was also a trial, and took quite a while to clear up. All those stricken with typhus – a tick-born illness that became prevalent after the troops began jungle exercises – required careful nursing, as there were no drugs with which to treat it, or them. Prickly heat, which was troublesome at first, was soon brought under control by a liberal and regular dusting of sweetly scented Johnson's baby powder, much to the disgust of the troops.

As soon as the troops arrived at their bases, they were sent on daily route marches to acclimatise and toughen them up. Three days later they commenced jungle training – the like of which not one of them, including senior officers, had ever experienced. Unused to the high humidity and salt depletion through excessive perspiration, both officers and men suffered greatly from fatigue and cramp. The many skin diseases they had heard about during their lectures were now experienced at first hand, but were brought more or less under control through a concerted effort by the medical staff.

To the consternation of the British garrison soldiers, who were accustomed to a nice siesta after lunch, afternoon rest for the Australians soon became a thing of the past. There was too much training to do and, in any case, as they were unused to such indulgences, trying to enforce them to rest was often a waste of time.

Although on the voyage the officers had lectured the men on what to expect when they arrived in Malaya, they were not prepared for the assault on their physical and emotional senses. Trained and outfitted for conventional open warfare, they found the jungle an eerie place, full of poisonous snakes, huge spiders and stinging insects. Unable to see these dangers, many imagined that death, in some form or other, lurked behind every tree and bush.

A booklet issued by Australian Army Headquarters warned that the Japanese were experienced, ruthless, highly trained, had few physical requirements and, unencumbered by non-essential gear, were able to move across the country at great speed. They also had a potentially large 'fifth column' at their disposal and a capacity to live off the land.

This frighteningly accurate analysis was completely contradicted in lectures conducted by staff officers, who maintained the Japanese were small, bandy-legged, very myopic and frightened of the dark. Their aeroplanes were made from recycled pots and pans and other scrap aluminium, their guns salvaged from the 1905 Russian war and their rifles obsolete. Aware that the Japanese had been fighting in China for years, some troops queried the veracity of these statements, only to have their questions brushed aside.

The booklet also emphasised the need for jungle training. To this end, the troops were put though an intensive training regime that included village fighting, wide enveloping manoeuvres, movement along narrow jungle defiles, ambushes, night attacks and tactics for fighting in vegetation ranging from thick jungle to rubber plantations.

CHAPTER 2

Halcyon days

As the workload was not demanding at first, I had plenty of time to explore the town centre, which was about 15 minutes from the hospital. Over many centuries, Malacca had been occupied by four different foreign powers, each of which had put its individual stamp on the place. The exotic-looking buildings and ruins were fascinating to our Antipodean eyes, especially as in Australia anything that had been standing for more than a century was regarded as old.

I discovered that the Chinese, who had first settled in the area in the 10th century, had occupied Malacca in greater numbers in the 15th, when the town became a major trading centre, and it was during this period that they had built the Cheng Toon temple, the oldest of its kind in Malaya. Portuguese adventurers, traders, soldiers and priests, who occupied the town in the early 16th century, had created an even more important trading port, and had constructed a fortification known as Fort a'Famosa, where the Portuguese missionary, St Francis Xavier, is buried.

However, Malacca's importance was on the wane, and when the Dutch East India Company took over in the mid-17th century and built the Stadhaus, or Town Hall, the port's status had been dramatically reduced. By the time the British, who didn't seem to build anything of note, gained control, the settlement had been further sidelined by the establishment of Batavia, in Java, as the centre of power for the East Indies.

The shops, providing a variety of local produce, were two-storey terraces that had residences above and were known as shop houses. They were mostly owned by Indians, Malays and Straits Chinese, or Baba Nonyas, as the descendants of the original Chinese immigrants are known. They spoke English, Chinese and a kind of Malay dialect, and were often the go-betweens between the British and Chinese traders. They also had created a very distinctive style of cuisine, using typical Malay spices, and adapted Malay clothing to their own style.

Chinese-run gem stores sold star sapphires, moonstones and jade, as well as jade and ivory figurines and attractive gold ornaments. Herbalists were in demand, their shopfronts displaying long lists of ailments and the recommended cure. In the side-street workshops we watched in fascination as Malay craftsmen tapped dimples into sheets of tin or pewter and then fashioned them into trays, tankards, coffee pots and other household items. As Royal Selangor pewter, it is much admired and said to be the best in the world.

Malacca in 1941

The softly spoken dusky Indians were superb tailors. Their shops were filled with the most beautiful silks and cottons. We didn't waste any time patronising them as we all had been issued with a grey Cesarine cotton button-through uniform with long sleeves. A red cape and white veil completed the ensemble. However, the cotton crushed terribly and the design was not suitable for the climate, so we were granted permission to have shirtdresses with short sleeves made in much lighter weight grey cotton. They were far more comfortable, but we had to wear petticoats as the fabric was so light that it became semi-transparent in strong sunlight. As a further concession to the tropical heat, we were also allowed to wear white shirtdresses when we went out and about.

A nearby kampong (village) was occupied mainly by Malay plantation workers and their families. The small-boned women, with their easy, fluid movements, were a joy to see in their colourful sarongs and blouses, especially when dancing to their own lonely, haunting music. There is no word other than delightful to describe the children. When a sudden shower sent us sheltering under the eaves of the village houses, they dashed through the puddles, their impish grins showing flashes of white teeth. Tiny tots, often quite naked and holding banana leaves over their heads, also joined in the fun.

We were also entertained, although in a far more restrained fashion, by members of the English community – the rubber planters and their wives, along with merchants and Colonial Service personnel. They invited us to their homes, to play golf and to swimming parties, and gave us introductions to people in the countryside whom we could visit on our days off.

Nurses at Malacca take time out to attend a swimming party

The nurses based at Malacca spent a great deal of time in the company of a local couple, Joyce Mary 'Doi' Chidson (nee Wilkinson) and her husband. Joyce, who was born in St Leonards, Tasmania, in 1894, but had spent many years in Sydney, had served as a nurse in England in World War 1. After completing her Midwifery Certificate in Melbourne in 1925, she had travelled to Malaya to help her pregnant sister, who was married to a tin miner and had a large brood of children.

While in Malaya, Joyce met and married Lowthian Hume Chidson, known as Hume, a King's Scholar from Cambridge University who was a barrister and partner in a law firm. In 1922, Hume, who had enlisted in the British Army in World War 1, joined the Straits Settlement Volunteer Reserve. His roots were evidently Scottish, as were his given names, and in 1929 he announced that his unit, 2 Battalion SSVF, was forming a Scottish Company. He was appointed commanding officer of its Machine-gun Platoon. He rose in rank and status and by 1940 was a lieutenant colonel, 2nd in command of the battalion, and a member of the advisory committee for the formation of land forces in Malacca.

When the Australian nurses arrived in Malacca, it is not surprising that Joyce (an Australian and an ex-nurse) and Hume (the most senior local army officer) made every effort to welcome them, creating an 'open house' and inviting them to functions on a weekly, sometimes daily, basis. In August 1941, when Joyce flew back to Australia to visit her family, she delivered messages from the nurses. The Chidsons' hospitality was appreciated, so much so that Bonny Howgate mentioned their names frequently in her diary.

Although the British regarded themselves as a cut above the rest, I was impressed by the caring attitude of the planters towards their workers. Many knew the names of all their rubber tappers, while their wives ran clinics for the workers and their families. It was like a kind of benign feudal system.

With plenty of servants to do their bidding, the lifestyle enjoyed by the European population was regarded as idyllic, provided they could stand the climate – hot and humid all year, with air-conditioning a rarity. Separation from family, friends and familiar places was another drawback for those posted to the Far East. As the climate was considered to be unsuitable for European children, many remained in Britain with grandparents, or were sent away to boarding school at a very young age.

Occasionally we received invitations from wealthy Chinese. I recall going to a dinner party at a beautiful home owned by a Chinese millionaire. It was said that when he had first come to Malaya as a young man he had worked as a coolie, engaged in menial labouring jobs. I think, when I met him, he owned several tin mines. His daughter, a slender, elegant creature who would have graced any salon, was our hostess. After dinner, watching our host playing the violin with such a happy, peaceful expression, I thought, 'There is a man at peace with himself and the world.'

The initial welcome from the citizenry for the ordinary soldier was a somewhat different experience from that enjoyed by the officers. On arrival at their various destinations, the troops were perplexed by the absence of women and children. The mystery was finally solved when they learned that stories had circulated that no female was safe while Australian soldiers were around and that they also kicked and beat children on sight. Such was the strength of the rumours that some Chinese women had fled, at the urging of their families, into the countryside. However, their fears were soon put to rest by the friendliness of the troops, who treated everyone as their equal.

Unused to Europeans behaving in such an egalitarian manner, the local people reciprocated by extending the warm hand of friendship. The Chinese community in Seremban opened an 'Oriental Garden', where troops could buy steak and eggs, fresh fish and Australian beer. Other non-European citizens invited the troops to dine in their homes and enjoy the hospitality extended by their clubs. Before long, the mere sight of an AIF convoy approaching a village or town was enough to ensure a road lined with smiling, shouting children. The soldiers soon learned to speak enough Malay to make themselves understood and, once they became familiar with the local currency, began organising successful two-up schools. Generous to a fault, they handed out treats to the children and outrageously overpaid the Chinese rickshaw coolies, much to the annoyance of some of the local Europeans.

This egalitarianism and total disregard for the well-entrenched British class system would create a lasting rift between the AIF and many British expatriates, especially in Singapore. Although there were instances of private hospitality, lavish at times, offered by Europeans, the troops often found themselves being counselled by their hosts, anxious to maintain 'the prestige of the white man', to refrain from fraternising with 'the natives'.

The Australians took no notice. Gregarious by nature, they had no problem in accepting acts of kindness, such as the offer of a ride into town from those considered 'inferior', especially when similar invitations were not offered by the 'superior' white community.

However, it was while on leave in Singapore that the AIF encountered the most overt prejudice. Notwithstanding the rumours that they would wreck the place, the level of animosity towards them was unexpectedly high.

In a society that pandered to trivial social niceties, and where one could be cut dead for a breach of etiquette no matter how unintentional, the presence of these brash Australians was, for many white civilians, an irritation that must be endured. For an ordinary soldier to address a European woman or girl or, in many cases, a man, anywhere in Singapore was to invite a most calculated snub. A simple request for directions could result in not only being cut dead completely, but a loud remark to the effect that these 'dreadful soldiers', who actually fraternised with the 'natives', were everywhere.

Starved of female company, the rank and file spent much of their leave at Singapore's amusement parks – the 'New', 'Great' and 'Happy' Worlds. Besides the usual sideshows, shooting galleries and refreshment stalls, there were dance halls where, for the price of a ticket, soldiers could dance for a few minutes with beautiful Chinese and Eurasian girls. Known as 'taxi dancers (possibly because they were hired), their English was limited and their services definitely did not extend beyond dancing – a regulation rigidly enforced and supervised by an army of older and most formidable women chaperones.

Apart from the amusement parks, which welcomed them with open arms, there were not many places that allowed patronage by the rank and file. Raffles Hotel, for instance, was completely out-of-bounds, as were the European clubs and better restaurants. Barred from these establishments, soldiers on leave were forced to patronise the sleazier parts of town. Consequently, when later criticised for their ostracism, some Europeans offered a defence that they would have liked to have been more hospitable to the Australian troops but it was so damnably difficult for one to do so – they were always hanging about the red-light district.

However, not all Singaporeans held the AIF's rank and file in such low regard. A few months after 22 Brigade arrived, an English resident donated land in the heart of the city, on which the ANZAC Club, a recreation facility for Australian soldiers, was erected 'as a mark of an Englishman's appreciation of the Dominion troops'. The club was the brainchild of Mrs Gretchen Howell, wife of the Attorney General for the Straits Settlement. After laying claim to a piece of prime real estate owned by the government, not far from Raffles, she persuaded a wealthy Chinese businessman to provide the necessary funds to build a clubhouse. The redoubtable Mrs Howell and a small band of Australian and New Zealand women living in Singapore staffed the club on a voluntary basis and the Australian Comforts Fund supplied the necessary goods. Similar instances of generosity were experienced in Malaya, where local Europeans ran Service Canteens and non-Europeans organised social clubs.

Quite early in the piece, someone further up the chain of command decided that all 2/10 AGH nurses should learn how to march – a facet of army life that had received no attention due to our unit being hastily assembled. Realising that it would be bad for discipline if the ORs (other ranks) saw officers, who should definitely know how to drill, being put through their paces, our senior staff decreed that marching practice should take place secretly and at dawn. In the tropics, daybreak is around 6 am, when we had roll call. The flat roof of our quarters, being well out of sight, was designated as the parade ground. The area was probably about 115 feet long and 50 feet wide (35 metres by 15 metres), with a parapet on all sides.

Our attempts at drill were hilarious. We were all sizes, from short and dumpy to tall and slender, and all shapes, from well-endowed to reed-like. One of our senior sisters, Pearl Mittelhauser, who was always called Mitzi, declared that she had taken short steps all her life and didn't intend changing now. None of us had ever swung our arms when we walked, and for the more buxom among us, to do so was harder than it looked.

We had no idea at all what to do, let alone how to respond instantly to commands. The poor sergeant major shouted, 'When I say 'alt, I want all of you to 'alt, not just arf of you.' As we approached the parapet, almost all in step, someone whispered, 'Do you think he'll say 'alt, or do we go over the top?' The reply, 'Would you blame him if he didn't?', sent ripples of laughter through the ranks.

I don't know whether our contingent ever managed to reach the standard of marching required by the drill sergeant, as in early May my friend Win Davis and I, along with two 2/4 CCS girls, were posted to the venereal disease section of the medical department of 2/4 Casualty Clearing Station (CCS), based at Kijang. We were there for the best part of three months.

The town is about 15 miles (25 kilometres) south of Kuala Lumpur and is in Selangor state.

2/10 AGH nurses at Malacca. Pat is far right, back row

Our commanding officer there was Colonel Tom Hamilton, a surgeon from Newcastle, who kept a tight rein on his team. The work was interesting, but not taxing, allowing plenty of time for sightseeing. The CCS ran smoothly and efficiently, with Major W E Fisher, an honorary physician from Sydney Hospital, the Colonel's able second-in-command. A number of the staff came from Tasmania, including two pharmacists, one of whom was keenly interested in insects and had built up a most interesting collection of bugs and beetles he found in the jungle.

Kuala Lumpur, only 12 miles (20 kilometres) away, was a small and pleasant city with an air of quiet affluence. Among the attractions were first-class swimming and golf clubs and also a racecourse, surrounded by casuarina trees. Englishwoman Mrs Langworthy, wife of the Senior Superintendent of Police, took us under her wing and showed us around the stables, cautioning us not to pat the horses, which she said might bite as many Asian owners and trainers did not care for their animals in the same way as Westerners. Most of the thoroughbreds I saw that had been shipped from Australia were either past their prime, or had failed to prove themselves on racecourses at home. Many of the jockeys were also Australian, and we were advised that, if we wanted a flutter, to bet on the jockey, not the horse.

The architecture of Kuala Lumpur was varied and extremely interesting. Some Europeans were scornful of the massive railway station, built in the Moorish style, with minaret-like towers and arched colonnades. The detractors thought it vulgar and ostentatious, but to me it was exotically picturesque. Directly opposite the station was the beautiful Hotel Majestic and the Royal Selangor Club, favourite venues among the Europeans for dining and dancing.

The railway station, built in 1910, consisted of a main terminal building with three glass-roofed platforms, two single and one double, servicing four railway lines. The main structure is primarily 'Raj' in style, a mix of Western and Mughal architecture, similar to Moorish Revival, which was popular in Colonial India at the end of the 19th century and early 20th.

The 51-room Hotel Majestic was the largest and grandest hotel in Kuala Lumpur, unrivalled for its prestige and luxury. Built in 1932, 'The Majestic', as it was also known, was constructed in a hybrid of Neo-classical and Art Deco styles and was set amid several acres on a hilltop. Featuring tall white Roman columns and detailed cornices, with a sweeping curved driveway and an impressive porte-cochere, the hotel boasted a first for Malaya – modern sanitation in all rooms, with hot and cold water, showers and, in some rooms, full-sized baths, considered to be the height of luxury.

With its custom-designed furniture, silverware and sumptuous furnishings imported from England, the hotel catered to every whim and fancy of contemporary society. A special and most popular feature was the roof garden, with a dance floor and seating for 350 guests. Entertainers from all over the world performed at the hotel, including popular acts from Hollywood and the Coliseum in London.

The Majestic, with its extravagant parties, Sunday curry tiffin lunches and traditional European-style tea dances, was a magnet to the colonial elite, the rich and the famous.

The nearby Selangor Club was equally exclusive, with membership determined by high educational or social standing rather than race or citizenship. Founded in 1884, the club started out as a tiny wooden building with an atap roof. In 1910 it was rebuilt in a mock Tudor style, using a design by the architect responsible for the railway station, Arthur Hubback. The main clubhouse, which overlooked a large padang, or green, on which a variety of sports was played by club members and visiting teams, was also known as 'The Spotted Dog', or simply 'The Dog'.

Some say that the unusual name stems from the nature of the club's mixed membership. Others attribute it to two Dalmatian dogs belonging to the wife of one of the club's founders, which sat guarding the front door whenever their owner was in attendance. Yet another theory is that the first emblem of the club was a leopard, so badly drawn that it was mistaken for a dog.

Whatever the origins of the Spotted Dog, it was definitely the place to see and be seen, and was an irresistible drawcard to Australian officers and nursing sisters stationed near Kuala Lumpur and looking for a welcome change of scenery.

I remember a beautiful Eurasian girl who frequently accompanied a British officer to the club. They danced superbly. I wonder what happened to them? They, the ubiquitous they, who always knew everything, said that, if they married, there would be no further promotion for him. And she, poor thing, would have been snubbed by all sides. It had been made very clear to us that Eurasians were not socially acceptable to either the British or the Asians.

While we were adjusting well to army life and the climate, home was often in our thoughts and we always looked forward to the arrival of letters, which were read and re-read. Censorship

Royal Selangor Club

was in force, with the ever-alert censor chopping out anything that didn't pass the security tests, but this didn't stop our more creatively minded friends and relatives from telling us that 'Mary's sister Elizabeth, had visited. She is much like Mary, only broader in the beam.'

Letters that arrived while I was at Kijang from nurses in the Middle East made me cringe with embarrassment when I compared my life of ease with theirs. Even so, their brief descriptions of the evacuation of Greece and Crete gave little real indication of the misery and wretchedness of the withdrawal of defeated troops, or the distress of knowing that those left behind would become prisoners.

We had quite a lot of news about the war situation because it was reported in the Australian papers. My father used to send me Saturday's *Sydney Morning Herald* regularly and also *The Bulletin*, a hard-hitting journal that had some very interesting opinion pieces. The local *Straits Times*, which was prevented from reporting on the situation in the East, was permitted, however, to publish some news on what was happening in Europe and the Middle East.

My embarrassment was not helped by newspaper and magazine journalists constantly filing reports on 'our troops in Malaya'. One female journalist wrote such glowing accounts of our lifestyle that they raised the ire of most of our service personnel.

The unpopular journalist was Adele Shelton Smith, who had arrived on the scene in April to collect 'human interest' stories for The Australian Women's Weekly. *Feted by the officers, she had also been given access to the troops, their training and facilities, and was invited to meals in the soldiers' messes, at which the food was of a much higher standard than normal. Her articles featuring 'first-hand news of how our boys are faring in the tropics' were published in Australia throughout May, June and July, under provocative headlines such as 'Sarong Siesta', 'Curry tiffin with 400 of the AIF' and 'Sunday Swimming Party'.*

Matron Paschke and 2/10 AHG nurses at Malacca

'Their quarters are more comfortable than at home', she gushed, 'and there are no flies, mosquitoes, or dust. They are receiving marvellous hospitality from the local people. Mails are arriving regularly, the canteens are cheap, and they are getting plenty of leave.' The hard-working nursing sisters at 10 AGH, who had naively entertained her, also came in for their share of publicity from Adele, with a piece entitled 'They treat us like film stars'. This unfortunate headline had been taken from a statement attributed to Matron Paschke: 'Some days we feel like film stars. The local residents send us huge baskets of orchids, presents of fruit and invitations to their homes or clubs.'

Although Adele mentioned that the nurses had air-raid drill, and even included a photo of them wearing tin hats and carrying gas masks, troop training received but a passing mention. The small snippets that did appear were supported by photographs – not of men up to their armpits in swamps, or battling their way cross-country guided only by a compass, but of clean-looking soldiers in open country or rubber plantations engaging in exercises, after which, she reported, they indulged themselves with ice-creams from the local vendors.

In the 12 April issue, an entire page of the Weekly was devoted to pictures of the AIF 'keeping cool' – in a huge private swimming pool owned by a Chinese millionaire, relaxing on the west coast's sandy beaches and even, in the case of Private Cecil Richardson, tipping a dipper of water over his body while sitting in a giant ceramic pot. The more staid newspapers were hardly any better, with the Sydney Morning Herald writing in a similar vein, accompanied by photographs of 'the boys' playing two-up, riding in rickshaws or 'on the job' with their rifles.

The exotic life that the AIF, known as the 'tid apa (no worries) boys', were supposedly leading in the mysterious Far East created a furore. The public and families at home, especially the wives and girlfriends, were most upset. Letters of protest about the 'holiday posting' were sent to the men who, having been dubbed 'Menzies' Mannequins' (after the Australian Prime Minister) by a tabloid newspaper, were referring to themselves as 'Menzies' Glamour Boys'.

When copies of the articles themselves, published in May, arrived in Malaya, some of the troops were furious, not only with the Women's Weekly journalist, but also with the officers who had invited her into the fold. When girlfriends at home became aware of the taxi dancers and wrote that they too knew how to have a good time, the situation became so volatile that senior officers were forced to issue statements refuting the allegations. As far as the troops were concerned, Adele Shelton Smith was the most reviled person on earth.

By the time copies of the Women's Weekly actually arrived in camp, the men were not simply fed up with hearing about her silly articles. They were fed up also with Malaya, the garrison duties, the heat, the humidity, the jungle, the gloom, the endless rubber plantations and, above all, the inability to come to grips with a real enemy. Aware of the situation, senior officers did everything in their power to combat the boredom and frustration. Weekend leave

April 12, 1941 The Australian Women's Weekly 11

THEY'RE KEEPING COOL: *Two kinds of bathing*

SUNDAY swimming party at seaside home of Mr. Chan, Chinese millionaire rubber planter, one of many wealthy Chinese hosts of A.I.F.

PRIVATES R. MELLOR and E. J. Hutchinson, of Victoria, chatting with one of their hosts. Cars go to camps to fetch troops to seaside.

BATHING Malayan fashion in Shanghai jar. Made of brown earthenware, it's glazed jade-green inside and decorated with native designs. Private Cecil Richardson likes it!

LIVELY AS MONKEYS, four A.I.F. lads climb a Malayan palm. In tropic heat frequent bathing is a lifesaver and residents see no soldier is without opportunity to swim on leave.

JUST LIKE HOME. It might be Palm Beach sands they're racing over. Training doesn't leave them short of energy.

Photographs by Wilfred ("Bill") Brindle, Australian Women's Weekly photographer.

was granted in Singapore, Malacca, Kuala Lumpur and other towns, and army transport laid on – an 'indulgence' that annoyed the British – on General Bennett's orders. Sporting teams and inter-unit competitions were also organised at his direction, along with concerts and other amusements, but these diversions did not resolve the underlying problem. Some men fretted that they might go 'troppo' if they stayed too long; others, realising that medical discharge was one way to get home, went to great lengths to convince doctors they had.

Some invented imaginary dogs that they took on imaginary walks on the end of an imaginary lead. Others began to ride imaginary horses around the camp or organise sheep musters, complete with imaginary sheep, sheep dogs and sound effects. Dog races were organised, with owners parading their dogs and bookmakers laying the odds. A course was laid out and the race called in a very exciting manner, as men yelled at their dogs to urge them on. Winners jumped up and down, and threw their hats in the air, while losers demonstrated their displeasure.

These antics were not confined to the camp. Pranksters who 'tripped' on the footpath while on leave in Singapore astounded passers-by by turning and saying 'What a stupid place to put a log'. Before long, Singapore-based journalists were writing that the heat had addled the brains of some members of the AIF who had 'gone troppo'. However, apart from one man who took the charade to extremes by punching a major who had 'kicked' his dog, no

A 2/19 soldier vents his anger

one managed to get a boat ticket home on the grounds of mental instability. Once the ruse was detected, it was back to the barracks and the parade ground.

During the year, Kath Neuss and I spent a couple of short periods of leave at Fraser's Hill, a hill (rest) station established by the British in the mountains north-east of Kuala Lumpur. Although we were anxious to escape from the heat and humidity of the city, it was a difficult place to get to – a journey of several hours in fact – so we had to wait until an army car could be made available. It was said that the road maker was Chinese and that he had been paid by the mile. Maybe it was true. The narrow road certainly followed a tortuous and hair-raising route. I could appreciate why Sister Betty Jeffrey, on reaching Fraser's Hill, contemplated sending a telegram to Matron saying, 'I'll be late back. I'm walking.'

Fraser's Hill was lovely – mountain ranges disappearing into the distance, mists rising in the gullies. Oh, the joy of fresh, cool air after the months in the steamy humidity of the lower areas. We golfed, played tennis and generally relaxed.

Fraser's Hill, about 65 miles (105 kilometres) by road from Kuala Lumpur, nestles on a high plateau in the Titiwangsa Range. It is surrounded by seven mountain peaks, none of which are less than 4,000 feet (about 1,220 metres) above sea level and, at the time of Pat's visit, all were linked by road. The hill station was named for Louis James Fraser, a Scottish pioneer who, in the 1890s, set up a tin-ore trading post at The Gap, on the lower slopes. The British army had not explored the ranges, so Fraser recruited guides and coolie labourers to accompany him to the summit on an expedition to prospect for gold or other valuable metals. On the cloud-enshrouded tops they discovered an ancient forest of moss-covered trees and ferns.

Fraser also found rich tin deposits, and opened a mine. A steep track was constructed for mules to transport the ore to The Gap and then to Raub, the nearest town. When Fraser vanished about 20 or so years later, a party led by the Bishop of Singapore went in search of him. They found no trace of the missing Scotsman, but they reported that the highlands were perfect for a Hill Station – a place to escape from the heat and humidity of the lowlands.

Work began on an access road, the open-cut mine was converted to a golf course and by 1922 Fraser's Hill was open to visitors. There were nine bungalows for government officials, four for ex-servicemen and women, three private homes, a country club, a golf course and a post office. By the time Pat Gunther and her friend took a break there in 1941, there had been considerable further development. Handsome bungalows, many of them in Mock Tudor style and with large open fires to ward off the chill of the evenings, dotted the slopes, and a spacious clubhouse, complete with numerous annexes, occupied the entire summit of one mountain.

The access road, however, was still very narrow and winding. As the last few miles were only one way, a timetable was in force for many years to control the traffic flow.

We also had occasional leave in Singapore, which I found fascinating in spite of the appalling stench from canals and monsoon drains that were little more than open sewers. The smell was terrible. We used to stay mostly at Raffles Hotel because it had that old-world sort of atmosphere and was very relaxed. We'd meet up with some of the air force or army officers for dinner and dancing, or just go sightseeing.

The harbour and Singapore River were packed with sampans, most of which provided accommodation as well as a living for entire families. Washing festooned the cramped deck area, which was littered with all kinds of paraphernalia. And no matter what time of day, someone on board always seemed to be cooking something, the acrid smoke from the small braziers and the smell of the exotic spices adding not unpleasantly to the general Singapore aroma. The sampans were arranged like sardines in a tin and almost completely covered the surface of the river, making it perfectly possible to move from one bank to the other without getting your feet wet. How the owners manoeuvred the boats free of the jam to reach open water was beyond me.

The Botanical Gardens, just to the north of Tanglin Village and opposite Tanglin Military Barracks, were a joy. Bright with colour, the flowerbeds were a perfect foil for the backdrop of tropical greenery and immaculate lawns, beautifully maintained by gardeners swinging fine-bladed scythes in a rhythmic, circular movement – so much less intrusive than the motor mowers and whipper snippers in use today. Cheeky monkeys scampered about the place, demanding titbits and quite obviously discussing us.

We also visited all the popular tourist spots including the Singapore Swimming Club, Haw Par Villa (owned by the manufacturers of Tiger Balm ointments), Change Alley (the foreign currency market) and the very pukka Tanglin Club.

The Tanglin Club and Raffles Hotel, built in a grand colonial style, were a mecca for officers, but both were definitely out of bounds to the rank and file. The very up-market Tanglin Club, founded in 1865, was created to provide an exclusive social venue for British residents. It quickly grew to become a pillar of Singaporean social life, with membership restricted to the well-heeled and successful European community. According to Chinese who lived in nearby villages, this exclusivity was maintained with signage declaring 'No Chinese or Dogs Allowed' – an edict that Chinese living in Penang also claim was prominently displayed at the Penang Swimming Club.

Raffles Hotel, named for Singapore's founder Stamford Raffles, had its beginnings in 1830 as a privately owned beach house on Beach Road. After changing hands, it was in turn a small hotel, then a house for boarders attending nearby Raffles College, before opening as the 10-room Raffles Hotel catering solely for a wealthy clientele. In the 1890s, additions and improvements were made, but a few years later, the building that is recognisable worldwide as Raffles Hotel was constructed. Besides the luxury and opulence that its guests expected from Raffles when it opened in 1899, the hotel was the first in the region to have electrically powered lights and fans. By 1931, various wings, verandahs and a billiard room had been added, and also the famous Long Bar, where the Singapore Sling cocktail was invented by a Chinese bartender, some time before 1915.

Raffles Hotel, a byword for luxury and synonymous with exceptional service, attracted many celebrities from around the world, including internationally acclaimed writers Somerset Maugham and Ernest Hemingway. While the hotel was off limits to all military personnel, apart from officers, no visit to Singapore for the rank and file was complete without the mandatory photograph standing in front of the distinctive Beach Road entrance, with its fan-like Travellers' Palms in the background.

In Kuala Lumpur and Singapore, the presence of servicemen was very evident. Uniformed English, Australians, tall turbaned Sikhs (often called Punjabis) and small, olive-skinned Ghurkhas from Nepal were everywhere. We took this abundance of military personnel as a sign that Singapore and Malaya were well prepared, should hostilities ever break out.

Some of the older soldiers, however, did not share our optimism. I recall one patient undermining my confidence by saying, 'Sister, if war does start, we'll be caught like rats in a trap.' A solidly built non-commissioned officer, who was staged in our ward awaiting transfer to Australia for parachute training only added to the worry. When I remarked, 'That's a dangerous job isn't it?', he replied, 'Sister, this is the danger spot.'

At around this time, the *Straits Times* reported that a Japanese delegation was visiting Thailand on the northern border of Malaya. Although we didn't know it, it was a portent of what was to come.

In September, 2/4 CCS moved to a small civil hospital of about 150 beds at Kluang in Johore state, which is on the Malayan side of the causeway linking the peninsula to Singapore Island. With the venereal section shut down, we were surplus to requirements and returned on 19 September to Malacca where, with the workload now averaging 400 admissions per month, the 2/10 had taken on reinforcements. Among the newcomers were Jenny Greer from Sydney, Betty Jeffrey from Victoria, and two South Australians, Betty Pyman and Nell Keats. In September, 10 nurses from 2/13 AHG, which had just arrived in Singapore, had also joined our staff to gain local experience. I knew two of them – Joyce Bridge, whom I'd met while nursing at St Luke's Hospital in Sydney, and Mona Tait from Canberra. [The others were Sisters Brewer, Bullwinkel, Clancy, Glover, Gunton, Harris, Kerr and Rayner.] They were quite surprised to find our accommodation was in such a large, modern building. However, some of the facilities were far from up-to-date – we had to sterilise our instruments by boiling them on Primus stoves.

The 2/13 Australian General Hospital had been dispatched from Australia in early September on the hospital ship Wanganella, *following the arrival the previous month of thousands of reinforcements for Singapore and Malaya – 8 Division's 27 Brigade.*

Its embarkation had been a complicated affair. Unlike 22 Brigade, not all troops left from Sydney. Some, including most of 2/13 AGH, joined the convoy in Melbourne, while others travelled overland by train from Bathurst to Fremantle. Those departing from Sydney, including 19 Queensland nurses, boarded three troopships berthed in Woolloomooloo Bay

– the Dutch liners Johann Van Olden-Barneveldt *and* Marnix Van Sint Aldegarde, *and an Australian vessel, SS* Katoomba.

As was the case for 22 Brigade, the departure was supposed to be a secret, but even without the presence of Queen Mary, *word quickly spread, fuelled, no doubt, by the knowledge that the escort was the cruiser HMAS* Sydney, *dear to the heart of the city, for which she was named. As the convoy made its way down the harbour, hundreds of small pleasure craft followed, adorned with large signs wishing 'Bon Voyage' to various units and individuals.*

In Melbourne, after more troops were embarked, the convoy proceeded west, detouring to 40 degrees south latitude owing to reports of German raiders. The potent combination of oily food served up by the Dutch Javanese cooks and the dark-green Antarctic seas of the Great Australian Bight saw many troops laid so low by seasickness that they were quite sure they would die. Instead of death, however, came bright, sunny, hospitable Fremantle and eight hours' leave. The welcome was warm, the people of Fremantle having been tipped off to the imminent arrival of troopships by the removal from the streets of all portable, and therefore souvenirable, traffic signs. There was no security crackdown, so phone and telegraph lines ran hot, relaying news of the convoy's progress to friends and families in the eastern states.

Despite exemplary behaviour by the troops, Western Command refused permission to grant further leave, although the ships were tied up at the wharf all the next day. Aware that 7 August would be their last day in Australia for some time, many took unauthorised leave, climbing out portholes and threading their way under the wharf supports, guided by sympathetic sentries who patrolled above them. Very few failed to return.

At Fremantle, Katoomba *was replaced by another Dutch vessel,* Sibajak, *and their escort HMAS* Sydney *by the heavy cruiser, HMAS* Canberra. *The 2/13 staff was also treated to the sight of seeing both* Queens *in port –* Elizabeth *and* Mary.

The convoy sailed on 9 August and, with 5,000 troops on board three small vessels, conditions for the rank and file were far from comfortable. Orders had been issued for the men to sleep below, but the overcrowded sleeping arrangements, combined with the nauseating odours from the galleys, overworked sanitation facilities and slimy bilges, forced many to abandon their hammocks and seek refuge on deck. They bunked down where they could, only to be awakened well before dawn by overzealous crewmen hosing down the decks.

There had been no official notification of the final destination but, by this time, the men were convinced that it must be the Middle East. Why else would the vehicles in the ships' holds be painted the colour of desert sand? However, a day or two out of Fremantle, speculation ceased with an announcement that they were to join 22 Brigade in the defence of Malaya. As if to emphasise the point, lessons in the Malay language immediately commenced and winter clothing was exchanged for tropical kit. Regulation dress was now shorts and shirts by day and long trousers by night. The turned-up 'jungle shorts' or Bombay bloomers, which these troops dubbed 'goon pants', were, mercifully, to be kept for field exercises.

Early on the morning of 15 August the convoy reached Singapore. As the ships were of a much smaller tonnage than Queen Mary, *they were able to berth in Keppel Harbour. Unlike 22 Brigade, the arrival was a very low-key affair, barely rating a mention in an official government handout. Either through disinterest, or sloppy attention to detail, the* Straits Times *reported the arrival of 31 ships from Australia. In complete contrast to the hoopla that had accompanied the disembarkation of 22 Brigade only six months before, there were no crowds of beribboned dignitaries to greet them, nor welcoming brass bands.*

As the men prepared to disembark, the heavens opened up. Their natural exuberance somewhat dampened, they were trucked to various camps and bases around the island. Despite the supposed secrecy, the Australians' arrival did not go entirely unheralded. As the trucks passed through the red-light district, the troops noticed that the girls in Lavender Street were ready and waiting, with a huge, boldly lettered banner, 'Welcome to the AIF', strung above the road. Once at their camps, which ranged from canvas tents to permanent barracks buildings, the men were addressed by senior officers with a list of dos and don'ts, and the most alarming 'fact' that 95 per cent of young Chinese women had venereal disease, a figure which was almost immediately upped to 99.9 per cent. It was rumoured that this astonishingly high rate was attributed not to unbridled promiscuity, but to an old Chinese belief that men suffering from gonorrhoea could be cured by sleeping with a young Chinese virgin.

When Wanganella *sailed from Melbourne on 2 September, it had a twofold aim – transfer the 212 members of staff of 2/13 AGH to Singapore and bring back troops requiring*

AIF troops arrive in Singapore

St Patrick's School, Katong

evacuation. Like 27 Brigade, just a few weeks before, all those on Wanganella *experienced a turbulent crossing of the Great Australian Bight that severely tested the most cast-iron stomachs. When the vessel mercifully arrived at Fremantle, seven more nurses came on board, and one disembarked, bringing the total to 52 – Matron Irene Drummond, 48 nurses and three masseuses.*

Unlike their 2/10 counterparts, the sisters were not on duty during the voyage as, being a hospital ship, Wanganella *had permanent staff. After leaving Fremantle, the nursing sisters filled balmy days sailing on a flat sea by looking after colleagues unfortunate enough to be confined to the sick bay and attending lectures on tropical medicine, the many temptations of the flesh in Singapore and the dangers of drinking the water or eating fruit that could not be peeled. A traditional 'crossing the line' ceremony also provided a welcome diversion, as did the sight of a volcano erupting on the island of Krakatoa.*

On arrival in Singapore, the 2/13 disembarked at Victoria Dock, Keppel Harbour. All, apart from the 10 sisters to be detached for duty with the 2/10 at Malacca, boarded open trucks in sweltering heat for a short ride to St Patrick's School, a Catholic College run by the De la Salle Brothers on the shores of the South China Sea at Katong, to the east of Singapore city.

After setting up a hospital literally from scratch and training orderlies for five weeks, other nurses were given the opportunity to volunteer for temporary detachment to the 2/10. As everyone wanted to go, a list of names was drawn up. Among them was Sister Duxie May Setchell, known as May, who had trained at RPA and had joined the army immediately after her graduation in 1939. She was keen to go to Malacca, not only to gain experience but also to meet up with nursing friends who had been posted to the 2/10.

While I was away, our senior surgeon, Dr Coates, had begun training medical orderlies and NCOs in operating theatre techniques so that, in a time of emergency, they could undertake tasks normally allotted to nursing sisters. This was not a scheme to replace us, but rather to have a backup plan in place for the worst-case scenario.

Albert Coates had been inspired by a civilian doctor at the Malacca General Hospital, who wanted to train orderlies and junior nurses to care for patients injured in air-raids. To make the training sessions more realistic, he obtained artificial 'wounds', made from papier-mâché, which he tied onto the 'patient'.

Impressed by what Coates termed 'gruesome-looking pieces of make up', he established a similar and highly successful scheme. As he later remarked, 'In the last days before Singapore fell, and in the long ghastly period of enslavement that followed, many a surgical operation was successfully carried out because there were on hand medical orderlies with the required technical training and ability.'

In early October, shortly after I arrived back in Malacca, Andrea, a well-known Sydney journalist, arrived on the scene to file exclusive reports for the *Sun* newspaper in Sydney. If anything, she was worse than Adele Shelton Smith.

Andrea's real name was Dorothy Hetty Fosbury Jenner (nee Gordon). She was born in 1891 on a station property at Narrabri, New South Wales. After completing her private school education and travelling to England, she established a dressmaking business in Sydney before heading to America, where she married and divorced Murray McEwen. After working as an actress for Paramount Pictures and obtaining small parts in various films, she resumed dressmaking and married George Jenner. The marriage lasted a scant two years.

During a tour of Europe, Dorothy attended a bullfight and cabled her impressions to the Sun *newspaper in Sydney, using the by-line 'Andrea'. This led to a weekly syndicated column – a mixture of gossip, royal news, fashion, character sketches and theatre reviews.*

Andrea's chatty wartime reports from Malaya and Singapore, simply signed 'Andrea' with a rounded, flourishing signature, were published in the paper over several weeks, with the last one appearing long after she had departed for Thailand, en route to Hong Kong.

The first story to appear after her arrival in Singapore was about a Highland Gathering she attended.

> The skirl of pipes floated over the steamy hills reaching far beyond into the jungle while the games were in progress. Great interest was centred in the reels – two, four, six and eightsomes – and tremendous was the prowess of the exponents of the various forms of Scottish dancing.
>
> One, Downs, a simple Digger belonging to the AIF, entered for all possible events. He walked away with every type of solo dancing, and stood out in all the partnered reels, so much so that the commanding officer of the Highland regiments asked to see him in order

> to congratulate him. The general told him that he had never seen finer footwork even in Scotland, and asked Downs's colonel if he might be attached to the Gordons as dance instructor for a period. The permission was granted.

The Scottish dancing exponent was Signaller Raymond Downs, of 2/19 Battalion, the New South Wales Highland Dancing Champion. His victory over expert Scottish dancers from the Gordon Highland and Argyll and Sutherland Highland regiments made national news in Australia. The Sydney Morning Herald *reported that his prowess and skill amazed not only judges and other dancers, but 'astonished born-and-bred Scots'.*

Andrea then ventured further afield – to the British garrison at Changi, where she interviewed a member of the Women's Royal Naval Service. Her report, and another published three weeks later, simply reinforced the stories published by Adele Shelton Smith months before.

> The WRNS' quarters, as are all the quarters for the women of the Forces, are as comfortable its any home in Malaya. Without being luxurious, they have enough of the home touch to help create that atmosphere of well-being, without which these brave young things would be useless.

Shortly afterwards, Andrea caught up with some of the Australian nurses, including Matron Drummond. Originally the Matron in Charge of 2/4 Casualty Clearing Station, she had been transferred to 2/13 AGH on its arrival in Singapore. Plumpish and with trademark owl-like spectacles, Irene Drummond looked after her nurses and their welfare like the proverbial mother hen.

Andrea gushed:

> On a strip of palm-girt shore, overlooking the grey-green sea, is a huge, gaunt clump of structures, which was a school. Now it is a transit hospital, where newly-arrived Australian nurses 'break' their journey before being detailed up country or to such large military hospitals as the Alexandra, in Singapore.
>
> I went out to tea with Matron Irene Drummond (of South Australia), 13th Australian General Hospital, who has served in Malaya in different posts for upwards of eight months. It certainly was as good as Benzedrine to meet with such a fine, happy and courageous lot of women. Many of them had been in the country only six weeks, but they were on for anything.
>
> This detachment of nurses will serve in Johore Bahru, being attached to the bulk of the rather more local troops, and whatever hardships present themselves, they're on. It was fun to find out just where that wide circle of girls came from — we sat in seance formation for tea — the Coast Hospital, St. Vincent's, St. George's, Kogarah, Prince Alfred, Launceston Hospital, Adelaide Hospital, Brisbane General Hospital, Western Australian Government Training School, Austin, Victoria, St. Luke's, in our own backyard. It is very amusing to watch their reactions to being the centre of attraction; to find themselves with a double-up of dates for every moment of leave in this Eveless Eden.

Matron Drummond (right) with Sister Gardham (left) and Sister Hannah

Although Andrea, later described as a 'war correspondent', wrote what are best described as gossipy puff-pieces, the journalist did notice a distinct air of apathy, despite the obvious military presence.

> To the newcomer from Australia the dogs of war seem to be barking furiously; so vivid is the defence set-up, and one is apt by comparison to compare our apathy with the noticeable steam-up. Concentrations of troops, mechanisation on the march and preparations appear in mushroom growth wherever one goes.
>
> But after settling in one discovers it is also only comparative. To the soldier, sailor or airman freshly arrived from the Middle East, or a bomber command in Britain, where death and destruction stalk by their sides, this Malayan picture is a happy valley in a fake paradise, and a land of plenty in which the Big Thing is still out of focus.

While in Malaya, Andrea insisted on observing an infantry battalion. The commanding officer, wanting to impress on her that life in Malaya was no picnic, took her on a route march with his soldiers through the jungle. Pointing to his sweat-drenched troops, he said, 'Look at their pants, see how wet they are'. To which the redoubtable Andrea quipped, 'And what do you think my pants are like?'

Two months later Andrea became a prisoner of war in Hong Kong.

CHAPTER 3

At war

About a month after Andrea left Singapore, two British warships, HMS *Prince of Wales* and HMS *Repulse*, arrived at the naval base, causing great excitement.

> *Ignoring Admiralty advice that they would be 'more of a bait than a deterrent' and that their dispatch was a 'major strategical blunder fraught with the gravest of risks', the elderly* Repulse, *launched in 1916, and the brand-new* Prince of Wales, *pride of the British Fleet, arrived from England on 2 December.*
>
> *To the people of Singapore and Malaya, the well-publicised arrival indicated that 'Britain meant business'. According to the onlookers who flocked to see the vessels, Japan had 'stuck her neck out too far and would now have to pull it in again'. What the civilians did not realise was that the rest of the 'fleet' defending Malaya and Singapore consisted of three small and outdated cruisers, seven destroyers (of which four were obsolete), three gunboats and a collection of small craft, ranging from motor launches to minesweepers.*

On 8 December, our relaxed lifestyle came to an abrupt end when, as they say, 'the balloon went up'. Japan, without any declaration of war, invaded northern Malaya, bombed Singapore, Hong Kong and other islands, and also attacked the United States' naval fleet at Pearl Harbor, with devastating effect. It was announced that Australia was at war with Japan.

> *At 4 o'clock that first morning of the war, the Japanese turned their attention on Singapore. Although it was three hours since enemy troops had stormed ashore at the Beach of Heavenly Passion at Kota Bharu in north-east Malaya, Singapore was ablaze with lights. Unopposed, squadrons of enemy planes unleashed their deadly hardware. Most bombs fell on Tengah and Seletar airfields, causing little damage, but others fell on the city itself. Chinatown took the brunt of the attack. According to the official figures, 60 were killed and another 133 were taken to hospital, but the death toll was undoubtedly higher. The European residents,*

unaware of the carnage taking place in the Chinese quarter, watched the show from their living room windows and gardens, believing it was a spectacular and very realistic air-force exercise. It was not until those near enough heard the anti-aircraft guns, and the crump of exploding bombs, that they realised it was not.

Apart from the introduction of total blackout regulations the next night, the early morning raid made little impression on the population of Singapore. After they had finished gawking at the damage and marvelling at the size of the bomb craters, life went back to normal and remained that way until the next raid, three weeks later.

Rumours now reached Malacca that the Japanese were coming through Burma, with claims that hospitals had been attacked, nurses raped and patients murdered. Although Dr Coates expressed the opinion that the nurses could be 'trapped like flies' if the Japanese moved south, higher authorities believed 2/10 AGH was ideally placed at Malacca, being far enough away from Singapore, the expected front line, for the wounded to be moved up there for treatment.

Although most people were taking what appeared to be a most unrealistic and relaxed view of the situation, the Royal Navy concluded it could not let the sea-borne landings go unchallenged. Prince of Wales *and* Repulse *would sail at once to the Gulf of Siam in a show of strength. With no air cover they were sitting ducks.*

An enemy reconnaissance plane spotted the ships.

Five torpedoes struck Repulse. Prince of Wales *was hit by two torpedoes, and then repeatedly attacked by bombs and torpedoes. The commanders of both vessels, a captain and an admiral, went down with their ships, along with 845 sailors.*

With the loss of the ships and so many highly trained naval personnel, all hope of the Navy impeding or preventing enemy landings in Malaya was gone. So, too, was the value of the magnificent naval base. When news of the disaster reached Churchill, he was devastated. 'Over all this vast expanse of waters Japan was supreme, and we everywhere were weak and naked.'

Despite this, there was no sense of urgency or anxiety among the Australian troops who, having been placed on third and then second degrees of readiness, had received the long-awaited signal that hostilities had commenced. Over at Batu Pahat, where 2/30 Battalion was keyed up and raring to go, word arrived that the newly arrived British Fleet had intercepted the Japanese convoy, which had turned tail and fled. On the strength of this, Lieutenant-Colonel Galleghan gave permission for a concert to be held, at which he made the announcement public. There was no panic either at 22 Brigade or at 2/10 AGH at Malacca, not even when the true situation became known. Life, in fact, went on as usual.

Meanwhile, as the Japanese thrust south into Malaya in a three-pronged attack, any hope of halting the enemy faded. For troops trained for conventional warfare, and for troops trained hardly at all, it was too big an ask. Even those who put up spirited resistance could not continue to do so indefinitely. Dog tired, and with no prospect of relief, even the most tenacious units had no option but to withdraw. Left without air cover, and with transport unable to use anything but sealed roads (of which there were few, apart from major trunk routes), they were constantly harassed by enemy aircraft and had to fight lightly clad enemy soldiers who rode bicycles, used tracks through the plantations and jungle, and lived off the land. The over-encumbered Allied army fell back repeatedly, until the whole of northern Malaya was in retreat.

At Malacca the 2/10th had been taking less urgent cases from 2/4 CCS and the 2/13th, but this ceased as the Japanese edged closer, and the hospital found itself in a forward position. On 15 December, all hospital personnel were ordered to wear Red Cross brassards on their left arms.

In preparation for possible bombing raids, the outer walls of our hospital had been sandbagged, but at this stage very few casualties had been admitted, as our own infantry troops had not yet engaged the enemy.

For the Australians, positioned way to the south and far removed from the scene of battle, Christmas Day passed with reassuring normality.

At Malacca, General Bennett hosted a cocktail party and for lunch we enjoyed roast turkey, ham, baked potatoes and peas, followed by fruit salad and ice-cream, with an optional bottle of beer to wash it all down. After a rest, it was time for tea – a traditional Yuletide dinner of roast meat, roast fowl, plum pudding and cream, followed by a very unconventional piece of durian, the odoriferous fruit so loved by the Malays. Known as the King of the Fruits, it is an acquired taste, and a week-long festival is held every year when the fruit is at its ripest. Legend has it that, if you eat durian while in Malaya, you will return.

We had scarcely digested our Christmas feast when more bad news arrived – the town of Ipoh had fallen to the Japanese.

On New Year's Day, Pat was among 20 nursing staff transferred from Malacca for attachment to 2/13 AGH, which, in November, had moved from Katong across the causeway to a brand new mental hospital at Tampoi, not far from Johore Bahru. In preparation for the move, the nurses on detachment to the 2/10th had been returned to their unit. The buildings were not completely finished, but the military had seized the initiative and commandeered them before the mental patients had a chance to move in.

The hospital was well established by the time Pat came on the scene, but when the 2/13th staff had arrived to set up the wards, May Setchell and her fellow nurses had discovered there were no beds and that the surgical instruments consisted of two pairs of artery forceps, a probe and a pair of scissors. An urgent call went out to nursing friends in Australia, who immediately dispatched any unwanted instruments.

Mental Hospital at Tampoi

By 4 January the defence position centred on Slim River, too close to Malacca for comfort. Colonel Derham, anxious about the safety of 2/10 AGH, which had 800 tonnes of equipment to move, ordered a total withdrawal to the 2/13th. By 10 January, all the patients had been moved from Malacca to Tampoi, along with most of the remaining staff, apart from some who were sent to 2/4 CCS at Kluang. They only just made it. The following day the Malacca hospital was bombed. By this stage, the Allies had little air cover, as most of the aircraft had been destroyed.

One of the patients at Tampoi was Charles Cousens who, on 23 December, had accidentally received second-degree burns during the firing of Jemaluang village on Malaya's south-east coast, in order to deny it to the enemy. He was admitted to Tampoi on Christmas Day and was still there when Bonny Howgate arrived on 5 January from Malacca. To her delight, she was able to spend a couple of hours each evening with her 'pal' until 14 January, when he was discharged and posted to the nearby General Base Depot.

The nurses transferred to the 2/13th were put on night duty and, as the Japanese moved further south like an unstoppable steamroller, we were soon very busy. Like most people who are sent from one hospital to another, most of us were put on night duty to relieve the regular staff during the day.

Daytime sleep was just about impossible because of aerial dogfights overhead. They created a distraction as well as a cacophony of noise as the few Allied planes we had left tried to intercept Japanese aircraft on their way to bomb Singapore or, having failed to do so, to chase them after they had dropped their deadly load. It was a one-sided contest. Our planes were hopelessly outnumbered and not nearly as good as theirs – but we were not told this until the war was over.

The hospital was very spread out, with huts for the staff scattered around the vast grounds. When trainloads of wounded were expected, some of the day staff rested on the patients' beds on the verandahs until alerted that the ambulances were on their way. Then it was 'all hands to the pump'. Some of the injuries were severe – mutilated limbs, gaping wounds in abdomens caused by bomb fragments and terrible disfigurement. Despite the carnage, I was most impressed by the quiet efficiency with which the doctors, nurses and orderlies worked.

The patients didn't say very much. It was tragic to see these beautiful young men coming in so badly wounded and having to patch them up. Quite a few of the fractures were multiple. Some patients had their legs in plaster or one leg in plaster and one up in extension, with weights on it. But no matter how bad the injury, they were always in very good spirits and never complained.

While at Tampoi, we had flights of planes constantly passing overhead on their way to bomb Singapore. As the nearby General Base Depot was a potential target, we were supposed to go into slit trenches or run through a gap in the fence and into the nearby jungle when the air-raid sounded. Those of us on night duty said we had to get some sleep somehow and slit trenches were just that. So we stayed in our beds listening to the planes pass overhead and the sound of the ack-ack of anti-aircraft guns.

Then, in about mid-January, we were all ordered to evacuate to Singapore.

Japanese radio warned the hospital to vacate Tampoi as, by 26 January, the buildings would be needed by the Japanese army. With front-line resistance fading, it certainly looked that way. A new home on Singapore Island had to be found for 2/10 AHG so, on 13 January, Colonel White and Matron Paschke inspected Oldham Hall, a boarding house in the Anglo-Chinese School, situated on Bukit Timah Road, about 3 kilometres from the city. Just two days later, in a remarkably short space of time, the old mission building, with indifferent sanitation facilities, was converted to a military hospital.

A few days later, Manor House, a large guesthouse several hundred yards away, was taken over to accommodate surgical cases. By 26 January, the staff had settled in to the new site and begun to receive battle casualties from Mersing and Jemaluang, on the east coast of Johore, in the area entrusted to 22 Brigade.

The wounded were coming in from 2/4 CCS, which was still on the mainland. Descriptions of the patients' injuries were written on cards tied to their shirts – a red one for the seriously injured, white for less serious wounds. Those who had been given morphine had a purple M marked on their foreheads in indelible pencil. At first, we had no gas connected and, with some of our equipment lost along the way, we had to sterilise our instruments by boiling billies of water on spirit stoves.

Meanwhile, the 2/13th, with its sister hospital temporarily out of action, had expanded from 600 beds to 1,200 in a very short space of time. On 24 January, as the battered remnants of the Allied forces prepared to cross the causeway in preparation for a final stand on Singapore Island, the hospital was ordered to move back to its original billet at St Patrick's School at Katong. The transfer of patients, staff and equipment took just 38 hours.

On 3 February, the 2/10th received a visit from General Bennett, who was 'shocked' by the overcrowding. He recorded that 'Every room was packed with beds, practically all of which were occupied. A few malaria patients were arriving and I was expecting more . . . The men, especially the wounded, were very cheerful.'

As more casualties arrived, the entire school and surrounding private houses were pressed into service. To make more room, medical cases were transferred to a convent, a kilometre or so away.

At the 2/10th's Oldham Hall-Manor House complex I was put in charge of a surgical ward that consisted of two tennis courts covered by a huge marquee – not the safest place to be with a war going on. We were placed 'on alert' and told to go to the trenches or bunkers, but this was completely impractical as the alert extended for the whole time. When we were given direct orders to take cover, we refused, as we had no intention of leaving our patients to seek shelter in the dank bunkers. We figured that we would not be put in detention for disobeying an order because, if we were, who would do the nursing?

Airstrikes came on a regular basis – 6 am, 3 pm, 9 pm and midnight – but there seemed to be almost a constant barrage of shelling and firing. However, we were so busy it didn't worry us and, in any case, I was in charge of a ward and couldn't show fear or worry. So I just kept on working.

The day-staff worked a straight 12-hour shift; the night-staff, two six-hour periods because of the heavy workload. With only two sisters rostered on each ward at night, they could not possibly cope, so at least two of the day staff extended their shift, often working until 10 pm, after a 6 am start. As the intensity of the Japanese attacks on the island and city increased, the locally

Oldham Hall

sourced staff, not at all keen to be caught in our employ if the Japanese arrived, packed up and left. With no one to serve meals in the dining room, we ate in the wards.

Betty Jeffrey, another sister assigned to 2/10 AGH, recalled:

> All the wounded just kept coming and coming, one ambulance after the other, day after day, night after night; it just didn't let up. We never had enough beds. When the hospital was full after a few days we had to start taking the houses down the street. They were all evacuated, empty, and we just took them and took them and took them. So the hospital staff was very spread out. But somehow or other we just coped. No person went without care.

I was dressing a wound on the leg of a soldier aged about 18 when shelling started on 30 January, destroying the kitchen. After checking with the senior orderly that the ward was 'secure' (which meant dropping the side flaps of the marquee and seeing if any of the patients were distressed or without a tin hat), I returned to my patient, who could not be moved as his other leg was in plaster and traction. As each shell went over, he and his companions said, 'Don't worry about that one Sister.' They assured me that the one we couldn't hear would be the one to worry about. I pretended not to hear their remarks as they joked about which part of their anatomies they were going to protect with their tin hats or bedpans, which were issued when we ran out of hats.

I then received a message that the senior pharmacist wanted to see me. I took the treatment sheets across to the dispensary, where the two pharmacists joked about what they had and hadn't done during the shelling. One of them then became quite serious and gave me a phial of morphia, asking if I knew what to do with it if things became grim. I replied, just as seriously, 'Yes, chew it up, glass and all.'

On 7 February, prior to invasion of the island the following night, the enemy began an intensive artillery barrage. Despite the large Red Cross laid out on the lawns of Oldham House, 15 shells dropped on the hospital grounds. One landed on the verandah, killing one patient and wounding others. The nurses remained calm, earning praise from General Bennett who wrote:

> The nurses were cool and courageous throughout the shelling, neglecting their own safety to protect their patients. These nurses are the nearest things to angels I can imagine. They never quarrel among themselves. They devote themselves wholeheartedly to the task, frequently working continuously for over twenty-four hours to deal with a rush of casualties. They never complain and always have a smile and kindly word for our wounded and sick men.

The only news we received was of retreats. We were inundated with patients. They were everywhere – in beds, on stretchers, on verandahs of the houses and in garages. On one occasion we worked a 48-hour shift without a break. We were so short staffed that Matron Paschke turned her hand to kitchen duty and made gallons of soup to feed the new arrivals, while we cut away their clothes to assess the extent of their injuries. Torrential rain only added to an already stressful situation. It was so heavy that the ground under the marquee became waterlogged, and the beds began to sink.

Despite the proximity of the battle, I was amazed at the calmness of the patients, even though many of them were so young. When dressing the leg of a 17-year-old, a sudden burst of machine-gun fire caught us unawares. The youngster calmly said, 'That's ours Sister.' I was always grateful my hands and voice remained steady, but I will admit that occasionally my knees felt a bit weak.

Despite the workload and the shelling, Pat's friend Kath Neuss took time out to write a letter to her family: 'Guess you will be thinking I've gone up in smoke. There is plenty of it about.'

There was also plenty of smoke at the 2/13th where, although the buildings were clearly identified with a large Red Cross, the hospital was bombed. Fortunately, it was night and the bomb aimer was off. Four missed. The fifth caused some damage to a ward, but no injuries. Almost as unnerving as enemy bombs were the great guns, installed by the British at nearby Changi. Whenever they opened up to fire on Johore, the ground shook, and the hospital buildings with it.

Bomb damage at 2/13 AGH at Katong

Smoke from burning oil tanks casts a pall over the city

Some orderlies and Sister Dot Freeman, who had miraculously escaped death herself, brought the injured men into the ward on stretchers. Major Furner then came by, telling me 'For heaven's sake Sister, get under the table'. I told him that there was no way that I could do my dressings under the table, or get my work completed. He then left, I think in disgust, as there was no point in talking to me. Our headquarters eventually made contact with the Japanese and the shelling stopped, but not before two staff members were killed and others wounded.

Late on the evening of 8 February, the Japanese swarmed across the Straits of Johore in their thousands, infiltrating the thinly dispersed Australian battalions and overrunning them. Once ashore, the enemy pushed on relentlessly towards the city.

We had been receiving wounded on alternate days from 2/4 CCS which, on crossing the causeway, had initially been relocated temporarily to Bukit Panjang English School, near Bukit Timah. However, with the Australians defending the north-western area, they had moved to the Swiss Rifle Club, which was much closer to the action.

With the big influx of wounded, we were informed on 10 February that six nurses were to be ready within 15 minutes to board one of the makeshift hospital ships. Matron had already drawn up the list, and I was pleased that I was not on it.

The original list was changed when Thelma McEachern discovered that she had been selected and her best friend, Molly Campbell, had not. Thelma was on duty that day with Pat's friend 'Mitzi' Mittelheuser, who had been chosen, and asked if she would swap with Molly. They flipped a coin to see who would go. Mitzi gathered it up quickly, saying it was tails, and that she had lost. The final six evacuees were Aileen Irving, Veronica Dwyer, Violet Haig, Iva Craig, Molly and Thelma.

The nurses were to accompany the wounded on a small hospital ship called Wah Sui. *Matron issued instructions before they left: they were to take as many men as they could, stay with their patients no matter what might happen and get them to safety.*

Wah Sui *was a Chinese vessel, requisitioned by the British and under the control of civil personnel. The nurses managed to get about 450 wounded soldiers aboard. However, many civilians, believing that Singapore could not possibly fall, had left it too late to leave and now, in a state of panic, poured aboard with their belongings, leaving no room for any more wounded. Fortunately, although spotted by an enemy plane as they steamed south,* Wah Sui *was a hospital ship, prominently marked with huge Red Cross emblems, which the pilot unexpectedly respected – giving a wave as he turned his aircraft away.*

The nurses had deliberately selected the most urgent cases for evacuation and their patients were seriously ill. However, no one appeared to be in charge and they received no help from the civil authorities, who denied them access to medical supplies. Thelma Bell recorded:

> There were only the six of us to look after those men, yet there were other women on board. They were all well spoken and must have considered that they were above it. They wouldn't help us in any way. On one occasion a little native lass was having a baby. We asked but they wouldn't give over a bedroom for her, so she had it on the deck and one of our girls delivered it. There was a lot of friction between the nurses and the authorities aboard. Our boys were going without.
>
> The men were fed mostly tinned food, which was no good for them at all because they were so sick. And we weren't allowed to change their dressings because we were told there was a shortage. The stench was terrible and the men were in a lot of pain. When we asked for supplies the answer was always, 'You can't have any of those. If the British can put up with it, why not the Australians?'

The nurses watched helplessly while civilian passengers were issued with the supplies, ate the food and drank the beer.

On Friday, 13 February, one of the wounded, a member of 2/30 Battalion, died and was buried at sea. That night the Captain spotted two burning ships and stopped in the hope of picking up survivors.

The following day Wah Sui *docked in Batavia, where the wounded were transferred to a hospital ship bound for Colombo in Ceylon (Sri Lanka), but no further provision was made to transport the nurses elsewhere. No one would take responsibility for them – in effect, they had been abandoned. Although they tried to board other ships, access was denied, and it was not until a week later that they managed to board* Orcades, *which had arrived to disembark Australian reinforcements from the Middle East, and finally sailed for Colombo.*

When they eventually reached Australia, they were forbidden to talk about their experiences for fear of upsetting the British.

Early on 11 February, we heard that a British artillery unit had placed a big gun practically on top of one of our red crosses. All army hospitals in war zones have red crosses on the roofs or nearby, but it is against the rules of warfare for combatants to use them as protection while engaging in battle. When our CO pointed out this irregularity to the artillery commander, the gun was moved a short distance away.

The gun was relocated the following day, 11 February, without further loss of life, but the same could not be said for the Alexandra Military Hospital where, three days later, retreating Indian troops erected machine-guns within the hospital grounds. The advancing Japanese troops, on whom they fired, considered that all bets were off, and used this breach of international law as an excuse to storm the hospital at 1 pm on the afternoon of 14 February. An officer holding a white flag of surrender at the entrance was the first to be killed.

Fortunately, all the female nurses had been evacuated, but the rampaging Japanese moved inside the building, killing not only doctors and nursing orderlies, but also two anaesthetised patients lying on operating tables – Corporal Robert Veitch, of the Federated Malaya States Volunteers, undergoing surgery to amputate his foot, and Corporal Gerald Holden of the Loyal Regiment, British Army. The invaders then entered the wards, herding about 200 patients and staff, tied into groups of eight, into three small rooms in a row of nearby buildings. The seriously injured were killed if they faltered.

The remainder, left without food, water or ventilation, suffered terribly and a number died during the night. At around 11 am the following day, the Japanese allowed the captives to leave the rooms in small groups, on the pretext that they were to be allowed access to water. However, the screams and cries of those just released soon made it clear to those remaining that the enemy troops were executing them. Providentially for those still left alive, a shell struck the building, interrupting the massacre and allowing some prisoners to escape.

About 11 am on the day that the gun was removed, Matron Paschke called us all together and said, 'I have been ordered to send half of the nurses out. Those of you who are prepared to stay move to my side.' We all moved as one body, giving her the wretched task of choosing who to send. Again, I was not one of them.

Casualties were coming in thick and fast at the 2/13th, among them a young machine-gunner awaiting surgery for the removal of multiple bullets, who asked for a cigarette. Putting it between his lips he inhaled deeply, only to have three plumes of smoke spiral from his bullet-ridden chest. With cases like this and many others requiring attention, none of the nurses wanted to hear that Matron Drummond had just received instructions that all 53 nurses and masseuses were to be evacuated.

However, before any actually left, the order was amended to send out 30 of the nurses, immediately, and the remainder the following day, as there was insufficient room for all of them on the two evacuation ships, Empire Star *and* Vyner Brooke. *Brooking no argument, Matron simply drew up a list, allowing 26 to return temporarily to the wards, much to the surprise of the male orderlies who had just bidden them farewell.*

Sister May Setchell, who had been on night duty at the convent annex and was asleep in one of the nearby houses, was hurriedly awoken and ordered to be ready to leave within the hour, taking whatever belongings she could squeeze into a very small suitcase. She, and all nursing staff who had been 'volunteered' to leave, were transferred to the harbour where their embarkation onto Empire Star *was delayed as an air raid was in progress.*

Empire Star *was a ship of almost 13,000 tons. The main decks were all but filled with vehicles and equipment, leaving little space for the more than 2,000 evacuees. The nurses were in a group of about 200 ordered into a cargo hold normally reserved for transporting frozen meat. In peacetime, the ship carried just 16 passengers. On this voyage, besides the 88 crew, there were 1,000 British airmen, 500 British soldiers and sailors, 53 Australian nurses and seven physiotherapists, a number of British nurses, about 140 Australian soldiers, approximately 70 specialised signal staff, 29 authorised civilians and about 200 other civilians. The 128 civilian women and 36 children were crammed into the few cabins and a small saloon.*

Also on board, packed in the nurses' luggage, was a 150-year-old heirloom bridal veil. Of Scottish origin, and beautifully embroidered with thistles at the corners, it had been entrusted to the nurses to take to Australia.

Nurses in the hold of *Empire Star*

Empire Star *set off for the wide, cliff-lined Durian Strait, where they were to await the arrival of three other vessels: SS* Gorgon *with 358 evacuees on board and two escorts, the Royal Navy's cruiser* Durban, *carrying just 57 passengers, and HMS* Kedah *with more than three hundred. During the night, 15 more ships joined the convoy – the British destroyers* Jupiter *and* Stronghold, *each with 150 evacuees, and 13 merchant vessels ranging from 200 to 6,000 tons.*

The convoy left at about 6 am on 12 February, protected from air attack by a thick haze, but this soon lifted. Durban, *in the lead, had just cleared the Durian Strait when, at 8.50 am, they were spotted by a reconnaissance aircraft. It took just 20 minutes for 17 dive bombers to appear, peeling off in waves for the attack.*

Empire Star *was well armed. Anticipating that attack was extremely likely, the captain had already deployed his crew and Royal Navy gunners to battle stations. The available firepower was strengthened considerably by Australian soldiers who, although they were not front-line troops, set up Bren guns in the three lifeboats on the boat deck and assisted the RAF manning various machine-guns. Others stood by to assist the crew with firefighting.*

Military personnel not engaged on deck were either taking cover behind the trucks, where they let loose with rifle and pistol fire, or sheltering in the holds along with most of the nurses and male civilians.

Picking off the weakest first, the planes concentrated their attack on the smaller craft at the rear, sinking some and disabling others. The four ships at the front were targeted next, but the concentrated anti-aircraft fire forced the enemy to release their bombs at an altitude of about 1,000 feet (300 metres), thereby reducing their accuracy. Gorgon, *whose machine-gunners were credited with shooting down an enemy plane, emerged from the encounter unscathed.* Empire Star, *the largest vessel in the fleet and the last to be attacked, did not.*

As six dive-bombers hurtled towards the ship, the guns on board opened up. RAF gunners on the starboard side brought down one plane and another, smoke pouring from the tail, was forced to abort its attack, but nothing could stop the onslaught. Empire Star *took three direct hits, killing 12 of the military outright. Fifteen others and two of the ship's crew were very badly wounded. One of the aft lifeboats, where six Australians had stationed themselves with their Bren guns, took almost a direct hit, killing five of them and critically injuring the other.*

With no thought for their own safety, two Australian Army sisters and close friends Margaret Anderson and (Audrey) Vera Torney of 2/13 AGH, ran to the wrecked wooden turret. As they lifted a limp and bleeding man onto the deck, the planes turned for a strafing run. Without hesitation, Sister Anderson threw herself across the wounded man in an attempt to prevent him incurring further injury as the bullets slammed and ricocheted around them.

The aircraft then peeled off, allowing him to be dragged to safety.

The pair also evacuated wounded men from a cabin, where fumes and smoke threatened to suffocate them, and took them onto the deck, believing the air-raid was over. When the planes returned, they remained beside their patients, shielding them with their bodies. For this outstanding bravery, Anderson received a George Cross for Gallantry, a non-combatant award equal in status to a Victoria Cross. Torney was made a Member of the British Empire.

By 9.30, the first attack was over, allowing nurses and RAF medical officers to set up a casualty clearing station in the main saloon to attend to the wounded. Lieutenant Denis Emerson-Elliott, British Secret Intelligence, who had been on the bridge throughout the attack, had gone below to check on the condition of the hull following a couple of very near misses. The iron plates were still sound, but below decks it was an absolute shambles, with casualties and blood everywhere. Although pale and distressed, the Australian nursing sisters were quietly and methodically attending to their patients.

The wounded, including those seriously injured, now totalled 37.

Sister Setchell recorded:

> We had very little equipment but we looked after the 37 wounded as well as we could. I do not remember having anything to eat. With so many on board it was impossible for the crew to feed us, but I do remember drinking tea from a Players cigarette tin. I also remember during the worst of the bombing, one of the air force personnel who was on board passed around a bottle of whisky, which we all just drank neat.

Despite the nurses' best efforts, the soldier shielded by Margaret Anderson and the critically wounded soldier from the lifeboat both died, bringing the death toll officially to 14. Throughout the attack, the nursing sisters had maintained their composure, singing wartime songs and that perennial Australian favourite, Waltzing Matilda, *to keep up morale and prevent panic from setting in among the passengers.*

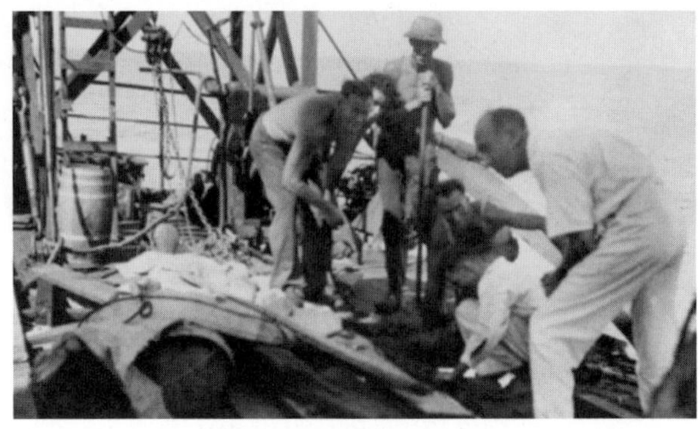

Crew members clear wreckage

At 10 am the enemy returned. This time it was a squadron of 20 heavy bombers, which circled the convoy at long range before splitting into three flights. Augmented by an additional nine aircraft, they maintained continuous high-level bombing attacks on all the ships from a height of 6,000–10,000 feet (1,800–3,000 metres). At 1.10 pm the attack was strengthened by another 27 aircraft which concentrated their bombs on Durban *and* Empire Star, *the two most attractive targets.*

Throughout the terrifying three-and-a-half hours that this second attack lasted, the captain kept his head, manoeuvring his ship from side to side as members of the crew relayed information on the movement of the enemy planes as well as the probable angle of attack. Although some of the bombs exploded only 3 metres from the vessel, lifting her hull from the water with great shuddering vibrations, the vessel came through safely. At 1.30 pm the bombers broke off the attack. It was all over.

Empire Star *suffered the worst damage, as two bombs had penetrated the deck. One killed several soldiers and injured about 18, with three more allegedly blown overboard. One badly wounded airman dragged himself to the railing and toppled into the sea. Most of the others were beyond help, having lost limbs or been disembowelled. One, who was still alive, was on fire and screaming for help. An Australian airman, Flight Lieutenant Charles Johnstone, tipped a bucket of water over him. The bomb that wiped out the Australian gunners also killed an RAF officer sheltering in a cabin. Fortunately, it missed the holds, but for those cowering below the noise was so tremendous that an Australian nurse had both her eardrums ruptured.*

The ship eventually reached Java safely, where the military were disembarked to continue the fight. After essential repairs were carried out, Empire Star *continued to Australia without incident. The nurses and the remaining passengers were the last to be successfully evacuated from Singapore.*

However, some of the nurses, far from being welcomed home, were treated with hostility by ignorant members of the public – when Sister Ada Morse and others alighted from trains, they were 'greeted' by people waving white feathers, the symbol of cowardice. Shortly after their return to Tasmania, Sisters Gunton and Rayner were stopped on a Hobart street and also presented with white feathers, leaving them stupefied with shock and disbelief.

The heirloom wedding veil survived the voyage. Unable to locate the owner, the nurses entrusted with its delivery decided to honour her by wearing it when they became brides.

Those of us still at Oldham Hall and Manor House stayed at our posts but, with half our workforce gone, we were spread even more thinly. Matron instructed me to take some orderlies and open up a couple more houses to receive casualties. She appointed Sister Jenny Greer to take over my ward. I didn't want to leave my patients and, as Jenny was a more senior nurse in terms of training, I protested. However, Matron told me that, as I had been longer in the army, I was more senior and must take the responsibility. Within a couple of hours, with the help of the orderlies, the beds were made up and half-filled with patients.

All that night, the big gun fired salvo after salvo, rattling the windows and sending flakes of plaster falling onto the beds. Exhausted troops tried to sleep, gaining some comfort from one of the soldiers, a pianist from Mario's nightclub in Melbourne, who played and replayed all the current popular tunes throughout the night.

Shortly afterwards, heavy transports pulled up outside our window. On hearing English voices, one of the sisters shouted, 'Drive on soldiers, this is a hospital.' A tired, shocked voice with a northern English accent said, 'Jesus, women!' They had survived a hazardous trip across the island and thought they had at last found a safe place to stop and rest. They couldn't stay, of course, but someone handed them a bottle of beer and they went on their way.

About 11 am the next day, 12 February, Dr Rod Jeffries came to the house where I was working. He asked me, 'Why are you still here? Don't you know the rest of the sisters are leaving?' I didn't. As we all knew, the Japanese were close, but I didn't want the patients to think I'd just disappeared, so I replied, 'No-one has told me. I'll just say goodbye to the patients.'

I can still recall his tired, exasperated voice saying, 'Do you always have to do the right thing?'

Leaving the hospital and my patients was the worst moment I had experienced in my life. We only had 30 minutes' notice and everyone was in tears.

We would have given anything to stay, not knowing the gravity of the situation, since the hierarchy, in their wisdom, had decided to censor all news from the general public. We were kept completely in the dark. Although people in Australia and Colonel Derham, our Director of Medical Services, knew of the horrors of Hong Kong, where nurses had been raped and murdered, we knew nothing of this in Singapore.

With the civilians also totally oblivious of the danger, three evacuee ships that had been sent out by England had left Singapore barely a third full. As things deteriorated, a very high number of young women with families were caught. It was too late by the time they realised the danger and there was a mad rush to board anything that could float. Consequently, nobody will ever know how many people were lost in small boats.

Aware of the outrages that had taken place when Hong Kong fell, the Colonel had wanted to evacuate us three weeks earlier, but was overruled by General Bennett and the British commander, Lieutenant-General Percival. They thought it would be bad for civilian morale and, like everyone else at that stage, they believed that Singapore would not fall. However, since then, Bennett had seen the writing on the wall and had ordered our evacuation several days previously. In hindsight, we would have been better off staying, as the survival rate among women internees who remained in Singapore was quite high. I later learned that, if we had stayed, and there was any indication the Japanese might harm us, the hospital orderlies were to shoot us.

As Rod walked with me to the ambulances, the patients called out 'Goodbye, and good luck Sister!' An almost inaudible voice then said, 'She'll need it!'

I never saw Rod again.

CHAPTER 4

Shipwrecked

Army ambulances took us to St Andrew's Cathedral where we reported to Matron Paschke and Colonel Glyn White, and met Matron Drummond and the other sisters from the 2/13th who were also being evacuated. Among them was Sister Vivian Bullwinkel, from Kapunda, in South Australia, who, at age 26, was one of the youngest nurses. Later, I heard that, while we were waiting in St Andrew's, Singapore had been subjected to one of the heaviest bombing raids of the war.

By the time Pat was relocated to St Andrew's Cathedral on Newbridge Road, not far from Raffles Hotel, those fighting for survival in the city were confined within a small perimeter. The 2/10th staff had moved into the Cathay Theatre, establishing hospitals in the adjoining Cathay Building, Singapore's only 'skyscraper', and in the Cathedral, with an annex in the Adelphi Theatre across the road.

Bomb damage in the city

Out at St Patrick's School, where there were officially 825 beds, 900 patients had been admitted. They were accommodated in the schoolrooms of the main block, the gymnasium, nearby houses and in the beautiful upper storey chapel, now minus its magnificent stained glass window of St Patrick, removed for safe keeping. As the hospital was outside the final defence line, red crosses were prominently displayed and the walls floodlit.

The remaining male staff and the patients were now at the mercy of Japanese forces advancing from the east. They arrived at St Patrick's at around midday on Friday, 13 February. As the walking wounded watched from the windows, five of the six Australian soldiers on guard duty at the gate were taken prisoner and beheaded.

When all was quiet, the doctors ventured outside to examine the carnage. They discovered that the sixth man, Private Bill Cooke from Queensland, was lying at the bottom of the gory pile. He was still alive, but only just. Evidently, the sword meant to decapitate him had hit a rock, deflecting the blade. He was very badly injured, but the medical staff managed to sew him up, giving strict instructions to keep the wound covered with a scarf, lest the Japanese see it and realise that he had survived an attempted beheading. Fortunately, although the Japanese soldiers who arrived to occupy the hospital looked fearsome, no further harm was done.

Meanwhile, Matron Drummond and the twenty-six 2/13th nurses reached St Andrew's safely, where they joined Pat and 37 others from 2/10 AGH and 2/4 Casualty Clearing Station, before being transported to the harbour.

Since we were driven almost all the way to the wharf area from St Andrew's in covered ambulances, we saw little of the devastation caused by the Japanese onslaught, until we left the vehicles to walk the last few hundred metres.

Carrying their equipment, they were escorted to HMS Laburnum, *the naval shore base at Telok Ayer Basin. Dead and decomposing bodies littered the streets, which Sister Elizabeth Simons described as 'indescribable ruin, blazing buildings, acrid smoke and abandoned or wrecked cars'.*

The previous day, Lieutenant Denis Emerson-Elliott had driven along the same shattered streets to board Empire Star. *As a British secret service agent and a member of the highly secret Oriental Mission, a cover name for SOE-Far East, Denis had a price on his head and his evacuation had been ordered lest he fall into enemy hands. He had about an hour to reach Number 4 Wharf in Keppel Harbour, about 6 or 7 kilometres from his office in the underground command bunker at Fort Canning, in the heart of the colonial district.*

However, with the city a shambles, he realised it would be a near thing. His small car had covered less than 2 kilometres when Denis saw a row of streetlamps directly ahead, falling like wheat stalks before a scythe. It wasn't until he saw people sprinting across the road to take cover in a monsoon drain that he realised it was an air-raid. Following their lead, he threw himself into the drain as a stick of bombs pulverised his car.

He made his way along desolate streets on foot, trying to get his bearings from familiar landmarks reduced to rubble and with the sun blotted out by billowing clouds of black smoke. Bomb craters pockmarked the streets and festoons of telegraph and phone lines dangled from teetering poles.

On reaching our destination at around 1 pm we were met by Major Tebbutt, an Australian intelligence officer, who said he had been sent to oversee our evacuation and accompany us to Java. However, we understood that he actually had some kind of connections to secret military intelligence, and this was a convenient cover story.

Major William Alston Tebbutt, a Sydney solicitor from the suburb of Roseville, was with a group of military specialists – radar technicians, cypher clerks, code-breakers and intelligence personnel. Tebbutt was actually the Australian liaison officer with the Far East Combined Bureau (FECB), a British organisation that had relocated to Singapore from Hong Kong. It appears that Englishman Cuthbert Tyrwhitt, also a member of FECB, was also on board.

The FECB was run by the Admiralty, which was in contact with the British secret service agency known as MI6. Officers from the British Army and Air Force were attached to the Bureau, along with officers from the Australian, American, Dutch and French military. A vital component of the Bureau was Y Section, which detected, intercepted and decrypted enemy wireless signals. Tebbutt, who knew of the rapes and massacres in Hong Kong, had discussed the evacuation of the nurses with General Bennett at Divisional Headquarters at Tanglin Barracks just a few days before. Neither Tyrwhitt nor Tebbutt could be allowed to fall into enemy hands. The former was on board masquerading as the ship's second engineer. The latter had been 'appointed' to oversee the evacuation, as a means of escape for himself and to provide a cover story.

However, with British naval staff asserting that there was no need to hurry, it was not until 11 February, when Captain Geldardt of Malaya Command made it clear that enemy attacks on the city were imminent, that the evacuation of both men was treated as a matter of urgency.

We were directed by the Major to board a lighter, towed by a tug, which took us out to the harbour proper and to *Vyner Brooke*, a small, ageing vessel flying a White Ensign. Formerly the Rajah of Sarawak's private 'yacht', it had definitely seen better days. As we left the wharf, watched by senior medical officers, some of the girls began singing 'The Maori Farewell', rather unsuccessfully. Drawing alongside, we boarded through a large steel door in the side of the ship.

Built in Scotland in 1928, the 'Royal Yacht' was a single-funnelled British-registered cargo vessel of 1,670 tons, named after the Third Rajah of Sarawak, Sir Charles Vyner Brooke.

Normally crewed by 47, it carried cargo in two holds, fore and aft, and up to 44 first-class passengers in cabins positioned on two levels amidships. Above these was the lifeboat deck and the bridge, its windows protected against bomb blast by mattresses. There were also two deluxe cabins and a private sitting room at the stern, normally reserved for the Rajah and Ranee.

In peacetime, the vessel had plied the waters between Singapore and Kuching, under the flag of the Sarawak Steamship Company. However, at the beginning of the war, Vyner Brooke *was requisitioned by the Royal Navy, crewed with naval personnel and local reservists (including the ship's captain), painted grey and converted to an armed merchantman with a four-inch deck gun, two Lewis guns and depth charges. It also had a wireless.*

As an evacuation vessel, the ship was equipped with enough lifeboats, rafts and lifebelts for 650 people. There were three lifeboats on each side of the vessel – one large and two small – capable of holding a total of 140 people. The two large and two of the smaller boats were on the top deck, either side of the bridge, with the two smaller boats and a quantity of life rafts on the stern deck, just above the staterooms.

As the voyage south through enemy-infested waters was fraught with danger, the ship's captain, Richard Edward (Tubby) Borton, now a lieutenant in the Malayan Royal Volunteer Naval Reserve, had been ordered to proceed to Java via the Durian and Bangka (Banka) Straits by night, and to lay up close to the coast by day.

The available cabin accommodation was given to civilian women and children, who made up the bulk of the 250 or so passengers and crew. The remainder of the European civilians packed the dining saloon, while the Eurasians were in the after-hold. The Chinese crew members were in the forward hold. Sister Mavis Hannah was offered the radio operator's cabin, but was told by Matron Paschke to give it to an elderly couple. On board there were 65 nurses, all told. Kath Neuss, Jess Doyle, Pat Blake, Win Davis and I found a quiet area on the port side, well forward.

The captain and crew, who had spent the last few days evading Japanese planes, had arrived in Singapore hoping to have a rest. Instead, the skipper was ordered to refuel the ship and prepare to sail to Sumatra. Rations had not been provided for the evacuees and the only food taken on board were our rations, supplied by the army. However, the big problem was drinking water as the vessel's supply was inadequate.

The entire island of Singapore was now under a pall of black smoke from the burning of the Shell Oil storage tanks, part of a 'scorched earth' policy to deny precious fuel to the enemy. Bombs were also constantly dropping on the island, igniting other fires. The harbour was under frequent attack and the ack-ack guns were responding, but we were too tired to care. The feeling of sadness and desolation was quite overwhelming.

When the ship slipped her moorings at approximately 4 pm, Jenny Greer gamely sang 'Wish me luck as you wave me goodbye'. However, we didn't go far. As we approached the middle of the harbour, the ship was intercepted by a naval launch. An officer, standing on the deck with a revolver in his raised hand, shouted 'Stop, and await further sailing orders'. What the hold-up was, we didn't know.

Sister Jean Ashton recorded that dinner that night was a scratch affair. With little food on board, the nurses were asked to organise and assist with a meal for the passengers, which they did, using their army rations of tinned meat and vegetables, followed by army biscuits. Forming a chain gang, they passed plates of food from the galley. The nurses ate their share sitting on the deck, which was devoid of creature comforts apart from a few rugs, chairs and stretchers.

It was agreed that strict rationing was essential, and that meals were to be restricted to two per day – breakfast and dinner, with tea and biscuits at noon.

All we had with us by way of personal items were our tiny suitcases or knapsacks, which we had been carrying to and from the wards for the last fortnight, knowing we could be ordered to leave. So, with nowhere else to bed down and the ship at anchor, we just curled up on the deck and went to sleep. We were woken when a lighter bumped up against the hull and we heard people scrambling aboard, but I don't know where they went – probably down into the hold or any space that they could find. At around 10 pm the ship slipped out of the harbour.

As Vyner Brooke *threaded its way through the minefield, other refugee-laden vessels followed, including the P&O Line's* Mata Hari, *on charter to the Admiralty. On board this ship, which was a little over 1,000 tons, were 483 passengers and crew. However, during the night the ships in the little convoy became separated.*

All the next day, *Vyner Brooke* hugged the offshore islands, seeking protection of the mangroves. That morning, Matron Paschke and Major Tebbutt had addressed the passengers, stressing the need to be very careful with water and food, both of which were in short supply. Lectures were also given on the ship's alarm system, lifeboat drill, the use of lifebelts, what to do if attacked and how to abandon ship. Nurses were assigned to various areas of the ship and given responsibility for the passengers in those zones. Kath, Win and I were assigned to the forward part of the ship. Should we be attacked, we were to muster our charges, try to keep them calm and move them to the lifeboats. As there were insufficient lifeboats, anyone who could swim was instructed to take to the water and use a life raft. All passengers were given lifebelts, which were altered to fit children.

My kit bag, containing my photograph album, had been tossed aboard and Kath had put her diary in her small case. As we had always spent leave together, we passed the time by indulging ourselves in some happy reminiscing.

On the morning of Friday, 13 February, at about 8 o'clock, Vyner Brooke, *having passed unhindered through the Durian Strait, anchored in the bay of a small island off the Lingga group. Japanese planes flew over at 9 am and again at 11, circling the ship but not attacking.*

Approximate route taken by *Vyner Brooke* from Singapore

At 11.30 the vessel proceeded cautiously on its way along the Lima Channel, close to Lingga Island. They were spotted again at 3 pm, but again the ship was not attacked.

At sunset the captain decided to make a run through the Berhala Strait for the Bangka Strait. However, prowling Japanese warships with searchlights seriously impeded progress and he was forced to hove to at 1.30 am off the Tudjuh Islands, in open waters between the Berhala and Bangka Straits. At first light, 6 am, an enemy plane spotted them. It signalled something indecipherable to the ship and, when there was no response, raked the deck with machine-gun fire, holing the lifeboats on the port side. Three hours later another plane circled, but there was no further attack.

The Captain now informed Tebbutt that he considered it suicidal to remain so close to the only land as the ship could be easily seen and would be a sitting duck for enemy bombers. He believed, however, that he might be able to take evasive action in open waters, so at 10 am he gave orders to raise the anchor and head for the Bangka Strait.

As we were steaming quietly along, trying to be as inconspicuous as possible, the siren sounded several warnings. Planes had been spotted by the lookout.

They were nearing the entrance to the strait when, shortly before 12 noon, a formation of nine bombers came into view. The planes flew over the ship several times before three peeled off, to drop their bombs from an altitude of about 300 feet (90 metres). The Lewis and anti-submarine guns fired, and the ship turned away at full speed, constantly altering course. The bombs missed, but only just, and shook the vessel. When the next three planes attacked, and then the next, the Captain again took evasive action. Then, at 1 pm, all nine planes attacked together.

Everyone took cover. We were ordered into the saloon below and told to lie on the floor, but Kath Neuss, Win Davis and I took shelter in an officer's cabin, well forward on the port side. From the portholes we watched in fascinated horror as the first few bombs fell. They just missed, as the ship was zigzagging, but it was no use. A bomb hit the gun on the forward deck, killing and injuring the gun crew and killing the elderly couple in the radio operator's cabin. Another went down a funnel into the engine room, killing the engine room staff and badly burning crew members. A third bomb hit the life rafts on the rear deck and exploded close to the saloon, killing some of those sheltering there and wounding two or three sisters, who were hit by shrapnel in the buttocks and legs. The ship was then rocked by several near misses, one of which blew a hole in the starboard side. Others sent huge waterspouts shooting into the air, drenching those on deck. With water entering the hold, the ship began to list to starboard.

The bridge had suffered considerable damage and was on fire. There was no hope of saving the vessel and the order to abandon ship was given at 1.20 pm. There was no panic among the nurses. As soon as the alarm had sounded, the sisters went into a well-rehearsed emergency evacuation procedure, methodically organising the passengers and treating the injured with dressings, bandages, hypodermics and morphine, pinned inside their uniform pockets. Each nurse also carried an additional bag of medical supplies. With no apparent thought for themselves, they moved among the wounded, giving assistance. Anyone too badly injured to survive or be evacuated was given an extra shot of morphine, to ease the way.

Some passengers, sliced open by shrapnel, were obviously beyond saving. The elderly man sitting beside Sister Sylvia Muir had his abdomen ripped open by flying shrapnel. Trying to keep his intestines from spilling out, he attempted to sing a few bars of 'Rule Britannia' before dying. The girl sitting on the other side of Muir was severely injured in the buttocks. The sister's hand was covered in blood, but it was not hers. She was bowled over by the force of the bombing but her injuries were confined to a cut elbow. As the nurses were under orders not to leave until every civilian was accounted for, about half a dozen began a search of the ship to ensure that no one able to be evacuated was left below.

As the ship was listing to starboard, orders had been issued to lower the lifeboats on the port side first, before the angle became too great. All had been strafed by machine-gun fire and bombarded with shrapnel from near misses, which had not only pockmarked the hulls but also partially cut the ropes attaching the boats to the davits. As the crew lowered the first boat, filled with women and children, one of the lines broke, spilling the passengers into the sea. The remaining line then gave way and the boat plunged into some of those struggling in the water below. A second boat, which broke completely free before it could be boarded, speared into the water and sank. The third, with two Malay sailors on board, also dropped into the sea rather rapidly, but remained upright.

The three boats on the starboard side were also damaged, but appeared seaworthy enough. Matron Drummond stepped aboard the larger one. With Matron Paschke on the deck supervising and with the assistance of the ship's first officer Sub-Lieutenant Bill 'Ginger' Sedgeman, the Royal Navy's Lieutenant-Commander James White, two sailors, the supplies and the injured were loaded aboard. The injured included a badly burned Malay seaman and Sister Flo Casson, who had been in the saloon and received serious shrapnel wounds to her legs. As the boat swung out, someone threw in some coats and blankets.

The smaller boat amidships was earmarked for other wounded, including Sister Rosetta Wight, also severely injured by bomb splinters while sheltering in the saloon, and Sister Florence Salmon, whose breast had been almost torn off by shrapnel. As the loading got underway, the attack aircraft circled high above like vultures, waiting to administer the final blow. One peeled away, plummeting downwards, machine-guns blazing. As the bullets lashed the water, panic-stricken survivors tried to push themselves under, hampered by the buoyancy of their life vests. For those on rafts or in the lifeboats, there was nowhere to hide. Fortunately, there were no further casualties either in the water or on board the ship. Once the second boat was lowered into the water, others climbed on board.

Wilma Oram and Mona Wilton of 13 AGH helped Kath, who was bleeding with a severe injury to her hip, out of the cabin and onto the promenade deck. I didn't have time to assess her injury, so I assisted her down a ladder, streaming with water from the near misses. Win Davis followed. I climbed into the lifeboat, but I could see that there would not be enough room for others, so Win and I helped Kath in, then relinquished our places. Before slipping into the sea, I gave my tin hat to Kath in case she needed to help bail water and told her that we would see her on the beach.

A third starboard boat, positioned aft, was only partially filled, due to the increasing list, which made boarding difficult. The crew attempted to lower it, but the lines became tangled, leaving it and its occupants suspended above the water. Meanwhile, other passengers scrambled down rope ladders, jumped overboard or slid down ropes to reach the available lifeboats and rafts, stripping the skin from their hands in the process.

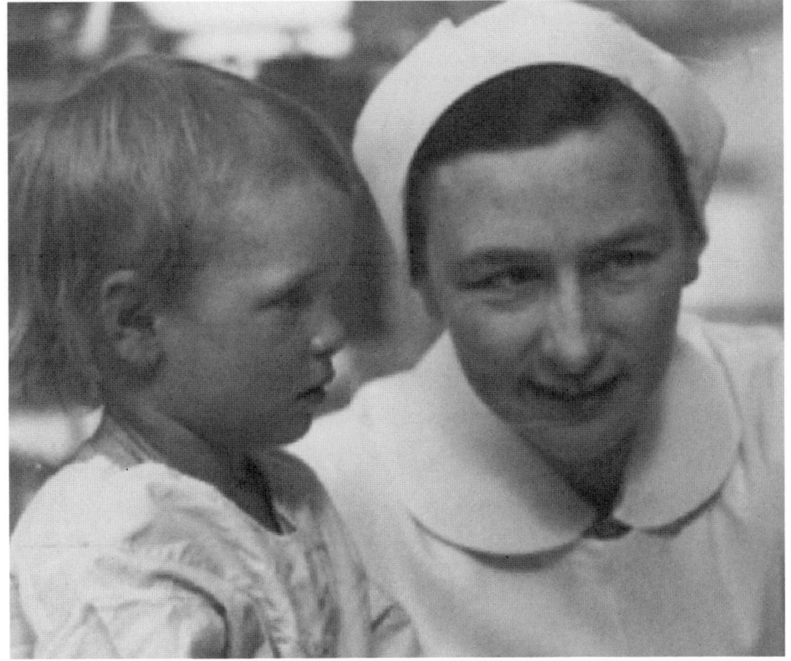

Pat's friend, Kath Neuss

Eric Germann, a powerfully built 31-year-old brewer from New York, made his way to Matron Drummond's partially submerged lifeboat with Izidore Warman, a three-year-old White Russian boy, before assisting a grossly overweight civil engineer and a wounded soldier. Six or seven others also managed to get to the boat before Eric cut the line tethering it to the ship. With the wounded lying in water in the bottom of the boat, and several people clinging to ropes along the side, Eric clambered on board himself, picked up an oar and started to row while others bailed furiously.

Matron Paschke, after checking that all her 'girls' were safely off the ship, was the last to leave. Removing her shoes, she climbed onto the railing of the now partially submerged vessel and called 'Here I come girls. Look out for me. Remember, I can't swim', before launching herself over the side. When she surfaced, willing hands pulled her onto a raft. On it, or clinging to it, were Sisters Caroline Ennis, Hilda Dorsch, Mary Clarke, Gladys McDonald and Annie Trenerry; a Chinese boy aged about three; a four-year-old English girl; two Malay sailors and five civilian women.

Win and I were soon joined in the water by Pat Blake. Win had been raised in the Clarence River area in northern New South Wales and was a good swimmer. I was a poor swimmer, but a good floater. We were within a reasonable distance of Bangka Island, which was about 12 miles (19 kilometres) away, and I could see a mountain [Mt Menoembing, 445 metres high] which acted as a landmark. As we had our lifebelts on, I was confident we could make it.

It had taken about 20 minutes from the time the first bombs found their mark to abandoning ship. The time of each individual evacuation was precise as everyone's watch, apart from mine, had stopped on hitting the water.

> *As Sister Betty Jeffrey was one of the last to leave the ship, her watch stopped at 2.40 pm. However, Captain Borton and Tebbutt put the time of the sinking at 1.40 pm, and of abandoning ship at 1.20 pm – a one-hour time difference caused by the passengers' watches not being adjusted from the current Singapore Time (7.5 hours ahead of GMT) to Northern Sumatra Time (only 6.5 hours ahead).*
>
> *At 1.40 pm,* Vyner Brooke *heeled completely over on the starboard side, crushing the women and children still in the stricken lifeboat. It remained bottom up for about two minutes, exposing the propeller, before it slid into the depths, bow first. Trapped air broke the surface in huge bubbles, bringing with it smashed wood, luggage, packing cases and bodies wearing lifebelts, which bobbed among the debris and fish, killed by concussion. The corpses of small children and babies, too small to be fitted with life jackets, floated briefly before sinking below the waves. Betty Jeffrey had the odd experience of bumping into dead sharks, also killed by the explosions.*

Dead bodies floated all around us – men, women, children and nursing sisters. Some had been machine-gunned or hit by shrapnel. Others had broken their necks on their lifebelts when they jumped into the sea. The belts were just four blocks of cork, covered with rough canvas. We had been told to hold them down if we had to jump in order to prevent them hitting our chins and breaking our necks, but some people must have forgotten. I turned the dead over to see if I knew

Castaways adrift

them, before struggling on. One of the floating victims was a very fat girl whose skirt had ridden up, exposing her pink bloomers. I knew she was dead, but I couldn't stop myself from making her decent by pulling her skirt down.

We kept getting caught in oil slicks, which not only covered our skin and clothes in sludge but had fatal consequences if inhaled. I wondered how could a small ship have so much oil. Win and I found a stretcher floating among the wreckage and clung to it. Betty Jeffrey and Iole Harper joined us until, being good swimmers, they struck out on their own. Not being a strong swimmer myself, I had just about had it when, at about 4 pm, a life raft reached us. On it were Elizabeth Simons from 13 AGH; a seaman named Stan, who had served on *Prince of Wales*; a Malay wireless operator and a very badly burned gunner, both from *Vyner Brooke*. It was Stan's fourth sinking – twice while serving in European waters, then *Prince of Wales*, and now *Vyner Brooke*. He and the others pulled me onto the raft for a rest. The gunner, who was practically naked and without any protection from the scorching sun, was in considerable pain, so Jessie took off her uniform and covered him, while I gave him some morphia tablets to swallow.

Later we were joined by Mrs Mary Brown, a very stout lady aged in her sixties, and her adult daughter Shelagh, a very sweet girl in her mid-twenties. There was a third woman with them, but she was unconscious and was swept away. As by this time I was well rested, I slid back into the sea to join the able-bodied, leaving Mrs Brown on the raft with the burn victim. Bangka Island was not far off now, but with no oars we had no way of steering the raft. We tried to head for land by hanging onto the rope with one arm and paddling along with the other. A few times we came within a hundred metres of the beach, only to be caught in rips and borne swiftly seaward. Island currents are contrary things.

The sisters who had survived the attack were now split into small groups. Some survivors, like Major Tebbutt, Betty Jeffrey and Iole Harper, who could all swim well, headed confidently for land. Others clung desperately to the side of a raft or a lifeboat, willing themselves to hang on and not to fall asleep. Vivian Bullwinkel, who could not swim, was one of a group of nurses ordered to take to the water by Matron Drummond. Jumping over the side, she dog paddled to a partially submerged lifeboat. In it or clinging to the sides were 12 sisters, including the injured Florence Salmon, Kath Neuss and Rosetta Wight; Thomas and Carrie Betteridge, an elderly British couple who were desperately holding onto each other; Miss Louise Beetson, a schoolteacher from St Andrew's School in Singapore; and Sub-Lieutenant Jimmy Miller, the ship's engineer and second officer.

Sister Jenny Greer and four colleagues from 2/10 AGH (Jessie Blanch, known always as 'Blanchie', Beryl 'Woodie' Woodbridge, Florence Trotter and Joyce 'Tweedie' Tweddell) showed indomitable spirit as they paddled off towards the distant shore, clinging to a length of wood and singing 'We're off to see the Wizard'. They then fought a battle to keep each other awake throughout the night.

Not everyone acts well in a life-or-death situation and there was an ugly incident on one raft when white European women ejected a Eurasian hairdresser named Marie, who swam towards Eric Germann's boat screaming for help. Threatening to capsize the raft, Germann forced the women to take her back. Shortly afterwards, Vyner Brooke's *First Officer, Bill Sedgeman, joined those clinging to Germann's boat and assisted in securing three empty rafts to it with a long line. After transferring the uninjured to the rafts, the boat headed for the nearest land.*

At around 5 pm we saw a bonfire on a beach. A lifeboat had reached the shore and the beacon had been lit to guide us in. But the current was against us and before long we drifted further south and lost sight of it. Smoke stacks then appeared on the horizon. Our hopes that they belonged to the British Navy were dashed – it was a Japanese invasion fleet. At midnight they anchored near us. Landing craft, laden with armed soldiers, slid out from the sterns of landing ships. We were obviously of no interest, as torches were flashed on us – but that was all. The boats then left and sped off to take possession of the island. By this time, I was close to exhaustion.

In our struggle to reach Bangka Island we did not notice that, in the darkness, the burned gunner had slipped off the raft. However, by this time we were too tired to really care. With our arms aching from hanging onto the ropes and the poor unfortunate gunner gone, we took it in turns to rest on the raft. As dawn broke, we were close enough to land to see that the Japanese troops from the invasion fleet were already in occupation on the island and that landing craft were ferrying supplies ashore.

No one paid us any attention. We tried to turn the raft away, but it was useless. We would have to land, Japanese or no Japanese. It was easier said than done, as none of us had the strength to swim ashore for help, although Win thought at one stage that she could try. We were still trying to struggle to the beach, probably only 200 yards (180 metres) away, when one of the boats changed course and stopped. Putting their hands under our armpits, the Japanese hauled us aboard.

Our rescuers would prove to be quite kind and gentle, but I was the first one they grabbed. I thought 'Well I'm not going to be the only one', so I immediately turned around to grab Win. Jessie, Mrs Brown and Shelagh followed, but the men stayed on the raft, which the Japanese tethered to their craft with a rope. The Japanese soldier who appeared to be in charge picked up a coconut from the bottom of the boat. With a parang (a heavy jungle knife), he chopped off the top and handed it to me. One after another, we drank the cool, soothing coconut juice – balm to our sore, parched throats. It was the best drink I had ever had in my life. On reaching the beach, Mrs Brown, who, besides being very overweight had a heart condition, found that her legs would not hold her and she collapsed on the beach.

Pat and her companions did not know how lucky they were. They had been rescued by members of the Akatsuki Detachment, a non-combatant barge and boat-landing unit, which was ferrying stores to a beach near Muntok, the island's main town at the northern entrance to the Bangka Strait. This unit had assisted in the movement from Hong Kong of 229 Infantry Regiment, 38 Division, whose troops had raped European and Chinese nurses at an emergency hospital at The Jockey Club at Happy Valley Racecourse. They had then moved on to another emergency hospital, St Stephen's College at Stanley, where they bayoneted 56 wounded British and Canadian soldiers in their beds and raped and murdered seven Chinese and British nurses. Two British officers who tried to protect them were also killed.

The only nursing sister in Hong Kong to successfully defend her patients was Elizabeth Mosey, from South Australia. Born in 1876, she had served with distinction in World War 1 and post-war as matron in country hospitals, before volunteering her services in World War 2. Now aged 65, Matron Mosey had been left in sole charge of wounded Scottish troops at the Repulse Bay Hotel. When marauding Japanese troops tried to force their way into her emergency ward, they were confronted by a stoic, white-haired lady, wearing her World War 1 medals, barring the doorway with her body and saying 'You'll kill me first'. For saving the lives of her patients by this outstanding act of defiance, Elizabeth Mosey was awarded an MBE in 1948.

Pat and her companions were helped ashore by Japanese clad in G-strings, who were busily unloading stores. As the women waited on the sand, an animated discussion took place between the rescue team and a member of the shore party. The castaways, who assumed their fate was being discussed, were relieved when their benefactor won the argument.

During this time, Mrs Brown, who had tied her handbag full of money and valuables to the raft, had recovered somewhat and began pointing imperiously to her handbag. One of the Japanese obligingly waded into the water, cut it free with a knife and, on examining the contents, calmly strolled off along the beach with it.

As Jessie's uniform had gone over the side of the raft with the burned gunner, she was now clad only in her bra, panties and petticoat. Her hair, which was cut very short, was plastered to her head with oil and water. Unable to determine if she was male or female, one of the Japanese looked down her chest, whereupon the Malay wireless operator immediately whipped off his shirt and gave it to her. Jessie's hands were raw from sliding down a rope; amazingly, I still had my lipstick in my pocket and used it as a salve. Being bright red, it looked really gruesome, but the lanolin in it seemed to help.

We were then taken into a large shed where the Japanese, despite their kindness, were very interested in our watches. The other sisters had large, 'sensible' ones, which had stopped immediately they hit the water. Mine was small, neat and inconspicuous. Despite being immersed in the sea, it was still ticking away. The metal band had broken a week before and, not having time to replace it, I had put on a white linen band, now covered with black oil. The broken metal band hung down. When the Japanese came to see what I had, I laughed and shook my wrist saying, '*Tidah biak, tidah biak*' – 'no good, no good'. The Japs, who understood Malay, laughed. Later I pinned the watch out of sight inside my uniform.

About 10 am, Allied planes were spotted and we took cover in some nearby jungle. One plane dropped a stick of bombs, which exploded harmlessly about 50 yards (45 metres) away. It felt very odd being attacked by our own side. The soldiers were very excited by the raid and asked 'Americano? Americano?' We had no idea who they were or where they had come from, and if we had we wouldn't have told them.

I pointed to my uniform and Red Cross armband and tried to explain to our captors in my limited Malay that, as non-combatants, we couldn't be taken prisoner. It was then that we discovered these Japanese spoke good English. Rather naively, we asked them to contact Victoria Barracks in either Sydney or Melbourne. When they said the Japanese had already taken both cities, it didn't seem worthwhile pursuing that objective any further.

The Japanese made no attempt to molest us in any way, but they did make us feel uncomfortable by placing their hands to our foreheads at intervals to check if we had a fever. We were given some rice and bottles of sarsparilla soft drink before being taken to a nearby house to get some clothes. A dead Indonesian, possibly the owner, lay nearby. Under the circumstances, we thought it best to ignore him. Our escort, who was a polite fellow, told us to take whatever we wanted from the house, which had already been looted. We had been instructed to remove our footwear before abandoning ship, so none of us had shoes, apart from Mitzi, a non-swimmer, who figured she would drown in any case, so what was the point of taking off her shoes.

We were not comfortable taking anything from the house, but as I have small feet I managed to find some sandals that fitted and an old sarong. Jessie also found a battered kettle and some other bits and pieces. The soldier removed a mirror from the wall and showed me my reflection, doubling over in mirth at my exclamation of horror. My eyes were scarlet, my face purple and my hair was hanging down and coated with sticky black oil. I was not offended that he laughed – I did look hideous and at least it showed he was human.

We were then led to a crude shower room. Some of the Japanese tried to peek at us over the top of the stall, but as we just turned our backs on them they didn't see much. After we had changed and tried to wash the oil from our clothes, we were escorted to an adjacent shed, which we knew from the grunts and the smell was home to some pigs. The pigs were in one half, behind a flimsy partition, and we were in the other. The floor was a mixture of broken concrete and dirt, but there was a narrow wooden bench along one wall, so we put Mrs Brown on it.

As the Malay wireless officer and Stan, the British sailor, had been taken away after the air raid and had not returned, we were now without our male protectors. However, I found an iron bar, about 15 inches (38 centimetres) long and 2 inches (5 centimetres) in diameter, and took up a position on the floor, nearest to the door.

After a while, Win and I thought we should find out what had happened to Stan and the sailor. We discovered them in a long line of men, Japanese and prisoners alike, unloading cargo from a ship which, due to the shallowness of the water, was anchored well out. As the day wore on, we began to wonder what fate had in store for us.

Win and I were sitting on a log when a young Japanese pilot came down the track. Pausing, he removed a pair of beautiful leather flying boots and then his socks, which he threw to me. I don't know why, but I thanked him very much in Malay, 'Terima kasih bunyah'. Win muttered, 'Put them on.' When I said, 'He might have tinea', she hissed, 'There are worse things than tinea.' I had been lucky enough to find the sandals in the house so, for the first and only time in my life, I wore 'bobby' socks with sandals.

In the late afternoon, while resting on the floor in the shed, we heard a hen squawking loudly. Less than an hour later, the Japanese, closely followed by our two male companions, arrived with delicious fried chicken and real, freshly brewed coffee.

Leaving Mrs Brown on the bench, we all settled down once more on the floor. I slept with the iron bar by my right hand. The radio operator lay across the doorway and Stan was next to him, with his head near my thigh. We all had a fairly restless night, particularly Mrs Brown, while trying to keep her balance on her hard, narrow bench, and Stan, who discovered the next morning that his head had been resting on the iron bar.

Shortly after daybreak, we were interviewed by a fat, sleazy-looking, middle-aged Japanese. On our insistence that the only work we could do was nursing, he looked at us slyly and assured us that there was 'always work for women'. When he asked where we wanted to go, Mrs Brown sensibly said 'where there are other women'.

At about 2 o'clock that afternoon, we set off on foot along a rough road leading through the jungle to Muntok, the island's main town. I had my socks and sandals on, but all the others with us were shoeless. Mrs Brown had never walked barefoot in her life, so I bandaged her feet with strips torn from rags we found in the house. However, it was not very successful as the material had no elasticity and every 30 minutes her feet needed to be rebound. The guard became angry each time we stopped until I had the bright idea of putting the airman's socks over the bandages. I was as glad to get rid of them as Mrs Brown was to receive them. At about 4 pm we reached a large corrugated-iron cinema, where we met other sisters from our group, held under guard with other survivors.

Among the nurses held at the cinema were the Wizard of Oz quintet – Jenny Greer, Jessie Blanch, Beryl Woodbridge, Florence Trotter and Joyce Tweddell – along with Blanche Hempsted, Eileen Short (known as Shortie) and Wilma Oram. Jean Ashton, Oram and her best friend Mona Wilton, who had all boarded the third lifeboat, had jumped into the water on the instructions of one of the sailors when it became stuck and the ship began to heel over. As it turned turtle, they avoided being sucked down by the sinking ship, but Oram and Wilton were struck by rafts cascading from the deck. Oram suffered a nasty head wound to the back of her head, but lost sight of Wilton, whose skull was crushed. She was last seen floating away by Jean Ashton.

Fortunately, Oram managed to find a raft, which she shared with a civilian woman, Dot Gibson, until the pair came ashore near Muntok Jetty. They were the first castaways to arrive. Before being transferred to the cinema, they were held in the courtyard of the nearby Customs House, where Oram learned that some Japanese occupation troops were not taking prisoners. A group of eight men told her they owed their lives to Veronica Clancy, whose group had provided a distraction by coming ashore just as the Japanese were about to shoot them.

Aircraftsman J E Barker also had a hair-raising tale. He had been manning a Royal Air Force air-sea rescue launch and had assisted in bringing survivors of Vyner Brooke *ashore. After finishing this task, he was taken into custody, lined up with a number of other Europeans and moved in single file to a small building. The two men in front of Barker were interviewed briefly before being escorted one by one to the other side of the building by a Japanese soldier. A shot rang out each time, and the soldier returned alone.*

The Japanese officer asked Barker to identify himself, before the soldier escorted him from the room. However, Barker had no intention of dying. As soon as he was alone with the soldier he delivered a solid punch, knocking him down. Barker then took to his heels, jumped into the sea, and swam out to a nearby wreck. He hid in the submerged part of the wreck, where there was a small air gap between the water and the ceiling. That night he swam ashore and, proceeding further along the coast, joined Major Tebbutt who had swum ashore on his own. He had landed some distance from where he had spotted the bonfire – on a beach roughly midway between Tanjung Oelar (Ular) and Tanjung Kelian. A section of this unnamed stretch of sand would later be referred to as Radji Beach. Tebbutt and Barker then wandered around in the jungle with another survivor for the best part of a fortnight before being taken prisoner.

Jean Ashton was with Veronica Clancy's group, which had been brought to shore by Aircraftsman Barker in his RAF air-sea rescue launch. After abandoning ship with Oram and Wilton, Ashton had found Mitzi and Sylvia Muir clinging to an overturned lifeboat – possibly the one on the port side that had broken free during the attempted launching and spilled the occupants into the water. The trio were then joined by Sisters Clancy, Gardam, Hughes and Raymont, along with Mrs Annabelle Bull and her six-year-old daughter Hazel, a couple of civilian men, a Malay sailor called Billy and several other women. Using their combined muscle power, they had managed to turn the boat over, plugging the shrapnel and bullet holes with various items of clothing. However, there were no oars and, despite furious bailing and rigging a sail of sorts, using two of the nurses' uniforms, they made no headway as the boat was settling further and further into the sea. Forced to abandon it, they were fortunate to be within reach of several rafts tied together.

Sitting or clinging to them was a good number of castaways, including Olga Neubronner, a former nursing sister who was in her late 30s and seven months' pregnant with her first child, and Mrs Evelyne Madden, aged 59, who had lost the skin off her hands when sliding down a rope and was highly traumatised. She had supported her husband, who was badly injured and had refused to don a lifebelt, until he died in her arms.

By general consensus, the group agreed that Mrs Madden and Olga should stay on the raft, with those in the water having a spell in rotation. On one of the other rafts, being propelled along by three nurses, were three British sailors, all of whom were uninjured, and Dr Anna Maria Goldberg-Curth – a German Jewess and paediatrician who, with her neurologist husband, had practised in Ipoh. When Veronica Clancy asked the doctor to get off the raft to make way for two of the nurses to have a rest, she refused point blank, claiming (untruthfully) that she was the mother of three children and her life was more important.

Putting her knee on the raft, an infuriated Veronica supported herself with her left arm and hit the doctor hard on the back with her fist. She didn't budge. Sister Blanche Hempsted then joined in, securing Goldberg in a headlock and pulling her into the water. Veronica had no luck in persuading the sailors to move an inch. Words failed to make any impression, and the nurses did not have the courage to physically attack them.

This life-raft group, numbering about 23, was eventually picked up by the RAF launch and taken to Muntok pier, where they surrendered. As they made their way down the jetty, Olga Neubronner suffered a miscarriage. The nurses did what they could, but the baby, a boy, was stillborn. Arriving at the Customs House, Veronica Clancy spotted an advertising sign on a mirror, exhorting those who could not return home to Europe for leave due to the war situation there, to 'Spend your Vacation in Sunny Australia'.

Many ships fleeing from Singapore had been attacked and sunk in what became known as 'Bomb Alley'. A large number of survivors made their way to Bangka Island, clinging to debris, rafts and lifeboats or managing under their own steam: British, Australian, Dutch, Irish, American, White Russian and Eurasian; old and young, injured and unharmed; civilian men, women and children, service personnel, government officials and nursing sisters.

One escape vessel that was not attacked was Mata Hari, *which had become separated from* Vyner Brooke *shortly after leaving Singapore. The ship had been allowed to surrender without incident and arrived under destroyer escort at Muntok, where the 400 passengers and their belongings were landed without having suffered so much as a scratch. Among the passengers were Doctor West and Lieutenant Surgeon John Reed, of the Malay Royal Naval Volunteer Reserve, who had a small case of medical supplies.*

Another vessel to surrender was a small launch of about 12 metres in length, Mary Rose. *On board were the Australian Trade Commissioner to Singapore, Mr Vivian Bowden, Assistant Trade Commissioner Mr Norman Wootton and political secretary Mr John Quinn. After capture, the Japanese escorted the launch into Muntok Harbour, where the passengers were marched under guard to the cinema. When one of the soldiers tried to take Bowden's gold watch and identity disc, the Commissioner, who spoke fluent Japanese, asked to speak to a senior Japanese officer so that he could explain his diplomatic status and request proper treatment for the captives. His request fell on deaf ears. He was taken outside, made to dig his own grave and shot.*

Other vessels captured at sea were also shepherded to the jetty where the passengers were unloaded. Unlike the oil-soaked castaways, who had only what they stood up in, these survivors had money and possessions. As they were unwilling to part with them, those who had nothing were forced to scrounge whatever they could – bits of old clothing, discarded mangy toothbrushes, half coconut shells for a food bowl, bits of wood and anything that could serve as eating utensils. Soap, shampoo and towels? These were now luxuries they had to do without.

We conducted a head count. Of the 65 nursing staff who had left Singapore on *Vyner Brooke*, at least 29 had reached the island. Many of the other girls, on being taken prisoner, had been slapped, hit or kicked and few had been given food. We realised how lucky we were to have been rescued by a medical and not an infantry unit. After a meal of rice and stewed vegetables prepared by the male prisoners, we lay down on the floor to sleep.

At mid-morning the next day, Tuesday, 17 February, we were all marched out of the cinema to a Chinese school, where we had a short rest before continuing to an internment camp, consisting of some tin-roofed, native-style atap (palm frond) huts, arranged around a square. Constructed before the war, they had been built by the Dutch as a quarantine station for their coolie labourers working in the tin mines. The front row was set aside for the guards and sick bay, with sleeping areas for the inmates along two sides of the square. At the far end was the cookhouse. A square of ceramic tiles, set in the middle of the square and covered by an atap roof, was designated for general purposes.

Running along the inner walls of the huts, which had been divided into rooms, were two cement bali balis, or sleeping platforms, about 3 metres wide, sloping towards a centre aisle. If sleepers slid down the slope to the edge of the platform during the night, the guard woke them up with a whack on their feet from his rifle butt as he passed through. We had no mosquito nets, and nothing to cover ourselves, other than our uniforms, so we were eaten alive at night. The one trickling tap – there was a severe shortage of drinking water – added to the general misery. A crude ablutions area with a filthy open drain served as a lavatory and a communal 'bathing facility'. This consisted of a long oblong tong (concrete tub) containing water and several battered dippers, which were used to pour water over our bodies. As there were no cubicles, the Japanese took advantage of what was, for them, a free peep show.

The quarantine depot's coolie-lines belonged to Bangka Tin Winning, a tin dredging company. Next door, connected by a barbed-wire run, was the men's camp, formerly the island's gaol and originally built to incarcerate life-term prisoners. When a new gaol made the building redundant, it had been converted to a pepper warehouse, only to revert back to a prison when the Japanese arrived. The male internees slept on pepper sacks in one half of the building, with 600 starved and ill Chinese coolies, all forced labour conscripts, occupying the other half. Captured in Hong Kong, they had been herded aboard ships, kept in the holds for six weeks and then dumped at Muntok to work on the airfield.

Well past their use-by date, their lives were of no consequence now that a new labour force had arrived. The shipwrecked newcomers were to take their place, marching at dawn each day to the airstrip, where they toiled all day before marching back at night.

There must have been several hundred people concentrated in the Muntok camps – men, women, children and servicemen. Most had been shipwrecked. The period immediately following our arrival was most distressing as people sought news of relatives and friends. We pooled our information and it was surprising how many we could account for. Not that any of us had any idea of how many lives had been lost. One report said that 28 ships had been sunk in the vicinity.

It is believed that between 4,000 and 5,000 evacuees perished in or around Bangka Strait on vessels that left Singapore between 12 and 15 February 1942. Vyner Brooke *was one of about 40 vessels sunk. Another 20 were captured. Only four reached safety.*

While most of our group were in relatively good shape, some were not so lucky and required medical attention. Mickey Syer, whose real name was Ada, and who had clung to a piece of wreckage until she was washed ashore, had her arm in a sling in an attempt to relieve an old spinal complaint, aggravated by her ordeal. Elizabeth Simons, although managing to obtain some ointment, was still very much handicapped by her raw hands, as was Veronica Clancy. As we had nothing with which to treat the burns, some had become infected and were pus filled. And Jenny Greer developed great weals on her skin after eating pieces of lily root that had been included in our stewed vegetables.

However, our most serious casualty was Jessie Blanch, one of the Queensland nurses, who developed a peritonsillar abscess – a severe infection of the tissue surrounding the tonsils, sometimes known as quinsy. A beautiful sari-clad Indian doctor, who was interned with us, attended her. She was very kind, but when the Japanese, under their philosophy of 'Asia for the Asians', allowed those who had been living under what they described as 'oppressive colonial rule' to go free, the doctor left. The rest of us had escaped rather lightly, apart from those who had spent a great deal of time in the water and had lost varying amounts of skin from underarms, chins and shoulders where the harsh canvas lifebelts had rubbed.

Life in the camp was very tedious. There was nothing to do and nothing to provide any diversion, other than playing cards, which someone fortunately had. The food was awful – just two so-called meals a day. For the first we lined up at 11 am for a dollop of rice, with some sugar or salt and a cup of lukewarm fluid that was supposed to be tea, but didn't taste like tea at all. The 'main' meal, another dollop of rice with a bit of vegetable matter or a tiny piece of meat, was at 4.30 pm. 'Supper' consisted of more hot tea at around 6 pm. The only drinking water available came in dribbles from the tap, and was rationed to a cup per day.

We nurses had no possessions, so we had to make do by scrounging for bits and pieces to serve as a bowl or cup or spoon. Slivers of wood served as eating utensils, empty tins as bowls – anything that was of the slightest use, even if it was originally designed as something completely different. If you couldn't find anything better, one hand became your rice bowl, the other your spoon.

Clothing was anything we could find lying about that could possibly be worn as is, or converted. Some of the internees had sewing machines, which we borrowed to fashion skimpy tops and shorts. Anything at all was cut up and refashioned, including some naval uniforms that we found in a storeroom. We thought the garments had been abandoned but they actually belonged to male prisoners sent out on a working party. They were not overly pleased to discover we had recycled their pants and shirts into sun-tops and shorts.

Bedtime was shortly after it got dark, at about 7 pm. Before trying to settle down on the hard, cold concrete for the night, we wrapped ourselves in anything we could find to use as protection from mosquitoes. Not that we got much sleep, with children constantly crying and guards patrolling up and down, flashing torches about and whacking anyone who was slipping towards the edge of the slab.

Things looked up a little when someone found some chipped rice bowls, discarded by the coolies and enough to supply all the nurses. We also acquired an old mattress, which I shared with Win Davis, Betty Jeffrey, Jess Doyle and Pat Blake. With five of us, it was a bit of a squeeze, but we didn't have it for long because two English army nurses, Margot Turner and Mary Cooper, arrived a couple of days later and they needed it more than we did. They belonged to the Queen Alexandra Imperial Military Nursing Service – QAIMNS, but commonly known as QA – and had been burned black by the sun after spending the best part of a week clinging to rafts. The pair had left Singapore with their hospital's nursing staff on the evacuation ship, *Kuala*, which was sunk by the Japanese off the coast of central Sumatra on 14 February.

Many of the survivors had made their way to nearby Pompong Island. Three days later, a rescue vessel, Tandjoeng (Tanjung) Pinang, *alerted to the situation by Dutch authorities in Sumatra, arrived and took off 200 women and children. After dropping about half the passengers in Sumatra,* Tandjoeng Pinang *sailed immediately for the supposed safety of Java. Late on the night of 18 February it was caught in a searchlight beam and sunk by enemy gunfire. With another nurse, Margot Turner assembled 16 survivors onto a makeshift raft. They included four children and two babies less than a year old. There was no water. Four days later, when found by a Japanese cruiser, Margot was the only one left alive. Her eyes were so sunken and her skin so blackened that there was confusion over her nationality.*

Mary Cooper was one of eleven who had taken to another raft. Five days later, when a Japanese ship picked up the survivors, only Mary and a young Australian woman named Molly Watts Carter, plus three Eurasians, were still alive.

Some survivors from Tandjoeng Pinang *reached Bangka Island only to be killed on arrival. Among them were the captain, New Zealander Basil Shaw, and crew-member Oswald Young who came ashore near the Tanjung Kelian lighthouse, a substantial structure at the entrance to the strait, where they were murdered on the beach on 21 February. The same fate befell survivors from other ships that had been sunk, including naval Commander Horace Vickers, whose decapitated remains were found in a plantation post-war.*

However, 76 castaways who survived the sinking of Kuala, *fared much better. Shortly after* Tandjoeng Pinang *had evacuated most of the women and children from Pompong Island, the rest were rescued by a small fishing boat, salvaged from Singapore by Australian mining engineer and master mariner Bill Reynolds, who also worked for the British undercover organisation, MI6.*

Among the refugees was Australian nursing sister Gwen Dowling, who was a couple of years ahead of Pat at Royal Prince Alfred Hospital. Gwen, who had been in England at the outbreak of war, had joined the QAs. Reynolds took his passengers, some of whom were hideously injured, to Sumatra's Indragiri River, where the British had established an escape route across the mountains to Padang, on the west coast. Although most of the wounded were ultimately captured, a good number reached Padang, where they were evacuated by British warships and Allied passenger vessels.

Reynolds handed over all those who were too badly injured to continue to Padang to Dr Albert Coates, who had left Singapore on Sui Kwong*, an auxiliary patrol vessel of just under 800 tonnes at around midnight on 13 February. Sixteen hours later the vessel was attacked. Coates was among the fortunate survivors rescued by* Tenggaroh*, a luxury launch owned by the Sultan of Johore, which was taking several senior Allied personnel, including Coates's fellow Australian officer, Colonel Broadbent, to the Indragiri River to join the escape route. On learning that many wounded would be arriving shortly, Coates and two of his medical staff, Sergeants Clancy and Hughes, left the launch and remained at Tambilihan on the lower reaches of the river. Here, with the help of Gwen Dowling, they converted a small village dispensary into an aid post.*

When Reynolds turned up again just on dusk four days later with another load of castaways, Coates was alerted to his arrival by a distinctly Australian voice bellowing from the water, 'Colonel Coates! Here is a new load of customers, plenty of them. Get your saw sharpened up.' He then left in search of other survivors.

After transferring the injured with great difficulty up a rickety ladder and along an equally decrepit jetty to a primitive room he grandly referred to as an 'operating theatre', Coates set to work. Using the most basic surgical instruments, including a meat chopper donated by a local, and with the help of his two sergeants (Gwen Dowling being 'all in'), Coates performed seven major operations that night. Two senior officers died, but he managed to save the life of Matron Jones, of the Singapore General Hospital, who had a bomb splinter lodged in her spine.

Once the numbers of wounded trickled to nothing, Coates and his helpers left for the west coast of Sumatra. Coates, who refused to leave his patients and escape on an evacuation ship, was captured. He was sent to the Burma-Thai railway, where his skills saved the lives of many prisoners of war.

We realised that we could be in the coolie-lines for some time and, because we needed something constructive to do, we decided to see what could be done in the way of providing medical services in the camp. There were several male doctors, civilian and military, and two British women with medical experience – Dr Smith, who was English, and Dr Jean McDowell, a Scot.

Dr Constance Smith, an antenatal and child welfare officer, came from Malacca, where Pat had been stationed. The doctor was a very down-to-earth type and Pat, who rarely swore, struck up a great rapport with her, despite the fact that every second word the doctor uttered was 'bloody'.

Although Dr Anna Maria Goldberg-Cluth, known simply as Dr Goldberg, had reached Muntok with Veronica Clancy's group, she was not interned in the coolie-lines. On arrival, she had immediately made herself known to the Japanese, declaring 'I am German. I am German. I am your friend.'

The nurses believed she had a German and a British passport but, if she did, the British one was certainly a fake, as she and her husband, Erich, certainly did not qualify as British citizens. In 1933 Erich Goldberg had emigrated from Germany to Italy, where he undertook further study before marrying Anne Marie Curth (as she was then known), who joined him in 1934. They both practised medicine in Florence until 1939, when anti-Jewish laws forced them to move to Ipoh, in Malaya.

In 1941, they came to the notice of Erich's superior medical officer at the Tanjung Rambutan Mental Hospital, who believed they were spreading anti-British propaganda among the native staff as well as showing great interest in shipping movements. Apparently threatened with internment if they did not leave Malaya, the pair went to Singapore, where Erich, suspected by Military Intelligence of engaging in Fifth Column activities, was interned. Somehow, Anna Maria managed to obtain a pass to enable her to board Vyner Brooke, *possibly by successfully applying to the Australian authorities for Jewish refugee status or as an internee. Somehow, just a week before the surrender, she also managed to ship 35 packing cases with her belongings to Fremantle, Western Australia, despite the fact that bona fide evacuees were limited to one suitcase each.*

The doctors from the men's camp commandeered three of our adjoining rooms to serve as a makeshift hospital. However, only about half of us were in a fit enough state to do any nursing. The rest were suffering from friction burns from sliding down the ropes into the water. Wilma Oram, despite her head wound, was one of the first to volunteer.

We shared duties with some English nurses, always working in pairs on either a morning or an afternoon shift, under the watchful eyes of two civilians – Matron Ena Castle from the Colonial Medical Service and Dr McKern, an Australian.

Dr Albert Stanley McKern was born in Sydney in 1885. After studying Divinity at Sydney University and then at Yale in America, he decided to take up medicine, graduating from Edinburgh University in 1917. He, his wife and two sons moved to Penang, where he established a flourishing practice as a general practitioner, gynaecologist and obstetrician. A third son was born in Penang in 1924.

When Penang was invaded in December 1941, the McKerns went to Singapore. With his wife safely evacuated to England, McKern stayed on as long as possible before boarding Mata Hari. *As the vessel was one of the few ships captured intact by the Japanese, Dr McKern arrived at Muntok with a suitcase full of clothing, along with some drugs and medical equipment.*

The women doctors looked after female patients not ill enough to be hospitalised. The hospital was actually more like a sick bay, as we had no proper equipment and very few supplies. With camp rations consisting of a measly portion of rice per day, some deaths were inevitable, in spite of our enthusiasm and best efforts.

One of the first patients was Flight Lieutenant Ronald Armstrong, of the Royal Air Force Volunteer Reserve, who had two shattered feet that required amputation. As Doctors West and Reid begged in vain to transfer him to a Japanese field hospital, they had no alternative but to operate themselves. Without an operation, the airman would die. They had some morphine, but their trunk of supplies contained no anaesthetic and few surgical instruments, so Mr Roberts, a civilian refugee, fashioned a saw from a barrel hoop by heating and straightening it, and then filing it to create the teeth. With British nursing sisters Alice Rossie and Phyllis Briggs acting as 'theatre' sisters, the patient was tied to a wooden table while his feet were amputated with the saw.

Three days after our arrival at Muntok, Betty Jeffrey and Iole Harper arrived in a very distressed state, after trying to swim ashore and becoming caught in mangroves. They were covered in mosquito and sandfly bites and their arms and legs were infected from puncture wounds made by the mangrove spikes.

After being knocked out with a hefty dose of morphine and sleeping for three days straight, they were able to confirm that they had been with Matron Paschke's raft for many hours, paddling with two pieces of timber throughout the night and then swimming beside it to try to propel it ashore. Harper had been a tower of strength. When not paddling she swam round the raft, keeping everyone together and giving words of encouragement. However, defeated by the swirling currents, the two women, along with the two Malay sailors, decided to swim to shore and find help. They had just left the raft when a fast-moving current carried it swiftly away to the south, with two nurses – Sisters Dorsch and Trenerry – in the sea holding onto trailing ropes. Shortly afterwards, Jeffrey and Harper also lost contact with the two sailors.

Caught in crocodile-infested mangroves at a river mouth, they had climbed into the higher branches to avoid being caught by rising tides and eaten by hungry crocodiles. Eventually, they made their way upstream where native fishermen found them. They took the girls to their village, where they were well cared for, before deciding to surrender.

One afternoon, when Win and I were on hospital duty, Dr McKern introduced us to an immaculately uniformed young Irishman, a surgeon commander, saying he was leaving him in our capable hands as he was taking the afternoon off. Without uttering a single word to either of us, the Irishman went immediately to the doctor's room. During the next hour or two there were three admissions. Although none required treatment, we followed normal hospital procedure and referred them to the medical officer. He came out, looked at each patient, and then, without speaking, returned to his room.

We felt there was something very wrong and, on Dr McKern's return, told him of our concern. He looked into the distance, then said, 'I think he'll be all right. I got a bit of pork from a hawker today, and an Irishman surely loves his bit of pig.' He then explained that the doctor was highly traumatised. He had been with a group that was captured and taken to a house where the Japs were having a party. One at a time, they had taken the captives out and beheaded them. As the doctor was led out, another group of Japanese arrived and put an end to their fun.

We were shocked. The old hands of the East had told us to be thankful we were prisoners of the Japanese, not the Chinese, as they were the cruel ones. Not surprisingly, we were very apprehensive about our future, half expecting to be taken out and shot at any time, and with good reason. Shortly after arrival, all the ships' captains in camp were ordered to line up. A Japanese officer addressed them, asking all those holding a Master Mariner's Certificate to step forward. No one moved. The officer laughed. The Japanese had their persuasive ways. Shooting members of his crew would soon make even the most stubborn skipper change his mind.

The RAF's Air Commodore Modin, who was in charge of the camp, told us how, shortly after he and the other male prisoners had arrived on Bangka, they had been driven out to the aerodrome and lined up in front of deep trenches dug across the landing strip. Manned machine-guns were evenly spaced along the other side. Expecting the inevitable, the prisoners shook hands with one another, saying goodbye and adding, 'I didn't expect it to end like this.' The Japanese were just playing mind games. They handed out shovels, ordering the prisoners to fill in the trenches, which had been dug by Allied soldiers to render the airstrip useless to the enemy.

With such stories, the thought of escape surfaced from time to time. Pat Blake and I learned from internees Huck Finlay (later to become head of the Australian Broadcasting Commission) and Mr Lambert, an English plantation manager from Sumatra, that they were planning to escape. Lambert, who knew how to get a boat, wanted to contact the Achinese, the indigenous people of Sumatra, reputed to be great fighters. We offered to go with them, saying we could manage an oar between us. They didn't seem very impressed and we heard nothing more. A couple of days later I saw Huck Finlay. As he was ill with dysentery, it was obvious that they had abandoned any thought of escape for the time being.

CHAPTER 5

On Radji Beach

Towards the end of February, about 10 days after our capture, we heard someone yell 'It's Bullwinkel. Bully's here. She's alive!' and looked up to see Viv hurrying towards us, her right arm outstretched and the other clutching to her bodice an army water-bottle slung crosswise over her shoulder.

Her legs were covered with infected mosquito bites. Although always slender, Viv now looked decidedly thinner, but otherwise seemed fine. When the excitement calmed down, we bombarded her with questions, asking where she had been and if she had news of the other girls.

She told us her lifeboat had reached the island on the night of 14 February, the day on which *Vyner Brooke* had sunk. Spotting the fires lit as beacons by survivors on the beach, Viv and some of the others had taken to the water to guide the waterlogged boat ashore and onto a beach, a mile or so away. Escorted by a ship's officer, Viv and a couple of nurses walked along the coastline towards the fire, where they found Matron Drummond with about 10 of the girls, along with a number of wounded, some military personnel, and civilian men, women and children.

Among the civilians were Marie, the hairdresser, and the women who had tried to eject her from the raft; Cuthbert Tyrwhitt, the bogus ship's engineer; and various occupants of

Vivian Bullwinkel

Eric Germann's life-boat-and-raft train which, guided by the bonfire, had reached Radji Beach safely at around 8.30 pm. In this group was little Izidore Warman, who would later be reunited with his very relieved mother, and the badly burned Malay sailor, who did not survive. Unfortunately, he had died with his arms and legs outstretched and, by the time Germann and others managed to bury him, rigor mortis had set in, making their task very difficult.

Germann, sitting on the sand by the fire, looked up to see Bullwinkel and two other nurses, accompanied by Jimmy Miller, the ship's second officer, walking towards him from the north. On learning that a nurse in their party was seriously hurt and could not walk, Germann and an English youth, who volunteered to help, fashioned a makeshift stretcher from a couple of oars and two buttoned shirts. No one else was willing to offer assistance, not even Dr Tay Soo Woon, a Singaporean Chinese civilian who, despite Matron Drummond's entreaties, refused point blank to accompany them. With an indignant Matron in tow, the group set off for the beach, where Germann loaded his patient, Florence Salmon, onto the makeshift stretcher. The other seriously wounded – Sisters Wight, Cassan and Neuss – were half-dragged, half-carried by the more able-bodied to Radji Beach – an agonising trip that took the best part of an hour and a half. It was close to midnight when they reached the main party.

The next morning Bullwinkel noticed that during the night a third lifeboat from Vyner Brooke *had come ashore, evidently the one that had hit the water rather rapidly with the two Malay sailors on board. In it were Sisters Peggy Farnamer, Lorna Fairweather, Esther Stewart, Ellen Keats and Clare Halligan, along with some civilian women and official evacuee Lieutenant Commander James White, Royal Navy. When the castaways awoke next morning, they discovered that White, the most senior in rank, had disappeared. He turned up later in the prison camp at Muntok. When Major Tebbutt later asked him why the lifeboats that reached Radji Beach were not used to go and search for other people in the water, he replied that 'everyone was too bewildered and exhausted'.*

With no reliable food source and few medical supplies, it was decided to send out three parties to seek help at first light: one party of men to go south along the beach towards Tanjung Kelian lighthouse; a second group under Miller to go in the opposite direction towards Tanjung Oelar; and a third to move inland, in the hope of finding a village. The latter party was the largest, numbering 13 in all: Sedgeman and four sailors, along with six able-bodied nurses – Sister Alice Rossie of the QA and the Australian Army's Clare Halligan, Ada Bridge, Janet Kerr, Mona Tate, Nancy Harris and Vivian Bullwinkel – and two civilian women, Mrs Kathleen Hutchings and Mrs Marion Langdon-Williams, a prominent member of Singapore society.

While they were away, Matron Drummond and the remaining nurses set about making the injured as comfortable as possible, within their very limited resources. The other able-bodied

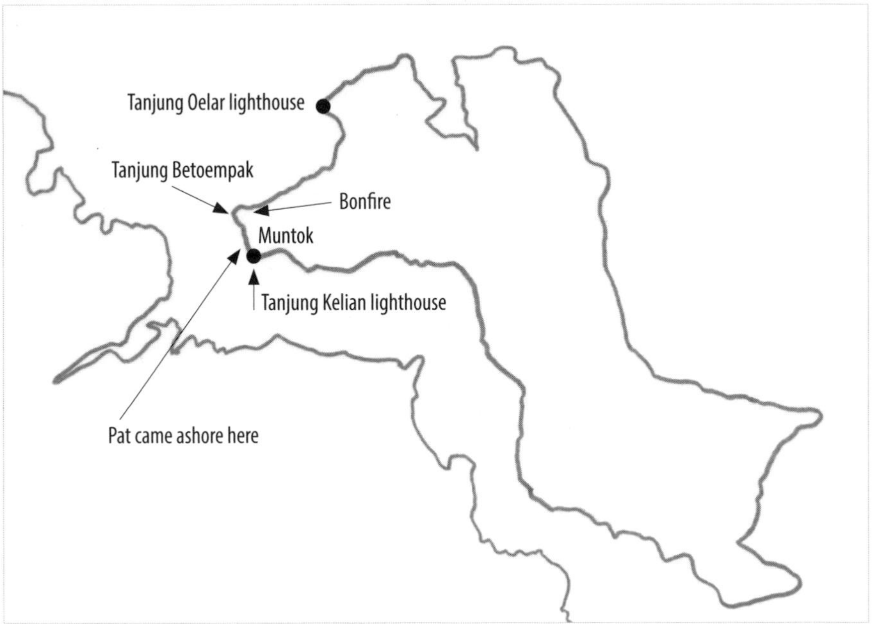

Where the boatrs came ashore on Bangka Island

foraged behind the beach for coconuts and pineapples, and materials to make stretchers for the severely wounded.

Miller's party returned to the beach first. They had located a small stream fed by a spring, but little else. The other party that had headed for Tanjung Kelian lighthouse did not return at all. It was later learned that they had been captured, possibly by a group of Japanese sent to ensure that the Malay lighthouse keepers did not allow its destruction. Sister Nesta James, who had come ashore there on a raft by herself, had also been detained. However, she was released unharmed after being held at bayonet point and relieved of her pay book and 100 Singapore dollars. She wandered around until she met up with other survivors who, on learning that the Malay lighthouse keepers were unwilling to help, decided to walk into Muntok and surrender.

When Sedgeman's group finally returned to the beach, they also had nothing to show for their efforts. After walking for two or three miles (3–5 kilometres), they had come to Mendjelang (Menjelang) village, where the women offered them a drink. However, as the Japanese were now in control of the island and the locals were fearful of retribution, the headman refused to allow the village women to provide any food or clothing and motioned the group to move on. In the late afternoon, some fishermen imparted the devastating news that all of Bangka Island was in enemy hands, and that the nearest food and habitation was in occupied Muntok.

That night, the survivors, who slept on the beach or in the ruins of a nearby fisherman's shack, heard the explosions and saw flashes of gunfire out to sea as enemy naval vessels attacked ships trying to run the gauntlet. A couple of hours later, a steel-hulled lifeboat came ashore, guided by the fires and holding about 20 military personnel, mainly from the British Army's Ordnance Corps. The newcomers included a sailor close to death and a very seriously injured soldier – Private Cecil Kinsley, a 33-year-old Yorkshireman. Most of the flesh of his left upper arm and shoulder had been blown away when his ship, Siang Wo, was attacked.

The sailor died shortly after arrival and was buried in the sand beside the burned Malay crewman, leaving about 80 or so people camped on the beach. As the castaways had no food, no medical supplies and no chance of escape, at first light Sedgeman called them together and advised that they should give themselves up. As everyone was in agreement, including the occupants of the steel lifeboat, he set off for Muntok, accompanied by two slightly wounded British sailors from Prince of Wales.

Matron Drummond suggested that, rather than wait on the beach, the civilian women and children should begin walking towards Muntok as their progress would be slow. An Australian miner, 62-year-old John Dominguez of Bright in Victoria, assumed responsibility for the party, which numbered around 15. An employee of Anglo-Oriental Tin Mining, he was a colleague of fellow miner and master mariner Bill Reynolds, who had rescued the castaways on Pompong Island. Accompanying Dominguez were Prince of Wales sailors Wallace Cake and George Noble, who had injuries to their arms and could not help as stretcher bearers, and Dr Tay, the Chinese medico who had infuriated Matron Drummond when he refused to help Sister Salmon and the other wounded from Bullwinkel's boat. On discovering that he was a person of interest to the Japanese, Tay later committed suicide.

Carrie Betteridge did not go with the women and children as her husband Thomas, to whom she had been married for 50 years, had been badly injured by a bomb fragment that had penetrated his kidney. She elected to remain behind with the nursing sisters who, in preparation for the expected journey to Muntok, had fashioned a flag from a stick and a Red Cross armband. Meanwhile, the men continued their work on making stretchers to carry the 10 or so wounded.

Among the stretcher cases were two civilian women, one of whom is believed to be Mrs Kathleen Waddle (Principal of Raffles Girls' School, friend of Mary Brown and another doyenne of Singapore society), who was wounded in the head and hand and had reached Radji Beach in the first lifeboat; Sister Florence Salmon; Private Kinsley and a 68-year-old British-born barrister from Ipoh, Ernest Watson, formerly a member of the Malayan judiciary.

At mid-morning Sedgeman returned with a party of Japanese soldiers, dressed in khaki shirts *and jodhpur-style pants, and carrying rifles. They were members of 1 and 2 Company, of 1 Battalion of 229 Infantry Regiment, 38 Division, which had landed on Sumatra. Number 1 Battalion, known as the Orita Battalion, was commanded by Captain Orita Masaru.*

The party that arrived at Radji Beach with Sedgeman was under the command of a sword-toting officer, 2nd Lieutenant Kohiyama of Orita Battalion's 2 Company. Somewhat smaller than his men, he was nattily dressed in a tailor-made uniform. He and his troops were from the same unit responsible for the outrages against the nurses in Hong Kong. They had passed the women and children making their way down the trail to Muntok and had ordered them to wait until they returned, but fortunately the women got tired of waiting and kept walking.

Arriving at the beach, Sedgeman tried to explain to the lieutenant that the women were nurses who were giving themselves up as prisoners of war but he was given short shrift.

Eric Germann later recalled:

> The officer ordered the men and women to form two lines, then barked at his men. Four soldiers took up sentry points on the flanks of the lines. The officer surveyed the group in silence for so long that, one by one, all but eight men broke rank and resumed working on the stretchers. The officer conferred with one of the soldiers and finally, by gesturing, ordered the men who were still standing in line to walk down the beach. He followed with six soldiers, two of whom carried a machine gun. The four sentries remained, bayoneted rifles at the ready.
>
> The soldiers and their prisoners climbed over a small promontory of rocks and driftwood about 200 feet away and disappeared. Three shots, exploding in quick succession, sounded from beyond the promontory. After a long silence, another shot was heard, but muffled, as though the gun muzzle had been pressed against something soft. Then another silence.
>
> The stretcher workers looked apprehensively at each other but, except for a murmured 'Afraid they're gone', no one spoke.
>
> Soon Kohiyama and two soldiers reappeared, climbing over the rocks. They returned to the stretchers and ordered the remaining ten men to march.

Sedgeman, Miller and another sailor, pointing to their epaulettes, protested that they were officers and expected treatment according to their rank. The Japanese officer shouted them down. Germann and Sedgeman were then ordered to carry Mr Watson, the former judge, whom the Japanese officer had noticed was sitting up in his stretcher. As the prisoners made their way towards the promontory, Germann desperately grasped at straws. He called to the officer and the procession halted. From his shorts, Germann pulled a swollen, water-soaked wallet containing his American passport and $900 in $20 bills.

> I hoped that the passport with its gold seal would impress him and he might change his mind. The officer studied it intently but ended by throwing it on the sand. In drawing out the

> passport, some of the twenty-dollar bills also came out with it. The sight of them caused the officer to burst into a furious tirade. Obviously he thought I had tried to bribe him.
>
> Picking up a piece of driftwood he swung it at my face. I warded off the blow with an upraised hand and threw the wallet and its contents after the passport, thinking 'I won't need the money any more'.

Sedgeman and Germann picked up Mr Watson and laboured down the beach. They had difficulty getting the elderly man over the rocky outcrop and driftwood so the officer motioned to leave him there. They propped him against a log, shook hands, said good-bye and climbed down over the rocks. Germann continued:

> We were in a small cove. At the water's edge, lying face down, sprawled the bodies of those who had gone before us. I saw only seven bodies. I wondered about the eighth but remembered the first quick shots presumed that the eighth had made a dash for the sea and been cut down by rifle fire. The last muffled shot must have been the coup de grace for someone who did not die quickly enough. The others had not been killed by bullets. That was obvious from the wound in the back of the body nearest to me, the young Englishman who had helped me carry the nurse to the fire. There was a short red wound under his left shoulder blade. The instrument that had made it, and similar wounds on the other bodies, was a bayonet.
>
> Three soldiers stood near the bodies, wiping their bayonets with rags; polishing them carefully as though anxious to have naught but the cleanest steal for the next job. A machine gun was ready to sweep the little strip of beach should anyone attempt to run.
>
> We were ordered to stand in line facing the sea. I noticed two men blindfold themselves with their handkerchiefs. No one spoke. I looked out over the water. The hazy sky and sea seemed especially beautiful that morning. 'What a stupid way to die', I thought. I began to pray 'Our Father, Who art in heaven, hallowed be Thy Name'.
>
> At that moment the first officer, standing at the other end of the line, dashed for the sea. The machine gun chattered. He fell to one knee, rose, stumbled again as the firing continued and slumped to a halt on his right shoulder, directly in front of me. He was dead, bleeding from a multitude of holes.
>
> I continued praying, slowly and with more fervour. I was saying 'deliver us from evil' when I was aware I was no longer standing but lying face down on the beach. My hands were clasped under me, pressing palm upward at the right side of my chest. My face was turned slightly to the left. My mouth was open and full of sand and water. I realised the reason – tiny wavelets on the outermost edge of the sea were surging and receding. On the incoming rise I could inhale slightly and quickly, and, as the wave receded, exhale slightly and slowly, but so minutely the Japanese could detect no movement. They were shooting men who moved.
>
> Metal struck against metal. Feet scuffed. Probably they were dismounting the machine gun. After that, only the lapping sounds of the water.

Germann waited, lapped by the waves, for what seemed an interminable time. It was just as well. Out of the corner of his eye he saw two Japanese appear on the rocks and survey the cove. One then waved a small flag in the direction of Radji Beach. Resisting the urge to move, Germann waited.

Back at the main beach, the women, who had heard the gunfire, had watched with mounting apprehension as the Japanese returned from the small cove, strolling along and cleaning their bayonets and rifles. The nurses had no doubt what was in store for them. Sister Nancy Harris now voiced what they all knew, but were too terrified to admit. 'It's true then. They're not taking any prisoners.'

Sister Lainie Balfour-Ogilvy suggested that, if they all went in different directions, good swimmers into the sea and fast runners into the jungle, some of them might be able to get away. However, Matron reminded them that, while there was life there was hope, and that the wounded were depending on them.

On reaching the women, the Japanese soldiers stood in a semi-circle and, using their bayonets, made them form a line, while another soldier set up a machine-gun under the trees, about 20 or 30 yards (18 to 27 metres) away. The serious stretcher cases were left where they were, but Sisters Neuss, Casson and Wight, although injured, were herded down the beach. Leaning on the able-bodied for support, they stood alongside Matron Drummond, who was first in the line on the right. At the far end was Alma Beard with Jenny Kerr and Vivian Bullwinkel beside her. Alma Beard remarked 'Bully, there are two things I've always hated in my life: the Japanese and the sea, and today I've ended up with both.'

Prodding them with bayonets, the Japanese forced the nurses and a weeping Mrs Betteridge to walk towards the water's edge. Anyone slow to respond was given a shove. Vivian Bullwinkel claimed there were no cries for mercy or shouts of anguish, no stifled sobs or indeed any sound at all, apart from Esther Stewart calling out 'Girls take it, don't squeal', and the soft voice of Matron Drummond who, with her last breath, said 'Chin up girls. I'm proud of you and I love you all.'

The machine-gunner then opened fire, moving from right to left and aiming for the middle

Selection of photos of nurses who were massacred.
From left to right: Flo Casson, Alma Beard, Lainie Balfour-Ogilvy, Janet 'Jenny' Kerr, Ellen Keats

of the victims' backs. The first bullet struck Matron Drummond, pitching her forward and knocking her glasses from her nose. As she scrabbled for them in the sand a second bullet finished her off. Flo Casson and Rosetta Wright and their helpers were all hit before they even reached the water's edge. The rest kept moving. Those at the far end of the line were up to their waists before the bullets found their mark. Vivian Bullwinkel was shot though the flesh, just above her left hip. The force pitched her forward. There was so much blood in the water she could taste it. She tried desperately not to cough, or vomit.

As she later said:

> I was hit in the sort of side, left side, and the bullet went just straight through and came out on the front ... The force of it knocked me over into the water and there I lay ... To my amazement, I remained conscious and found that I wasn't dying at all. Then my next fear was that the Japanese would see me moving, because by this time I was being violently sick from having swallowed a fair amount of sea water ... The waves brought me back on to the edge of the water. I lay there 10 minutes and everything seemed quiet. I sat up and looked around and there was no sign of anybody.

When she realised that she was still alive and that the enemy soldiers had left, Bullwinkel made her way to the edge of the jungle where she passed out and then slept for the next two days. When she awoke, she was about to break cover and make her way to the stream when a group of Japanese soldiers appeared without warning, and made their way to the beach. They had apparently come to dispose of any bodies still on the beach. As they were not there for long, they evidently pushed the corpses out on the tide.

Bullwinkel made her way to the beach a day or two later to see if there were any emergency rations left in the lifeboats. She picked up an army water-bottle lying on the sand and a couple of lifebelts, but there was no food, and no sign of any corpses, although later some floated in on the tide. However, while she could see that some of them were nurses, she could not identify any and did not think to gather any identity discs.

She was on her way back to the jungle when a voice called to her from a small fishing hut. It was Private Kinsley, who had been among the stretcher patients left on the beach. After shooting the nurses, the Japanese had bayoneted the wounded, bringing the total number of deaths to around 70. Kinsley had been struck in the middle of the chest, but the blade had missed his vital organs. The Japanese had then departed, leaving the wounded on the stretchers where they had been killed.

After dressing Kinsley's wounds as best she could, using fibre from a nearby coconut palm for bandages, Viv helped him into the jungle where she propped him up on a lifebelt while she went to the village to seek help. The headman refused to offer assistance. However, in defiance of their village chief and in spite of the danger of reprisals from the Japanese if they found out, some women followed her back into the jungle and gave her food – pineapple, dried fish and rice as I recall – wrapped in banana leaves. The women returned again with more food but, as Kinsley's wounds needed proper medical attention, Viv realised that they must give themselves up.

> *It was now 25 February, nine days since the massacre on the beach. After discussing the situation with Kinsley, Bullwinkel agreed to wait a little longer before surrendering themselves to the Japanese, as the following day was Kinsley's 33rd birthday, and he wanted to spend it in freedom.*
>
> *The next morning, after giving Kinsley his present – a small mound of rice wrapped in a banana leaf, with a twig on top to represent a candle – Bullwinkel dressed his wounds with fresh coconut fibre. After washing her uniform, she scrubbed Kinsley's shirt with sand to fray the edges of the bayonet holes and make them less obvious.*

Viv was lucky. There was a gap between her hip and ribs where the bullet had hit her. When she arrived, we didn't know she had been shot as she had covered the tell-tale bloodstains on the front of her dress with her army water-bottle. She was taller than most of the others so the bullet, which was supposed to strike her in the middle of her back, hit her lower down. As it went straight through her side at waist level, it missed all her vital organs. A little bit further left and it would have missed her completely. Had her intestines been nicked, she would not have survived.

Of the 65 nurses who had left Singapore on 13 February, we now knew that 12 were presumed drowned and 21 shot. Only 32 were left alive. My friend, Kath Neuss, who had reached Radji Beach with Vivian, was not among them.

> *Once the village headman learned that Bullwinkel and Kinsley intended to give themselves up, he became far more friendly, giving them tea and biscuits and putting them on the right track to Muntok. Shortly afterwards, they met an English-speaking Malay who told them that concentrated in the town was a large number of people, some of whom were women wearing a Red Cross armband. Heartened by this news, the pair continued on their way, only to be stopped by a Japanese officer in a car, searched at gunpoint, offered a banana and some cigarettes and driven to naval headquarters. After questioning, Bullwinkel was given some refreshments and asked to bandage the foot of an officer. She was then driven to the coolie-line camp, which was crowded with prisoners and refugees, including the 15 civilian women and children who had set off for Muntok from Radji Beach.*
>
> *On 28 February, Bullwinkel and the 31 nurses who had landed at different points on Bangka Island were finally reunited. At first, she did not recognise them as all were dressed in sarongs, scrounged pieces of civilian clothing or shorts and sun-tops made from the sailors' uniforms they had found in storage. However, as she entered the compound, she was spotted by Sisters Jenny Greer and Beryl Woodridge who yelled 'Bully! She's alive!', leaving her in no doubt that she was back with friends.*
>
> *Realising that, if the Japanese discovered she had survived the massacre, it would mean certain death, Bullwinkel had sworn Kinsley to secrecy, intending to tell no one at all of her*

miraculous escape – not even her fellow nurses. However, the emotion of their reunion and the persistent questions about what had happened to their colleagues weakened her resolve, and she told them her story. It was dangerous knowledge that she had shared. Total secrecy was now vital to their survival.

Sister Nesta James, now our most senior nursing sister, informed Mr Quinn and Mr Wootton about Viv's miraculous escape. Aware that people had been taken from the camp and had not come back, Wootton warned 'Well, for God's sake don't talk about it. Don't say anything. Just forget it. If the Japs get an inkling, you'll all be taken out and killed.'

There was no danger that Kinsley might inadvertently spill the beans. The Japanese refused to provide proper medical care for his injuries and he died a couple of days after arriving at the camp. Bullwinkel, who was summonsed to his bedside in the makeshift hospital, was with him when he died, about 20 minutes later.

*Kinsley was buried in the Dutch cemetery, about a mile from the camp. Several days later, Ronald Armstrong, the flight lieutenant whose feet had been amputated, succumbed to dysentery and was laid to rest beside him in a coffin made by three Australian soldiers from the door of the Tin Winning company office.**

Bullwinkel recorded that, by the time she reached the camp, her wounds 'had practically healed by then and didn't need much attention at all. Being in the salt water had helped, and I'd had absolute rest for I don't know how long after being shot.' However, as the fabric around the bullet hole at the front was still quite bloodstained, Wilma Oram washed the uniform to remove the worst of the marks. She also took over the complete care of Bullwinkel, bandaging her infected mosquito-bitten legs and making sure that her wounds were kept clean until the healing process was complete. The only available clothing, apart from Bullwinkel's uniform, was on the skimpy side, so, in order to ensure the scabs remained well hidden, Oram gave her a pair of men's silk pyjamas, which she had received only that morning from a New Zealand colonel.

Pat and the other nurses were unaware that Vivian Bullwinkel was not the sole witness to the events that had occurred on Radji Beach. They were also unaware that senior members of the men's camp – including Australians John Quinn and Norman Wootton, colleagues of the murdered Trade Commissioner Vivian Bowden – already knew about the massacres.

Their informants were Eric Germann and Stoker Ernest Lloyd, who had both survived the massacre in the cove; Corporal Robert Seddon, a Royal Marine whose evacuee vessel Yin Ping *had been sunk by shellfire and who was making his way alone towards the shore near Radji Beach; and Leading Seaman William Wilding, shipwrecked when* Li Wo *sank and who reached the island in a damaged lifeboat the day after the massacres.*

Stoker Lloyd was with Eric Germann and the second group of men taken around the headland to the small cove. He was able to provide Wootton and Quinn with details that Germann had not noticed or witnessed, as he was unconscious. Lloyd reported that the Japanese had motioned his group along a beach and lined them up, with their backs to the sea. Signs were then made for the men to remove their insignia and shirts, tear strips from the latter and use them as blindfolds. When some difficulty was experienced in making the captives understand what was wanted, the Japanese officer became angry, drew his sword, and cut one man across the face. The men were then ordered to turn and face the ocean. Some tried to run into the jungle, but were shot. Lloyd reported:

> The man next to me, who was a seaman I had known in Singapore – I think his name was 'Jock' McGlurk [Hamilton McGlurg, from Glasgow] – said 'This is where you get it Ernie, right in the back'. I said 'Not for me, Jock' and we both dived into the sea with one other man, as the Japs opened fire with a machine-gun. They mowed down the others first and then turned the gun on the three of us.

By the time the stream of bullets reached the final man on the beach, Lloyd and his companions were some 30 yards (27 metres) out to sea. Then Jock cried out, 'I'm hit, Ernie', and both he and the other man sank out of sight. Lloyd, who was a powerful swimmer, plunged on and kept swimming, assisted by a strong easterly current, but a bullet struck him on the shoulder, and another in the head, causing momentary unconsciousness. As he came to, he continued swimming until finally the current and his efforts took him out of the danger zone and further along the coast, where he came ashore.

Lloyd returned to the scene of the tragedy, and saw the bodies of his companions. At Radji Beach the corpses of the nurses and others were still strewn about, some partly in the sea. About 50 yards (47 metres) from the others were the bodies of Bill Sedgeman and a nurse, who had apparently tried to flee. After 10 days at large, Lloyd was recaptured.

The third witness, Corporal Robert Seddon, had been in the sea for 24 hours when he neared the island. As he floated offshore, supported by his lifebelt, he heard screams and gunfire and saw men and women being bayoneted. He reported that a few men attempted 'to rush into the water but they were shot and killed before they were able to swim out of range'. Drifting ashore, he was kicked in the face by the Japanese, stabbed and left for dead. Some hours later, when he was sure that the danger had passed, he made his way to the jungle where he spent the night. The next morning, he returned to the beach where he saw the bodies of 15 nurses, 15 British service personnel, 5 merchant seamen and 7 sailors.

The fourth witness was William Wilding, who reached Radji Beach on 16 February shortly after the killings with a Malay naval telegraphist named Abdullah. Fluttering on a stick pushed into the sand was the Red Cross flag that the nurses had made and near it they found a dozen bodies – all women except for two. Some were scantily dressed in civilian clothing, some in nurses' uniforms and some naked. Wilding examined two of the women's bodies. One had been shot. The other had been killed with a sword. Walking further along the beach, they found Mr Watson, propped against the log, with critical head injuries and near to death. At the cove they came across another 20 bodies – mostly servicemen – also shot and bayoneted. They then made their way inland, where they linked up with Eric Germann.

After lying doggo in the water for some time, Germann had finally decided it was safe to move. He could see that the beach was now empty, apart from the dead. As he moved off, one corpse in particular took his attention. It was the overweight civil engineer, sitting upright, his sightless eyes staring out to sea.

Following the coastline for about a mile, he had turned inland, where there was a small stream, and assessed his injuries. Blood was oozing from a wound in his lower right chest. When he found a corresponding wound in his back, he realised that the bayonet thrust had gone right through. He spent the night there and next morning, hoping to find a village, had headed south.

After meeting Wilding and Abdullah, Germann returned to the cove. Mr Watson was dead and the civil engineer was still in the upright position, surrounded by the bodies of his companions. Scattered on the sand of the main beach were some of Germann's $20 bills. He didn't bother to pick them up – what he wanted right now was food, not money.

The bodies of some of the nurses lay scattered along the water's edge – Germann presumed that the rest had been taken by the outgoing tide. Lying further up the beach was a red-headed nurse, whose skull had been crushed. The stretcher patients too were dead – Mr Betteridge and three women had been bayoneted in the chest. Two stretchers were empty – one belonged to Mr Watson, the other to Kinsley. Thinking the latter may have survived the bayoneting and crawled into the jungle, the three men searched the immediate area, calling his name, only to be met with silence.

Abandoning their search, the trio moved further north, where some Malay fishermen gave them water and told them that the nearest food was at Muntok. With no other option, they gave themselves up.

When Tebbutt arrived in the camp two days later, he learned from Quinn and Wootton of Bullwinkel's miraculous escape. Tebbutt, who saw Bullwinkel in the camp, did not interview her for fear of drawing attention to her, but made notes and took statements from the male eyewitnesses to be used as evidence against the Japanese when the war ended.

I saw Major Tebbutt in the camp, but made no attempt to speak to him as we understood that being in charge of the nurses was only a cover for his real mission – to collect and take vital intelligence to Australia. When I didn't see him again I feared the worst, but learned many years later that he had been taken away for interrogation and then sent to another POW camp.

On the day Viv arrived, word circulated that some inmates, at least, were to be transferred to Singapore. Sister Nesta James, now our most senior sister, compiled a report of our situation along with a nominal roll giving details of known survivors, which she entrusted to Air Commodore Modin, who was leaving with the first group, in the hope that he could deliver it to 8 Division HQ.

Before the men left, they received a mascot, tossed over the wall by nurses from 2/4 CCS. Using scraps of material, they had crafted a kangaroo, complete with a pouch and joey, and an Australia-shaped card – 'Greetings from nurses of the 2/4. Cheerio. Will see you soon.'

Three days after Modin departed, we too left Bangka Island.

** The official dates of death ascribed to Kinsey and Armstrong are at odds with information supplied by Bullwinkel and others. Kinsley's official death date of 24 March 1942 was taken from a handwritten camp record, by which time the men were no longer in Muntok. Bullwinkel, who was with Kinsley when he died, was transferred from Muntok to Palembang on the morning of 2 March. It therefore appears that Kinsley most likely died in the early hours of 2 March 1942.*

Armstrong's death is officially recorded as 16 February 1942. This is a presumed date of death. Armstrong died after Kinsley, and was buried alongside him in the coffin made by Australian POWs from the Tin Winning Company's office door. As he died after Kinsley's death on 2 March and before the Australians were transferred to Palembang on 12 March, his death occurred some time between 2 and 12 March.

Although the two men were properly buried and their graves marked, post-war search parties failed to locate them, probably because the official dates of death were incorrect. The names of Private Cecil Gordon Kinsley, 7654688, Royal Army Ordnance Corps, and Flight Lieutenant Ronald Armstrong, 77799, Royal Air Force Volunteer Reserve, are inscribed on the Singapore Memorial at Kranji War Cemetery on columns 109 and 411.

CHAPTER 6

Bukit Besar and Irenelaan Camps, Palembang

2 March 1942 – 18 September 1943

The male prisoners were not sent to Singapore. Their destination was much closer – Palembang, just across the Bangka Strait on the island of Sumatra. Before being transferred to various camps there, the inmates at the coolie-lines and the old gaol were divided into groups. The first of the men left with Air Commodore Modin on 28 February, with others following on various dates until mid-March.

The women, children and the sick made the move on 2 March, along with Dr West and a party of civilian men. The latter were to be imprisoned in Palembang Gaol where, for the first month, the able bodied would be put to work unloading ships at the Shell Oil refinery across the river at Pladjoe (Pladju) before being split into smaller camps. The Australian military prisoners, including Major Tebbutt and Lieutenant Reed, the senior medical officer, did not leave Muntok until 12 March. Tebbutt remained in Palembang until May 1945 when he and 1400 male prisoners were transferred to Changi Camp in Singapore on the 1150-ton vessel, Sibolga. *In Changi, Tebbutt handed in statements obtained on the death of Mr Bowden and compiled a lengthy written report on the massacres at Radji Beach.*

We shifted camp at dawn. It didn't take long to pack because we didn't own much and the internees who were well equipped were jealously hanging on to their clothing and possessions.

After the usual rice breakfast, we were given more rice – just a small amount wrapped in a banana leaf to sustain us on our journey – before being trucked to Muntok pier. It was said to be about half a kilometre in length but, by the time we reached the far end, the distance seemed closer to three.

Muntok jetty (Muntok Peace Museum)

We spent the night sleeping on the rough timber planks of the wharf, and awoke to a beautiful sunrise and a magnificent rainbow, which I took to be a good omen. Motorboats then transferred us in relays – men on one, nurses and civilian women on the other – to a small, decrepit-looking riverboat, moored about a mile offshore. With about 200 crammed on board the upper and lower decks, we steamed slowly through the wrecks of sunken ships and debris floating in the shallow waters of the Bangka Strait. A machine-gun mounted on the upper deck made sure that no one tried to escape.

Toilet facilities were very crude and very basic – a fruit packing case with one side removed to make a kind of booth, suspended out over the deck. The middle slat of the three-slatted base had been removed to create a narrow toilet 'seat'. It was a most uncomfortable and very public contraption and, for anyone overweight, like Mrs Brown, squeezing into it was difficult.

A voyage of about 20 miles (32 kilometres) across the Bangka Strait brought us to the entrance of the Moesi (Musi) River. The muddy, oil-slicked waters did not look inviting and we were a little unnerved by the strange cries of birds and monkeys hidden in the thick jungle lining the banks. Now we had left the open sea, the air was very humid and, as we had no shade, it was extremely hot – until it rained. The relief was short-lived as, when the sun came out again, it was like a sauna. However, despite our physical discomfort, the poor sanitation facilities and our alien surroundings, it was wonderful to be out in the open air.

After passing several native villages and sailing for seven hours up the river, at about 5 pm we finally arrived at our destination – the town of Palembang where, after a considerable wait lining up for inspection and *tenko* (a head count), we climbed into cattle trucks – standing room only – for a drive through the township and along rough roads to our next destination.

As an act of humiliation, the Japanese had rounded up some of the locals to watch us pass by.

Most ignored us, but a few, probably feeling it would put them in the good graces of the Japanese, jeered and yelled, until some of the nurses retaliated by shouting back and even sticking out their tongues, shocking the onlookers into silence.

The trucks stopped at a Chinese school, our accommodation for the night. Male prisoners who had left Muntok earlier were already in residence and, as we had eaten nothing all day other than the banana-leaf rice ration given to us the day before, we greatly appreciated the meal of rice and vegetables, cooked at the direction of Air Commodore Modin.

The women had arrived at Mulo School, which was to become one of three men's camps in Palembang. Vivian Bullwinkel took the opportunity to tell Modin about her experiences and, in the hope that rumours of a prisoner exchange might be true, gave him a list of the nurses who had been shot, in case she herself did not survive captivity.

Although the Air Commodore was a high-ranking prisoner, who warranted special attention, there was to be no prisoner exchange. On 17 July 1942, after spending just over five months at Mulo Camp, Modin was transferred to Changi Camp in Singapore where he presumably delivered to the Australian camp authorities the lists given to him by Sisters James and Bullwinkel. Five weeks later, Modin was shipped to Karenko, in Formosa (Taiwan), where he joined other senior Allied officers, including Britain's Lieutenant-General Arthur Percival.

We spent the night on the floor between the school desks, our sleep disturbed frequently by fretful children and hungry mosquitoes. Air Commodore Modin did his best to persuade the Japanese that the Australian nurses should be regarded as military prisoners of war, not internees, and therefore should remain with the military, but the Japanese would not have a bar of it.

About mid-afternoon we were marched off to a new destination, a couple of miles away, again watched by curious locals. As we walked along, we kept our eyes peeled for anything that might come in useful – bits of fabric and discarded clothing, bowls, empty tins and other containers. We eventually stopped at a row of European-style houses, where we were split into groups.

The homes, 20 in all, belonged to Dutch people who had been interned. The Australian nurses were allocated two adjoining houses. I was with the 2/10 AGH girls in Number 24, while those of the 2/13th and the CCS were in Number 26. The houses were quite habitable, but Number 26 had virtually no furniture, apart from a baby's bath and a wardrobe that was full of adults' and children's clothing – all of which was eagerly seized upon. Mickey Syer found a pleated cretonne lampshade trimmed with a length of cord. She gave the cord to me and unpicked the lampshade, which was long enough for her to make a dress.

In the house assigned to my group the furniture was sparse – a double bedstead minus its mattress, a couple of chairs and a couch – but there was also an electric stove that actually worked and three tea chests packed with silver, much of it hallmarked. As we had no eating utensils, we each picked a spoon. I chose a small jam spoon – hallmarked, of course, as things always taste better when eaten with solid silver cutlery, and also small in size, as I wasn't expecting to be given much to eat. I kept this spoon with me throughout my captivity. I cannot recall being given any rations by the Japanese, but Indonesian women who had worked for the Dutch and who were living in the two houses next door gave us flour and palm oil, which we used to make fried scones.

On the nurses' arrival at the housing estate, known as Bukit Besar or Big Hill, the next-door neighbours also provided rice, fruit and a kettle filled with coffee, as well as clothing, toothbrushes and other useful items looted from the abandoned houses. Other Dutch people who had yet to be interned also dropped by, bringing bread, onions, packs of cards, chess sets and even some cushions. The nurses also found half-empty bottles of pickles and sauces, along with a nanny goat and kid, in the backyard. With one nurse holding the goat's head and another the forelegs, a third managed somehow to milk her. The only downside to the new accommodation was the Japanese, who were prone to wander in and out of the bungalows unannounced, even into the bathrooms. They didn't attempt to touch any of the occupants, but they certainly did lots of looking.

After about 10 days or so, the Japanese had the bright idea that 32 healthy young Australians would make good prostitutes. After evicting the occupants from the two adjoining houses, the Japanese ordered us to move in, as our houses had been earmarked for their new officers' social club – right next-door to our new accommodation!

When told to relocate on 13 March, the nurses took with them anything that was not nailed down – the electric stove, any furniture they had managed to acquire and even flywire from the windows. They were then set to work refurbishing the interior of the club buildings and scrubbing and cleaning six houses in a small adjoining street, from which the occupants had been evicted, that were to serve as the actual brothel. In honour of Singapore's notorious red-light thoroughfare, the nurses named it 'Lavender Street'. While they had not the slightest inclination to arrange so much as a stick of furniture at either the club or the Lavender Street annex, the knowledge of what had happened on Radji Beach was sufficient to make them comply.

While they were busy attending to the interior decorating and cleaning, a British woman, Mrs Chan Joo Kim, who lived in house 11, tried to drum up business. Mrs Chan had survived the sinking of Vyner Brooke, *along with two of her three sons – John and baby Denys (also recorded as Daris), who died at Muntok in February 1942. Her husband, a Chinese doctor, had perished on Radji Beach and her third child, said to be named Peter, was almost certainly the boy aged about four who was saved by Iole Harper and put on the raft with Matron Paschke. A statuesque brunette, Mrs Chan began canvassing for women to 'entertain' the Japanese officers at their new club, with the promise of one dollar per attendance, 30 cents of which was to be retained by her as commission. There were no takers, forcing the Japanese to resort to other means.*

The following day, 14 March, the nurses were informed that the grand opening of the club would be in four days' time and that they were to entertain the officers. When they refused point blank to consider such a proposal, the entire camp was given no rations for the next four days. However, Dutch civilians managed to supply each of the houses with a sack of Australian flour, enabling the occupants to make bread and scones, but clearly the situation could not continue. When the four days were up, the Japanese issued an order for three sisters to attend a meeting to 'discuss their living'.

On 18 March, Jessie Blanch's birthday, she, along with Sisters Nesta James and Win Davis, reported to the Japanese as instructed. They were ushered one at a time into an interview room where they were informed that they were to work for the Japanese. When each replied that the only work they were capable of doing was nursing, they were told 'there was other work to be done', leaving them in no doubt as to what was meant. Blanch recorded:

> I went in and here was a Japanese sitting at a table who could speak perfect English, and an officer lounging in an easy chair next to him, with his sword well bared. He told me to sit down at this table. He gave me a piece of paper and told me that they wanted me to sign it. I read it, and as far as I got was, 'The Japanese want you to work for the Japanese.' I refused to sign. I said, 'I K.N.O.W. – and the answer is N.O!'. I yelled at him, and he yelled at me. We argued about this, and I said I wouldn't sign. He said, 'If you don't sign, you'll starve to death. We're going to starve all the Sisters.' And I said, 'As far as I'm concerned I'm not signing it. I'll die first.' He said, 'How will you die?' I said, 'I'll lie down and die', which was so stupid because I was so well at the time.

The Japanese then informed us that six nurses were to attend a cocktail party to celebrate the opening of their new club. Fully aware of what our hosts were up to, we decided to go en masse, assigning the prettiest in our group to stay behind and look after anyone who was sick, leaving 27 to attend the party. We all wore our uniforms and spent some time making ourselves as unattractive as possible by rubbing wood ash into our hair and onto our faces, and only partly washing it off. Most were barefoot, and one clumped along in men's boots. I realised I had done a good job on my appearance when someone asked 'Who's that?'

At 8 pm the nurses entered the first of the two houses that comprised the Officers' Club. The Japanese issued instructions for six to go to the house next-door but were thwarted when the group defied the order by splitting in two. Worried about the nurses' welfare, two British internees, Mr Tunn and Mr Stevenson, stationed themselves in each house to act as barmen and keep an eye on everything.

We behaved in a most prim and proper manner, telling our Japanese hosts that Australian nurses didn't drink alcohol – only milk. We demolished the savouries though, and pocketed anything else on offer. After an hour or so, we were told that we could go but that some of the group in the other clubhouse had to stay. Four brave lasses volunteered. The rest of us went back to our houses, too upset to do anything.

Mr Myachi, a Japanese civilian in charge of the club, had advised that, as the Japanese had control of the food supplies, it would be prudent if four or five nurses volunteered to stay behind. Four did so – Mavis Hannah, Eileen Short, Val Smith and Blanche Hempstead. Despite a further attempt at coercion by an English-speaking Japanese doctor, the remainder refused to return to the club, stating that they would rather starve to death.

After some small talk, each of the four women who stayed behind was led from the club by an officer, who attempted to steer them towards the annex in Lavender Street. However, the nurses refused to cooperate and walked up and down in front of their quarters. The situation was at an impasse when Sister Smith, who was a heavy smoker, broke into a hacking cough, which Blanche Hempstead also imitated. Terrified that the two women had tuberculosis, their Japanese escorts clamped handkerchiefs over their mouths and quit the scene. Eileen Short got rid of her tipsy and very overweight companion by telling him that he needed a brisk walk up the hill to sober him up. The exercise proved to be too much for him, and he also beat a retreat. The fourth and final nurse, Mavis Hannah, dealt with her problem more directly – by simply giving her would-be paramour a good shove, which caused him to trip over his own sword and crash to the ground. As he lay on the roadway, his limbs flailing, Hannah made a strategic exit.

After what seemed an age, there were knocks on our windows and a couple of cheerful voices said, 'It's OK. You can go to sleep. We got rid of them!' I guess that, when the Japanese officers got back to their quarters, they said to their peers, 'You should have seen them. You wouldn't touch any of them with a barge pole.'

The resourceful Mrs Chan found a solution to her 'staffing' problem by recruiting some Eurasian women who were prepared to provide 'comfort' to the officers.

Fortunately, Dr Smith and Dr McDowell were both members of the Colonial Service. They were able to ask Mrs Holwegg, who lived nearby and whose Dutch husband was a doctor at the native hospital in Palembang, to take a message to Air Commodore Modin on the doctor's next visit to the men's camp. Modin, in turn, informed the general at Japanese Headquarters, who shut the club down, and we were mercifully left in peace.

There were no repercussions for the rest of the camp for our non-compliance, but rations to all our nurses were cut for several days, forcing us to go on scrounging expeditions. While out foraging, a couple of the girls passed a house that was not only fully furnished but had a wireless. The Dutch owners invited them in, lending them 10 guilders to buy food and saying, 'You might like to listen to the news.' The girls came back elated to tell us that the sisters who had left Singapore the day before us on *Empire Star* had arrived safely in Australia. This news was a great relief.

Just before dawn on 1 April, about 10 days or so later, to the accompaniment of banging doors and a great deal of shouting, the Japanese guards told us we had to leave. It was no April

Fool's Day joke. We walked up the hill to the town padang, an open grassed area, where we joined other internees. After waiting all day in the scorching sun, the men were separated from the women and marched away – to where, we didn't know. In the late afternoon, after a further wait, the women and children were marched to what would be our next camp.

We were hopeful that we were on our way to Singapore as we were supposedly stopping for one night only. However, when trucks arrived the next day to install a barbed wire fence around the houses, and erected a guard box at the entrance, our hopes were dashed, and we knew we were in for a long haul.

The camp was in a much poorer part of town, at Talang Semoet (Semut, meaning 'ant'). It consisted of 18 Dutch-style houses on two streets, Bernhardlaan and Irenelaan, named after members of the Dutch royal family.

The houses were much smaller than those at Bukit Besar. Twenty-four people – 7 civilians and 17 Australian army nurses from the 2/10th – were assigned to our house at Number 6 Irenelaan. The other 15 girls from 2/13th and the CCS were similarly squashed into Number 7 with two civilian women, three children and a piano.

The piano, scrounged from some Dutch women, was dragged by the nurses past six houses and up the slope to Number 7. Owing to the shortage of space, one of them slept on it at night.

Garages were also used as accommodation for 10 people. Each house had two bedrooms, a combined lounge–dining room, a bathroom and a kitchen, with a go-down (storeroom) at the back and a small porch at the front entrance. With two dozen people living in a house designed for four, at most, the septic tank overflowed and poured into the street drains.

Above left: Irenelaan houses, pre war. Above right: Houses 6 and 7, Irenelaan, prior to Japanese occupation

With so many women of disparate backgrounds kept in fairly close confinement, there were bound to be ructions. The nurses were a very cohesive group, and it appears that this irritated some of the internees. There was an attempt by the civilian women in Number 7 to take over the largest bedroom, claiming that the nurses had not only taken the largest room for themselves but also kept the best of the rations. Accusing them of being 'officers' playthings', the ringleader began throwing the sisters' possessions into the living area before physically attacking Wilma Oram, raking both cheeks with her fingernails.

At this point, two other civilian women burst in and grabbed the hair of another nurse, escalating what had been a minor fracas into an all-out brawl. The situation reached crisis point when another civilian, holding a knife and shouting expletives, pushed her way to the centre of the room declaring that she would use it.

At that point, Dr McDowell appeared on the scene and in an authoritative voice shouted, 'That will be enough.' To the annoyance of the nurses, she then resolved the dispute by allocating the larger room to the civilians.

The electricity was on, but not connected, and no water came from any of the taps. The furniture in our house consisted of a dining-room table, a cot and a broken-down cane lounge. Nesta James, being about five feet nothing, laid claim to the cot. Bedding for the rest of us was very basic – a rice sack mattress filled with grass collected from the banks of the drains, then dried, and a kapok-filled pillow if you were lucky. If you weren't, you had to make do with a lifebelt. Once again, we slept on the floor but, as it was covered in ceramic tiles, at least it was easy to keep clean.

The Japanese provided no cooking or eating utensils. All we had were the tins and bits and pieces we had scrounged from the coolie-lines at Muntok or found along the way. At first, we cooked communally over a fire using an old Mobil Oil Company tin, which tainted the rice and the tea, but later we divided into smaller groups, which we found easier to manage. Wood, however, was very scarce. We scrounged what we could from roof timbers and even the back door which, in hindsight, was not a sensible thing to do as it allowed the Japanese and light-fingered locals and others to wander in and out at will. It was not until the Japanese eventually delivered a load of timber – long planks that had to be chopped up – that there was an improvement.

Until the electricity was reconnected, our crowded conditions made it difficult for people to find their way to the bathroom at night. When Mickey Syer trod on my face in the darkness, I decided to move and joined Beryl Woodbridge on the small porch. She slept on the cane lounge. I was on the floor. We had no mosquito nets, but fortunately the Dutch colonial government had introduced strict malaria control and Sumatra at that time was virtually malaria free.

Camp commandants for the British and the Dutch were elected, causing almost as much interest and amusement as general elections do at home. These leaders dealt directly with the Japanese. We elected Sister Nesta James as our spokeswoman. Mitzi was appointed team leader for our house, and Jean Ashton for the other.

Dr McDowell was the commandant for the British camp but, due to the pressure of her

How prisoners were forced to bow, before Mrs Hinch's ploy worked

medical work, she relinquished her role for some time to Mrs Gertrude Hinch, her deputy and a woman of impeccable manners and great tact. When dealing with Captain Miachi, a quite handsome and incredibly conceited Japanese officer who was in charge of the camps, Mrs Hinch flattered his ego.

Gertrude Bean Hinch, aged 51, was born in Milwaukee in the United States. Her husband was the principal of the Anglo-Chinese School in Singapore and she was the only American in the women's camp. Prominent in the YWCA, she was a natural leader, and received an OBE from the British government in 1942. Described as dynamic and a 'thoroughbred patrician', she 'took nothing from the Japs but, rather, kept them on the defensive'.

It was Japanese policy for all civilians and prisoners to show their obeisance to them by bowing from the waist. The commandants dealt directly with the Japanese so that we had no need to have any contact with them, but the guards of course marched up and down and back and forth and we were supposed to bow to them as we passed. Mrs Hinch, however, suggested to Miachi that a man as erudite as he would know that, in England and most Western countries, a man raised his hat and a lady inclined her head in greeting when they met one another. Consequently, instead of lining up in front of our houses at 7 am and 5 pm each day for tenko and bowing to the guards, we just inclined our heads. On passing a guard, we did likewise.

There are few gestures more condescending than a gentle inclination of the head and, although there were a few incidents of face slapping for imagined or intended snubs, I cannot recall any such incident involving an Australian nurse.

The Dutch camp commandant was Mrs Tine Muller, a tall, handsome woman with an imposing presence, who had studied Japanese when her husband was Naval Attaché at the Dutch Embassy in Japan. She tried her Japanese on the guards, but could not understand their

Charitas Hospital, Palembang

responses. It was only in our last two camps that she realised the Japanese had been answering her in 'coolie' Japanese in order to show their contempt for women prisoners.

Mrs Muller's able assistant and adviser was Mother Laurentia, the most senior of the two groups of nuns – one was Charitas, a nursing order, and the other a teaching order. Tall, elegant, good-looking and dignified, she floated through the camp in her long habit, her face showing the strain of the circumstances in which she and her sisters were now held.

The hospital run by the Charitas nuns in Palembang was allowed to remain open and to admit both male and female internees. As we had a number of pregnant women in camp, and had other women who became very ill, after a time the Japanese provided a weekly ambulance service.

The camp doctors also arranged for people suffering from severe fatigue to be admitted to hospital, where the food was better, for a week's rest. Wednesday was outpatients' day. The wily nuns and doctors organised appointments to allow some of the married women to undergo treatment at the same time as their husbands, with whom there was normally no contact as they were segregated in the men's camp. The men took the opportunity to pass on news – mainly rumours – but if it was good we liked to believe it.

> *As the Japanese patrolled the corridors and clinic rooms to prevent any contact between male and female outpatients, most of the meetings took place in the solitary lavatory at the far end of the building – the one place not under surveillance. After the consultations were over, far more than rumours entered the women's camp. Every opportunity was taken to smuggle in medicines, money and messages. On one occasion, Sister Mavis Hannah was able to bring in letters, held against her body with a sanitary pad.*

Not long after our arrival, we received a visit from a very senior Japanese official. He was quite gentlemanly and spoke with Mrs Hinch, Sister James and some of the senior sisters. Afterwards, we were given papers to fill in with all our details, to be sent to Japanese headquarters. We hoped the form-filling might mean repatriation – we grasped at any straw! Later we were given yellow cards on which to write a message home, using just 25 words. Our families received the cards about 18 months later. They were the only messages to be delivered during our period as guests of the Japanese Emperor.

The official took time out to see the Australian Army nurses. Before he left, he promised that he would broadcast their names from Singapore and, to Sister James's astonishment, he did so. He also promised them better rations but, apart from a small increase in the supply of tea and sugar and the inclusion of waterlily roots and leeks in the rations, there was little discernible improvement. After the visit, some Dutch and Eurasian women were freed from the camp to return to their farms in an effort to improve the vegetable supply.

The Japanese were very disorganised, forcing the inmates to take over the internal running of the camp themselves. However, it soon became obvious that, whenever there was work to be done and a call was made for volunteers, the same people put up their hands. To force malingerers to pull their weight, Dr McDowell physically examined everyone to determine exactly what they could and couldn't do.

In order to ensure that the camp functioned as well as possible, various committees were formed, including squads of British, Australian and Dutch (BAD) nurses, to inspect the houses weekly. Our main role was to advise and assist in the maintenance of good hygiene as, in such crowded conditions, an outbreak of infectious disease was a distinct possibility. A roster was drawn up for emptying septic tanks, cooking, supervising rations, additional food gathering, drain clearing, general cleaning and entertainment. The Australian nurses also carried out 'district nursing', offering nursing advice or assistance to anyone who needed it and manning an aid station set up in the garage of a nearby house, where our two medical practitioners now lived.

Dr Goldberg, who had not been interned initially, was not in camp. She had come into the Bukit Besar Camp in April 1942, where she continued to receive preferential treatment, before being released to take up paid work in the Charitas Hospital in town. The hospital was new and very large, but it was not long before the Japanese appropriated it for their own use, forcing the nuns to move to much smaller premises. They were allowed to move only the beds and the operating table, but fortunately Mother Alacoque and her nurses received sufficient notice to enable them to hide much-needed drugs beneath their voluminous robes.

According to Mickey Syer, Dr Goldberg was always dressed in a white starched uniform, never contracted malaria, was never sick and, when working in the camps, slept on an innerspring mattress under a mosquito net in a room of her own. The nurses did not trust her and never discussed anything with her, as she had shown an unhealthy interest in Vivian Bullwinkel, trying to pump her and several of her friends for information.

The food-rationing committee was responsible for sorting and sharing the meagre supplies for distribution – the most thankless task of all, as dealing with hungry people is not easy. Betty Jeffrey was the representative for our house. On arrival, the food was tipped from the open truck onto the roadway. The rice was often mouldy, and if it wasn't, it was because lime sulphur, used to control fungi, had been added to the bags. This chemical gave off a smell like rotten egg gas and, as the lime was inedible, the rice had to be washed to get rid of it, as well as the taste and the smell. On the rare occasions when meat was included, it was usually wild boar or buffalo. We received only a handful to be shared among 24 or more, and the committee had to beat off hungry dogs, left behind by their owners.

The meat, when it came, was thrown in one lump onto the roadway by the Japanese delivery man, who would then use his boot to steady it as he hacked off portions with a pen knife. Any eggs in the delivery were deliberately smashed.

Gho Leng, a trader with a bullock cart, also came into camp each Sunday bringing food, pencils, paper and other small items. Occasionally, he also had lengths of material and even sandshoes. Each house was allowed access to him in rotation. As black marketeering had been conducted via the barbed-wire fence, it was a relief to have a legal supply of goods available as black marketeers, when caught, were severely punished.

Those attempting to provide goods were dealt with even more severely. A frail elderly man, who had been caught by the guards while attempting to sell duck eggs to the internees, was badly beaten before being dragged to the centre of the compound and tied to a post with barbed wire. The women were warned not to attempt to give him any water or food, as anyone who did so would share the same fate.

As the sun beat down on his battered body, he became semi-conscious and began to hallucinate. His pleas for water continued until well into the night when, mercifully, he lapsed into total unconsciousness.

At around noon the following day, screams brought the Australian nurses running from their houses. A middle-aged woman, a British internee unable to withstand the old man's suffering, had attempted to take him some water, only to be discovered by the guard. She was lying spread-eagled on the ground, with a Japanese soldier standing astride her, wielding a sheathed sword that he brought down with some force, opening up the side of her head. As he raised the weapon again, Sister Ashton, followed by the other nurses, strode out and, in a voice that indicated she would brook no opposition, ordered him to stop. Pausing, the soldier delivered one more blow before stalking off.

Although the Japanese were determined to stamp out illicit trading, they allowed Milwani, an Indian tailor, to call in from time to time, bringing with him lengths of fabric, cottons and sewing materials, which were sold at highly inflated prices. Two customers at a time were allowed to go outside the wire under escort to make purchases, so his visits lasted most of the day.

Every now and then a few more people came into camp, and each time 32 pairs of hopeful eyes scanned the newcomers' faces anxiously. The first lot arrived shortly after we moved in. They had come from Muntok and had been captured after we left. No more of our nurses ever arrived, but a number of British nursing sisters did, and three came to live in our house. I also remember, particularly, three beautiful Dutch girls named Colijn and a French woman and her exquisitely dressed children. There was also a large, lovely and very pregnant Dutch girl, Rita Wenning. I asked her rather stupidly, 'Why didn't you leave, go home, before the Japanese arrived? Anything is better than this.' Her reply was, 'But Sister, this is my home. My grandmother was Chinese.' Her husband was Dutch, who were far more tolerant of mixed marriages than the British. Rita was a very good artist and had brought her equipment with her. Later, when her supplies ran out, she switched to charcoal.

Most of the internees tried to look neat and tidy. This was not so hard for those whose ships had been captured without any serious damage, as they had been able to come ashore with whatever they could carry. For those of us who had been shipwrecked and salvaged nothing, it took effort and ingenuity to keep ourselves looking decent. Some of us were given frocks by other internees – I had a green one that I seemed to wear for ages. We were also given a nun's habit, which provided enough fabric to make several pairs of shorts. Win Davis was a good cutter and did a sterling job. However, our usual outfits were shorts and sun-tops, often made in a patchwork pattern from scraps. As our clothes wore out, we patched them, and then patched the patches.

Clergyman Vic Wardell, who had brought clothing belonging to his wife and daughters when he was evacuated in the hope of meeting up with them, donated items to the impoverished women, along with some of his own clothes. The formerly corpulent Mrs Brown, whose weight at captivity was 15 stone (95 kilograms), made herself a dress from the Reverend's striped pyjamas, and topped off the ensemble with a hat made from a discarded umbrella. Sister Wilma Oram, using cotton string and needles made from two pieces of fencing wire, knitted a sleeveless vest, and crocheted a matching striped beret with a crochet hook, also fashioned from fencing wire.

A much thinner Mary Brown (Muntok Peace Museum)

To earn money, we undertook various tasks. Pat Blake, who was minding a small Chinese boy, knitted for him, while I sewed his clothes. I also made a number of hats from woven-rush mats, including an Akubra-style bush hat for the little boy. His father was a wealthy Englishman and his Chinese mother wouldn't allow him to wear the popular conical, coolie-style hat, which was easy to make. Other nurses undertook various other tasks. Elizabeth Simons and Mavis Hannah made and sold soya-bean cakes. These were tasty and nutritious when fried in a little palm oil and provided the two sisters with a regular income for some time.

However, not all our work was enjoyable, or voluntary. The water pressure was so poor that houses in the upper area of the camp received no water at all. Consequently, we were impressed as water carriers, a backbreaking task that was to plague us for the rest of our imprisonment.

Camp life was very hard on the nuns who had lived such disciplined and cloistered lives. However, Sister Paula, a member of their community, had a small box of watercolours and was able to provide a welcome distraction by giving drawing and painting lessons to anyone who was interested. I was, and was fortunate to find a bottle of black ink lying in the garden. Sister Paula was sweet and most helpful, but after a few weeks she became ill and the lessons stopped. However, I continued to sketch, taking refuge from the world with my pencil and paper. I was able to sell a few of the sketches later on.

In the evenings, when the moon was bright, we gathered together outdoors in our street to listen to various people giving talks on interesting incidents in their lives. Mrs Joan Maddams, a splendidly forthright and cheerful person, who was clever with her hands and a tower of strength in the camp, gave an interesting and amusing account of a bus trip she and her husband had taken across the United States in the 1930s.

Mrs [Helen] Dixey talked of life in the Seychelles. It sounded an idyllic place, where the water was so pure there was no need for cosmetics. I think most of us decided to go there, one day. Iole Harper and Eileen 'Shortie' Short both spoke about the trials and triumphs of living on outback cattle stations – Iole in Western Australia and Shortie in Queensland. Both talks were interesting and quite different. Mrs 'Gillie' [Georgette] Gilmour, a Frenchwoman married to an Australian, told us about her life on a leper island, where her husband had been superintendent. At the end of her talk, a clear, bell-like voice rang out, 'What do you do with the toes and fingers that fall off?' Gillie replied, 'We curry them.'

Norah Chambers recounted the hazardous trip she and her husband had made from northern Malaya through enemy lines before she joined the ill-fated *Vyner Brooke*, while Helen Colijn, the eldest of the three Colijn girls, spoke of climbing Mont Blanc in the French Alps, with a nonchalance not expected from one so young. She was only 21 and the grand-daughter of the Prime Minister of Holland. We listened with great interest and admiration, but I doubt if anyone was tempted to follow in her footsteps.

The very attractive Colijn sisters, Helen, Antoinette and Alette, were the grand-daughters of Hendrikus Colijn, the Dutch Prime Minister. They, along with their mother and father Anton, who worked for the Dutch Petroleum Company and was also a member of the Dutch army reserve, had tried to escape to Australia on board Pulau Bras, *which had been subsequently bombed and sunk off Sumatra's coast.*

Margaret Dryburgh, a former schoolteacher, was the head of a team of Presbyterian missionaries. A person of many talents, she started up a choir and produced a monthly magazine, which contained a variety of news items, helpful hints and even a crossword puzzle. She also started a serial entitled 'Alice in Internment Land'. We followed the saga with great interest and amusement as she brought subjects of topical interest into the story, such as the 'Mythical Goat'. One of the guards had promised to bring a nanny goat into the camp so the children could have fresh milk. The goat never appeared, hence the story.

Margaret Dryburgh, born in Sunderland in northern England in 1890, was the daughter of a Presbyterian clergyman. After gaining her degree in education and music, she taught at a girls' grammar school in England, where she also trained the school choir, before working as a missionary in China. She then went to Singapore to work among the Teochow Chinese, whose language she spoke fluently, becoming the first principal of Kuo Chuan Girls' School.

Aged 52 when she was captured and one of the older women, she appreciated the effect that stress could have on the lives of the internees and realised the value of maintaining morale. She organised a weekly church service in the garage where Shelagh and Mrs Brown lived and one of her first tasks was to write the words of 'The Captives' Hymn'. Performed for the first time by her newly formed choir on 5 July 1942, women sang the hymn throughout their captivity and today it is an important component of many ex-POW memorial services.

Helen Colijn, who wrote the book, Song of Survival, *recalled:*

> When I first met Miss Dryburgh, she had struck me as a rather dull bird: eyes peeping through thick round lenses, brownish hair in a tight bun at the back of her head, a short stocky figure wearing the sensible loose-fitting cotton dress and Mary Jane-type shoes... But I soon discovered that Miss Dryburgh was not at all a dull woman.

Margaret Dryburgh

Regular singsongs were held next door at Number 7, which had the piano. We had several excellent pianists, including Miss Dryburgh and Mrs Jennings, a former nurse who also had a glorious singing voice. These get-togethers were so well attended that we had trouble fitting everyone in. We also organised several variety concerts, which were very popular and included solo vocal items by Mickey Syer. Mrs Brown and her daughter often joined in the entertainments, decked out in whatever finery they could find, which included chilli earrings and pumpkin-seed necklaces.

One day, Margaret Dryburgh and her helpers dragged out a small travelling organ, which she had brought with her into captivity and somehow managed to retain. With two little boys lying flat on their stomachs and pumping the bellows, she pounded away at the keyboard. As a musical event it was hardly remarkable but, as a gesture, it showed courage, determination and humour.

A library was formed and the joining fee was a book – a condition that was later dropped. I could join at once as I had picked up a copy of *Pride and Prejudice* in our previous house. It was nowhere near as heavy as Boccaccio's *Decameron*, but as I picked it up and leafed through it, Mrs Maddams saw me and said, 'Highly overrated'. I was tempted to say I had read it when I was about nine and perhaps I should now find out what it was all about. Knowing what a diverse group we were, I decided that maybe discretion was the better part of valour and chose instead one of Simon Templar's 'Saint' books. Light, racy and amusing, it was an easy read. Books took us into another world, and provided a very necessary diversion.

The Japanese allowed copies of their local newspaper in the camp but, as they had full editorial control, it was full of stories about fantastic claims of naval victories in the Pacific and little else.

A young and pretty Indonesian internee, who had noticed me reading *Pride and Prejudice* at the padang while we were awaiting transportation to the camp, asked if I had handed it in. I found it for her and complimented her on her English. She then told me she and her husband had married while studying law in Holland, and had honeymooned cycling along the dykes. She had two delightful children – Billie, whose grin split his face wide open and was aged about three or four, and Meikie, a sweet light-brown cherub.

The Japanese, conscious of the need to be respected by such lowly creatures as women prisoners, had instructed us to call them Nipponese and their homeland Nippon. I loved the fair-haired Dutch boys who strolled casually about the camp saying quite distinctly 'Der Yap'. The Japanese had a great affection for children and never reprimanded or punished them – apart from allowing them to slowly starve to death.

Among the children was Mischa, an orphaned boy. A self-confident little fellow, he strode purposefully about the camp. We laughed and said, 'If we are here for twenty years, Mischa will own the place.'

Mischa, meaning bear, was the pet name of Izidore Warman, who was rescued from the sinking Vyner Brooke *by Eric Germann. When the first bombs had hit the ship, Mischa's father, Stephen, had panicked and leapt overboard. Alerted by the screams of Mrs Warman that her husband could not swim, a British soldier jumped into the sea to save him. He reached the frightened man who seized his rescuer around the neck and both men disappeared below the surface.*

Mischa's mother collapsed and was helped into another lifeboat. She reached Radji Beach where she was reunited with her son, whom she always called Mischa. However, although Mrs Warman and Mischa reached the safety of Muntok with the women's group, she developed pneumonia and died in Palembang on 9 March 1942, shortly after transfer from the Muntok camp. Mischa, who spoke no English at first, was cared for by internees Mrs Mary Jenkin, a member of the Medical Auxiliary Service, and Mrs Mamie Colley, a former schoolteacher.

When doing rounds with the BAD squad, one of the joys was seeing Rita's son Bill (the Dutch called him Wim), who had been born shortly after our arrival. Sitting in his cot, clad only in a napkin, a wide toothless grin on his dribbling mouth, he loved playing 'Klappen einie handjes' with Gillie, who lived in the same house. Bill's hands never missed a beat. He was a lovely little fellow. I hoped that, later, life would be kinder to him.

Mrs Werkmann, the Dutch nurse on our BAD squad, always asked us to stay for morning tea when we finished our round at the house in which she lived. She didn't have to press too hard. It was a world away from what we were used to. The house was furnished. We sat on chairs, had coffee from real cups and scones served on a plate. It was almost too civilised.

For our own amusement and to relieve the tedium of the days, we made playing cards from a large photograph. I think it was Betty Jeffrey who borrowed the necessary cutting instruments and ruler from either the nuns or the missionaries. 'Jeff' was the most outgoing of us all and, as a member of the ration committee, had more contact with other internees. We also made mah jong sets at the urging of Cecilia 'Del' Delforce, who had played as a child. Soft wood from the cot was cut into small rectangular pieces, which we rubbed smooth with abrasive leaves from a clump of sandpaper fig trees growing in the compound. They were then beautifully decorated using the paints Paula had left with us. Sister Blanch and Del, who pulled down part of the house to make a particularly beautiful set, held a raffle. A nun won it and with the money they bought extra food.

We also made toys, some of which we sold. A small kangaroo with a joey in its pouch netted me 50 cents. It was amazing what could be done with a little piece of cloth and some filling. Del's mah jong set, a kangaroo made by Sylvia Muir, my pack of cards and several of my small drawings are now in the Australian War Memorial in Canberra.

There was no attempt made by the Japanese at Irenelaan to open up a 'Club', but that did not mean that they had given up the idea of coercing the nurses to work as comfort women.

One day, Captain Miachi called a meeting to discuss the need for internees to work for the Japanese. When I said I wasn't going, it was the down-to-earth, ever practical Gillie who said, 'Don't do anything to annoy them, they are only asking for us to attend the meeting.'

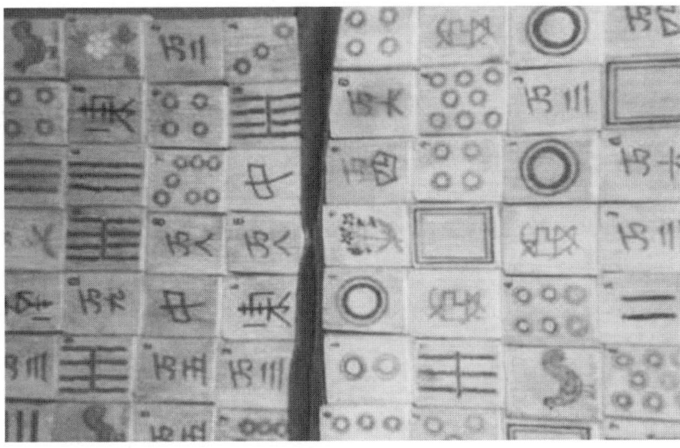

A mah jong set (Muntok Peace Museum)

So I went with the others to the meeting, held in one of the larger houses, which had some quite decent furniture. Captain Miachi strode into the room, looking very pleased with the good response. He unbuckled his handsome sword, placing it across the front of a very nice desk. Sitting down, he spoke at great length of his need for hospital workers, as the Dutch and British prisoners working at the Pladjoe oil refinery were ill and had requested white nurses to look after them. We smelled a rat, so when he asked for volunteers we slipped out the doors and through the low-silled windows.

Miachi's face darkened and was savage with rage. He was so angry that we felt it would not take much to have him unsheathe his sword and slash out at a few people. Gillie and her friend, Mrs Layland, both middle-aged, went forward to offer their services to give us a chance to get away. They were rudely brushed aside. It was young women he wanted – not matrons who were past their prime! Later, when Mrs Hinch, Dr McDowell and Sister James asked permission to see and inspect the premises where the volunteers would be living and working, their request was refused.

However, some women did leave camp to work for the Japanese. As we assumed they provided 'comfort' to our captors, we called them 'The Girl Friends'. After that, we had no further bother with requests to work for the Japanese. However, in October that year, Margot Turner and Mary Cooper, both QAs, along with Colonial Service nurses Olga Neubronner and Jenny Macalister, left the camp to work with Dr Holwegg in the native hospital in Palembang.

Meanwhile, we continued our daily routine – washing the filthy rice, separating pebbles and grubs from the edible grains, and preparing semi-rotten vegetables for our meals. In the evenings, we walked regularly along our street, stopping occasionally to chat with others. During the daytime, after we had finished our household chores, we played cards and mah jong.

Woodchopping was a constant chore and a very dangerous business. When the axe head flew off, which it did at every third hit, we clasped our arms around our heads, yelled 'fore' and ran for cover. At one stage we were issued with a load of very springy wood. When we chopped it, pieces flew off and hit people in the face, which resulted in a few black eyes among the civilian women and three of the sisters as well.

I thought I had mastered the technique of woodchopping until a chunk flew up and knocked me unconscious. I came to as Win and Mitzi carried me into the house. Certain that my face had been smashed to pieces, I gasped 'Mirror! Mirror!' They placed me on the floor and someone produced a piece of broken mirror. To my amazement, my nose was still intact, but I was bleeding from cuts on my right cheek and eyebrow, which were already swelling. I must have floated off again, as the next thing I knew, Dr Smith was kneeling on the floor beside me.

She said, 'I'll just put a few stitches in both cuts.' Stitches! As I was unsure about the standard of asepsis practised in the camp I was hysterical. In a split second I had a deep-seated infection, osteomyelitis, the whole works. I gasped, 'No stitches, no stitches!'

'All right, I won't bloody well stitch them,' said Dr Smith, getting to her feet and stalking off in a huff. I think I faded out again for a while. When I next opened my eyes, Win was sitting on the floor near me laughing. 'What's so funny?' I asked. 'You are,' she answered.

So I joined the black-eyed brigade. I don't know why it is called a black eye, because the bruise is almost every colour of the rainbow. I was not alone. Dot Freeman wore a line of Michell (surgical) clips across her forehead until the cut healed, while Jenny Greer, who had received a very nasty blow, suffered headaches for some time afterwards. Later, the men received permission to send us ready-cut wood. Their gesture was greatly appreciated, especially when they concealed notes in the pile for their wives and friends, containing whatever news was available.

With no reliable news coming in from the outside world, rumours were always rife. It was said that the Japanese had killed their non-Japanese spies and informers as they took the Malayan Peninsula and Singapore. Another rumour was that they had turned the V for Victory signs, which most of the British had placed on the bumper bars of their cars as a fundraising idea, upside down, added a bar across the centre and promoted the 'A' symbol as 'Asia for the Asians'.

We periodically received 'war news' from the Japanese. It was always good news for them and bad for us. They said that their submarines had destroyed the Sydney Harbour bridge, which we were inclined to believe until they added that they had torpedoed the non-existent 'centre pylon' and the bridge had fallen down.

Some time in the latter months of 1942, we were called together and informed that we were all to sign a 'no escape' agreement, promising not to run away or plot means of escape. Should we attempt to do so, we were to agree to accept any punishment handed out. We were uncertain what to do about this until a message came from the men's camp telling us to sign as it would be regarded as signed under duress and therefore not binding.

In September 1942, POWs at every camp in South-East Asia were issued with similar forms to sign. When those still in the main Changi Camp in Singapore refused to comply, they were herded onto the confined space of the parade square at Selarang Barracks, defying the order to sign until the Japanese threatened to bring out the sick from the hospital. Assured by senior officers that the agreement was not binding, all signed – not in their own names but those of movie stars or cartoon characters.

There was always a number of dogs around the camp and, if rations tipped onto the ground contained meat, we would have to beat the dogs off. All they got to eat was food that was too bad for us to eat, and that was very little. Always hungry, they tended to become savage, snarling at the Japanese guards who mistreated them. The Japanese said, if we took them down to the guardhouse, about a couple of hundred yards along the road from the camp, they would shoot them. As it was the only sensible thing to do, a sad procession took about 20 of them away. In about 10 minutes or so, quite a few of the dogs struggled back into camp, bleeding from bayonet wounds. They had to be caught and taken back to the guardhouse, and this time they did not return.

A number of women fainted at the sight of the injured animals and I doubt if any internee was dry-eyed. Our distress was completely beyond the understanding of the Japanese, who said, 'We tell you of our battles and how many of your men we have killed and you only laugh.' We also heard that the Japs amused themselves by tying bricks around dogs' necks and tossing them into a swimming pool. Each time a dog surfaced, their tormentors pushed it under with a long pole until it drowned.

There were a few schoolteachers among the British, including Louise Beeston and Miss Dorothy Moreton, who held classes for the children. This was great as, with the children occupied for a few hours, their mothers had a chance to do their work without interruption. As Christmas approached, the teachers, along with Gillie and a few of the other prisoners, were kept busy making cloth books and toys from fabric samples obtained from the Indian tailor.

With most commodities unavailable, Christmas of 1942 presented a particular culinary challenge. The nurses normally pounded the rice into a kind of flour to make bread in a tin. On Christmas morning, they woke very early and made 'toast' out of this quasi bread before going to church. The men sent in some meat, which was added to vegetables to make a stew. Christmas pudding was dough made from rice flour, with brown beans added to look like raisins, topped with custard made from coconut milk thickened with overcooked rice.

Christmas presents were exchanged, as were cards, both made from anything we could lay our hands on.

As the Japanese paid as much regard to Christian religious principles as they did to the Geneva Convention, the men were sent out to work as usual. However, stopping at a spot where we could see them, they sang Christmas carols and hymns and we, regardless of voice, sang to them. It was a very emotional experience. With the extra food sent in by the men, that night we went to our sacks with full stomachs, for the first time since becoming prisoners.

New Year was also celebrated. We wished each other a happier new year, but I doubt if anyone had the strength to see the old year out. At Easter we received very belated Christmas greetings from Mr Curtin, our Australian Prime Minister. His message, mailed from Australia and handed to Mrs Hinch by the Japanese commandant, ended with the exhortation 'Keep smiling girls'.

We tried to keep busy in our spare time – the usual things, playing bridge, mah jong, reading or pursuing our money-making activities – but boredom had become one of our greatest enemies. So we thought of different things to discuss and do as a group. I think it was Betty

Jeffrey's suggestion that, if we were to take the best features of our group, we could make one good-looking person. Mitzi's facial bone structure was chosen, Pat Blake's smile, Jenny Greer's complexion and eyes, my hair, Jeff's beautiful long legs, Win Davis's graceful movements, Dot's dimpled knees. This simple game amused us for a few hours.

I sketched our house, sitting on the fence of the house opposite. Then I drew the house opposite, from our porch. If the guard saw me, he took no notice. I also sketched a kitchen Rene Singleton and Dot Freeman had constructed, just outside the fence of our house at number 6. They had built it when we broke into smaller groups for our cooking, and it was indeed an exercise in ingenuity. I had by this time bought myself a 4B pencil – my pride and joy. For paper, I cut the blank section of pages from books. Sacrilege, but I chose only German and Dutch books. It was good quality vellum. Otherwise, I used any blank paper I could get.

Mrs Layland, Gillie's good friend, was admitted to hospital sometime after Easter. She was very ill and died a few weeks later. It was the first death of someone we knew well, and we were very distressed.

Kathleen Layland, who came from Vancouver, Canada, died on 12 May 1943.

As the year wore on, we settled into a set routine, with the Australian and English nurses taking their turns on the district roster. Due to the poor quality and quantity of the food, the health of the internees was steadily and quite obviously deteriorating. Dysentery affected many. Beriberi was manifest in swollen feet and abdomens, with the inevitable peripheral neuritis (damage to nerves that affected sensation). The weekly ambulance bringing discharged patients from the hospital always went back full.

The doctors did their best to see that everyone, particularly the most destitute, had a week or more in hospital, where the food was much better and they were freed from daily chores. Usually, two or more of the nurses were in hospital at any one time. I felt particularly sorry for the older women, some of whom had come from poor, beleaguered England to relatives in the east, thinking they would be safe, only to be taken prisoner by the Japanese. Others, who had led a pampered life in Singapore, surrounded by servants and luxury, found prison life extremely hard.

Australian-born Mrs Geraldine Harding was one of them. Married to Major Frank Leonard Harding, a wealthy racehorse trainer, she had lived in Singapore for 20 years. Life at her home Irwellbank – a 20-acre (8-hectare) property with 27 racehorses, a string of polo ponies, nine Alsatian dogs, four cars and a legion of servants – had ill prepared her for captivity. Admitted to hospital with malaria and beriberi shortly after capture, she had the resources to stay there throughout most of her captivity, as she had been evacuated on Mata Hari *and was among those who had arrived with money and belongings. One day she bought a pot of pepper, wrapped in newspaper, and was shocked to read that three of her racehorses were now owned by Japanese officers and had won races in Singapore.*

On 13 September, Dr Goldberg and the Charitas hospital staff, along with all their equipment and patients, including Mrs Harding, were transferred, without warning, from the town premises to an empty house outside the camp.

The Japanese had discovered some time before that subversive elements in Sumatra were involved in an underground organisation backed by the Dutch, and had swooped on Ambonese and Manadonese civilians (people from the islands of Ambon and Sulawesi) in the Palembang area. On learning that messages and money from male internees were being channelled through the Charitas hospital to the women's camp, they deduced that some of the money was being used to aid and abet the underground movement. Declaring that Charitas staff were engaging in anti-Japanese behaviour, the Japanese shut down the hospital and sent everyone to either the men's or women's camps. The new owners promptly turned the building, which had a clear view down the river, into a military facility.

It was widely believed that Dr Goldberg, through whose hands money was being passed to the nurses from the men's camp, had informed the Japanese. The suspicions seemed to be well founded – Goldberg was the only person working at the hospital to escape attention. Sister Hannah, who had been involved in the smuggling, was taken out and interrogated.

The repercussions against hospital staff for the alleged subversive activities were savage. Dr Tekelenberg, the surgeon, and 171 Ambonese and Manadonese suspects were sent to a kempei tai military gaol at Soengei (Sungei) Liat on the east of Bangka Island, where it was reported the doctor's hands were cut off. He and 165 of the civilians arrested with him died there, together with most of the other inmates. Reverend Mother Alacoque was removed from the women's camp. Tortured by the kempei tai, she was sent with four Ambonese women to a military prison in Palembang, where she spent the months until the end of the war in prayer, refusing to speak to her captors.

Dr Ziesel and nine Ambonese were beheaded on 9 November. Had the Japanese discovered that Dr Tekelenburg had a secret radio, he too would have been executed.

The hospital's transfer from town had cut our link with the outside world but, in spite of this, rumours and news flourished – most of it, I think, the product of the internees' overactive imaginations. As always, we pretended to believe the good news. However, the advantage of having the hospital in our compound was that ill patients could be admitted any day of the week. Dr Goldberg, who had kept a low profile while in town, was now in sole charge. Wondering if the axis powers were winning the war in Europe, we accepted her appointment with some reservation.

The reservations were justified. For the next 12 months Goldberg was the only doctor permitted to enter the camp hospitals, over which she had total and absolute control, prompting the Australian nurses to keep a close eye on her. Mrs Holderness, a Jewish internee, acted as her handmaiden – cleaning her shoes, fetching water for her to bathe in and attending to her every need, apart from laundry and cooking, which were done by the nuns in the hospital.

As noted by the nurses, apart from being very friendly with the Japanese guards, Goldberg would refuse to attend to patients at night but gave preferential treatment to anyone with money by allowing them to be admitted to hospital on the slightest pretext. Anyone who was penniless and fell ill had no chance of a prolonged period in hospital, as Goldberg admitted only those who could pay – in cash, gems or jewellery – the huge amounts she demanded for tending and feeding them. None of the money she accumulated was used to buy food for herself or Holderness, who dined on superior hospital rations purchased from a special fund. Goldberg also fed precious powdered milk, intended for the children, to her cat.

Shortly before the hospital was relocated, a message from the men's camp came via the woodpile telling us to 'Get ready to move. We are moving soon.'

This was followed by a second message, also delivered via the woodpile, on 18 September. 'Leaving today – destination unknown'.

We were ready. We had very little to pack.

CHAPTER 7

The 'Men's Camp', Palembang

18 September 1943 – 15 October 1944

The new camp was at Poentjak Sekoening (Puncak Sekuning), a 15-minute drive away. To their amazement, the women discovered that they were to occupy the camp just vacated by the male internees, who had been transferred to their old camp at Muntok Gaol on Bangka Island. The recently relocated hospital, which also made the move, remained under the control of Dr Goldberg.

A convoy of rattletrap trucks took us to our new camp. The men, not knowing we would soon be in occupation, had left it in a filthy, disorganised mess, saying, 'The Japs can clean this up.' However, the wily Japs moved us in and we cleaned it up. The camp was in a fairly confined area but it still took us almost a week. We were amused at the size of some of the wooden scuff-type sandals, known as trompers, which the men had left behind. They were far too big for our feet, so we used them for firewood.

Trompers were made by carving shoe-shaped soles from solid pieces of wood. A strip of rubber cut from an old tyre was then hammered across the instep area to create a scuff. Women without footwear, which was most of the nursing sisters, had been forced to make their own trompers when the septic tanks overflowed at Irenelaan.

The 'Men's Camp', as it continued to be called, was in a low-lying area, surrounded by marshland, and consisted of an irregular square of wooden huts with atap roofs, surrounded by the usual barbed wire. The central padang had two wells and a square, general-purpose open-sided building with an atap roof that served as a kind of community centre. The earth in the middle

Trompers

of the padang had been rolled to make a playing field. In the rainy season it was a quagmire and in the dry, as hard as cement.

The entrance was in the front row of huts. One side had been reserved for the hospital. Opposite the hospital were the guardhouse, accommodation for Dr Goldberg and the nuns, and a storeroom. On the far side of the padang and opposite the entrance were two cookhouses – one for the British and one for the Dutch – with huge iron kwalis (woks) set into elevated brick fireplaces for cooking the communal rice and vegetables. There were also areas set aside for individual cooking.

The British and Dutch nationals were housed opposite each other in the two remaining wings. As in the coolie-lines at Muntok, the huts were split into sections, with the usual bali balis on each side and a wide aisle separating them. There were about 60 crammed into each hut. A single electric bulb gave some light, but provided more sparks than light when the weather was wet and windy. The atap roofs, sloping towards the padang, had wide eaves, providing shelter over wooden mess tables and benches where we ate our meals or played cards and mah jong. The ablution blocks adjoining the sleeping quarters had a cement floor with a large tong in the middle. A row of cubicles lining the outer wall housed oriental squatting-style lavatories. Thankfully, the cubicles had doors.

The Australian nurses were allocated the same hut. The men had removed a single 8-inch (20-centimetre) wide board from the wall facing the padang. We removed another to create easier access and used the discarded board to keep our trompers off the dirt floor. The sleeping space for each person was about 24 inches (60 centimetres) wide – totally inadequate, even though we had all lost weight.

Palembang 'Atap' camp (M Dryburgh)

Mrs Mary Austin, a charming Australian who came from the Sydney beachside suburb of Manly, had a lightweight pine door which she had used to keep her bedding off the floor in the first camp. She couldn't use it on the bali bali, so she gave it to me. We had tables under the eaves where we ate our meals and bench-like stools on which to sit, so at night I balanced the door on the stools and slept outdoors. Mary was one of the few civilians happy to share what she had. I am sorry to say that two other Australian women in the camp, who had plenty of clothes, were not nearly as charitable.

It was fortunate that the nurses had one another. According to Betty Jeffrey, of the 200-odd British women in the camp in July 1944, no more than 20 passed muster. The rest, which included 'slum cats, prostitutes and spies' were 'the world's worst shockers'. Some internees, who were well off, rejected any idea of carrying out camp duties or relying on camp rations, saying that they had never worked like that in their lives, had never eaten food like that and were not going to start now. One Dutch woman excused herself from engaging in hard labour, such as chopping down trees for much needed firewood, by saying 'That's all right for you Australians. You're used to this sort of thing.'

We had only been in the new camp for a short time when the four British nursing sisters, who had left Irenelaan to work in the native hospital in Palembang, returned. Thin, distressed and utterly wretched, they were relieved to be back with familiar faces. After working in the hospital for six months, they had spent the next six months in a filthy gaol, much of it in solitary confinement and living in fear of being taken away and executed. Why they had been imprisoned, they didn't know. Each day they were allowed out of their cells to walk in the inner grounds for a short period, always accompanied by a guard to prevent them escaping. Escape! To what? And to where?

The sisters, who were broken in health and generally in a poor mental state, had evidently been caught up in supposed anti-Japanese subversive activities. Two of them were QAs – Irish-born Mary Cooper and Margot Turner, who survived the sinking of Tanjoeng Pinang. *The other two were Olga Neubronner and Janet 'Jenny' Macalister, previously employed by the Medical Department at Seremban, Malaya, who had been captured when her ship* Mata Hari *surrendered. The return of the four sisters also heralded the arrival of a number of Dutch and German women who, although previously free, were now interned. They were well equipped with pillows, sheets and clothes and a good supply of guilders, sewn into children's stuffed dolls and toys.*

The Girl Friends were also returned to camp. They looked well fed and well dressed. I remember how Gillie had lectured us when they left the camp, 'You younger ones needn't look down on them. They are your protection.'

She was right of course. If we had to provide medical assistance to one of the Girl Friends, we didn't treat them any differently from anybody else. Naturally, when we were sponging them, we might have had a bit of a conversation, but we never talked about what they had been doing. It seemed pointless. It was their lifestyle. It was their business. As long as we didn't get involved, we didn't worry too much about it.

A lovely young Russian woman had gone out of the camp with the Girl Friends as she was anxious about her husband, of whom she had had no news since being interned. She was severely traumatised and, on her return, went straight to Mother Laurentia. She remained with the nuns until the war ended.

I was on duty the day the Girl Friends came back to camp. Dr Smith told me that the youngest of the group, a Eurasian girl now aged 17, had given birth to a baby boy while working at the brothel. The Japs had told her that, if she named the father, they would 'arrange a marriage and all would be respectable'. When the streetwise girl refused to divulge a nationality, let alone a name – after all, the baby could be Japanese or Chinese or Indonesian – she was subjected to 'bastinado', a severe caning on the soles of her feet. Unable to walk, she had to be brought back by ambulance.

Poor little girl. When I walked in with a bowl of warm water to sponge and soak her bruised and battered feet, she looked at me with a fear almost bordering on hatred. After washing her feet with scented soap and dusting them with the talc that she had brought back with her, I dressed her in one of her pretty nighties. The fear had now gone, because I had treated her like any other patient. We heard later that the Japs had sent the baby to Japan.

Some of the Girl Friends became quite friendly with the camp guards. We were grateful as it diverted attention away from us, although, by this time, I doubt we were in any danger as our youthful looks had evaporated. We didn't realise to what extent we had aged until a new arrival at the camp told us that we looked like 'a lot of withered peas'. The other advantage from the Girl Friends' liaisons with the guards was that they were able to bring in food from the black market, which in turn flourished due to increased demand. Through the good graces of the Girl Friends, some goods filtered through to other internees – at high prices, of course. Unfortunately, they also told the guards that we had nicknames for them – 'Seki the Sadist', 'Bully' and 'The Snake'.

'Bully' was a large, very ugly man. One day during tenko, evidently made aware by the Girl Friends of our contempt for him and his fellow guards, Bully read out a statement in English: 'We who are your conquerors will not admit you are a superior race if you do not show us more respect. We will not tolerate your silent contempt and silent insolence.' Far from intimidating us, Bully's declaration helped sustain our morale. A few months later, Val Smith made a rag-doll version of Bully for Betty Jeffrey's birthday. It was a work of art, dressed in a Jap military uniform made from a khaki shirt-tail she had scrounged.

Morale was further improved when civilian internee Norah Chambers approached Margaret Dryburgh with the idea of forming a 'vocal orchestra'. Born Norah Hope to Scottish parents in Singapore in 1905, this talented woman had been educated in England and had studied violin, piano and chamber music at London's prestigious Royal Academy of Music. She had played in the Academy's orchestra, under the baton of Sir Henry Wood, a meticulous taskmaster. However, when she left the Academy, she found that 'fiddlers were two-a-penny' and that there were very few openings in professional orchestras for female musicians, unless they were harpists. She returned to her family, married an engineer and eventually settled at Kuala Terengganu in north-east Malaya, from where she had made her hair-raising escape after the Japanese landed. Although Norah had taught violin to members of her small white community, it was not until she became an internee and created the vocal orchestra that she discovered just how great her musical talent was.

We had not been able to bring the piano with us from Irenelaan, but Margaret and Norah didn't need it. Voices were used to reproduce the orchestral pieces, with each person humming to represent a different stringed instrument – violin, viola, cello and double bass. Margaret and Nora were amazingly talented and could detect the slightest deviation in pitch.

In the early days of our imprisonment we were allowed to have get-togethers in the evenings, but gatherings after dark were now banned, forcing the girls to practise in the cookhouse hut at night. The Japs must have heard them, of course, but they evidently appreciated the music and turned a blind eye.

Between them, Norah and Margaret were able to recall and record the scores of many classical pieces, which were meticulously copied by Antoinette, the second of the Colijn girls. She and Alette, the baby of the trio, were also in the vocal orchestra. In an amazingly short time, the 30 members of the orchestra, which included Mickey Syer, Flo Trotter and Betty Jeffrey, had developed an excellent repertoire. I regretted that my lack of vocal talent precluded my becoming a member but, like all others in a similar position, I thoroughly enjoyed listening to the practice sessions, and particularly the concerts.

The repertoire of the orchestra, under the baton of Norah Chambers, was extensive. Norah and Margaret had transcribed all the music from memory – no less than 30 classical pieces – into four-part harmonies, allowing the orchestra to perform at four concerts with no item repeated. The first concert, held in the all-purpose 'community' shed in the centre of the camp on 27 December 1943, was a gala event. The nurses wore whatever passed for their best clothes, which wasn't much, but other patrons who had access to a trunk-load of clothes dressed to the nines. Ribbons appeared in the hair of the little girls and some women even managed to find some lipstick.

The audience was treated to Dvorak's Largo *from the* New World Symphony *(a classical piece popularised in 1922 when it was adopted as the tune for the song,* Goin' Home*), Tchaikovsky's* Andante Cantabile, *Mendelssohn's* Songs Without Words, *a Brahms waltz, the sentimental favourite* Londonderry Air (Danny Boy), *Debussy's* Reverie, *Beethoven's* Minuet *and* To a Wild Rose. *Mrs Ena Murray, Norah Chamber's sister, had a magnificent soprano voice and sang* Faery Song *from* The Immortal Hour.

Even the guards stopped to listen. We sat in silence, entranced. All too soon, the performance was over, but the memory of the music at this concert, and at others that followed, sustained us in the months to come. However, while the music was excellent, the food was as bad as that in our previous camp. The vegetable ration was often in a state of advanced decomposition, so the weaker and some of the elderly women were given the unpleasant task of sorting out the edible bits.

The well on the Dutch side had clean, fresh water. It probably would have been safe to drink, but no one was prepared to risk it. The well on the British side had muddy water and was used for cleaning and sloshing out the ablution block. There were taps installed over the tongs but, as there was no water connected to them, there was no running water at all in the camp. All water for drinking, cooking and bathing was collected in buckets from a hydrant near the Japanese army barracks, over half a mile away.

Water carrying was performed between 1 pm and 3 pm, the hottest part of the day and, before collecting water for our own use, we had to fill all the tongs and baths used by the Japanese. We were supposed to pour all water we brought to the compound into the tongs in the ablution blocks. By this time, however, most of us had acquired large soft-drink bottles, which we carried in our water-filled buckets. As we returned to camp, we slipped the filled bottles under our bench stools before tipping the buckets' contents into the tongs.

Del and I joined the workers who cleaned the ablution block. Our turn came around every couple of weeks and we were assisted by two English women who offered to be our water carriers – Mamie Colley, a kind and gentle woman who later took over the responsibility of raising Mischa, and Valda Godley, a small, delicately pretty Dolly Varden-type woman, with large violet-blue eyes, a pale face and a pointed chin. We pleaded with Mrs Godley not to carry water, but she insisted she was quite strong and wanted to work with nice people. The only thing we could do to ease her load was to carry as much water into the blocks ourselves before we started our cleaning, using large yard brooms.

Separated by the padang, the English and Dutch saw less of each other than had been the case at our previous camps. 'English and Dutch', incidentally, is somewhat of a misnomer – it seemed that every European nationality was represented in the camp. Among the English was a slender, dark-haired woman whose cousin had been a friend of the Duchess of Monaco. The

Duchess had been in the habit of passing on clothes to her cousin who, in turn, passed some to our fellow internees. The cousin was well off and had come ashore from a beached ship, bringing all she could carry. As she could afford to pay, others were employed to carry her belongings from camp to camp. She was always perfectly dressed. When she returned to normal life in Singapore, it was almost too much for the recently-arrived expatriate English community, who had become accustomed to the drabness of life with coupons, utility clothes and rationing.

In the evenings we got into the habit of taking a walk around the compound. We usually teamed up in the same pairs, but I occasionally walked with Ruth Russell-Roberts. A most interesting and elegant woman, and a former model for couturier Norman Hartnell, she was determined to keep slim. As the daughter, and then the wife, of an army officer, she had seen quite a lot of India and Malaya. Her three-year-old daughter Lynette had left for England in the care of a friend on one of the evacuee ships, but Ruth had received no news of her or of her husband Denis, whom she had last seen in Singapore.

Ruth, nevertheless, had managed to smuggle a letter to her husband, via the lavatory window, during a visit to the outpatients' clinic in town in May 1942, shortly after the women moved into Irenelaan. She had learned from Gho Leng, the trader, on one of his weekly visits, that a Chinese man named Ah Wong sailed a junk to Singapore once a month. However, Gho Leng told her that he was uncertain when the next sailing would be as Ah Wong had a poisoned foot and was undergoing treatment at the Charitas hospital.

By feigning toothache, Ruth managed to attend the next outpatients' clinic, only to discover from patients lined up outside the lavatory window that Ah Wong had left. However, they promised to make contact with him and did so, but it was not until her third bogus visit to the dentist that she was able to pass her precious letter out the window to Ah Wong. He promised that, on reaching Singapore, he would give it to one of the British soldiers who were trucked in from Changi Camp each day to work on the wharves. However, although the letter reached its destination, it would be more than two years before Ruth received any news of her husband and child.

The official food ration was poor, so on Christmas morning 1943 we were startled to see a Chinese man, who had slipped past the guards at the entrance, running as fast as he could towards the cookhouses pushing a wheelbarrow in which there was a dressed pig. Hot on his heels were the guards who, having belatedly spotted the pork, wanted their share. They took a hind leg. Our portion, shared among the entire camp, was the only extra food we had for Christmas that year.

The food was less than festive, but the children were not forgotten. The indefatigable and creative Joan Maddams made a pack of 'Snap' or 'Happy Families' cards for each child. Lucky adults received pictures she had embroidered, using threads drawn from coloured fabrics.

The hair salon (J P L Kickhefer)

A couple of days later, the vocal orchestra put on a concert. The recital was superb, a splendid effort that showed the ability, ingenuity and dedication of the performers, as well as their sheer hard work in bringing each piece to near perfection. Their brilliant performance, and Miss Dryburgh's little organ, reminded us that there was another world outside. And the kindness of the Chinese man reassured us that we had not been entirely forgotten.

By February, a shop had been opened, with supplies brought in by a local Chinese. The destitute nurses, who had no funds, used their ingenuity to make various items that they offered for sale. Betty Jeffrey cut hair with a pair of nail scissors, and she and Iole Harper created what they termed banana fritters, made from a kind of flour and overripe squashed bananas. Pat later used her creativity to make very passable hats. The sisters also performed menial tasks, took over roster duties or babysat for internees who were relatively flush with funds, or who had items they could sell to support their superior lifestyle.

In late March it was announced that the Japanese military police, or kempei tai, were taking over the camp administration from Captain Miachi. On 1 April the internees gathered in groups according to their nationality to meet the new team – Captain Seki Kazuo, described as 'an awful individual' and who became known as Seki the Sadist, and his offsider, a grossly overweight sergeant who was immediately dubbed 'Fatty' or 'Ah Fat'. Besides the new hierarchy, the nurses had to contend with a group of 'hei-hos', a quasi-military organisation of local collaborators who were quartered in the camp while they underwent training and performed guard duties. The upside was that the hei-hos liked children, didn't like their Japanese masters, and tended to fall asleep while on duty.

Some internees earned money by doing menial tasks for those who could pay (J P L Kickhefer)

With the new administration, there was a slight improvement in quality and quantity of the rations – sacks of clean rice, enough for three-quarters of a cup a day per person, instead of just half a cup, sugar and salt (a teaspoon per day) and half a cup of tea leaves a month. A kerosene tin of red palm oil – to be shared among 500 – also arrived, giving welcome relief to the fat-deprived diet, as well as 10 sacks of filthy weevil-ridden corn. However, after the corn was washed and dried, it was palatable enough and, when pounded, made passable porridge. Water, however, remained a problem.

When Captain Seki replaced Miachi, things became more difficult. Before we could bring any water into the camp for our own use, we had to fill the tong at the house belonging to Ah Fat. The accepted procedure was for each person to spit into the tong as the bucket was emptied. I could never quite do it, but I'm pleased to say there was always a certain amount of froth on the top of the water when the tong was full.

Three weeks after the new administration took over, there was great excitement when some European women arrived from a camp at Djambi (Jambi), to the north of Palembang. Among them was Violet Pulford, formerly Matron of the British General Hospital at Malacca, where Pat and the 2/10 AGH nurses had been based, three Dutch ladies, some Eurasians and Dr Margaret Thompson, a Scot, bringing the number of doctors in the camp to four. On the same day that the newcomers arrived, the Australian nurses received some news from home.

The Japanese called us to the general-purpose area in the padang, as they had something 'good' to tell us. We went, thinking that their idea of what was 'good' was probably somewhat different from ours. When we arrived, we were confronted by several fairly high-ranking officers, all with pleased grins on their faces. They told us that Japanese submarines had been sunk in Sydney Harbour and that the Australian Government had sent the ashes of the dead crews back to their homeland. They spoke at great length, telling us that, because of our government's generosity, something good would come to us. What it might be, we had no idea.

As we walked silently away thinking that repatriation was the only thing we wanted, Iole Harper, witty and pretty, suddenly stopped. 'I know, I've worked it out,' she said. 'They're going to send our ashes back.'

The 'good things' promised to Pat and her friends never eventuated. However, in a prison camp at Sandakan, in British North Borneo, the commandant there was so impressed with the goodwill shown by the Australian Government in honouring the sailors with a full military funeral, and returning their ashes to Japan, that he not only supplied a dugong (sea cow) to supplement the rations but also gave the Australian POWs a holiday.

Captain Seki and Ah Fat, the overweight sergeant of the guards, usually attended our concerts. Seki enjoyed the classical items very much, but Ah Fat was far more impressed by the 'leg shows'. However, neither could understand satire, at all. They appreciated a simple dance performed by Ena Murray, Norah's sister, but a 'take off' or skit, performed by Norah and Audrey Owen, which we found funny and nonsensical, left them very puzzled.

One of the new internees, a neatly dressed Dutch woman, wandered around the camp like a lost soul. We learned that after months of house arrest she had been taken to see her husband, whom she thought was still alive. When confronted with his emaciated corpse, lying in a coffin and showing signs of obvious torture, she had a mental breakdown.

After she had been in camp for some weeks and shown no sign of improvement, the Japs decided she must go to an asylum for the insane. They also decided that Mrs Gravenmaker, who had been matron of a psychiatric institution before the war, should accompany her. I met Mrs Gravenmaker on my way to the hospital and held out my hand, saying, 'I hope it won't be too bad.' She hugged me so tightly I thought my ribs would break. Her face had the expression of one who knew she was facing death. The camp, while in no way good, would have been heaven compared to where she was going.

Not long after we had been told that good things would be coming our way, a pair of Japanese nurses stepped into the ablution block. Del and I, who were on roster that day, were at the other end. When two buckets of water sloshed along the floor towards them, they were forced to make a hasty retreat. It was a small victory, quite childish, but it lightened our day as there was not much to laugh about.

The increased rations did not last long, so the Japs, never short of ideas to keep us occupied, decided we could dig up the area in the middle of the padang. They supplied us with changkuls (cangkuls) – very heavy hoes with handles over 6 feet in length – but the ground was so hard that the blades bounced off it.

The guard in charge of our working party, whom we nicknamed 'The Dancing Master', took my hoe from me and proceeded to show us how to dig. We then stood in a line and practised what we called 'government stroke'. The following day, a working party was taken outside the camp to clear a drain running from the ablution block. As The Dancing Master leapt gracefully back and forth across the drain, exhorting the workers to put more zeal into their efforts, they silently prayed, 'Make him fall in, make him fall in' but, to their great disappointment, the prayers went unanswered.

Eventually, the ground in the padang was dug up and planted with sweet potatoes, which had to be watered with water lugged in buckets from the well. The water needed for the gardens, along with that required for the Japanese tongs, had priority. There was barely enough left for drinking and cooking purposes and we were limited to less than two pints (about a litre) a day each for bathing and washing our clothes.

Fertilised by the contents of the cesspool, the sweet potato vines flourished. The women on the fertiliser squad were paid for this work, but the rest of us did not receive anything. As the plants matured, we were shocked to hear that some of the internees were stealing tubers at night. However, the thieving came to an abrupt end when the Japs harvested the crop, leaving us the spent vines and wondering about the benefits of honesty.

After about six months in captivity on a reduced diet, we had stopped menstruating. Some girls were lucky and stopped earlier. Until this happened, we had to cope with bits of towelling or rag, a couple of pins and a makeshift belt. The rags had to be reused, so we boiled them in special tins. It was not until long after everyone had ceased menstruating that the Japanese issued some cottonwool and voile pads, as 'ladies require them'.

By this time, all cooking was communal and small private fires were a thing of the past. When cooked, the rice we received to go with our meagre vegetable ration amounted to three small bowls a day. It was of poor quality and much of it looked like, and probably was, floor sweepings, containing grit, mice droppings, weevils and grubs. When the cooks complained, The Snake told them they weren't cooking it properly, as they boiled all the goodness out of it. He then demonstrated how rice should be cooked, by placing some in a cellophane bag and tossing it into a cauldron of boiling water. Not surprisingly, the cellophane disintegrated, to the great amusement of the cooks and quite a few onlookers who just happened to be in the kitchen. So ended our first and only cooking lesson given by the Japs.

One night in early August we were awakened by the sound of bombing. Someone said, 'The Allies are bombing Pladjoe oil fields.' We got up and cheered and hugged one another. Then came the sickening realisation that bombing only meant that people were being killed.

Bully was on guard duty that night. To our amazement, he behaved impeccably, quietly ordering us back inside the hut. Pointing to my bed board, still outdoors under the eaves, I said as snootily as I could, 'Saya tidur sini' (I sleep here). Val Smith said quietly, with a grin on her face, 'I wouldn't offer any invitations, Pat.'

The internees watched in excitement as waves of planes flew overhead until almost dawn. The next day, the Japanese declared that it was a practice raid. Two nights later there was another 'practice', followed by several more throughout the month.

The planes were American B29s, known as Liberators, which flew from Tricomalee in Ceylon, 6,370 kilometres away, making it the longest non-stop mission of WW2 – 170 kilometres further than similar bombing raids on Singapore. Because of the distance and the need to carry extra fuel, each plane had a payload of two 1,000 pound (450 kilogram) bombs, or mines of equivalent weight, to seed the mouth of the Moesi River.

With the advent of the bombing raids, the nurses wondered if the rumour that they would be moved to Muntok might be true. This notion strengthened on 21 August when everyone was ordered to line up for typhoid, dysentery and cholera vaccinations. This was not a one-off occurrence. The Japanese, terrified of catching diseases themselves, had vaccinated the camp on a regular basis since March 1943.

Air-raid alerts increased. This, along with a talk delivered entirely in Japanese by Seki, gave rise to a rumour that we would shortly be moved to Muntok. About a week after Seki's talk, Veronica Clancy and Mary Cooper became ill and were admitted to hospital. Mary was a dear girl, proud of her Irish heritage and the fact that her passport had been signed by de Valera, leader of the 1916 Easter uprising, which led to Ireland becoming a republic. I realised she had a temperature when, flushed and cross-looking, she split wood with a parang, at the same time singing what I assumed to be the Irish version of 'There'll always be an England'. I can remember only two verses:

There'll always be an England
My bible tells me so
Because God's chosen people
Have nowhere else to go

There'll always be an England
While money holds the reins
While Ireland's in rebellion
And India's in chains

After a couple of weeks in hospital, both nurses returned to us, feeling much better. Some cases, however, were far more serious. I was the 'on duty' nurse for the huts one morning when Dr Smith asked me to prepare one of our cooks, a young South African woman, for transfer to hospital in Palembang. She had woken that morning to find that her body was paralysed from the hips down. As she had a history of tuberculosis, the Japs were worried in case she had TB meningitis. The patient was quite cheerful as she waited for the ambulance, but a few days later we heard that she was dead.

The attack on Pladjoe was a great boost to the morale of the camp, but trying to stay alive was as hard as ever. Jessie Blanch exercised her ingenuity and made what she called a 'sparrow trap'.

It consisted of a box (I think two sides were wire netting) with a few grains of rice inside, and a door, which was supposed to drop down when the bird walked in. It didn't work.

A few of our nurses tried working for the Dutch, but soon found that the money they earned did not compensate for the extra drain on their health. I continued drawing, and amused myself by designing tennis and golf outfits. I also copied pictures of local scenes. As paper was impossible to get and my pencil was steadily wearing away, I had to draw my sketches in miniature. I was finally forced to give up when I didn't have the physical strength to sit up and draw and, in any case, by that time I didn't have any paper and the pencil had worn out.

It was not long before Dr Smith told me that I looked far too pale and insisted I should go to hospital. I only made a feeble protest, lured by the thought of a proper rest plus the better food served at the hospital. Once in bed, I pulled the sheet over my face to shut out the light and slept. I was woken when the nun lifted the sheet and squealed, 'The same face! The same face!' I had no idea what she meant until I sat up and looked at my neighbours, Mrs Holwegg and Mrs Van der Nuit. Until that moment, I had not realised how closely I, also being of German descent, resembled them. I explained that one of my great-grandfathers, who had been born in Germany, had settled with his English wife in the New South Wales country town of Mudgee in the 1800s. I was immediately struck by the incongruity of war. Here we were, two German nationals and an Australian army nurse, talking and sharing a joke in hospital in a Japanese internment camp.

Generally, the atmosphere in camp was fairly relaxed, but one never knew when a guard would become nasty and so, as far as was possible, we avoided them. However, one day, Val Smith, of 2/13 AGH, and Wilhelmina 'Ray' Raymont, of 2/4 CCS, were upbraided by a guard. They were then made to stand about 100 yards (100 metres) apart in the sun with two civilian women for a couple of hours. They had no idea what they had done to make the guard so angry. Ray collapsed at the end of the punishment and took a long time to recover.

In early September, Sister Raymont was sitting in her bedspace quietly sewing when she was accosted by the guard, Ishimara, known as Rasputin, who had noticed a small notch of wood missing from the timber slat in the wall on the far side of the hut. Raymont was accused of damaging military property and, for some reason, Sister Val Smith and two British women, Mrs Helen Dixey and Mrs Marjorie Jennings, were also implicated. Although Smith and the other two women were strong enough to withstand the punishment, Raymont had been in failing health for some time and was not. When one of the sisters took her a hat, Rasputin snatched it away and slapped Raymont so hard across the face that she fell into a patch of sweet potato. Entreaties for mercy were useless. She was forced to remain in the sun until unconsciousness brought a merciful end to her ordeal.

Standing in the sun for long periods for real or perceived misdemeanours was not uncommon. Vivian Bullwinkel and Wilma Oram, when returning to their hut from gardening duty, failed to notice Ah Fat and therefore failed to deliver the mandatory bow of acknowledgement. Ah Fat, whose real name was Sergeant Major Mizumoto, chastised them severely in Malay before standing them in the sun for an hour. When Norah Chambers refused to add a

Wilhelmina 'Ray' Raymont

Japanese song to the vocal orchestra's repertoire, she too was forced to undergo this form of punishment for several hours.

The days went by and there seemed no hope of improvement in the quality of the food supplied by the Japanese. Some maize was brought in, but when we shook the kernels a powdery substance fell out. The weevils had been there before us. Nevertheless, we boiled the maize, weevils and all, with the vegetables.

Fortunately, the black market was flourishing so, whenever possible, we persisted with our money-making efforts – sewing, minding children and hat-making. Until my materials ran out, I also continued to sketch, sitting quietly and peacefully under the eaves. Occasionally, Mrs Anderson would sit nearby, and sometimes we'd talk, but mostly we just maintained a restful silence. She told me she envied me – I seemed so calm and untroubled. I knew it wasn't so, but didn't bother to contradict her.

Mrs Frances Anderson, who had lived in Penang before the war, was the complete opposite of Pat – a large, strongly built woman known for her booming voice. Pat's quiet demeanour, and her ability to sketch in such unlikely surroundings, evidently had an impact.

Occasionally a sale of goods was held, providing an outlet for people who had items to sell and were short of money. I usually put in a couple of drawings, for which I received 40 cents each. An egg on the black market cost 50 cents. I called them my 'almost-an-egg' drawings. I think some of the money was given to a fund for the really destitute, particularly those with young children.

The main currency in use, by this time, was Japanese occupation money which, due to rampant inflation, had very little purchasing power. As the design on the notes included a bunch of bananas, they were dubbed 'pisang' (banana) money, a term that became synonymous with worthless currency.

Rita also kept up her artwork. I remember a painting that is best described as mixed-media, as she used quite a lot of charcoal. She called it 'Danny Boy' – a dead, nude black soldier, perfectly drawn and sensitively portraying the poignancy and beauty of the subject. Beauty was in short supply in the camp, apart from the tropical sunsets, each one seemingly more beautiful than the last. Such soft, delicate, opalescent colours that seemed to last a long time before fading into the darkness of the night.

In mid-September, American Red Cross parcels arrived. Before they were distributed, the guards helped themselves to the cigarettes, cheese and canned meat, along with boxes of medical supplies including dressings, medicine, bandages, cottonwool and a vast amount of quinine tablets. To torment the internees, the hei-hos flamboyantly lit cigarettes, took a couple of puffs and then threw the remainder away, only to immediately light a fresh one.

The pickings were lean. Each person received six prunes, one tablespoon each of rancid butter, cream and jam, a small amount of cheese and a few teaspoons of tea and sugar. One of my prunes was bad, but I cracked the stone and ate the kernel. I saved some of my rice and patted it into a scone shape, dried it on a piece of tin over the fire and, with the butter, cream and jam, made myself a Devonshire tea.

Early on we had been permitted to send postcards to our families. Unlike in other camps, we were not restricted to just a few words or given pre-printed cards with phrases on them, which could be struck out if not applicable.

Some of the cards reached Australia. One, written by Mavis Hannah, sent the news that there were 32 nurses in the camp, naming the four who were from her home state of South Australia. She also put in a request for shoes or sandshoes, size four and a half, soap, sewing cotton, toiletries, vitamin B tablets, sunglasses, dried fruit, vegetable seeds (especially carrots, parsnips, lettuce, tomatoes, beans, peas and onions), tinned goods or anything edible, clothing, books (especially Shakespeare and English history, plus novels), sheets, towels and anything else useful. No parcels ever arrived or, if they did, they didn't reach the intended recipients.

Some of us received mail – the first since our captivity, and the first of the three deliveries we had as prisoners. The letters, which we shared with each other, were at least 12 months old. However, some of the sisters and other internees received no mail at all during their imprisonment.

More mail was delivered shortly afterwards, and there was a further distribution from the pilfered Red Cross parcels. This time each internee received 22 cigarettes, an inch (2.5 centimetres) of mouldy chocolate, half a cup of powdered milk, four sugar cubes, half a pound (250 grams) of jam, an inch of cheese, a spoonful of coffee essence, a spoonful of butter, a small tin of meat and another of salmon to be shared among 15, and a small packet of soup powder to be shared by three. Later, each internee received 11 guilders from the American Red Cross but, with commodity prices so highly inflated, the money did not go far.

On 4 October, a dentist arrived.

He set up his clinic in a room adjoining the hospital and, as I had been plagued with toothache, I decided to pay him a visit. On the way I met Jeff and a friend carrying Iole, semi-conscious after 'treatment'. Only the memory of my previous nights of discomfort forced my feet onwards. I sat on the hard chair, gripping the seat with both hands, and opened my mouth. The so-called dentist dabbed something on the offending tooth, and said something like 'Huh, huh'. Realising that he was about to perform an extraction without anaesthetic, I shot out of the chair like greased lightning. On my way across the padang, I met Jess Doyle and Win, who were on their way to carry me back. Poor Iole – the wretch had pulled her tooth without an anaesthetic.

Whatever the dentist had dabbed on my tooth worked and my first night without toothache was heaven. Next day, however, a throbbing pain behind my right ear started. Always fearing the worst, my self-diagnosis was mastoiditis, a very serious complication of untreated middle-ear infection that results in inflammation and then disintegration of the mastoid bone. Recalling that we had been issued with a kilo of coarse salt to be shared among four, I heated some, put it in a sock and placed it behind my ear. It gave me considerable relief and, after several days, the pain ceased.

For the past few weeks, there had been strong rumours that we were to be moved again. Our confidence somewhat restored by the fact that the Japanese hierarchy had not forgotten us, we told each other, 'Well, it couldn't be worse.' How wrong we were.

We assumed that, as had been the case on previous occasions, the move would come with little notice. As we had no illusions about the quality and quantity of food we were likely to receive for the journey, those who had 50 guilders bought a black-market egg, which was then hard-boiled for 10 minutes so that it would keep. I had dropped my watch some weeks earlier and, as no amount of shaking would make it go again, I sold it. To my amazement, it fetched 50 guilders.

Rumours continued about our anticipated transfer, the most persistent being that our destination was to be Bangka Island. 'We'll be easy to dispose of there', said one of the cheerful ones, but it was not until mid-October that we finally moved.

CHAPTER 8

Muntok New Camp, Bangka Island

16 October 1944 – 8 April 1945

The confirmation that a move was definitely in the offing came at midday on 5 October when eight of the nurses were ordered to join a 40-strong advance party. Betty Jeffrey was with the group, which left in the early evening in an open truck for the wharf, some miles away. From there the group boarded a triple-deck riverboat for a short journey across the river to pick up more than 120 women internees. They were mainly Dutch and Eurasian, and had been imprisoned at Benkoelen (Benkulen) on the western side of Sumatra. Another four women had been interned at Pangkal Pinang Camp on Bangka's east coast.

After the nurses spent a day loading the boat with stores – bags of rice and an ominous number of coffins, also filled with rice – the group set off for Muntok, where they made preparations for the arrival of the main parties. One of their tasks was to erect a barbed-wire and pole fence around the perimeter.

The remainder of the Palembang camp was then moved in two separate groups. Pat went with the first group. The hospital patients and their carers followed.

We bundled up our few possessions and clambered into the trucks that took us to two ships waiting at the Palembang wharf. The journey down the Moesi River once again promoted a pleasant feeling of freedom, despite the severely overcrowded conditions. Amenities, as usual, were non-existent. The lavatory on our ship was an arrangement of bars, rather like a cage, extending from the stern. Those in occupation had a good view of the sea below, at the same time providing a not so pleasant view of themselves to the other passengers.

We steamed very slowly across the strait to Bangka Island. It was dark when we arrived, but small boats took us to the beach, where we were pleased to see a Red Cross prominently displayed. Our hopes were dampened, however, when a weary English voice said, 'Don't put your faith in that. The Swiss Red Cross representative is married to a Japanese.'

Shouting and screaming, the guards hustled us into trucks, which took us to Muntok and our camp. We Australian nurses always travelled together, wearing our uniforms and Red Cross armbands for easy recognition, but this time we had been split into smaller groups. We hated being separated because, although we didn't see eye to eye on everything, we were very supportive of one another.

The huts in the compound were dimly lit. We had bali balis for sleeping, but this time there was far more space than in the other camps. The downside was that the platforms were neither sawn timber nor cement, but roughly hewn planks. The advance party had been provided with rush mats, but there was no sign of any for us. Our thinning mattresses – the sacks we had stuffed with dried grass in our first permanent camp – were inadequate padding on such an uneven surface. To make matters worse, some of the dysentery sufferers, exhausted by the long journey, became incontinent.

Next morning, we examined the camp more closely. Unlike our other camps, this one was large and brand new. Situated on the top of a hill where it caught the breezes, it was enclosed by two fences, about 20 feet (6 metres) high and about 20 feet apart. Guards patrolled up and down in the space between.

The long accommodation huts, built of sawn timber, were divided into three sections. The half walls, made of timber planks, were only about waist high, creating an open space that extended to the atap roof. Each hut had its own pit latrine and a small cookhouse, separated by a cement-lined well. The wells were very deep, 50 feet (15 metres) or so, but ours rarely had any water in it. There was no ablution block, so we washed at our sleeping space. The main cookhouse area, in the centre of the compound, had its own well – by far the best in the camp.

The hospital was the largest to date but Dr Goldberg, although still in charge, was no longer the sole practitioner, on the instructions of the Japanese who had ordered the other three doctors to report for duty. The main ward was capable of holding about 20 patients on one long bali bali, made from rubber-tree limbs bound together. Infectious cases were housed in four separate rooms and children in another room furnished with two old cots. There was also a convalescent ward that could take up to 30 people. The only drugs supplied to treat malaria in the camp of 700 people were 100 quinine tablets per week.

We began our first day trekking some distance down a steep slope to the creek to collect water for the camp. It was a pleasant walk and the creek, a crystal-clear stream, widened into a waterhole, around which the Japs had erected an attractive bamboo fence. It actually looked quite artistic. Negotiating the steps cut into the bank with a full bucket of water on the return journey was more than a little tiring, and I cannot recall how many times we went back and forth.

The chronically ill and their nurses left the Palembang Camp for Muntok on 23 October.

Top to bottom: Muntok Women's Camp huts, kitchen and hospital (M Dryburgh)

> *Crammed into a small boat, they waited for 12 hours before sailing, sustained only by a small amount of rice and a few slices of cucumber. Apart from some tea, the women had nothing to drink for the 24 hours that they were on board. Sanitation facilities did not exist. When they arrived at the camp, they discovered that all their baggage had either been 'lost' or rifled and that everything of value – money, jewellery and carefully hoarded sugar – was missing.*

The rations, as always, were small in quantity and poor in quality. As before, they were tipped onto the ground and left in the sun until the Japs decided that the ration committee could collect them. Nothing that could possibly be consumed was wasted. All egg shells and bones were dried, ground to powder and eaten. Occasionally, tiny fish were brought in and, after sitting in the broiling sun for some time, were rationed out to the huts, rather than the communal kitchen. We gave them a squeeze to disgorge the contents of the alimentary canal and fried them in oil. They were quite tasty.

> *Those who still had money or goods that could be sold or traded made use of a flourishing black market. The main go-between was Nellie, an Ambonese internee, who risked death or severe punishment to make contact with the locals. Dressed in black pyjamas, and with her naturally dark skin and black hair, she was able to slip past the guards under cover of darkness. She was never caught, but it was a near thing one night when the alarm on a clock she was about to trade went off, alerting the guard who, fortunately, did not discover the source of the noise.*

In the afternoon during siesta hour, some of the teenage girls would sit on the edge of the bali bali and say, 'Can we talk to you, Sister?' They were very concerned that they were not developing as they expected. I assured them that, once free and on a decent diet, all would be well, adding, 'Pretty little things like you will soon marry and have babies.' Their gratitude was touching. I pitied them being exposed to such a cruel and ugly side of life at such a tender age. One girl, noticing I was reading *All Quiet on the Western Front* in German, brought me some magazines. Pat Blake was shocked that I could read such trash, so I read the most romantic lines to her.

The influx of about 200 or so internees from other camps had raised the camp population to 714. Next day, deaths had reduced the tally by two – a trend that was, unfortunately, to continue. We were shocked by the appearance of the new arrivals. They were mostly Dutch, or of Dutch extraction, with a sprinkling of other European races, and obviously had been subjected to much worse conditions than we had experienced. However, within four to six weeks, we would look just as gaunt, haggard and ill.

With so little quinine, most of us had malaria within weeks of arrival at Muntok. So many were ill that the Japs generously gave the hospital a small crate containing quinine tablets in glass bottles. However, the gift was not as magnanimous as it had appeared as the crate had been badly smashed, reducing the contents to a mash of broken glass and tablets. Undeterred, the nuns boiled and strained the mess until the fluid was free of glass particles, then used it in the hospital. The Japs also sent in a quantity of thick brown cinchona bark, used to extract quinine. I chewed my way through a cupful, all to no effect. I think the quinine had already been extracted.

The 'rigor' period during a malaria attack, when the body is wracked by uncontrollable shivering, is the most hellish. New arrivals who had possessions loaned us blankets to help us over the worst but, as they had also brought lice, bed bugs and scabies with them, we soon acquired all three. One sister thought she was too refined to get lice. I told her that in some countries it was considered an honour, as the lice only chose to live on, and with, generous people. A couple of days later, when she discovered that she too had lice, she repeated my remark to another sister, who laughed and said, 'Isn't that interesting, so-and-so hasn't got any!'

> *As there was nothing available to treat the lice, those suffering from an infestation were forced to call on the services of Flo Trotter and Betty Jeffrey and have their hair cut off. This eventually brought the outbreak under control. According to Pat, the lice died out because the internees' blood was too poor a quality.*

The bali balis had rows of people ill with malaria lying helplessly on their mattresses. As the high ceilings and open half walls, designed to combat the heat and humidity, made the huts too cool for fever-ridden patients, the Japanese allowed the open sections to be filled with woven rush mats. A guard – a tall, handsome Eurasian fellow who looked more European than Oriental – installed them. He was said to be sadistic. However, considering the way Eurasian guards were treated by their Japanese masters, it is not surprising that some of them treated prisoners brutally.

His assistant was a Yugoslavian nun, a delicate, pretty creature who had come into camp with a batch of Dutch internees. They worked quickly and precisely together. Even though we had become accustomed to sudden and unexpected deaths in camp, we were shocked to learn the next day that the nun had died – from exhaustion. Her heart just gave out. She was 25 years old.

I was deeply upset and, although ill, I staggered across to the clump of rubber trees where some of the fallen limbs had produced lovely autumn-toned leaves. I gathered several small branches and took them to the Charitas nuns at the hospital, asking them to put them on the coffin. They accepted with a graciousness that seemed from another world.

On my way back, as I passed through one of the wards, Mrs Maddams sat up and spoke to me. I was shocked by her appearance and suddenly realised what people meant when they said someone's eyes were like 'two burnt holes in a blanket'. She died the next day. I was so stunned by her appearance that I could never recall what she said to me. Even the Japanese were upset by her death. She had exuded confidence and had been a tower of strength to the British internees, as well as to the two camp leaders, but not even her strong constitution could withstand the rigours of the Bangka Island camp.

Christmas came a few days after Mrs Maddams died. We thought God would forgive us if we didn't celebrate the birth of Christ in 1944.

> *There was a half-hearted effort to organise a concert but the plans were shelved as the women were too weak to bother. Nor were presents exchanged among the nurses that year, not even a handmade card, as there was not a scrap of paper to be had. The day was, nevertheless, marked by a stir-fried meal of rice, flavoured with the flesh of two small pigs that the Japanese had seen fit to provide to the inmates for 'being good'.*

The nuns were granted permission for their priest to visit them from the men's camp at the old coolie-lines and gaol and to conduct a special service. We did not recognise the thin, aesthetic-looking man in clerical garb as the well-fed and kindly fellow we had met before.

On New Year's Day I developed a violent headache, the worst I'd ever had. It felt as if my head would split. Even so, when a call came from the kitchen staff for volunteers to draw up water, Del and I volunteered. After we had managed to fill the required 20 buckets, I felt so sick that I went back to the hut to lie down.

I concluded that I was suffering from the so-called 'Bangka fever', which we thought was some form of malaria or possibly a kind of typhus. However, we didn't ever use the word typhus, because it's a very serious disease and a rather frightening term for lay people. When Dr Smith called on her rounds, she gave me a tablet of quinine – there was nothing else to prescribe. As she had discovered that some of her patients were keeping their tablets in their cheeks, drying them and selling them to buy food on the black market, she sat on the edge of the bali bali until I swallowed mine.

I had a bad reaction to the tablet, which induced a feeling of hysteria. I was able to quell any outward signs, but vowed never to take quinine again. Always fearing the worst, I worried that the hysteria was a prelude to an epileptic fit, which occurred in patients suffering from malignant tertian (MT) malaria – a severe form of malaria that can lead to death. I admit I could have been wrong about the quinine, but was not prepared to find out. Furthermore, I could not be bothered arguing the toss with Dr Smith, who had made it mandatory that anyone with a temperature of 104 degrees Fahrenheit (40 degrees Celsius) or over must take quinine.

As my temperature was certainly hovering around the 104-degree mark, whenever the doctor was due on her rounds Jess Doyle placed a coconut shell of cool water on my chest. After wetting my face washer, now reduced to a piece of grey towelling, I placed it alternately under each armpit. When Dr Smith produced her bath thermometer, I held it in a pocket of air in my armpit, making sure it didn't touch any skin. With this subterfuge, I always managed to show a reading of just under 104. Occasionally we had a difference of opinion regarding the reading, but I told her my eyesight was superior to hers.

By January 1945, the ration consisted of 150 grams of rice a day and jack fruit, a rich tasting tropical fruit that was prone to induce vomiting. Too much also resulted in diarrhoea. Four teaspoons of sugar and salt were also issued fortnightly. On such a meagre diet, weight loss was rapid. By the end of the month, most of the older women were dead, including Mrs Brown, who died on 17 January from a combination of starvation, beriberi and malaria, her ample form reduced to skin and bones. All but one of the 32 Australian sisters were suffering with malaria. Six were in hospital. Sisters Raymont, Hempsted, Gardham and Singleton were very ill.

January 1945 was a dreadful month. The hospital wards were full; dysentery patients could not be nursed in the huts; Bangka fever and malaria raged. The most tragic victims of all were children and their mothers. The children's thin, haunted, little old faces are still a troublesome memory. Without proper food, their mental and physical development was severely retarded. Toddlers, unable to even crawl, let alone walk, were the size of babies, and four-year-olds the size of toddlers. Mothers who had starved themselves to see their children fed saw their little ones fade away before their very eyes. Death often came quickly. One poor woman lost four of her five children from malnutrition in the space of one week.

There were one or two deaths each day. One of the many who died in January was Ruth Russell-Roberts, our glamorous ex-model. She had everything to live for. She had received news that her husband was interned in Singapore's Changi Gaol and her young daughter had arrived safely in England.

The strongest women dug the graves and carried out the coffins. Wilma was in this squad, but I've no idea how they managed as I was virtually hut-bound.

By December 1944, 210 women and children had contracted Bangka fever, including Margaret Dryburgh. In the following weeks, the death toll would reach 70. Funeral squads, composed of the strongest women, were detailed to dig the graves using changkuls, while the young boys were put to work making coffins. When the timber ran out, the internees were forced to use packing cases, many of them still bearing the logos of the original contents. The deceased were then carried by internees to the local cemetery, accompanied by a guard who usually allowed the mourners to detour a little to pick a bunch of wildflowers.

The pit latrines had to be emptied and the Japs 'generously' supplied tins. They were carried into the scrub some distance from the camp and emptied by latrine workers, who were paid a pittance by the Japs for their efforts.

The sanitation workers at this time were Betty Jeffrey, Iole Harper, Vivian Bullwinkel, Wilma Oram and Jean Ashton, who were paid 80 cents a day from a fund created by internees unwilling to carry out the task. Their equipment consisted of two kerosene tins, two half-coconut shells nailed to sticks to form a scoop, and a long pole to carry the contents of the tins to a dump site, about 800 metres away. On one of these many trips, the pole slipped and speared into Iole Harper's chest, breaking a rib.

Latrine duty (J P L Kickhefer)

For some months the Japanese had been weighing us on a regular basis and the practice continued on Bangka Island for the first few months, but was then discontinued. I assume the Japs did not want further records to be kept as everyone had lost a lot of weight. By February, I tipped the scales at just over 5 stone (33 kilograms).

Some of the women were so thin that they slipped through the slats that served as a seat on the latrine and fell into the pit below. When screams alerted a nearby hut, the person was hauled out, buckets of water were thrown over her and she was taken to hospital. Not one of the women who fell into the pit survived.

Sometime in January 1945, the Japanese ordered the internees to take over guard duties at the huts at night. The official reason was that there was a lot of thieving among the prisoners. However, it is far more likely it was simply a face-saving excuse as the guards were afraid of coming down with the fever.

Policing the huts involved patrolling the outside and then walking down the aisle at regular intervals. At about 4 am, when my fevered blood felt it was at boiling point, I whispered to the person on guard that I would take her place. When word spread that I was happy to do the 4 am round, I no longer had to volunteer. However, I didn't put my name on the list of official 'guards' as it would mean another argument with Dr Smith, and I had enough altercations with her already about my temperature.

I moved along my beat, supporting myself on whatever was available, until I reached the tables and bench seats under the eaves. The cool air soothed my skin and was infinitely preferable to the foetid air of the hut. Seeing me seated outdoors, a Japanese guard, sent to check on whether we were doing our duty, would invariably appear from the shadows and mutter something unintelligible. My reply, 'Saya jaga' (I'm a guard), evidently satisfied him, for he would continue on his way.

When people appeared restless or distressed, I sat beside them on the edge of the bali bali, saying 'I'm an Australian nurse', sometimes placing my hand on their feet. It was amazing how soon they settled down. I never went around the outside of the hut, or to the far side, as I always felt evil lurked there in the darkness. Thank goodness only the patients on the near side seemed in need of help.

Feeling brave, I ventured one day to walk to our cookhouse, which meant traversing about 20 feet (6 metres) without anything to hold on to. On my way back, a line of living cadavers sitting on stools clapped and smiled at me. I'm ashamed to say I was concentrating so hard I couldn't acknowledge them, but I was very touched.

One day in February, Del shouted for me to come to her aid as the woman lying next to her was having an epileptic fit. I held her jaw open to stop her biting her tongue while Del went to the hospital to fetch a stretcher and bearers. However, the woman had cerebral malaria and died the next day.

On 8 February, Sister Wilhelmina 'Ray' Raymont died. She was the first of our nursing sisters to die in captivity. I don't think she ever fully recovered from being forced to stand in the sun in the Men's Camp.

The day before Sister Raymont's death, she had received a visit from Dr Goldberg, who had

Funeral procession (J P L Kickhefer)

slapped her across the face before declaring that the patient, who was actually unconscious, was hysterical and that there was nothing wrong with her. She refused to administer any medication. Within hours, Raymont's condition deteriorated and by 6 am she was dead.

I was too weak to attend the funeral. The sisters who were well enough to go wore their army uniforms which, we had agreed, must be worn when attending the funeral of one of our colleagues, when moving from camp to camp, when we were buried and when we were liberated.

Ray's friend, Val Smith, who had also been forced to stand in the sun, was in hospital herself when Ray suddenly became critically ill. Although too sick to attend her friend, Val felt that she should have been there, and I doubt if all our reassurances ever relieved her sense of guilt. Ray's funeral was the first military-style funeral held in the camp. The Japanese, in a rare show of respect, removed their caps as the solemn cortege passed their quarters on the way to the cemetery.

At about this time, Dot Freeman and Rene Singleton, of 2/9 Field Ambulance, came to visit our hut. Rene looked desperately ill. Her blue eyes seemed even larger but, for all that, she was still the same Rene, with her wonderful sense of humour and sense of the ridiculous. I think she had come to say goodbye – she died of beriberi on 20 February. Margaret Dryburgh, although ill and weak, delivered a eulogy in the general-purpose block.

By the middle of February, my Bangka fever had burned itself out. I was still too weak to attend any funerals, but I was able to do a few things for some of the others in the hut, such as compiling the attendance roll for tenko, bed bathing and helping people with their meals.

One morning, Matte Bakker, the Dutch member of the BAD squad who worked with Jess Doyle and Pat Blake, came looking for Pat. She was shaking with shock as her friend Bep, a cheerful fresh-complexioned woman, hard-working and seemingly never ill, had died suddenly. She left behind three children – Hans, about seven years old, Pinkie, his five-year-old brother, and little Lucy, younger still. Their inconsolable grief was heartbreaking to see.

The older women were another heart-wrenching group. At least two were in their 70s, and a good number in their late 50s and 60s. No elderly person should spend their last days under such appalling conditions. However, the will to survive can be strong and some managed to cling on with a stoicism that probably surprised even themselves. Others simply gave up the fight and quietly slipped away. During our time at this camp, the death toll from malaria and Bangka fever was about 150.

On 19 March, Blanche Hempstead, of 13 AGH, died after repeatedly apologising to the hospital staff for taking so long about it. Her death was followed on 4 April by that of Shirley Gardam, of 2/4 CCS. Like her friend Ray, Shirley was a tall, fair and rather frail-looking girl. She received no letters during captivity and did not know that her mother had died in 1942. By this time, we no longer had the strength to give our dead colleagues the funeral with full military honours they deserved.

> *Shirley Gardam had been sick for many months. In mid-March her condition deteriorated but, although she was now seriously ill, Dr Goldberg refused to admit her to hospital as she was penniless. It was only when Gardam was at death's door that Goldberg finally relented, but by then it was too late.*

A distressed Mavis Hannah was now the only surviving member of 2/4 CCS.

CHAPTER 9

Belalau Plantation, Loeboek Linggau

8 April 1945 – 15 September 1945

By 20 March life at the Muntok camp had been reduced to the barest existence. Food was so scarce that the women were eating banana skins and rubber tree seeds. When the day's essential work was complete, they had only enough energy to drag themselves to the bali balis, where they remained until morning.

With so many ill and dying, concerts, charades and sing-songs were a thing of the past. The vocal orchestra had lost 19 of its 30 members. Those who survived were too weak to continue and, with Margaret Dryburgh ill, it too was disbanded. On 22 March, Olga Neubronner died. One of the four British sisters sentenced to solitary confinement, she had never really recovered from her ordeal.

The women had been informed that they were to move to a new camp in Sumatra where there would be plenty of deer, wild boar and unpolished rice, replacing the white rice that had very little nutritional value and was responsible for the high incidence of beriberi – a debilitating and often fatal disease caused by a lack of Vitamin B.

A few days before the supposed date of departure, 20 March, some chairs, a battered piano, half a dozen scrawny-looking goats, a few chickens and some pigs were brought into the camp, prior to a visit by a representative of the Japanese Foreign Minister. According to Seki, the purpose of the visit was to distribute Red Cross parcels.

In anticipation of the visit, the camp was stripped of weeds, small bridges were constructed over ditches and drains and the hospital scrubbed. In order to make a good impression,

Sister Flo Trotter, who was on duty at the hospital, donned her uniform and found a veil to wear, in honour of the occasion.

With a flourish of tooting horns, no less than nine large sedans arrived, holding the guest of honour and an entourage of 16 lackeys. They walked straight to the far end of the camp, ignoring the rows of bowing internees who had been assembled and waiting for the last hour. They then left, without laying eyes on the hospital, Flo Trotter's finery, the goats (one of which had died), the piano, the pigs, the chairs or the little bridges.

They had brought no Red Cross parcels – these, the internees were told, were to be transported to the next camp to save them the bother of carrying them. They had, however, brought a message all the way from the Minister in Tokyo – 'My kind regards to the women and children and I'll give them a present when they get to their new camp'.

Within the hour, the specially imported props had vanished, apart from the goats, which were not worth removing.

When we heard we were to be moved to another camp – Loeboek Linggau (Lubuklinggau), in Sumatra – no-one dared say, 'It couldn't be worse.' In fact, we wondered why the Japanese bothered moving us at all. Surely their objective to eliminate all prisoners was well on the way to being achieved as our camp population was now around the 500 mark. One suggestion, received with grim amusement, was that they were worried about our death rate.

An advance party went first, to prepare the camp for the rest of us. Jess Doyle, Win and I were ordered to go with the next group, which was for all internees still able to walk. I went to the hospital to tell Pat Blake that we were going and she looked at me as if we were deserting her. However, I assured her we'd keep her a spot at the new camp.

We left in the late afternoon of 8 April and, once again, trudged along the Muntok pier for transfer by boat to our waiting steamers. I have no recollection of being issued with any food, but we had our water-bottles with us. After spending the night on board, we set sail next morning – no rainbow to farewell us this time. The small ship wallowed in the seas, which seemed rougher than before, and many of the passengers were seasick. The weather didn't help – sudden showers followed by hot sunshine – but at least it dried our clothes.

It was better once we reached the calm waters at the entrance to the Moesi River, where we anchored overnight. The next morning at daybreak, we set off again and after a journey of four hours or so disembarked at Palembang, where shouting, screaming Japs hustled us to board a train waiting at a nearby station.

Despite all the seeming urgency, the train sat at Kerta Putti station all day. No drinking water had been provided so, apart from an issue of weak tea, boiled in unwashed containers that had previously been used to cook vegetables, the internees had only what they had brought with them. As toilet facilities were non-existent, those wishing to relieve themselves were obliged to do so in ditches beside the rail line, in full view of passers-by and under the interested gaze of the families of hei-hos, quartered in nearby barracks.

With darkness approaching and no sign of the train going anywhere soon, the passengers were instructed to close the shutters and bed down for the night. For the first time in days, the internees were able to stretch out, and slept like the dead, not caring one whit about the hordes of mosquitoes.

Finally, at 7 am the next day, the engine struggled into life and they were off.

Dr Smith, Win and I lay on the floor of the guard's van at the end of the train with three very ill women. As the train lurched its way along the track, we were swamped in black tea when two over-full buckets sloshed across the floor. Early next morning, when Win and I were relieved by two other nurses, we found quite comfortable cane seats in a carriage.

The day's food ration was heavy 'bread', made from tapioca flour, sugar and water and shaped like an old-fashioned domed loaf. It weighed about 8 ounces (220 grams). Solid and rubbery, it was impossible to bite into, but when we eventually got it down, by sucking and licking, we discovered it was surprisingly satisfying.

The rail line followed a river valley that led west into the interior. The train lurched and rattled its way along the uneven track, passing through several tunnels, crossing over arched bridges and snaking at times along the sides of steep gorges. The scenery was beautiful. Trees, ferns and bushes covered the hills and gullies – a joy to eyes accustomed to the barren dreariness

Location of the women's POW camps

of a prison camp. Even the rhythmic clickety-clack of the wheels was a happy sound.

It took about 12 hours to reach Loeboek Linggau, situated at the end of the railway track on the eastern side of the Barisan Mountains, which run like a spine down the western side of Sumatra. We passed through several stations on the way, but I have no idea what they were as the Japanese insisted on closing the shutters whenever we approached a station. There was only one stop, at around noon, when we were given a very welcome meal of rice and fish.

It was quite late when we reached Loeboek Linggau, so we spent another night on the train. Just before dawn we were herded into trucks for the 15-mile (25-kilometre) journey along a very rough road through jungle, rubber trees and small farms to our new camp at Belalau, a derelict rubber plantation.

Belalau was in the foothills of the mountains, about 2000 feet (600 metres) above sea level and much cooler than Muntok. The camp area, encircled by barbed wire, was large, overgrown and very run down, with broken and rusting machinery lying about. Buildings that had once housed plantation workers were scattered among the rubber trees. The main accommodation huts were on the top of a small hill. There was plenty of bed space, as each hut held just 12 internees. Every hut had its own pit latrine and there were the usual bali balis, this time made from lengths of timber laid loosely over a bamboo frame. The floors in most of the huts, including ours, were dirt. Almost without exception, the atap roofs leaked when it rained, which was often, and soon the earth floors were ankle-deep mud.

From the main accommodation area, the ground sloped steeply down to a creek, spanned by a bridge. On the far side was a flat area, on which there were a number of huts reserved for the hospital and staff, and the cookhouse and cooks.

The 18 nuns were housed in Number 12, a one-roomed cottage with a small balcony. Next door was Number 13, which had a concrete floor and a corrugated iron roof that didn't leak. It was put aside for 10 Australian nurses working at the hospital. The others, who were rostered for district nursing, were up on the hill.

The previous occupants of the huts had left behind an unwelcome legacy – bali bali boards infested with fleas and bed bugs. The only way to try and eliminate them was to carefully search for the pests in the cracks between the boards and in the seams of the mattresses and to air all bedding in the sunshine each day.

The hospital consisted of two huts – one with a concrete floor and the other earthern. The creek, which meandered gently and curved around the hospital, was our sole water supply for the main hut area and all water had to be lugged up the slope in buckets. If it rained heavily, the creek flooded, cutting off the hospital and cookhouses from the rest of the camp.

There were no ablution facilities, but two rows of atap had been placed across the stream to make a kind of communal bathing area. The stream was shallow, but after heavy rain we could take a plunge and wash our hair, provided we had the energy to walk down from the huts and then climb back up the hill. As the Japanese guards' camp was upstream from our pool, it was best not to think about what floated down.

Hospital building Loeboek Linggau (Muntok Peace Museum)

On arrival, we immediately set to work, scrounging for useful items – boards on which to store our outdoor footwear, or to serve as shelves. Balanced on a framework of bamboo sticks hammered into the ground with lumps of wood, they kept our bowls, water-bottles and rations off the muddy floor. We used stones and bits of scrap iron to create small fireplaces on which to boil our water. Later, when we discovered that the food cooked in the communal kitchens was cold by the time we negotiated the bridge over the creek and struggled up the hill with it, we used the fires to reheat our meals, adding any vegetables we had managed to grow.

We had only just settled into the new camp when the remainder of the hospital staff, patients and other internees arrived.

It was not until 12 April, four days after the first group departed, that the rest of the camp, numbering around 400, had received instructions to leave Muntok. They were told that they were going to a camp where food was plentiful and where they could regain their health.

As some of the patients were critically ill, the Japanese had given the camp administration the option of allowing them to remain at Muntok with a doctor and volunteer nurses. However, the consensus was that the Japanese were not to be trusted, and that the entire camp would move.

The Australian nurses assigned to this party were ordered to load the stretcher cases onto trucks and transfer them to the pier and then onto the ship at the other end of the journey – work that was always allocated to the sisters on the basis that they were 'young and unmarried'.

The sick, some of whom were dying – from malnutrition, tuberculosis and dysentery – were left lying in the sun on the foreshore until the vessel was ready for boarding. The body of one woman who died during this period was loaded unceremoniously onto the tray of a truck where it bumped about, uncovered, all the way to the camp where the women still awaiting transfer had to bury her.

Once on board the small steamer, patients and hospital staff occupied the open deck space, while the rest of the group was consigned to the overcrowded hold. The boat pitched and tossed so much that the nuns had to lie across the stretcher patients to prevent them rolling overboard. Almost everyone was suffering from diarrhoea, but no sanitation facilities had been provided, forcing the passengers to use tins and bottles they had brought with them. The more fortunate were able to make use of a few bedpans belonging to the Dutch nuns. These were collected and were emptied tirelessly by Iole Harper, who clung precariously to a small ledge in order to dispose of the contents overboard.

The voyage took about 36 hours. About 12 patients died from sunstroke and illness. Mrs Mary Austin, aged 43, the Australian who had given Pat the door to use as a bed and was now critically ill with beriberi, died off the coast of Bangka Island and was buried at sea. As there was nothing with which to weigh down her wrapped remains, they bobbed along in the wake of the ship. The others were buried on reaching Palembang.

Once ashore, the guards had trouble reconciling the numbers at the mandatory tenko until one of the women reminded them that some had died en route. The internees were then ordered to board the train, with the stretcher patients assigned to enclosed vans. There were no lavatories, and excreta could only be disposed of through an opening, set high in the wall. Several people, including Hyda Scott-Eames, aged 42, a nurse with the Malayan Aid Society, died before the train left the station. Antoinette Colijn, one of the stretcher patients confined to the enclosed vans, reported that another five died en route. Sister Nester James, who was with this group, recorded:

> We remained that night at Palembang with all the shutters down, in the stifling heat, and sanitary conditions ghastly. Next day we set off and were allowed between stations to have the shutters up a few inches. The odour of sweating humanity became terrible. On this journey we were given scarcely any food – just a small amount of rice and a drink of coffee ... We arrived at Loeboek Linggau having lost several more patients on the way. [They] ... were left for several hours dead in the vans. Some were carried more or less strung under the train. All these people were buried somewhere en route – I do not know where.

Win and I made a billy of camp 'coffee' (scorched rice grains) for the new arrivals. Some accepted gratefully, others walked by with unseeing eyes. Many hospital patients were very ill and the stretcher-bearers struggled to carry the bed patients down the steep slope, then across a narrow plank spanning the creek to the wards. Pat Blake appeared, walking slowly, but her face brightened on seeing us. As we had finished distributing the coffee, we escorted her to our new abode.

Someone suggested, as we were all together again, that we have a game of bridge. After the first hand, Pat said, 'Make me dummy. I'll have to lie down.' When playing the third hand, we all lay down in a row, calling our cards as we played them. Then we gave up and packed the cards away.

There was no improvement in the ration scale, but for the first couple of weeks sweet potatoes and tapioca replaced some of the rice and a variety of vegetables was issued. There was also an increase in the palm oil ration, which allowed the internees to vary their diet by making chipped potatoes. Within a few weeks, however, the women were subsisting on rice and sweet potatoes, with an occasional additional vegetable and, on two occasions, 5 pounds (2 kilograms) of bullock meat to be shared among 64. Flourishing pawpaw and banana trees grew inside the compound, but these were totally out of bounds, with dire punishment threatened for anyone caught pilfering them.

All our nurses suffered from recurring bouts of malaria, apart from Jessie Blanch, who seemed to have a natural immunity, and many of the women were stricken with chronic dysentery. Beriberi was rife and affected the children in particular. Appeals by our Dutch and British camp leaders for better food and housing fell on deaf ears.

Those of us who were well enough continued with district nursing, and several worked in the hospital with the Charitas nuns and some of the English nurses. Bangka fever, thank goodness, stayed on its own little island.

As the effects of prolonged starvation began to take hold, the death rate mounted and burials became more frequent. The internees, including the sisters, dug graves with changkuls and made crude coffins from roughly sawn timber. When the time came to move to the cemetery, it took 20 people just to deal with the coffin.

The box was placed on three long poles, but everyone was now so weak that it took 18 to lift it. Another supported the rear end, as we were worried that someone might stumble and the coffin and its contents would slide off. The twentieth person walked in front, holding her hands behind her to steady the coffin and keeping her eyes on the track for fear of walking on someone's grave. A formal service was conducted with great dignity by the missionaries and nuns, while we ragged remnants of humanity stood with heads bowed. The sad little mounds were then marked by wooden crosses, onto which Norah Chambers and Audrey Owen had burnt the names.

The burials took place any time after 3 pm. The usual 'Sumatra', the local name for a short, sharp electrical storm with strong winds, frequently blew up as we finished filling in the graves. On our way back to camp, we spread out to collect wood. The Japanese guard accompanying the burial party always screamed and raged at us but, as he did not take his rifle with its fixed bayonet off his shoulder, we continued foraging for sticks until we had as many as we could carry. As the weeks went by we exhausted what wood was available and squads were formed to go outside the camp to fell trees for the kitchen fires.

The only water available had to be lugged back to the camp from the creek. The young boys, including Bill Wenning, Rita's small son, stood mid-stream to fill our buckets. Now all of three years old, Bill would say demandingly, 'Seester, I feel your bucket', and I always made a point of letting him. When we lacked the strength to make the journey to the creek and back, we often had no water at all in the huts.

None was wasted on bathing and, unless the women had the energy to collect a bucket from the creek, or it rained, ablutions and the washing of clothes were severely restricted, along with general cleaning. Fortunately, the hospital and cookhouses were beside the creek and, as there was a concrete-sided well nearby, the water supply there was not a problem.

A squad of the 'strongest' women was now formed to dig graves and also to dig the pits outside the camp, into which they emptied the contents of the latrines. Those undertaking these tasks were given extra food – they certainly earned it.

There was a black market in operation, with most transactions carried out in Dutch guilders. However, few nurses had any saleable items left and were too weak or too worn out by a gruelling workload in the hospital to earn money by hiring out their labour. Even for those who had money, the prices were sky high and commodities scarce.

In the first week of May, the promised Red Cross parcels from America arrived, but were not distributed. According to the Japanese, delivery was withheld as the Japanese ship carrying the receipt had been sunk by the Americans.

Margaret Dryburgh died a couple of weeks after our arrival. She bequeathed a knitted yellow top to me. Her death brought a great sadness to the entire camp for, apart from her musical talent, she had been an inspiration to all with her creative ability, her steadfastness and faith, and her 'Captives' Hymn'. On 31 May, six weeks after Margaret died, we lost another of our nurses – Gladys Hughes, of 13 AGH.

The death of Mrs Dorothy McLeod, just before we left Muntok, had also been a great blow. A small, attractive woman aged in her late 50s, she was a former teacher and a well-known singer. Dorothy loved to sing and her strong contralto voice always lifted our spirits. She left me a brand-new man's shirt. Although my two sets of shorts and sun-tops were more patches than original material, my first thought was food as I figured I could get 60 guilders for it on the black market. So, when the need for money was pressing, I offered it for sale. Marie de Souza, my go-between, brought it back, saying it had been cut down to fit Mrs McLeod and was too small to fit any of the slightly built hei-hoes – not even the smallest ones. She could only get 12 occupation dollars for it and assumed, quite rightly, that I wouldn't want to sell it for as little as that.

An unexpected break in the tedium of camp life was preceded by an announcement from the Japanese, about six weeks after our arrival, that a band was coming to entertain us – news that was greeted with annoyance rather than pleasure. We needed food for the body, not the soul, so many of us decided to boycott the event. On the appointed day, we were lying down in the hut, determined not to go, when a guard [newly appointed and dubbed Gold Teeth] stormed in, shouting and yelling and ordering us to attend. As we walked to the area where the concert was being held, the music of *Poet and Peasant* floated through the air. We pricked up our ears. This sounded good.

> The Poet and Peasant Overture *by Franz von Suppe, a late 20th-century composer, had been popularised by two animated cartoons made many years after his death in 1895. The first, released in 1930 by Walt Disney Studios, featured Mickey Mouse, Clarabella the Cow and Horace the Horse dancing to the music at a concert. The second was screened in 1935, when Fleischer Studio recycled it as* The Spinach Overture, *featuring Popeye the Sailor Man.*

An immaculately uniformed band stood to attention on a slight slope before taking their seats on chairs they had brought with them. As the music they played was mostly German, the Dutch and German women joined in the singing. Ironically, although the Germans were supposed to be allies of the Japanese, this fact had evidently not penetrated as far as Sumatra – all German nationals, apart from Dr Goldberg who enjoyed a special status, had been interned.

The concert was actually a beautiful experience. The music was superb, the grass was a brilliant green and the sun was filtering through the rubber trees, which were in their full glory with autumn-toned leaves. We, who had been prepared to be scornful, silently wept.

Walking back to the hut, I really appreciated for the first time the beauty of the surrounding area, with its gentle grassed slopes, bubbling creek and small streamlet that joined it after passing under the barbed wire. I also wondered about the life and fate of the coolies, whose huts we now occupied.

The most beautiful dragonflies floated through our huts. When they settled on an outstretched finger, their delicately coloured transparent wings quivering in the air, someone would say 'It means a letter'. Another, 'No, a kiss'. However, we would all reply 'We'll settle for the letter.'

We did get some mail in this camp, mostly old and of the prescribed 25 words. Some of the more recent letters contained news of demobilisation of some of our troops. We wondered what was happening. Could the war really be drawing to a close?

> *One of the sisters who received a letter from home was Jenny Greer. Her correspondent was Sister May Setchell, who had reached Sydney safely on* Empire Star.

The Chinese woman whose son Pat Blake had minded each morning, and for whom she had knitted and I had sewn, came to us in great distress. Her dear friend, the pretty Indonesian lass who had borrowed *Pride and Prejudice* in our first camp, had died suddenly. She was very distressed and agitated and, as she was a widow, was worried about the future of her son, should anything happen to her.

She told us she was a very wealthy woman and had made a will, naming us joint trustees and giving us Power of Attorney of her estate. We were appalled. We did not want to have the burden of such a responsibility. Assuring her that we had no business acumen, we implored her to find someone else. She was adamant. 'No, no, no, you are the two best people in the camp. I know you will look after my Johnny.'

We looked at each other askance. Apart from handling her estate, the possibility of our arriving in Australia with a small Eurasian child filled our shallow hearts with horror. No one would believe he did not belong to one of us. I brewed some 'coffee' and we both made placatory noises, avoiding any commitment and inviting her to visit us each afternoon. She made her daily visits, which we greatly enjoyed as she was witty, interesting company and talked about her life before the war.

The two Pats were not called upon to fulfil their obligations as their Chinese friend survived. She was Katherine Efford who, prior to moving to Singapore, had lived at Sandakan, British North Borneo, where her husband, Thomas, worked as an accountant for the trading firm, Harrison and Crosfield. Her son, John, known as Johnny, was only three months old when he and his mother entered captivity. His father died at the Padang Internment Camp on Sumatra's west coast in November 1944.

The Indonesian hei-hoes, who patrolled the camp carrying guns with obligatory fixed bayonets, were usually smiling and pleasant. One day, when Barbara La Follette saw a pig in the lower section of the creek, she asked the nearest guard to shoot it to provide food for the camp. He smiled and said he had a gun, but no bullets. Undaunted, Barbara walked up to the guardhouse, but the Japanese guards ignored her and she returned to the creek almost in tears. In the meantime, the pig had finished his ablutions and trotted away.

We were intrigued to learn that the hei-hos were not armed. In fact, none had ever been properly armed and in some places they were even issued with dummy wooden guns. It was just as well for our morale that we did not realise the hei-hos were just for show. We now figured that, as the Japs were not game enough to arm the indigenous people, the war must be almost over.

Although the Australian nurses had not been subjected to brutal treatment as prisoners, other than the incident when the two sisters had been made to stand in the sun, the guards could be very cruel. One day, one of the nuns took a group of small orphaned children outside the barbed wire to collect wood. A Japanese guard who had been at our previous camp spotted them. The young children took off down the ridge to the exit point, where the barbed-wire fence crossed the creek, but the guard caught the nun and repeatedly beat her upper arms with his baton. She took the punishment stoically, but we knew her arms would be useless for some time. We also knew that any attempt to help her would only worsen the situation.

I've said little about our rations at this camp because it still sickens me to think about the food situation, which became so desperate that people ate virtually anything.

Although none of the nurses ate rats, other internees did, until the medical staff put a stop to it in July. A good-sized rat could fetch $2.50. Val Smith and Jessie Blanch had no qualms about gathering edible ferns and also shellfish from the creek until Dr Smith found out and forbade it, saying that, if they became ill, she would not treat them. Although the nurses knew that the Japanese latrines discharged into the creek, they were so hungry they were prepared to eat anything. Better rations – such as duck eggs, chickens and ducks – were *available for hospital patients, as long as they had funds to pay for them. Sister Mickey Syer, who was very ill, traded her gold watch for a not-so-fresh egg.*

We rarely saw any meat in the rations, but in the nearby men's camp there was a Dutch Eurasian doctor who was a very good hunter. The Japs escorted him on hunting trips, but he was allowed only one bullet. He had to almost touch his quarry before he pulled the trigger. Through his efforts we had bear and deer, but only very occasionally, and the Japs, of course, took more than their fair share. One day the doctor shot a monkey, which the Japs magnanimously gave to our camp. Each person received three pieces of flesh, no bigger than the tip of my little finger. Food was food, but when the others told me that it smelt to high heaven and tasted worse, I was thankful I was too ill that evening to eat my share.

The male internees had moved from Muntok to Balabau on 5 March and had endured a journey remarkably similar to that of the women. They were imprisoned a mile or so (2 kilometres) from the women's camp in coolie-lines, where Seki now had his headquarters. On 27 May, a week or so after the doctor shot the monkey, word filtered through to the women's camp that the war with Germany was over. Although no one knew the source of the story, or even if it were true, the nurses nevertheless celebrated in the hope that it was.

There was no clandestine radio in the camp, or in the men's camp, although news that Germany was crumbling had been discovered in January from a newspaper wrapped around goods brought in by a Chinese contractor. It is likely that the news of Germany's surrender on 8 May came from one of the Japanese guards and was brought into the women's camp by one of the Girl Friends.

Some of us tried to grow our own food. The soil was beautiful, so I planted some pumpkin seeds from our rations and grew the healthiest vine I've ever seen. Covered in magnificent golden blooms, it climbed the wall of the hut, came in through the window opening and entwined itself around the entrance. To my disappointment, every single flower was male.

Mary White, one of the English Colonial Service nurses, had grown a similar vine over a large stump. There were no bees to be seen and Mary's vine, like mine, was not bisexual. One day, as I walked to the creek to get water, I saw her assiduously attempting to cross-pollinate her blooms using a piece of long grass. I was very amused, but she said, 'Well something might happen.' It did. The vine grew a crinkled little black object which, after a few months, was still only the size of a cricket ball. One day it was missing. When I asked Mary what it tasted like, she said, 'Horrible!' We also grew some of the local spinach, known as kang kong, but, driven by hunger pangs, we always picked it too early.

In July, Pat Blake and Win Davis were admitted to hospital with dysentery. Win, who was very ill, was convinced she would die before her thirtieth birthday in a few days' time.

As Jess Doyle had an infected foot and had gone to live with some of the English and Australian nurses living near the hospital, I took over the care of Win with the help of Louise Beeston, the English schoolteacher, who also had some nursing experience. I sold the yellow knitted top that Margaret Dryburgh had left me, and used it to buy eggs and potatoes for Win.

I was by this time living in the English sisters' hut. It was closer to the hospital than mine and, as I had malarial rigors every 23 hours, I needed to be near my bed space. On 19 July, 12 days after Win's birthday, Val Smith came to see me as I came out of a rigor. She told me that Win had just died. Val and Louise were attending her when she suddenly collapsed. I was very upset that I had not been with her and my only consolation was that she would no longer have to suffer.

I spent the entire day after Win's death resting and sewing her mattress to mine. It had been a gruesome joke between us that whichever one of us lived the longest would have a thick, decent mattress at last. The Japanese also provided 14 live pigs for the camp that day, but it was a one-off and within days everyone was hungry again.

By this time, we looked like old crones, with our washboard ribs, thin lifeless hair and missing teeth. It was getting increasingly hard to stay live and we had now reached the stage when we envied those who had been lost at sea, and even those who had been massacred. The end had come quickly for them and they had not been forced to slowly die, suffering the misery and wretchedness of life in a Japanese internment camp. It became all too hard for some internees, who simply gave up the will to live, even those who had children. Many years have now passed, but time has not eased the painful memories of all those who died, and the appalling conditions in which we lived.

With Win gone, and my special nursing no longer needed, I decided to go back to my own hut. When I arrived, I was shocked to see that Pat Blake was no longer in hospital but lying in her old bed space. She wept and pleaded with me not to send her back, although I told her what she already knew – that there were no facilities to care for dysentery cases outside the hospital.

After the usual appalling meal of watery vegetables and rice, we settled down to fitful sleep as she was very restless and was so ill that I had to turn her every two hours. In the morning, I could see that a rat had chewed her toe. No blood oozed from it – I guess she didn't have enough to reach her extremities.

After I had sponged her, I took her mattress outside in the sun to be aired. I was shocked at its thinness. Most of us had used the kapok from the pillow we had been given to make one small pillow, and used the rest to pad out the top 6 inches (15 centimetres) of the sack. The remainder, sealed off from the kapok with a row of stitching, was filled with dried grass. Pat, however, had spread the kapok evenly in sewn-off segments of her sack. After three-and-a-half years of use, there was no padding left in her mattress. I gave her mine.

Dr Smith arrived on her rounds at 9 am. On the defensive, she abruptly asked, 'How are you?' Before I had time to answer, she added, 'How's Blake? You know she has to go back to hospital?' I replied, 'I did not discharge her, nor would I have. You did. I don't see how you can discharge a person one day, readmit her the next and expect her to survive under these conditions.' Dr Smith reacted very angrily to my response. Storming off, she went to see Pat and then continued her rounds in the British section of the hut.

She came back a little later, upset and almost contrite, saying, 'I don't know what to do. When I suggested to Blake that she should go back to hospital, she cried. I've never seen her cry before.' I was the only person available to care for Pat but, as I lacked the energy to do so, Dr Smith injected me with an iron supplement, instructing me 'not to bloody well tell anyone'. After that, she visited Pat each day and gave me an injection once a week.

Despite the extra work and worry Pat created, I was thankful for her company. We were able to discuss so many things. We talked of the theatre, books, art – anything to keep our minds off food. We discussed John Galsworthy's *Forsyte Saga*, with its descriptions of the Forsyte family's dinner parties, deciding the book should be banned. Our topics also included more philosophical matters and we agreed that that the tragedy of war, with its unprecedented scale of death and destruction, would promote an upsurge of religious fervour.

We also went on trips down memory lane – to the coast south of Sydney along the Princes Highway, passing Missenden Road where Royal Prince Alfred Hospital, our old training school, is located. We stopped off at the hospital to reminisce, reviving memories of friends and wondering what they were now doing.

We laughingly recalled our jaunts from RPA to Bondi Beach with Con, who ran a hire-car service. Depending on the number of girls who wanted to go, he would send one or two cars to collect us. The vehicles were also used as mourning coaches for funerals and were very roomy. We managed to squeeze 12 into one car – not so bad on the way to the beach, but a little trying on the return journey when we were all sandy and sunburnt.

Continuing our nostalgic trip along the Princes Highway, we called in at Bill the Oyster King's shop at Georges River to buy oysters. Then on to Audley in the Royal National Park for a picnic lunch and perhaps a row on the river before driving down the winding coastal road to Bulli, laughing at the signs 'Beware of falling rocks'. With the steep mountain escarpment on one side and a sheer drop to the ocean on the other, we always wondered what we should do if the 'falling rocks' fell.

Deciding to go further afield, we embarked on an imaginary trip to the centre of Australia and were appalled by our ignorance. We had little knowledge of the outback. Other than a few placenames, we knew only that it was hot and arid and that Ayers Rock was an outstanding landmark.

We all faced the reality that death was a distinct possibility and in our previous camp we had all made wills, leaving our possessions to one of our friends. This was necessary because, if a will could not be produced, the Japs took the lot, and the beneficiaries had to buy their intended legacy back. Many of us also wrote a 'farewell' letter to our families, setting out the facts of our life since we became prisoners. I wrote:

> Dear Family
>
> Please don't worry about me. I enlisted of my own free will, knowing I could be going into a war zone and we nurses who have been prisoners of the Japs for so long have always been with other women. I have not been raped, bashed or tortured. If I die, it will be due to malaria and starvation.

I think a few others wrote letters. I don't know how many. It's not the sort of thing we talked about. It's sort of something to do privately and then ask a friend 'If you get home, please send this to my father.'

Staying alive had become very difficult and death, had it come, would have been a welcome release. I was so weary that each night when I settled down to sleep, I prayed, 'Please God, don't let me wake up tomorrow.'

I dreamed one night that I had died and was walking up a hill to the place where I knew I had to go. A young RAF officer helped me up the last few yards. He was so clean and healthy. I laughed and said, 'Well, you died in the full flush of beautiful youth.' He said, 'And you died in a prison camp.' We entered a building and studied the noticeboard. I laughed again and said, 'They've had my name down three times and at last they've got me.' He replied, 'Three times? Me too.' My name was down on 15 February 1942, in January 1945, and now.

He said, 'You go that way and I go this way', adding 'They're pretty hard on you at first, so I'll come back and collect you, we'll go through it together'.

I walked towards a group of women, dressed in Grecian clothes and standing on a raised, curved dais, surrounded by graceful columns. Kath and Win were among them. They all looked so well and happy. Kath smiled her crooked smile and said, 'You're older than I am now.' The difference in our ages had always irked her. Win said, as I knew she would, 'We knew you'd be late.' We stretched out our hands to one another, and then I woke up. I couldn't believe it, I was still in the camp.

I closed my eyes and tried to get back into my dream. When I opened them again, Pat said, 'You were smiling in your sleep. Did you have a nice dream?' For a fleeting moment, I thought perhaps I should tell her the truth, that death was much nicer than life. Instead I said, 'I dreamed I walked down Castlereagh Street and bought 10 frocks.' As I sponged her, we talked frocks and fashions. I treasured my dream and pretended that it was reality and that reality was fantasy. In a funny way it helped me.

With the deterioration in our health and the worsening of the conditions and rations, it was interesting that kindliness and gentleness towards one another increased. Vi McElnea brought in some tobacco, which was issued regularly as part of our rations. It had to be washed and dried three times before any of us could use it. It helped somehow to deaden the hunger pains. For me, though, it was a matter of one puff, then one hiccup.

Humour, thank goodness, was still with us. Iole dropped by, wanting our opinion on a terrific idea she had that might improve our situation. Recalling Mr Curtin's admonition in his 1942 Christmas message to 'keep smiling', she wanted to ask the Japs' permission to send a cable to him, asking, 'Can we take the grin off our faces now?'

It was now the end of July, and we were completely without money. Food was very short and difficult to obtain, even on the black market. However, the suppliers had their regular customers, who still had goods to trade or sell. I had sold Mrs McLeod's cut-down white shirt, thinking I would probably not have any use for it, and the money had long since gone. Things were looking very grim until Pat decided to sell her engagement ring. Our Chinese friend negotiated the deal and got quite a lot for it, so we were able to purchase enough food to keep us going for a little bit longer.

I received a message that Dot Freeman wanted to see me. I walked up to her hut to find her lying in the foetal position. She told me she couldn't straighten her legs. She couldn't remember

Rubina 'Dot' Freeman

how long she had been like that, so I assumed she must have been sleeping. I told her not to worry as I would arrange a hospital admission for her right away and, once there, she'd be all right.

In the late afternoons when I wasn't suffering a malaria attack, I usually helped out with the coffin carrying, and collected wood on the way back. A few days after Dot's admission, I said I couldn't be a carrier, but would lead out. Holding my head up to keep to the track between the graves, the first cross I saw was Dot's. It was like a slap in the face. No one had told me that she had died on 8 August.

CHAPTER 10

Free at last

Towards the end of August, there was a change in the atmosphere of the camp and the attitude of the guards. Rumours that the war was over were rife.

The first real indication that something was up was when the children, who were old enough to walk the distance, were allowed to visit the male members of their families at the men's camp.

> *Dressed in the best clothing that could be found, with their faces scrubbed clean and sporting new haircuts courtesy of Flo Trotter and Betty Jeffrey, the children lined up at the gate. However, their excitement dissipated completely when the guards read out the names of those who would not be going – their fathers were dead.*

Nevertheless, it was a memorable occasion for those old enough to remember their fathers and older brothers, who had been transferred to the men's camp on reaching puberty. However, others who were accustomed to the small-statured Japanese and Indonesians were afraid of the big, hairy white men. One small family reported that 'Daddy just cried all the time when we told him Mummy was dead'.

Certain that the war was over, Sister Catherina now smiled more than ever and wore the Dutch colours as she walked about the camp. As I passed her on my way to collect water, she smiled mischievously and pulled a lovely thick plait of fair hair from under her wimple. I was filled with envy. Before the war, nuns cut off their hair on taking their vows. However, when the Germans overran Holland, they forced the nuns to abandon their long, traditional habits and veils and dress as ordinary women. To avoid embarrassment, since one of the punishments meted out to women who collaborated with the enemy was to shave their heads, all nuns had been given permission to grow their hair.

Our unpredictable captors then announced that a 'very important general' was coming to visit the camp the following day. Consequently, the vegetables that had just been delivered were stockpiled. The heap was left in the sun and the next day's issue dumped on top. The following day the same thing happened. To a visitor, it would appear that the camp was receiving an adequate supply of rations. However, by the afternoon of the third day, the unpleasant aroma of rotting vegetation wafted through the camp. When there was still no sign of the general, the Japs gave permission to distribute the vegetables. We lined up with our buckets and the ration committee shoved their spades into the heap and filled them. Carefully going through our issue, I retrieved one tablespoon of edible food.

The very important general finally came the following day, dressed in full uniform. We realised that we knew him, as we had seen him quite a few times before, strolling through the camp in a boiler suit. As on previous visits, he talked to the children and some of the women.

A few days later, we were told Captain Seki would address us. While we felt sure he would tell us the war was over, no-one could remember him ever telling us anything that brought joy to our hearts. Standing on a table and looking grim, Seki spoke briefly, telling us that the war had ended and, that now there was peace, we would all soon be leaving Sumatra. He optimistically ended his speech with the words, 'If we have made any mistakes in the past we hope you will forgive us, and now we can all be friends.'

Although we were expecting the news, it seemed unbelievable. At first there was just a stunned silence. It was just too much to take in. Someone fainted. I think most of us cried and laughed at the same time – I know I did. When the news finally sank in, the relief was wonderful, our joy unbounded. An English internee who had a Union Jack hidden away got it out and put it on the end of a stick. The only thing to dampen our euphoria was that we had lost so many of our companions.

Japan had surrendered unconditionally on 15 August, but the announcement was not made at our camp until the 24th. Sister 'Mitzi' Mittelheuser, from Bundaberg, Queensland, who had always wanted people to call her Pearl, her real name, was not with us to share the joy. She had died on 18 August, three days after the surrender, unaware that she was free.

The Japanese allowed the men to come over from their camp. There were many happy reunions, and some sad ones. Some of the men who, by the good graces of the guards, had been sending vegetables they had grown to their wives, found out they had died months before. The men, or most of them, seemed to have withstood camp life better than most of us, although some of them were very ill. They mended leaking roofs, chopped down trees for firewood, built duckboard paths across the muddy patches and took over all the heavy duties, leaving the care of the sick to us. Sadly, it was too late for some of our patients.

Immediately after Seki's big announcement the rations improved, in quality and quantity. We also received some presents – a lipstick between two, a bottle of scent and some strong-smelling Chinese hair oil. This was followed by a distribution of the much longed for Red Cross supplies. Much of the food had deteriorated, but anything still usable was distributed.

With a better diet and less arduous work, our health improved and we quickly gained weight. For my birthday on 31 August, which I shared with Queen Wilhelmina, we had a real feast as the natives gave us a huge bullock, which the men skinned and cooked. However, the day came and went with no sign of liberating forces, shattering my hopes that on my birthday I would be truly free. Allied planes en route to Palembang flew over the camp but, as the days went by and no one came for us, we wondered when, or if, we would be released and taken home.

Meanwhile, teams were combing Sumatra in search of Allied prisoners of war.

Before hostilities had ceased, a five-man party had parachuted from a Catalina flying boat into Japanese-occupied territory 60 miles (100 kilometres) from Medan, in north-eastern Sumatra. They had come from Ceylon and were members of Force 136, the code name for the SOE-Far East, a sub-division of the covert British Special Operations Executive (SOE) organisation. The group was under the command of South African-born Major Gideon Jacobs, a young Royal Marine with extensive commando training. His orders were to gather intelligence prior to an anticipated invasion and to transmit the information to Lord Louis Mountbatten's South East Asian Command (SEAC) Headquarters in Ceylon.

Jacobs' party comprised two Australian signallers, Sergeants Earlsford Bates and Roy Gillam, and two members of the Royal Netherlands East Indies Army, Sergeant Albert Plesman and Javanese–Chinese signaller Tjoeng Suet, who had lived in Sumatra.

Several days after their insertion, Japan surrendered and Jacobs was instructed to make contact with Japanese Command Headquarters in Medan. On learning of the appalling conditions in Sumatran POW camps from the Swiss Consul, Mr Amsler, and two male internees who had just been liberated – the Governor of Sumatra, Dr Beck, and Mr Fenton, the senior British representative – Jacobs ordered Colonel Okada, the Chief Staff Officer, to arrange to take him to every camp, and issued instructions to Allied teams to begin gathering evidence for anticipated war crimes trials.

Jacobs and his men, accompanied by a Colonel Yoshida, were flown in Japanese aircraft to access camps dotted all around Sumatra. After visiting the Padang area on the west coast, they drove to Pekan Baroe (Pekanbaru) in central Sumatra, where Allied POWs had been used as slave labour to build a 'death railway'. Jacobs then returned to his base at Medan to coordinate a relief effort by RAPWI (Repatriation of Prisoners of War and Internees), an organisation that Mountbatten had established the previous February. On 2 September, RAPWI launched Operation Mastiff, which began dropping supplies into the Sumatran camps.

It was early September before Jacobs and his team flew to Palembang, the last of the camps listed by Yoshida. On his visit to the POW camp there, Jacobs was amazed to discover that the inmates were well informed as one prisoner had a radio, made from various bits and pieces and concealed in the lower half of his water-bottle.

As had been the case at Pekan Baroe, Jacobs organised the camps into panels to facilitate the collection of evidence for war crimes trials. Captain Corrie, one of the senior British POWs, handed over statements already made by POWs and internees. Noticing that one was signed by a Royal Marine, Jacobs paused to read it. The deponent was Robert Seddon, the corporal who had drifted offshore at Radji Beach and had witnessed the massacre of the nurses.

Searching through the pile for corroborative evidence, Jacobs came across a report by Ernest Lloyd, the Royal Navy stoker who had escaped death by diving into the water when the

Japanese opened fire on his group. He too had seen the bodies of the murdered nurses when he returned to the beach.

Although Tebbutt had reported the story of the massacre to Changi Administration when he had arrived in Singapore the previous May, nothing had been made public. However, press reports on 22 August had revealed that, of the 65 nursing sisters who had left Singapore on Vyner Brooke*, 32 were interned somewhere in Sumatra. The other 38, including two matrons and the sister in charge of the Casualty Clearing Station, were presumed dead.*

Certain that neither he nor any of his men had come across any Australian nurses at any of the camps they had visited, and aware that there was a considerable shortfall between the number of internees supposedly in the camps and the number actually located, Jacobs and his men canvassed the prisoners. Apart from vague suggestions that some Australian nurses had been moved into the interior and had all died from malaria, and that other women had been held at a camp at Benkulen on the west coast (another camp not mentioned by Yoshida), no one could shed any light on the matter.

Jacobs finally confronted Yoshida. Telling him that it was not true that his team had seen every camp in Sumatra, Jacobs demanded to be taken immediately to the camps he had not yet seen. Non-compliance, Jacobs threatened, would result in Yoshida's duplicity being reported to his general and to Lord Mountbatten.

A few hours later, after checking with his superiors, Yoshida reported to Jacobs, explaining that there had been a mistake. There was a camp at Loeboek Linggau. In effort to save face, Yoshida said that it was not included in the list because he thought Jacobs would not want to travel so far and because the Japanese intended to bring the internees to Palembang.

Discovering that the nearest airstrip to Loeboek Linggau was at Lahat, Jacobs forced Yoshida to fly him there immediately. The Japanese were reluctant to obey as the disused airstrip was overgrown, but they touched down without incident. After making further enquiries at Lahat, the party went by road to Loeboek Linggau, where Bates and Gillam established communication with SEAC HQ. By this time, Jacobs had been reinforced by another Force 136 team, which included three Dutch paratroopers – Corps Officer Wilhelm, Sergeant Major C B Hakkenberg and Sergeant Van Hasselt. On 6 September, Wilhelm, Hakkenberg and Van Hasselt, along with Signaller Tjoeng, made contact with the men's camp.

The next day they went to the women's camp, where their arrival created a sensation. An ecstatic Betty Jeffries recorded: 'The Allies have arrived!'

Major Jacobs drove to the camp from Loeboek Linggau late that afternoon. After a very brief inspection, he returned to Loeboek Linggau to report to SEAC and to prepare for a more thorough investigation.

Jacobs was back at the camp the next day for a closer inspection of what he considered to be the worst camp in Sumatra. However, it was only on this second visit that he realised some of the European women were the missing Australian nurses. After forcing the Japanese to distribute their stocks of military clothing, lengths of fabric, sewing implements and shoes to the internees, he returned to Loeboek Linggau, where the signallers transmitted a new message to SEAC, with a request to relay it to the Australian ambassador in India and to Australian army headquarters in Melbourne.

> Have encountered among 250 repeat 250 British female internees in Loebuk Linggau camp Sister Nesta James and 23 other surviving members of the Australian Army Nursing Services remnants of contingent AANS evacuated from Malaya in *Vyner Brooke* STOP In view of their precarious health suggest you endeavour arrange air transport direct to Australia from here soonest STOP Am collecting particulars of massacre of members AANS on Bangka Island for later transmission.

On 9 September, the Japanese, on Jacob's orders, distributed the contents of their storehouses to the internees. After taking whatever they wanted in the way of clothing and footwear, the nurses and the other women spent the next two days bartering for food with the locals, who had plenty of food, but virtually no clothing, and were only too keen to make the exchange. The nursing sisters also made clothes from lengths of fabric and mosquito nets to replace their worn-out sun-tops and shorts.

On 11 September, the two Australians, Bates and Gillam, arrived at the camp with Jacobs, causing great excitement. Vivian Bullwinkel was the first to spot the Rising Sun badges and rushed to spread the exciting news to her companions that 'Australians are here!'

On seeing the nurses' pitiful condition, the reaction of the two sergeants was one of profound shock. However, when one of the sisters told Gillam that a guard called Moonface had tried to rape her, the shock turned to rage. Lining the dozen or so guards up along the fence, Gillam demanded that Moonface identify himself, making it perfectly clear that he intended to shoot him. He was only prevented from doing so by Jacobs' assurances that the perpetrators of all war crimes would be brought to trial.

Before returning to Medan, the signallers sat on the bali balis while the nurses eagerly bombarded them with dozens of questions. They, in turn, told the women of some of the huge changes that had occurred in the outside world and of the powerful destruction of the atomic bombs dropped on Hiroshima and Nagasaki, bringing a sudden end to the war.

Local Indonesian vendors now arrived with fruit, vegetables, eggs, dried fish and live fowls. Foolishly I bought a chook, a long-legged thing. It hung limply in my hand and, when I looked down at it, curled its neck up and looked at me. I knew I couldn't kill it, so I took it along to an English woman and asked her to do it. She said, 'Gawd, sis, you're a nurse and you can't kill a chook! 'Ere, give it to me!' In a second, she had wrung its neck.

On the morning of 13 September, in accordance with RAPWI's Operation Mastiff, two four-engined Liberator bombers, based at the Cocos Keeling Islands in the Indian Ocean, flew in at treetop height to drop 78 packages into the camps. The internees, who had existed on so little for more than three years, were now showered with boxes of medical stores containing bandages, quinine, vitamin tablets and serum, along with powdered milk and eggs, tinned butter and bacon, cigarettes and newspapers.

That evening the nurses revelled in the luxury of drinking hot cocoa and eating bread baked on Cocos Island the day before. They were treated to half a slice each, topped with butter and Vegemite – a salty, tangy yeast spread beloved by Australians.

Two days later, on 15 September, word came through that the nurses and very ill patients would be flown to Singapore the following day. We were overwhelmed with happiness, but sad to be leaving behind the many friends we had lost in Sumatra.

Of the 714 women interned in the Muntok Camp in October 1944, there were just 545 alive on 23 August. Of these, about 250 were British. For the Dutch women, who had entered captivity with belongings, cash and jewellery, the death rate was 20 per cent. The British, many of whom arrived on Bangka Island with the clothes they stood up in, lost 30 per cent. The Australian nurses had lost 8 of their party of 32 – four at Muntok and four at Balabau – a death toll of 25 per cent. The nurses attributed their better survival rate to the fact that they were disciplined, stuck together and worked as a team.

The last woman internee to die at Balabau was an Australian, Mrs Millicent 'Molly' Watts-Carter who, having miraculously survived days floating on the life raft after her ship Tanjoeng Pinang *was sunk, succumbed to the effects of starvation on 27 August. She was 34. Her parents, George and Daisy Osborne, lived in Killara, on Sydney's north shore. Her husband Jeffrey, an Australian planter, survived his internment in Singapore. Aware that the war was over, Molly had whispered to a friend that she was happy to have lived long enough to know that everyone would soon be free.*

At around 9.30 on the evening of 15 September, Seki informed Sister Nester James that the nurses were to be evacuated the next day. Shortly afterwards, Mrs Hinch arrived to tell her that she was wanted on the phone. A phone? What phone? The nurses in her hut, who had settled down for the night, were now wide-awake. After taking the call at the guard house, Sister James returned with the news that a Flying Officer Brown had advised that arrangements had been made to transfer the nurses and the stretcher patients to the aerodrome at Lahat for evacuation to Singapore.

Despite the lateness of the hour, the sisters in the other Australian hut, who were plucking ducks and chickens in preparation for the birthday of an internee, joyfully spread the news to the hospital patients and the Dutch nuns, who joined in an impromptu celebration supper of fried rice washed down with black coffee, laced with sugar.

Early next morning, while it was still dark, we left for Loeboek Linggau in two trucks. Before we left, Pilot Officer Ken Brown, of the RAAF, arrived. With him was Haydon Lennard, an Australian war correspondent.

On 10 September Jacobs had received a signal that RAWPI would begin airlifting Allied prisoners from the three main camp areas at Padang, Paken Baroe and Palembang. The air evacuation unit, comprising 10 RAAF nursing sisters, British and Australian army doctors and a number of DC3 aircraft under the command of Wing Commander John Game, had swung into action. The first of the 2000 to be rescued were women and children living in 'unbelievable squalor' at Padang, who were evacuated to the equally unbelievable comfort of Singapore's Raffles Hotel.

Once Padang had been cleared of all POWs and internees who were strong enough to be moved, the RAWPI teams moved to Paken Baroe. Palembang, the most distant of the centres, was left until last. Each of the evacuation areas had been given an identifying code. The name assigned to Loeboek Lingga was Operation Aspect.

Meanwhile, Haydon Lennard of the Australian Broadcasting Commission had been reporting on the recovery of POWs in Singapore. In recent days, he and other journalists had received copies of an official report on the Bangka Island massacre, compiled by Major Tebbutt. The report also listed the names of all the Vyner Brooke *nurses, 32 of whom were known to have been in Palembang. However, as this information was embargoed until such time as the nurses were located, Lennard, a well-known and experienced war correspondent, was keen to chase the story for himself.*

It is evident that neither Lennard nor the RAPWI evacuation team had any idea that Jacobs had already made contact with the nurses at Balabau plantation. Determined to find them, and on learning that a team was flying to Palembang to organise the recovery of POWs there, Lennard successfully prevailed upon the authorities to allow him to join them. At 8 am on 14 September he boarded a DC3 aircraft, piloted by RAAF Squadron Leader Fred Madsen. Also on board were co-pilot Ken Brown, British army doctor Lieutenant-Colonel Hayes, Major (Doctor) Harry Matthew Windsor, of 2/14 AGH, Major Clough, Private Frederick Prott, of 20 Field Ambulance, and RAAF nursing sister Beryl Chandler.

When the plane touched down on the Palembang airstrip at 10.15 am, Madsen had no idea if the strip was mined, or if the Japanese flagging him in might turn on a hostile reception. Disembarking, the team was confronted by about 30 fully armed Japanese, brandishing swords and demanding to know why they had landed at Palembang. Major Windsor's reply, that they had come in search of POWs and Australian nurses imprisoned there, elicited no response until a quick-thinking Lieutenant Colonel Hayes said they were there on the express orders of Lord Louis Mountbatten.

This certainly struck the right chord, and the team was escorted to a nearby pavilion where they were offered coffee and cigarettes. The officer in charge telephoned his headquarters and within 15 minutes staff cars had arrived to transfer them into town, 16 kilometres distant, saluted along the way by Japanese soldiers standing to attention.

At Buys Hotel they met the Japanese area commander. After questioning him on the whereabouts of the POWs and internees, they were escorted to the prison hospital, where a large number of Dutch soldiers were in the last stages of starvation. Among the sick were just five Australians, but in the prison, which Windsor visited next, he located another 57 who were in good spirits and good condition. However, the Japanese would not, or could not, give him any information about the missing nursing sisters.

Two POWs, however, had heard that the women were in a camp 'up Lahat way'. With the help of a British POW, five Dutch civilians who were known to have been with the Australian nurses were located and interviewed, all to no avail. It was not until they met Reverend Mother Alacoque that they had a breakthrough. She told them that Australian nurses had been with her in Palembang until September 1943, when she had been arrested, but had since moved to Loeboek Linggau, 250 miles (400 kilometres) to the west.

On receipt of this information, the party split up.

The plane and all but four of the team returned to Singapore, taking with them a load of ill POWs from the prison. Major Windsor and Sister Chandler, who remained behind at Palembang overnight, took the opportunity to visit the POW camps. During this time, Windsor learned of the massacre at Radji Beach from Lieutenant Bull, an Australian artillery officer who had managed to escape from Singapore with several others, and who had helped collect the eyewitness accounts. He also heard of the deaths of the doctors arrested for their involvement in the local underground and of the terrible torture inflicted by the kempei tai. The details so sickened him that, after describing their torture in his report, he tossed the accepted protocols to the winds and wrote 'I recommend that all kempei be forthwith slowly and painfully butchered'.

It had been arranged that the next morning the plane would return at 8.30 am to collect Major Windsor and Sister Chandler and then fly them to Lahat, 150 miles (240 kilometres) to the south-west. To ensure that there were no problems, Lennard and Brown were instructed to drive to Lahat immediately and check out the condition of the airfield, which the Japanese had said was a grass strip about a mile outside the town, 250 metres wide, 1,500 metres in length, and running north-south.

Ordered to locate the sisters and to transfer them to the Lahat airstrip by whatever means possible, the pair left at 3 pm in a truck, accompanied by an English-speaking Japanese officer, a driver, and 20 armed Japanese 'just in case'. At Lahat they were met by one of

Jacob's Dutch officers, who persuaded the Japanese to provide a train to take him and Lennard north to Loeboek Linggau. After commandeering mattresses and sheets, which were placed in an enclosed van to create a makeshift hospital car, the pair departed, leaving Brown to follow in the truck with the Japanese.

The train and the truck both arrived at Loeboek Linggau at 4 am. Climbing aboard the truck, Lennard and the Dutchman left for the camp, leaving Brown to follow with additional vehicles. However, they arrived to find that two of the Dutch paratroopers were already there and were loading 62 evacuees onto 'every type of transport'.

Five of the seriously ill were children, one of whom was little Mischa Warman. As the last of the stretcher patients was loaded, Dr McDowell waved them off, saying 'Thank God you've cleared all the sick from the hospital'.

The convoy left in pouring rain, with the Australian nurses in two trucks, driven by guards Tanaka and Amana. It took three hours to travel the short distance to Loeboek Linggau as Amana, evidently as an act of pure malice and rebellion, made sure that his truck 'broke down' repeatedly. Finally, the passengers transferred to another truck to complete the journey.

It was a much better journey going back – this time the Japanese had provided couches in the back of the trucks for us to sit on.

At Loeboek Linggau station, Ken Brown and Haydon Lennard told us of their search and that two planes from Singapore were coming to Lahat to evacuate us. We all boarded the train but, although it was a 'special' train, the train driver would not start the engine as the departure time for the normal service was not until 8 am. While we waited, one of the Dutch paratroopers raided the refreshment room and handed out cakes. Amid cheers from male internees who had come to see us on our way, and very dirty looks from the Japs, we finally set off for Lahat.

About four hours later we arrived at Lahat, where obsequious Japs brought us food and drinks [bully beef, rice, fruit, tinned milk and coffee, looted from the food drops], but most of us were too excited to eat. After waiting for an hour in the train, we boarded the trucks again for the short ride to the airstrip, where our former hosts provided us with chairs and an atap shelter. Here we waited and waited, while a Japanese officer shouted repeatedly into a phone 'Banga, banga', or something that sounded like that.

Despite expectations, there was only one plane coming that day. On its arrival, the evacuees were told that it had been assigned to the 24 Australian nurses, Mrs Harding and two other stretcher cases, and three other very ill patients. The remaining 32 members of the group were taken to a Chinese Hotel in Lahat, before transferring to a Dutch hospital to await the arrival of additional aircraft the next morning.

The plane that eventually arrived to transport the nurses had been delayed by a flat tyre and had not touched down at Palembang to pick up Major Windsor and Sister Chandler until 12.30 pm, four hours after the expected arrival time. There was then a further delay while the Japanese pumped up the tyre before the plane flew on to Lahat.

There were two unexpected passengers on board – The Australian Women's Weekly *war correspondent A E (Eddie) Dunstan and the kangaroo mascot made by the 2/4 CCS sisters, thrown over the wall to the male POWs in the first weeks of captivity. The POWs had given it to Sister Chandler when she visited Palembang prison. Bayoneted by the Japanese, it now looked rather the worse for wear, but the card tied around the mascot's neck had miraculously survived, along with its now faded greeting, written in red ink.*

At last, we heard the drone of an engine and a speck of silver appeared in the sky. When the plane landed, a young, handsome officer was first off. He was Major Harry Windsor, who would later perform the first heart transplant in Australia. He had been given copies of our enlistment photos. He looked around and, seeing no faces that he recognised, asked, 'Where are the Australian nurses?' We laughed and said, 'We're here', then realised how thin we were and how drab and worn we must have looked in our faded uniforms.

The next to disembark were two officers dressed in grey safari jackets with pips on their shoulders denoting their army rank, long pants, gaiters and boots. It wasn't until they came a bit closer that we realised they were women! We looked at the trousers in amazement. Someone said, 'Who are you?' The more senior of the two stepped forward with her arms outstretched and replied, 'I'm the mother of you all.'

Matron Annie Sage and Sister Floyd at Lahat

She was Matron Annie Sage, Principal Matron of the Australian Army Nursing Service. She told us that, ever since she had taken the position, her greatest wish had been to find us. She looked at the 24 nurses clustered round her or lying under the shelter and asked, 'Where are the rest of you?' There was silence for a moment, then a voice said, 'They're all dead.'

We boarded the plane, the stretcher cases lying end to end along the aisle, while we occupied bench-type seats on either side of the fuselage. Jenny Greer and another sister, who were very weak, were carried on board. Sister Chandler, who came from Queensland and knew a number of our nurses, flew back with us. Major Windsor, Matron Sage and her companion Sister Jean Floyd, a Salvation Army Officer who had been attached to 10 AGH for a few weeks before Singapore fell, went to Lahat hospital to help care for the group that was flying out the next day.

It was after 5 pm when we arrived in Singapore. I later learned that we blew a tire on landing. At the airfield, we were greeted by members of the Red Cross, who served us with very welcome cups of tea in real cups and saucers, and a less welcome barrage of war correspondents, all clamouring for our stories. We were told that we could speak to them, as people at home were anxiously awaiting news of our rescue. Although tired, excitement ran high, keeping our weariness at bay while we answered the reporters' questions.

Heydon Lennard was already one jump ahead of everyone else. On the four-hour train journey to Lahat, he had also taken the opportunity to talk to the nurses who, in accordance with their pact, were dressed in their uniforms. Vivian Bullwinkel, when recounting the details of her ordeal to Lennard, showed him the bullet holes in her dress, laughingly adding that 'the Japs never even gave us a needle and cotton'.

The nurses also spoke freely about their experiences during the brief press conference. As soon as it was over, Lennard and his fellow journalists dispatched a series of telegrams with news of the rescue and that some nurses had been drowned at sea or massacred. However,

Nurses arrive in Singapore from Palembang

the news of the massacre was not news at all. The embargo on Tebbutt's report had already been broken.

On 15 September, the day before the nurses were rescued, a garbled 'first-hand' story of the massacre appeared in Melbourne's Age *and Adelaide's* Advertiser *under the headlines 'Frightful Deeds. Nurses Killed by Japanese' and 'Nurses' fate revealed. Party shot in back by Japanese'. The accounts were identical, and had been filed by someone in Bangkok – for the* Age *by its 'Special Correspondent', and for the* Advertiser *by its 'Special Representative'.*

According to the newspaper articles, the informant was supposedly a sub-lieutenant in the New Zealand Navy, supposedly imprisoned in Java, where he supposedly 'met' Bullwinkel:

> A first-hand story of the fate of Australian nurses with the 8th Division in Malaya was told by Sub-Lieutenant R J Murray, a New Zealand naval man from Penang, who was in a hospital in Java after Singapore's fall. There he met an Australian nurse survivor of a ship sunk in Bangka Straits. The nurse told him she left Singapore just before the fall on a ship carrying 60 Australian nurses. When the ship was bombed by Japanese planes it was sunk, and about a third of the nurses drowned, with many of the crew.
>
> A group of officers got ashore with nurses, but ran into a Japanese naval patrol in the islands off the coast of Java. The Japanese took the naval officers into the jungle, and returned without them.
>
> They next marched a group of nurses away from those who reached the shore, ran them into the water, and machine-gunned them. One nurse survived from this group, with bullet wounds in the shoulder. She escaped to Java, where Japanese found her again, working in a village hospital, and tried to make her their officer 'geisha' girl. She refused, and a German woman doctor in the same village made secret arrangements with friends and had her removed to another hospital at Bandoeng (Bandung), where Lieut. Murray met her and heard her story. Certified statements of this atrocity have been made, and are now in Singapore.

Evidently in response to this hopelessly inaccurate account, the embargo on Tebbutt's official report was lifted on 16 September. Reporters were now free to send full details of who had been rescued, died at sea, massacred or died in the camps. The next day the ABC broadcast the details of the massacre. The first to publish a print edition was Innisfail's Evening Advocate, *followed by morning editions of the* Cairns Post *and Murwillumbah's the* Tweed Daily *– all country papers that had received the information from Australian Associated Press. Others followed and by the 18th the story was front-page news all around Australia.*

Newspaper editors in capital and regional cities and country towns also scrambled to find a 'local' connection with the rescued nurses, hurriedly putting short biographies together accompanied by photographs – not of the nurses in their present state, but portraits of healthy young women, taken on enlistment. Photos of Pat and Jenny Greer, with the caption 'Nurses freed from Sumatra', appeared in the Sydney Morning Herald *on 18 September.*

However, it didn't take long for images of the emaciated nurses, taken on their arrival in Singapore, to also be published by the press, causing outrage among readers and distress to their families.

We were taken to 2/14 AGH, which was at St Patrick's School at Katong in the same buildings occupied by the 13th in 1942. There were flowers everywhere and there to greet us were Major Ida Brown, the Matron, and the smiling, familiar faces of nurses who had been evacuated on *Empire Star*.

Among them was Sister May Setchell. After reaching Australia, she had served in various hospitals before requesting a return to active service in 1945. She was posted to 2/6 AGH on Labuan Island, Borneo, shortly after the Australian 9th Division had landed there on 10 June to retake Sarawak, Brunei and British North Borneo.

When Japan surrendered, May was transferred from Labuan Island to Singapore for attachment to 2/14 AGH. She arrived four to five days before the ship bringing the unit's commanding officer, matron, staff and equipment from Australia. While waiting for them to arrive, May paid a visit to the POW hospitals at Kranji and Changi.

> My first visit was to Kranji. Never will I forget it! Line after line of our boys lying on palliasses (straw-stuffed mattresses) on the floor, each palliasse almost touching the other and so thin one could easily count their ribs. As I walked down the ward I heard my name called, which surprised me greatly. I stopped to speak with the soldier and found that I had nursed him in Malacca in 1941. As I moved on to speak with other boys, he caught my hand, and thanked me for coming back. This was too poignant. Tears were streaming down both his cheeks and mine.
>
> My second visit was to Changi jail. At the entrance I was stopped by a lad looking almost as ill as the boys at Kranji who asked where I came from. I told him NSW. He then asked me where I had trained and when I replied Royal Prince Alfred Hospital, he asked if I knew a certain trainee. 'Yes,' I replied. 'And do you know where she is now?' he asked. 'No, but I do know she had married.' 'Who did she marry?' he queried, 'I don't really know but I think he was a dentist.' To my horror he replied 'No she didn't. I'm the dentist. I was engaged to her.' I was very upset and wished the ground would open and swallow me.
>
> Changi was almost as bad as Kranji. In the first ward I entered I met two of the doctors from Prince Alfred. One was Colonel Bye who had been our service physician in 2/13 AGH. He was so weak that my first task was to feed him evil smelling dried fish called belachan. The second doctor was Roy Mills who did a marvelous job in Thailand while a prisoner of war. He had tuberculosis and was in a room alone.

When Pat and the surviving sisters from Vyner Brooke *arrived at Katong, May received an unexpected shock.*

> I had written to three of my friends while prisoners, only the 25 words permitted, and had

The condition of the POWs reduced May Setchell to tears

seen two of them since their release, when another sister came out and threw her arms around me and said, 'It's lovely to see you.' I hadn't a clue who she was. She weighed just over 3 stone (19 kilograms). At last she said 'Thanks awfully, for writing,' I realised it was Jenny Greer, with whom I had trained and worked with at 10 AGH.

While at St Pat's, May also met the man who was to become her husband, Mervyn James (Jim) Hamilton, of 2/10 Field Regiment, who had spent the best part of three years slaving on the 'death Railway' in Thailand. They were married in the historic Anglican sandstone

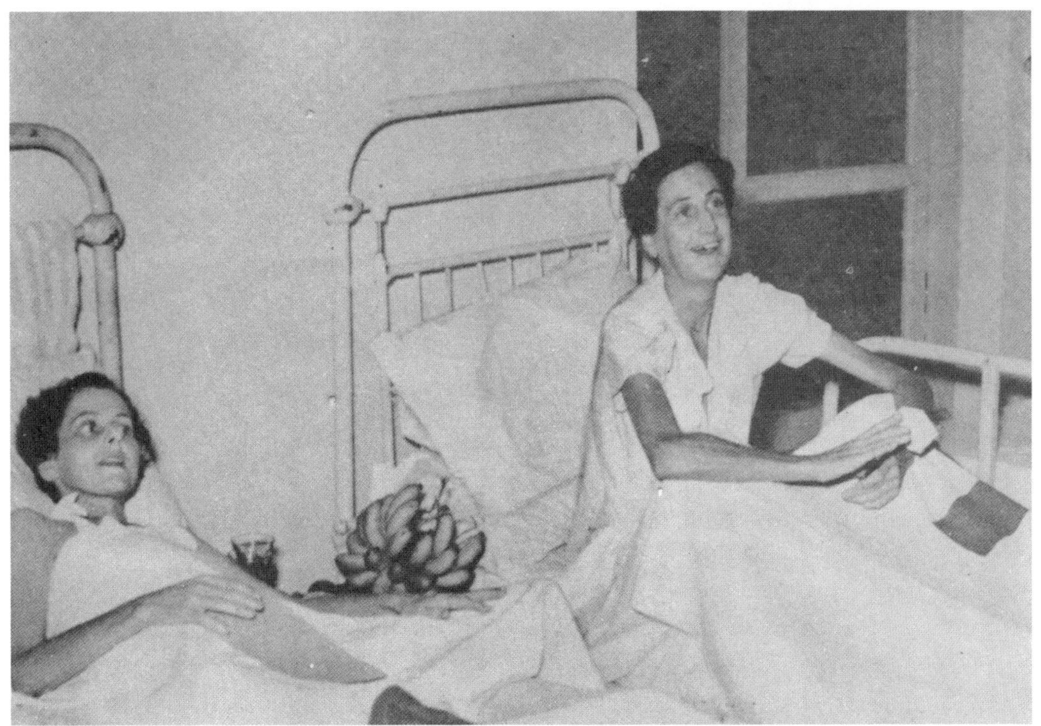

Jenny Greer and Betty Jeffrey in hospital at Singapore

church in the tiny New South Wales village of Wiseman's Ferry in September 1946. At her wedding, May wore the beautiful heirloom bridal veil that the nurses had been entrusted to take to Australia.

May left no record of who owned the veil, other than to tell a journalist covering her wedding that it had belonged to an unnamed 'elderly lady' in Singapore who had left it behind when she was evacuated. It was believed at the time of May's marriage that the evacuation ship had been bombed and that the veil's owner had not survived the war.

However, research shows that the 'elderly lady' was almost certainly 42-year-old Mabel (Mab) Chidson, sister-in-law of Joyce Chidson, the Australian ex-nurse who had been so kind to the 2/10th girls in Malacca. Mab had married Richard Chidson, a British army officer, in Surrey in 1930. It was described as a great love match and the pair, who had no children, were devoted to each other.

Richard was posted to Singapore in 1938, and in 1940 Mab went to Australia for an extended visit. However, she and her husband missed each other so much that she flew back to Singapore in October 1941, despite the fact that the threat of war with Japan was very real – so much so that Hume Chidson had insisted that his wife, Joyce, remain in Australia with their son, John, after visiting their two daughters who were in boarding school in the northern Sydney suburb of Wahroonga.

In February 1942 Mab was still in Singapore. Desperate to get her out, Hume managed to find a berth for her on a ship bound for India. Mab, an incurable romantic all her life, was allowed to take only a small case containing hurriedly packed essentials. There was no room for something as frivolous as a wedding veil, no matter how precious.

The chances of her ever seeing it again were slim, unless someone could take it to Joyce in Australia. Although security was tight, her brother-in-law, Hume, a lieutenant colonel, was in a position to not only locate the 2/10 nurses, whom he knew by name, but also gain access to them and ask them to take the veil to his wife.

It is not known if Mab, who risked attack from enemy ships to sail from Bombay to Sydney in May 1942, was ever reunited with the veil. In early 1946 she and her husband, who had been interned in Singapore, returned to England. May Setchell, the only nursing sister definitely known to have worn the precious heirloom, was still alive in 2018, but her memory had failed. Aged 103, she is believed to be the last surviving 8th Division nursing sister.

Several medical officers, who had been POWs in Changi and Thailand, also arrived at St Patrick's to see us. They had waited all day at the airport, only to be ordered to return to their quarters at 5 pm, 15 minutes before we touched down.

Also waiting to welcome them were POWs recovered from Burma and Thailand. Although

> *thin and weak themselves, they were appalled at the condition of the nurses, some of whom were skeletal; others moved like old ladies, barely able to walk. As they shuffled up the stairs, some of the men became hysterical, shouting, 'Give us guns. Let us at these bastards.'*

We were taken upstairs where those suffering from scabies were given a disinfectant bath. Once that was over we were let loose. Oh, the joy of showers, unlimited hot water, scented soap and soft towels! Pretty night dresses and underclothes, face washers, talc, face creams, nail files, brushes, combs and mirrors – items we had once taken for granted and had done without for so long. Toothbrushes and toothpaste were so much better than a shared brush with worn-down bristles rescued from a rubbish heap, or fibre from coconut husks and charcoal. It was almost too good to be true.

Then came the joy of sleeping in real beds with clean sheets, although some girls who were unused to such comfort slept on the floor. During the night, I was woken by rain dripping through the ceiling, so I immediately hopped out and pulled my bed out of the way, startling the poor night sister who told me I'd wake the whole ward. Someone giggled and said, 'It's raining on Pat.' A sleepy voice answered, 'She should be used to that.'

To the sisters who did not know us, we were evidently something of a handful. We certainly were not what they had expected. They had been warned that, because of our protracted imprisonment, we might be sullen, uncooperative and resentful.

Instead, laughter came easily to us.

We had survived.

We were flying high.

We were free.

CHAPTER 11

The aftermath

Five of the nurses admitted to 2/14 AGH were in such poor condition that, had they not been rescued, they would have died within a few days. Fourteen were treated for scabies and five had wasted muscles that required physiotherapy. Betty Jeffrey was suffering from tuberculosis. After a month-long stay in hospital on a vastly improved, protein-enriched diet supplemented by vitamins, most of the nurses were back to normal weight. It was anticipated that the few who were still underweight would add the lost pounds during the three-week voyage to Australia.

Pat Gunther and Jess Doyle in hospital in Singapore

Sisters Simons, Hannah, Oram and Bullwinkel after 'fattening up'

On 5 October, after three weeks of innumerable medical tests, vaccinations, medical examinations and visits from the world press and VIPs, including Lord Louis Mountbatten and his wife, Edwina, Pat embarked on the hospital ship Manunda *for home. To Matron Sage's disappointment, new uniforms had not arrived in time, so she and her companions were dressed in clothing borrowed from the 2/14th sisters.*

Eddie Dunstan had done a fine job with his coverage in the Australian Women's Weekly, *and at every port the returning nurses were treated like film stars, showered with flowers and gifts, and cheered by crowds lining the streets. On reaching Sydney on 26 October, Pat and Pat Blake were taken to Yaralla, a magnificent estate on the shores of the Parramatta River at Concord. Built in 1886 as a Convalescent Hospital using bequests from Thomas Walker, a wealthy merchant and banker, and his daughter Eadith, Yaralla was taken over by the military in 1943 to become 3 Australian Women's Hospital. Here the two Pats were finally reunited with their families.*

After further medical checks, they were interviewed by the Principal Matron, who gave them three months' leave, adding that the sooner they got back to work, the better.

Pat Blake, who had sold her precious engagement ring to buy food for herself and Pat, spent the first part of her leave organising her wedding. She and her fiancé, Lieutenant Keith Dixon, were married in Sydney on 1 December that year. Less than two weeks later, Sylvia Muir also tied the knot.

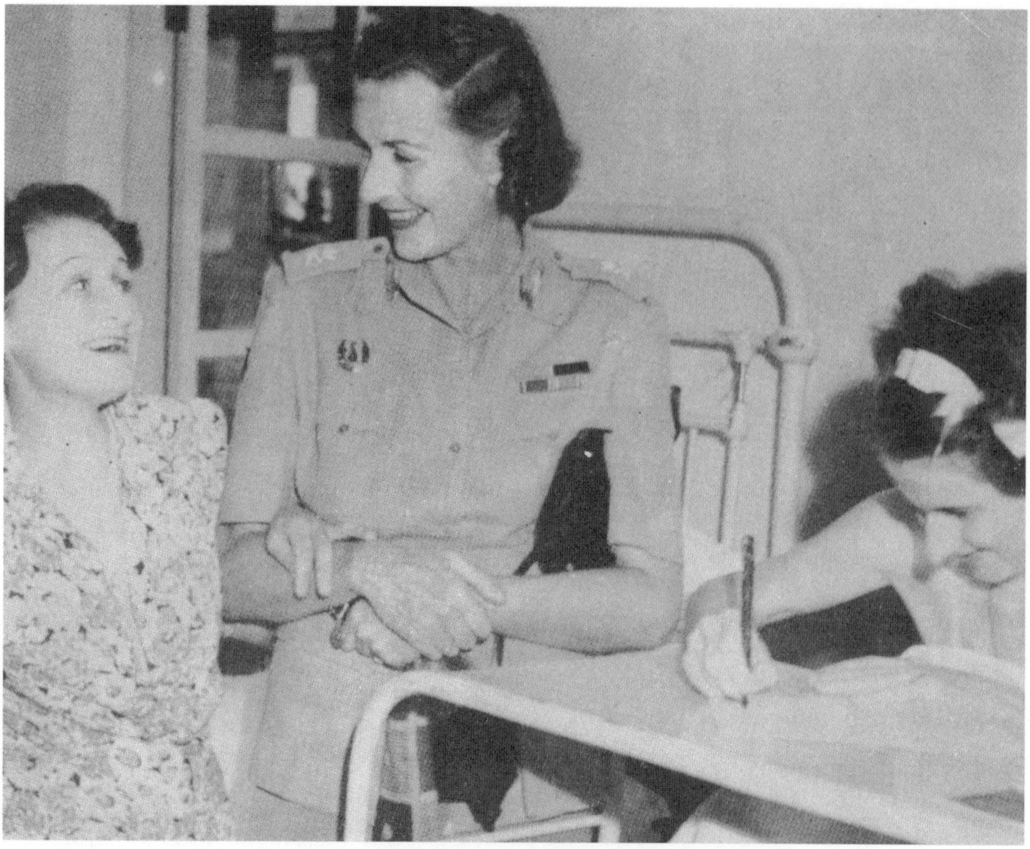

Above: Lady Moutbatten with Sisters James and Doyle. Below: *Women's Weekly* article, 6 October 1945

Nurses' terrible years in Sumatra prison camps

Cruel Jap guards are on their war criminals' list

Australian nurses, survivors of three and a half terrible years in Sumatra prison camps, were flown to Singapore for hospital treatment. The story they told of the sinking of the Vyner Brooke, the massacre of 21 nurses on the beach of Banka Island, the deaths of eight in camps is by now known to the world.

In Singapore, our correspondent, A. E. Dunstan, interviewed the girls who survived. They told him more of their struggle for existence with other women internees in the unspeakable Jap camps.

By A. E. DUNSTAN

Kept up spirits

Dazed by news

Jessie Blanch, Veronica Clancy, Cecelia Delforce, Jess Doyle, Jenny Greer, Mavis Hannah, Iole Harper, Nesta James, Sylvia Muir, Wilma Oram and Chris Oxley all married, most of them within a couple of years of returning home. Vivian Bullwinkel and Elizabeth Simons, who were late starters, married in the 1970s. In November 1947, Flo Trotter became Sister Mickey Syer's sister-in-law, when she married Mickey's brother.

Although the nurses belonged to a profession that they all loved and which offered them emotional security in the ordered and predictable routine of hospital life, they found it difficult to adjust to the normal world. Being prisoners of war with no material possessions had radically altered their outlook. They dismissed as trivial the things their mothers thought important, such as borrowing beds for unexpected visitors when there was a perfectly adequate floor, and washing clothes in the laundry, not the bath, in an effort to make full use of the water. They felt guilty about not eating everything served to them at meal times and throwing away items that were still serviceable. Some even hoarded food. They kept in constant contact with each other by letter and by phone, finding comfort and support from their tightly knit circle, as so many things had happened in the years of their imprisonment, and so many things had changed. They found it impossible to follow conversations that referred to events of the past three years, and it would be years before they caught up. As Elizabeth Simons so aptly put it: 'history passed us by'.

In late 1946, Vivian Bullwinkel, who had been posted to Heidelberg Military Hospital, was called to testify before the War Crimes' Tribunal in Tokyo. She delivered her account of the massacre faultlessly. Individual trials had not yet commenced, but before she left she learned that Captain Orita, the officer in charge of 1 Battalion of 229 Regiment, had been taken prisoner by the Russians and was in a Siberian prison camp.

In 1948 he was released by the Russians and returned to Japan, where he was promptly

Welcome home!

arrested by the Australians and transferred to Sugamo Prison in Tokyo. However, on 13 September that year, the night before he was due to be interrogated by war crimes investigators, Orita committed suicide by cutting his throat with a glass cutting tool that he had smuggled into his cell from the prison workshop. With his death, any chance of bringing to trial those responsible for the massacres was lost, as many of the troops on Bangka Island had been killed in fighting on the islands around New Guinea. In 1947, Captain Randal Watts had located 23 members of 229 Regiment in Rabaul, but only one, a sergeant major, had been on Bangka, and he had not left Muntok.

In February 1947, following her return to Heidelberg, Bullwinkel was a VIP guest at a ceremony in Adelaide to unveil a memorial to South Australian nurses. Here, she met another VIP – the feisty Elizabeth Mosey, the World War 1 and 2 nursing sister who had stood up to rampaging Japanese troops in Hong Kong.

The following month, Bullwinkel received the Royal Red Cross Medal, followed in May by the prestigious Nightingale Medal, also awarded to Matron Annie Sage and a Red Cross officer for their distinguished service. Bullwinkel graciously accepted hers on behalf of her courageous colleagues who had been 'left behind in other lands', paying particular tribute to Matrons Drummond and Paschke. Other honours followed. She was made a member of the British Empire (MBE) in 1963 and appointed to the Order of Australia (OA) in 1993.

Four months after receiving her Nightingale Medal, Bullwinkel resigned her commission as army captain to accept the position of Matron at Melbourne's Fairfield Infectious Diseases Hospital, a post she held for 16 years. In 1955 she joined the Citizen Military Forces (reservists), retiring in 1970 as Lieutenant Colonel of 3 Royal Australian Nursing Corps Training Unit, Southern Command.

After resigning as Matron in 1963, she remained at Fairfield as the Director of Nursing until 1977, when she married Colonel F W Statham and moved to Perth. On 2 March 1993 she was one of seven nurses to attend the dedication of a bronze plaque on Bangka Island, honouring those who had sailed on Vyner Brooke. *Twenty-four years later, in March 2017, another memorial was unveiled on Bangka Island in memory of all those who had died at sea or on the island.*

Vivian Bullwinkel died in Perth in July 2000, at the age of 84. Despite her high profile, it was not until 1999 that her biography was published. Unfortunately, although interviewed many times over the years, she did not ever put pen to paper herself.

Betty Jeffrey also maintained a high profile throughout her life. After spending the best part of two years in hospital recovering from tuberculosis, in December 1947 she and a group of nurses, including Bullwinkel, Jenny Ashton and Beryl Woodbridge, began raising money for a Victorian-based appeal to honour all Australian nurses who had lost their lives in World

War 2. They eventually raised more than £120,000, and in May 1949 the Nurses' Memorial Centre on St Kilda Road, Melbourne, was opened.

The following year Jeffrey and Bullwinkel left on an extended visit to London, where they were presented to King George VI, Princess Elizabeth and the dowager Queen Mary, who questioned them at length about their POW experiences. On her return, Jeffrey became the Centre's administrator, but continuing ill health forced her retirement in 1954.

In March that same year, Jeffrey's best-selling book, White Coolies, was released. This was followed in May by Elizabeth Simons's While History Passed (republished in 1985 as In Japanese Hands). However, excellent publicity and extracts from White Coolies that appeared in the press before the actual release date ensured that Jeffrey's book overshadowed that of Simons, which was very well written and told almost the same story.

More than 40 years later, the film, Paradise Road, some of which was very loosely based on Jeffrey's book, was released in 1999. The 1995 book about the vocal orchestra, Song of Survival Women Interned, by Helen Colijn, is not listed in the film's credits as being a source for this film, although Helen is thanked for her help. The highly fictionalised movie version of life in the Sumatran camps and the vocal orchestra, which claimed to be a 'true story', received a mixed reception. Historian Hank Nelson, who wrote a lengthy critique, was particularly scathing. When asked to comment, Pat dryly remarked that, had the film been a true portrayal, it would have been very boring.

Following the successful publication of her book, Betty Jeffrey did not return to nursing. Always a keen recreational golfer, she became a caddie to her friend, well-known operatic soprano and champion golfer Dame Joan Hammond. Jeffrey died in September 2000 at the age of 92.

The publicity in Australia that followed the safe arrival of the Sumatran nurses ensured that when Dr Goldberg unexpectedly surfaced in Perth in late 1945, the authorities took notice.

Not surprisingly, Anna Maria Goldberg-Curth survived the war and in November 1945 boarded a RAAF transport plane in Singapore for a flight to Australia. Stating that she was of German nationality and was born in Trebnitz, Austria, she registered as an alien pending acceptance of an application for permanent residency, based on her 'medical work' in Sumatra.

When word circulated that Dr Goldberg was in Australia and wanted to make it her home, the nurses were outraged. In February, Nesta James denounced her as a collaborator, resulting in an official inquiry, at which Sisters Hannah, Simons, Harper, Oram and Bullwinkel also testified. They made it clear that not only had she collaborated with the Japanese but she had failed in her duty as a doctor, lining her own pockets at the expense of the sick and destitute, whom she refused to treat.

Goldberg countered by producing statements from those who had benefited from their association with her. Although some involved in the inquiry wanted her to be investigated for war crimes, the statements were enough to forestall the execution of a deportation order. However, with her reputation in tatters, Goldberg came to the conclusion that she no longer wanted to remain in Australia. After being granted residency in the Dutch East Indies, she moved to Java, where she had applied successfully for a medical post, only to have her residency and job cancelled when the Dutch authorities made their own enquiries.

Her next port of call was Singapore, where her husband had been declared dead, allowing her access to his substantial estate. She then returned to Australia on a temporary visit in July 1947, armed with an emergency certificate issued in Singapore in place of a passport. On her registration form, she now declared that she was Polish and that her birthplace was Magdeburg in Germany.

In February 1948 Goldberg quit Australia for good, sailing for Singapore on Gorgon *and taking with her the crates of belongings that had been held in storage in Fremantle for her since 1942. A woman of independent means, she moved into the upmarket Goodwood Park Hotel on Scott's Road, and filled in some of her time as a voluntary doctor at St Andrew's Mission Hospital.*

Surrounded by 6 acres of parkland, her new and luxurious home had started out life as The German Club in 1900 but, when World War 1 broke out, the property was seized by the Custodian of Enemy Property. It was purchased in 1918 by three Jewish brothers whose family still owned it at the time of Goldberg's occupancy.

In October 1952 she applied for residency in Singapore and within two months had gained it, along with a title and a husband, when she married Sir Charles Murray-Aynsley, a widower and Chief Justice of Singapore. The pair lived in Singapore until Sir Charles's retirement three years later. He died in Florence, Italy, in 1974 at the age of 74. Dr Goldberg-Curth, now Lady Annemaria Eleanor Murray-Aynsley, the ultimate survivor, outlived him by 23 years. She died at Chobham, Surrey, on 13 April 1997, aged 90.

Not all of Pat's medical colleagues survived their imprisonment. Shortly after becoming a POW, Dr Roderick Lionel Jeffrey, who had worked beside her at Manor House in the last desperate days before Singapore's fall, was transferred to Sandakan, in British North Borneo. In October 1943, when most of the officers were transferred to a camp in Kuching, Sarawak, Rod was one of only three Australian doctors to remain behind at Sandakan to look after the men.

In February 1945 he was placed on a draft of 455 POWs to march 250 kilometres through the jungle-covered mountainous interior to Ranau. Anyone who could not keep up was shot. Rod survived the ordeal and subsequent appalling conditions at Ranau, but became overwhelmed by the circumstances of his captivity, refusing to treat his fellow prisoners. He died from illness on 6 May 1945. Only six of the more than a thousand POWs who marched into the interior survived the war. The 1,400 prisoners who remained at Sandakan all died, making it Australia's worst atrocity of World War 2. Throughout the years of Rod's captivity, his fiancée, Claire Westbury, never gave up hope that he would return.

After being released in late 1945 from the Women's Hospital at Concord, Pat returned to her hometown of Casino, which turned on a grand civic welcome with flowers and a speech by the Mayor, followed by morning tea. Her leave over, she returned to Sydney where she was posted to 113 AGH, also known as Yaralla, which also formed part of the Walker estate and was just a short distance away from the Women's Hospital. After spending a most rewarding year in charge of a surgical ward caring for returned servicemen and women, Pat resigned her commission in February 1947.

That same year Pat, Jean Ashton, Jess Doyle, Flo Trotter and Elizabeth Simons were awarded a Mention in Despatches (MID) by the army in recognition of their work in the camps while prisoners of war.

Some Japanese responsible for various crimes against the women internees were brought to trial by Dutch authorities at Medan in Sumatra, but neither the proceedings nor the sentences were published in the press. Based on the sworn statements of Sisters James and Bullwinkel, Dr Smith, and two civilian women, Mrs F Briggs and Mrs D Frompton, the court sentenced three of the culprits, Captain Seki Kazuo, Sergeant Tarutani Mitsuji and Corporal Shigemura Takeshi to 15, 5 and 6 years' gaol respectively.

Despite concerted efforts by investigation teams, tracking down those responsible for the Radji Beach massacre proved far more difficult, as 229 Regiment had suffered heavy losses. There was insufficient evidence to bring to trial any of the survivors of 1 and 2 Battalions eventually rounded up and, as Orita committed suicide before he could be interrogated, no Japanese ever stood trial for the massacres.

In the meantime, Pat and her colleagues got on with life. After leaving the Army, Pat spent the next two years studying obstetrics at Crown Street Women's Hospital, Sydney. With her midwifery certificate under her belt, she was able to realise her long-held dream of travelling to England, her 'spiritual home', where she worked for a couple of years. In November 1952 she returned to Sydney to take up a post with the New South Wales Department of Public Health, in its tuberculosis unit. Five years later, at the age of 44, Pat married widower Colin Darling and set up home at Mt Keira near Wollongong, on the New South Wales south coast. Over the next few years, the Darlings, who were keen gardeners and founding members of the Illawarra Garden Festival, established a magnificent garden, which they opened to the public each year.

Pat never forgot the nursing sisters who had lost their lives. Like many others, she suffered from survivor guilt, and the death of her friend Kath Neuss, who had taken Pat's seat in the lifeboat, haunted her all her life. In 1993, when she visited the Australian War Memorial to place a red poppy beside Kath's name, she told a reporter, 'I gave her my tin hat, telling her she might need it to bail water, and I swam away. I sent her to her death.'

After Colin Darling's death in 1983, Pat moved to Manor House, the retirement village at Mosman where she spoke to me about her wartime experiences, enjoying the final years of her life pottering in the garden and jotting down her memories.

But not all of them.

She died in 2007 at the age of 94, never revealing the biggest secret of all.

EPILOGUE

Unravelling The Secret

Whenever I talked to Pat Gunther or her fellow nurses, it was the elephant in the room. It was the topic no outsider wanted to raise – until the early 1990s, when two Japanese academics, who had examined documents released by the Japanese government as well as archival material in Australia and Holland, asked the questions that no one had dared to ask – at least not publicly. Had any of the nurses who were captured by the Japanese on Bangka Island been raped or forced to work as comfort women?

Yoshimi Yoshiaki was the first to float the possibility that the nurses were forced to become comfort women and in 1992 went to print with Jugun Ianfu Shiryoshu (Documents on Military Comfort Women).

When interviewed by reporters from the Australian *and the* Age *newspapers in December 1992 and January 1993, the surviving AANS members denied any sexual involvement with their Japanese guards. Given their denials, a statement that suggested otherwise took me by surprise when, in 1994, I was sent a copy of the diary of Charles Stewart Johnstone, the Australian flight lieutenant who had thrown a bucket of water over the burning bomb victim on* Empire Star.

In 1940 Charlie, as he was known, had volunteered for service in the Far East with the RAF in order to release British pilots to fight closer to home. He sailed for Singapore on Zealander *in May 1941, along with various troops and additional nursing sisters bound for 2/10 AGH in Malacca. When RAF personnel were ordered to evacuate to Java in February 1942, Charlie had boarded* Empire Star *where he again came into contact with members of 2/10 AGH. At Batavia they had parted company – the nurses to continue to Australia and Charlie to take up battle stations in Java, where he was captured a few weeks later.*

He spent the rest of the war in POW camps in Borneo, firstly at Sandakan and then in Kuching. Throughout his imprisonment, he kept a record of events which, in 1983, he consolidated into a typescript covering 45 foolscap pages. He stated that 'everything written here is true in every respect, most incidents indelibly engraved on my memory and supported by notes written on thin airmail paper, which has disintegrated somewhat, and also in a small diary and inside playing cards, which were carefully split and stuck back again with latex.'

After his recovery from Kuching, Charlie received medical treatment at 2/6 AGH on Labuan Island. On 28 September he was discharged and sailed on the hospital ship Manunda *for Singapore where he thought he would have a better chance of speedy repatriation to Australia. The ship docked in Singapore on 1 October.*

On page 43 of his diary Charlie recorded:

> On the 1st October we anchored in the roads at Singapore and the matron and two senior medical officers went ashore. We saw them come aboard a few hours later with matron weeping. One of the colonels told us they had gone ashore to see a number of Australian nurses recovered from POW camps up-country. They were in a shocking state physically and mentally. All had VD [venereal or sexually transmitted disease] and some had children.

When the nurses sailed for Australia on Manunda *three days later, Charlie was not on board and therefore did not see them. As he had joined the RAF, he had to travel to the UK for discharge.*

My reaction on reading such a definitive statement in Charlie's diary was one of shock. Could there be any truth in it? Or was it complete fiction? However, the latter seemed unlikely as it was hardly something Charlie would invent and I had not come across any inaccuracies in the rest of his diary, which at times is very detailed.

Apart from the denials from the surviving nurses issued in 1992–93 following Yoshini's revelations, the only reference to sexual interference by the Japanese was in the form of an official denial, made almost 50 years before. It was contained in a signal sent in September 1945 by the Commander of 2 Australian Prisoner of War Reception Group in Singapore to the Adjutant General in Canberra.

> For peace of mind of relatives of 24 sisters recovered and now in 2/14 AGH all well cared for are happy and making good progress. None were molested by the Japanese. This information supplied by Matron in Chief who returned with them from Sumatra and assures me of this fact. Recommend that relatives be informed.

I had always assumed that the very definitive statement referring to molestation had been included in the message to allay any fears that the nurses had been subjected to this kind of treatment, which had occurred in other areas and had been reported in the press.

The first reports were in September 1942 when an Australian newspaper revealed that Dutch nurses had been raped at Tarakan in Borneo, and in June 1943 that British nurses had been 'attacked' in Hong Kong. The precise nature of the attack did not become clear until February 1944, when internees repatriated to South Africa reported nurses in Hong Kong had been raped and that white women had been forced into brothels.

However, it was not until 12 September 1945, four days before the Sumatra nurses were rescued, that other instances of rape were reported – this time by an Australian woman missionary rescued from a village near Kowloon, Hong Kong. Within days, other internees in Hong Kong were released, and what had happened to the nurses there became only too clear, giving rise to headlines such as 'Hong Kong Horror. No Penalty Too Severe for Japs'.

Until Johnstone's diary surfaced, the motive for stating that the Sumatra nurses had not been molested seemed cut and dried: to put the minds of family and friends at rest. However, was there now a possibility that it had been included to forestall any suggestion that they **had** *been molested?*

On the one hand, there was a second-hand statement attributed to Matron Annie Sage allegedly stating that the nurses had not been molested, and on the other a second-hand statement attributed to the weeping Matron of the hospital ship Manunda *that they obviously had, as they were suffering from VD.*

Information exists relating to the causes of death of the nurses who died in captivity in Sumatra. However, it does not appear that there are any individual reports available on the medical condition of the nurses recovered, although there is a generalised 'Medical Points of Interest' in regard to various diseases suffered during their internment. In any case, even if individual reports had been compiled, the official denial that anyone had been molested would preclude any mention of sexually transmitted diseases being recorded.

A report by Major Harry Windsor, Officer Commanding the Surgical Division of 2/14 AGH, covering the period 12 September to 20 October 1945, sheds no light on the matter other than to state that a total of 111 POWs (gender not stated) were admitted to hospital suffering from VD. The majority (106) had gonorrhoea and responded to treatment.

The irreconcilable statements attributed to the two matrons is a worry, as is the inclusion of the word 'Australian' in Charlie Johnstone's diary, especially as Charlie had an association with the AANS that went back to 1941. However, is it possible that British nurses liberated from other camps may have brought orphaned Eurasian children with them? Or did Charlie mean that the nurses seen by the Australian officers had borne children? And if the nurses were not Australian, why were senior Australian medical staff visiting them?

It has proved impossible for me to obtain clarification of any of these questions as Charlie Johnstone died in July 1994, shortly after I received his diary. Interestingly, in a version published in 1995 entitled To Sandakan: the diaries of Charlie Johnstone, Prisoner of War 1942–45, *the entire statement relating to the nurses was purged by the editor, Christopher*

Dawson. However, if it was done to avoid awkward questions being asked, it was a useless gesture. That same year, the possible sexual exploitation of the Sumatra nurses arose again when Yoshimi published Comfort Women. *Given the opinions expressed by him and, as a copy of Johnstone's original typescript is easily accessible at the Australian War Memorial in Canberra, perhaps this matter warrants further investigation to determine if there is any truth at all in Johnstone's statement.*

Notwithstanding the nurses' denials, it is interesting that not one of them referred to the attempted rape of one of their group by Moonface in any affidavit, post-war debriefing, interview, autobiography or biography. The dramatic scene at Loeboek Linggau Camp, when Sergeant Gillam wanted to shoot Moonface, is not recorded anywhere, by any of them. The sole account is that of Major Gideon Jacobs, who heard the ruckus and difused the situation on the basis that the Japanese would face justice for their actions. Does the failure of the nurses to ever allude to this incident indicate that they had agreed to never mention any incident of this nature to anyone? Was this one of the secrets they had vowed never to reveal? If so, what else might they be hiding? Was there any chance that the nursing sisters on Radji Beach had been raped before being murdered?

As the troops involved in the massacre were from the same battalion that had raped and killed the nurses in Hong Kong, this was also a question that many had wondered about but were too reticent to voice. However, Yoshini's fellow academic, Yuki Tanaka, raised it in 1993 in a paper delivered in September that year to an international conference on Japan, held at the Australian National University in Canberra.

The Canberra Times *reported:*

> Yuki Tanaka, now teaching at Melbourne University, says evidence suggests that Sister Bullwinkel 'did not tell the truth at the investigation in order to save her dead colleagues from the disgrace as being known as victims of rape' ... Mr Tanaka says it is significant that the bodies of bayoneted British soldiers were left on the beach, but that the Japanese had made sure that the evidence of the women's bodies would not be left behind.

He repeated his claim to a much wider audience in 1996 in his book Hidden Horrors: Japanese war crimes in World War II, *in a chapter entitled 'Rape and War: The Japanese Experience'.*

Although Tanaka concluded that it was unlikely that the nurses had volunteered to work as comfort women, he again put forward the suggestion that the nurses on Radji Beach may have been raped. Not only were the perpetrators members of the same group that had raped and murdered the nurses in Hong Kong, but they were under the command of the same officer, Captain Orita Masaru – a person Tanaka identified only by his initials, in order to protect the officer's identity! As Tanaka pointed out, no attempt had been made to dispose of the men's corpses, so why had the killers covered up the massacre of the women by making them walk into the sea?

However, there was a further and very deliberate attempt by the Japanese to eliminate all evidence of their crime – one that Tanaka did not mention.

After Vivian Bullwinkel was shot, she had retreated to the safety of the jungle where she lay unconscious or semi-conscious for a considerable time – a couple of days she thought. When she awoke, she saw a contingent of Japanese soldiers moving past her towards the beach. Some time later, when she ventured down to the beach to see if there might be some emergency rations left in the lifeboats, she found no trace, at all, of any of the bodies. This included the stretcher patients who had been murdered away from the water and those who had tried to escape. The only conclusion that can be drawn from her observations is that the corpses remaining on the beach were disposed of by the Japanese on an outgoing tide. As Bullwinkel did not report seeing any digging implements, and as she said that the soldiers were only on the beach for a short time, it does not seem likely that the corpses were buried in the sand.

Tanaka, at the time of writing his book, was evidently not aware that there were various male eyewitnesses, who had gone to Radji Beach shortly after the nurses were killed and had made statements. One of them, Stoker Lloyd, had reported:

> When I came to it was dark; my head and shoulder throbbed and it was raining. The next day I started to look for food and luckily found some coconuts and a fresh water stream. I lay like this for a few days and then thought I ought to walk back along the beach to see if any of the others had survived. It was quite horrible. All the male bodies had been piled on top of one another in one big heap. Then I went further along and found the bodies of the Australian nurses and other women. **They lay at intervals of a few yards – in different positions and in various stages of undress**. They had been shot and then bayoneted. It was shocking.

This supports the statement by William Wilding, who had seen 10 female bodies on the beach, some scantily dressed in civilian clothing, some in nurses' uniforms and some naked.

Two years after the publication of Tanaka's book, a New Zealander, James MacKay, released Betrayal in High Places, *which chronicled the work of Captain James Gowing Godwin, a tenacious war crimes investigator attached to 2 Australian War Crimes Section (2 AWCS) in Tokyo. He was there from 1947 until 1950, when investigations ceased.*

On returning home to New Zealand, Godwin took with him copies of many of the war crimes he had worked on, along with non-official reports summarising various cases. On the unofficial reports, he had also recorded the frustrations experienced in tracking down suspects and the demands by the United States that Australia put an end to its investigations, in the name of political expediency.

Supplemented by an 18-page typed account of his time as a prisoner of war, and a handwritten diary he had kept in an old exercise book, Godwin had intended to use this material to write a book. The documents brought from Tokyo were stored for years in a tea-chest at his mother's house in New Zealand, where rising damp from a concrete floor affected a substantial number of papers at the bottom and middle of the pile.

Between 1961 and 1965, Godwin and his Asian wife Sally, whom he met in Kuala Lumpur, visited Tokyo three times. Sally, who knew very little about his time in Japan, was surprised at the level of his conversational Japanese, although he was not by any means fluent.

The couple settled down in Sydney. In 1975, three years after the death of Godwin's mother, they received a visit from his sister, Moyra, who brought with her a large pile of papers that had been stored in the tea-chest. To make sure that they were not subjected to further damp, Godwin later put them in cardboard folders, tied them together into a bundle with cotton tape and stored them, along with his POW account and the exercise book containing his diary, in a cupboard above the oven of his Sydney apartment.

Godwin did not speak to his wife about his wartime experiences, except in passing, and told her not to read the contents of the bundle, which contained distressing accounts of atrocities. However, she had a cursory look and was aware that it contained office folders full of reports from his time in Tokyo, typed on thin foolscap paper, and his handwritten diary in an old, grey-covered exercise book of about 100 pages or so.

Despite his good intentions, Godwin did not ever write his book. After suffering a stroke, he developed dementia in 1989 and died in May 1995 at the age of 72. However, before he became incapacitated, he sorted through his bundle and sent carbon copies of various wartime reports, including some of those affected by damp, to Doris Heath, one of the clerks who had typed them. Following her death in 1990, Beverley Durrant (formerly Floyd), a clerk who had worked at 2 AWCS for about 12 months in 1948–49, lodged them with Australian National Archives in Canberra. The documents are no longer issued to researchers, due to the fragile state of the damp-affected pages, but photocopies are available.

In June 1995, Godwin's sister arrived back in Sydney to attend his funeral. When she was returning home, she took with her the bundle of documents, including the exercise book. She gave them to writer James MacKay, who was collating material on wartime atrocities.

Some of the paperwork was in excellent condition, but many of the damp-affected sheets, especially the 'unofficial' reports, were in a poor state, with some literally crumbling to pieces. In order to preserve the contents, MacKay laboriously typed copies on a manual typewriter. Unfortunately, he later passed these off as photocopies of 'original' documents, a claim that would later cast doubt on their authenticity.

The contents of the bundle confirmed that Godwin had investigated a large number of war crimes. One, designated as File 152, involved the murders of Mr Bowden and the Australian nurses. When Godwin arrived in Tokyo, the investigation of these two crimes had been in abeyance for some time because of a lack of leads, but in November 1949 he reactivated the file and called for various Japanese to present themselves to 2 AWCS for questioning.

On 28 November, Godwin's offsider, Sergeant Arthur H Weston, interrogated Hikosaka Tadeo. He was not able to contribute any pertinent information himself, but mentioned the name of someone who might be able to help – Leading Private Tanemura Kiyoshi (also listed elsewhere as Hiyoshi), a runner with 2 Platoon in 2 Company of Orita's 1 Battalion. Interrogated that same day, Tanemura identified the officer in charge of the group that had murdered the nurses and other POWs as Lieutenant Kohiyama, whose name had appeared on the list of suspects during investigations carried out in Rabaul in 1947 by Captain Randal Watts. Kohiyama had been listed by Watts as possibly 'missing', but Tanemura confirmed that he had been killed in action in the Admiralty Islands in early 1944.

Despite Tanemura's assertion that Kohiyama was dead, the investigation continued. Godwin, who believed that Tanemura was being very evasive, recalled him for questioning six weeks later on 13 January 1950. Godwin noted in his weekly report that the results of the interrogation would be reported in Sergeant Weston's weekly report. However, although Weston alluded to Tanemura's interrogation in general terms, he noted that a 'copy of his report appears in File 152'. It doesn't. There is no trace of Weston's report or the file, because all investigation files that did not result in a trial were destroyed in 1951, when 2 AWCS closed down. As the investigation into the murders of Mr Bowden and the nurses did not lead to a prosecution, File 152 was culled.

However, when MacKay's book was published, it included an 'unofficial' account of Tanemura's interrogation, conducted by Godwin and typed by a clerk named Barbara Elizabeth Jupp, whose initials appeared at the head of the report as part of the identification process. Under closer questioning, Tanemura had revealed that he had been with a group of soldiers who had rounded up some men and a number of Australian nurses on Bangka Island. Tanemura, who had not fully recovered from a malaria attack, claimed that he had obtained permission from Sergeant Furakawa (believed to be Sergeant Fukagawa Shintaro) to rest in the shade of some trees. As he lay there, he heard screams and was told that some officers and NCOs were 'pleasuring themselves' (raping) the nurses and that it would soon be the platoon's turn. Claiming that he took no part in the proceedings, he went on to say that he had heard that the nurses were herded down to the beach and ostensibly forced to bathe, whereupon a machine-gun had opened fire.

This account tallies with that of Corporal Robert Seddon, who heard screams as he floated offshore, but there is one detail mentioned by Tanemura that seems to be rather odd – his assertion that the 'pleasuring' took place in the houses of a nearby village. As the nearest village, Mendjelang, was about 4 kilometres away, it has been suggested that this account, if true, could refer to another group of men and nurses. However, it is common in South East Asia for villagers to cultivate fruit and other crops on land a considerable distance from their village. This certainly appears to have been the case at Radji. Eric Germann reported that some of the castaways at Radji had gathered coconuts and pineapples growing nearby, and a villager, interviewed in 2018, stated that there were huts near the beach, used by village people when tending their gardens.

In 1999, two or three years after I read Tanemura's account in MacKay's book, I was guest speaker at a dinner held at a Sydney RSL Sub-Branch. As my topic was about war crimes committed against POWs in Borneo, my host had seated me next to an ex-serviceman who had worked on war crimes investigations. To my astonishment, he was Arthur Weston from 2 AWCS. He in turn was astounded to discover that my most recent research work focused on the massacre of 110 wounded Australians at Parit Sulong in Malaya – one of the cases he had worked on with Godwin. In fact, Arthur had attended the trial of General Nishimura, who had given the order to kill the prisoners – a crime that resulted in his execution at Manus Island in June 1951.

As I was conversant with many of Weston's investigations and knew the names of most of those with whom he had worked, we had plenty to talk about. During the course of the evening, the conversation turned towards James MacKay's book. Although the author was not as exacting as he should have been when it came to fine detail, and had included imagined conversations in his narrative, making some parts of his book factionalised rather than fact, Weston endorsed it as pretty accurate on the whole.

He certainly did not dispute Godwin's report of Tanemura's interrogation or, indeed, any other of Godwin's 'unofficial' reports. In order to try and draw him out, I remarked that it was a pity that the massacre of the nurses on Bangka Island had never gone to trial. However, unlike other cases we had discussed, Arthur Weston refused to be drawn on this one, other than to remark, 'There are some things about that case that I had to keep secret and cannot talk about'. I did not press him further.

Although Weston had no argument with MacKay's book, others have cast doubt over the veracity of some of the reports – a claim that was strengthened by the fact that MacKay tried to pass off material he had retyped as 'authentic' photocopies and had made exaggerated claims about his connections to various prominent people.

It was also alleged that MacKay had fabricated a report of a massacre on Sado Island where, on 2 August 1945, more than 300 POWs supposedly had been entombed in a mine – a story, it was claimed, that could not possibly be true. However, in 2003 Sterling and Peggy Seagrave published Golden Warriors, *in which they stated that thousands of slave labourers, after stashing away Japanese gold bullion in booby-trapped mines and caves, were entombed as Allied forces approached, and that 1,000 Korean labourers in a Mitusbishi owned gold mine on Sado Island had 'disappeared' – a fact that only came to light in 1991, when Mitsubishi company records relating to wartime cigarette rations were released.*

The possibility that the POW entombment story may have been a hoax perpetrated by the Japanese 'informant' was evidently not considered, although it had similarities with a massacre at Loa Kula in Indonesian Borneo on 30 July 1945, when Japanese troops beheaded 144 men, cut their wives to pieces and hurled their children 180 metres into a mine shaft.

At first Godwin was accused of falsifying the Sado Island report, and then MacKay, despite the fact that such a deception based on the 'facts' as presented could not possibly be sustained. Furthermore, MacKay, who evidently believed that this atrocity had occurred, had written to the then president of the New South Wales RSL, Mr Rusty Priest, asking for his assistance in building a memorial to honour those who had been entombed.

It was further claimed that the file cited for this investigation, 125M, was also a fabrication, as there was no trace of it in Australian Archives. However, because it was not archived, it does not mean that such a file did not exist. Thousands of war crimes were reported at the end of the war, generating thousands of files. The numbering for the 125 series went from 125A to 125Z. When 2 AWCS closed down, all cases or investigations in the 125 series that had not gone to trial (about 75 per cent) were culled.

As further proof that MacKay fabricated evidence, it has been claimed that two majors mentioned in Godwin's unofficial reports were figments of James MacKay's imagination. However, a brief search of war crimes files shows that one major was a highly regarded legal officer attached to 2 AWCS until 1951 and that the name of the other, who left the army in 1948 shortly after Godwin arrived in Tokyo, had evidently been mistyped or misinterpreted. By whom, it is not possible to say. James MacKay made numerous transcription errors, especially when dealing with the water-damaged pages, and it is not uncommon to find that clerks at 2 AWCS also made mistakes, which makes tracing Japanese (and even Allied personnel) 'named' in some documents difficult.

After the allegations were made against MacKay, who died from cancer in May 2004, his family sent me a large parcel of documents, including a number of pages from his original typescript – material that had not been included in his book. The details in the unpublished and retyped 'unofficial' reports I received tally with details appearing in the official reports, and include names that could only be known to someone involved in a particular investigation. There is no reason, therefore, to believe that the unofficial consolidated reports are forgeries, especially since details included in some of them can only be discovered after days of trawling through investigation files. As MacKay published his book a scant 12 months after taking custody of Godwin's material, it is simply inconceivable that he came to Australia, spent weeks locating and combing hundreds of files in order to extract obscure facts, and then had time to incorporate them into fabricated reports. Australian Archives staff in Melbourne, where files relating to war crimes' trials occupy many metres of shelving, confirmed that no one by the name of MacKay had sought access to any files during that 12-month period.

It was at this point that I decided to undertake further research into the work undertaken by 2 AWCS. I sifted through every war crime that Godwin and his colleagues had investigated. In the course of this research, I discovered that the papers of Major Harold Stannett Williams, who had spent a considerable amount of time in Japan pre-war, spoke fluent Japanese, investigated war crimes at 2 AWCS and had been an adviser on Japanese affairs, were held in the National Library in Canberra. Among the many items in the collection was a 10-page typed account by his wife Jean of her husband's background and work.

Of the many appalling crimes with which her husband had been confronted, she was particularly proud of two that he had investigated. The first was the massacre of the nurses at Bangka Island, who had been walked into the sea and machine-gunned. The second concerned the cannibalisation of two American and three Australian airmen. After capture in New Guinea, they had been forcibly tied down on mess tables, vivisectioned and their livers removed. Two were cut up for the officers' evening meal. The other three were dried over a fire and two were sent to the doctor's parents in Japan to be used as special medicine.

In due course, the doctor who had dissected the airmen while alive and the sergeant who had tied them to the mess table were located. Williams, who was investigating the case, went to the home of the doctor's parents where he recovered a hard, dark substance with grate marks on it. It was identified as the liver of a Caucasian. Despite efforts by the doctor's colleagues to bribe Williams, who was offered a huge amount of money, justice prevailed and the doctor was executed. The sergeant received eight years' imprisonment. Mrs Williams added that her husband never ate liver again.

I had read many shocking war crimes files during my years of research, including those that involved cannibalism and vivisectioning, but never one quite as repulsive as this. Of the many stomach-churning crimes that her husband had investigated, I wondered why Mrs Williams had identified the Bangka Island massacre as being on a par with the story of the airmen. The story of the nurses was tragic, but there were far worse atrocities that had taken place during the war, and which he had investigated. Unlike the wounded killed at Parit Sulong, who had been machine-gunned, doused in petrol and set on fire while still alive, the deaths of the nurses had been quick. I turned back a page and re-read the account. It was, like the rest of the document, typed on loose-leaf paper, and it was only now that I realised that the narrative on the nurses stopped short in mid-sentence at the bottom of the page. There was nothing more on the next page. I then realised that this particular page was much shorter than the others. Mrs William's narrative had continued overleaf, but someone had crudely hacked off the top 5 centimetres with a pair of scissors.

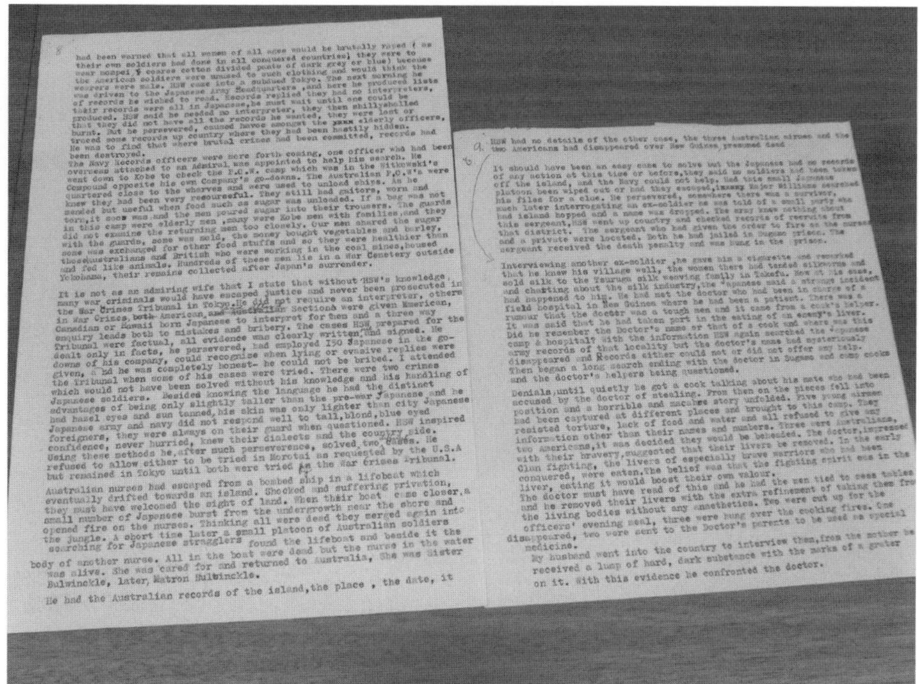

8

had been warned that all women of all ages would be brutally raped (as their own soldiers had done in all conquered countries) they were to wear mompei & coarse cotton divided pants of dark grey or blue) because the American soldiers were unused to such clothing and would think the wearers were male. HSW came into a subdued Tokyo. The next morning he was driven to the Japanese Army Headquarters ,and here he produced lists of records he wished to read. Records replied they had no interpreters, their records were all in Japanese,he must wait until one could be produced. HSW said he needed no interpreter, they then shillyshallied that they did not have all the records he wanted, they were lost or burnt. But he persevered, caused havoc amongst the elderly officers, traced some records up country where they had been hastily hidden. He was to find that where brutal crimes had been committed, records had been destroyed.
The Navy Records officers were more forth coming, one officer who had been overseas attached to an Admiral was appointed to help his search. He went down to Kobe to check the P.O.W. camp which was in the Nitkowski's Compound opposite his own Company's go-downs. The Australian P.O.W's were quartered close to the wharves and were used to unload ships. As he knew they had been very resourceful. They still had gaitors, worn and mended but useful when food such as sugar was unloaded. If a bag was not torn,it soon was and the men poured sugar into their trousers. The guards in this camp were elderly men ,many were Kobe men with families,and they did not examine the returning men too closely. Our men shared the sugar with the guards, some was sold, the money bought vegetables and barley, some was exchanged for other food stuffs and so they were healthier than those Australians and British who were working in the coal mines,housed and fed like animals. Hundreds of these men lie in a War Cemetery outside Yokohama, their remains collected after Japan's surrender.

It is not as an admiring wife that I state that without HSW's knowledge, many war criminals would have escaped justice and never been prosecuted in the War Crimes Tribunal in Tokyo.He did not require an interpreter, others in War Crimes, both American and Australian Sections were given American, Canadian or Hawaii born Japanese to interpret for them and a three way enquiry leads both to mistakes and bribery. The cases HSW prepared for the Tribunal were factual, all evidence was clearly written and signed. He dealt only in facts, he persevered, had employed 150 Japanese in the go-downs of his company, could recognise when lying or evasive replies were given, and he was completely honest- he could not be bribed. I attended the Tribunal when some of his cases were tried. There were two crimes which would not have been solved without his knowledge and his handling of Japanese soldiers. Besides knowing the language he had the distinct advantages of being only slightly taller than the pre-war Japanese and he had hazel eyes and sun tanned,his skin was only lighter than city Japanese Japanese army and navy did not respond well to tall,blond,blue eyed foreigners, they were always on their guard when questioned. HSW inspired confidence, never hurried, knew their dialects and the country side. Using these methods he,after much perseverence, solved two cases. He refused to allow either to be tried in Morotai as requested by the U.S.A but remained in Tokyo until both were tried at the War Crimes Tribunal.
Australian nurses had escaped from a bombed ship in a lifeboat which eventually drifted towards an island. Shocked and suffering privation, they must have welcomed the sight of land. When their boat came closer,a small number of Japanese burst from the undergrowth near the shore and opened fire on the nurses. Thinking all were dead they merged again into the jungle. A short time later a small platoon of Australian soldiers searching for Japanese stragglers found the lifeboat and beside it the body of another nurse. All in the boat were dead but the nurse in the water was alive. She was cared for and returned to Australia, She was Sister Bulwinckle, later, Matron Bulwinckle.
He had the Australian records of the island,the place , the date, it

9

HSW had no details of the other case, the three Australian airmen and the two Americans had disappeared over New Guinea,presumed dead

It should have been an easy case to solve but the Japanese had no records of any action at this time or before,they said no soldiers had been taken off the island, and the Navy could not help. Had this small Japanese platoon been wiped out or had they escaped, Major Williams searched his files for a clue. He persevered, somewhere there was a survivor, much later interrogating an ex-soldier he was told of a small party who had island hopped and a name was dropped. The army knew nothing about this sergeant,HSW went up country and checked records of recruits from that district. The sergeant who had given the order to fire on the nurses and a private were located. Both he had jailed in Sugamo prison. The sergeant received the death penalty and was hung in the prison.

Interviewing another ex-soldier ,he gave him a cigarette and remarked that he knew his village well, the women there had tended silkworms and sold silk to the Tsurugu silk weaving family in Takefu. Now at his ease, and chatting about the silk industry,the Japanese said a strange incident had happened to him. He had met the doctor who had been in charge of a field hospital in New Guinea where he had been a patient. There was a rumour that the doctor was a tough man and it came from a cook's helper. It was said that he had taken part in the eating of an enemy's liver. Did he remember the Doctor's name or that of a cook and where was this camp & hospital? With the information HSW again searched the Japanese army records of that locality but the doctor's name had mysteriously disappeared and Records either could not or did not offer any help. Then began a long search ending with the doctor in Sugamo and camp cooks and the doctor's helpers being questioned.
Denials,until quietly he got a cook talking about his mate who had been accused by the doctor of stealing. From then on the pieces fell into position and a horrible and macabre story unfolded. Five young airmen had been captured at different places and brought to this camp. They resisted torture, lack of food and water and all refused to give any information other than their names and numbers. Three were Australians, two Americans,it was decided they would be beheaded. The doctor,impressed with their bravery,suggested that their livers be removed. In the early Clan fighting, the livers of especially brave warriors who had been conquered, were eaten.The belief was that the fighting spirit was in the liver, eating it would boost their own valour.
The doctor must have read of this and he had the men tied to mess tables and he removed their livers with the extra refinement of taking them from the living bodies without any anesthetics. Two were cut up for the officers' evening meal, three were hung over the cooking fires. One disappeared, two were sent to the Doctor's parents to be used as special medicine.
My husband went into the country to interview them,from the mother he received a lump of hard, dark substance with the marks of a grater on it. With this evidence he confronted the doctor.

Pages 8 and 9 of Mrs Williams' account, showing where the top of page 8 has been crudely cut off

Enquiries made of the library staff could not shed any light on when this was done or who may have done it. It was not possible to determine if the page was tampered with before it was deposited in the library or after. However, it was evident that whatever else Mrs Williams had written about the nurses had been removed by someone determined that no one else should see it.

As I harboured strong suspicions about the content of the excised portion of Mrs Williams' account, I maintained more than a passing interest in the Bangka Island story. On one of my frequent visits to the research centre at the Australian War Memorial, I stopped off at the World War 2 gallery and looked closely, for the first time, at the uniform Vivian Bullwinkel had been wearing when she was shot.

Bullwinkel's short-sleeved, pale grey uniform is a button-through, waisted, shirt-maker style. It had seven buttons – two above the waist and five below – with a press-stud at the waistline, which is covered by a wide fabric belt. Buttons 6 and 7, at the hemline, are missing.

Bullwinkel stated several times that the bullet had passed straight through the flesh just above her hip, a fact endorsed by both Wilma Oram and Pat Gunther. The hole in her uniform – made by the bullet as it entered her back, just above the waistline – is small but clearly visible, and is where I expected it to be. The exit hole, however, is not. It is not on the left side, but almost in the centre of the bodice. This did not make sense to me, as the injury

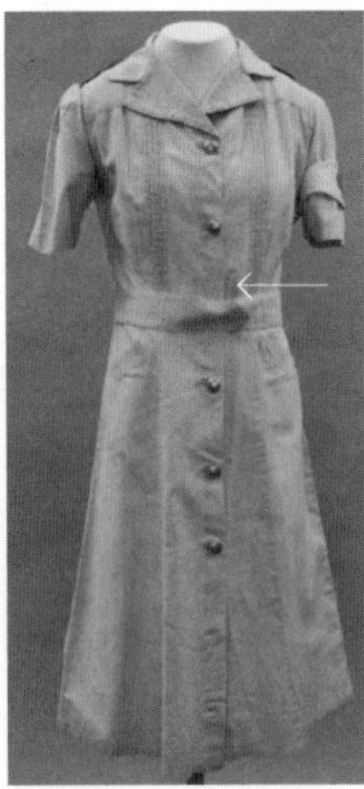

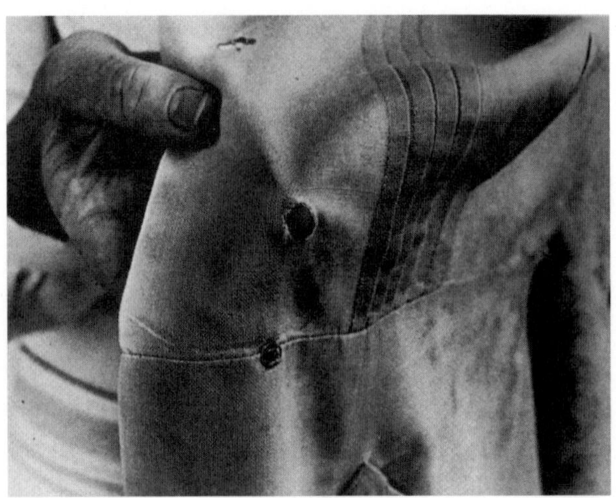

Vivian Bullwinkel's uniform, with two missing buttons and showing the exit hole from the bullet

was always described as a flesh wound on the left side that had practically healed by the time Vivian Bullwinkel gave herself up.

I then discovered that some time after the war Bullwinkel had changed her story, claiming that the bullet had entered her back just above her hip but had then perforated her diaphragm, miraculously doing no damage to her internal organs. My knowledge of anatomy was not extensive, but I could not see how she could have survived a bullet wound to that area without expert medical attention, let alone recovered quickly – so quickly that she hurried to meet her friends in the camp with no discernible discomfort. It was a puzzle that I could not resolve until the like-minded Barbara Angel undertook a forensic examination of the uniform.

In 2003 Angel, who first met Wilma Oram in 1991, published her biography, A Woman's War. *Like me, Angel had met Oram's fellow nurses and had also wondered about the secret that they were so obviously protecting – something that they all knew about, but had agreed never to divulge.*

Referring to the secret, Angel recorded:

> Tangible evidence to support this arrived when a friend of mine was driving Wilma, with Betty Jeffrey and Vivian Bullwinkel, to a function. It was during what transpired to be the last year of all three remarkable lives. While the group was travelling, they started to discuss the fact that I was writing Wilma's biography. After a while, a silence fell. It was broken abruptly when Betty Jeffrey said to Wilma, stressing the words: '**You won't tell our story, will you**.' Wilma replied with a short, 'No', and a brisk shake of her head.

Oram had told Angel that 'Vivian was shot here, like this', using a thumb and forefinger to pinch a small area of flesh on her left side, just above her belt. Whereas I had simply wondered about the bullet holes and the discrepancies in Bullwinkel's story, Barbara Angel took direct action, applying and receiving permission from the Australian War Memorial curators to examine the uniform closely.

Now that Angel had access to the uniform, she noted that buttons 1 and 2 on the bodice had been removed at some stage and replacements sewn on with thick aquamarine thread. As buttons 6 and 7 are missing, it is likely that they were used to replace the missing buttons on the bodice. Jane Peek, the Australian War Memorial's curator of heraldry, also examined the uniform and recorded precisely where the bullet holes were located:

> Entry. Left back – 50 mm from left side seam and 10 mm above waist seam
>
> Exit. Left front – 35 mm above waist seam and 5 mm from centre front.

Angel then contacted Professor John Hilton, at the New South Wales Institute of Forensic Medicine in Sydney. As a fellow Member of the Australian and New Zealand Forensic Society, I knew the professor quite well and had sought forensic advice from him myself when investigating war crimes.

Based on the trajectory of the entrance and exit holes, Hilton advised that the bullet would have entered Bullwinkel's body just below the left kidney, and would have then passed through the stomach cavity. Depending on the amount of visceral (intestinal) damage, he concluded that with a wound of this nature it would be possible to live for some days, but the victim would be severely incapacitated and only able to move around in a limited capacity.

Although Oram had described on numerous occasions where Bullwinkel had been wounded, as had Bullwinkel herself, Angel wanted to be sure. The two women and Bullwinkel's husband were now deceased, so Angel contacted Marie Thompson, who had cared for Bullwinkel in the last years of her life. Thompson confirmed that the entry and exit scars made by the bullet, although very faded, were 'almost together on the left-hand side of Vivian's torso'.

The evidence – that the wounds had been minor and healed quickly, the holes in the uniform, the conclusions drawn by Hilton and the scars left by the injury – seemed irreconcilable until Angel conducted a simple practical experiment.

By undoing the buttons of a similar garment and pulling the open bodice back, to simulate the movement of the fabric as Bullwinkel waded waist-deep through the water, Angel discovered that the position of the exit hole in the front of the uniform was now lying back along the waistline and was aligned with the entry hole.

There was no doubt about it. Vivian Bullwinkel had entered the water with her bodice undone and open to the waist.

The buttons on the skirt of Bullwinkel's uniform are attached to the fabric with matching thread. The two on the bodice, however, have been sewn in place with aquamarine thread, indicating that her uniform bodice was ripped open so forcefully that the buttons were torn off and lost, making it necessary to replace them with buttons 6 and 7 on the skirt.

While Bullwinkel was able to replace the torn buttons, the entrance and exit bullet holes in her uniform were a dead give-away to anyone who had more than a passing acquaintance with human anatomy. Her fellow sisters, who fell into this category, were also experienced in treating gunshot wounds to the abdomen. As Pat had remarked, had the bullet nicked Vivian Bullwinkel's intestines, she would have died from peritonitis. The nurses, on seeing the exit hole in the uniform, would have realised at once that there was no way Bullwinkel could have survived such an injury.

Furthermore, those who saw the actual wounds would have known immediately that the exit hole in the uniform did not line up with the exit wound. This fact, rather than the need to answer questions about the fate of her companions on Radji Beach, is probably the reason why Bullwinkel was forced to tell them the full story – not the sanitised version she later told to everyone else.

It would not be hard to have all the nurses agree to enter into a conspiracy of silence. To be raped in those days was considered to be 'a fate worse than death' and was a crime so serious that in New South Wales it was punishable by death until 1955. As Pat Gunther so succinctly put it: if she had been bashed during her captivity she would have been humiliated; if raped, suicidal.

It was tragic enough that 21 nurses had been massacred. For families to know they had also been violated was a burden that the surviving nurses were not willing to share. They made a pact that those who made it back home would cherish and keep alive the memories of those who had been murdered.

While Angel's forensic work was compelling evidence that Vivian Bullwinkel had been roughly handled and sexually molested, if not raped, there was still one more vital piece of evidence to emerge. It was not made known publicly until February 2017 and the informant was Vivian Bullwinkel herself.

Before she died in 2000, she had spoken confidentially with Tess Lawrence – a broadcaster, journalist advocate and specialist in ethical media services. The two women had previously met in Melbourne on several occasions at the Naval and Military Club, where they had mused on the different course Bullwinkel's life may have taken, had she not had flat feet and been rejected by the RAAF.

Bullwinkel intended to speak out, to tell others what she had told Lawrence, but death intervened. Seventeen years later, on the 75th anniversary of the Bangka Island massacre and no longer bound by confidentiality, Lawrence revealed what Bullwinkel had told her.

> I can't recall if it was there [the Naval and Military Club] or at the nearby Windsor Hotel when she told me in confidence about two things she was keeping secret for the time being – but said there would be a time when she would speak publicly about both.
>
> She was tortured by these secrets and her sense of justice was offended by keeping them locked in.
>
> The first matter was that she confirmed the ill-kept secret that most 'of us' – meaning she and the women who had been gunned down – had been 'violated' by the Japanese soldiers beforehand.
>
> The second matter related to this violation and it more than irked her. It caused her great mental and emotional anguish and distress.
>
> She had been ordered by the government not to say anything about the rapes.
>
> She wanted to put this in her statement before the war crimes tribunal but was ordered not to by the Australian Government.

This confession not only confirmed what many had suspected for so many years. It also explained why there was no mention of rape in any of the archival files. Furthermore, it was not only Bullwinkel who had been gagged. Sergeant Weston and James Godwin, who interviewed Tanemura, had also been silenced. This explains why Tanemura's interrogation, giving details of what had occurred on Radji Beach, do not appear in Weston's weekly report and why, although many years had passed, Arthur Weston felt bound to obey the government's directive to keep the nurses' secret.

There was no danger that Weston's interrogation report, lodged in File 152, would give anything away, as the entire file was destroyed. The only record of Tanemura's interrogation is the one that Godwin wrote and took back with him to New Zealand.

It has taken more than 75 years for the truth about what occurred on Radji Beach to be fully revealed. Although Vivian Bullwinkel said she would speak out, she took her secret, ill-kept though it may have been, to the grave. Some may say that it would be best to follow her example and to let sleeping dogs lie. However, social attitudes have changed since 1945 and rape victims no longer suffer the social disgrace or stigma that was so prevalent decades ago. To continue to deliberately ignore the facts, no matter how unpalatable they may be, is to deny not only that it happened, but also to deny moral justice to those who suffered at the hands of the Japanese.

The 21 Australian nursing sisters who died so bravely on Radji Beach on 16 February 1942 deserve better than this.

Telling and knowing the truth does not in any way denigrate their memory.

Maintaining the silence, however, protects no one but the perpetrators.

APPENDIX 1

WHERE IS RADJI BEACH?

The first time the name Radji Beach was used in reference to the location where the nurses were massacred was in a newspaper article in November 1945. It did not surface again for another 40 years, when it appeared in Hank Nelson's book, *Prisoners of War Australians Under Nippon*.

As the original reference related to a memorial event organised by Colonel Hamilton, the commanding officer of 2/2 CCS, it seems likely that the name may have been coined and given to him by a member of the post-war investigating teams. As investigators often used nearby geographical features to identify unnamed locations, Radji may be a corruption of Korang Hadjie, a coral reef near Muntok, which would have been marked on maritime maps. If the Australians met up with local people, it could also be derived from an Indonesian word 'rajah', meaning cut to pieces, which in turn comes from the root word 'raja', which is associated with stabbing, murder, torture or physical punishment.

Radji Beach, despite its notoriety, and the many published accounts in which it has featured, has never been officially or positively identified. There are several clues provided by survivors, but descriptions are not precise, and when Vivian Bullwinkel returned to Bangka in 1993 she could not locate it.

According to various eyewitnesses, Radji Beach was midway between the two lighthouses, which are 8 miles (about 13 kilometres) apart, and were visible to the survivors on the beach; the beach was about '2-3 miles' (in one account) or 4 miles (in another) from Mendjelang village; Muntok was a further 4 miles (6.5 kilometres) away; coconuts grew along the shoreline, and pineapples nearby; there were two freshwater springs, which were large enough for Bullwinkel to bathe in; 200–300 feet (60–90 metres) to the south of the bonfire area was a rocky headland/bluff/promontory, separating the beach from a 'small cove' where the men were killed; there was a stream 1 mile (1.6 kilometres) south of this cove; Vivian Bullwinkel came ashore about a mile (1.6 kilometres) to the north; and Mangeris (Mengerris) Bay is also known locally as Inggris (English) Bay.

Using wartime maps and satellite images, it is possible to identify two beaches that more or less satisfy this criteria.

The first, and the one that ticks most boxes, is the stretch of sand on the northern side of Tanjung Betoempak (Betumpak), the most northerly of three small capes on the coast just to the north-west of Muntok, and equidistant between the two lighthouses. Since this cape is also the most easterly point on the entire coastline, the lighthouses to both the north and south would have been visible to the two groups that set off in opposite directions on the morning of 15 February.

From Tanjung Betoempak, a long stretch of beach runs uninterrupted to the north, almost all the way to the Tanjung Oelar lighthouse. Satellite images show a fairly large outcrop of rock at Tanjung Betoempak, creating a bluff or headland, and shielding a 'small' cove to the south (about 60 metres wide), as described by Eric Germann. Sixty metres is certainly 'small', but large enough to dispose of a small group of men standing in line. The cove is delineated by a second outcrop at the far end, while there is a third, even larger outcrop, a little further south again.

Wartime military maps show coconuts growing along the shoreline at Tanjung Betoempak and also a small swampy area just to the north, fed by Rulong and Betoempak Creeks. A foot track led to Mendjelang village, about 2.5 miles (4 kilometres) away – the distance cited by Vivian Bullwinkel (in another she cited a distance of 4 miles). This track provided access from the village to the beach for fishing and to tend gardens.

From the village, a vehicular road led to Muntok, roughly 4 miles (6.5 kilometres) further on, a distance also cited by Bullwinkel. About a mile south of the small cove is a stream, marked as the

Mangeris on wartime maps, which gives its name to the present-day Teluk Mengerris (Mengerris Bay). According to Eric Germann, when he walked south from the small cove he came to a stream about a mile away, where he cleaned his wounds.

According to Bullwinkel, her lifeboat came ashore a mile to the north of the bonfire – the same distance cited by Germann, who carried the injured nurse to Radji Beach on a stretcher.

The second contender for Radji is a beach about a mile (1.6 kilometres) south of Tanjung Betoempak, to the north of Tanjung Sabadjau and not far from where Mangeris Creek runs into the sea. The lighthouse at Tanjung Kelian (3 miles to the south) would be visible from this cape, but the one at Tanjung Oelan (5 miles to the north) was masked by a 25–30 metre high jungle-topped ridge running inland from Tanjung Betoempak. Coconuts also grew at Tanjung Sabadjau and there was also a foot track from Mendjelang, only 1.5 miles away (not 2–3 miles as stated by Bullwinkel), leading to the beach and gardens. About a mile down the coast is a waterway known as Mendjelang Creek, which also ties in with Eric Germann's account.

Satellite images show a small outcrop of rock at Tanjung Sabadjau creating a small cove to the south, about 60 metres across. However, the outcrop does not appear to be of sufficient size to be described as a bluff, headland or promontory. Nor does it appear to be large enough to have been used as a vantage point by the Japanese to survey the cove after the murders, or to create an obstacle like that encountered by Eric Gormann, who had to leave Mr Watson propped against a log in order to climb over and down the rocks.

Unlike the long stretch of sand to the north of Tanjung Betoempak, the coastline for a mile to the north of Tanjung Sabadjau is not unimpeded. About 500 metres away is another cape, Tanjung Besajap, which has a rocky expanse of about 80 metres in length. This cape would not only have made it impossible for Bullwinkel's group to see a bonfire burning on the beach at Sabadjau, but neither Bullwinkel nor Germann made any reference to climbing over rocks in the dark with seriously injured nurses, one of whom was on a stretcher. Note: If Bullwinkel landed more than a mile to the north of Radji (beyond Tanjung Betoempak), to reach a bonfire at Tanjung Sabadjau her party would have had to negotiate three substantial rock outcrops.

'Radji' is a name not known to local people or to Vivian Bullwinkel. Assuming that Bullwinkel's estimated distance to Mendjelang village (2–3 miles) is correct, the beach at Tanjung Betoempak, from which both lighthouses can easily be seen, is midway between the two and from which a fire could be seen for a considerable distance to the north, rendering it more likely to be the site of the massacre than the beach to the north of Tanjung Sabadjau, which is much closer to the village, is not midway between the lighthouses, is masked by Tunjang Besajap from the north and has obstacles when approaching from that direction.

However, local people also refer to a bay, Teluk Mangeris (Mengerris), as Teluk Inggris or English Bay, because of the number of 'English' bodies strewn along the beach. Whether they were the bodies of the massacred nurses, or the remains of some of the hundreds of people lost at sea, is not able to be determined.

Mr Idris, an 84-year-old villager from Mendjelang, who was 8 years old at the time of the massacre, was interviewed by researcher Judy Balcombe in March 2018. He stated that a few days after the ships were attacked and sunk, one or two villagers who wanted to go fishing came across many corpses on 'the beach'. They informed the other villagers but, as they were afraid of the Japanese, they did not go to look and did not dare bury any bodies, apart from a few that were lying near their farm huts. After a few days, the corpses on the beach disappeared.

The beach where the bodies were seen was not identified by Mr Idris and could be one of three, since three paths led from the village to three separate beaches – one at Tanjung Betoempak (2.5 miles away), a second at Tanjung Sabadjau (1.5 miles away) and a third further to the south, not far from the mouth of the Mendjelang Creek (1 mile away).

As corpses were strewn all along the coast to the north-west of Muntok, Inggris Bay may have referred to a much larger expanse of coastline, not just the area around Mengaris Creek.

Mr Idris's parents also told him that survivors had scavenged for food in the gardens – information that is consistent with that of Eric Germann – and that one or two 'white people' had sheltered in huts near 'the beach'. Who these survivors were is not possible to determine, but they could be any one of a number known to have wandered into the area before giving themselves up.

As Radji Beach could not be identified by Vivian Bullwinkel, a memorial honouring the murdered nurses was unveiled in 1993 near Muntok. In 2017, another memorial, dedicated to all those who died at sea or on land was placed at Tanjung Betoempak – not because the stretch of sand beach immediately to the north had been identified as Radji, but because it was accessible by vehicle, was believed to be in the vicinity of the massacre sites and overlooked the area where so many had perished at sea in February 1942.

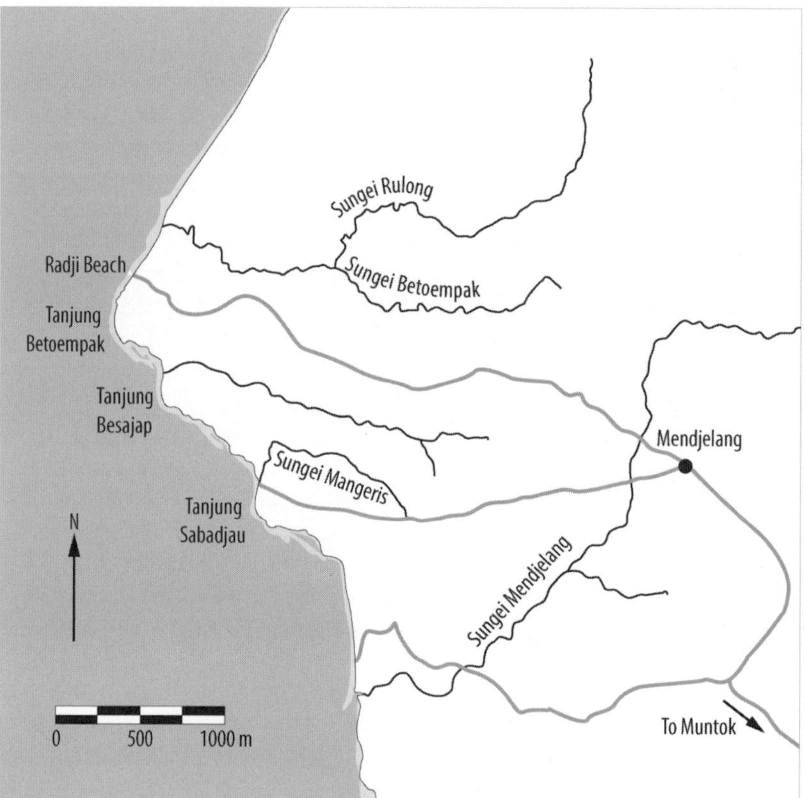

Above: Coastline and tracks leading to Mendjelang village. Right: Sattelite map and army map 1945

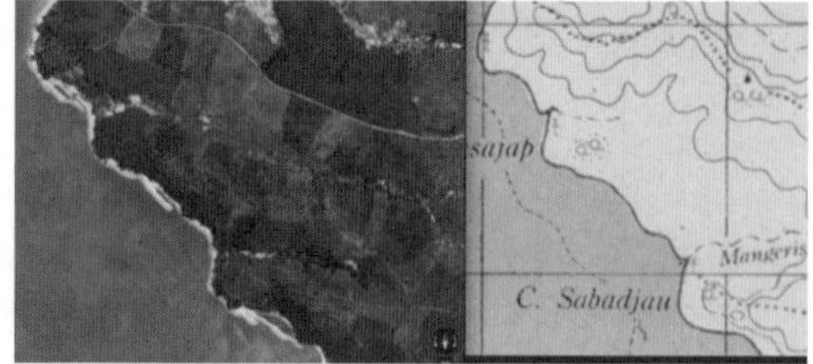

APPENDIX 2

THE FATE OF OTHER INTERNEES

Pat had met many people in Malaya and during her three years of captivity. The following documents the fate of some of them.

Andrea (Dorothy Jenner): In January 1942, Andrea was interned in the Stanley prisoner-of-war camp, Hong Kong, where she managed to keep a diary, written on tough toilet paper. Quick thinking prevented her from being raped by a Japanese officer and she invoked dysentery as an excuse not to make propaganda broadcasts to Allied forces in the Pacific.

Following her repatriation to Australia, she returned to journalism, writing for various newspapers and appearing on ABC TV in a panel show before moving to radio, where her greeting 'Hello Mums and Dads' became her trademark.

Well connected in elite social circles, Andrea maintained a high profile. She was a tireless worker for charity and in 1968 was awarded an OBE. Her memoir *Darlings I've had a Ball*, published in 1975, became a best seller and was serialised. She died in Sydney in March 1985.

Beeston, Louise: Louise, the schoolteacher with nursing experience, survived her imprisonment. She was repatriated to England, but later returned to Singapore to teach at St Andrew's School, before accepting an appointment as supervisor of Singapore's three Anglican schools. In 1960 ill health forced her retirement and she returned to England, where she died in Barnstaple, County Devon in 1983.

Bennett, Major-General Henry Gordon: General Bennett, Commander 8 Division, along with two Australian officers, made a hair-raising escape from Singapore in a small boat on the night of 15 February 1942, two hours after the surrender. On reaching Sumatra, they transferred to a motor launch and made their way up the Djambi River before continuing by road across the mountains to Padang, on the west coast. On 25 February the party was picked up by a Dutch plane and flown to Java, where Bennett boarded another plane for Australia. He arrived in Melbourne on 2 March.

Although publicly praised by the Prime Minister for effecting an escape, and promoted to lieutenant general, some senior elements in the Army were highly critical of his actions, claiming that he should not have left his troops. The rank and file, however, supported his decision to escape, pointing out that he was the only Australian commander who had any experience in fighting the Japanese and asking of what use was a general in captivity.

Despite the terrible privations experienced in POW camps, Bennett's troops remained staunchly loyal. Returning from more than three years' captivity, they sailed into Sydney Harbour with a huge banner over the side of the ship declaring 'We want Bennett'. The general, deeply concerned for his men, was at the wharf to meet them. When an enquiry was held a few months later to determine if Bennett had left Singapore without authorisation, his men created a campaign fund and paid for his defence. Although the findings at the enquiry went against him, they continued to remain loyal to their controversial general until his death in 1962, following him in the thousands as he proudly led his Division through the streets of Sydney every Anzac Day.

Brown, Dorothy Shelagh: Shelagh, as she was always known, survived the war. Reunited with her father Edwin, who had been interned in Changi Gaol and then Sime Road Camp, she returned home to England. After her marriage in 1946 she went to Canada, but returned to the UK following the death of her husband in 1988. Shelagh died in 2005 at the age of 89. Her memoir is preserved in the

Imperial War Museum, London.

Bull, Annabel: Mrs Bull, wife of Harold Robert Bull, a District Judge in Singapore, survived the war along with her daughter Hazel. Two other children, Millie, aged 12, and Robin, aged 10, had become separated from their mother when *Vyner Brooke* sank and were believed to have been killed. However, when enemy machine-gun fire raked their lifeboat, they had jumped into the water and reached a raft. With them was a Thai woman, believed to be fellow passenger Mrs Pearson. After spending some days at sea, the raft came ashore in Java, where local people cared for the castaways for a few months. When the three were interned, Mrs Pearson claimed that her name was Stanton, and that the children were hers, evidently in an attempt to protect them. It is said that they were renamed Joan and Peter but, according to another source, they were known as Betty and David. In the camp they came under the care of Miss Leila Bridgeman, of the Singapore YWCA and, in September 1945, were reunited with their mother, sister Hazel and their father, who had spent the war interned in Singapore.

Castle, Edith Evangeline (Ena): Edith, the Colonial Nursing Service Matron, was one of the many victims who succumbed to the Bangka fever epidemic that broke out in the latter months of 1944. She died at Muntok 'new camp' on 19 November 1944, at the age of 50.

Chambers, Margaret Constance Norah: Norah and her husband John, an internee in Palembang, survived their imprisonment. They were repatriated to England, but in late 1946 returned to Malaya where John, an engineer, accepted a post with the Public Works Department. On his retirement, the couple returned to England, to live in St Helier, on the Isle of Jersey. Norah died in 1987.

Chan, Joo Kim: Mrs Chan, who procured 'comfort women' for the Japanese, survived the war, along with John, her son.

Chidson, Joyce: Joyce, who had befriended the nurses at Malacca, spent the remainder of the war with her children, Mary, Joan and John, in Wahroonga, on Sydney's upper north shore. After Japan's surrender in 1945 they were reunited in Sydney with Hume, who had been interned in Changi Gaol and Syme Road Camp in Singapore. The family then moved to London. Following Hume's untimely death there in December 1946, Joyce returned to Australia with her children. She died in Sydney in 1993 at the age of 99.

Coates, Dr Albert: After caring for hundreds of castaways at his makeshift clinic on the Indragiri River, at the end of February Coates moved west to Padang, which was occupied by the Japanese three weeks later. Although Bill Reynolds, who had delivered many of the injured to his clinic on the lower Indragiri, had urged Coates to sail with him to India, Coates refused to leave his patients.

Now a prisoner of war, he was transferred to Burma and then to Thailand where he cared for hundreds of prisoners working on the Thai–Burma railway. Conditions were deplorable and medical equipment basically non-existent but, due to his innovative surgery and treatment, he saved many lives.

At the cessation of hostilities, Coates was repatriated to Melbourne in October 1945. He was awarded an OBE the following year and knighted in 1955. A prominent figure in medical circles, he held several important posts in Australia and overseas until his retirement in 1971. He died in 1977 at the age of 82.

Colijn, Alette, Antoinette, Helen: The three Coljin girls and their mother survived the war. In 1995, at the age of 65, Helen, the eldest, wrote a book entitled *Song of Survival Women Interned*, which records the story of the vocal orchestra. Their father was Antonie (Anton) Hendrikus Colijn, a Dutch amateur mountaineer who led a 1936 expedition to climb Ngga Pulu which, at that time, was snow covered and the highest peak of the Carstenzgebergte Range in Dutch New Guinea. He died of illness at Muntok in March 1945.

Cooper, Mary: Mary, the Irish nurse from Carrickmacross, County Monoghan, who left the camp to work at the native hospital in Palembang, did not survive the war. She never fully recovered from the hardships suffered during her six months in solitary confinement and died at Balalau Camp at Loeboek Lingga in June 1945.

Cousens, Major Charles Hughes: Cousens was taken POW when Singapore fell and was sent to Japan where he made propaganda broadcasts on Radio Tokyo. Although he claimed this was under duress, post-war he was committed to trial for treason. The charges were dropped, but in January 1947 the Army stripped him of his rank – an action that was perceived as vindictive by the members of his battalion who showed their support by inviting him to lead them at the ANZAC Day march that year. He died in 1964, still married to Grace. Five years after Cousen's death, his close friend Edith Howgate married for the first time at the age of 61. The groom was Cecil Ariossion Johnson. She died in 1989.

Dixey, Helen: Mrs Dixey, who spoke so eloquently about life in the Seychelles with her husband Arthur, and who was also forced to stand in the sun with Sisters Raymont and Smith, died at Muntok on 28 February 1945.

Germann, Eric Harrison: After the war, Eric returned to his career as a brewer, firstly in New York and then in Ecuador, in 1947, where he married his wife, Connie. He also worked in Costa Rica, Puerto Rica, Spain, Rotterdam and Nigeria, before retiring to America in 1974 to live in Florida. The story of his wartime experiences was included in the book *By Eastern Windows* by William H McDougall, published in 1949.

Gilmour, Georgette Gabriel: Gillie survived the war and settled in Australia. She died at Bentley, Western Australia, in 1981 at the age of 79.

Hinch, Gertrude Bean: After her liberation, camp leader Gertrude Hinch was reunited with her husband, Thomas, who had been interned in Singapore. They returned to Singapore the following year – Mrs Hinch to take up the position of President of the YWCA and her husband to resume his career as Principal of the Chinese-Anglo School. Following his retirement, the couple returned to England in 1948 where Gertrude died in 1971.

Howgate, Edith Emily: Edith Howgate was evacuated safely on *Empire Star* to Australia, where she was posted to various hospitals and medical units. In August 1945, she went to Singapore with 2/14 AGH. On discharge from the Army, she lived in Sydney's eastern suburbs and continued to work as a physiotherapist. It is not known if she continued her liaison with Charles Cousens, who also lived in Sydney. He died in 1964, still married to Grace. Five years after his death, Edith married for the first time at the age of 61. The groom was Cecil Ariossion Johnson. She died in 1989.

Jacobs, Major Gideon Francois: Dubbed 'the man who came from heaven' by the many internees and POWs he located and liberated, 23-year-old Jacobs took control of the 80,000 Japanese troops who had surrendered and became military governor of Sumatra during a time of great political upheaval. Returning home, he had a distinguished career in South Africa as an academic and politician. He was awarded an Order of the British Empire (OBE) by King George VI in 1947 for 'outstanding work in Sumatra, immediately following the Japanese surrender'.

Langworthy, H B: Mrs Langworthy, who had entertained Pat in Kuala Lumpur, was fortunately in England with her husband when hostilities broke out in Malaya. Post-war they returned to Malaya where she was appointed Red Cross Commissioner. Her husband, formerly a Police Superintendent, was appointed the first Police Commissioner of the Federation of Malaya.

Macalister, Janet (Jenny): Jenny Macalister was one of the four nurses who left the internee camp to work in the native hospital in Palembang, where she was gaoled and spent six months in solitary confinement. She survived the war and returned home to Bunlarie, in Scotland.

McDowell, Dr Jean: Dr McDowell arrived back in the UK in November 1945 and returned to her hometown of Port William, in Scotland.

McKern, Dr Albert Stanley: Two months before the war ended, on 16 June 1945, Alfred McKern, aged 60, died of amoebic dysentery at Balabau camp. There were no drugs to combat the disease as the Japanese had not issued any and McKern had lost his suitcase containing all his clothes, along with a bottle of emetine used to stave off previous attacks. He was buried in a rough plank coffin among the rubber trees.

Before he died, he drew up a complex will, ensuring that his considerable property portfolio and other assets would be properly managed, and not sold until 10 years after the last of his immediate family had died. In 2007, 10 years after the death of his youngest son, McKern's estate, valued at more than $12 million, was sold and the money distributed evenly between the three universities he had attended – Sydney, Yale and Edinburgh. His instructions were very specific. The proceeds of his property empire were to establish 'research scholarships for investigation into the causes, prevention and treatment of mental and physical pain and distress during pregnancy'. Unfortunately, Pat Gunther, who would have approved heartily of McKern's actions, was not alive to learn of his amazing legacy.

Modin, Air Commodore: Despite high hopes, Modin was never transferred to Singapore. From Karenko Camp in Taiwan, he was moved to Tamazto and Shirakawa Camps, also in Taiwan, and then to Tai Tun and Mukden Camps in Manchuria, where the prisoners were liberated on 16 August 1945 by an American six-man special forces team, which parachuted into the camp.

Moreton, Dorothy Emily: Dorothy Moreton was formerly headmistress of the Methodist Anglo-Chinese Primary School for Boys, Penang. She survived the war and on liberation sailed for the UK. In 1977, she wrote a biography of John Lowe, entitled *An Irishman In Malaya*. She had met Lowe, a solicitor, in Ipoh, Malaya, while she was working there as a missionary and had been impressed by his efforts to establish a home for destitute boys, abandoned by their families during the Depression. She died in Wales in 1984.

Quinn, John Paul: Mr Quinn, who joined the Department of External Affairs at the age of 21, was only 23 years old when he became a prisoner of war. A brilliant linguist, he spoke seven languages fluently and lectured on language and phonetics while interned. Quinn survived the war and returned to Australia to resume his career. He married Josephine Paton in London in August 1949 and held various diplomatic posts overseas and in Australia until September 1961 when, while serving as Ambassador to the short-lived alliance known as the United Arab Republic, the Air France Caravelle plane on which he was travelling from Paris to Casablanca crashed near Rabat, Morocco. All 78 passengers and crew were killed. He was survived by his wife, two daughters and a son, John, who entered the Australian diplomatic service in 1979.

Sage, Matron Annie Moriah: Annie Sage accompanied the Australian military contingent to London for the Victory Parade in 1946, but left the Army the following January to take up an appointment as Superintendent of the Melbourne Women's Hospital. However, she continued part-time as Matron-in-Chief, Citizen Military Forces (reservists), until ill health forced her to retire in 1952.

She maintained an active interest in nursing, holding several senior honorary positions and was an Honorary Colonel of the Royal Australian Nursing Corps from 1957 to 1962. She died in April 1969 at the age of 73.

Smith, Dr Constance Blangdon: After her release from the prison camp, Constance Smith resumed her welfare and antenatal work in Malaya. On her retirement she returned to England, where she lived in Bromley, Kent. She died in 1976.

Tebbutt, William Alston: The nurses were correct in their belief that Major Tebbutt was not simply acting as their escort. Born in 1898, he had served in WW1, landing at Gallipoli with the first troops in 1915, and had fought on the Western Front, where he was wounded in 1917. Promoted to lieutenant, he had risen to the rank of captain in the Militia between the wars, before joining the 2nd AIF and sailing for Malaya in April 1941. A practising solicitor, he was appointed intelligence officer to 8 Division Headquarters in Kuala Lumpur, but in September was attached to the highly secret Far East Combined Bureau, which dealt with codes and cyphers – hence the need for his evacuation.

Liberated from Changi in September 1945, he returned to his home on Sydney's north shore, where he was reunited with his wife Gwendoline, whom he had married in 1928, and their two daughters. Returning to his law practice, he was engaged by General Bennett to act as his solicitor during the enquiry into Bennett's escape. He died in June 1960 at the age of 62.

Turner, Margot Evelyn Marguerite: Margot, one of the four nurses sent to work in the native hospital in Palembang and kept in solitary confinement for six months, resumed her career with the QAs with a succession of overseas postings in Malta, Libya, Cyprus, Egypt and Eritrea. Now a major, she led the QA contingent in the 1953 Coronation Parade.

Margot received an MBE in 1946. In 1964 she was appointed Matron-in-Chief and Director, Army Nursing Service, a post she held for four years until her retirement in 1968, when she became Colonel Commandant of Queen Alexandra's Royal Army Nursing Corps. In 1965 she was made Dame of the British Empire.

In 1978 she was featured on the highly popular program, *This Is Your Life*, where she was joined by many of the internees, whom she had not seen since war's end. To conclude the program, they sang Margaret Dryburgh's 'The Captives' Hymn', which indirectly led to the development of the internationally acclaimed TV series, *Tenko*, screened in 1981. Margot died in Brighton, England, in 1993.

Warman, Izidore (Mischa): On liberation, the orphaned Mischa went to England, escorted by Mrs Mamie Colley and missionary Sarah Cullen. The only life he could remember was in the prison camps, so when he was taken for a drive round Singapore, prior to embarkation for the UK, he asked when they would reach the barbed wire. On arrival in Liverpool, Sarah took Mischa with her to Bebington, Merseyside. As Sarah was engaged to be married, she wanted to adopt him, but the Jewish Society in London insisted that he go to Shanghai, where he was handed over to the care of a distant relative.

Windsor, Major Harry: Irish-born Dr Harry Matthew John Windsor remained in Singapore as the 2/14th AGH surgeon until November 1945. Returning home to his wife and family, he rose in prominence as a thoracic surgeon and in 1968 pioneered heart transplants in Australia at St Vincent's Hospital, Sydney. By the time he died in 1987, heart transplants had become standard procedure. His memoir, *The Heart of a Surgeon*, was published the following year.

Wootton, Alfred Norman: Mr Wootton survived captivity but suffered from impaired health. He served with the Australian Trade Legation in China, and then as Trade Commissioner to Calcutta before taking up a similar post in Paris in 1952. In June 1954, he was found dead in his car on a deserted track in Senlis Forest, outside Paris. He was 52.

OTHER AUSTRALIAN WOMEN INTERNEES

Coates, Dorothy: Dorothy, who came from Adelaide in South Australia, was married to Claude Coates, a headmaster in Malaya, and had left Singapore on board *Mata Hari*. She survived the war and was repatriated.

Harding, Geraldine Inez: The wealthy Mrs Harding was reunited with her husband, who had been taken POW, and her son and daughter, who were at boarding school in Australia at the time of Singapore's fall. She and her husband returned to their former privileged way of life at their palatial property, Irwellbank, 'the only place I want to be'. She died in 1964 at the age of 54.

Reid, Marie: Marie was married to J H 'Jock' Reid of the Malayan Public Works Department. She and her five children – Erica, Jane, James, Dirk and Roy – all left Singapore on board *Vyner Brooke*. The family was repatriated to the UK, but later returned to Penang to live.

Thane, Pamela: Pamela, aged 21, was the daughter of Colin Thane, an Australian planter, and Phyllis (see below). A Voluntary Aid Detachment nurse, she left Singapore on *Mata Hari*. Pamela survived the war, married a merchant seaman and, after living in the UK until 1990, returned to Australia, where she settled in the Sydney suburb of Mt Pritchard.

Thane, Phyllis: Phyllis, who was a Voluntary Aid Detachment nurse, came from Sydney and was the wife of Colin Philip Thane, an Australian planter. Their son, Colin Tarleton, who was born in Malaya but joined the AIF, was badly wounded during the fighting and was evacuated on *Empire Star*. He recovered, and died in 2013 at the age of 95. Phyllis left Singapore with her daughter Pamela (see above) on *Mata Hari*. Phyllis died on 20 April 1945, shortly after reaching Loeboek Linggau Camp.

APPENDIX 3

THE FATE OF THE NURSES EVACUATED FROM SINGAPORE

Evacuated on *Vyner Brooke*

Sixty-five members of the Australian Army Nursing Service were evacuated from Singapore on *Vyner Brooke* on 12 February 1942.

Lost at sea (12)

NAME	STATE	AGE	UNIT	DATE
Bates, Louvima Mary	WA	32	2/13 AGH	14/02/42
Calnan, Ellenor	QLD	29	2/10 AGH	14/02/42
Clarke, Mary Dorothea	NSW	30	2/10 AGH	14/02/42
Dorsch, Millicent Hilda Marie	SA	29	2/4 CCS	15/02/42
Ennis, Caroline Mary	VIC	28	2/10 AGH	14/02/42
Kinsella, Kathleen	VIC	37	2/13 AGH	14/02/42
McDonald, Gladys Myrtle	QLD	32	2/13 AGH	14/02/42
Paschke, Olive Dorothy	VIC	36	2/10 AGH	14/02/42
Russell, Lavinia Jean	NSW	32	2/10 AGH	14/02/42
Schuman, Marjorie	NSW	31	2/10 AGH	14/02/42
Trenerry, Annie Merle	SA	32	2/113 AGH	14/02/42
Wilton, Mona Margaret	VIC	28	2/13 AGH	14/02/42

Massacred on Radji Beach on 16 February 1942 (21)

Balfour-Ogilvy, Elaine Lenore	SA	30	2/4 CCS
Beard, Alma May	WA	29	2/13 AGH
Bridge, Ada Joyce	NSW	34	2/13 AGH
Casson, Florence Rebecca	SA	38	2/13 AGH
Cuthbertson, Mary Elizabeth	VIC	31	2/10 AGH
Drummond, Irene Melville (M)	SA	36	12/3 AGH
Elmes, Dorothy Gwendoline	NSW	28	2/10 AGH
Fairweather, Lorna Florence	SA	29	2/13 AGH
Farmaner, Peggy Everett	WA	28	2/4 CCS
Halligan, Clarice Isobel	VIC	37	2/10 AGH
Harris, Nancy	NSW	31	2/13 AGH
Hodgson, Minnie Ivy	WA	33	2/13 AGH
Keats, Ellen Louisa	SA	26	2/10 AGH
Kerr, Janet	NSW	31	2/13 AGH
McGlade, Mary Eleanor	NSW	38	2/13 AGH

Neuss, Kathleen Margaret	NSW	30	2/10 AGH	
Salmon, Florence Aubin	NSW	26	2/10 AGH	
Stewart, Esther Sarah Jean	NSW	37	2/10 AGH	
Tait, Mona Margaret Anderson	NSW	27	2/13 AGH	
Wight, Rosetta Joan	VIC	33	2/13 AGH	
Wilmott, Bessie	WA	28	2/4 CCS	

Died in captivity at Muntok Camp, Bangka Island (4)

Gardam, Dora Shirley	TAS	34	2/4 CCS	04/04/45
Hempsted, Pauline Blanche	QLD	36	2/13 AGH	19/03/45
Raymont, Wilhelmina Rosalie	TAS	33	2/4 CCS	08/02/45
Singleton, Irene Ada	VIC	36	2/9 Fld Amb	20/02/45

Died in captivity at Loeboek Linggau Camp, Sumatra (4)

Davis, Winnie May	NSW	30	2/10 AGH	19/07/45
Freeman, Rubina Dorothy	VIC	32	2/10 AGH	08/08/45
Hughes, Gladys Laura	VIC	36	2/13 AGH	01/05/45
Mittelheuser, Pearl Beatrice	QLD	41	2/10 AGH	18/08/45

Survived captivity (24)

Ashton, Carrie Jean (Jean)	2/13 AGH
Blake, Kathleen Constance (Pat)	2/10 AGH
Blanch, Jessie Jane (Blanchie)	2/10 AGH
Bullwinkel, Vivian (Viv, Bully)	2/13 AGH
Clancy, Veronica Ann	2/13 AGH
Delforce, Cecilia May	2/10 AGH
Doyle, Jess Gregory	2/10 AGH
Greer, Jean Keers (Jenny)	2/10 AGH
Gunther, Janet Patteson (Pat)	2/10 AGH
Hannah, Ellen Mavis (Mavis)	2/4 CCS
Harper, Iole	2/13 AGH
James, Nesta Gwyneth	2/10 AGH
Jeffrey, Agnes Bettina (Betty)	2/10 AGH
McElna, Violet Irene (Vi)	2/13 AGH
Muir, Sylvia Jessie Mimmi	2/13 AGH
Oram, Wilma Elizabeth Forster	2/13 AGH
Oxley, Christian Sarah Mary	2/10 AGH
Short, Eileen Mary (Shortie)	2/13 AGH
Simons, Jessie Elizabeth (Elizabeth)	2/13 AGH
Smith, Valerie Elizabeth	2/13 AGH
Syer, Ada Corbitt (Mickey)	2/10 AGH
Trotter, Florence Elizabeth (Flo, Trot)	2/10 AGH

Tweddell, Joyce (Tweedie)	2/10 AGH
Woodbridge, Beryl (Woodie)	2/10 AGH

Evacuated to Australia aboard *Wah Sui* (6)

Bell, Thelma May	2/10 AGH
Campbell, Mary Cecelia	2/10 AGH
Dwyer, Veronica Agnes	2/10 AGH
Grigg, Iva Evelyn	2/10 AGH
Haig, Violet	2/10 AGH
Irving, Aileen	2/10 AGH

Evacuated to Australia aboard *Empire Star* (60)

Adams, Monica	2/10 AGH
Aiken, Nancy Muriel	2/10 AGH Physio
Anderson, Margaret Irene (Madge)	2/13 AGH
Atwood, Bennos Jean	2/10 AGH
Baldwin-Wiseman, Sarah Catherine	2/13 AGH
Bell, Joyce Eva Lockhart (Joy)	2/10 AGH
Bentley, Nellie Pearce	2/13 AGH
Brewer, Harley Rosalind	2/13 AGH
Clough, Mavis Alice	2/10 AGH
Cosgrove, Marion	2/10 AGH
Crick, Marjorie Louisa	2/10 AGH
Cullen, Frances Ann	2/13 AGH
Daley, Sheila Merid	2/10 AGH
Drover, Naomi Theo	2/10 AGH
Duthie, Lorna Constance	2/10 AGH
Floyd, Jean Elizabeth	2/10 AGH
Forsyth, Beryl Gethla Jouise (Gethla)	2/13 AGH
Garrood, Betty Hampden (Bettie)	2/13 AGH
Gibson, Thelma Jean	2/10 AGH Physio
Glover, Trixie Alice	2/10 AGH
Gordon, Celia Josie (Bon)	2/13 AGH
Gunton, Mollie Marie	2/13 AGH
Higgs, Merrilie Nancy	2/10 AGH Physio
Hildyard, Hilda Mavis	2/13 AGH
Hill, Marjorie	2/13 AGH Physio
Holden, Mary Elizabeth	2/10 AGH
Howgate, Edith Emily	2/10 AGH Physio
Hurley, Marie Evelyn	2/13 AGH
Jacob, Helen Bertha Mary	2/10 AGH
Marden, Mary Elizabeth	2/10 AGH

McMahon, Mary Eileen	2/10 AGH
McManus, Gertrude Mary (Netta)	2/13 AGH
McMillan, Kathleen	2/10 AGH
Moriarty, Ellen Mary	2/10 AGH
Morse, Ida Arundal	2/10 AGH
Muldoon, Annie Susan	2/13 AGH
Mulvihill, Mavis Valerie	2/13 AGH
Olliffe, Margaret May	2/10 AGH
Powell, Julia Elizabeth Blanche	2/13 AGH
Pugh, Phyllis Bronwyn	2/13 AGH
Pump, Bertha (Betty)	2/10 AGH
Pyman, Elizabeth Berle (Betty)	2/10 AGH
Ralston, Irene Dorothy	2/10 AGH
Rayner, May Eileen (Maisie)	2/13 AGH
Russell, Mary Elizabeth	2/10 AGH
Seebohm, Loris Irene	2/13 AGH
Selwood, Margaret Constance	2/13 AGH
Setchell, Duxie May McLean (May/Margaret)	2/13 AGH
Sheehan, Dorothy Mary	2/13 AGH
Simpson, Audrey Katherine Allen	2/13 AGH
Skeat, Belinda Rosalind	2/13 AGH
Spehr, Maude Lyall	2/13 AGH
Sturgess, Dorothy	2/10 AGH
Sutton, Cynthia Myra	2/13 AGH Physio
Taprell, Veronica Jean	2/10 AGH
Taylor, Frances Grace Lavinia	2/10 AGH
Torney, Vera Alexandria	2/13 AGH
Wittwer, Elvina Minna	2/13 AGH
Zouch, Winsome Throsby (Zouchie)	AANS Physio

NOMINAL ROLLS

The following rolls are restricted to doctors and nursing sisters known to have served in World War 2. They do not include members of the Voluntary Aid Detachment (VAD), orderlies, physiotherapists, dental nurses, occupational therapists or laboratory and other support staff.

AUSTRALIAN ARMY MEDICAL CORPS

The following 29 women served as doctors in the Australian Army Medical Corps (AAMC) in World War 2.

ABRAHAMS	Elsie Louisa
BERTRAM	Mary Nicholl
BOWEN	Janet Mora
BRAYE	Helen Margaret
BURFITT	Barbara Joyce
CROSIER	Joan
DIXON	Margaret Mary
FRANCIS	Shirley Elliston
GILLESPIE-JONES	Margaret Ruth
GROGAN	Gertrude Urquhart
HENDERSON	Annis Macalister
HOLLAND	Llonda
HOLT	Dorrie Alfreda
IRVINE	Mary Clarenza
KERSHAW	Hilda Burn
KIEL	Dorothy May
LATIMER	Thelma Lottie
LAURIE	Elizabeth Frances
LEE	Clara
LUSBY	Mary Gwenyth
MACKAY	Margaret Eleanor
MACKENZIE	Winifred Iris
MACKERRAS	Mabel Josephine
MCLEAY	Leslie Margaret
REFSHAUGE	Joan Janet
SCOTT-YOUNG	Eileen
SCOTT-YOUNG	Margery
TAYLOR	Helen Margaret
VOSS	Florence Mary

ROYAL AUSTRALIAN NAVY

The following 67 women served as nursing sisters with the RAN in World War 2.

ANDERSON	Joyce
BARR	Mary Holtom
BARROW	Nell Margaret
BERTRAM	Barbara Nicholson
BOVELL	Eileen
BRUCE	Pauline Drummond
BUSH	Eleanor Mary
CAHILL	Margaret Mary
CAREY	Mary Elizabeth
CLEGG	Ellaline Jessie Cope
COBCROFT	Elizabeth Rose
DANIELS	Judith Louise
DAVIES	Dorothy Darling
DUFF	Margaret
DURDIN	Muriel Eva
EMMS	Eileen
FLOOD	Patricia Amelia Mary
FREEBAIRN	Gwen
GODDARD	Lettie Alexa
GRANT	Margaret Campbell
GUNDLACH	Jean Spence
HAUXWELL	Joan Mary
HEALY	Margaret Mary
HUTCHINS	Marjorie
JEFFREY	Edna Florence
JONES	Margaret
JONES	Teifi Mary Nesta
KELLY	Violet Emily
KENTWELL	Grace Muriel
KYLE	Audrey Carmen
LAIDLAW	Annie Ina
LAKEMAN	Roslyn Glanville
LAURENCE	Kathleen Mignon
LINDON	Mary Margaret
MCBEATH	Agnes Doreen
MCDONALD	Kathleen Mary
MCKAY	Jean Mary
MORGAN	Doris Elizabeth Margaret
MOSES	Florence
MOUNSTER	Oenone Dacia
NANKERVIS	Joan Bernard
NEUMANN	Lois Sylvia
NEWMAN	Lillian Caroline
NICHOLLS	Enid Ursula Elizabeth
NICOL-HALL	Joyce Lorraine
O'HAIR	Patricia Theresa
ORFORD	Hilda Bell
PARKER	Mavis Irene
PLUMMER	Jean Eliza
PRESTON	Mary Isabel
QUIN	Eileen Veronica
QUINEY	Helen Elizabeth
RAE	Mabel Lucy
ROACH	Emmeline Gordon
ROGGIERO	Beatrice Edna
SCHERGER	Myrtle Jean
SCHINCKEL	Muriel Eily
SOPER	Betty Yvonne Howard
STAMMERS	Eva May
STAPLETON	Gweneth Thelma
SWALLOW	Beryl Victoria Lenard
TAME	Joan Elizabeth Woolacott
THOMAS	Jean Edgar
TONKIN	Lilian Josephine
WEBB	Margaret Elsie
WILSON	Cherry Spence
YOUNG	Betty Scott

ROYAL AUSTRALIAN AIR FORCE

The following 612 women served as nursing sisters with the RAAF in World War 2.

ADAM	Frances Marina
ADDERLEY	Vera May
ADENEY	Mary
AHLSTON	Edna
ALLAN	Nora Alexis
ALLBUTT	Brenda Lily
ALLSHORN	Cecelia Ada
ALLSHORN	Daphne Amelia
AMPS	Ida May
ANDERSON	Elsie Harriet
ANDERSON	Margaret Florence
ANDREW	Nancy Jean
ANGUEY	Phyllis Bertha
ANNETTS	Joyce Elizabeth Naomi
ARMSTRONG	Edna
ASHBEY	Florence Alice
ATKINS	Edith Mary
AUMANN	Doris Lilian
AUSTIN	Ellen
BACON	Julia Agnes
BAILEY	Alice Joyce
BAKER	Edith Clarice
BALDWIN	Elizabeth Helen
BALE	Elma Anne
BALFOUR	Daisy Miller
BARBOUR	Florence Margaret
BARKER	Ray Millicent
BARLIN	Nancy Joan
BARNES	Patricia Margarita
BARTER	Pearl Isabel
BARTLETT	Margaret Lucy
BATEMAN	Mary Cecil Lindsay
BEATTY	Dulcie Mary Jean
BECKETT	Dorothy
BEGG	Erna Margaret
BELL	Joan Grace
BENNETT	Audrey Evelyn
BENNETT	Nancy Powell
BICE	Hilda Joan
BIGGINS	Eileen
BIRD	Margaret Elizabeth
BIRT	Barbara Rosalind
BLACKWOOD	Helen Isabel
BLANCH	Maisie Fay
BLAND	Margaret
BLIGH	Dorothy Norma
BOAS	Naomi
BODEY	Shirley Margaret
BOLGER	Eleanor Mary
BOLT	Winifred Nance
BOND	Isabella Mary
BOND	Lavinia Rosamond
BOWER	Marjorie Agnes
BOWIE	Eunice Octavia
BOYD	Alice Joyce
BRADY	Mary Bridget
BRAID	Ailsa Rae
BRAID	Margaret Alice
BRAY	Elizabeth
BROTCHIE	Esther Grace
BROWN	Evelyn Peace
BROWN	Lillian Lorraine
BROWNLEE	Beryl Sara Arnold
BRUCE	Winifred Jean
BRUMMITT	Olwen Jean
BRYANT	Phyllis Isabel
BUCHANAN	Margaretta Jean
BUCKLEY	Annie Georgina
BUDD	Alice Mary
BUDD	Kathleen Agnes
BUTEMENT	Stephanie Catherine
BUXTON	Grace Constance

CAHILL	Norah Catherine
CAHILL	Jean Mary
CAIRNCROSS	Grace
CALLAGHAN	Catherine Joan
CALLAGHAN	Mary Eileen
CAMERON	Barbara Marshall
CAMERON	Jean Callart
CARNE	Ivy May Peggy
CATCHLOVE	Mavis Estelle
CHANDLER	Beryl Olive
CHARLTON	Rose Christina
CHEGWIDDEN	Sylvia
CHIPPERFIELD	Joyce Edith
CLARK	Enid May
CLARKE	Ada Frances
CLEARY	Agnes Theresa
CLEARY	Helen Agnes
CLODE	Thelma Oenone
COCKER	Victoria Mabel
COLEMAN	Doris Lillian Edith
COLVIN	Rita Jane
CONFEGGI	Marie Elizabeth
CONN	Eileen Edith
CONNELL	Joan
CONSIDINE	Mary Catherine
COOK	Constance Grace
COOK	Georgina Ida
COOK	Helen Joyce
COOKE	Elaine Whitthorn
COOLEY	Adelaide Mary
COOMBES	Dorothy Mavis
COOMBES	Nancy Beatrice
CORNISH	Nola Eileen
COTTER	Helen Mary
COULSON	Hilda
CRAIG	Marie Eileen
CRAIG	Violette Charlotte
CRANSWICK	Mary Harvard
CROCKETT	Marjorie Alison Bruce
CROWHURST	Emily Joyce
CUMMINGS	Elizabeth Hannah
CUNNINGHAM	Mary May
CUNNINGTON	Marion Jean
CUTTS	Edith Lorraine
DALTON	Lesley Margaret
DALZIEL	Margaret Beattie
DANIEL	Helen Margaret
DARLING	Margaret Hudson
DAVIES	Ellinor Kathleen
DAVIES	Hester Amey
DAVIES	Mavis Joyce
DAVIS	Hilda Maud Olga
DAVIS	Jessie Christena
DAVIS	Lilah Evelyn
DENHAM	Eldred Elizabeth
DEXTER	Marie Maude
DIBBS	Elisabeth Gloria
DICKFOS	Marjorie Grace
DISHON	Grace Barbara
DOBB	Audrey Enid
DOBBIN	Gladys Eileen
DOCKER	Betty Bristow
DOHERTY	Betty Joan
DOHERTY	Elizabeth Rose
DOHERTY	Muriel Knox
DOHNT	Lynley Eva
DONELAN	Doris Constance
DONNELLY	Madeleine Agnes
DONOGHUE	Margaret Mary
DOUGLAS	Phyllis Irene
DOWARD	Irene Constance
DU MOULIN	Teresa Mary Grace
DUE	Gloria Blanche
DUNCAN	Evelyn Isobel
DUNN	Elizabeth Fulloon
DUTTON	Mary Doreen
DYKES	Maria Patricia
EAGERTY	Nancy Margaret

EARL	Edith Mary
EATON	Aileen Beatrice
ECHLIN	Naomi Constance
EDDY	Joyce Lorraine
EDGAR	Annie
EDWICK	Jean Olive
EINSPORN	Joyce Pauline
ELLSON	Ailsa Margaret
ESPERSON	Elizabeth Madeline
EVANS	Ivy Evelyn
EVANS	Mavis Myra
FAIRBAIRN	June Emily
FALLON	Betty
FERGUSON	Ethel Susannah Middleton
FEWKES	Phyllis Ann
FIEDLER	Alice Isabel
FILSELL	Vera Hampton
FISHER	Deidre Noel
FISHER	Kate
FLEMING	Nancy Sheila
FLETCHER	Elsie Jean
FOLEY	Mary Grace
FORAN	Agnes Mary
FORBES	Mary
FORREST	Jessie Beryl
FORRESTER	Rita Mary
FOSTER	Evelyn Ellen
FOWLER	Myrtle Phyllis
FOX	Patricia Mary
FRAME	Dorothy May
FRANKLIN	Thelma Victoria
FRENCH	Hilda Mary
FUREY	Betty Doreen
GALL	Victoria Ann
GAMBLE	Laura Louisa
GAMBLE	Nance Alexander
GARDNER	Nellie May
GARDOLL	Hazel
GEDDES	Margaret Grace
GEERING	Edith Jean
GIBBS	Betty Mary
GILBERT	Audrey Esther
GILDING	Joy
GILLESPIE	Mary
GLASS	Betty
GOBBART (MCIVER)	Mary Isabell
GODFREY	Gwladys May Victoria
GODSON	Louisa Winifred
GOODALL	Vera Edith
GOODE	Helen Jessie
GOODE	Janet Mary
GORE	Joan Kathleen
GOYDER	Gertrude Gilmartin
GRAHAME	Margery Myra
GRANT	Ailsa Douglass
GRAY	Sara Margaret
GRAY	Ursula Jean
GREENING	Mary Gay
GREENLAND	Margaret Olive
GRIFFIN	Mary Joan
GRILL	Roma Alice
GRIMES	Leola Evaline
GULLQUIST	Joan Hilda
HACK	Grace Marion
HAIRE	Patricia Noeline
HALING	Elsie Caroline Sivyer
HALL	Edna Stuart
HALL	Shirley
HALSE-ROGERS	Lorraine Winifred
HAMBLETON	Beryl Evelyn
HAMBLY	Eileen Muriel
HAMILTON	Audrey Evelyn
HAMMILL	Alice Margaret
HANCOCK	Mary Amelia
HANNAH	Florence Margaret
HANNAH	Annie McMillan
HANSEN	Ena Amanda

HANSEN	Doris May	HUMPHREYS	Margaret Gladys
HARBISON	Margaret Fyfe	HUTCHEON	Frances Newnham
HARBISON	Margery Jean	HUTCHINGS	Marjorie Lilian
HARBOURD	Veronica Evelyn	HUTTON	Margaret Ethel Harold
HARDIE	Emily Annette Margaret	IRVIN	Annie
HARDING	Elsie May	ISBISTER	Mary
HARLEY	Jean Newell	JACKSON	Heather
HARLEY	Margaret Elizabeth	JACKSON	Mary Una
HARRISON	Florence Mayvis	JACKSON	Sylvia Beryl
HARRISON	Isabel Grace	JAMES	Violet
HASKING	Mary Kathleen	JEFFERY	Alma Louise
HATELEY	Martha Madge	JEMMETT	Doris Margaret
HATFIELD	Joan Ada Sarah	JENNINGS	Zena Jose
HAUG	Mary	JOHN	Constance
HAYCOCK	Eileen Rosemary	JOHN	Mavis Winifred
HEADING	Doris	JOHNSON	Amy Isabel
HELLYER	Eunice Winifred Reid	JOHNSON	Beatrice Mary
HENEY	Jean Roma	JOHNSON	Nancy
HESTER	Jean Hope	JOHNSTON	Mary Arthur Alexandra
HEWETT	Joan Elliott	JOINER	Dorothy Evelyn
HIGGS	Jean Marjorie	JOLLY	Kathleen Islay
HILL	Phyllis Gertrude	JONES	Ada
HILL	Shirley McCracken	KAVANAGH	Mary Sybil
HIND	Clarice Elizabeth	KELLY	Dorothy Evelyn
HINES	Irene Beatrice	KELLY	Edythe Mary
HODGE	Elvie Phyllis	KELLY	Ellen Mary
HODGMAN	Lucie Kathleen	KELLY	Susan
HOGAN	Eileen	KELLY	Joan Helmore
HOPE	Alice Steuart	KELLY	Lucy Ann
HOPWOOD	Sheila Mary	KELSALL	Dorothy Mary
HORSFALL	Rita Patterson	KEMMIS	Olive Mary
HOWARD	Nancy De Vere	KENDRICK	Nancy Irene
HOWARD	Patricia Mary	KENNEDY	Patricia Eileen
HOWELL	Patricia Joan	KEOGH	Helen Jean
HUDDLE	Elaine	KERR	Dorothy
HUGHAN	Isabel Myra	KESSELL	Rosemary Joan
HUGHES	Jessie Isobel	KIRTON	Lyrian Jean
HUGHES	Marjorie Irene	LANE	Mary Dennis
HUGHES	Annie Margaret	LANG	Margaret Irene

LANGFORD	Ida Mabel
LARKIN	Mary Irene
LAW	Jean Catherine Victoria
LAWLER	Veronica
LAWLOR	Mary Catherine
LEE	Una Mary
LEGGE	Heather Elizabeth
LEWIN	Joyce Ellen
LEWIS	Elizabeth Maude
LINDLEY	Ainslie Dora Mary
LITHGOW	Isabel Emma
LOCKETT	Melva Muriel
LOLLBACK	Eileen Myrtle
LOMAX	Joan Clayton
LONG	Sheila Mary
LOUTIT	Joan Medway
LOVEBAND	Mary Frances
LOWRY	Mary Isobel
MACAULEY	Elsie Leah
MACDONALD	Barbara Sugden
MACINTIRE	Clare Rothwell
MACKAY	Jean
MACKENZIE	Grace
MACKENZIE	Lucy Georgia
MACKENZIE	Margaret Joy
MADDISON	Lois Margaret
MAHER	Norah
MAHER	Eileen Edna
MANN	Joan Catherine
MANNING	Margaret Campbell
MANSFIELD	Elizabeth
MANTON	Frances Mary Jervis
MANTON	Violet Isobel
MARENDAZ	Marion Jean
MARLOW	Beryl Dawson
MARS	Florence Mary
MARSHALL	Lucy Thelma
MARSHALL	Marjorie Leam
MARSHALL	Martha McDonald
MASON	Peggy
MASON-JOHNSON	Betty
MATHEWS	Lynette
MATSON	Irene Myrtle
MATTHEWS	Elizabeth Lilian
MAXWELL	Eileen Josephine
MAY	Mavis Merle Crompton
MCALLISTER	Gladys Wilson
MCANALLY	Mabel Marjorie
MCBEAN	Nancy Mortimer
MCCLYMONT	Mary Joan Alloway
MCCORMACK	Noreen
MCCORMICK	Patricia
MCCRACKEN	Agnes Heather
MCCRIMMON	Sarah
MCDONALD	Constance Clare
MCDONALD	Christina
MCDONALD	Heather Jean
MCDONALD	Marion Joan
MCDOWELL	Matlida Ritchie
MCGOVERN	Marion Claire
MCINNES	Dulcie May
MCINTOSH	Mary Winifred Lyle
MCKEE	Margaret
MCKELVIE	Dorothy Gwendoline
MCKELVIE	Violet Elsie Mary
MCLEOD	Jean Grace
MCMAHON	Nancy Josephine
MCMASTER	Jean Edith
MCNAMARA	Mary Dellis
MCNAMARA	Glenda Josephine
MCNAUGHTON	Annie Catherine
MCNEILL	Mary Teresa
MCPHEE	Margaret Jean
MCRAE	Charlotte Joan
MCWILLIAM	Joan Agnes
MEDLYN	Agnes Joy
MEIKLEJOHN	Jean Mavis
MELLOR	Dorothy Winifred

MENZIES	Lillian Jean	ORTON	Marjory Isabel
MESLEY	Joan	OSBORNE	Gweneth
MESLEY	Madge	OVERTON	Gladys Daureene
METHVEN	Molly	OWEN	Dorothy Grace Lilian
MILBURN	Thelma June	PARSONS	Flora Mary
MILLER	Eleanor Grace	PASCOE	Amelia Bertha
MILLER	Iris	PATERSON	Helen Marjorie Lukin
MILLIKEN	Joan Crawford	PATERSON	Jean
MILLS	Elma Joyce	PATRICK	Margaret Gladys
MILLS	Joyce Irene	PATTERSON	Dorothy May
MITCHELL	Zelma May	PATTERSON	Joyce Catherine Anne
MOLLER	Ellen Jean	PATTISON	Dorothy Grant
MOLONEY	Margaret Jean	PAYNE	Edith May
MONGER	Norma Margaret Forrest	PAYNE	Mary Elizabeth
MOONEY	Thelma	PAYTEN	Lesley Ann
MORAN	Mary	PEARCE	Leta Gertrude
MORELL	Jessica Enid	PEARSE	Alma Sarah Jane
MORGAN	Ethel Livingstone	PEARSON	Edna May
MORRIN	Una Agnes	PEGRUM	Ursula May
MORRIS	Jessie Olive	PENFOLD	Joan Marion
MOXHAM	Thelma Minnie	PERGER	Ruth Annie
MUNRO	Pauline May	PERMEWAN	Audrey Florence
MURPHY	Dorothy Frances	PERRETT	Daphne
MURPHY	Irene Margaret	PICKERING	Margaret Mary
MURRAY	Jean Samson	PICKUP	Edna Ainsworth
MURRAY	Alison	PITTMAN	Phyllis Margaret
MUSGRAVE	Jean Downton	POLAND	Annie Olive
NALL	Helen Spencer	POTTER	Audrey Annie Evelyn
NEILSON	Elsie Florence	POUSTY	Marguerite Ethelwyn
NEUENKIRCHEN	Margaret Collard	POWELL	Florence Theodosia
NEVILLE	Gertrude Eleanor	POZZI	Carina Margherita
NEWTON	Peggy	PRICE	Edith Eveline
O'DOHERTY	Ida Elizabeth	PROVIS	Florence Nancy
O'DONNELL	Joan Ingrid Marea	PRYDE	Winifred Mary
OHLMEYER	Ada Miriam	PUCKRIDGE	Dorothy Florence
OLIFENT	Joan Elwyn	PURSEHOUSE	Cecelia Mary
OLSEN	Faith	PURTILL	Eileen Stephanie
O'MALLEY	Inez	RAE	Madeline Farquharson
O'NEILL	Rosemary Mabel	RAMSDEN	Florence Ethel

RAYNER	Jean Annie Primrose
READ	Esmay Myra
READ	Nancy Jean
REEVES	Elizabeth Haslett
REID	Patricia Le Roux
REID	Ada Mary
RENKIN	Lucy May
RENNIE	Margaret Jessie
RENWICK	Agnes Taylor
REYNOLDS	Mabel
RICHARDS	Margery Cullen
RICHARDSON	Isabel Bessie Spencer
RITCHIE	Millicent Estelle
ROBERTSON	Gwendoline Hope
ROBERTSON	Lorraine Winifred
ROBERTSON	Olive Kathleen
ROBIN	Mary De Quetteville
ROBINS	Lorna Davies
ROBINSON	Gwendolyn Murial Bradley
ROBINSON	Joan Mildred
ROBINSON	Mary Thelma
RODDA	Emma Matilda
RODWELL	Mavis Joan
ROGERS	Doris
ROUGET	Beatrice Margaret Anne
ROWLEY	Dorothy Marie
RULE	Lucy Eyrie
RULE	Catherine Ida
RYAN	Catherine Mary
RYAN	Colleen
SAMPSON	Constance Eva
SAWTELL	Trissie May
SCANLON	Mary Patricia
SCHACHE	Gwenneth Ruby
SCHOLZ	Phyllis Reta
SCHUH	Janet Valeria
SCHULTZE	Nellie Constance
SCOTT	Marjorie Elizabeth
SCOTT	Margery Kathleen
SCOTT	Marjorie Allan
SCRIVEN	Ethel Everlyne
SCULLEY	Monica
SEATON	Mary Kathleen
SEYMOUR	Nora
SHAND	Edna Mabel
SHANN	Hilary
SHANNON	Irene Elizabeth
SHAW	Audrey Ailsa
SHAW	Beryl Sabina Mary
SHAW	Florence Edna
SHEAH	Verdun Beatrice
SHEPHERD	Mary May
SIMMONDS	Ruby May
SIMMONS	Mary Agnes
SINCLAIR	Patricia Annie Elizabeth
SIRL	Marjorie Bernice
SISSONS	Marjorie Mary Hall
SKERRITT	Winifred May
SLEEP	Evelyn Victoria
SLOMAN	Zara
SMAIRL	Lilian Gladys
SMALLHORN	Stella Joan
SMITH	Ila Mary
SMITH	Jean Stuart
SMITH	Edna Lilian Merle
SMITH	Elizabeth Catherine
SMITH	Gweneth Alma
SMITH	Marjorie Beatrice
SNOOK	Irma June
SOULIE	Dolace Frances
SPARK	Elsie Rennie
SPENCER	Ada Helen
SPICER	Catherine Lyell
STAFFORD	Betty Muriel
STANLEY	Mary Blyth
STARR	Alice Evelyn
STEPHENSON	Lois Minna

STEWART	Alma Doris
STRANG	Sheila Joan
STRICKLAND	Alison Ann
STRINGER	Jean Francis
SULLIVAN	Mary
SUMERSFORD	Lorraine Alberta
SWAN	Florence May
TALBOT	Florence Isabel
TALLENT	Annie
TARLINTON	Patricia Ann
TAYLER	Ellen Stace
TAYLOR	Alix Jessamine
TAYLOR	Marjorie Hamlet
TAYLOR	Josephine Elsie
THOMAS	Annie Beatrice
THOMAS	Megan Gredwin
THOMPSON	Elizabeth Rae
THOMPSON	Phyllis Doreen
THOMPSON	Barbara Beresford
THOMPSON	Patricia Edna
THORNTON	Edith
THORNTON	Esme Margaret
THRELKELD	Gwenneth Grace
THROSBY	Jessica Douglas
TOBIAS	Frances Elizabeth
TOMLINSON	Rita Helen
TONKIN	Edna May
TOPHAM	Nellie Grace
TREWIN	Grace
TURNBULL	Winifred Mary
TYSON	Mary Ellen
VANCE	Mary Doris
VINES	Dorothy Gertrude
VIRGO	Joan Eva
WADDELL	Marion Moffatt
WALKER	Grace Nellie
WALSH	Jeanne Marie

WALTER	Eula Lorraine
WARBY	Leila Jeffery
WARD	Evelyn Ellen
WARD	Delia Loris
WARR	Margaret Ann
WARREN	Florence Evelyn
WARRILOW	Margaret Mary
WASS	Valerie Eveline
WATCHORN	Pauline
WATERS	Theresa May
WATT	Constance Lockyer
WEBER	Edna May
WHEATLEY	Alice Jean
WHITE	Marie
WHITE	Amber Florence
WHITE	Joan Nell
WHITLOCK	Beatrice Mary Elizabeth
WILLIAMS	Gladys Myrtle
WILLS	Elizabeth Niven
WILSON	Greta Mary
WILSON	Molly
WILSON	Elizabeth Jane
WILSON	Nalda Lilla [Lillian]
WINNING	Iris Evelyn
WINTER	Phyllis Jean
WISEMAN	Bessie Beryl
WISEMAN	Thelma Elizabeth
WITCOMBE	Marion Pozieres Gertrude
WOOD	Margaret Emily Ettie
WOODHILL	Frieda Crisford
WROE	Margaret Honora
WYNNE	Shirley Verna
YOUNG	Joyce Courtney
YOUNG	Mabel
YOUNG	Maysie Matilda
ZAPPA	Deborah Frances
ZEUNERT	Frieda Pauline

AUSTRALIAN ARMY NURSING SERVICE (AANS)

The following 3414 women are known to have served as nursing sisters with the AANS in World War 2.

ABBERFIELD	Daisy Aline
ABBERTON	Anastasia Ellen
ABBOTT	Agnes Jean
ABBOTT	Dorothy Lilian
ABBOTT	Joan Stevenson
ABBOTT	Phyllis Mary
ABBOTT	Yvonne Patricia
ADAMS	Doris
ADAMS	Ellen Mary
ADAMS	Margaret Lamont
ADAMS	Monica
ADAMS	Rose Catherine
ADAMS	Ellen Mary
ADCOCK	Alice
AGAR	Patricia Maud
AHERN	Mary Gladys
AIK	Alma Jean
AINSWORTH	Evelyn Harris
AITKEN	Dorothy Alix Nancy
ALAND	Mabel Adelaide
ALCHIN	Lilian Brooks
ALCORN	Joan Iris
ALCORN	Mary Edith
ALDOM	Frances Amelia
ALEXANDER	Jessie Elizabeth
ALFREDSON	Bertha Meta
ALLAN	Jean Leah
ALLEN	Daphne Gladys
ALLEN	Edith Muriel
ALLEN	Elsie Grace
ALLEN	Freda May
ALLEN	Gweneth Helen
ALLEN	Marjorie Joyce Oxtoby
ALLEN	Nancy Nora
ALLENDER	Betty
ALLINGHAM	Joyce Ethel
ALLISON	Flora Milne
AMOUROUS	Elsie May
ANDERSEN	Mary Adele
ANDERSON	Alice
ANDERSON	Ella Irene
ANDERSON	Georgiana Maude
ANDERSON	Ida Muriel
ANDERSON	Ivy Lillian
ANDERSON	Lorna Mary Graeme
ANDERSON	Margaret Irene
ANDERSON	Marion Naples
ANDERSON	Marjory Jean
ANDERSON	Olga Marcella
ANDERSON	Phyllis Mary
ANDERSON	Rita Gweneth
ANDERSON	Robina Margaret
ANDERSON	Ruth
ANDERSON	Stella Grace
ANDREW	Jessie
ANDREW	Mary Douglas
ANDREW	Myra Joyce
ANDREWS	Gwendoline Marion
ANDREWS	Phyllis Isobel
ANSTEAD	Beatrice Annie
ANSTIS	Mary Elizabeth
ANTHONY	Hilda Jane
ANTONELLI	Dorothy
APPLEFORD	Alice Marion
APPLEFORD	Alice Ross
APPLETON	Hilda Mary
ARBUCKLE	Elizabeth Colquhoun
ARCHER	Laird Meredith
ARCHER	Lois Eileen
ARLISS	Marjorie Edith

ARMITAGE	Ivy May Marguerite	BAINES	Marjorie Catherine
ARMSTRONG	Bessie	BAKER	Alice May
ARMSTRONG	Dorothy Mary	BAKER	Anna Ruth
ARMSTRONG	Stella Joan	BAKER	Enid Ivy
ARNDELL	Janet Mary	BAKER	Enid McLachlan Joy
ARNOLD	Patricia	BAKER	Geraldine Mary
ARTHUR	Thelma Winnie	BAKER	Helen Shirley
ARTHUR	Thora Jean	BAKER	Jessie Balmain
ARTIS	Dixie Josephine	BAKER	Mary Furner
ASHE	Grace	BAKER	Rhoda Florence
ASHENDEN	Ruby Esther	BALD	Edna Winifred
ASHTON	Carrie Jean	BALDOCK	Constance Louise
ASHTON	Molly	BALDWIN-WISEMAN	Sara Catherine
ASMUS	Dorothy Margaret	BALES	Eloise Marcia
ATHERTON	Letitia Charlotte	BALFOUR	Betty Christine
ATKINSON	Dorothy Anne	BALFOUR-OGILVY	Elaine Lenore
ATKINSON	Dorothy Mary	BALL	Phyllis Marion
ATKINSON	Marguerite May	BALLANTINE	Jessie Frances
ATWOOD	Bennos Jean	BALLARD	Rosalind Eva
AUSTIN	Nola Lynton	BANKS	Essie May
AVELING	Frances Brenda	BANKS	Grace Eileen
AVERAY	Coralie Violet	BANNEAR	Dorothy May
AXFORD	Doris Jean	BANNERMAN	Jean Victoria
AYRE	Maida Emily	BANNON	Mary Josephine
AYRTON	Alma Hilda	BARAGWANATH	Dorothy Ruth
BACK	Mina Margaret	BARCLAY	Catherine Mary
BACK	Phyllis Mary	BARCLAY	Daisy
BACKHOUSE	Betty Daveney	BARCLAY	Jean
BACON	Bessie Joan	BARDWELL	Jean May
BADCOCK	Marjorie Esther	BARLING	Enid Elizabeth
BADOCK	Adela	BARNARD	Jean Burnside
BAGLIN	Elizabeth Constance	BARNARD	Margaret Gordon
BAILEY	Daphne Grace	BARNES	Kathleen Hope
BAILEY	Dora Elizabeth	BARNES	Nell Isobel
BAILEY	Edna Agnes	BARNES	Sheila Doreen
BAILEY	Hazel Frances	BARNETT	Fanny Louise
BAILEY	Marjorie Effie	BARNETT	Jean Marie
BAILEY	Marjorie Lavinia	BARNETT	Marjorie Taylor
BAILLIE	Barbara Joyce	BARNS	Ivors May

BARRATT	Gwenyth Morris	BENNETT	Cordelia Helen
BARRETT	Stella Mitchell	BENNETT	Eva Louise
BARRETT-LENNARD	Prudence	BENNETT	Joan Mercy
BARROT	Jean	BENNETT	Marion Alice
BARROW	Jessie Blanche	BENNETT	Mavis Eileen Ruth
BARROW	Joyce Waterton	BENNETT	Millicent Celeste
BARTHOLOMEW	Edith Jean	BENNETT	Phyllis Ethel Maud
BASTIN	Audrey	BENNIE	Rosemary
BATE	Wilma Jean	BENNIE	Violet Audrey
BATES	Louvinia Mary Isabella	BENNY	Dorothy Constance Marion
BATHGATE	Mairi Fraser	BENOIT	Muriel Joyce
BAUTOVICH	Olga Sylvia	BENSON	Agnes Ivy
BAXTER	Ethel Adelaide	BENSON	Beryl Leonie
BAXTER	Mary Margaret	BENSON	Edna Phyllis
BEACH	Esma Margaret	BENTLEY	Nellie Pearce
BEACROFT	Edna Ann	BENZIE	Jean Kennedy
BEARD	Alma May	BERE	Eileen Mary
BEARD	Margaret Ellen	BERESFORD	Rosemary De La Poer
BEATTIE	Ruth	BERMINGHAM	Mary Elizabeth
BEATTON	Jane Mary	BERRIE	Ruth Kathleen
BEAVEN	Eileen Grace	BERRY	Vera Alexandra
BEBBINGTON	Marion Ruth	BERRYMAN	Joyce Irene
BECKETT	Catherine	BERTALLI	Nellie
BECKETT	Winifred Frances	BERTRAM	Joan Margaret
BEDDOE	Olive Marjory	BEST	Kathleen Annie Louise
BEDFORD	Victoria May	BETTS	Bessie
BEER	Mavis Claire	BETTS	Daphne
BEER	Melanie Doreen	BETTS	Louisa Kathleen
BEETHAM	Eileen Gertrude	BEULKE	Dorothea Jean
BEGGS	Elizabeth Rosaline	BEUZEVILLE	Alma Edna
BEGGS	Mona	BEVERLEY	Jane
BELL	Doris	BEWGLASS	Shena Campbell
BELL	Edith Margaret	BIGGIN	Frances Helen
BELL	Joyce Lockhart	BIGNOLD	Violet Baron
BELL	Margaret Forbes	BILLING	Ella Bulstrode
BELL	Vera Isabel	BILNEY	Madge
BELLERT	Mary Brown	BINGHAM	Evelyn Annie
BELLINGHAM	Doris Grace	BINNIE	Alice
BENEKE	Zelma		

BINNS	Eva
BIRCH	Regina May
BJERRING	Maren Cecilie Kristensen
BLACK	Kate Ruth
BLACK	Pauline Merle
BLACKER	Evelyn Edith
BLACKER	Jean
BLACKLOCK	Reta Alma
BLACKWELL	Margaret De La Tour
BLAKE	Audrey Joan
BLAKE	Jessie Mary
BLAKE	Kathleen Constance
BLANCH	Jessie Jane
BLANCH	Myra Rose
BLANCHARD	Olive Marie
BLANSHARD	Lesla Meddy
BLEECHMORE	Nora Mary
BLENEY	Agnes Winifred
BLIGHT	Lorraine May
BLOMFIELD	Nancye Margaret Nivison
BLOSS	Doris Ada
BLOW	Lorraine Stewart
BLOWFIELD	Madge
BLUNDELL	Beatrice Olive May
BLYTH	Jessie Lorraine
BOAG	Elizabeth
BOAG	Olive Isabel
BOATFIELD	Muriel Grace
BOLITHO	Anne Riffel
BOLTON	Marie Isobel
BOLTON	Mary Julienne Grace
BOLTON	Nora
BOND	Marie Ruth
BONDFIELD	Bessie Agnes
BONFIELD	Beryl Beatrice
BONNER	Anna Ruth
BONNIN	Kathleen Patricia
BOOCOCK	Mavis Helena
BOOLER	Joan Irene
BOONE	Joan Louisa
BOONE	Patricia
BOOTH	Ethel Winifred
BOOTH	Jean Mcpherson
BOOTH	Joan
BOULLY	Nancy
BOUNDY	Mary Gwendoline
BOURCHIER	Gladys Jean
BOURKE	Florence Agnes
BOURKE	Winifred Eva
BOWDEN	Doris
BOWE	Ethel Jessie
BOWEN	Rosetta Elizabeth
BOWER	Dulcie
BOWER	Grace Elizabeth
BOWMAN	Isobel Mary
BOWMAN	Joyce Devlin
BOWMAN	Kathleen Mary
BOWMAN	Noel Henrietta
BOWMAN	Shirley Bessie Macarthur
BOX	Constance Clara
BOX	Jessamine
BOX	Joan
BOXSELL	Maris Stella
BOYD	Mollie Irene
BOYS	Catherine Alice
BRADSHAW	Anastacia Veronica
BRADSHAW	Jean Ellen Mary
BRADY	Alice Muriel
BRADY	Eileen Nancy
BRADY	Irene Mary
BRAID	Margaret Younger
BRAITHWAITE	Mary Alice
BRAKELL	Jessie Estella
BRAMMER	Joyce
BRAND	Thelma
BRANDT	Hilda Margaret

BRANLEY	Sheila Patricia	BROOME	Ida Merle
BRASEN	Doris May	BROOMFIELD	Doris
BRATT	Eva Winifred Lilian	BROOMHEAD	Mary Phyllis
BRAY	Joan Mary	BROPHY	Noreen Mary
BRAY	Winifred Enid	BROSNAN	Betty Agnes
BREARLEY	Alice	BROSNAN	Florence Jocelyn
BREEN	Deborah Margaret	BROSNAN	Gerard Joan
BRENNAN	Elizabeth Stuart	BROWN	Eloise Mary Jeffery
BRENS	Louise	BROWN	Ethel Marjorie
BREWER	Harley Rosalind	BROWN	Evelyn Mary
BREWIN	Alice Dorothy	BROWN	Grace Evelyn
BREWIS	Hazel Mary	BROWN	Ida Madge
BRIANT	Margaret Kate	BROWN	Jean
BRIANT	Muriel Elizabeth	BROWN	Jean Darvall
BRIDGE	Ada Joyce	BROWN	Jean Isabele
BRIGGS	Hilda Florence	BROWN	Jessie Elma
BRIGHT	Margaret Brailsford	BROWN	Joan
BRINDAL	Audrey Evelina	BROWN	Kathleen Patricia Mary
BRINDLEY	Gertrude Elizabeth Middleton	BROWN	Leone Marie
BRISKEY	Gwendolyn Gladys	BROWN	Mabel Ivy
BRISKEY	Margaret Helen Henrietta	BROWN	Madge Ellen
BRITTEN-JONES	Hannah May	BROWN	Margaret Annie
BRITTINGHAM	Marjorie Constance	BROWN	Marie Frances
BROADHEAD	Racheal Rebecca	BROWN	Melna Isobel
BROADHURST	Kate Kirkland	BROWN	Olive Madeline
BROADSTOCK	Elsie Winifred	BROWN	Ruth
BROCKETT	Frances Vivienne Mary	BROWN	Ruth Auschau
BRODIE	Mary Clement	BROWN	Ruth Henshall
BRODRIBB	Mary Emily	BROWN	Vera Grace
BRODSKY	Isadore Irvine	BROWN	Vera Joyce
BROGAN	Eleanor Elizabeth	BROWNE	Barbara Esther
BROOK	Irene	BRUCE	Dorothy
BROOKE	Lawrence Amy Margery	BRUCE	Gertrude Kathleen
BROOKE	Nora Selma	BRUMMITT	Gladys Valmai
BROOKER	Thelma Jean	BRUNTON	Olive
BROOKING	Betty Mena	BRUS	Iris Neva
BROOKS	Sylvia Edna	BRYANT	Ellen May
BROOM	Isabelle Alfreda	BRYANT	Violet Jean
		BRYANT-SMITH	Carmen Leila

BRYCE	Alvie Nerida
BRYCE	Daphne Adell Hollingshead
BRYCE	Jeanie Mercer Horne
BRYCE	Vera May
BRYDON	Lorna Jane
BRYDON	Mary Elizabeth
BRYDON	Morveen Ruth
BRYSE	Mavis Amy
BUCKLAND	Marjorie
BUDGE	Dorothy May
BULGIN	Minnie Beatrice Maud
BULLWINKEL	Vivian
BURBIDGE	Beryl Emma
BURBURY	Eleanor Christina
BURCHILL	Dora Elizabeth
BURGESS	Dorice Mary
BURGESS	Gladys Margaret
BURGESS	May
BURKE	Mary
BURNETT	Dorothea Anne
BURNS	Agnes Mary
BURNS	Edna
BURNS	Eileen Cecilia
BURNS	Thelma Clarice
BURNSIDE	Jean Elsie
BURRELL	Nellie Mayo
BURRIDGE	Aileen Travers
BURRIDGE	Lucy Travers
BURT	Iris Dosia
BURZACOTT	Kathleen Helen
BUSH	Dorothy Reavley
BUTLER	Edith Dorothy Kate
BUTLER	Lucy Marion
BUTTON	Clara Ray
BUTTON	Louisa Maud
BUTTROSE	Merle Mary
BYRES	Joan
BYRNE	Mary

BYRNES	Doreen Theresa
CADELL	Jean Mary
CAFFYN	Lavinia Martha
CAHILL	Gertrude Hyacinth
CAHILL	Kathleen
CAIN	Hanora Elizabeth
CAIN	Phyllis Christina Wearne
CAIRNS	Lucy Margaret
CAIRNS-HILL	Molly
CALDECOAT	Vera Isabel
CALDERWOOD	Doris May
CALDWELL	Myee Kathleen
CALLAGHAN	Eileen Mary
CALLAGHAN	Lorna Mary
CALLEN	Sheila Veronica
CALLINAN	Eileen Mary
CALNAN	Ellenor
CALVERT	Pauline Willis
CAMERON	Agnes Bah Hunter
CAMERON	Alice Clementine Alison
CAMERON	Bessie Agnes Thora
CAMERON	Edna Beryl Yvonne
CAMERON	Flora Alison Collier
CAMERON	Joan Agnes
CAMERON	Joan Margaret
CAMERON	Joyce Adele
CAMERON	Kathleen Patricia Lyndsay
CAMERON	Kathleen Sheila
CAMERON	Mary Gertrude
CAMERON	Mary Monica
CAMERON	Myth Kenaway
CAMPBELL	Annie Towns
CAMPBELL	Bernice Leila
CAMPBELL	Betsy Jane Ann
CAMPBELL	Dorothy Janet
CAMPBELL	Lesley June
CAMPBELL	Mary Cecilia
CAMPBELL	Ruth Margaret Letitia

CAMPBELL-SMITH	Kathleen Millicent
CANDLISH	Frances Jessie
CANNING	Barbara Scott
CAREY	Alice Martha
CAREY	Myrtle Myra
CARMICHAEL	Evelyn Hay Drummond
CARMICHAEL	Margaret Constance
CARPENTER	Nancy Jean
CARROLL	Agnes May
CARROLL	Deborah
CARRUTH	Adele Mary Ellen
CARSELDINE	Doris Constance
CARSELDINE	Effie Mary
CARSON	Alice Elizabeth
CARTER	Ethel
CARTER	Gladys
CARTER	Helena Betty
CARTER	Marjorie Frances
CARTER	Miriam
CARTER	Muriel Maude Langhorne
CARTER	Verna Lesley
CARTER	Zerah Emma Jane
CASEY	Ellen Lorraine
CASEY	Joffrette Bridges
CASH	Isabel Vallance
CASHMAN	Sheila Mary
CASSON	Florence Rebecca
CASTLE	Evelyn Maud
CATCHLOVE	Ruby Adelaide
CATHIE	Peggy Cynthia
CATRON	Virginia May
CAVANAGH	Clarice Esther
CAVANAGH	Florence Mary
CAVENAGH-MAINWARING	Patricia
CAVILL	Audrey Dunsmore
CAWTHORN	Margaret Jean
CHAD	Joyce Rosalie
CHADWICK	Elizabeth Alexandria
CHADWICK	Eva Madge
CHADWICK	Irene Constance
CHALINOR	Freda Florence
CHALLINOR	Edith May
CHALMERS	Catherine Margaret
CHALMERS	Clair Drummond
CHALMERS	Hannah Elizabeth
CHALMERS	Joan Violet
CHAMBERLAIN	Violet Gwendolen
CHAMBERS	Doris Maude
CHAMBERS	Emily Ellen
CHAMPION	Joan Avril
CHANCE	Gladys Emily
CHAPMAN	Isabelle
CHAPMAN	Kathleen
CHAPMAN	Mary Patricia
CHAPMAN	Patricia Coleman
CHARLES	Devina Alice
CHARLTON	Enid Rachel
CHARTERS	Enid Marjorie
CHEERS	Lille Elizabeth
CHEGWIDDEN	Ruth Georgia
CHESSELL	Jean Miller
CHESSWAS	Mary Lillian
CHESTERMAN	Barbara Edith
CHEW	Mavis Catherine Banvill
CHILD	Cecily Imelda
CHIPPER	Kathleen Maud
CHISHOLM	Bonnie Mary May
CHOMLEY	Patricia Downes
CHRISTOE	Marie Elizabeth
CHURCH	Leila Eileen
CHURCH	Loris Irene
CLANCEY	Helen Mary
CLANCY	Janet
CLANCY	Veronica Ann
CLARK	Cecily Rowell
CLARK	Doris Jane
CLARK	Edith Fraser

CLARK	Gwen Elizabeth	COGHLAN	Eva Muriel
CLARK	Joan Doreen	COGHLAN	Veronica Magdalene
CLARK	Louise Olive	COLCLOUGH	Vivian Betty
CLARKE	Beryl Irene	COLE	Bessie France
CLARKE	Clarice Isabel	COLE	Joan Margaret
CLARKE	Erica Lace	COLE	Thelma Fenetta
CLARKE	Jean Victoria	COLEBATCH	Marion Frances
CLARKE	Mary Dorothea	COLEMAN	Dorothy May
CLARKE	Mary Rogers	COLEMAN	Greta Gladstone
CLARKE	Nancy Elizabeth	COLEMAN	Jean
CLARKE	Patricia Edith	COLEMAN	Judith Barbara
CLARKE	Pauline Mary	COLES	Iris Jessie
CLARKSON	Ethel Mary	COLLETT	Kathleen Alice
CLATWORTHY	Millie	COLLIE	Sydney Jane
CLAY	Irene Mildred	COLLINS	Gwendolyn Florence
CLAYTON	Isadore Melville	COLLINS	Joan Gertrude
CLEARY	Joyce Ellen	COLLINS	Kathleen
CLEGGETT	Irene Muriel	COLLINS	Mary Alma
CLEMENS	Nuria Evelyn	COLLINS	Ruby May
CLEMENTS	Eadyth Grace	COLLIS	Naomi Gray
CLEMENTS	Joyce Emily	COLLYER	Jessie Hope
CLEMENTS	Margaret Esther	COLVIN	Thecla Eugenie Gleeson
CLEMENTS	Phyllis	COLWELL	Dorothy Jean
CLEMENTS	Ruby	COMINS	Nancy
CLEMSON	Ena Muriel	COMMINS	Elizabeth Ida
CLENNETT	Natalie Elsie	COMPTON	Gladys Emily
CLIFF	Mary	COMPTON	Hanna Violet
CLIFFORD	Ida Lucy	COMTESSE	Margaret Agnes
CLIFT	Alice Alma	CONCANNON	Kathryn
CLIFTON	Rosina Jean	CONDON	Margaret
CLINCH	Dora Miriel	CONDON	Marjorie Alberta
CLINCH	Ethel Mary	CONDON	Mary Elizabeth
CLISSOLD	Millicent Amy	CONDON	Thelma Jean
CLOHESSY	Marcia Jessie	CONNAUGHTON	Mary
CLOUGH	Mavis Alice	CONNOLE	Monica Mary
CLOWES	Dulcie Estelle	CONNOLLY	Myra Gwendoline
COCKING	Frances Mary	CONNOR	Elvy Agnes
COE	Louisa Mary	CONNOR	Jean May
COGAN	Eileen Teresa	CONNOR	Maggie Beryle

CONNOR	Sarah Gwendolen	COTTON	Doreen Mary
CONOLE	Jean Margaret	COTTRELL	Louisa Millicent
CONRAN	Robina Ida	COUCHMAN	Jean Constance
CONROY	Marjorie Alberta	COULSELL	Phyllis Mary
CONSTABLE	Irene Beryl	COUTTS	Isabella Mary
CONSTANTINE	Percia	COWAN	Flora Wishart
CONWAY	Amy Christina	COWAN	Jeanne Meredith
CONWAY	Kathleen Monica	COWAN	Margaret Harkes
COOK	Dorothy	COWELL	Evelyn Vera
COOK	Freda Marjorie	COWELL	Jessie May
COOK	Gladys Elizabeth	COWELL	Una Beryl
COOK	Janet Lyall	COWIE	Janet
COOK	Joan Seymour	COWPER	Barbara Croisdale
COOK	Vera Mary	COX	Ellen Bertha
COOKE	Evelyn	COX	Elsie May
COOKE	Vera Patty Robinson	COX	Florence Adelaide
COOMBES	Dorothy Irene	COX	Gladys Emily
COOMBS	Marie Jean	COX	Vacy Clarendon
COOPER	Elvie Elizabeth	CRAGG	Lorne Margaret
COOPER	Joan Mary	CRAIG	Blanche
COOPER	Kathleen Ruth	CRAIG	Hazel Ruth
COOPER	Leila May	CRAMERI	Jean Frances
COOPER	May Ruby	CRANE	Mary
COOPER	Muriel Winifred	CRAVEN	Joan Isabel
COOPER	Ruby Isabella	CRAWFORD	Anne Ethel
COOTE	Margaret Ann	CRAWFORD	Dorothy Enid
COPE	Marjorie Jean	CRAWFORD	Jean Elizabeth
COPLEY	Isabel Mary	CRAYSON	Mena Josephine
CORBETT	Mary Lorraine	CREAGH	Anne Odonnell
CORCORAN	Angela Sarah	CRESP	Ethel Ada
CORDEROY	Valorie Florence	CRESSALL	Thelma May
CORKER	Nancy Maynard	CRETTENDEN	Ruby Lillian
CORNFORD	Betty	CRICK	Marjorie Louisa
COSGROVE	Marion	CRISP	Ivy Mabel
COSTIGAN	Barbara Jane	CRISP	Muriel Ethel
COTTELL	Gladys Myrtle	CRITTENDEN	Jean Hilda
COTTER	Mary Eileen	CRITTENDEN	Moira Ann
COTTERILL	Hazel Clarice	CROCKETT	Margaret Hannah
COTTON	Betty	CROKER	Lilian Mary

CROKER	Olga	CUSSEN	Audrey Patricia
CROLL	Hope	CUTHBERT	Margaret Blyth
CROMARTY	Elizabeth Stella	CUTHBERTSON	Mary Elizabeth
CRONE	Pauleen	CUTLER	Agnes Hester
CROOME	Elsie May	CUTLER	Janie Margaret Lillian
CROSER	Olive May	DAER	Eileen Beatrice
CROSS	Marion Lawson	DAER	Emily Frances
CROSSAN	Margaret	DAINTON	Florence Alberta
CROSTHWAITE	Majorie Kestell	DAKIN-WARD	Eileen
CROTHERS	Roma Constance	DALBY	Eileen Millicent
CROUCH	Joan	DALE	Agnes Hamilton
CROUCHER	Mary Kathleen	DALE	Phyllis Nell Leo
CROUCHER	Thelma	DALE	Ruth
CROUDACE	Jean Alderford	DALEY	Margaret Teresa
CROUGH	Monica Mary	DALEY	Mary Agnes
CROW	Corelli Una	DALEY	Sheila Merid
CROWLEY	Helen Jean	DALLEY	Mary Alison
CROWLEY	Valerie Margaret	DALWOOD	Sylvia Ailsa
CRUDGINGTON	Alma	DALY	Doris
CRUICKSHANK	Patricia Margaret	DALY	Enid Philomena
CRUMP	Adele Mascot	DALY	Kathleen
CRUMP	Violet Mary	DANCE	Eleanor Mavis
CUDDIHY	Eileen May	DANSON	Lorraine Frances
CUFFE	Mary Honor	D'ARCY	Maureen Kissane
CULLEN	Frances Ann	DARE	Judith Joan
CULLEN	Mavis Claudia	DARLING	Eleanor
CULLY	Annie Mary	DARVENIZA	Annie
CULMSEE	Bertha Dora	DAVEY	Joan Mary
CUMMING	Dora May	DAVID-MOSS	Viola Muriel
CUMMING	Gertrude Mallaby	DAVIDSON	Betty Woodford
CUMMING	Mary Josephine	DAVIDSON	Edna May
CUMMINGS	May Alison	DAVIDSON	Hazel Rosalind
CUMMINS	Kathleen Mary	DAVIE	Phyllis Leah
CUNNINGHAM	Isma Alma	DAVIES	Dorothy Joan
CUNNINGHAM	Teresa Marian	DAVIES	Havrena Fon
CUNNINGHAM	Winifred Harrison	DAVIES	Joyce Maitland
CUPIT	Joan	DAVIES	Joyce Mary
CURTIN	Maureen	DAVIES	Kathleen Bridget
CUSKEY	Elizabeth Margaret	DAVIES	Lois Fanny Loughman

DAVIES	Mabel Betty	DEBNEY	Emily Ellen
DAVIES	Marjorie Catherine	DECKERT	Vera May
DAVIES	Patricia	DEEN	Alvina Safurah
DAVIES	Shirley Helen	DEIGNAN	Esme
DAVIS	Charlotte Victoria	DELANEY	Nora Kathleen
DAVIS	Estelle Janet	DELFORCE	Cecilia May
DAVIS	Irene Norma	DELMONT	Caroline May
DAVIS	Janet	DELPRATT	Elinor Wynne
DAVIS	Mabel Hope	DEMPSEY	Ellen
DAVIS	Mary	DEMPSEY	Marie Sylvia
DAVIS	Nora Pleasance	DEMPSEY	Ola Marie
DAVIS	Ruby Eileen	DENGATE	Iris Hilda Ellis
DAVIS	Winnie May	DENHAM	Una Gwendoline
DAWES	Lorna Caroline	DENMAN	Jean Leighton
DAWSON	Ethel Elizabeth	DENNETT	Doreen Edna
DAWSON	Eugenie	DENNIS	Mary Catherine
DAWSON	Ilena	DENT	Margaret Alencon
DAWSON	Jean Christina	DENTON	Alice Ann
DAWSON	Jean Elizabeth	DENTON	Doris Irene May
DAWSON	Mana	DEVLIN	Elsie May
DAWSON	Mavis	DEVOS	Marcia Elizabeth
DAWSON	May Elaine	DEW	Helen
DAWSON	Sadie Gertrude	DICKESON	Audrey Margaret
DAY	Margaret Jean	DICKIE	Audrey Margaret
DAY	Patricia Florence	DICKIE	Elizabeth Lilian
DE BRACY	Myra Elizabeth	DICKIE	Marie Eugene
DE MESTRE	Margaret Augusta	DICKINSON	Anne Hannah
DE OBERITZ	Josephine Mary	DICKSON	Ella Douglas
DEACON	Dulcie Hazel Bassett	DICKSON	Jean Catherine
DEALL	Dorothy Joyce	DIEKMANN	Joyce
DEALL	Florence Gwendolen	DILLON	Barbara Helen
DEAN	Alice Winifred	DILLON	Margaret
DEAN	Edna May	DINGLE-MITCHELL	Marie Margaret Veronica
DEAN	Ellen Alice	DISHON	Muriel Beatrice
DEAN	Jean Alice	DITTY	Sheila Margaret
DEAN	Mavis Edith	DIXON	Alice
DEAN	Phyllis Lesly	DIXON	Kathleen Margaret
DEANE	Sarah Elizabeth	DOBBYNS	Ida Ella Grace
DEAR	Mona Elizabeth		

DOCKSEY	Anne Dorothy	DOYLE	Jess Gregory
DODD	Jessie Anne Gwendolene	DOYLE	Veronica Louisa
DODD	Jessie Lillian	DRABSCH	Edith May
DODD	Nancy May	DRAKE	Joyce
DOHERTY	Margaret Mary Rita	DRENNAN	Ivy May
DOHNT	Gwendoline Mary	DREWE	Dulcie Vera
DOIDGE	Doris Irene	DRINAN	Minna Doralice
DOIG	Edna Nell	DROVER	Naomi Theo
DOLLAHAN	Lucy Mary	DRUITT	Ruth Evelyn
DOLLARD	Aileen Veronica	DRUMMOND	Irene Melville
DOLLARD	Nancy Kathleen	DRUMMOND	Jean
DONALD	Agnes Joyce	DRUMMY	Robina Maria
DONALD	Ina Margaret	DRYLIE	Winifred Hazel
DONALDSON	Florence May	DRYNAN	Kathleen Cecelia
DONEGAN	Helen May	DRYSDALE	Mary Helen
DONNELLY	Helen Mary	DRYSDALE	Vida
DONOGHUE	Elizabeth Austin	DUANE	Patricia Margaret
DONOHUE	Ellen	DUDLEY	Ruth
DORAN	Johanna Maria	DUFF	Veronica Mary
DORMER	Mary Veronica Sophia	DUFFIELD	Alice Mary
DORNAN	Grace	DUFFIELD	Edith Merle
DORSCH	Millicent Hulda Maria	DUFFY	Annie Catherine Sheila
DORWARD	Joyce	DUFFY	Heather
DOUCH	Sheelah Strachan	DUFFY	Josephine Eileen Teresa
DOUGHENEY	Anne	DUFTY	Phyllis
DOUGLAS	Jean Isobel	DUGGAN	Miriam
DOUGLASS	Audrey Mavis	DUKE	Sylvia Coral
DOUGLASS	Dulcie Thelma	DULY	Violet Lillian
DOVEY	Enid Marion	DUMAS	Mary Edna Florence
DOWDLE	Freda Mary Eliza	DUMBRELL	Emmeline Beatrice
DOWIE	Jean Isabel	DUN	Beatrice Jean
DOWLING	Beatrice Lorraine	DUNBAR	Jessie Norma
DOWN	Ruth	DUNCAN	Eileen Ethel
DOWNE	Marjorie Florence	DUNCANSON	Nellie Cathrine
DOWNEY	Kathleen	DUNHILL	Vera Anne
DOWNIE	Claire Edith	DUNMAN	Maude Leslie
DOYLE	Catherine Ellen	DUNN	Mary
DOYLE	Elizabeth	DUNN	Shiela Mary
DOYLE	Eveline Mary	DUNSTONE	Mary Josephine

DURR	Joan	ELLIOTT	Violet Isabel
DURUZ	Jessie Louise	ELLIS	Joan Mary
DURWARD	Annie Mabel	ELLIS	Nancy Theodora
DUTHIE	Lorna Constance	ELLISON	Helen Duthie
DWANE	Beryl Edith	ELMES	Dorothy Gwendoline Howard
DWYER	Elizabeth Jean	ELWORTHY	Nancy Madge
DWYER	Ellen Maizey	EMBREY	Theresa
DWYER	Gwenyth Merle	EMMS	Marie Allen Walker
DWYER	Veronica Agnes	ENDEAN	Stella
DYER	Grace Alice	ENGELBRECHT	Mary Jean
DYER	Stella	ENGLAND	Moreen Cecilia
EADE	Marie Phillipa	ENGLUND	Ella Roddam
EADES	Mary	ENNIS	Caroline Mary
EADIE	Clare	ENNIS	Iris Mathews
EASTON	Nancy Lorraine	ERRINGTON	Marie Elizabeth
EASTWOOD	Eunice Marion	ERRINGTON-ESSEX	Pauline Mary
EDIS	Margaret Dorothy	ERSKINE	Margaret Ramsay Young
EDMONDS	Marjorie Marion	EUNSON	Margaret Fulton
EDWARDS	Ethna Joan	EUNSON	Marion Watt
EDWARDS	Isabel Ivy	EVANS	Annabella Gertrude
EDWARDS	Jean Beryl	EVANS	Bronwen
EDWARDS	Jean Ravenshaw	EVANS	Daisy Mona Eileen
EDWARDS	Kathleen Mary	EVANS	Doris May
EDWARDS	Leila Alexina	EVANS	Mabel Dorothy
EDWARDS	Lucy Hamnett	EVANS	Margaret Muriel
EDWARDS	Norma Rose	EVANS	Norma Adeline
EDWARDS	Violet Alma	EVANS	Shirley
EGAN	Gertrude Mary	EVANS	Zoe Winifred
EGAN	Joy Margaret	EVENNETT	Gwendoline Joyce
EGAN	Mary Agnes	EVENSON	Signe Christobel
EGAN-LEE	Dorothy Yvonne	EVERARD	Kathleen Mary
EGERTON-WARBURTON	Elizabeth	EVERETT	Dorothy May
EGGER	Honor Jean	EVERETT	Muriel Grace
EGGLESTON	Lois Cathleen	EVERINGHAM	Kathleen
ELLERAY	Thelma Mary	EWAN	Charlotte Alexandra
ELLIOT	Nancy Amelia	EWART	Margaret Archibald
ELLIOTT	Kathleen	EWERS	Gladys Audrey
ELLIOTT	Ola Maree Teece	EWING	Audrey

EWING	Frances Peace	FIELD	Gwladys Parker
EWING	Lorna	FIELDER	Muriel Inez Annette
EWING	Mona Eugenie	FIELDING	Edna Mary
EXTON	Ada Margaret	FIELDING	Jean Elizabeth
FAGAN	Wilhelmina Margaret	FINCH	Nancy Mary
FAHEY	Iris Edith	FINDLAY	Agnes Joy
FAHLE	Mary Dorothy	FINDLAY	Mary Ann
FAIRCLOUGH	Jean	FINLAYSON	Margaret Mackenzie
FAIRFAX	Desma Ryan	FINLAYSON	Susan Terris
FAIRHALL	Constance Grace	FINLAYSON	Viva
FAIRWEATHER	Lorna Florence	FISCHER	Ada Ruth
FAKHRY	Maureen Matilda	FISK	Margaret Elsie
FALL	Constance Amy	FITZGERALD	Frances Monica
FALLICK	Rae	FITZGIBBON	Ursula Myra
FALLON	Reta Hazel	FITZHUGH	Amy Hope
FANE-DE-SALIS	Una Lesley	FLETCHER	Dorothy Elizabeth
FARMANER	Peggy Everett	FLETCHER	Edith Mary
FARQUHAR	G'Lenton June	FLETCHER	Esme Kathleen
FARRACY	Kathleen Molly	FLETCHER	Joan Patricia
FARTHING	Gladys Jean	FLETCHER	Lilian
FARTHING	Grace Catherine Melba	FLETCHER	Margaret Weld
FAULKNER	Gertrude Ivy	FLETCHER	Mary Agnes
FAULKNER	Helen Linda	FLETCHER	Phyllis
FAULKNER	Irene May	FLETCHER	Sybil Jean
FAVALORO	Florence Margia	FLETT	Doreen Bertram
FAVALORO	Jean Florence Maria	FLETT	June Neruda
FAWCETT	Elizabeth May	FLOWER	Diana Hickson
FAWCETT	Hazel Florence	FLOWER	Margaret
FECHNAY	Jean Adeline	FLOYD	Jean Elizabeth
FELSTEAD	Elsie May	FOGARTY	Mary Nancy
FENNELLY	Janet Ellen	FOGARTY	Sheelah
FENNER	Ellen Margaret Bobbie	FOGARTY	Winifred
FENWICK	Anne Therese	FOLDER	Edith Millie
FERGUSON	Edith Mary	FOLEY	Bridget Mary
FERGUSON	Isobel Alexandra	FOLEY	Lorna Mary
FERGUSON	Jean Elsie	FOLEY	Margaret Elsie
FERGUSON	Marjorie Jean	FOLLAND	Ena Azalia
FERNIE	Isobel Thomson	FOLLENT	Sheila Mary
FERRIS	Ethel May	FOOTE	Patricia

FORBES	Ethel Jean	FREEMAN	Emma Lycett
FORBES	Jean Marion	FREEMAN	Esther Meta
FORD	Joyce Christine	FREEMAN	Jeanne Neste Willgress
FORD	Mary Patricia	FREEMAN	Mena
FORDHAM	Ethel Grace	FREEMAN	Rubina Dorothy
FOREMAN	Barbara Joan	FRICK	Madeline Nance
FORREST	Elizabeth Grace	FRICKER	Clara Elsie
FORRESTER	Elsie Charlotte	FRIEBE	Marjorie Campbell
FORRESTER	Ethel Jean	FRIEDLIEB	Lorna Carmel
FORSTER	Jean Marion	FRINSDORF	Helen Day
FORSTER	Mary Kathleen	FROST	Alice
FORSYTH	Beryl Gethla Louise	FROST	Florence Ethel May
FORSYTH	Marcelle Watson	FRY	Edith Richenda Elizabeth
FORWOOD	Bettie Hampden	FRY	Patricia Eve
FOSTER	Laura Adeline	FRY	Ruth
FOSTER	Phyllis Mae	FULLARTON	Ellen Clive Victoria
FOULKES	Francesca Mary	FULLARTON	Joyce Bonnin
FOUNTAIN	Gwendoline	FULLER	Patricia Clare
FOWLE	Alice Patricia	FULLERTON	Jessie Irma
FOWLER	Ismay Marjorie	FULTON	Ella Mary
FOWLES	Winifred Ellen	FULTON	Lilian Mary
FOX	Elsie Frances Newton	FUREY	Phyllis Isabelle
FOX	Jean Elizabeth Keenan	FURLONG	Katherine Lucy
FRANCIS	Doris Edith	FURLONGE	Laura Elizabeth
FRANCIS	Dorothy Gwennith Mary	GAGGIN	Coralie Alice
FRANCIS	Margaret Olive	GALE	Linda Mary
FRANKLIN	Elizabeth Kathleen Mary	GALLAGER	Annie Ella
FRASER	Beryl	GALLAGHER	Kathleen Julia
FRASER	Edith Helen	GALLEN	Jessie Irene
FRASER	Elizabeth Hutchinson	GALLOWAY	Winifred Katherine
FRASER	Gladys Merle	GALWEY	Agnes
FRASER	Jean	GAMBLE	Jean Dorothy
FRASER	Jean Estelle	GANE	Miriam Edith
FRASER	Ruby Evelyn	GANIM	Leila May
FREDERICKS	Colma	GANT	Beryl Alice Mary
FREDERICKS	Mary Eileen	GARBUTT	Nancy Elizabeth
FREEBAIRN	May Isabel	GARDAM	Dora Shirley
FREEMAN	Clare Winifred	GARDINER	Agnes Margaret

GARDINER	Barbara Helen	GILES	Lavinia Ellen
GARDINER	Cynthia Catharine	GILES	Nella Margaret Kathleen
GARDINER	Joan Mary	GILES	Sarah Palmer
GARDINER	Olive Jean	GILL	Clare Kathleen
GARDNER	Gertrude	GILLAM	Betty
GARDNER	Kathleen Carew	GILLANDERS	Margaret Dolina
GARDNER	Muriel Augusta	GILLETT	Nellie May
GARLICK	Lucy Isobel	GILLIES	Catherine Brown Meikle
GARRATT	Dorothy	GILLIES	Catherine McPherson
GARRETT	Doris Edna	GILMORE	Lydia Grace
GARRETT	Lilla Victoria May	GILMORE	Thelma Joyce
GARTNER	Joyce	GILMOUR	Isobel Hislop
GARVEY	Madeleine Claire	GILMOUR	Mary Margaret
GAUL	Ruth Genevieve Boyce	GILMOUR	Nance
GAVENLOCK	Olive Ida May	GINTY	Joyce Alison
GAY	Jean Margaret	GLASGOW	Mary Margaret
GAYLARD	Isla Anne	GLASSON	Winsome Betty
GEHRIKE	Ruby Dorothea	GLEADALL	Amy Winifred
GEISLER	Hildegarde Meta	GLEESON	Dulcie Bridget
GEORGE	Margaret Alice	GLEESON	Isabelle Mary
GEORGE	Monica Mary Silles	GLEESON	Madge Eileen
GERAGHTY	Mary Patricia	GLEN	Ida Melrose
GERAGHTY	Monica	GLEN	Myra Joan
GERLACH	Alma Margrita	GLENNIE	Irene Josephine
GERRARD	Kathleen	GLOVER	Trixie Alice
GIBBONS	Mavis Esme	GLUCKMAN	Irene Bessie
GIBSON	Charlotte Travis Lynn	GLYNN	Ellen Frances
GIBSON	Emily Jean	GOFF	Elsie May
GIBSON	Joan Grace	GOLAND	Olga Olive
GIBSON	Margaret Elizabeth	GOLDEN	Rhoda Joyce
GIBSON	Rose Margaret	GOLDEN	Ursula Mary
GILBERT	Edna May	GOLDFINCH	Doris Edna
GILBERT	Joan Russell	GOLDNEY	Edna Marion
GILBERT	Joyce Helena	GOLDSMITH	Isobel Imogene
GILBERT	Martina Agnes	GOLDSMITH	Mona Sara
GILBY	Marjorie Valerie	GOLDSTEIN	Minnie Sutherland
GILCHRIST	May	GOLIK	Agnes Marion Cecily
GILES	Beryl Aphra	GOLLAN	Jeanie
GILES	Laurie Gwendoline		

GOLOMB	Joyce Leona	GRAINGER	Febe Irene
GOOCH	Kathleen Hope	GRANT	Marjorie Alice
GOODE	Agnes Nancy	GRANT	Mary Matilda
GOODE	Dorothy Jean	GRANT	May Louise
GOODE	Helen Marston	GRANT	Winifred Florence
GOODES	Jean Margaret	GRAY	Audrey Ethel
GOODGER	Gladys Lilywhite	GRAY	Beatrice Phillimore
GOODIN	Wilhelmina Edna	GRAY	Myee
GOODMAN	Hilda Margaret	GRAYLING	Frances Eunice
GOODSIR	Makiri Kathleen	GREAVES	Margaret Victoria Mary
GOOS	Johanna Wilhelmina	GREEN	Edna Mary
GORDON	Celia Josie	GREEN	Gwendoline Alice
GORDON	Eunice	GREEN	Joyce Margaret
GORDON	Geraldine Clare	GREEN	Mavis Emmeline
GORDON	Jean Isabel	GREEN	Shiela
GORDON	Millicent Eden	GREENE	Lorna Leland
GORMAN	Hazel	GREENING	Dorothy Grace
GORMAN	Marjorie Leila	GREENWOOD	Alice Constance
GORMAN	Mary Gladys Katherine	GREENWOOD	Laura Bessie
GORMAN	Mary Patricia	GREER	Catherine Mary
GORRIE	Jessie May	GREER	Jean Keers
GORRY	Margaret Jean	GREET	Jean Katherine
GORTON	Leila Mavis	GREGERSON	Pearl
GOULD	Kathleen Alice	GREGORY	Beryl Enid
GOULD	Vida Mary	GREGORY	Laura Lindsay
GOULDEN	Ethel Francis	GRIEVE	Jean Alice
GOYDER	Elizabeth	GRIFFIN	Margaret White
GRACE	Josephine	GRIFFIN	Thelma Janet
GRACE	Thurza Anne	GRIFFITH	Helen Roberta
GRACEY	Catherine Jean	GRIFFITH	Margaret Elizabeth
GRADY	Imedla Bridgid	GRIFFITHS	Bernice May
GRAHAM	Beatrice Lilian	GRIFFITHS	Ethel Mabel
GRAHAM	Betty Evelyn	GRIGG	Iva Evelyn
GRAHAM	Dulcie Ellen	GRIMES	Muriel Adelaide
GRAHAM	Evaline Elizabeth	GRIMES	Winifred
GRAHAM	Gwenda Hamilton	GROSVENOR	Lucy Margaret
GRAHAM	Irma Edith	GROTEFENT	Isabella Mary
GRAHAM	Laura Marguerite	GRUBB	Margaret Beaumont
GRAHAM	Maud Ada	GRYLLS	Edith Melva

GUICE	Edna Mavis	HAMLYN-HARRIS	Margery Bertha
GUILD	Betty Ariell	HAMMILL	Marjorie Rebecca
GUILFOYLE	Bridget Mary	HAMMOND	Joan Howison
GULLY	Margaret Martha	HAMMOND	Lyla Smiley
GUNTHER	Janet Patteson	HAMPTON	Marjorie
GUNTHORPE	Elsie Emily	HANCOCK	Mary Beatrice
GUNTON	Mollie Marie	HANCOCK	Mildred Florence
GUTHRIE	Lorna	HANLON	Isobel Ada
GUYE	Violet Sylvia	HANMER	Beatrice Walden
HACK	Charlotte Helen	HANNA	Margaret Jean
HADLEY	Norma Woodfield	HANNAH	Ellen Mavis
HAEBICH	Eva Frances	HANRAHAN	Ethel Frances
HAIG	Violet	HANSCOMBE	Rita Ann
HAILEY	Joyce Mary	HANSEN	Kate Isobel
HAINES	Brenda	HANSON	Margaret Jean
HAINES	Ethel Lucretia	HARBEN	Dorothy Anne
HAINES	Susan Jean	HARBISON	Anna Graeme Agnes
HALE	Margaret Theodosia	HARBORNE	Christina May
HALE	Mollie Antoinette	HARDCASTLE	Kathleen May Selwyn
HALES	Doreen Marie Jacqueline	HARDWICK	Mary Clare Louise
		HARDY	Honor
HALES	Nora Hope	HARLER	Edith Elizabeth
HALL	Alma Jean	HARPER	Iole
HALL	Eleanor Margaret	HARRINGTON	Agnes Janet
HALL	Florence Mary	HARRIS	Alice Ismay
HALL	Gladys Irene	HARRIS	Brenda Irene
HALL	Phillipia Judith	HARRIS	Doris Irene
HALLETT	Bernice Robertson	HARRIS	Elizabeth Josephine
HALLIGAN	Clarice Isobel	HARRIS	Hazel Mary
HALLOWS	Sylvia Frances	HARRIS	Nancy
HAMBLETON	Daphne Agnes	HARRIS	Vera Philomena
HAMBOUR	Angelina	HARRISON	Dorothea Mary
HAMILTON	Ann Elanor	HARRISON	Dorothy Florence
HAMILTON	Helen Margaret	HARRISON	Dorothy Mabel
HAMILTON	Lorraine Myrtle	HARRISON	Ella Jean
HAMILTON	Mary Kathleen	HARRISON	Kathleen Narelle
HAMILTON	Nella Isabel	HARROP	Lorna Hayward
HAMILTON	Vera Frances	HART	Audrey Harriett May
HAMILTON-FOSTER	Adelaide Clara	HART	Edna May

HART	Lillian	HEATHCOTE	Eileen Jane
HARVEY	Catherine Edwina	HEATHWOOD	Irene
HARVEY	Florence Elsie	HECTOR	Katie Christina
HARVEY	Jean Ogilvie	HEDGES	Christine
HARVEY	Joan Rosemary	HEERS	Hazel Omega
HARVEY	Vera Simms	HEFFERNAN	Patricia
HASENKAM	Selma Freda	HEGARTY	Margaret Rachell
HASKING	Jessie	HELE	Rita Mary
HASLUCK	Rosa Hope	HELLICAR	Letritia Jocelyn
HASTIE	Lillian Marie	HELY-WILSON	Una
HASTIE	Margaret Jean	HEMMINGS	Oenone Louise
HATCH	Millicent Christina	HEMPSTED	Pauline Blanche
HATELEY	Doris May	HENDERSON	Beatrice Amelia
HATFIELD	Joyce Frances	HENDERSON	Edna Ruby
HAULTAIN	Helen Frances Jane	HENDERSON	Gwendoline Dinah
HAUSER	Nancye Franziska	HENDERSON	Janet Elizabeth
HAW	Ena Doreen	HENDERSON	Janet Hall Scott
HAWKES	Elizabeth Maud	HENDERSON	June Bronte
HAWKES	Thora Dorothy May	HENDERSON	Marie Anketell
HAWKINS	Katherine Doreen	HENDERSON-WILSON	Laura Mary
HAWKSLEY	Mary Rebecca	HENDRA	Grace Lettie May
HAWORTH	Mary Cecelia	HENDY-POOLEY	Margaret Mary
HAWTHORNE	Dorothy	HENLEY	Joyce Alice
HAY	Dorothy Jean	HENNESSY	Dorothy
HAY	Marjorie Grace Rivers	HENNESSY	Valmai Amy
HAY	Miriam Victoire	HENNING	Mona
HAY	Peggy Hamilton	HENRY	Catherine Margaret
HAYES	Beatrice Isabel	HENRY	Frances Elizabeth
HAYES	Margaret Veronica	HENRY	Leonie Trace
HAYES	Mary Mackenzie	HENRY	Mona Violet
HAYES	Patricia Marie	HENSCHKE	Gladys Elma
HAYNES	Barbara	HEPWORTH	Florence Ella
HAYNES	Mary Christina	HERMAN	Ellen Elizabeth
HAYTON	Edna Phyllis	HERRIDGE	Ilma Joan
HAYWARD	Lorna Alice	HERRIOT	Mary Elizabeth
HEADBERRY	Jean Evelyn	HEWISH	Annie Joyce
HEALEY	Gwendoline	HEWISON	Catherine
HEAPHY	Kathleen	HEWSON	Bertha Alma
HEARD	Rita Madge		

HEWSON	Jean Osborne
HEWSTON	Stella Jessie
HEWTON	Daphne Ross
HEYBROEK	Sonja
HEYER	Margaret Veronica
HIATT	Bessie Frances
HICKSON	Jean
HIGGS	Gwenneth
HIGH	Marian
HILDYARD	Hilda Mavis
HILL	Adeline Louisa
HILL	Bessie Douglas
HILL	Elizabeth Ashton
HILL	Gabrielle Mary
HILL	Hazel Ruby
HILL	Mary Phillips
HILL	Nell Culmer
HILL	Rita Florence
HILL	Veronica Mary
HILLMAN	Doreen Madge Alison
HILLS	Kathleen Margaret
HIMMELHOCH	Enid Sylvia
HINDS	Jean
HIRSCH	Constance Marie
HIRSCHBERG	Joan Marie
HITCHINGS	Matilda Ellen Florence
HITCHINS	Irma Robina
HOARE	Mary Madeline
HOARE	Nellie
HOBBS	Mary Dorothy
HOBBS	Victoria Alexandra May
HOBILL	Avis Rhoda
HODGSON	Ethel
HODGSON	Minnie Ivy
HODSON	Frances Charlotte
HOEY	Iris
HOGARTH	Isobel Hilary
HOGBEN	Elizabeth Cole
HOLCOMBE	Valerie Winifred Vernon
HOLDEN	Mary Elizabeth
HOLDING	Betty Alice
HOLDING	Marjorie Olive
HOLLAND	Mildred Grace
HOLLINGSWORTH	Alma Edna
HOLLOW	Faith
HOLLOWAY	Nancy Howarth
HOLLOWAY	Vera Louise
HOLMES	Creslie Elizabeth
HOLMES	Jessie Ellen
HOLMES	Joan
HOLMES	Margaret
HOLMES	Nancy Millicent
HOLT	Lucy Myrtle
HOLT	Lynda Elma
HOLTZE	Kathleen Isobel
HONEY	Gertrude
HONNER	Margaret Mary
HONNER	Mona Bridgid
HOOD	Jean Ethel Grieve
HOOD	Reta Myra
HOOKE	Helen Fanny
HOOKE	Joan Sybilla
HOOPER	Kathleen Elizabeth Moore
HOOPER	Roma Patricia
HOPE	Ina Althea
HOPE	Sheila Ellen
HOPKINS	Ada Caroline
HOPKINS	Evelyn Victoria
HOPTON	Nance Vivian
HORAN	Eileen
HORDER	Avril Marian
HORSTMAN	Dorothy Jean
HORTON	Elizabeth Mary
HOSKING	Violet Adelaide
HOUSTON	Audrey Ellen
HOUSTON	Catherine Josephine
HOUSTON	Elizabeth Joy

HOWARD	Joyce Priscilla
HOWER	Veronica Jean
HOWLETT	Alexandria Lavinia
HOWSON	Violet
HUBERT	Beryl May
HUDSON	Jennet Collier
HUDSPETH	Margaret Vera
HUETT	Eileen Beryl
HUGHES	Aileen Mary
HUGHES	Doris Helen
HUGHES	Dulcie May
HUGHES	Gladys
HUGHES	Gladys Laura
HUGHES	Lucy Winifred
HUGHES	Olive Emilene
HUGO	Joyce Lillian
HULL	Denise Mary
HUNGERFORD	Ruth Lois
HUNGERFORD	Victoria Iris
HUNT	Marcia Emma
HUNTER	Bridget
HUNTER	Doreen
HUNTER	Joan
HUNTER	Lorna Frances
HUNTER	Sara Ruth
HUPPATZ	Rosa Zelma
HURFORD	Catherine Maude
HURLEY	Evelyn Joyce
HURLEY	Frances Ferguson
HURLEY	Marie Evelyn
HURST	Mabel
HUTCHISON	Betty Stewart
HUTCHISON	Doris Edna
HUTTON	Iris Grace
HUTTON	Mary Margaret Honorah
HYLAND	Esme Rutherford
HYLAND	Margery Rutherford
ILLINGWORTH	Marjorie Beryl
ILLINGWORTH	Phyllis Hannah
IMHOFF	Rachel
IMS	Olive Annie
INGLIS	Dorothy Mary
INGRAM	Florence Barbara
INGRAM	Rhoda Anderson
INKPEN	Esme
INSKIP	Iris May
IRBY	Elspeth Douglas
IRELAND	Elsie Grace
IRVINE	Della Mary
IRVINE	Edith Grace
IRVINE	Jean Agnes
IRVINE	Mabel Elsie
IRVING	Aileen
IRWIN	Mary Johanna
IRWIN	Veronica Francis
ISON	Ethel Margaret
JACKSON	Beverley Francis
JACKSON	Deliah Theresa
JACKSON	Dorothy Agnes
JACKSON	Margaret Lawrence
JACKSON	Marjory Florence
JACKSON	Muriel Haydn
JACOB	Helen Bertha Mary
JACOBS	Rachael Miriam
JAFFER	Audrey Alice
JAKINS	Freda
JAKINS	Nancy
JAMES	Ethel Mary
JAMES	Katherine Magdeline
JAMES	Kathleen Mary
JAMES	Nesta Gwyneth
JAMES	Ruth
JAMESON	Gladys Jean
JAMIESON	Ida Mary Dickson
JARMAN	Rene Laura
JEFFERY	Edna Haynes
JEFFREY	Agnes Betty

JELBART	Ida Rose	JONES	Georgia Betty
JELBART	Lorna Edith	JONES	Gwendoline Lilian
JELLEY	Fay Christina	JONES	Gwendoline Marion
JENKIN	Ruby	JONES	Gwenyth Farrar
JENKINS	Harriet May	JONES	Laurie Charlotte
JENKINS	Ida Verina Grace	JONES	Mary Patricia
JENKINS	Marion Rose	JONES	Mavis Kathleen
JENKINS	Marjorie	JONES	Millicent Hilda
JENKINS	Mollie Agnes	JONES	Mona Doris
JENKINS	Patricia Estelle	JONES	Norma Dorothea
JENNINGS	Gertrude May	JONES	Olive Catherine
JENNINGS	Margaret Ada	JONES	Viola Ilma Pryce
JENSEN	Doris Maida	JONES	Violet Margaret
JENSEN	Joy Augusta	JONES	Winifred Alvera
JENSEN	Marion Joyce	JOSEPH	Ray Alberta
JEPSON	Olive Alvia	JOSEPHS	Margaret Elizabeth
JESSEN	Marie Doreen	JOUBERT	Kathleen
JESSURUN	Olive Marion	JOYCE	Eileen Finlay
JEWELL	Sarah Ann	JOYCE	Lilian Mary
JIEAR	Patricia	JUNOR	Dora
JOHNS	Elizabeth Francis	JURY	Lillian Constance
JOHNSON	Agnes Muriel	JURY	Marian
JOHNSON	Eileen Blanche	KABLE	Coral Rose
JOHNSON	Elizabeth Vera	KAMP	Myrtle Olive Whilemine
JOHNSON	Elsie Mavys	KAVANAGH	Florence
JOHNSON	Kathleen Mary	KAY	Alice
JOHNSON	Margaret	KAY	Joyce Dudley
JOHNSON	Mary Frances	KAY	Muriel
JOHNSON	Nona Gertrude	KAYLER-THOMSON	Olive Una
JOHNSON	Phyllis	KEALY	Kathleen Teresa
JOHNSTON	Anne Margaret	KEAMY	Beanie
JOHNSTON	Jean Margaret	KEAREY	Elizabeth
JOLLEY	Thelma May	KEARNS	Gwenneth
JOLLY	Norma Frances	KEARNS	Margaret Alice
JONES	Alice Saint David	KEARNS	May Lorraine
JONES	Edna Lucy	KEARNS	Miriam Victoire
JONES	Eileen Mary	KEARY	Hilda Ethel
JONES	Ethel Jean	KEAST	Daisy Cardin
JONES	Eva Ethel	KEATS	Ellen Louisa

KEEBLE	Gwyneth	KING	Ellen Irene
KEETLEY	Marion Elizabeth	KING	Evelyn Veronica
KELAHER	Gwendoline Thelma	KING	Gladys Elizabeth
KELIHER	Johanna Mary	KING	Josephine Margaret
KELLY	Aileen Mary	KING	Julie
KELLY	Avoca Mary	KING	Mary Ellen
KELLY	Beatrice Maud	KING	Muriel Christabel
KELLY	Marie Stewart	KINGSFORD	Maureen Norma
KELLY	Mary Goldsack	KINSELLA	Kathleen
KELLY	Phyllis Nein	KIRCHNER	Thekla Elisabeth
KELLY	Sheila Mary	KIRK	Constance Sheila
KELLY	Winifred May	KIRKWOOD	Norma De Lange
KEMP	Eily May	KIRWAN	Catherine
KENNEDY	Patricia Curran	KIRWAN	Mary Alice
KENNY	Eileen Veronica	KISSANE	Imelda Anne
KENT	Dulcie Maud	KITTO	Jessie Alice
KENT	Marion Young	KLOSE	Norma Dulcie
KENTWELL	Helen May	KLUCK	Agnes Ann
KENYON	Alison	KLUG	Doris Margaret
KENYON	Eileen May	KNAPPSTEIN	Vera
KERR	Audrey Joan	KNECHTLI	Nancy Cranstoun
KERR	Janet	KNIGHT	Barbara Marjorie
KERR	Gwendoline May	KNIGHT	Bertha Olive
KERR	Marcella Watson	KNIGHT	Helen Maud
KERR	Stella Marion Agnes	KNIGHT	Edith Nellie
KERVILLE	Nancy Una	KNOWLES	Marie Beryl
KESTEL	Olive Ada	KNOWLES	Muriel Elizabeth
KEVIN	Sheila Kathleen	KNOX	Doris Ruby
KEYS	Lorna Elsie	KNOX	Rae
KIDD	Dorothy Annie	KNUDSEN	Vida Maysie
KIEL	Mary Evelyn	KOCH	Constance Adelaide
KIEL	Maude Elaine	KOCHEVATKIN	Mary
KIERNAN	Elizabeth	KOZLOWSKI	Gabrielle Dorothea
KIERNAN	Kathleen Una	KRAUSS	Beatrice Mary Louise
KILDEA	Mavis	KREMER	Kathryn Jessie
KILLMISTER	Mary Constance	KUHLMANN	Audrey Olive
KILMINSTER	Cecelia Rose	KUHLMANN	Dorothy Jean
KINANE	Therese Alacoque	KUNKLER	Marjorie
KING	Beverley Graham	LACEY	Dorothy Grace

LADE	Sheila Isabel	LEANE	Mary Bridgid
LAFFER	Lorna Florence	LEAR	Martha Alice
LALOR	Charlotte Eileen	LEAVERS	Ruth
LALOR	Enid Adelaide	LEE	Hazel Mary
LAMBELL	Unee Florence	LEE	Joan
LANCASTER	Eileen Alma	LEE	Midj
LANDERS	Doris Kathleen	LEECH	Vera Florence
LANDRIGAN	Nora Jessie	LEFROY	Margaret Grace
LANE	Veronica	LENAGHAN	Minnie Joyce
LANG	Victoria Carlisle	LENNON	Jessie Scott
LANGFORD	Leslie Margaret	LEONARD	Ellen Margaret
LANGHAM	Jessie Margaret	LEONARD	Sheila Alice
LANGHAM	Natalie Charlotte	LESLIE	Jean Mary
LANSKEY	Elizabeth Anne	LESLIE	Kathleen
LANYON	Honor Agnes	LESLIE	Lois Beatrice
LARSEN	Eva May	LESLIE	Nancy Barbara Mary
LATTA	Avis	LESTER	Gwenda May
LAUGHREN	Ethel Frances	LETCH	Jeannette Esme
LAVIS	Mabel	LEWIN	Helen Eunice
LAW	Ellen Angela	LEWIN	Joyce Mary
LAW	Grace Marion	LEWIN	Melva Laura
LAWLER	Rita Frances	LEWIN	Rosalind Blanche
LAWRENCE	Beatrice Pearl	LEWINGTON	Lucy Alma
LAWRENCE	Katherine Ethel	LEWIS	Hazel Joyce
LAWRENCE	Kathleen Ross	LEWIS	Heather Elizabeth
LAWSON	Betty Constance	LEWIS	Lorna Newton
LAWSON	Marjorie Emily	LEWIS	Lydia
LAY	Ella Marion	LEWIS	Margaret Winifred
LAYCOCK	Lily Gertrude	LEWIS	Mary Geraldine
LAYTON	Beulah Unita Lillian	LEWIS	Mary Quita
LAYTON	Emma Mildred	LEYS	Margaret Constance
LAZARUS	Hilda Grace	LIDDY	Anne Angela
LE CORNU	Marguerite Phyllis	LIDDY	Christina Catherine
LE VARING	Jocelyn Andrew	LIGHTOWLER	Pearl Elizabeth
LEAHY	Catherine	LINDNER	Alvera Dora
LEAHY	Mavis Margaret Catherine	LINDSAY	Emily Hilda
LEAKE	Mildred Amy	LINDSAY	Margaret Isabel
LEAMON	Jean Alderford	LINDSAY	Mary Florence
		LINDSAY	Ruth

LINGFORD	Lucy Bowman
LINN	Mabel Esmee
LINNELL	Alice Joyce
LIPSETT	Adeline
LIPSTINE	Audrey Rosa
LITTLE	Elsie Agnes Constance
LIVINGSTONE	Wilhemina
LLOYD	Freda Margaret
LLOYD	Mary Leila
LLOYD	Thelma Jane
LOAN	Marie Daisy
LOCKE	Ethel Maude
LOCKE	Macrina Josephine
LOELLER	Barbara Joy
LOFTUS	Olga Lucy
LOGAN	Eleanor Mary
LOGAN	Eliza Mary
LOGAN	Margaret Crew Gourley
LOGAN	Nancy Olive
LONG	Betty Robilliard
LOOKER	Margaret Francis
LORD	Mary
LORD	Thelma Joan
LORENZ	Kathleen Theresa
LORES	Florence Joyce
LORKING	Hazel Maryanne
LOSCHIAVO	Helen Francis Marie
LOTT	Barbara Doreen
LOUGHLIN	Nellie
LOVE	Ida Dorothy
LOVELOCK	Peggie Elizabeth
LOVETT	Edith
LOWDER	Margaret
LOWE	Constance Thelma
LOWREY	Edna Minnie
LOWRY	Marjorie Forbes
LOWTHER	Eileen Mary
LUCAS	Mary Kennedy
LUCAS	Olive Ruth
LUCAS	Verna Patricia
LUCE	Mary Margaret
LUCK	Dorothy Mavis
LUCOCK	Miriam Cregeen
LUDDY	Mary Beatrice
LUKE	Marjorie
LUMBUS	Kathleen Mary
LUMSDEN	Doreen Margaret
LUSCOMBE	Audrey Pearle
LUSCOMBE	Wilhelmina
LYCETT	Edith Edna Sherlock
LYNAS	Una Florence
LYNCH	Lillian Elizabeth
LYNCH	Mary Clare
LYNCH	Nancy Edith
LYNDON	Flora Beryl
LYNN	Joan Patricia
LYON	Agnes Crawford
LYON	Elizabeth Wilson
LYTTLE	Joan Marie Purves
MACARTNEY	Elinor Macartney
MACAULEY	Violet Grace
MACCALLUM	Roma Faith
MACDONALD	Doris Kyle
MACDONALD	Georgina Margaret Murray
MACDONALD	Maisie May
MACDONALD	Mary Margaret
MACDONALD	Olive Annie
MACFARLANE	Cecilia
MACGREGOR	Helen Jean
MACHON	Ivy Frances
MACINNES	Mary Catherine
MACKAWAY	Alma Lucy
MACKAY	Jessie Isabelle
MACKENZIE	Elsie Elaine
MACKENZIE	Margaret Martin
MACKEY	Margaret Vivian
MACKIE	Gwendolyn Dorothy

MACKIE	Helen Beatrice	MARKS	Isabella Annette
MACKLEY	Norah Frances	MARMONT	Honora Alma
MACKRILL	Kathleen Lois Read	MARRIE	Mary Winfield
MACLEAN	Dora Mary Hamilton	MARSDEN	Lois Irene
MACMILLAN	Mina Isabel	MARSH	Ruth Ruby
MACQUEEN	Nancy Florence	MARSHALL	Grace Beatrice
MACTAVISH	Thelma Jean	MARSHALL	Margaret Anne
MADDY	Ida Lilian Margurite	MARSHALL	Mavis Gwendoline
MAERSCHEL	Joan	MARSHALL	Nellie
MAGOR	Marjorie Olive	MARSHALL	Nellie May
MAHER	Mary Grace	MARSHE	Esme Maysie Alleta
MAHONEY	Mary	MARTIN	Alison Mabel
MAHONY	Aileen Dorothea	MARTIN	Egyptsia Ivie
MAIDENS	Anne Lee Alice	MARTIN	Elsie
MAIN	Winifred Violet Louise	MARTIN	Elsie Beatrice Sheilah
MAINWARING	Eileen Margaret	MARTIN	Ermyntrude Mary
MAINWARING	Mary Anne	MARTIN	Gwen Garnet
MAKIM	Alice May	MARTIN	Isabel Taylor
MALCOLM	Mary Mercia	MARTIN	Jean Tait
MALCOLM	Suzanne Lillian	MARTIN	Lexie Laura
MALE	Margaret Elizabeth	MARTIN	Lorraine
MALE	Mary Adelaide	MARTIN	Mamie Elizabeth
MALEE	Mary Josephine	MARTIN	Marion Catherine
MALING	Marie Coverley	MARTIN	Mavis Nellie
MALINS	Dorothy Grace	MARTIN	Ruth Elizabeth
MALLETT	Florence Costello	MARTIN	Sylvia Patricia
MALONE	Kathleen	MARTYN	Mary Kathleen
MALONEY	Teresa Ellen	MARUM	Mary Frances
MANGAN	Patricia Elizabeth	MATHERS	Winifred Monica
MANN	Marion Banbury	MATHESON	Annabella Johanna Caroline
MANN	Stella Lorraine	MATHESON	Gladys Grace
MANSFIELD	Florence Hazel	MATHESON	Laura Jean
MANSFIELD	Joyce Mary	MATHEWS	Audrey Rewa Burlton
MANTOVA	Edna	MATHEWS	Kathleen
MAPSTONE	Eileen Mary	MATHIESON	Ethel Clara
MARDEN	Mary Elizabeth	MATTHEWS	Alma Mary
MARFELL	Mirth Amelia	MATTHEWS	Esme Mary Stuart
MARKHAM	Ilma Joan	MATTHEWS	Phyllis
MARKMAN	Mily Nell		

MATTHEWS	Yvonne	McCOY	Annie Margaret
MATTINSON	Alice Jean	McCREADY	Eileen Norah
MAURICE	Helen Bourne	McCREDDEN	Ellen Marguerta
MAWSON	Marjorie	McCRUM	Dorothy Elizabeth Jean
MAXWELL	Lucy Anderson	McCULLA	Adeline Annie
MAY	Beryl	McCULLOCH	Ada Helen Faith
MAY	Eunice Dorothy	McCUMSTIE	Lillie
MAY	Margaret	McCUTCHEON	Holly
MAYFIELD	Helen Bliss	McDERMOTT	Joan Isabel
McALARY	Margaret	McDERMOTT	Sheilah Alice
McALLISTER	Charlotte	McDONAGH	Marjory Alice
McALLISTER	Margaret Gilliland	McDONALD	Annie Fedora
McALPINE	Helen Bayne	McDONALD	Elizabeth
McARTHUR	Evelyn Christina	McDONALD	Fanny Raines
McAULAY	Mary	McDONALD	Gladys Myrtle
McBEAN	Bertha	McDONALD	Jean Alexandra
McBEAN	Madge	McDONALD	Jean Bainden
McBRIDE	Dorothy Dennis	McDONALD	Margaret Esther
McBRIDE	Laura Ilma	McDONALD	Marjorie Mary
McBRIDE	Veronica Sara	McDONALD	Marjorie Naida
McCABE	Hilda Mccabe	McDONALD	Norma Mary Beatrice
McCAFFREY	Mary Victoria	McDONNELL	Margaret Mary
McCALLUM	Agnes Elizabeth	McDONNELL	Una Grace
MvCALLUM	Mary Elizabeth	McDOUGALL	Mary
McCARTHY	Dorothy Louisa	McDOUGALL	Myra
McCARTHY	Irene Mary	McEACHERN	Thelma May
McCARTHY	Mary Agnes	McELNEA	Dorothy Jean
McCARTHY	Norah Philomene	McELNEA	Edith Muriel
McCARTHY	Perditta Marjorie	McELNEA	Violet Irene
McCASKILL	Jean Florence	McENTEE	Margaret Rose
McCAULEY	Kathleen	McFADYEN	Edna Florence
McCAUSLAND	Connie	McFADYEN	Frances Jean
McCLELLAND	Ethel	McFARLANE	Hazel Violet
McCLYMONT	Isabelle Hazel	McFARLANE	Mary Gaetana
McCLYMONT	Jessie Isabella	McFARLANE	Mary Hamilton
McCOLE	Grace Laura	McGHIE	Elizabeth Ruth
McCONNEL	Amy Beatrice	McGILLIVRAY	Agnes Mary
McCORMACK	Eugena Angela	McGILLIVRAY	Kitty Elizabeth Dallas
McCORMACK	Imeida Elizabeth	McGIRR	Veronica Alice

McGLADE	Mary Eleanor
McGOVERN	Mabel Ella
McGRATH	Doris May
McGRATH	Jean
McGRATH	Sheila
McGUIGAN	Blanche
McILRATH	Mary Garnham
McILWAINE	Doris Anna
McINNES	Margaret Mary
McINNES	Mary
McINTOSH	Irene Margaret Bethel
McINTOSH	Jocelyn Frances
McINTOSH	Mary Elizabeth
McINTOSH	Olivine Joan
McINTYRE	Jean Margaret
McINTYRE	Margaret Sinclair
McINTYRE	Nance
McINTYRE	Vivien Langdon
McKAY	Marjorie Ella
McKAY	Violet Isobel
McKEAN	Mavis Gladys
McKEE	Jessie Nicholson
McKELL	Florence Mary
McKELLAR	Catherine Jean
McKENNA	Jean Lorna
McKENZIE	Dorothy Margaret
McKENZIE	Josephine Margaret
McKENZIE	Mary Lindsay
McKENZIE	Olive Esther May
McKENZIE-McHARG	Margaret Jean
McKERROW	Mary
McKINLAY	Jean Brownell
McKINLEY	Yvonne Gertrude
McKITTRICK	Emilie Marion
McLACHLAN	Margaret Jean
McLAREN	Janet Agnes Lillian
McLAREN	Myra May
McLARTY	Violet Ann
McLEAN	Dorothy
McLEAN	Jean Annie
McLELLAN	Ruth Emily
McLENNAN	Fay
McLENNAN	Jean Gray
McLENNAN	Oriel Nancy
McLEOD	Betty May
McLEOD	Christina Annie
McLEOD	Doris Maude
McLEOD	Katherine May
McMAHON	Bernadine Theresa
McMAHON	Doris Blanche
McMAHON	Doris Mary
McMAHON	Helena Elizabeth Monica
McMAHON	Mary Eileen
McMAHON	Mary Margaret
McMANUS	Florence May
McMANUS	Gertrude Mary
McMARTIN	Alice May
McMASTER	Gertrude Agnes
McMEEKIN	Nancy Naomi
McMENAMIN	Marjorie Iris
McMENAMIN	Veronica
McMILLAN	Beryl Eveline
McMILLAN	Kathleen
McMURRAY-WALLACE	Catherine Jeane Margaret
McNAB	Elsie Lillian
McNAIR	Vera Gwenifer
McNALLY	Nancy
McNAMARA	Johanna Mary
McNEARY	Annie Maureen
McNEE	Martha
McNEIL	Doris Jean
McNEILL	Olive Jean
McNICOL	Emily Alice
McPADDEN	Isobel Lily
McPHAIL	Lilian Elaine
McPHEE	Elizabeth Mary

McSHANE	Mary
McVICAR	Phyllis Blanche
McVIE	Mary Marion
McWILLIAM	Enid May
McWILLIAM	Joan Louise
McWILLIAMS	Elizabeth Rowley
MEAD	Cordelia
MEAD	Doreen
MEAD	Phyllis
MEANEY	Ellen Dorothy
MEANEY	Ruth
MEATES	Edna
MECKLEM	Constance Hope
MEEHAN	Margaret Elizabeth Norah
MEEHAN	Mary Elizabeth
MEHAN	Helen
MEHAN	Marjorie
MELANO	Constance Joyce
MELLAR	Gwendoline Mary
MELLETT	Marion Olive
MELROSE	Edith Blair
MELVILLE	Gwyneth Marjorie
MELVILLE	Una Alison
MELVIN	Winifred Jessie
MEMBREY	Elsie Gertrude
MENZIES	Jean Joan
MENZIES	Winifred Alicia
MEREDITH	Dorothy Crossman
MEREWEATHER	Constance Alice
MERRIGAN	Margaret Honorah
MERRIGAN	Thelma Helen
MERRION	Gladys Gertrude Evelyn
MESSITER	Dorothy Mary
MESSITER	Florence Woolford
MESTON	Joyce Toressa
METZKE	Letitia Anne Sylvie
METZNER	Haidee Margaret
MEYER	Elizabeth Pride
MIDDLETON	Irene Constance
MIDDLETON	June
MIDDLETON	Margaret Viveash
MIDGLEY	Anne Grace
MILBURN	Beryl May
MILBURN	Betty Wilhelmina
MILBURN	Elwyn Mary
MILLARD	Barbara Mary
MILLER	Christina Dora
MILLER	Edith Lorna
MILLER	Elaine Gowan
MILLER	Elaine Gowan
MILLER	Hope Anne
MILLER	Isabel Mary
MILLER	Kathleen
MILLER	Mary Ellen
MILLER	Phyllis Berenice
MILLER	Violet Sophia
MILLIKAN	Annie Jane
MILLINER	Mavis Alma
MILLS	Alyson Manning
MILLS	Dorothy Mary Mackenzie
MILLS	Hetty Mary
MILLS	Una Clara
MILNE	Laura Martha
MILNE	Joyce Madeline
MILNES	Ruth Mary
MILSOM	Romola Beedham
MILSON	Ruby Henrietta
MILSTEAD	Joy Cumming
MINHARD	Patricia Furner
MINOGUE	Clare
MINTORN	Maisie Winifred
MITCHELL	Elsie
MITTELHEUSER	Pearl Beatrice
MOAD	Ursula Elizabeth
MODEN	Linda May
MOFFAT	Mary Cecelia

MOLE	Gladys Elva
MOLE	Moira Margaret
MOLLARD	Margaret Florence
MOLONEY	Sheilah Ellen
MONAGHAN	Mona Maria
MONAHAN	Laura Mavis Mary
MONGER	Alice Irene
MONK	Judith Dunmore
MONKIVITCH	Edna Hope
MONKS	Mollie Humble
MONTGOMERY	Joyce Elizabeth
MONTGOMERY	Nancy Mirla
MOODIE	Myrtle Olive
MOORE	Beatrice
MOORE	Betty May
MOORE	Clara May
MOORE	Ellen Mary
MOORE	Enid Clare
MOORE	Eveleen Dowson
MOORE	Gladys Clare
MOORE	Joyce
MOORE	Joyce Violet
MOORE	Kathleen Mary
MOORE	Mary Elizabeth
MOORE	Olive May
MOORE	Olive Winifred
MOORE	Rona
MOORHOUSE	Cecile May
MOORS	Helen Estelle
MORAN	Laureen Carmel Mary
MORAN	Mary Agnes
MORAN	Mary Rebecca
MORAN	Patricia Mary
MOREY	Phillis Eileen
MOREY	Rachel Isabel
MORGAN	Hannah Evelyn
MORGAN	Margaret Isabel
MORGAN	Thelma Lenore
MORGAN-PAYLER	Barbara
MORIARTY	Ellen Mary
MORIARTY	Kathleen Agnes
MORIESON	Mavis Christina Anne
MORLEY	Joan Elizabeth
MORPHETT	Gladys Gertrude
MORRIS	Bernice Merle
MORRIS	Ivy Estelle
MORRIS	Patricia Adeline
MORRIS	Sheila
MORRISBY	Isabel Margaret
MORRISON	Beryl Mary
MORRISON	Maggie
MORRISON	Mary
MORRISSON	Neita Lillian
MORRISSY	Hanora
MORSE	Ida Arundel
MORTON	Edith Mary
MORTON	Vera May
MOSEY	Elizabeth
MOSS	Grace
MOSS	May
MOSTON	Myrle
MOULTON	Cecilie Catherine
MOUNSEY	Edna May
MOXHAM	Bessie Violet
MOY	Janet Doris
MOYES	Sheila Ellen
MUDGE	Grace Isobel
MUDGE	Jessie Isabel
MUIR	Isabelle Rose
MUIR	Muriel Harriet
MUIR	Sylvia Jessie Mimmi
MUIRHEAD	Margaret Elizabeth
MUIRSON	Katherine Emma
MULDOON	Annie Susan
MULDOON	Bessie Christina Ellen
MULES	Edna Lavinia
MULES	Mary Catherine
MULHEARN	Dulcie Mary

MULHEARN	Mary Caroline	NAYLOR	Joan Jackson
MULLALY	Cecelia Eleanor	NEAGLE	Eileen Margaret
MULLALY	Doreen	NEAL	Mary Isabel
MULLANE	Margaret Mary	NEALE	Katharine Constance
MULLENS	Eileen Cecily	NEILL	Clodagh
MULLENS	Phyllis Katherine Fraser	NEILLEY	Elizabeth Joyce
MULLER	Gertrude Catherine	NELSON	Lilian May
MULLINS	Dorothia Elizabeth	NETTERFIELD	Moya Millie
MULLNER	Minnie Charlotte	NETTLEFOLD	Jean Phyllis
MULVIHILL	Mavis Valerie	NETTLEFOLD	Winsome Mary
MUMFORD	Edith Jean	NEUMANN	Lois Sylvia
MUMFORD	Joyce Elizabeth	NEUSS	Kathleen Margaret
MUMME	Lillian Annie	NEUSS	Philippa Eveleen Mary
MUMMERY	Cynthia Rose	NEVELL	Linda
MUNRO	Dorothy	NEVILLE	Jean Pauline Lobie
MUNRO	Grace Louise	NEWELL	Margaret Mary Ursula
MURCH	Kathleen Jamieson	NEWING	Dulcie Lela
MURDOCH	Marjorie Agatha	NEWITT	Ella Isabel
MURNANE	Catherine	NEWLYN	Marie Aileen
MURNANE	Mary Hannah	NEWMAN	Constance
MURNANE	Mary Magdallene	NEWMAN	Henrietta Josephine
MURPHY	Catherine Margaret	NEWMAN	Jessie Isabel
MURPHY	Ellen Frances	NEWMAN	Marjorie
MURPHY	Eva May	NEWNHAM	Madge Murray
MURPHY	Gladys Mary	NEWTON	Daphne Alice
MURPHY	Margaret Mary	NEWTON	Dorothy Joyce
MURRAY	Edith Hildebrand	NEWTON	Lucy
MURRAY	Edith Winifred	NEWTON	Marjorie
MURRAY	Effie May	NICHOLAS	Dorothy Margaret
MURRAY	Helen	NICHOLLS	Margery Francesca
MURRAY	Mabel	NICHOLLS	Mavis Catherine
MURRAY	Mary Heaford	NICHOLS	Beryl Thirza
MURRAY	Mollie Winifred	NICHOLSON	Berenice Mavis
MURRAY	Nancy May	NICHOLSON	Frances Mary
MURRAY	Thea Mary	NICHTERLEIN	Dora Elisabeth
MUSGRAVE	Elizabeth Mary	NICKOLL	Emily Mary
NALDER	Rosemary	NICOL	Helen Shields
NAPIER	Mary Joan	NICOLSON	Florence
NASH	Marjorie Constance	NIELSEN	Ida Josephine

NIVEN	Mary Esther	OLIVER	Marjorie Elvine
NOBBS	Emmeline	OLLIFFE	Margaret May
NOBLE	Mary Florence	O'LOGHLIN	Marie Blanche
NOONAN	Alberta Mary	O'LOUGHLIN	Doreen Catherine
NOONAN	Mary Margaret	O'LOUGHLIN	Marie Bernette
NORMAN	Elwyn Theodora	O'LOUGHLIN	Mary Ellen
NORMAN	Johanna	OLSEN	Emily Margrethe Cummings
NOTT	Gwenyth Maude	O'MALLEY	Mabel Clarice Catherine
NUNAN	Rita Margaret	O'MALLEY	Pauline Norma
NUTTER	Amy Joyce Howard	OMAN	Lesley Margaret
NUTTING	Phyllis Esme	O'MARA	Dorothy Cleeve
OAKESHOTT	Joyce Marjorie	O'NEIL	Catherine
OAKLEY	Mary Dorrell	O'NEILL	Georgina Meryle
O'BRIEN	Mary Clare	O'NEILL	Grace Mary
O'BRIEN	Patricia	O'NEILL	Jane Beryl Eugene
O'BRIEN	Patricia Margaret	O'NEILL	Mary Bridget
O'BRYAN	Kathleen	ONGE	Ella Blair
O'CONNOR	Catherine	ONSLOW	Helen Jane May
O'CONNOR	Kathleen Cecily	OPPATT	Verna Anna
ODDIE	Margaret Jean	ORAM	Wilma Elizabeth Forster
ODDY	Freda Alma	O'REILLY	Annie Theresa
O'DOHERTY	Kathleen	ORIGLASSO	Mary Ellen
O'DONAHOO	Beryl Irene	O'ROURKE	Bridget Josephine
O'DONNELL	Alice Margaret	O'ROURKE	Gertrude
O'DONNELL	Mary Agnes	O'ROURKE	Linda Grace
O'DONNELL	Mary Helena	ORR	Dorothy Jean
O'DONNELL	Nora	ORR	Ida Millicent
O'DWYER	Bridget Hazel	OSMOND	Una Mary
OFFICER	Olive Adele	O'SULLIVAN	Norma
O'GORMAN	Jean	O'SULLIVAN	Sheila
O'HALLORAN	Margaret Elizabeth	O'TOOLE	Kathleen Dorothy
O'HALLORAN	Mary Anastasia	O'TOOLE	Norah Clarke
O'HANLON	Nora	OUTRED	Ruth Marion Windsor
O'HARE	Mary Johanna	OWEN	Jean Gertrude
O'KEEFE	Eileen Margaret	OWEN	Nancy Estelle
O'KEEFE	Ellen Rose	OWENS	Bernice Louisa
O'KEEFE	Mary	OXLEY	Christian Sarah Mary
OLDHAM	Gwendolen Bertha	PAIGE	Beatrice Joan
OLDHAM	Rebecca Beatrice		

PAINE	Doreen Leonore	PAYZE	Marjorie Alice
PALMER	Alice Elizabeth	PEACOCK	Edith Alma
PALMER	Florence Anne	PEACOCK	Jean Amy
PANNAN	Eileen Maude	PEACOCK	Mona Rene
PARISH	Winifred Marie	PEAKE	Elna Audrey
PARK	Gloria Wallace	PEARCE	Ida Elizabeth Horton
PARKER	Bessie	PEARCE	Jean Margaret
PARKER	Deborah Ross Symons	PEARLMAN	Celia
PARKER	Eileen Edna	PEARS	Lilian Brightie
PARKER	Elberta Bessie	PEARSE	Alice Thelma
PARKER	Kathleen Isabel Alice	PEARSE	Jean Ursula
PARKER	Mary Beatrice	PEARSE	Marjorie Elizabeth
PARKER	Vera Victoria	PEARSON	Bernadine
PARKER	Vida Margaret	PEARSON	Elizabeth Dodd
PARKINSON	Gertrude	PECK	Eleanor Mary
PARR	Joan Kathleen	PEEL	Alice Clara
PARROT	Tasma Josephine	PEGG	Gwendolyn Nellie
PARRY	Mena Rose	PEGLER	Eileen Nora
PARRY	Mona Foulkes	PELLIZZER	Hilda
PARSONS	Emily Lorraine	PEMBERTON	Constance Annie
PARSONS	Phyllis Eva	PEMELL	Joan Amelia Shepherd
PASCHKE	Olive Dorothy	PENDER	Dulcie May
PASKINS	Elizabeth Mary	PENNEFATHER	Kathleen
PATEN	Eunice Muriel	PENNY	Helen Rosina
PATERSON	Isobel Elizabeth	PERCY	Myra Royce
PATERSON	Jean Marjorie	PERRIN	Kathleen Mary
PATON	Sheila Christine	PERRIN	Veda Irene
PATRICK	Eva Elizabeth	PERRY	Agnes Joyce
PATTERSON	Catherine Ursula	PERRY	Hilda
PATTERSON	Isabella Annie	PERRY	Myrtle Elsie
PATTERSON	Jean Moncur	PERRYMAN	Dorothy Alice
PATTERSON	Kathleen Patricia	PERSSE	Elizabeth Downes
PATTERSON	Mary Jeffries	PETCH	Mary Paisley
PATTERSON	Sarah Rachael	PETERSEN	Evelyn Alice
PAUL	Beryl May	PETERSON	Florence Mary
PAVY	Kate	PETRICH	Florence Mary
PAYNE	Elwyn Joyce	PETTIGREW	Jessie Margaret
PAYNE	Kathleen Mary	PETTIT	Madge
PAYNTER	Ailsa Jean Mary	PFAFFLIN	Dorothy Helene

PFITZNER	Adele Francis
PHILIP	Margaret Tenison
PHILLIPS	Cara Elizabeth
PHILLIPS	Dorothy Joy
PHILLIPS	Dulcie Alice
PHILLIPS	Mabyn Margaret
PHILLIPS	Mary Ellen
PHILLIPS	Phyllis Clair
PHILLIPS	Stella Mona
PHILP	Betty
PHIPPS	Margaret Mary
PICKERING	Loveday Edith
PICKERING	Olwen Eleanor
PICKERSGILL	Audrey Helen
PIDCOCK	Ivy Evelyn
PIDDINGTON	Pamela Alice Maberly
PIERPOINT	Doris May
PIKE	Ida Madge
PILKINGTON	Catherine
PIPER	Cavell Edith
PIPER	Decima Enid
PITMAN	Dulcie Emma
PITT	Mary Winifred
PITTS	Ethelwyn Violet
PLAIN	Flora Macdonald
PLANTE	Isabel Erskine
PLAYFAIR	Jean Maskell
PLOWMAN	Marjorie Ethel
PLUM	Erica
POCOCK	Dulcie May
POLLACK	Gwenyth Patricia
POLLARD	Beatrice Isabel Fox
POLLOCK	Evelyn Mavis
POLLOCK	Gladys Isobel
POLLOCK	Marjory Isobel
POLMEAR	Ivy Hannah Jane
PONTEY	Laura Mary Noelle
PORTER	Clarissa May
PORTER	Daphne May
PORTER	Patricia Yvonne
POTTER	Dorothy Agnes
POTTER	Dorothy Gwendoline Maude
POTTS	Jean Ella
POULGRAIN	Celestine May
POULTER	Mary Elizabeth Jean
POWELL	Alison Mary
POWELL	Julia Elizabeth Blanche
POZZI	Beatrice Isabel
PRESTON	Eileen Winifred
PRESTON	Marie Rose
PRICE	Beryl Gladys
PRICE	Lilian Claire
PRICE	Martha May
PRICE	Mary Eliza
PRICE	Phyllis Amy Millard
PRICHARD	Bertha Louise
PRICHARD	Margaret Moline
PRIDEAUX	Mildred Lucy Kenrick
PRIDEAUX	Nita Alice
PRINCE	Edna Muriel
PRINDABLE	Mona Josephine
PRITCHARD	Dorothy Victoria
PROSSER	Marion Ivy
PROVIS	Barbara
PROWSE	Honor May
PRUNTY	Mary Lillian Patricia
PRYDE	Agnes Nelson
PUGH	Phyllis
PULLMAN	Melba Magdalene
PUMP	Bertha
PURCELL	Joan Therese
PURDIE	Iris Lorraine
PURNELL	Fernie Erica
PYE	Iris Esme
PYMAN	Elizabeth Merle
QUEALY	Catherine Mary
QUICK	Violet Adelaide

QUIN	Winifred	REILLY	Bridget
QUINLAN	Eileen Mary Frances	REILLY	Frances Mildred
QUINLAN	Nancy Elizabeth	REILLY	Maisie Leola
QUINN	Gwendoline Rose	REILLY	Mavis Joan
QUINN	Margaret Florence	REILLY	Nora Muriel
QUIRK	Bertha Winifred	RENDELL	Nancy Jean Annie
RAE	Lilian Grace	RENFREE	Gwenneth Mavis
RAFFERTY	Joan Mary	RENKIN	Lettie Mary
RAGLAND	Bridget Agnes	RETALLACK	Elizabeth Elfrida
RALSTON	Irene Dorothy	RETSCHLAG	Doris Marie
RAMAGE	Muriel May	REYNOLDS	Margaret Lyla
RAMSEY	Mary Jeanie Ferguson	RICE	Rose Catherine
RANSOM	Mary Janet	RICHARDS	Mary Joan
RATCLIFF	Enid Edmeades	RICHARDSON	Elsie May
RATTLEY	Margaret Effie	RICHARDSON	Helena Mary
RATTRAY	Catherine Mary	RICHARDSON	Janet Lindsay
RAVEN	Florence Edith	RICHARDSON	Nellie Maude
RAWLINGS	Sylvia Maud	RICHARDSON	Phoebe Hayton
RAY	Philippa Campbell	RICHES	Catherine Eleanor
RAYMENT	Jessie Gwendolin	RICKETTS	Edith Maud
RAYMONT	Wilhelmina Rosalie	RIDDELL	Gwendoline Elaine
RAYNER	Enid Susannah	RIDDLE	Ellen Dora
RAYNER	May Eileen	RIDE	Winifred Muriel
READ	Beatrice May	RIDEOUT	Thelma Jean
READ	Eleanor Euphemia	RIGGS	Clara Elizabeth
REDDAN	Sylvia Doris	RILEY	Ellen Agnes
REDMAN	Elsie May	RILEY	Elsie May
REECE	Mildred Daphne	RILEY	Elva Mabel
REES	Jean Florence	RILEY	Mary Veronica
REEVE	Elsie Freda Merle	RILEY	Patricia Elsa
REGAN	Dorothy Lorna	RIMMER	Phyllis
REID	Bella	RINGHAM	Joy Marjorie
REID	Constance Jean	RISELEY	Lila Wilhelmina
REID	Edith Heron	RITCHIE	Ruby Enid
REID	Elsie Margaret	RITCHIE	Una
REID	Mabel	RIXON	Agnes Joan
REID	Muriel Vivienne	ROACHE	Joan Mary
REID	Rebie Alison	ROBB	Sheila Isabel
REID	Thelma	ROBBINS	Marjorie Rose

ROBERTS	Constance
ROBERTS	Minnie
ROBERTSON	Alice Blair
ROBERTSON	Alma Mabel
ROBERTSON	Avis Nancy
ROBERTSON	Betty Alexandra
ROBERTSON	Elsa Merton
ROBERTSON	Frances Ethel
ROBERTSON	Jean Agnes
ROBERTSON	Rita Maxine Ruby
ROBERTSON	Vida Lesley
ROBINSON	Georgina Hanna
ROBINSON	Irene Gray
ROBINSON	Isobel Louise
ROBINSON	Ivy Rachel
ROBINSON	Joan Elaine
ROBINSON	Joyce Violet Mary
ROBINSON	Olive Edna
ROBISON	Mildred
ROCHE	Mary Vie
ROCK	Nina Jessie Beatrice
ROCKLIFF	Irene Katie
ROCKLIFF	Katharine Nancy
RODEN	Elvera Marguerite
RODGERS	Lorna
ROE	Dorothy Grace
ROGERS	Dilys Joyce
ROGERS	Dorothy Phyllis
ROGERS	Jean Margaret Lucy
ROHAN	Margaret Alice
ROHR	Eva Lomer
ROLFE	Clarice Yvonne
ROMAIN	Gwendolene May
RONAYNE	Gertrude Lilian
ROOME	May
ROOTER	Agatha Marion
ROSE	Margaret Elizabeth
ROSS	Cynthia Catherine
ROSS	Emmaretta Mary
ROSSITER	Norma Gertrude
ROTHWELL	Aileen Marea
ROUSCH	Bridget Linda
ROWE	Aileen Mary
ROWE	Edna Dorothy Hanoria
ROWE	Elsie Marie
ROWEN	Kathleen
ROWLAND	Joan Irene
ROWLAND	Lorna Jessie
ROWLEY	Lila Mary
RUDD	Edith Annie
RUDD	Elizabeth Joy
RUMSEY	Iris May
RUNGIE	Emily Langridge
RUSE	Daisy Noble
RUSSELL	Lavinia Jean
RUSSELL	Mary Elizabeth
RUTHERFORD	Eileen Mary
RUTLEDGE	Sheila Joan
RUTTER	Muriel Grace
RYALLS	Mary Carmel
RYAN	Bidelia
RYAN	Edith Mary
RYAN	Marie Benedetta
RYAN	Marjorie Mavis
RYAN	Vera Grace Helstead
RYRIE	Gwendolyn Granville
RYRIE	Selma Morven
SADLER	Elsie May
SAGE	Annie Moriah
SAINSBURY	Sybil Ray
SAINTY	Emily Edith
SALAN	Esther Clara
SALMON	Florence Aubin
SAMBELL	Charlotte Burnell
SAME	Beatrice May
SAMSON	Linda Edna
SAMUEL	Elsie June
SANDERS	Mary Winton

SANDERS	Rose Elizabeth
SANDISON	Joan Ilma
SANDLAND	Rita Nancy
SANDWITH	Laura Isabel
SANSOM	Eileen Gwenyth
SAUNDERS	Ailsa
SAUNDERS	Edna May
SAVAGE	Ellen
SCALA	Jane Gertrude
SCALES	Mollie Gweneth
SCANLAN	Carlene Mary
SCANTLEBURY	Mignon Magdalen
SCHAEFER	Lillian Grace
SCHINCKEL	Frances Charlotte
SCHNEIDER	Margaret
SCHNEIDER	Myra Jean
SCHNEIDER	Rita Margaret
SCHOFIELD	Anna Elizabeth
SCHOLES	Dorothy
SCHRODER	Naomi Grace
SCHULTZ	Ivy Bartz
SCHUMAN	Marjorie
SCOBIE	Elaine Warren
SCOBIE	Esther
SCOBLE	Marjory Clara Calland
SCOTLAND	Melita Grace
SCOTT	Aldyth Evelyn
SCOTT	Beryl Elizabeth
SCOTT	Edith Ogilvie
SCOTT	Gwendoline Ella
SCOTT	Isabella Jean
SCOTT	Lilian Clare
SCOTT	Ruth Kathleen
SCOTT-YOUNG	Beryl Elizabeth
SCRAGG	Beatrice
SCRUBY	Edna Jean
SEABROOK	Dorothy Lilian
SEARL	Daisy Aline
SEARLE	Marion Agnes
SEARS	Kathleen Anne
SECKER	Joan Stewart
SEE	Kathleen Clare
SEEBOHM	Loris Irene
SEELEY	Edna Ivy Millicent
SEERS	Ada May
SEIFFERT	Amy Christina
SELLER	Iris Ruby
SELWOOD	Margaret Constance
SENIOR	Constance Muriel
SENIOR	Marjorie Barbara Crawford
SETCHELL	Constance Edith
SETCHELL	Duxie May Mclean
SEVIL	Marjorie Ellen
SEWARD	Norma Doris
SEWELL	Christina Elizabeth
SEXTON	Annie Kinsman
SEYMOUR	Gladys May
SHACKLEFORD	Janet Affleck
SHAMBROOK	Mabel Alice
SHANAHAN	Carmel Annie Maria
SHANAHAN	Helen Noreen
SHANAHAN	Kathleen Amy
SHANNON	Phyllis
SHAW	Edna Alice
SHAW	Enid Mary
SHAW	Florence Ella Wager
SHAW	Grace Maud
SHEAHAN	Cordula
SHEAHAN	Grace Irene
SHEEHAN	Aileen Dorothy
SHEEHAN	Dorothy Mary
SHELLEY	Kathleen Maysie
SHEPHERD	Alice Mary
SHEPHERD	Betsy Eileen
SHEPHERD	Elizabeth Mary
SHEPLEY	Agnes Roma
SHEPPARD	Edna

SHERIDAN	Cornie Ella	SKERMAN	Evelyn Lucy
SHERIDAN	Kittie Wallace	SKERMAN	Mabel Alice
SHERWOOD	Aileen Margaret	SKETCHLEY	Norma Veronica
SHERWOOD	Norah Joyce	SKIPPEN	Enid Rita
SHERWOOD	Ruth	SKIPWORTH	Emma Agnes
SHIRLEY	Irene Pearl	SKUTHORP	Elizabeth Margaret
SHORT	Eileen Mary	SKYRING	Thora Alaque
SHORT	Patricia Constance	SLATER	Violet Patricia
SHORT	Winifred Olga	SMARTT	Una Mary
SHUMACK	Clara Jane	SMEETON	Freda Mary
SIDES	Olive Forsyth	SMIRTHWAITE	Lillias Nellie
SIER	Edith Joan	SMITH	Agnes Annie
SILLAR	Jean Hazel	SMITH	Alwyn Merle
SIMCOCKS	Daphne Elizabeth	SMITH	Auriol Millicent
SIMKIN	Margaret Jean	SMITH	Betty Eleanor
SIMMONS	Dorothy Evelyn	SMITH	Betty Margaret
SIMON	Lorna Helene	SMITH	Daisy Ethel
SIMON	Violet Alma	SMITH	Edna Marjorie
SIMONS	Jessie Elizabeth	SMITH	Elizabeth
SIMPKINS	Phyllis Leeton	SMITH	Elizabeth Dorothy May
SIMPSON	Beryl Catherine	SMITH	Elizabeth Rylice
SIMPSON	Elizabeth Jean	SMITH	Ethel Mary
SIMPSON	Mary Geraldine	SMITH	Gladys Irene
SIMPSON	Vera Myrtle	SMITH	Helen Mary
SIMS	Marjorie	SMITH	Hilda Vilera
SIMSON	Margaret	SMITH	Isabella Jane
SINCLAIR	Irene Isobel	SMITH	Jean Anderson
SINCLAIR	Iris	SMITH	Jean Christabel
SINCLAIR	Jean Campbell	SMITH	Josephine Ellen
SINCLAIR	Lucille Ann	SMITH	Lillian Winifred
SINCLAIR-WOOD	Janet	SMITH	Marjorie McLaurin
SINDELL	Marie Phillipa	SMITH	Marjorie Moira
SINGLETON	Irene Ada	SMITH	Mary Innes
SINGLETON	Rita Gwendoline	SMITH	Merlie Wilhelmina
SINGLETON	Sylvia Jane	SMITH	Neta Maude
SINNOTT	Sheila Evelyn	SMITH	Patricia Maude
SKEAT	Belinda Rosalind	SMITH	Phyllis Grace Bridget
SKEHAN	Kathleen	SMITH	Phyllis Gwen
SKELLY	Margaret Geraldine	SMITH	Primrose Mary Viner

SMITH	Thelma Rose	STEEL	Frances Mary Isobel
SMITH	Valrie Elizabeth	STEEL	Lucy Violet Margaret
SMITH	Thelma Alice	STEEL	Myrtle Mary
SMITHENBECKER	Clarice Jean	STEELE	Nancy Harding
SMITHERS	Meryl Colvin	STEEN	Margaret Letitia
SMYTH	Constance Esther	STEERE	Doris Annie Leslie
SMYTH	Elizabeth Flora	STEINBECK	Mary Leith
SMYTH	Gwendoline May	STENBERG	Mary Cecilia
SMYTH	Norma Mclennan	STENBORG	Mavis Veronica
SMYTHE	Annie Lilian	STENT	Maud Annie Violet
SNADDON	Elizabeth Whitehead	STEPHEN	Ethel
SNOWBALL	Dorothy Frances Mary	STEPHENS	Dorothy Kate
SOLLING	Elizabeth Edna	STEPHENS	Millicent Mary
SOMERFIELD	Nell Josephine	STEPHENSON	Joan Brewer
SORENSEN	Thelma Elizabeth	STEPHENSON	Millicent Mary
SOUTER	Helen Ross	STEPHENSON	Nellie Kathleen
SPARGO	Evelyn Maud	STEVENS	Dorothy May
SPEARRITT	Amy	STEVENS	Marjorie Elwyn
SPEEDING	Margaret Macleod	STEVENSON	Florence Evelyn
SPEHR	Maude Lyall	STEVENSON	Frances Amy
SPENCE	Agnes Riley	STEVENSON	Heather Lillian
SPENCE	Mary Frances	STEVENSON	Sadie Agnes
SPENCER	Amy Theresa	STEWART	Esther Sarah Jean
SPENCER	Gertrude Elizabeth	STEWART	Heather Mary Isobel
SPENCER	Marion Violet	STEWART	Olive May
SPICKLER	Ruth Yvonne	STOBERT	Florence
SPRING	Lilian May	STOCKWELL	Catherine Daphne Alice
SPURGIN-SMITH	Vera May	STOCKWELL	Margaret Emma
STACY	Muriel Hamlyn	STOKES	Dorothy Marie Maude
STALKER	Ethel Marian	STOKES	Lucy Florence Joy
STANDISH	Daisy	STONE	Jean Margaret
STANLEY	Elaine Blyth	STONE	Joan Cleveland
STANLEY	Lorna Isabelle	STONE	Sheila
STANMORE	Rose	STORCH	Vanda Louise
STANTON-COOK	Jean Isali	STOREY	Constance Evelyn
STANWELL	Catherine Muriel	STOREY	Natalie
STANWELL	Isla Margaret	STORMONTH	Magdalene Jasemine
STATON	Lucy Agnes	STORRER	Ailsa Marion
STEED	Dorothy Joan	STORRIE	Alva Kelway

STORY	Florence Ethel May
STRAIN	Dorothy Gertrude
STREAM	Marjorie Taylor
STRETCH	Margaret
STRICKLAND	Helen
STRONACH	Gwenneth Ada
STROUD	Maisie Elizabeth
STUCKEY	Dorothy Alice
STUHMCKE	Maidie Phyllis
STURGESS	Dorothy
SUFFREN	Beryl Lorraine
SULLIVAN	Elsie Louise
SULLIVAN	Florence Grace
SULLIVAN	Margaret Doreen
SULLIVAN	Mary Elizabeth
SULZBERGER	Edna Florence
SUMMERS	Jean Elizabeth
SUTCLIFFE	Audrey Jean
SUTCLIFFE	Margaret Ruth
SUTER	Isabel Roberta St Margaret
SUTHERLAND	Edna Charlotte
SUTHERLAND	Molly Jean
SUTTIE	Clarice Maud
SWALLOW	Grace
SWAN	Beryl Isis
SWANSON	Ethne Doris
SWEANEY	Florence Joan
SWEENEY	Emily Charlotte
SWEET	Phyllis
SWINEY	Lexie
SWINSON	Dorothy Elizabeth
SYER	Ada Corbett
SYME	Jean Calder
TAINSH	Alice Isabel
TAIT	Jessie Mcpherson
TAIT	Mona Margaret Anderson
TALBOT	Helen Maude
TALBOT	Lorna Hope
TANNER	Constance Adelaide
TANNER	Shirley Livingstone
TANWAN	Annie
TAPP	Elsie May
TAPRELL	Veronica Jean
TARLINTON	Elizabeth Florence
TARRANT	Patricia Elsie
TASKER	Alpha Isobel
TAYLER	Ruth
TAYLOR	Frances Grace Lavinia
TAYLOR	Gwendolyn Merle
TAYLOR	Helen Katherine
TAYLOR	Mary Jean
TAYLOR	Myrtle Annie
TEDDER	Hazel Ethel
TEEL	Elvor Helena
TELFORD	Lola Madge
TEMPLE-SMITH	Winifred
TEMPLETON	Lesley Grace
THEAKER	Heather Rose
THEODORE	Florence Jean
THIEDEKE	Cynthia Mabel
THOM	Edna May
THOMAS	Alma Jean
THOMAS	Annie Irene
THOMAS	Annie Joyce
THOMAS	Beryl Ella
THOMAS	Diana Langslow
THOMAS	Elizabeth
THOMAS	Florrie
THOMAS	Grace
THOMAS	Grace Mary
THOMAS	Gwladys Margaret
THOMAS	Ruby Kathleen
THOMAS	Sadie Annette
THOMAS	Violet May
THOMPSON	Annie Ethelwyn
THOMPSON	Elizabeth
THOMPSON	Grace Constance

THOMPSON	Ivy
THOMPSON	Kathleen Bridget
THOMPSON	Margaret Jessie
THOMSON	Catherine Elsie Evelyn
THOMSON	Elizabeth Ann
THOMSON	Elizabeth Jessie
THOMSON	Jessie Robertson McFarlane
THORBURN	Alice
THORNE	Marguerite North
THORP	Doris Alexander
THUMPSTON	Sarah Jane
THURLOW	Isley Edna
THURLOW	Mona Johanna Catherine
TICEHURST	Marjorie Jean
TICKLE	Muriel
TIDD	Gwendoline Vincent
TIERNEY	Kathleen Mary
TIMBS	Catherine Alice
TIMBS	Heather Joan
TIMPSON	Florence Ross
TINDALE	Daryl Kathleen
TINGATE	Elsie
TINNEY	Hazel Angela
TINNEY	Marie Isabel
TINSON	Katie Ithilma
TIPPER	Eva Jane
TIPPET	Lotus Vyvyan
TIPPETT	Lorna Winifred
TIPPETT	Marjory Ethel
TISDALL	Enid Mary
TOLMAN	Joan Audrey
TOMLINS	Daphne May
TOMLINSON	Hazel Russell
TOMLINSON	Marjorie
TONKIN	Sasie Anne
TOOTELL	Elsie May Caroline
TORBETT	Isabel Annie
TOTTEN	Elsie Margaret
TOZER	Patricia Grace
TRANTER	Eileen May
TRANTER	Florence May
TRAVIS	Olga Mary
TREBECK	Jean
TRELIVING	Ruth Kathleen
TRELOAR	Olive Ida
TREMBATH	Alice May
TREMBATH	Dorothy Mary
TRENERRY	Annie Merle
TRESIDDER	Edith Kathleen
TRETHEWIE	Dulcie May
TRINDER	Isabella
TRIPLETT	Grace
TROEDSON	Thea Celeste
TROTT	Abbey Elizabeth
TROTT	Marjorie Winifred
TROTTER	Florence Elizabeth
TROTTER	Josephine Winifred
TRUDINGER	Margaret
TRUSCOTT	Joan
TRYHORN	Dorothy Emma
TUFREY	Alice Anne
TULLOCH	Beryl Gwendoline
TUPPER	Frances Edith
TURNBULL	Annie Matilda
TURNER	Doris Jean
TURNER	Florence Muriel
TURNER	Joan Lowick
TURNER	Margaret Constance
TURNER	Marie Patricia
TURTON	Mollie Hallett Wilson
TWEDDELL	Joyce
TWOHILL	Eileen Monica
TWYNAM	Dorcas Mabella Gayor
TYLER	Jean
TYMMS	Joan Frances
UMPHERSTON	Thelma Lily
UNDERWOOD	Cassandra Alice

UREN	Elizabeth Irene
VALENTINE-BROWNE	Desda Madoline
VARY	Beryl Jean
VASEY	Marjorie Hope
VAUGHAN	Lorna Elsie
VEARING	Ruth Mavis
VEITCH	Ruth Margaret
VEIVERS	Georgina Marjory
VENABLES	Kathleen Imelda
VENNING	Marion Jean
VICKERS	Annie
VICKERS	Bessie Hannah
VICKERS	Phyllis
VIGAR	Ella Jeanie
VINALL	Laura Lillian
VINES	Dorothy Alexander
VINEY	Gladys Eileen
WADE	Evangeline Mary
WADE	Linda Dorothea
WAHLHEIM	Aina Armas
WAINWRIGHT	Phyllis
WALCOTT	Lucy Beatrice
WALDEN	Elizabeth Annie
WALKER	Elsie Gladys
WALKER	Jean Lauder
WALKER	Jenny Wendy
WALKER	Marjorie Florence
WALKER	Ruth Gertrude
WALL	Kathleen Patricia
WALL	Marjorie
WALLACE	Mary
WALLACE	Phoebe
WALLIS	Margaret Joan
WALLIS	Mona Olive
WALPOLE	Marion Rewa
WALSH	Bernice Agnes
WALSH	Betty Patricia
WALSH	Jean Phyliss
WALSH	Margaret Isobel
WALSH	Mary Josephine
WALSH	Sheila Mary
WALSH	Veronica Clare
WALTER	Isabelle Mary
WALTERS	Ada Catherine
WALTERS	Joyce
WALTERS	Winifred May
WALTON	Joan Wilton
WARBY	Jean Edmund Noble
WARD	Alice May
WARD	Dorothy Joan
WARD	Evelyn
WARD	Joyce Lorna
WARD	Lilian
WARD	Mary
WARD	Patricia
WARFIELD	Norma Margaret Anne
WARK	Marcia Finch
WARNECKE	Edna May
WARNER	Elsie Isobel
WARNER	Pauline Nicholson
WARNER	Ruby Inez
WARREN	Hazel
WARREN	Helen
WARREN	Kathleen Maude
WARREN	Margaret Emma Brough
WASHINGTON	Jean Louisa
WASLEY	Eunice Marguerite
WASSON	Joyce Isabel
WATERFORD	Marie Josephine
WATERMAN	Winifred Evelyn
WATERS	Daphne Doreen
WATERS	Joyce Elaine
WATERS	Morna Eileen
WATKIN	Nina Isabel
WATSON	Doris Miriam
WATSON	Frances Downie
WATSON	Irene Ella

WATSON	Leila Elizabeth	WESTBURY	Imelda Catherine
WATSON	Mary Jean	WESTCOTT	Georgina Louise
WATSON	Olga	WESTCOTT	Joan Ellen
WATSON	Pauline	WESTLEY	Mona Mary
WATSON	Royale Mary	WESTON	Joan Kathleen
WATT	Grace Mcclure	WESTON	Olive Muriel
WATT	Irene Ruth	WESTON	Ruth May
WATTERS	Esther	WESTWOOD	Betty Rutherford
WATTERSON	Ruby Ida	WETTENHALL	Editha
WATTS	Barbara Jeanie	WHEATLEY	Florence Marie
WATTS	Madeline Adele	WHEELER	Maisie
WAUGH	Doreen Joyce Turner	WHEELER	Margaret Olive
WAY	Elsie Constance	WHELAN	Jean Annie
WAYCOTT	Rosa Layton	WHITE	Annie Gwendoline
WAYMOUTH	Kathleen Mervynne	WHITE	Edith McQuade
WEATHERHEAD	Elizabeth Jean	WHITE	Edna Alice
WEATHERSTONE	Elma Florence	WHITE	Josephine Mary
WEAVER	Elinor Joan	WHITE	Lily Agnes
WEBB	Annie Sarah	WHITE	Mary Josephine Hilda
WEBBER	Joyce	WHITE	Mary Maxwell
WEBSTER	Esther Clare	WHITE	Mary Shiela
WEBSTER	Marjorie Garcia	WHITE	Mavis
WEDESWEILER	Mary	WHITE	Merle Eloise
WEETMAN	Joan Galbraith	WHITE	Philomene Amelia Marie
WEIDENHOFER	Jessie Mabel	WHITE	Sheilah Josephine
WEIDENHOFER	Joyce Harriet	WHITE	Stella
WEIGHT	Valmai Doris	WHITE	Viola Clarice
WEIR	Catherine	WHITEHEAD	Grace Claris
WEIR	Emily Frances	WHITEHEAD	Hilda Madeleine
WEIR-SMITH	Gwynneth	WHITEHEAD	Margaret Ethel
WELCH	Florence	WHITELAW	Audrey Lillian
WELLER	Gladys Margaret	WHITELAW	Rita Mary
WELLMAN-MARSH	Patricia	WHITFIELD	Annie Irene
WELLS	Iris Evelyn Sarah	WHITFIELD	Doris May
WELLS	Margaret Lillian	WHITFIELD	Idamay Lucy
WELLS	Thelka Maitland	WHITFIELD	Violet Elsie
WENTWORTH	Winsome May	WHITFORD	Joan Morrell
WEST	Marjorie Ann Simm	WHITING	Evelyn
WEST	Stella May		

WHITTENBURY	Isabel Blanche
WHYTE	Aleen Mary
WHYTE	Lorna Margaret
WIDDICOMBE	Kathleen Jessie
WIDDOWSON	Annie Ethelwyn
WIGHT	Rosetta Joan
WILDING	Helene Joyce
WILKIN	Dora Jean
WILKINSON	Emily
WILLANS	Margery
WILLIAMS	Constance
WILLIAMS	Elsie Ellen
WILLIAMS	Jean Ferguson
WILLIAMS	Mary Winifred
WILLIAMS	Isyabell Ann
WILLIAMSON	Elizabeth Anne
WILLIAMSON	Lucia D'Esterre
WILLIAMSON	Nancy
WILLIAMSON	Winifred Grace
WILLIS	Eleanor Pearl
WILLIS	Kathleen Vera
WILLMOTT	Hope
WILLOUGHBY	Valerie Louise
WILMOTT	Bessie
WILSHIRE	Anna Oakes
WILSON	Doris
WILSON	Ellen Jean
WILSON	Elsie Charlotte
WILSON	Girlie Marguerite
WILSON	Grace Margaret
WILSON	Heather
WILSON	Helen
WILSON	Jean Fogo
WILSON	Jean Nancy
WILSON	Joan De Caurcy
WILSON	Lilian Jessie Rae
WILSON	Mabel Inez
WILSON	Mary Aroha
WILSON	Mary McLennan
WILSON	Mary Rees
WILSON	Nancy
WILSON	Shirley Cameron
WILSON-HAY	Agnes Dorothy
WILTON	Mary
WILTON	Mona Margaret
WINCHESTER	Dorothy May
WINNALL	Eleanor Manley
WINNING	Mary Howit Wills
WINTER	Elsie Verdun
WINWOOD	Nina
WINZAR	Mary Catherine Joyce
WITTIG	Elsie Umina
WITTUS	Nancy Jean
WITTWER	Elvin Minna
WOLFE	Elsie
WOOD	Athola Yvonne
WOOD	Eliza Ellen
WOOD	Joan Gillian
WOOD	Kathleen Mavis
WOOD	Olga Mary
WOOD	Tessie
WOODBRIDGE	Beryl
WOODGATE	Isabel Mary
WOODS	Ellen May
WOODS	Norma Grace
WOODWARD	Edna Lavinia
WOODWARD	Norma Evelyn
WOOLFE	Ellen Noreen
WOOLLACOTT	Joy
WOOLLEY	Alice
WOOLLEY	Lillian Jane
WOOLNOUGH	Mary Flexmore
WOOLNOUGH	Winifred
WORTHLEY	Ray Lyall
WREN	Helen Gwenyth
WRIGHT	Clarice Irene
WRIGHT	Dorothy May
WRIGHT	Dorothy Miriam

WRIGHT	Ethel May
WRIGHT	Frances Helen
WRIGHT	Frances Una
WRIGHT	Phyllis May
WYATT	Anne Hinemoa
WYLD	Lillian May
WYLIE	Eleanor Mabel
WYLLIE	Annie Blumer
WYLLIE	Doris Joyce
YEOMAN	Beryl Gladys
YOUD	Elsie
YOUMAN	Ethel
YOUNG	Dulcie Lillias Berthe
YOUNG	Eleanor Ruth
YOUNG	Elizabeth Gratton
YOUNG	Mary Jean
YOUNG	May
YOUNG	Ruth Merle
ZANKER	Phyllis Janet
ZIELKE	Joyce Beryl
ZILLMAN	Phyllis Gertrude

The following 88 women have been identified as serving either with the AANS or in an army hospital in WW2, but in precisely what capacity is not known.

AANS (47)

ANDERSON	Doris May
BURKE	Annie
BURKE	Francis Margaret
BYRNE	Edna
CHRISTIE	Dorothy May
CONNELL	Josephine Phyllis
COOK	Betty
CROUCH	Ruth
DALL	Ailsa Zilpah
DONALDSON	Ivy Lorraine
DOUGHTY	Letitia Edith
GLAVIN	Jessie
GOUGH	Joan
HALLIDAY	Veronica
HOWELL	Margaret Patricia
JACKSON	Ethel May
KEENAN	Stella Ignatia
KENDALL	Marjorie
KENNEWELL	Ada Isabel
MANNING-SMITH	Ethel
MCLEAN	Jean
MEAGHER	Lilian Bacchi
MILLS	Australia May
MURRAY	Lala May
NANCARROW	Margaret
O'BRIEN	Bridget
PARKS	Vera
PEARSALL	Iris
PEIRCE	Margaret Louise
PICKEN	Margaret Wilson
POTTER	Nancy May
RYAN	Elizabeth Michael
SCOBIE	Shirley Venessa
SIMONS	Mary Joan
SIMPSON	Clara Mabel
SMITH	Marjorie Inglis
SMITH	Ruth Emma
SPEER	Mary Margaret
STEWART	Mary
STEWART	Mary
SYKES	Joyce Hilda
THOMPSON	Doris
THOMSON	Yolande Mary
TUCKER	Florence Mary
WALTON	Marjorie Violet
WILSON	Ruby
WRIGHT	Dorothy Burns

ARMY HOSPITAL (41)

CAMPBELL	Margaret
CAMPBELL	Phillis May
CARR	Nancy Warburton
CLANCY	Alice Mary
CLARK	Helen Goldthorpe
CRAWFORD	Joan Davis
DAVIES	Elsie May
DOYLE	Mary
FERGUSON	Elsa
FITZPATRICK	Kathleen
FOLEY	Mary Teresa
FRASER	Mavis
HARVEY	Joy Johnston
HOPKINS	Maude Emily
KAY	Margaret Patricia
KENNEDY	Jean
KENNEDY	Margaret Mary
KENNY	Eileen Thelma
LE PAGE	Blanch Marion
MACKAY	Sheila Farquhar
MACKIE	Alice Mary
MALONE	Ellen Mary
McMEEKIN	Marjorie Helen
O'BRIEN	Constance Elizabeth
PATRICK	Janet Mabel
PHELPS	Olive Adelaide
PHILLIPS	Mary
RANKIN	Jane Margaret Anderson
REILLY	Annie
SHARPE	Iris Lillian
SHIER	Dorothy Mary
TEMBY	Evelyn Irene
THOMSON	Marjory Francis Adam
THORN	Edna Lorna
TURTON	Judith Vivienne
WATTERSON	Maude
WILLIAMSON	Mary Innes
WILSON	Jacqueline Marie Henrietta
WILSON	Margaret Alice Stuart
WILSON	Sylvia
YOUNG	Margaret Helen Jean

SELECT BIBLIOGRAPHY **BUSH NURSE**

Official Records

Births, Deaths, Marriages, NSW

Published books and journals

Cameron, W J, *Bourke: A History of Local Government*, 1978
Cameron, W J, *Bourke, A Pictorial History*, 1982
Far West Children's Health Scheme, *Annual Report, 31 October 1936*
Far West Children's Health Scheme 1932–33
Maclean, Meta, *Drummond of the Far West*, 1947
Old Moore's Almanac, 1934
Royal Far West Children's Health Scheme, *Golden Jubilee 1924–1974*, 1974
Royal Far West Children's Health Scheme, *Diamond Jubilee 1924–1984*, 1984
Royal Far West Children's Health Scheme, *Reflections*, 1984
Santa Gertrudis Annual, 1976
Walton, Nancy Bird, *Born to Fly*, 1961
Walton, Nancy Bird, *My God it's a Woman*, 1990
Wearn, Polly, *The Magic Shoulder*, Far West Children's Health Scheme, 1966

Newspapers, periodicals

Advertiser (Adelaide), 28/5/1936; 29/5/1936; 2/6/1936
Australian Women's Weekly, 15/6/1966; 7/9/1966; June 1988
Barrier Miner (Broken Hill), 27/5/1936; 15/1/1937; 11/3/1937; 17/3/1937
Country Life, 10/1/1935
Courier-Mail, 29/5/1936; 29/1/1938; 10/6/1975
Daily Examiner (Grafton), 24/2/1936; 13/5/1936
Daily Mirror (Sydney), 03/8/1929; 7/3/1930; 19/12/1930; 17/2/1931; 24/2/1931; 13/11/1931; 10/6/1932; 25/10/1932; 16/6/1933; 28/07/1933; 15/5/1935; 31/12/1937
Daily Telegraph, 3/9/1936; 6/7/1937; 22/5/1986; 24/8/1989
Dubbo Liberal and Macquarie Advocate, 7/11/1935; 5/12/1935; 14/3/1936
Farmer and Settler, 12/12/1935
Forbes Advocate, 12/6/1936; 10/7/1936; 15/9/1936; 9/4/1937; 4/2/1938
Gilgandra Weekly and Castlereagh, 11/6/1936; 10/2/1938
Glen Innes Examiner, 5/5/1936; 3/2/1938; 28/4/1938
Henty Observer and Culcairn Shire Register, 4/2/1938
Hillston Spectator and Lachlan River Advertiser, 23/4/1936; 22/10/1936,
Inverell Times, 16/10/1935; 2/2/1938
Katoomba Daily, 13/6/1936; 17/9/1936; 9/4/1937; 5/2/1938
Labour Daily, 28/12/1934
Lachlander and Condobolin and Western Districts Recorder, 8/7/1936; 9/9/1936; 8/4/1937; 7/2/1938
Land, 8/11/1935; 10/7/1936; 4/9/1936
Maitland Daily Mercury, 4/9/1936
Moree Gwydir Examiner and General Advertiser, 21/10/1935; 31/10/1935; 11/11/1935; 16/4/1936; 9/7/1936; 7/9/1936; 15/10/1936
Mudgee Guardian and North-Western Representative, 3/2/1938
Murrumbidgee Irrigator (Leeton), 1/5/1936
Muswellbrook Chronicle, 14/4/1938
Narromine News and Trangie Advocate, 8/11/1935; 10/9/1936; 15/10/1936; 7/2/1938

National Advocate (Bathurst), 9/7/1936; 13/10/1936; 2/2/1938; 3/2/1938; 4/2/1938
Newcastle Sun, 27/12/1935
News (Adelaide), 5/6/1936, 4/8/1938
North Western Champion (Moree), 10/10/1935; 31/10/1935; 7/11/1935; 11/11/1935; 14/11/1935; 7/9/1936; 27/2/1938
North Western Courier (Narrabri), 9/7/1936
People Magazine, 7/5/1952
Queensland Country Life, 18/11/1976
Riverina Recorder, 18/4/1936
Saga World, September 1991
Scone Advocate, 11/10/1918; 10/2/1920; 31/08/1921; 9/11/1923; 10/6/1932; 2/8/1932; 10/12/1935; 24/4/1936; 16/4/1937; 26/4/1938; 19/12/1952; 29/3/1960
Sun (Sydney), 23/12/1935; 24/12/1935; 13/4/1936; 15/4/1936; 28/1/1937; 12/4/1938; 14/4/1938; 19/4/1938; 17/10/1987
Sydney Morning Herald, 28/13/1934; 2/4/1935; 2/5/1935; 7/12/1935; 12/12/1935; 24/12/1935; 24/2/1936; 9/3/1936; 19/3/1936; 15/4/1936; 16/4/1936; 21/4/1936; 3/6/1936; 6/6/1936; 6/7/1936; 2/9/1936; 8/10/1936; 8/10/1936; 11/12/1936; 31/12/1936; 25/1/1937; 7/11/1998; 21/6/2000; 27/5/2005
Telegraph (Brisbane), 29/5/1936
Tumut and Adelong Times, 8/9/1936
Warialda Standard and Northern Districts Advertiser, 14/10/1935
Wellington Times, 11/6/1936; 7/9/1936; 12/10/1936; 3/2/1938
Western Age (Dubbo), 29/11/1935; 20/3/1936
Western Herald (Bourke), 9/1/1934; 8/2/1935; 8/11/1935; 13/12/1935; 20/12/1935; 6/3/1936; 13/3/1936; 27/3/1936; 3/4/1936; 5/6/1936; 12/6/1936; 31/7/1936; 28/8/1936; 4/9/1936; 16/10/1936; 9/4/1937; 14/5/1937; 21/5/1937; 6/8/1937; 20/8/1937; 11/2/1938; 17/6/1938; 28/8/1938; 15/12/1967
Western Mail (Perth), 18/8/1938; 21/8/1938
West Wyalong Advocate, 16/6/1936; 16/6/1936; 10/7/1936; 8/9/1936; 9/4/1937; 4/2/1938
Women's Day, 26/10/1988

Correspondence, interviews, private papers
Bourke Shire Council, correspondence (Silver Papers)
Cameron, Bill correspondence (Silver papers)
Henderson, George Papers (Mary Turner Papers)
Pike, Robyn correspondence (Silver Papers)
Silver Family, private papers
Turner, Mary, interview and correspondence (Silver Papers)
Walton, Nancy Bird, transcripts of interviews 27/2/1992; 12/6/2002 (Silver Papers)
Walton, Papers of Nancy Bird (newspaper cuttings, scrapbooks, photographs, correspondence, pilot logbook, licence, manuscripts, diaries, etc), ML MSS 6490/ 1, 2, 3, 4 (Mitchell Library, Sydney)
Weiss, Charles, private Papers (Silver Papers)
Weiss, Marjorie, memoir (Silver Papers)

SELECT BIBLIOGRAPHY WAR NURSE

Primary sources

Australian War Memorial (AWM)
National Archives of Australia (NAA)
National Library of Australia (NLA)

Official records

Birth, Death, Marriage Records, various Australian states
Bullwinkel, V, Affidavit, AWM54 1010/4/24 (AWM); sworn statement, AWM54 553/6/2 (AWM) and MP742/1 336/1/1976 (NAA)
Bullwinkel, V, Report, MP742/1 336/1/1976 (NAA)
Census, 1911, England
Commonwealth War Graves Commission
Department of Veteran Affairs Nominal Roll WW2
Dixson, K M, Report, MP742/1 336/1/1976 (NAA)
Germann, Eric Harrison, MP742/1 336/1/1289 (NAA)
Goldberg-Curth, Dr Anna Maria A472 W30744 (NAA)
James, N, Statement, MP742/1 336/1/1289 (NAA); AWM10104/78 (AWM)
Lennard, Haydon, Release of nurses and civilian internees, SP300/3 637 (NAA)
Maps, pre-war and 1945, Bangka Island, National Library of Australia (NLA)
Pritchard, R J, Zaide, S M, Watt, D C (ed.), Transcripts, *The Tokyo War Crimes Trials* (pp. 13,454–76; 40,196, 1981
Register, Civilians, 1939, England
Ross, Colonel, Report, MP742/1 336/1/1289 (NAA)
Sage, Annie, Report, MP742/1 336/1/1289 (NAA)
Tebbutt, W A, Report, MP742/1 336/1/1976 (NAA); Report on Prisoner of War Camps Banka [sic] and Palembang, B3856 144/1/346 (NAA)
War Crimes, Banka [sic] Island, MP74/1 336/1/1976 (NAA)
War Crimes Investigations, 229 Infantry Regiment, AWM 54 1010/6/128 (AWM)
War Crimes, Weekly Investigation Reports, Captain J G Godwin, MP742/1 336/1/1965 (NAA)
War Crimes, Weekly Investigations Reports, Sergeant A H Weston, MP742/1 336/1/1965 (NAA)
War Service Dossiers (NAA)
Windsor, Major, Report on 2/14 AGH, Aug–Sept 1945, AWM54 403/7/1 (AWM)
Windsor, Major, Sumatra 1: Basic documents relative to war crimes, MP742/1 336/1/1289 (NAA)

Private records

Arthurson, Lex, article, 'The Story of the 13th Australian General Hospital', no date (Silver Papers)
Balcombe, Judy, 'Interview with Mr Idris, Bangka Island' (copy in Silver Papers)
Bullwinkel, Vivian, Papers, AWM PR01216 (AWM)
Chidson Family Papers
Clancy, Veronica Ann, AWM MSS 1086 (AWM)
Clancey, Veronica, article, 'You Learn a Lot', 1946 (Silver Papers)
Emerson-Elliott, Denis (Emerson-Elliott Family Papers)
Godwin, Sally, interviews (Silver Papers)
Gunther, Janet, memoir and interviews (Silver Papers)
Jeffrey, Betty, Papers, diary etc., AWM PR01780 (AWM)
Jeffrey, Betty, 'Obituary', *The Times*, London (Silver Papers)
Hannah, Mavis, AWM MSS 1486 (AWM)

Henning, Peter, *Finding the Nurses in Sumatra* (Silver Papers)
Howgate, Edith Emily, PR91/045 (AWM)
MacKay, James, Personal papers, correspondence, unpublished sections of manuscript (Silver Papers)
McEarchan, Thelma (nee Bell), Memoir, AWM PR90/050 (AWM)
Moffatt, Jonathan, Papers and correspondence (Silver Papers)
Priest, Rusty, Correspondence (Silver Papers)
Setchell, Margaret (Setchell Family Papers)

Autobiographies

Colijn, Helen, *Song of Survival: Women Interned*, 1996
Jacobs, G F, *Prelude to the Monsoon – Assignment in Sumatra*, 1982
Jeffrey, Betty, *White Coolies*, 1954
McDougall, William H, *By Eastern Windows: A story of a battle of souls and minds in the prison camps of Sumatra*, 1949
Simons, Jessie Elizabeth, *In Japanese Hands* (also published as *While History Passed*), 1954

Sound, film recordings

Bowden, Tim, *POW. Australians under Nippon: An Ordinary Bunch of Women*, (various nurses), 1992
Bowden, Tim, *Survival, I Could Never Ever Trust Them* (Vivian Bullwinkel), 1987
Gunther (Darling), Janet, AWM S02024 (AWM), Australians at War Film Archive
James, Nesta, AWM S03014 (AWM)
Syer, Ada Corbitt, AWM S04098 (AWM)

Published books, articles

Angel, Barbara, *A Woman's World: The Exceptional Life of Wilma Oram Young AM*, 2003, updated edition 2011
Australian Dictionary of Biography (adb.anu.edu.au/)
Bassett, Jan, *Guns and Brooches: Australian Army Nursing from the Boer War to the Gulf War*, 1992
Coates, Albert and Rosenthal, Newman, *The Albert Coates Story*, 1977
Fletcher, Angharad, 'Sisters behind the Wire: Reappraising Australian Military Nursing and Internment in the Pacific during World War II', Cambridge Journals, *Medical History*, vol. 55, no. 3, July 2011
Kenny, Catherine, *Captives: Australian Army Nurses in Japanese Prison Camps, 1986*
Lodge, A B, *The Fall of General Gordon Bennett*, 1986
MacKay, James, *Betrayal in High Places*, 1996
Manners, Norman G, *Bullwinkel*, 1999
McKie, R C H, *This was Singapore*, 1942
Morrison, Ian, *Malayan Postscript*, 1943
Nelson, Hank, *Prisoners of War: Australians Under Nippon*, 2001
Pratt, Ambrose, *Magical Malaya*, 1931
Sandilands, J, *Women Beyond the Wire: A Story of Prisoners of the Japanese 1942–45*, 1982
Seagrave, Sterling and Peggy, *Gold Warriors: America's Secret Recovery of Yamashita's Gold*, 2003
Silver, Lynette Ramsay, *The Heroes of Rimau*, 1990
Silver, Lynette Ramsay, *Krait: The Fishing Boat that Went to War*, 1992
Silver, Lynette Ramsay, *Sandakan: A Conspiracy of Silence*, 4th edn, 2010 (first published 1998)
Silver, Lynette Ramsay, *Deadly Secrets*, 2004
Silver, Lynette Ramsay, *The Bridge at Parit Sulong*, 2004
Tanaka, Yuki, *Hidden Horrors, Japanese War Crimes in World War II*, 1996
Walker, A, *Medical Services of the RAN and RAAF (The Official History of Australia in the War of 1939–1945)*, 1961
Wigmore, L, *The Japanese Thrust (The Official History of Australia in the War of 1939–1945)*, 1957

Newspapers, journals

Advocate (Burnie), 20/11/1945

Apa Khabar, Journal of Malay Volunteers Group, April 2018, 54th edn, Judy Balcombe, 'Visit to Muntok, Banka Island, Indonesia, February 2018'
Argus, 21/9/1945, 27/9/1945, 6/12/1945, 30/4/1947
Australian Women's Weekly, 3/5/1941, 29/9/1945, 27/10/1945
Barrier Miner, 17/9/1945
Beaudesert Times, 18/9/1942
Burra Record, 8/9/1942
Cairns Post, 18/9/1945
Canberra Times, 22/9/1993
Daily Mercury (Mackay), 3/10/1945
Evening Advocate (Innisfail), 17/9/1945
Independent Australia, 19/2/2017, Tess Lawrence, 'Vivian Bullwinkel, the Bangka Island Massacre and the Guilt of the Survivor
Journal of the Australian War Memorial, Issues 7, 32
Kalgoorlie Miner, 23/3/1942
Longreach Leader, 17/11/1945
Mercury (Hobart), 19/9/1945, 16/12/1945
Newcastle Morning Herald, 17/9/1945
Newcastle Morning Herald and Miners Advocate, 15/9/1945, 12/11/1945
Riverine Grazier, 29/7/1949
Straits Times Singapore, 1932–1942
Sun, 29/8/1946
Sydney Morning Herald, 25/9/1942, 18/9/1945, 11/12/2007
Tasmanian Times, 25/5/2009
The Advertiser (Adelaide), 15/9/1945, 27/2/1946
The Age, 15/9/1945
The Mail (Adelaide), 11/1/1947
The Telegraph (Brisbane), 17/9/1945
The Times (London), 14/9/1961
Townsville Daily Bulletin, 3/10/1945
Tweed Daily, 18/9/1945, 19/10/1945
Women's History Review, 1966, Bernice Archer and Fedorowich Kent, 'The Women of Stanley: Internment in Hong Kong 1942–1945', 1966

Websites

http://www.abc.net.au/news/2017-02-14/bangka-island-massacre-remembered-75-years-on-nurses/8269344
https://www.ancestry.com/
www.angellpro.com.au/women.htm
https://applegidley.wordpress.com/tag/empire-star/
http://docplayer.net/38495612-Sumatra-internees-compiled-by-jonathan-moffatt-michael-pether-becca-kenneison.html
https://earth.google.com/web/
https://www.encyclopedia.com/women/encyclopedias-almanacs-transcripts-and-maps/women-pows-sumatra-1942-1945
http://grahamhancock.com/phorum/read.php?2,383398,383398,quote=1
https://gwulo.com/comment/31202#comment-31202
http://www.manfamily.org/wp-content/uploads/2015/06/Judy-Balcombe-letter-re-Muntok.pdf
http://muntokpeacemuseum.org/
https://www.tandfonline.com/doi/pdf/10.1080/09612029600200119
http://the-history-girls.blogspot.com.au/2017/12/a-nursing-tragedy-massacre-at-radji.html
https://www.smh.com.au/news/national/in-a-pows-will-words-to-benefit-a-future-generation-of-women/2008/05/11/1210444244318.html

INDEX